Northeast India

Joe Bindloss

Lindsay Brown, Mark Elliott, Paul Harding

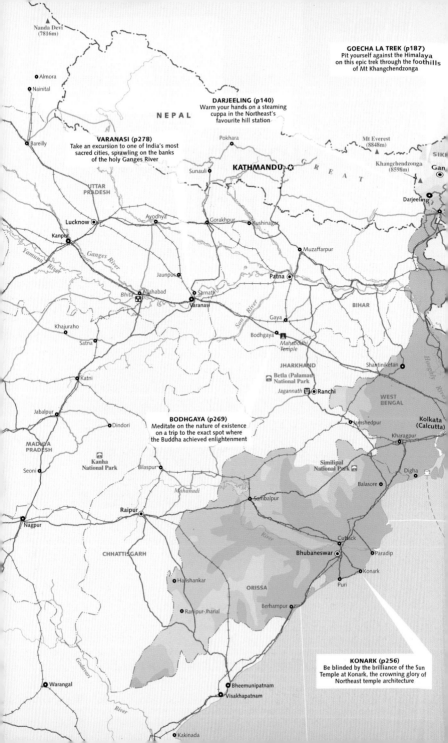

GOECHA LA TREK (p187)
Pit yourself against the Himalaya on this epic trek through the foothills of Mt Khangchendzonga

DARJEELING (p140)
Warm your hands on a steaming cuppa in the Northeast's favourite hill station

VARANASI (p278)
Take an excursion to one of India's most sacred cities, sprawling on the banks of the holy Ganges River

BODHGAYA (p269)
Meditate on the nature of existence on a trip to the exact spot where the Buddha achieved enlightenment

KONARK (p256)
Be blinded by the brilliance of the Sun Temple at Konark, the crowning glory of Northeast temple architecture

Nanda Devi
(7816m)

Almora
Nainital

NEPAL

Mt Everest
(8848m)

Khangchendzonga
(8598m)

SIK

Gan

Darjeeling

Bareilly

Pokhara

KATHMANDU

G R E A T

UTTAR
PRADESH

Sunauli

Lucknow
Kanpur

Ayodhya

Gorakhpur
Kushinagar

Muzaffarpur

Yamuna River

Ganges River

Jaunpur

Patna

BIHAR

Houghly River

Bhita
Allahabad
Sarnath

Varanasi

Son River

Gaya

Bodhgaya
Mahabodhi
Temple

Shantiniketan

Khajuraho

Satna

JHARKHAND

Betla (Palamau)
National Park

Jagannath Ranchi

WEST
BENGAL

Kolkata
(Calcutta)

Katni

Jabalpur

Dindori

MADHYA
PRADESH

Kanha
National Park

Seoni

Bilaspur

Jamshedpur

Kharagpur

Similipal
National Park

Digha

Mahanadi

Balasore

Raipur

Sambalpur

Nagpur

CHHATTISGARH

River

Cuttack

Bhubaneswar
Paradip

Hajishankar

ORISSA

Puri
Konark

Ranipur-Jharial

Berhampur

Godavari

River

Warangal

Bheemunipatnam
Visakhapatnam

Kakinada

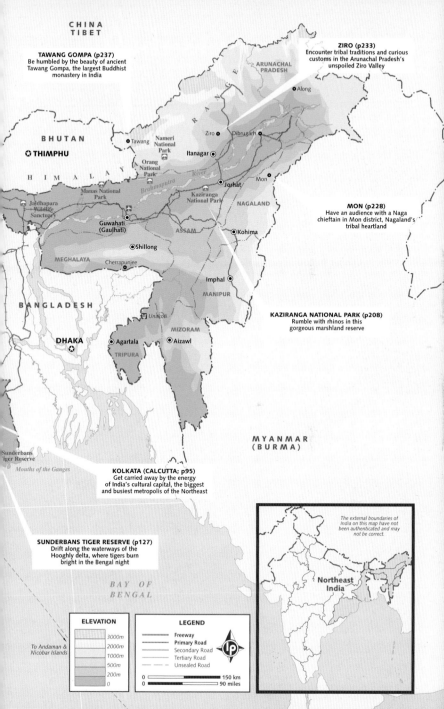

CHINA
TIBET

TAWANG GOMPA (p237)
Be humbled by the beauty of ancient Tawang Gompa, the largest Buddhist monastery in India

ZIRO (p233)
Encounter tribal traditions and curious customs in the Arunachal Pradesh's unspoiled Ziro Valley

ARUNACHAL PRADESH

Along

BHUTAN

⊙ THIMPHU

Tawang   Nameri National Park   Ziro   Dibrugarh
                    Itanagar ⊙
HIMALAYA   Orang National Park   Mon
Manas National Park   Brahmaputra River   Jorhat ⊙
Jaldhapara Wildlife Sanctuary   Kaziranga National Park   NAGALAND

Guwahati (Gauhati)   ASSAM   Kohima ⊙

Shillong ⊙

MON (p228)
Have an audience with a Naga chieftain in Mon district, Nagaland's tribal heartland

MEGHALAYA   Cherrapunjee ⊙

BANGLADESH   Unakoti   Imphal ⊙

                    MANIPUR

DHAKA   MIZORAM   **KAZIRANGA NATIONAL PARK (p208)**
⊙   Agartala ⊙   Aizawl ⊙   Rumble with rhinos in this gorgeous marshland reserve

        TRIPURA

Sunderbans Tiger Reserve

Mouths of the Ganges

KOLKATA (CALCUTTA; p95)
Get carried away by the energy of India's cultural capital, the biggest and busiest metropolis of the Northeast

MYANMAR (BURMA)

SUNDERBANS TIGER RESERVE (p127)
Drift along the waterways of the Hooghly delta, where tigers burn bright in the Bengal night

The external boundaries of India on this map have not been authenticated and may not be correct.

BAY OF BENGAL

Northeast India

ELEVATION

3000m
2000m
1000m
500m
200m
0

To Andaman & Nicobar Islands

LEGEND

Freeway
Primary Road
Secondary Road
Tertiary Road
Unsealed Road

0   150 km
0   90 miles

Northeast India Highlights

Providing a range of unforgettable highlights, the Northeast offers a travel experience unique from the rest of India. From fascinating tribal groups to breathtaking Himalayan panoramas, quaint and relaxed hill stations, fabulous wildlife-spotting opportunities and mystical Buddhist temples, the Northeast is sure to reward those who love to escape the tourist trail.

RICHARD I'AN

1

TREKKING THROUGH AWE-INSPIRING SCENERY

Taking a breather at the base of Khangchendzonga (8598m), the world's third highest mountain, while trekking through Dzongri (p187), Sikkim

PILGRIMAGES

Pilgrims gather at Dakshineswar Kali Temple in Kolkata for the Makar Sankranti (p302), to celebrate the winter rice harvest

GREG ELMS

RICHARD I'ANSON

2

COLOURFUL HINDU FESTIVALS

Celebrating the end of the Durga Puja festival (p97) in Kolkata (Calcutta), pilgrims set about the ritual of placing statues and effigies of Hindu gods in rivers and lakes

3

4

JOE BINDLOSS

TRIBAL DANCING

Naga dancers in full-warrior costume celebrate the annual week-long Hornbill Festival (p227) in Kohima, Nagaland

SACRED SITES
Snapping up religious artefacts and goods, on sale in the market stalls surrounding Kali Temple (p109) in Kalighat, Kolkata

RICHARD I'AN

6

5

HIRA PUNJABI

SUN TEMPLE
Illuminated at dawn, the impressive Sun Temple (p257) is one of Northeast India's signature, must-see buildings, Konark, Orissa

JOE BIND

7

SPIRITUAL NORTHEAST
Find some spiritual enlightenment at the stunning Tawang Gompa (p237), Tawang Valley, Arunachal Pradesh. It is the second largest Buddhist temple in the world, behind the Potala in Tibet.

MAJESTIC BENGAL TIGERS

Be lucky enough to spot one of these beautiful creatures in the Sunderbans Tiger Reserve (p127) in West Bengal, which has one of the highest concentration of tigers in the world

9

JOHN HAY

DENNIS JONES

RHINO SPOTTING

Eye off rare one-horned rhinos from the safety of an elephant-back safari, Kaziranga National Park (p208), Assam

10 ROOFTOP OF THE WORLD

Witness one of the most inspiring sunrises you will ever see, from Tiger Hill (p144) overlooking the Himalaya, near Darjeeling

RICHARD I'ANSON

FASCINATING TRIBAL GROUPS

Visit the Konyak people in the villages around Mon (p228) in Nagaland, one of the few remaining semi-traditional tribal groups

12

11 TRIBAL VILLAGES

Experience the tranquillity of village life in Central Arunachal Pradesh (p230), home to intriguing, colourful tribal groups

13 RIVER LIFE

Observe the peacefulness of daily life along one of India's great waterways, the Brahmaputra River (p197), while kicking back on deck during a boat trip in Assam. Be sure to keep an eye out for the rare Gangetic dolphin.

Contents

Regional Map Contents

Sikkim (p161)

Northeast States (p193)

West Bengal (p128)

Kolkata (Calcutta) (pp98–9)

Orissa (p242)

The Authors

JOE BINDLOSS
Coordinating Author

Joe first visited India in the early '90s, and something clicked. He's been back a dozen times since, dividing his time between the high mountain passes, the southern jungles, the backwaters of the Northeast and India's steamy cities. Joe was born in Cyprus and grew up in England, and he's since lived and worked in half a dozen countries, including the USA, Australia and the Philippines, writing for Lonely Planet, newspapers and magazines. When not scouring India for the perfect *kali mirch* kebab, Joe lives in London with his partner Linda and a growing collection of carpets and musical instruments.

Life on the Road

The first thing that struck me when I stepped off the plane in Assam was how few foreigners there were on the flight. The next day, walking through Guwahati's busy bazaars, it became apparent that I was quite possibly the only leisure traveller in town. A few days later, pushing a jeep through knee-deep mud with a group of machete-wielding Nagas, I felt like the only tourist in the country. Although I eventually bumped into other adventurers, this sense of being at the travel frontier has pervaded every trip to the Northeast states. Travel here involves going against the gradient, which was part of my inspiration for becoming a travel writer.

LINDSAY BROWN
West Bengal, Orissa

After completing a PhD on evolutionary genetics and following a stint as a science editor and a sojourn on the subcontinent, Lindsay started working for Lonely Planet. A former publishing manager of the Outdoor Activity Guides at Lonely Planet, Lindsay returns to the subcontinent to trek, write and photograph whenever possible. He has also contributed to Lonely Planet's *South India*, *Nepal*, *Bhutan* and *Pakistan & the Karakoram Highway* guides, among others.

LONELY PLANET AUTHORS

Why is our travel information the best in the world? It's simple: our authors are independent, dedicated travellers. They don't research using just the internet or phone, and they don't take freebies in exchange for positive coverage. They travel widely, to all the popular spots and off the beaten track. They personally visit thousands of hotels, restaurants, cafés, bars, galleries, palaces, museums and more – and they take pride in getting all the details right, and telling it how it is. Think you can do it? Find out how at lonelyplanet.com.

MARK ELLIOTT   Kolkata (Calcutta), Sikkim, Northeast States

Mark Elliott has been making occasional forays to the subcontinent since a mad 1984 trip that lined his stomach for most eventualities. Delighted to finally have the excuse to explore the Northeast, Mark was bowled over by the human warmth of Sikkim, Kolkata and Mizoram, and fascinated to compare mythical Tawang with equivalent Tibetan temples on 'the other side'. Between researching travel guides for countries as diverse as Azerbaijan, Indonesia, Greenland and Slovenia, Elliott lives in blissfully quiet suburban Belgium with his beloved wife Danielle, who found him at a Turkmenistan camel market. A camel would probably have been cheaper.

CONTRIBUTING AUTHOR

Paul Harding Ever since arriving wide-eyed in Delhi a decade ago, Paul has been drawn back to India regularly, each time finding it the same but so completely different. A journalist, travel writer, and sometime photographer, for more than 15 years, he has backpacked around much of Asia and Europe, travelled overland from Kathmandu to London and spent plenty of time hopping around the subcontinent, particularly in South India. This time around he headed north again and indulged his admiration of the mountains in Uttarakhand's Himalaya, saw a great deal of the Ganges, and picked his way through Varanasi's illuminating old city. Paul has contributed to numerous guides for Lonely Planet, including *India, South India* and *Goa*. He lives by the beach in Melbourne, Australia.

Destination Northeast India

Even the Mughals failed to dominate India's wild Northeast, a patchwork of former princely states and proud provinces squeezed between Nepal, Bhutan, Bangladesh, Myanmar and the snowcapped mountains of the Himalaya. From the plains of Bengal to the beaches of Orissa and the tribal villages of the Northeast states, the Northeast is perhaps the least explored part of India – it's also one of the most fascinating and diverse places in the subcontinent.

For travellers, the Northeast is a mix of famous sights and unexpected delights. Konark in Orissa is arguably the most famous Hindu temple in India, while the Rath Yatra chariot festival in Puri is one of Asia's wildest celebrations. West Bengal boasts sultry swamps and serene hill stations, as well as mighty Kolkata (Calcutta), India's fast-paced cultural capital. In the north, mountainous Sikkim is a spyglass onto the Himalaya, while Assam is blessed by sprawling tea gardens and national parks full of rumbling rhinos.

The states of the far Northeast are something else again – a cluster of tribal homelands, sprawling over mountains, hills and plains. Permit restrictions make this one of the trickiest regions of India to visit, but the rewards speak for themselves: medieval monasteries, tumbling waterfalls, magical markets and the villages of India's hill tribes, preserving a way of life rarely seen outside the pages of *National Geographic*.

Tourism is only just taking off in the Northeast – for every sight in this book, there are a dozen more waiting to be uncovered by travel pioneers. The Northeast is still a place where maps have gaps and trails can be blazed – pack your pith helmet and see what you can discover…

ANTHONY PLUMMER

Getting Started

The Northeast is perhaps the least explored part of India. From the crowds of Darjeeling to the peace of the Himalaya, this is India at its most undiluted – an evocative, energising roller-coaster ride of sights, sounds, smells and sensations. Kolkata, Darjeeling, Sikkim and Orissa have earned their place on the traveller map, while the tribal states curving east around Bangladesh are only just being discovered.

Few places in India can match the northeast for diversity – there are beaches and jungles, rivers and mountains, Buddhist monasteries and tribal totem poles. And as tourists are still something of a novelty, there are refreshingly few scams waiting for foreign visitors. However, you still need to prepare yourself for the challenges that India can deliver.

India is the second-most populous nation on earth and the crowds and congestion can turn even a short journey across town into a long, draining ordeal. Travellers will have to get used to being stared at, photographed and engaged in deep conversation by complete strangers on a regular basis. Then there's the infamous Indian bureaucracy – at times it can seem like nothing gets done without a complicated form, countersigned and filled out in triplicate.

But this all adds to the intensity of travel on the subcontinent. The energy and pace of life is strangely addictive – after visiting India, other countries can feel like they have the sound turned down. And the mix of noise, bustle and crowds just make the moments of tranquillity seem even more sublime.

If this is your first trip to India, take a few days to acclimatise before you head off to the sticks. Read up about India before you go and pay particular attention to the cultural and religious framework. Start your planning at least a month in advance to make time for immunisations and applying for visas.

Two essential virtues for travel in India are patience and flexibility, particularly when using public transport. Delays and cancellations are par for the course and you'll have a much more relaxing time if you accept that in India, you get there when you get there. Always build some flexibility into your plans and be prepared to change your itinerary if anything off route catches your attention.

Above all else, give yourself some time to relax. Every now and then, find a quiet spot to sit back and smell the jasmine – then when you're ready, throw yourself back into the wonderful, energetic maelstrom that is India.

THE INDIA EXPERIENCE

India is not a country you just see, it is a country you experience. As well as sight seeing make some time for the following:

- Festivals (see p301)
- Shopping (see p307)
- Volunteering (see p316)
- Activities (see p75)
- Courses (see p297)

WHEN TO GO

Climate plays an important role in deciding when to visit the Northeast. Different areas are affected by different climatic patterns and local topography can also affect the climate – the foothills of the Himalaya have a totally different climate to the swamps and deserts on the plains.

Generally speaking, the climate is defined by three seasons – the hot, the wet (monsoon) and the cool. The most pleasant time to visit the lowlands is during the cool season from November to mid-February. However, this is also the coldest time of year in mountainous Sikkim and northern Arunachal Pradesh.

See the 'Fast Facts' box at the start of regional chapters for the best times to visit specific regions, and Northeast states on p194. Apart from the weather, you may also want to time your visit to coincide with the best festivals and special events – see p301.

See Climate (p296) for more information.

The Hot

After the cool winter, temperatures start to climb through February and March, peaking just before the breaking of the monsoon rains in May or June. This can be an unbelievably sticky and uncomfortable time to visit the lowlands and many people retreat to the hill stations in West Bengal and the Northeast states. Late in May the first signs of the monsoon appear – high humidity, electrical storms, sudden rain showers and dust storms that turn day into night. Carry an umbrella just to be safe.

The Wet

Most of the rain in the Northeast comes from the heavy southwest monsoon. Showers become more frequent and heavier in June and temperatures fall a few degrees, but the cooling effect doesn't last long – the period from July to September is marked by persistent high temperatures and massive humidity.

Although it doesn't rain solidly all day, it rains virtually every day. National parks turn into quagmires and roads through the hills are frequently blocked by landslides. On the flip side, this is the quietest, cheapest – and arguably most interesting – time to visit.

The Cool

Around October the monsoon rains slow to a trickle. This is the peak season for tourism and there is plenty of competition for rooms and tourist quota seats on trains. November and December are the best times to visit national parks in the plains, and the slightly chilly weather in Sikkim and Darjeeling is offset by the fabulous mountain views.

COSTS & MONEY

Travelling around the Northeast can cost as much or as little as you like, depending on the level of luxury that you crave. Accommodation ranges from cut-price backpacker dormitories to luxurious suites in former palaces. A meal can cost pennies at a roadside stall or hundreds of rupees at a top-end restaurant. Transport is astonishingly cheap if you travel by public bus and train, and not much more expensive if you fly with the new budget airlines.

However, costs vary considerably as you travel around, particularly when it comes to hotel rooms and transport. The best way to assess the costs for your trip is to read the relevant regional chapters of this book. Expect to spend considerably more in popular tourist destinations and large cities such as Kolkata (Calcutta), if only because there are more things to spend money on.

HOW MUCH?

A sweet paan Rs 5

A thali (plate meal) Rs 40 to Rs 80

Three-hour bus ride Rs 40 to Rs 100

Budget hotel Rs 100 to Rs 500

Jeep tour per day US$20 to US$50

DON'T LEAVE HOME WITHOUT...

- Getting a visa (p315) and travel insurance (p303).
- Seeking advice about vaccinations (p335) and anti-malarial drugs (p339).
- Nonrevealing clothes – see p42 for more advice on Indian etiquette.
- A well-concealed money belt (p299).
- Sunscreen lotion and sunglasses, particularly in the mountains.
- A small torch for poorly lit streets and power cuts.
- Good-quality earplugs – for noisy hotels and sleeping on night trains and buses.
- A portable alarm clock – clocks are rare and hotel wake-up calls are unreliable.
- Flip-flops (thongs) for grungy bathrooms.
- A universal sink plug – plugs are rare except at top-end hotels.
- Tampons – sanitary napkins are widely available but tampons are rare outside of big cities.
- Mosquito repellent (a mozzie net can also come in handy).
- The eye mask from your flight – light pollution is a major problem in budget hotel rooms.
- Your sense of humour – your first line of defence against the trials and tribulations of India!

How does this all translate to a daily budget? As a rough indication, shoestring travellers can get by on Rs 450 to 600 per day, staying in dorms or rooms with shared bathrooms, travelling on cheaper classes of bus and train, and eating at local restaurants.

It's worth spending a little more for hotel rooms with hot water and private bathrooms, the occasional restaurant splurge, more comfortable seats on buses and trains, and local transport by autorickshaw and taxi. Midrange travellers can get by on Rs 900 to 1700 per day, or less in smaller, not so touristy towns.

At the top end, the sky is the limit. Kolkata has some truly extravagant five-star hotels, and there are upmarket resorts and old colonial hotels across the Northeast. A budget of $US200 per day will open up the most luxurious accommodation and the fastest and most comfortable classes of long-distance travel – including internal flights – allowing you to see the sights on your own timescale.

In all classes, accommodation prices fluctuate with demand. During the peak tourist season and major festivals, many hotels charge at least double the normal rate. Air-conditioning will also increase your accommodation costs. Most hotels in the Northeast fall somewhere within the following ranges:

Budget: Single rooms Rs 100 to 400; doubles Rs 200 to 600
Midrange: Single rooms Rs 300 to 1300, doubles Rs 450 to 1800
Top End: Single and double rooms Rs 1800 upwards

Eating is one of the unadulterated pleasures of travel in India and you can find inexpensive *thalis* (plate meals) for less than Rs 60 in most towns. At the other end of the scale, a meal in an upmarket restaurant can cost upwards of Rs 600 per head. Again, prices vary regionally, so see the Eating sections of individual chapters.

Travel costs will depend on the class and speed of travel. Domestic flights cost much more than buses or trains, but you can travel huge distances cheaply if you don't mind the discomfort of slow 'ordinary' buses and fan-cooled sleeper carriages on trains. Air-conditioning will boost up the price of all tickets.

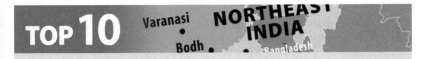

TOP 10

GREAT READS

There are some fascinating novels offering cultural insights into India. The following provide a solid introduction – for additional recommendations, see p59.

1 *Midnight's Children* by Salman Rushdie
2 *A Suitable Boy* by Vikram Seth
3 *A Fine Balance* by Rohinton Mistry
4 *The Inheritance of Loss* by Kiran Desai
5 *The Romantics* by Pankaj Mishra
6 *City of Joy* by Dominique Lapierre

7 *White Mughals* by William Dalrymple
8 *Hullabaloo in the Guava Orchard* by Kiran Desai
9 *The Raj Quartet* by Paul Scott
10 *The Calcutta Chromosome* by Amitav Ghosh

MUST-SEE MOVIES

Mumbai may be the home of Bollywood, but Kolkata (Calcutta) is the capital of Indian art-house cinema. Bengali directors such as Satyajit Ray and Ritwik Ghatak are some of India's finest, producing epic dramas about ordinary lives. The following list offers a mix of classic and modern treats – to find subtitled versions of these films outside India, try art-house video shops or the video libraries at local Indian grocery stores. See p58 for more on Indian cinema.

1 *Pather Panchali* by Satyajit Ray
2 *Pyaasa* by Guru Dutt
3 *The Cloud-Capped Star* by Ritwik Ghatak
4 *Ek Din Pratadin* by Mrinal Sen
5 *Gandhi* by Richard Attenborough

6 *Mother India* by Mehboob Khan
7 *Lagaan* by Ashutosh Gowariker
8 *Sholay* by Ramesh Sippy
9 *Bose: The Forgotten Hero* by Shyam Benegal
10 *Devdas* by Sanjay Leela Bhansali

FESTIVALS & EVENTS

Indian festivals are national spectacles, showcasing the Indian love of ritual and celebration. For comprehensive details, see p301 and the 'Festivals In…' boxed texts at the start of the regional chapters.

1 Gangasagar Mela – January: Sagar Island (p130)
2 Losar (p302) – February/March; Sikkim, West Bengal & Arunachal Pradesh
3 Holi/Dol Yatra – February/March; India-wide (p302)
4 Ambubachi Mela – June; Guwahati (p197)
5 Rath Yatra – June/July; Puri (p254) and Kolkata (p97)

6 Durga Puja/Dussehra – September/October; Bengal-wide especially in Kolkata (p97)
7 Diwali – October/November; India-wide (p302)
8 Kolkata Film Festival – November; Kolkata (p97)
9 Hornbill Festival – December, Kohima (p226)
10 Losoong – December/January, Sikkim

Full-service domestic airlines charge elevated US dollar fares for foreigners – to save money, book seats online with the new budget airlines. To work out the costs of specific journeys, see the Transport chapter (p325) and browse the Getting There & Away sections in the regional chapters.

Most towns have inexpensive suburban trains or buses; it costs more to travel by rickshaw, autorickshaw and taxi. Renting a car with a driver can seem expensive, but costs plummet if you split the fare with other travellers. For more information, see the Transport chapter (p325).

When it comes to sightseeing, foreign tourists pay elevated entry fees (set in US dollars but payable in rupees) at many monuments and museums. There may also be additional charges for still/video cameras; you can often get around this by leaving your camera in the lockers provided at the front desk.

TRAVEL LITERATURE

Kolkata has spawned a dozen travelogues all by itself. The essential reading list should include *Calcutta* by Geoffrey Moorhouse, Simon Winchester's *Calcutta,* and *The Weekenders: Adventures in Calcutta,* featuring the musings of Monica Ali, Irvine Welsh, Tony Hawks and others.

In *The Sorcerer's Apprentice,* Tahir Shah tells of his travels through India to learn the art of illusion under the guidance of a mysterious master magician from Kolkata. Every traveller to India should read *No Full Stops In India* and *India in Slow Motion* by Mark Tully, the BBC's correspondent for India for 25 years.

The backpacker scene in India is entertainingly sent up in William Sutcliffe's *Are You Experienced?*. Misadventures of a darker sort are explored in Anita Desai's *Journey to Ithaca,* the tale of a young European couple who lose their way on a quest for spiritual enlightenment.

Gita Mehta's *Karma Cola* amusingly and cynically describes the collision between India looking to the West for technology and modern methods, and the West descending upon India in search of wisdom and enlightenment.

The Northeast states fall off the radar of all but the most intrepid travel writers. Mark Shand describes an epic voyage along the Brahmaputra River in *River Dog.* In Alexander Frater's *Chasing The Monsoon,* the author races after the monsoon from Kovalam (Kerala) to Meghalaya (Northeast states).

INTERNET RESOURCES

123 India (www.123india.com) India-wide portal for news, sports and culture.

Best Indian Sites (www.bestindiansites.com) Gateway site for the most popular websites in India.

Incredible India (www.incredibleindia.org) The official government tourism site.

Khoj (www.khoj.com) Extensive India links from one of India's biggest ISPs.

Lonely Planet (www.lonelyplanet.com) Online travel information, hotel bookings and reader comments – post your own questions on the India thread of the Thorn Tree.

Maps of India (www.mapsofindia.com) A handy assortment of regional maps.

Northeast of India.com (www.northeastofindia.com) Tourism portal with information pages on each Northeast state.

Rediff (www.rediff.com) An extensive India portal, particularly good for news.

Itineraries

CLASSIC ROUTES

A SHORT HOP THROUGH THE HILLS   One Week

A week is a tight schedule, but the following itinerary will tick off some memorable experiences in the Northeast. To save time, book flights in advance (see p325).

Devote day one to exploring Kolkata (Calcutta), making time for the glorious **Victoria Memorial** (p102) and a **posh dinner** (p118) on Park St. Next morning, visit the **Indian Museum** (p105), then fly north to Bagdogra and take a jeep to the green hills of **Darjeeling** (p140).

On day three, catch the sunrise over Khangchendzonga from **Tiger Hill** (p144), then arrange your permit for Sikkim. In the afternoon explore Darjeeling's **gompas** (p145) and **tea gardens** (p145). Next day, travel by jeep to **Jorethang** (p172) and then **Namchi** (p171) to see the giant statue of Padmasambhava.

On day five, connect through Jorethang to **Pelling** (p174) for more epic Himalayan views. Spend day six exploring famous **Pemayangtse Gompa** (p176) and the ruins of **Rabdentse** (p176).

On day seven, take the bus or jeep to **Siliguri** (p133), before picking up the afternoon flight back to Kolkata, just in time to catch the sunset over the **Howrah Bridge** (p109).

A whirlwind tour from the Bengal plains to the foothills of the Himalaya, taking in the sights of Kolkata, the tea gardens of Darjeeling, vivid mountain vistas and the historic Buddhist monasteries in Sikkim.

ONCE AROUND THE BRAHMAPUTRA   One Month

This grand tour starts and ends in bustling Kolkata, taking in most of the famous sights of the Northeast as it criss-crosses the Northeast's mightiest river – the Brahmaputra. To maximise your time, arrange train travel in advance at the **Foreign Tourist Bureau** (p123) in Kolkata.

Devote the first few days to the sights of Kolkata, including the cultural centres founded by **Ramakrishna** (p111) and **Rabindranath Tagore** (p111). Fly on to **Agartala** (p220), the sleepy capital of Tripura, and visit the **Tripura Sundari Mandir** (p223) and **Neermahal Palace** (p223).

Providing things are secure, take the overnight bus to **Shillong** (p214), the green and pleasant capital of Meghalaya. Haggle for tribal artefacts at the **Iew Duh market** (p215) and detour east to **Cherrapunjee** (p217) to witness the thundering waterfalls.

For week two, connect through **Guwahati** (p197) – the Assamese capital – to **Kaziranga National Park** (p208) for an intimate meeting with wild rhinos beside the Brahmaputra. Continue west to **Majuli Island** (p210) and the temples and Ahom relics of **Sivasagar** (p211), then retrace your steps to Guwahati to visit atmospheric **Kamakhya Mandir** (p198).

Start week three with the overnight train ride to **Siliguri** (p133) and visit **Kalimpong** (p153) on your way north to **Gangtok** (p163) in Sikkim. Pop across to the **Rumtek** (p169) and **Lingdum** (p170) monasteries, and then head west to **Pelling** (p174) for knee-knocking mountain views. Take a few days to visit the gompas of the **Monastery Loop** (p185).

For the last week head south to **Darjeeling** (p140), taking time for a ride on the famous **toy train** (p145), and then roll south again by jeep and train to Kolkata, for a well-deserved slap-up meal. Spend your last few days exploring the Hooghly delta, with trips to **Sagar Island** (p130) and **Sunderbans Tiger Reserve** (p127).

A circuit right around the Northeast, starting and ending in Kolkata; see the backwaters of Tripura, the Shillong hills, temples, river islands and wild rhinos in Assam, and the magnificent monasteries of West Sikkim.

ROADS LESS TRAVELLED

NORTH & SOUTH   Three Months

This itinerary offers a broad sweep across the Northeast, including tribal tours to Arunachal Pradesh, so be sure to arrange the necessary permits (see p192).

First, take your time over the sights of **Kolkata** (p95) – don't miss the magnificent chintz of the **Marble Palace** (p110). Detour southeast for a tiger-spotting boat cruise through the waterways of **Sunderbans Tiger Reserve** (p127).

Returning to Kolkata, ride the rails south to **Bhubaneswar** (p244) and explore the city's many **temples** (p244), and day trip to the Jain caves at **Udayagiri** and **Khandagiri** (p245). Take a loop through **Konark** (p256) and **Puri** (p251) for more classic temple architecture and some of the Northeast's best beaches.

Continue south to **Chilika Lake** (p258) to see droves of migratory birds, then head inland to **Similipal National Park** (p264) for tigers, deer and wild elephants.

Crossing back into West Bengal, visit **Bishnupur** (p131), famed for its terracotta temples, then make for **Malda** (p133) to explore the ruins of **Gaur** and **Pandua** (p133). Your next stop is **Siliguri** (p133), gateway to the Bengal hills.

Head up to the hill stations at **Mirik** (p138) and **Kurseong** (p139) on the way to **Darjeeling** (p140). Then cut north to **Gangtok** (p163) to arrange a jeep trip to the northern villages of **Lachen** (p189) and **Lachung** (p190) for mountain vistas.

Return to Siliguri, then thunder east to **Guwahati** (p197) in Assam. With advance notice (one month or more), travel agents can arrange trips into wonderful Arunachal Pradesh. Highlights include spectacular **Tawang Gompa** (p237) and the tribal loop through **Ziro** (p233).

There should be time to catch the highlights of **upper Assam** (p209) – described in the Once Around the Brahmaputra itinerary (opposite) – before returning to Guwahati for the flight back to Kolkata.

From the beaches of Orissa to the rain-drenched Sunderbans Tiger Reserve, this three-month epic offers the best of the Northeast – tribal tours, wonderful wildlife, terrific temples, ruined civilisations and mountain villages in the lee of the Himalaya.

ALL THE NORTHEAST AND MORE...   Six Months

The six-month tourist visa gives you time to get deep into the Northeast, and even take some excursions to surrounding areas. Once again, **Kolkata** (p95) is the easiest starting point, and you can fly or take the scenic overland route through **Bangladesh** (p288) to reach **Agartala** (p220) in Tripura. Catch the local sights, then take your time exploring Meghalaya from the capital, **Shillong** (p214).

Continuing to Assam, combine well-known sights, such as **Guwahati** (p197), **Sivasagar** (p211) and **Kaziranga National Park** (p208), with off-the-beaten track destinations, like the peaceful ecocamp at **Potasali** (p207), little-visited **Dibrugarh** (p212) and the tea plantation getaways around **Jorhat** (p209).

With advance planning, you should have time for several trips into tribal areas of the Northeast states – see the dedicated Tribal Circuit itinerary later in this section (opposite). As you continue west, visit **Manas National Park** (p204) and **Jaldhapara Wildlife Sanctuary** (p137) for more unspoiled nature.

In West Bengal, ramble through the hill stations of **Mirik** (p138), **Darjeeling** (p140) and **Kalimpong** (p153), then head north for a contemplative sojourn in Sikkim. Be wowed by Buddhist monasteries and Himalayan viewpoints in **Gangtok** (p163) and **Pelling** (p174), then steel yourself for the testing **Goecha La trek** (p187) from **Yuksom** (p185).

Next, cut east across Bihar to **Patna** (p276) and walk in the footsteps of Buddha at **Bodhgaya** (p269). Roll on to the sacred Hindu city of **Varanasi** (p278) in Uttar Pradesh, and visit nearby **Sarnath** (p284) before taking the overnight train to **Bhubaneswar** (p244) for a circuit around Orissa. As well as famous **Konark** (p256) and **Puri** (p251), make time for **Gopalpur-on-Sea** (p260), tribal tours near **Jeypore** (p262) and wildlife-spotting at **Similipal National Park** (p264)

Finish off your Northeast odyssey with a trip to the **Sunderbans Tiger Reserve** (p127) before some well-earned rest and recreation in Kolkata – what a trip!

A Northeastern odyssey, taking a broad sweep across the Northeast. Highlights include trips around Tripura and Meghalaya, Assamese backwaters, tribal tours, Sikkim's favourite trek, hill stations in West Bengal, famous temples in Orissa, and excursions to Varanasi and Bodhgaya in the central plains.

TAILORED TRIPS

A NORTHEAST SAFARI

The Northeast is the least developed corner of India and unspoiled nature lurks around every corner. Species include tigers, leopards, elephants, deer, rare birds, like the great Indian hornbill, and the endangered one-horned Indian rhino, found only in the Northeast and remote parts of Nepal.

Starting from **Kolkata** (p95), head southeast to seek tigers in the rain-drenched creeks of **Sunderbans Tiger Reserve** (p127). Take a hop south to the bird-watchers' paradise of **Chilika Lake** (p258) and explore the little-seen wildlife sanctuaries of **Debrigarh** and **Badrama** (p264) near Sambalpur. Continue north through the hills to see wild elephants at **Similipal National Park** (p264).

Next, head north through Kolkata to **Darjeeling** (p140) to organise a trek through **Singalila National Park** (p152). Further north in Sikkim, elusive red pandas and monal pheasants roam free in **Maenam Wildlife Sanctuary** (p173) near **Ravangla** (p173). Species from the high Himalaya can be spotted on the **Goecha La trek** (p187), which passes through Khangchendzonga National Park.

Returning to **Siliguri** (p133), visit lush, green **Jaldhapara Wildlife Sanctuary** (p137) and take a wildlife-spotting river-boat ride through Assam's **Manas National Park** (p204). Make time to commune with one-horned Indian rhinos at **Kaziranga National Park** (p208). Enthusiasts can squeeze in **Nameri National Park** (p207) near Tezpur or a gibbon-spotting trek through Meghalaya's **Nokrek Biosphere Reserve** (p219), before flying back from **Guwahati** (p197) to Kolkata.

THE TRIBAL CIRCUIT

With a few months to spare, you can push deep into the tribal heartlands of the Northeast. Be sure to make the necessary permit arrangements (see p192 for a list) and check the security situation before you travel – see p298.

Start in **Kolkata** (p95) before flying to **Agartala** (p220) to explore Tripura, then ramble north to see primitive Hindu rock art at **Kailasahar** (p224). Head southeast to **Aizawl** (p239) in Mizoram, and explore surrounding **Mizo villages** (p240).

Roll north through the **Jaintia Hills** (p218) to **Shillong** (p214) in Meghalaya. Visit **Smit** (p217) and **Cherrapunjee** (p217) for Khasi culture, and drop in on Garo tribal villages in the **Garo Hills** (p219). Connect through Guwahati to **Upper Assam** (p209) to observe rural Assamese life.

Next, take a tribal odyssey through the Naga villages around **Mon** (p228) in Nagaland. Continuing to Arunachal Pradesh, explore Adi and Apatani villages near **Ziro** (p233) and Monpa villages near **Tawang Gompa** (p237).

To continue the tribal theme, visit Assam's **Manas National Park** (p204), deep in Bodo country. More tribal encounters are possible in **North Sikkim** **(p188)** and on tours to Adivasi areas near **Jeypore** (p262) in Orissa – best arranged in Bhubaneswar (p244) or Puri (p251).

THRILLS OF THE NORTHEAST

The Northeast is a giant-sized adventure playground for fans of action and adrenaline. Most activities are seasonal, so check the Activities chapter (p75) for the best times to get stuck in. As well as physical thrills, there are plenty of unique cultural experiences waiting for adventurers.

Kick off your quest by flying from **Kolkata** (p95) to **Shillong** (p214). Rumble east to rain-drenched **Cherrapunjee** (p217) and go canyoning over living tree bridges with Khasi tribal guides. Experienced spelunkers can explore India's longest cave system in the **Jaintia Hills** (p218) – make arrangements with agents in Shillong.

From Shillong, head north to **Guwahati** (p197) and immerse yourself in Tantric ritual at **Kamakhya Mandir** (p198), a major centre for animal sacrifices. Make advance arrangements for a tour to the Naga villages near **Mon** (p228), where you might end up eating dinner with a tattooed Naga chieftain.

Finish off your Assam explorations with an elephant ride in **Kaziranga National Park** (p208) and go wildlife-spotting by raft in **Manas National Park** (p204). Next, meander west to **Gangtok** (p163) in Sikkim to make arrangements for the **Goecha La trek** (p187) through the foothills of Khangchendzonga.

From Sikkim, rumble south to **Darjeeling** (p140) to arrange a trek along the **Singalila Ridge** (p152). Finally, thunder down to the plains on a **white-water rafting trip** (p147) on the Teesta River – book with agents in Darjeeling.

SPIRITUAL SITES

Spirituality pervades every aspect of life in the Northeast. The following circuit takes in the spiritual highlights – from Buddhism to Animism – starting in **Guwahati** (p197), where you should prearrange a permit for Arunachal Pradesh (see p192).

Start your spiritual journey at Guwahati's **Kamakhya Mandir** (p198) devoted to the worship of female spiritual power, then follow the Brahmaputra to **Majuli Island** (p210), home to tranquil Vaishnavite *satras* (monasteries), and **Sivasagar** (p211), the temple-strewn capital of the Ahom kings.

With a permit from Guwahati, begin your trip into rugged Arunachal Pradesh by touring the tribal totem poles between **Daporijo** (p233), **Ziro** (p233) and the Buddhist gompas of the **Tawang Valley** (p236). Head on by train and jeep to **Gangtok** (p163) and **Rumtek** (p169), the official seat of the 17th Karmapa of Tibetan Buddhism.

Visit **Pelling** (p174) and perform a circuit of **Pemayangtse Gompa** (p176), **Khecheopalri Lake** (p185) and the Buddhist coronation throne at **Yuksom** (p185). Complete the loop via **Tashiding Gompa** (p188).

Cutting south, you can tour more Buddhist gompas in **Kalimpong** (p153) and **Darjeeling** (p140). Trains run from **Siliguri** (p133) to **Kolkata** (p95), home to the famous Kalighat **Kali Temple** (p109).

Finish off in Orissa, with a trip to **Bhubaneswar** (p244), city of 7000 temples. Admire the stunning **sun temple** (p257) at Konark, then wind up your travels at the **Jagannath Mandir** (p253) in Puri – arrive in June/July to witness the riotous **Rath Yatra** (p253) chariot festival.

Snapshot

The Northeast often makes the headlines for the wrong reasons – most of them associated with ongoing separatist conflicts – but there have been positive developments. The ceasefire signed in 2005 between the Indian government and Bodo guerrillas in Assam seems to be holding well, helped by the creation of the Bodoland Territorial Council. In the 2006 Assam assembly elections, former rebels from the Bodo Liberation Tigers formed a successful alliance with the Indian National Congress to take over several district councils – only the second time in Indian history that rebels have successfully been brought into the political process (the first was the Mizo Accord, signed with separatist rebels in Mizoram in 1986).

Since seizing power in the 2004 elections, the Congress Party government has made a string of overtures to insurgents in the Northeast, including a meeting with Naga rebels in Delhi to discuss the formation of a semi-autonomous Naga district encompassing parts of Nagaland, Manipur and Arunachal Pradesh. Despite claims that the government has been dragging its heels, the rebels extended their ceasefire in 2006. The other big event in Nagaland that year was the uproar that greeted the release of the film *The Da Vinci Code* – no, they weren't protesting about the wooden acting and thin plotline; the film was judged offensive to Christians and banned, along with Dan Brown's book, by the state government.

Further west, new tensions appear to be rising in Meghalaya, with tribal leaders demanding the departure of all migrants from Nepal and Bangladesh – linked to an upsurge in immigration by refugees from the war in Nepal. Understanding politics in Meghalaya is further complicated by the names of the candidates – many Meghalayans choose comic names for their children and the Meghalaya Legislative Assembly contains such surprising politicians as Boldness L Nongum, Tony Curtis Lyngdoh and, until recently, Frankenstein W Momin and Adolf Lu Hitler Marak. Few raise eyebrows at these names inside Meghalaya, but they ruffle feathers in central government.

In another unusual development, 218 followers of the Bnei Menashe sect were granted permission to move from Mizoram to Israel in 2006. Around 1000 Mizo Jews have emigrated to Israel since the 1970s but migration was halted in 2003 when Orthodox rabbis questioned the Jewish credentials of the sect, which is founded on the belief that the Mizo people were descended from one of the 'lost tribes' expelled from Israel in the 8th century BC.

Meanwhile, in Bengal, car enthusiasts recently uncovered a lost collection of 1950s Land Rover jeeps being driven as taxis in Darjeeling. Only about 500 of the vehicles are still in existence worldwide, with just a few dozen in working order. Kept mechanically sound to deal with Darjeeling's pitted roads, these jeeps could be worth upwards of US$38,000 each to collectors. You may get to ride in one of these museum pieces while travelling around Darjeeling.

The news is less positive in the plains – central Bengal has seen growing unrest among peasant farmers, triggered by the confiscation of land by the Communist state government for new industrialisation projects. The shooting dead of 14 protesting farmers by police in early 2007 led to a series of state-wide strikes; which even halted production of India's famous Ambassador motor cars.

The big news in Sikkim is the reopening of the Nathu-la border crossing with China, which closed after the 1962 Indo-China war (see p170). Thus far only local villagers have been allowed to cross, but the move suggests a

FAST FACTS

Population: West Bengal 80,221,171, Orissa 36,706,920, Sikkim 540,493, Northeast states 38,495,089 (2001 census)

GDP growth rate: National 8.5%, West Bengal 8.5%, Assam 4.5% (2006)

Rural unemployment rate: National 6.7%, West Bengal 11.1%, Arunachal Pradesh 0.8% (2001)

Female participation in labour: National 25.6%, Orissa 24.7%, Sikkim 53%

National inflation: 5.2%

National population growth rate: 1.4%

National literacy rate: 53.7% (women) and 75.3% (men)

National proportion of females to males: 933:1000 (2001 census)

National life expectancy: 65.6 years (women) and 63.9 years (men)

relaxing of the Chinese position on Sikkim, which it officially claims as part of all lands formerly administered by Tibet. If the border fully reopens for trade, it could mark a dramatic rise in the fortunes of Sikkim, providing a direct route for Chinese goods to enter the Northeast, as well as a new overland route for travellers between India and China.

The environment in the Northeast has been thrust into the spotlight by the controversial hydroelectric projects in Arunachal Pradesh (p73). Despite providing much needed cash for state coffers, the projects are causing massive upheaval for locals – tribes are being displaced, forests are being submerged and freshwater is being trapped in the hills, increasing the salinity of coastal waterways. To make things worse, silt build-up caused by deforestation has clogged several major dams. At the Gumti HEP project in Tripura, falling water levels have exposed new land that has been snapped up by landless tribal farmers, to the great chagrin of the state government.

Water has also been an issue in the hills of Meghalaya. Once the wettest place on earth, the town of Cherrapunjee has recently faced a string of winter droughts. Again, the main cause is deforestation, which reduces the ability of the thin topsoil to retain rainwater. If the droughts continue, they could cause the demise of the state's main tourist attraction – Cherrapunjee's thundering waterfalls (see p217).

Environmental concerns have also been raised at the Sunderbans Tiger Reserve in West Bengal (p127) and Similipal National Park (p264) in Orissa. Wildlife experts have claimed that the tiger counts at both parks are heavily exaggerated, which seems likely considering the massive increase in human activity around the parks' boundaries. The construction of a new steel plant in Orissa has also led to protests, this time from tribes who will be displaced from their lands by the project. However, there has been one encouraging development: the first ever lesbian wedding in India was approved by Orissan religious leaders – if not the state government – in 2006.

India-wide events have also had an effect in the Northeast. The growing Indian economy – linked to smart fiscal policies by Prime Minister Manmohan Singh and the relentless rise of the information technology and outsourcing industries – has brought new investment to the Northeast. India's new budget airlines are now offering flights across the region, providing a cheaper, and arguably safer, way to get around than the ageing aircraft of Indian Airlines and Pawans Hans helicopters.

...the first ever lesbian wedding in India was approved by Orissan religious leaders – if not the state government – in 2006.

History

Visitors often struggle to conceive Indian history in its entirety, overwhelmed by the myriad characters in this epic play of human endeavour. Spanning more than five millennia, the history of India has been a constant process of reinvention and accumulation, with each successive culture leaving its own indelible mark on the subcontinent. Here's an introduction to the forces that shaped it.

INDUS VALLEY CIVILISATION

Straddling the modern India–Pakistan border in the northwest of the country, the Indus Valley was the cradle of civilisation on the Indian subcontinent. The first inhabitants were nomadic tribes but by about 3500 BC, permanent cities started to appear. The next 1000 years were dominated by Harappan culture, centred on the city of Harappa in what is today the Pakistan Punjab. By the middle of the 3rd millennium BC the Indus Valley culture was the equal of other great civilisations emerging at the time, with huge cities at Harappa, Moenjodaro (in Pakistan) and Lothal (in India's Gujarat).

Many elements of Harappan culture would later become assimilated into Hinduism: clay figurines found at these sites suggest worship of a Mother goddess (later personified as Devi, Durga and Kali), and black stone pillars and images of bulls hint at the origins of Shiva worship.

EARLY INVASIONS & THE RISE OF RELIGIONS

The Harappan civilisation fell into decline from the beginning of the 2nd millennium BC, which also saw the rise of Aryan Vedic culture and the appearance of the first distinct culture in the Northeast – the ancient kingdom of Pragjyotish.

According to one theory, the Harappans were defeated by an invasion of Aryans (from a Sanskrit word meaning noble) from the West. However, there is growing evidence that this was an invasion of ideas rather than a physical invasion. What is certain is that northern India came to be dominated by Aryan language and culture from central Asia.

The ethnic divide in India is first recorded from this time, with the north dominated by the paler-skinned Aryans and the south dominated by dark-skinned Dravidian peoples. The Hindu sacred scriptures, the Vedas (see p50), were written during this period of transition (1500–1200 BC) and the caste system became formalised, as Hinduism came to dominate the subcontinent.

Meanwhile, a new civilisation was emerging in the Northeast. By the first millennium BC, a kingdom known as Pragjyotish ('Land of Eastern Light') had risen in modern-day Assam, with its capital in Pragjyotishpura (now Guwahati). Known later as Kamarupa, this early kingdom may have stretched as far west as Nepal and West Bengal.

As the Aryan tribes spread across the Ganges plain in the late 7th century BC, four large states began to take shape on the subcontinent. In Bengal, the powerful kingdom of Magadha rose to prominence, covering much of West

Harappa (www.harappa.com) provides an illustrated yet scholarly coverage of everything you need to know about the ancient Indus Valley civilisations.

The Wonder That Was India by AL Basham offers detailed descriptions of the Indian civilisations, major religions, origins of the caste system and social customs.

The Assamese kingdom of Pragjyotish (Land of Eastern Light) is first recorded in the Mahabharata – composed around 1000 BC.

Bengal, Bangladesh and Bihar. In around 563 BC, Prince Siddhartha Gautama – later the Buddha – was born in the neighbouring province of Kapilavastu in modern-day Nepal. After abandoning a life of luxury, the prince went on to meditate under a Bodhi tree at Bodhgaya in Bihar where he achieved enlightenment, giving birth to Buddhism (see p53).

Equally tumultuous events were taking place in other parts of India. Near Patna in Bihar, a Hindu ascetic called Mahavira founded a rival faith to Buddhism – Jainism – based on similar concepts of liberation from the earthly plane and a rejection of the Hindu caste system (see p54).

Meanwhile, the western kingdoms faced two invasions which, if successful, could have significantly altered the path of Indian history. First, Persian king Darius (521–486 BC) annexed Punjab and Sindh (on either side of the modern India–Pakistan border), then Alexander the Great advanced to India from Greece in 326 BC, pushing as far as the Indus Valley, before a rebellion among his soldiers forced him to turn back.

THE MAURYAN EMPIRE & THE GUPTAS AFTERMATH

The first pan-Indian empire rose at Patna under king Chandragupta Maurya. In 321 BC, Chandragupta annexed Magadha and the neighbouring kingdom of the Nandas, soon expanding his empire to include the Indus Valley and most of the east coast.

The empire reached its peak under Emperor Ashoka (see the boxed text, opposite), a warlike conqueror who converted to Buddhism after a particularly brutal battle with the kingdom of Kalinga in Orissa. Under Ashoka's influence, Buddhism spread across the subcontinent, becoming the dominant religion in Pakistan, Bangladesh, Afghanistan, Sri Lanka and Nepal. Ashoka was a hard act to follow – his successors were weak and Mauryan empire collapsed altogether in 184 BC. In Orissa, Buddhism was slowly displaced by Jainism.

Despite the collapse of the Mauryan empire, this was a period of intense development across India, and the Northeast was no exception. The Chinese explorer Chang Kien wrote of trade between China and Assam in 100 BC. Assamese silk was sold in Rome in the pre-Christian era and the Egyptian scientist Ptolemy marked Kamarupa on his world map.

The early medieval period was marked by a patchwork of small kingdoms across the subcontinent. Another huge empire rose in AD 319, under king Chandragupta I, ruler of the Gupta tribe. At its height, the Gupta empire stretched from Pakistan in the west to Nepal and Bangladesh in the east. The Chinese pilgrim Fahsien, visiting India at the time, described a people 'rich and contented', ruled over by enlightened and just kings.

Towards the end of the Gupta period, Hinduism saw a massive revival, eclipsing Jainism and Buddhism, which went into slow decline. The end of the Gupta era came in AD 510, when the massed Gupta armies were defeated by the Hun leader Toramana.

THE MEDIEVAL NORTHEAST

With the passing of the Guptas, India again dissolved into a sprawl of separate kingdoms. During this period, South Indian culture blossomed under the Cholas, Pandyas, Chalukyas, Cheras and Pallavas, while the Northeast saw the rise of a distinct Bengali identity.

Emperor Ashoka's ability to rule over his empire was assisted by a standing army consisting of 9000 elephants, 30,000 cavalry and 600,000 infantry.

321–184 BC	AD 319–510
The Mauryan empire and the birth of Buddhism and Jainism	Golden age of the Gupta empire

> ## AN ENLIGHTENED EMPEROR
>
> The Mauryan empire was the largest kingdom ever to rise in ancient India. The domain of the Emperor Ashoka (304–232 BC) once extended over most of Pakistan, Bangladesh, Nepal and almost all of northern India. Although hungry for power and territory, Ashoka always had philosophical leanings. He embraced Buddhism in 262 BC, declaring it the state religion and cutting a radical swathe through the caste traditions put in place by Hinduism.
>
> Ashoka's rule was characterised by flourishing art and sculpture, and the emperor left a series of rock-hewn edicts carved into the sides of mountains as a record of his moral teachings. Evidence of his rule can still be seen at Buddhist sites such as Sarnath in Uttar Pradesh and Lumbini in Nepal. Ashoka also sent missions abroad – he is revered in Sri Lanka because he sent his son and daughter to carry Buddhism to the island.
>
> The long shadow that Ashoka casts over India is evident from the fact that Ashoka's standard, the lion-topped column, is now the Indian seal and national emblem: four lions sitting back-to-back atop an abacus decorated with a frieze of animals and the inscription 'truth alone triumphs' – chosen to reaffirm the ancient commitment to peace and goodwill.

In around AD 606, the first recorded independent king of Bengal – Shashanka – came to power. The tribes and kingdoms around the Brahmaputra River delta were unified, and the first Pala king of Bengal, Gopala I, came to power in AD 750 by democratic election. The Pala empire ruled over parts of Bengal, Bihar and Assam for 400 years, with Hindus and Buddhists granted equal rights and status.

Hinduism replaced Jainism in Orissa in around the 7th century with the rise of the Kensari kingdom, centred on Bhubaneswar (p244), known in the medieval period as the city of 7000 temples. The Kensaris were succeeded by the Ganga kings, who created some of India's finest temple architecture at Konark (p256) and founded the cult of Jagannath worship at Puri (p253).

During this same period, the Indian monk Padmasambhava (Guru Rinpoche) travelled from northwest India to Tibet, sowing the seeds of Tantric Buddhism as far afield as Nepal and Bhutan. After the decline of the Buddhist civilisations on the plains, monks from Tibet reintroduced Buddhism throughout the Himalaya.

Back in Bengal, the Palas faced a growing threat from the neighbouring Gaur kingdom, and were later defeated by the Buddhist Chandra dynasty from southern Bengal in the 11th century. A century later, the Sena dynasty from Karnataka introduced orthodox Hinduism and spread their language (which was the the prototype for Bengali) deep into Bengal, Orissa and Assam.

Visit the website www.cs.colostate.edu/~malaiya/ashoka.html for a translation of Ashoka's famous rock-carved edicts.

India: A History by John Keay is an astute and readable account of subcontinental history spanning from the Harappan civilisation to Indian independence.

INVADERS FROM THE NORTHWEST

From the 11th century, India encountered waves of Muslim invaders from the northwest. The first wave was led by Mahmud of Ghazni (971–1030), a notorious Afghan warlord who looted the treasures of North India and carted them back to Afghanistan. A century later, Mohammed of Ghur seized Delhi, appointing his general, Qutb-ud-din, as governor and later, sultan.

The forces of Qutb-ud-din pushed out across northern India in a devastating wave. Bihar fell in 1193, and the last Sena king of Bengal, Laxman Sena, was defeated in around 1204. The Devas dynasty clung on in eastern

Bengal for another century, but most of Bengal was incorporated into the Sultanate of Bangala.

Simultaneously, a new dynasty was rising in Assam. In 1228, Sukaphaa, a Shan prince from Burma (Myanmar) defeated the Naga tribes, extending his control to the Brahmaputra Valley. There, he made allegiances with local chieftains and founded a new capital at Charaideo near present-day Sibsagar in 1253. Thus began the Ahom dynasty, one of the longest lived kingdoms in Indian history.

The Ahom dynasty of Assam was one of the longest-lived empires in Indian history – the descendents of Sukaphaa ruled for 589 years.

Over the following centuries, the Ahom pushed west, defeating a series of smaller kingdoms, including the Chutiya and Kacharis of central Assam. The westwards expansion was checked by the kingdom of Koch, which controlled the western part of Kamarupa, extending from West Bengal to western Assam, Meghalaya and Tripura.

Half a country away, the Muslim dynasty founded by Mohammed of Ghur faced its own trials. In the 13th century, Ala-ud-din Khilji and Mohammed Tughlaq pushed the borders of the empire deep into the Hindu heartland of the south, while simultaneously fending off attacks by Mongols from the north.

The last of the great sultans, Firoz Shah, died in 1388 and the fate of the sultanate was sealed when the Mongol leader Tamerlane (Timur) made a devastating raid from Samarkand (in Central Asia) into India in 1398. Tamerlane's sacking of Delhi was truly merciless; some accounts say his soldiers slaughtered every Hindu inhabitant.

The following centuries were marked by unbelievable bloodshed as a succession of rival Muslim rulers sought to conquer the remaining Hindu, Buddhist and Jain strongholds in India, sowing the seeds for the communal violence that still wracks Indian society today.

THE MUGHALS

After the barbarity of the 14th century, a more enlightened age was ushered in by the Mughals. The founder of the Mughal line, Babur (r 1526–30), was a descendant of both Genghis Khan and Tamerlane. In 1525, he marched

MEANWHILE IN THE MOUNTAINS...

The dramatic events unfolding in the plains had a knock-on effect in the mountains of Sikkim, Bhutan and Arunachal Pradesh. Many of these areas were first settled by refugees from the surrounding conflicts. The original settlers of Sikkim were Lepcha tribal people from Assam and Myanmar, who came here in the 13th century, followed by Bhutias (Khambas) fleeing religious strife in Tibet during the 15th century.

The Nyingmapa form of Mahayana Buddhism was brought to Sikkim by Tibetan lamas in 1641. At the height of their powers, the chogyals (kings) ruled over a kingdom extending from eastern Nepal to Darjeeling and the Bengal Hills. However, most of this territory was later lost in wars with Bhutan, Nepal and the British, though Sikkim was nominally ruled by a chogyal right up until 1975.

Bhutan and Arunachal Pradesh have a much older Buddhist history. Padmasambhava introduced Nyinmapa Buddhism to Bhutan in the 8th century, and the Tibetan lama Shabdrung Ngawang Namgyal unified the nation in around 1616. The Monpa tribe came to dominate western Arunachal Pradesh from around AD 500, converting to Gelukpa Buddhism a thousand years later under the influence of lamas from Tibet.

1526	1600
Babur becomes the first Mughal emperor	Britain's Queen Elizabeth I grants a trading charter to the East India Company – the Calcutta depot opens in 1690

into Punjab from Kabul and defeated the sultan of Delhi at the Battle of Panipat in 1526.

Thus was founded the Mughal line, which ruled over much of India until the arrival of the British. Babur was succeeded by Humayun (r 1530–56), who was briefly defeated by Sher Shah of Bihar in 1539 and forced to withdraw to Iran, before returning to conquer Delhi in 1555. His successor Akbar (r 1556–1605) extended the empire until he ruled over a mammoth area. Bengal was seized from the descendents of Sher Shah in 1576 and placed under the rule of appointed governors, before passing to the Nawabs of Murshidabad – local Muslim rulers who accepted the authority of the Mughals.

True to his name, Akbar (which means 'Great' in Arabic) was probably the greatest of the Mughals. As well as being a man of culture, the Great Mughal also had a reputation for fairness in an era of brutality. He saw that the number of Hindus in India was too great to defeat, and sought instead to incorporate the Hindu population as subjects of Mughal India. He also appointed followers of other religions as advisers, generals and administrators.

Nevertheless, the tolerance of Akbar was relative. Throughout his reign, Akbar waged war against kingdoms that refused to bend to his will, and perpetuated the imperialist agenda of his predecessors. Hindus were granted certain rights but forced to live under foreign laws – even today, many Hindus, Buddhists and Jains regard the Mughal era as a time when their culture was under siege.

As in South India, the people of the Northeast continued to resist Mughal expansion. Akbar faced repeated rebellions in the Northeast, and Bengal, Bihar and Orissa swapped hands more times than a stage magician as rival warlords squabbled for control of the eastern frontier. Another ongoing thorn in the side of the Mughals were the Ahom, who were fighting the Koch for control of parts of West Bengal and Assam.

The 16th century also saw the first European interest in the Northeast. Portuguese traders established a trading post in Hooghly in West Bengal in 1579 with permission from the emperor Akbar. Unfortunately, the Portuguese enthusiasm for piracy and siding with rebels against Mughal rule proved too much to bear and the Portuguese were driven from the area in 1666.

Akbar was succeeded by Jehangir (r 1605–27), who dispatched his generals to confront the Ahom in Assam. Despite the disparity in numbers, the Ahom roundly defeated the first invasion attempt in 1615 and allied with the Koch to drive the Mughals from Kamarupa. Jehangir's son Shah Jahan (r 1627–58) – of Taj Mahal fame – faced similar problems in the Northeast, waging a series of campaigns against the Ahom in Assam and Kamarupa. The Mughals finally gave up their expansion into Assam during the reign of Aurangzeb (r 1658–1707), after the Ahom defeated the Mughals in an epic naval battle on the Brahmaputra at the Battle of Saraighat (near Guwahati).

Back in the plains, Aurangzeb faced a growing threat from the Marathas, a warlike Hindu dynasty founded by the charismatic Chhatrapati Shivaji. Between 1646 and 1680 Shivaji confronted the Mughals across most of central India, reclaiming the majority of the Indian plains for Hindu India. At its height, the Maratha kingdom stretched from Karnataka to the Punjab and east as far as Orissa.

With Aurangzeb's death in 1707, the Mughal empire's fortunes rapidly declined. The Mughals lost Delhi in 1739 to Persia's Nadir Shah and successive

The Emperor Akbar formulated a new religion, Deen Ilahi, which combined the best parts of all the faiths he encountered in India.

1707	1757
Aurangzeb, the last of the great Mughal emperors, dies	English forces recapture Calcutta from local nawab in Battle of Plassey

Mughals ruled over smaller and smaller kingdoms. The Maratha expansion westwards was halted in 1761 by Ahmad Shah Durani from Afghanistan, but by then a new power had arrived on the scene – the British Empire.

THE RISE OF EUROPEAN POWER

The British were not the first European power to arrive in India, nor were they the last to leave – both of those 'honours' go to the Portuguese (Goa was only formally handed to India in 1961). However, the Portuguese lacked the resources to maintain a worldwide empire and they were quickly eclipsed by the arrival of the British and French.

Plain Tales from the Raj by Charles Allen (ed) is a fascinating series of interviews with people who played a role in British India on both sides of the table.

The British established their first trading post at Surat in Gujarat in 1613, under the auspices of the East India Company, but the first foray into Bengal – a factory founded at Hooghly in 1651 – was only a limited success. The Muslim Nawabs granted permission for the East India Company to establish a formal trading post in Calcutta in 1690, joining the more established depots at Mumbai (Bombay) and Chennai (Madras).

During the early stages of the colonial era, the British were as much at war with the French and Portuguese as with the rulers of India. The French used their base at Puducherry (Pondicherry) in South India as a base for raids on British depots on the east coast, but the French East India Company scaled down its operations in 1750, effectively removing France as a serious influence on the subcontinent.

BRITISH INDIA

By the early 19th century, India was effectively under the control of the British Raj, although a patchwork of tiny 'princely states' remained nominally independent and governed by their own rulers, the maharajas (or similarly titled princes) and nawabs (Muslim ruling princes or powerful landowners). British bureaucratic models were soon replicated in the Indian government and civil service – a legacy that still exists today – and the British established faithful reproductions of home at hill stations across the subcontinent.

White Mughals by William Dalrymple tells the true, tragic love story of an East India Company soldier who married an Indian Muslim princess, interwoven with harem politics, intrigue and espionage.

From 1784 onwards, the British government began to take a more direct role in supervising affairs in India, although the territory was still administered by the East India Company until 1858. Calcutta (Kolkata) became the capital of British India and the British trade machine went into overdrive. Iron and coal mining were developed, tea plantations were established in the Bengal hills, and spices, coffee and cotton became key crops elsewhere in the country.

Like the Mughals, the British exploited the Bengali system of *zamindars* (landowners) to ease the burden of administration and help with tax collection. While a handful of Bengali families grew fabulously wealthy, the impoverished and landless peasantry were pressed to work as indentured labour, living in vast shantytowns surrounding Calcutta.

The British era also marked the demise of the Ahom dynasty in Assam, which finally succumbed to a Burmese invasion from Mandalay in 1817. Although the Burmese occupation only lasted nine years, it was marked by terrible atrocities against Assamese civilians. Meitei forces from Manipur eventually succeeded in driving the Burmese back, and the British finished the job in 1826.

1817	1858
The Ahom dynasty is defeated in Assam	British government assumes formal control over India; Mohandas (Mahatma) Gandhi is born a year later

Back in Bengal, the first railway in the Northeast started operating out of Calcutta in 1845. Even today, Indian Railways is the world's second-largest employer, providing a living for 1.6 million Indians. The British were also responsible for the postal service, irrigation schemes, drainage programmes to combat malaria, and increased law and order.

Another broadly welcomed development was the abolition of human sacrifice, which was widely practiced by devotees of Shakti (Kali) in the Northeast. The fanatical Thuggee sect is thought to have strangled some 30,000 travellers over a 300-year campaign of terror before they were hunted down by the colonial police in the 1830s. The British also imposed English as the local language of administration, critical in a country with so many different languages. However, this also kept the new rulers at arm's length from the Indian populace.

In 2003, Bengali landowners obtained a high court ruling that the British trader Job Charnock should no longer be officially regarded as the founder of Kolkata.

THE ROAD TO INDEPENDENCE

The desire among many Indians to be free from foreign rule remained. Opposition to the British began to increase at the turn of the 20th century, spearheaded by the Indian National Congress, the country's oldest political party, also known as the Congress Party and Congress (I).

BRITAIN'S SURGE TO POWER

The transformation of the British from traders to governors began almost by accident. After being granted a licence to trade in Bengal by the Mughals, the British East India Company turned its depot at Calcutta (Kolkata) into one of the great success stories of the British Empire. Before long, the 'factories' were starting to take on an increasingly permanent (and fortified) appearance and the local nawab (Muslim ruling prince or powerful landowner) decided that British power had grown far enough.

In June 1756 he attacked Calcutta and locked his British prisoners in a tiny cell – the infamous 'Black Hole of Calcutta' – where many died. In retaliation, Robert Clive, an employee in the military service of the East India Company, led an expedition to retake Calcutta and overthrew the nawab at the Battle of Plassey (now called Palashi) in June 1757. A Muslim general who assisted Clive was placed on the throne, on the understanding that he looked favourably on future British trade deals.

With the British effectively in control of Bengal, the company's agents engaged in a period of unbridled profiteering. When a subsequent nawab took up arms to protect his own interests, he was defeated at the Battle of Baksar in 1764, a victory that confirmed the British as the paramount power in east India. The East India Company took control of Dhaka in 1765, and soon gained control of all the main ports in the Northeast.

The early years of British rule were not happy ones. Between 1769 and 1773, a major drought caused crops to fail across Bengal, leading to a massive famine that killed up to a third of the Bengali population. Expansion of British control began in earnest in 1771, when Warren Hastings was made governor in Bengal. Aided by the implosion of the Mughal empire, Hastings set out to increase the influence of Britain across the subcontinent.

The only serious challengers to British expansion were the Marathas, the Hindu dynasty that drove the Mughals from central India. Ever the statesman, Hastings concluded a series of treaties with local rulers, leaving British soldiers free to pursue their campaign against the French and the Muslim rulers of Mysore before returning to confront the Marathas. The struggle with the Marathas was concluded in 1803, leaving only Punjab (held by the Sikhs) outside British control. Punjab finally fell in 1849 after the two Sikh wars (1845–46 and 1848–49).

1885	**1942**
Founding of the Congress Party	Mahatma Gandhi launches the Quit India campaign, demanding Indian independence

The National Congress met for the first time in 1885 and soon began to push for participation in the government of India. A highly unpopular attempt to partition Bengal in 1905 resulted in mass demonstrations and brought to light Hindu opposition to the division; the Muslim community formed its own league and campaigned for its own say in any future political settlement. As pressure rose, a split emerged in Hindu circles between moderates and radicals, the latter resorting to violence to publicise their aims.

With the outbreak of WWI, the political situation eased. India contributed hugely to the war (over one million Indian volunteers were enlisted and sent overseas, suffering more than 100,000 casualties). The contribution was sanctioned by Congress leaders, who believed that this loyalty would be rewarded after the war was over. No such rewards materialised and disillusion followed.

A wonderful collection of works and teachings by Mahatma Gandhi can be viewed on the websites www.mahatma.org.in, www.mahatma.com and www.gandhiserve.org.

Disturbances were particularly persistent in Punjab and, in April 1919, following riots in Amritsar, a British army contingent was sent to quell the unrest, killing over 1000 unarmed protesters. News of the massacre spread rapidly throughout India, turning huge numbers of otherwise apolitical Indians into Congress supporters.

At this time, the Congress movement found a new leader in Mohandas Gandhi (see the boxed text, p37), who led a brilliant campaign of nonviolent resistance to British rule. However, there were voices calling for more direct action – most notably former Congress leader Subhash Chandra Bose, who created a militaristic opposition party in Bengal, the All India Forward Bloc.

The mass movement led by Gandhi soon gained momentum, but once again communal rivalries rose to the surface. As former rulers, the large

---

THE FIRST WAR OF INDEPENDENCE: THE INDIAN UPRISING

The true causes of the 1857 Indian Uprising – known at the time as the Indian Mutiny but later relabelled as the First War of Indian Independence – have been muddied by subsequent rhetoric. Key factors included the influx of cheap goods, such as textiles, from Britain that destroyed many livelihoods, the dispossession of territories from local rulers, and taxes imposed on landowners.

The uprising started quite unexpectedly at an army barracks in Meerut in Uttar Pradesh on 10 May 1857. A rumour leaked out that a new type of bullet was greased with cow fat or pork fat, taboo to Hindus and Muslims respectively. Since loading a rifle involved biting the end off the waxed cartridge, these rumours provoked considerable unrest. With a singular lack of judgement, the British officers lined up the Indian troops and imprisoned anyone who refused to bite the ends off their bullets.

The following morning, the soldiers of the garrison rebelled, shot their officers and marched to Delhi. Of the 74 Indian battalions of the Bengal Army, seven (one of them Gurkha) remained loyal, 20 were disarmed and the other 47 mutinied. The soldiers and peasants rallied around the ageing Bahadur Shah Zafar – the last ruler of the Mughal dynasty – in Delhi, but the campaign was poorly coordinated and the mutineers were soon suppressed and the nawab deposed.

Almost immediately the East India Company was wound up and direct control of the country was assumed by the British government, which announced its support for the existing rulers of the princely states, claiming they would not interfere in local matters as long as the states remained loyal to the British.

---

15 August 1947	October 1947
India becomes independent and its territories are split between India and Pakistan (later subdivided into Pakistan and Bangladesh)	First India-Pakistan War over Kashmir; three months later Mahatma Gandhi is assassinated in Delhi by a Hindu extremist

Muslim minority retained a degree of autonomy and power under the British, but fears grew that Muslims would be powerless and vulnerable in a Hindu-dominated India.

As in other parts of the empire, the British stoked the flames of communal unrest as a pretext for remaining in India. By the 1930s Muslims began to raise the possibility of a separate Islamic state and the Independence movement became increasingly divided. Political events were partially disrupted by WWII when large numbers of Congress supporters and Independence activists were jailed to prevent disruption to the war effort.

India's Struggle for Independence by Bipan Chandra expertly chronicles the history of India from 1857 to 1947.

For Subhash Chandra Bose, the time had come to fight. Escaping from prison, Bose fled to Germany and sought backing from the Axis powers for a military strike against the British in the Northeast. In 1943, he led the Indian National Army (INA) against the British in Burma and later in Manipur and Kohima. Unfortunately, Bose's strategy was based on desertions from the regular Indian army that failed to materialise, and the campaign foundered. After the defeat of the Japanese at Imphal and Kohima – two of the bloodiest battles of the Pacific campaign in WWII – Bose fled towards Japan. Official reports state that Bose died en route in a plane crash over Taiwan in 1945, though many nationalists refute the claims.

INDEPENDENCE & THE PARTITION OF INDIA

The Labour Party victory in the British elections in July 1945 dramatically altered the political landscape of India. For the first time, Indian independence was accepted as a legitimate goal. By this stage, however, the Independence movement was split into two clear camps. Mohammed Ali Jinnah, the leader of the Muslim League, championed a separate Islamic state, while the Congress Party, led by Jawaharlal Nehru, campaigned for an independent greater India.

You've probably seen *Gandhi,* starring Ben Kingsley and 300,000 extras, but watch it again because few films capture the grand canvas that is India in tracing the country's path to independence.

In early 1946 a British mission failed to bring the two sides together and the country slid closer towards civil war. A 'Direct Action Day', called by the Muslim League in August 1946, led to the mass slaughter of Hindus in Calcutta, which prompted reprisals against Muslims. With their plans to 'divide and rule' coming apart at the seams, the nervous British government made the momentous decision that independence would come by June 1948.

To appease the Muslim League, a decision was made to divide the country; Gandhi was the only staunch opponent, correctly prophesying the bloodshed that would follow. Faced with increasing civil violence, the British viceroy Lord Mountbatten made the precipitous decision to bring forward Independence to 15 August 1947.

The decision to divide the country into separate Hindu and Muslim territories was immensely tricky. Some areas were clearly Hindu or Muslim, but others had evenly mixed populations, and there were isolated 'islands' of communities in areas predominantly settled by other religions. Moreover, the two overwhelmingly Muslim regions were on opposite sides of the country and, therefore, Pakistan would inevitably have an eastern and western half divided by Hindu India.

The BBC radio series *This Sceptred Isle* provides a vivid description of the fall of British India. A CD of the series is available online from www.bbcshop.com – request Empire Volume 3.

Predictably, Partition was a disaster. Calcutta, with its Hindu majority, port facilities and jute mills, was divided from East Bengal, which had a Muslim majority, large-scale jute production, no mills and no port facilities. One million Bengalis became refugees in the mass movement across the new border. The Muslim League also attempted to claim the entire Northeast states, but in the end only the Muslim-majority district of Sylhet joined East Pakistan.

The problem was far worse in Punjab, where communal tensions were already running at fever pitch. The creation of West Pakistan led to ethnic cleansing on an unprecedented scale. Trains full of Hindus and Sikhs fleeing east were held up and slaughtered by Muslim mobs, and Muslims, fleeing westward, suffered the same fate.

The army that was sent to maintain order proved totally inadequate and, at times, all too ready to join the sectarian carnage. By the time the Punjab chaos had run its course, more than 10 million people had changed sides; at least 500,000 were killed in communal violence and Pakistan emerged as an almost purely Muslim state.

The Proudest Day – India's Long Road to Independence by Anthony Read and David Fisher is an engaging account of India's pre-Independence period.

INDEPENDENT INDIA

Jawaharlal Nehru, independent India's first prime minister, tried to steer India towards a policy of nonalignment, balancing cordial relations with Britain and Commonwealth membership with moves towards the former USSR – a response to the growing belligerence of communist China and US military support for Pakistan.

Railway buffs should visit the website of the Indian Railways Fan Club (www.irfca.org), which includes a video gallery on the world's largest rail network.

Former British Assam was crudely chopped up into the seven Northeast states, sowing the seeds for much of the tribal unrest that was to follow. In 1962, India and China went to war over the North-East Frontier Area (NEFA; now the Northeast States), claimed by China as part of its dubious claim to all lands formerly occupied by Tibet. Although China eventually withdrew its forces, the Chinese government still refuses to acknowledge the Indian claim to Sikkim and Arunachal Pradesh.

Wars with Pakistan in 1965 (over Kashmir) and 1971 (over Bangladesh) also contributed to a sense among many Indians of having enemies on all sides. In the midst of it all, the hugely popular Nehru died in 1964 and his daughter Indira Gandhi (no relation to Mahatma Gandhi) was elected as prime minister in 1966.

Perhaps the most momentous event in her reign was the 1971 war with Pakistan. Since Partition, West Pakistan had steadily increased its power, while East Pakistan was increasingly treated as a vassal state. In response to growing calls for separation West Pakistan began a brutal military campaign against East Pakistan, killing as many as three million people – labelled genocide by Bengalis. India stepped in on the side of East Pakistan and Bangladesh finally won its independence on 16 December 1971.

The Nehrus and the Gandhis is Tariq Ali's astute portrait-history of these families and the India over which they cast their long shadow.

However, Indira Gandhi was a controversial leader, and many of her policies became notorious – most famously a forced programme of sterilisation for the poor. In 1975, facing growing unrest, she declared a state of emergency (which later became known as the Emergency), boosting the economy, but causing even more unrest through slum clearances and the arrest of political opponents.

Her government was bundled out of office in the 1977 elections in favour of the Janata People's Party (JPP), led by Jaya Prakash Narayan, an ageing Gandhian socialist who died soon after. With no viable leader to replace 'JP', the Janata party fell apart and the 1980 election brought Indira Gandhi back to power with an even larger majority.

1992	1998
Hindu hardliners destroy mosque in Ayodhya, unleashing riots across the country	Bharatiya Janata Party (BJP) wins national elections and conducts nuclear tests, almost triggering war with Pakistan

CONTINUITY IN CONGRESS

In 1984, Indira Gandhi was assassinated by her Sikh bodyguards, following an ill-considered decision to send in the Indian army to flush out armed Sikh separatists from Amritsar's Golden Temple. The following Hindu-Sikh riots that left more than 3000 people dead (mostly Sikhs) effectively ended the quest for a Sikh homeland.

Indira Gandhi's son Rajiv, a former pilot, became the next prime minister, with Congress winning in a landslide victory in 1984. However, after a brief golden reign, he was dragged down by corruption scandals and the inability

MAHATMA GANDHI

One of the great human beings of the 20th century, Mohandas Karamchand Gandhi was born on 2 October 1869 in Porbandar, Gujarat. After studying in London (1888–91), he worked as a barrister in South Africa, where he rallied against discrimination towards non-Whites and soon became the spokesman for the Indian community.

Gandhi returned to India in 1915 to spread his doctrine of *ahimsa* (nonviolence). Within a year, Gandhi had won his first victory, defending farmers in Bihar from exploitation, which earned him the title 'Mahatma' (Great Soul). The passage of the Rowlatt Acts in 1919 – which allowed political cases to be tried without juries – spurred him to further action and he organised a national protest, which was curtailed by the shocking massacre at Amritsar.

By 1920 Gandhi was a key figure in the Indian National Congress, and he coordinated a national campaign of noncooperation or *satyagraha* (passive resistance) to British rule. In early 1930, Gandhi defied the hated salt tax – introduced by the Mughals but perpetuated by the British to raise money from the native population – leading several thousand followers on a march to the coast of Gujarat, where they made their own salt. Not for the first time, he was imprisoned.

Released in 1931 to represent the Indian National Congress at the second Round Table Conference in London, Gandhi won the hearts of the British people but failed to gain any real concessions from the government. He was jailed again on his return to India and immediately began a hunger strike, aimed at forcing his fellow Indians to accept the rights of the Untouchables (the lowest caste or 'casteless', for whom the most menial tasks are reserved; formerly known as Harijan, now Dalit). A new policy on the Untouchables was eventually hammered out, but not before Gandhi was on the verge of death.

Disillusioned with politics, Gandhi resigned his parliamentary seat in 1934 and devoted himself to rural education. He returned spectacularly to the fray in 1942 with the Quit India campaign, in which he urged the British to leave India immediately. His actions were deemed subversive and he and most of the Congress leadership were imprisoned.

In the bargaining that followed the end of WWII, Gandhi was largely excluded and watched helplessly as plans were made to partition the country – a decision that he knew would lead to generations of bloodshed. While the rest of the country was celebrating, Gandhi returned to Calcutta to calm intercommunity tensions and promote peace. His last political action was a fast almost to the point of death to protest against intercommunal violence.

Gandhi stood almost alone in urging tolerance and the preservation of a single India, but he was perceived by many Hindus as too willing to make concessions to Muslims. On his way to a prayer meeting in Delhi on 30 January 1948, he was assassinated by a Hindu zealot.

Today, Gandhi is best remembered for his incredible bravery and steadfast adherence to the principles of nonviolence. Conceived at the height of the struggle for Independence, one quote from Gandhi adroitly sums up the philosophy of *ahimsa*: 'There are many causes that I am prepared to die for but no causes that I am prepared to kill for.'

May 2004	24 May 2005
Congress Party wins national elections and Manmohan Singh is installed as prime minister	Indian government signs a ceasefire with Bodo separatists in Assam, ending 19 years of conflict

to quell communal unrest. In 1991, he was assassinated by a gunman from a Sri Lankan armed separatist group in Tamil Nadu.

Narasimha Rao led the Congress Party to victory at the polls in 1991. In 1992 the economy was given an enormous boost after the finance minister, Manmohan Singh, floated the rupee against a basket of 'hard' currencies. The economy was opened up to foreign investment, with multinationals drawn by an enormous pool of educated professionals and relatively low wages, particularly in the fields of Information Technology (IT) and the call centre business, which now employs thousands of Indians.

For an introduction to the complex rebellions of the Northeast States, read *Strangers of the Mist* by Sanjoy Hazarika.

After the 1996 national elections, the Hindu-revivalist Bharatiya Janata Party (BJP) emerged as the largest party, but secular parties banded together to defeat its attempts to build a viable coalition. However, with the upsurge of Hindu nationalism, the BJP won the elections in 1998 and again in 1999, becoming the first nonsecular party to hold national power in India.

Communal relations deteriorated even further during the BJP era. In 1992, Hindu hardliners destroyed the Babri mosque, thought to be constructed over

SEPARATIST CONFLICTS

The merging of the princely states into mainstream India at Independence created a whole new set of problems. Granted considerable autonomy by the British, most of the princely states were reduced to the status of neglected backwaters in independent India. Tribes who had previously governed their own affairs suddenly found themselves bound by Indian laws and taxes and marginalised in local politics. The aftermath of Partition also cast a long shadow – Hindu and Muslim communities across India were wracked by mutual mistrust and resentment and other minorities began to campaign for increased representation and autonomy.

Frequently, these campaigns spilled over into violence. Facing neglect from central government and competition for resources from migrants spilling over the border from Bangladesh, many tribal groups in the Northeast took up arms to fight for independent homelands. From the late 1950s onwards, Naga tribals in Manipur and Nagaland began a brutal independence campaign that continues to this day, despite ceasefires with many of the main rebel groups.

Assam has faced a separatist struggle from the Bodo people in the west (now mainly resolved) and a separate campaign for a socialist Assamese homeland in the east, with continuing violence from the United Liberation Front of Asom (ULFA). Meghalaya and Mizoram saw their own tribal rebellions before the rebel groups were bought into the political fold. Tripura continues to face regular attacks by tribal rebels from the National Liberation Front of Tripura (NLFT) and All Tripura Tiger Force (ATTF). Almost all of the insurgents operating in the Northeast are thought to receive clandestine backing from Pakistan.

In Kashmir, the violence erupted immediately after Independence. Despite ruling over a predominantly Muslim population, the local maharaja refused to sign up with either India or Pakistan until an invasion of Pakistani Pashtun tribes persuaded him to throw in his lot with India. The first India-Pakistan War began just a few months after Independence and the violence only ceased when the UN divided Kashmir in half at the 'Line of Control'.

Both India and Pakistan still claim Kashmir in its entirety, and Muslim unrest in Indian Kashmir spilled over into armed rebellion in 1989. Since then, nearly 80,000 people have been killed in attacks by armed militants and raids by the Indian Army. Most of the deadly militant bombings taking place around India today are linked to the Kashmir cause. Kashmir is still an issue that divides Indian society, with most Hindus supporting the status quo and most Muslims supporting Kashmiri independence or union with Pakistan.

8 October 2005	July 2006
Thousands killed in a devastating earthquake in Kashmir; in the aftermath, India and Pakistan increase cooperation.	The Nathu pass between Sikkim and China reopens after 44 years, marking a thaw in Indo-Chinese relations.

the ruins of a Hindu temple marking the birthplace of Rama. Rioting flared across the country, egged on by extremist Hindu politicians, with Muslims bearing the brunt of the violence. Simultaneously, Muslim radicals began a deadly campaign of bomb attacks against Hindus and the Indian government, citing the riots and events in Kashmir as motivation. Another wave of anti-Muslim violence flared in Gujarat after dozens of Hindu pilgrims died on a train fire at Godhra – blamed, with no real evidence, on Muslims by Hindu activists.

In 1997 KR Narayanan became India's president, the first member of the lowest Untouchable Hindu caste to hold the position.

Meanwhile, India-Pakistan relations reached a new low in 1998 when the BJP government detonated five nuclear devices in the deserts of Rajasthan. Pakistan responded with its own nuclear tests, then launched an incursion into Kashmir at Kargil. The spectre of nuclear conflict loomed until the UN talked the two countries back from the brink.

The Congress Party eventually swept back to power in 2004 under the leadership of another Gandhi – Sonia, the Italian-born wife of the late Rajiv Gandhi – and former finance minister, Manmohan Singh, who went on to become prime minister.

Of the 545 seats in the Lok Sabha (Lower House of India's bicameral parliament), 120 are reserved for Scheduled Castes and Tribes.

Singh made a personal mission of easing relations with Pakistan and quelling the conflicts in Kashmir and the Northeast states. Massive investment was funnelled into industries in the Northeast – including hydroelectricity – and a ceasefire was signed with the Assamese Bodo rebels (see p205) in 2004. An existing ceasefire with Naga rebels was strengthened and overtures were made to rebel groups to quell the ongoing violence.

In 2004 Sikh Prime Minister, Manmohan Singh, became the first member of any religious minority community to hold India's highest elected office.

Talks with Pakistan initially produced positive results, with the two sides bought together by the devastating Kashmir earthquake in October 2005. However, talks took a setback following a series of deadly attacks by Islamic militants in 2006, including train bombings in Mumbai that killed 200 people. Events in 2007 followed a similar pattern, with another devastating train bomb on the Delhi–Lahore express. With Pakistan seemingly unable – or unwilling – to rein in the militants, hopes for lasting peace remain distant and insubstantial.

---

11 July 2006

Bomb attacks on commuter trains in Mumbai set back negotiations between India and Pakistan.

March 2007

Police suppress farmers' protests in West Bengal leading to massive strikes

The Culture

THE NATIONAL PSYCHE

Travellers often comment that the Northeast is the least 'Indian' part of India. Dozens of different tribal, religious and ethnic communities are spread out across the Northeastern states and, as a result, the sense of national identity is less coherent here than in other parts of India.

The people of the Northeast tend to define themselves primarily by their tribe or ethnic group, and the sense of being part of greater India decreases the further east you travel. Most Bengalis and Orissans are happy to call themselves Indian, whereas tribal people from Nagaland or Manipur see themselves as Nagas first and Indians second, if at all.

Nevertheless, certain common traits unite people across the region. One of the first things travellers will notice is how tightly everyday life is intertwined with spiritual life. Ritual and rites govern most aspects of day-to-day life, from the morning *puja* (prayers) to the way shopkeepers thank the gods for the first transaction of the day.

Along with religion, family lies at the heart of Indian society. Marriage and children are the most important goals in life for men and women. Although growing numbers of young Indians are choosing to marry for love, especially in larger cities, the majority of marriages are arranged by parents, though this process is often misunderstood in the West.

India is still a profoundly male-dominated society. Men – usually the breadwinners – are considered the head of the household, and the extended family also plays an important role in family decisions. The Western-style nuclear family, living independently of the previous generation, is rarely seen outside of Kolkata (Calcutta) and other metropolitan areas in the Northeast.

With religion and family considered so sacrosanct, travellers can expect to be grilled constantly about these subjects, especially in rural areas. As well as being asked about your home country, you may be asked about your religion, marital status, age, qualifications, profession and income, and often how much various items in your luggage cost in your home country. Most of this is natural curiosity, and it is perfectly acceptable to decline to answer or to ask the same questions back.

National pride is another India-wide characteristic, though in tribal areas this is often replaced by regional or tribal pride. Indians are justly proud of their history, their cultural and social achievements, and their growing status as a world power. This can occasionally spill over into overt nationalism, particularly where relations between India and Pakistan are concerned.

India's nuclear arsenal is another source of national pride, though the relationship between Indians and nuclear weapons is less enthusiastic than on the Pakistan side of the border. Relations with Bangladesh tend to be more cordial, though economic migration into India has led to growing resentment in some parts of the Northeast.

One thing that can be disconcerting is the enthusiasm Indians have for everything modern. Fads like American fast food and mobile phones are sweeping across the country and many locals have a rather rose-tinted vision of what life is like in the West. Don't be surprised if you get drawn into some convoluted conversations about the relative merits of India and your home country – with you standing up for India!

Nevertheless, the speed of change in Indian society is quite breathtaking. The last decade has seen a seismic shift in the lifestyles of tens of millions of Indians, with growing wealth and increasing disposable income. Gadgets and

The Indian Constitution recognises 573 Scheduled Tribes – there are 23 tribes just in Assam and 65 in Arunachal Pradesh.

Human sacrifice was common in the Northeast until the colonial era, linked to the ancient cult of *shakti* (female spiritual power) worship.

air travel have finally come into reach of the masses and people are throwing themselves into the 21st century with gusto.

LIFESTYLE
Traditional Culture
MARRIAGE, BIRTH & DEATH

Marriage is seen as the pinnacle of personal achievement in India and choosing the right partner is the most important decision in life. Although 'love marriages' are becoming common in larger cities, arranged marriage is still the norm. However, the process is rarely one-sided – although parents play the major role in selecting candidates for marriage, prospective brides and grooms usually have a say throughout the proceedings.

Typically, discreet inquiries are made within the local community. If a suitable match is not found, families turn to professional matchmakers, or place advertisements in newspapers or on the internet. Horoscopes are checked and, if propitious, there's a meeting between the two families. If all goes well, the couple are allowed to meet to see if they get on before things proceed to marriage.

The legal marriage age in India is 18, though girls marry earlier in many rural areas. Dowries are still a key issue in many arranged marriages, despite being illegal under Indian law. Many families plunge into debt to raise the required cash and there are tragic reports of brides being murdered over inadequate dowry payments – India saw 6787 registered dowry-related deaths in 2005.

In Hindu weddings, the ceremony is officiated over by a Brahmin priest and the marriage is formalised when the couple walk around a sacred fire seven times. The celebrations tend to be quite energetic – in traditional weddings, the groom leads the wedding party through the streets on horseback and musical accompaniment is provided by a raucous marching band who wear lanterns on their hats to illuminate the procession.

Islamic weddings have their own special rules. On the eve of the wedding ceremony, henna patterns known as *mehndi* are drawn on the hands and neck of the bride by female relatives. For the actual *nikaah* (wedding ceremony) male and female guests are separated and passages are read from the Quran. The wedding is formalised when the bride and groom read aloud from the *nikaahnama* (wedding contracts).

Other religions have their own unique rites. Buddhist weddings are presided over by a senior lama (monk) from the local monastery; two candles are lit

Matchmaking has embraced the cyber age with websites such as www .shaadi.com and www .bharatmatrimony .com catering to tens of millions of Indians and Non-Resident Indians (NRIs).

Based on Rabindranath Tagore's novel, *Chokher Bali*, directed by Rituparno Ghosh, is a poignant film about a young widow living in early-20th-century Bengal who challenges the 'rules of widowhood' – something unthinkable in that era.

TWO BOYS FOR EVERY GIRL?

Like neighbouring China, India is facing a shortage of women. In many states in the Northeast, there are more boys than girls, causing severe problems when male suitors go looking for brides. In parts of Arunachal Pradesh the sex ratio is just three females to four males – ie 25% more boys than girls.

In more developed parts of India, this disparity in numbers has been put down to selective abortions of females, but the sex ratio has been skewed for centuries in tribal areas by the high death rate of women from disease and complications in childbirth. Several tribes have come up with a unique solution: polyandry – women marrying more than one husband.

Most common in Buddhist tribes like the Lepchas of Sikkim and the Monpas, Khambas and Membas of Arunachal Pradesh, fraternal polyandry involves several brothers marrying the same wife. Among other advantages, polyandry keeps family agricultural estates intact from generation to generation and ensures that a man is always around to help the family while the other brothers are away herding yaks in remote parts of the countryside!

symbolising the union of the two families and the couple read out their responsibilities to each other from a Buddhist text called the *Sigilovdda Sutta*.

In big cities, such as Kolkata, the average cost of a wedding is pegged at around US$12,000.

The tribes of the Northeast states have their own rituals. In Tripura, the groom must enter the house of his prospective bride and serve her family for up to a year to prove he has the skills to care for their daughter. Naga weddings are nominally Christian, but tribal customs persist, including the passing of goods between families to seal the marriage contract.

Divorce is permitted by Indian law but condemned by society. Divorced men suffer few consequences, but women may be completely ostracised, even by their own families. Among the higher castes, widows are expected not to remarry and are admonished to wear white, and lead pious, celibate lives – see p55 for more on the role of women in India. By contrast, many tribes in the Northeast grant divorced women an automatic settlement of land and property.

As a rule, most Indian women live with their husband's family once married and assume the household duties outlined by their mother-in-law. Not surprisingly, the mother-daughter-in-law relationship can be a prickly one, as reflected in the many Indian TV soap operas that revolve around this theme.

DOS & DON'TS

Like the rest of India, the Northeast has many time-honoured traditions, and things get even more complicated when you factor in tribal customs. You won't be expected to get everything 'right', but common sense and courtesy will take you a long way. If in doubt, watch what the locals do, or simply ask.

Dressing conservatively (both women and men) always wins a warm response from locals – women should also read p317. Refrain from kissing and cuddling in public as this is frowned upon by Indian society. Nudity in public is definitely not on, and you should cover up (eg with shorts and a T-shirt) even when swimming.

Religious Etiquette

Whenever visiting a sacred site, always dress and behave respectfully – don't wear shorts or sleeveless tops (this applies to men and women) and refrain from smoking. Loud and intrusive behaviour isn't appreciated, and neither are public displays of affection.

Before entering any holy place, remove your shoes (tip the shoe-minder a few rupees when retrieving them) and check if photography is allowed. It does no harm to ask if it's OK to enter before stepping over the threshold. You're permitted to wear socks in most places of worship. Religious etiquette advises against touching locals on the head, or directing the soles of your feet at a person, religious shrine or image of a deity. Touching any image of a deity is frowned on if not done with the proper respect.

Head cover (for women and sometimes men) is required at some places of worship (especially gurdwaras), so carry a scarf just to be on the safe side. There are some sites that don't admit women – particularly mosques – and some that deny entry to non-adherents of their faith – inquire in advance. Women may be required to sit apart from men and some shrines have dedicated entrances only to be used by women. Some Jain and Hindu temples request that leather items are left outside, and menstruating women may also be forbidden from entering.

Greetings

The handshake is the most common greeting between men in India, though there are certain rules. Because the left hand is used for personal ablutions, always shake with the right. Generally, women bow with the hands brought together at the chest or head level instead of shaking hands.

When Indians greet someone older they will often touch their feet as a sign of respect, but foreigners are not expected to follow this ritual. Before entering tribal villages in the Northeast

The birth of a child is another momentous occasion, with its own set of special ceremonies, which take place at various auspicious times during the early years of childhood, including the casting of the first horoscope, name-giving, the first solid food and the first haircut.

Hindus cremate their dead, and funeral ceremonies are designed to purify and console both the living and the deceased. An important aspect of the proceedings is *sharadda* – paying respect to one's ancestors by offering water and rice cakes – repeated annually. After the cremation the ashes are collected and, 13 days after the death (when blood relatives are deemed ritually pure), a member of the family scatters them in a holy river or the ocean.

Indian Buddhists also cremate their dead, while Muslims bury the dead in graves with a formal service of Islamic verses. All of the tribes have their own funeral rites, linked to religion and tribal customs.

THE CASTE SYSTEM

Although the caste system is weakening, it still wields considerable power in India, especially in rural areas. The caste that Hindus are born into will largely determine their social standing, as well as their vocational and

---

states, you may need to seek an audience with the local chieftain – the rules are complex, so it's best to travel with a guide who can make the arrangements.

Eating Etiquette

When visiting someone's home it's considered good manners to remove your shoes before entering the house and to wash your hands before the main meal. Wait to be served food or until you are invited to help yourself – if you're unsure about protocol, simply wait for your host to direct you.

It's customary to use your right hand for eating as the left hand is used for unsavoury actions. In many Indian communities, food that has touched someone else's mouth is ritually impure – never offer someone anything that you have put to your lips. When drinking from a shared water container, hold it slightly above your mouth (thus avoiding contact between your lips and the mouth of the container).

When eating in a restaurant, there is an etiquette to paying the bill. If you are invited by someone else, the assumption is that they will pick up the tab. Conversely, India is famous for hangers-on who befriend foreigners in the hope of a free drink or meal – you'll have to use your judgement depending on the situation.

Photography Etiquette

Exercise sensitivity when taking photos of people, especially women, who may find it offensive. Be sure to obtain permission in advance. Taking photos inside a shrine, at a funeral, at a religious ceremony or of people publicly bathing (including rivers) can be offensive – so once again, ask first. Flash photography may be prohibited in certain areas of a shrine, or may not be permitted at all.

Other Traveller Tips

Because of the cultural gap, many locals may be unsure what kind of information you are after when you ask questions. Always try to phrase questions to encourage the exact response you are looking for. When seeking directions, ask 'which way' rather than 'is this the way'. When checking transport times, ask what time is the 'next', 'first' or 'last' service, rather than just saying 'what time is the bus'. It's also worth noting that the commonly used sideways wobble of the head can mean anything from yes to no, maybe, or I have no idea.

marriage prospects. Castes are further divided into thousands of *jati,* social communities that are often linked to specific occupations. Conservative Hindus will only marry someone of the same *jati.*

Caste is the basic social structure of Hindu society. Living a righteous life and fulfilling your *dharma* (moral duty) raises your chances of being born into a higher caste and thus into better circumstances. Hindus are born into one of four *varnas* (castes): Brahmin (priests and teachers), Kshatriya (warriors), Vaishya (merchants) and Shudra (labourers).

Beneath the four main castes are the Dalits (formerly known as Untouchables), who hold menial jobs such as sweepers and latrine cleaners. At various times, the Dalits have also been known as the 'Depressed Classes' and 'Other Backward Classes', which gives some indication of their status in society. Most of the Adivasis (tribal people) of the Northeast also fall into the catch-all grouping of 'Scheduled Castes and Tribes' under the Indian Constitution.

Over the centuries, many Dalits have sought to change their status by adopting another faith. The low status of many Indian Muslims today is largely a consequence of their historic origins as low-caste converts from Hinduism. Even today, Muslim communities in India are bound by the same notions of *jati* that govern Hindu society.

To improve the Dalits position, the government reserves a quota of public-sector jobs, parliamentary seats and university places exclusively for members of the Scheduled Castes and Tribes, accounting for almost 50% of sought-after government jobs. Although greatly appreciated by Dalits, the system is often criticised for unfairly blocking jobs and college places to people who would otherwise have got these positions on merit.

At the bottom of the social heap are the Denotified Tribes – a diverse group of tribal people condemned as being 'addicted to the systematic commission of non-bailable offences' under a perverse British colonial law. These people were known as the Criminal Tribes right up until 1952. Many are nomadic or seminomadic tribes, forced by the wider community to eke out a living on society's fringes, particularly in rural areas of Bihar and Orissa.

PILGRIMAGE
Devout Hindus are expected to go on *yatra* (pilgrimage) at least once a year to implore the gods or goddesses to grant a wish, to take the ashes of a cremated relative to a holy river or to gain spiritual merit. The Northeast has hundreds of pilgrimage sites linked to geographical locations from Hindu legends, and pilgrims from the Northeast make journeys across the country.

Muslims make pilgrimages to shrines within India, and also try to make the trip to Mecca in Saudi Arabia once in their lifetime. You can recognise *hajis* – pilgrims who have been to Mecca – by their henna-dyed beards. Pilgrimages are less important to the Northeast's tribes, but Buddhists often travel to sites associated with the Buddha, both in India and across the border in Nepal, Tibet and Bhutan.

Most festivals are a magnet for pilgrims, and the resulting crowds can be unbelievable. Every year, hundreds of people are crushed to death in stampedes at religious gatherings – see p297 for information on visiting festivals safely.

Contemporary Issues
SEPARATISM
All seven Northeast states were originally part of the British administrative district of Assam, but the boundaries set in place at Independence have been a source of conflict ever since. Most of the tribal groups in the Northeast face

---

Two insightful books about India's caste system are *Interrogating Caste* by Dipankar Gupta and *Translating Caste* edited by Tapan Basu.

High-caste Indians may refuse to shake hands with anyone who is not a Brahmin – this is a result of taboos about ritual purity and is not intended to be rude.

discrimination from mainstream society, and many are directly persecuted by larger ethnic and religious groups. Separatist movements have sprung up across the Northeast, with dozens of insurgent armies fighting for an independent tribal homeland.

The problems have been exacerbated by competition for resources from economic migrants from Bangladesh and money flowing to rebels from Pakistan. The Indian government has also fuelled the unrest through heavy-handed policing and by failing to represent the interests of tribal communities.

Some conflicts have been resolved as rebels have been integrated within the political framework – most notably in Mizoram, which was wracked by violence throughout the 1980s. The Bodo separatist movement in Assam and the Naga rebellion in Nagaland also seem to be moving towards a political solution.

However, dozens more conflicts remain unresolved and rebel attacks pose an ongoing risk to travellers – see p298 and p194 for information on safe travel in the Northeast states.

For an introduction to the diverse tribes of the Northeast, read *The Seven Sisters of India* by Peter van Ham and Aglaja Stirm – it's widely available in India.

HIV/AIDS

According to the latest reports, India has the world's highest number of people with HIV – there are currently 5.7 million reported cases across the country, though infection figures may be much higher as many people do not come forward for treatment. Apart from sex workers and truck drivers, intravenous drug users also fall into the high-risk category, particularly in the Northeast, which is flooded with drugs from Myanmar's 'Golden Triangle'.

As in Africa, the problem is made worse by poverty, lack of education and the refusal of men to use condoms, a position reinforced by the teaching of

---

TRADITIONAL INDIAN ATTIRE

The most distinctive piece of clothing for Indian women is the sari, a single piece of cloth between 5m and 9m long that is ingeniously tucked and pleated into place without the need for pins or buttons. Indian women wear the sari with a *choli* (tight-fitting blouse) and drawstring petticoat. Saris come in myriad colours and styles, but tying the sari is an artform and travellers tend to buy saris as souvenirs rather than daily wear.

An easier piece of attire for foreigners is the *salwar kameez,* a long dresslike shirt and loose flowing trousers accompanied by a dupatta (long scarf). This is the most popular piece of female clothing in Indian cities and *salwar kameez* come in a wonderful range of fabrics and designs. Wearing one can be a great way to break down the divide between travellers and locals.

Traditional attire for men includes the dhoti – a loose white garment pulled up between the legs like a loincloth – and the lungi – a simple sarong in plain white or coloured checks. The lungi is particularly associated with South India; people wearing lungis in the Northeast are usually migrant workers from the south or immigrants from Bangladesh.

Different religions have their own costume – Muslim women often wear the all-enveloping black burka or the *niqab* (face veil), linked to a strict interpretation of the Islamic requirement for modesty. There is a growing debate about whether covering the face is actually a requirement of Islam or just a custom perpetuated by male-dominated societies.

Buddhists tend to wear modern clothing, except for monks, who wear dark red robes over a saffron-coloured shirt. The tribes of the Northeast are rapidly abandoning their traditional way of life, but you can still find villages where traditional costume is the norm. Tribal costume focuses on handloom fabrics, traditional jewellery, and grass or basketware hats and bags. Many tribes carry ceremonial swords, and tattoos and tribal piercings are still common among the older generation – see the Northeast States chapter (p191) for more information.

Christian missionaries. Sexually transmitted hepatitis infections are also soaring and India's outmoded anti-gay laws (see below) hamper treatment and education. See also p338.

CHILD LABOUR

Despite national legislation prohibiting child labour, India is believed to have 60 million child labourers – the highest rate in the world. Poorly enforced laws and the lack of a social security system are cited as major causes of the problem. Child labour is driven as much by poverty as by exploitation; many families cannot afford to support their children and hence are forced to send them out to work to avoid starving.

Around 53% of India's child labourers work in agriculture, the main livelihood in the Northeast, and others are pressed into work on construction sites or in factories picking rags and making cigarettes, fireworks, bricks and carpets. A particular problem in the Northeast is young girls being traded as prostitutes or used to make pornographic films to provide money for insurgents.

Most attempts to target employers have failed through lack of enforcement, but children (aged below 14) were banned from working as labourers in households and the hospitality trade in 2006 – expanding on an existing ban on children in 'hazardous jobs'. Employers can be punished with fines and the government has started a programme of rehabilitation for displaced child labourers.

However, many are sceptical about this 'rehabilitation'. Without compulsory education and an economic alternative to child labour for the poor, these laws may just move children from one industry to another, or drive them onto the streets as beggars or criminals.

GAY & LESBIAN ISSUES

India is believed to have between 70 and 100 million gay, lesbian and transgender people, but Section 377 of the national legislation forbids 'carnal intercourse against the order of nature' (that is, anal intercourse). The penalty for transgression can be anything up to life imprisonment plus a fine. Although there are few prosecutions, the law is widely used to harass and blackmail gay people.

While the more liberal sections of society in Kolkata and other big cities are becoming more tolerant of homosexuality, gay life is still largely suppressed. Avoiding marriage and children is a major taboo, and most gay people stay in the closet for fear of being disowned by their families and society.

In 2006 more than 100 high-profile personalities, including Nobel prizewinning economist, Amartya Sen, and writers Vikram Seth and Arundhati Roy, signed an open letter supporting a legal challenge to Section 377 at

Children contribute 33% of household income in tea-producing areas of West Bengal and Assam.

The government-run National AIDS Control Organisation has more information on India's AIDS crisis – see www .nacoonline.org.

Read more about hijras *in* The Invisibles *by Zia Jaffrey and* Ardhanarishvara the Androgyne *by Dr Alka Pande.*

HIJRAS

India's most visible nonheterosexual group is the *hijras,* a caste of transvestites and eunuchs who dress in women's clothing. Some are gay, some are hermaphrodites and some were unfortunate enough to be kidnapped and castrated as children. In Indian society, *hijras* operate as a third sex, working mainly as prostitutes and as wandering entertainers for Hindu weddings and family celebrations. However, discrimination is widespread and *hijras* are one of the groups most at risk from HIV/AIDS. A number of Indian and international NGOs have recently taken up the cause of educating *hijra* communities about HIV/AIDS, and promoting understanding of *hijras* in mainstream society – see www.saathii.org/hiv_services/glbtq.html for a list.

INDIA'S BOOMING ECONOMY

According to some studies, India's GDP could overtake France and Italy by 2020 – partly a result of the meteoric rise of Information Technology (IT) and outsourcing, where Western call centres relocate to India to take advantage of low labour costs. The IT industry already employs one million Indians, with a further two million benefiting indirectly, and the outsourcing industry was valued at US$10 billion in 2006.

The new wealth created by these industries is creating a revolution in a country that previously depended on agriculture and handloom textiles as its main industries. However, wealth has been concentrated in boom cities such as Bengaluru (Bangalore) and Hyderabad, nicknamed 'Cyberabad' by locals. The main benefits to the Northeast have been increased services on budget airlines and massive investment in hydroelectricity to provide power for all the new computers.

---

the Delhi High Court – however, the court deliberations are likely to roll on for years.

For details about gay support groups and publications/websites, see p302.

POVERTY

Although the quality of life for most Indians has increased massively since Independence, India remains one of the most impoverished countries in the world. An estimated 350 million (and growing) Indians live below the poverty line, most in rural areas.

According to government figures, India's three worst performing states (in economic terms) are Bihar, Orissa and Assam. The main causes of poverty are illiteracy, dependency on subsistence agriculture and overpopulation. Despite the massive fall in child mortality since the arrival of modern medicine, the average family in India still has four children. Unless something is done to control this rate of increase, the Indian population may reach 1.4 billion – nearly four times the population at Independence – by 2010.

Although India's middle class is ballooning, 35% to 40% of the population survive on less than US$1 per day, and people living in rural areas earn around four times less than city dwellers. Although state governments set a minimum wage for many occupations, the average daily wage in the Northeast is just Rs 60, and many workers earn much less, particularly women.

The social ills caused by poverty are plain to see in the Northeast, particularly in larger cities. Levels of begging and crime are soaring, and many people are driven into the arms of the insurgents by poverty and desperation. In rural areas, debt is the hidden killer – because of poor harvests, many farmers spiral into debt, leading to hundreds of suicides every year.

For foreign visitors poverty is often the most confronting aspect of travelling in the subcontinent. Whether you give to beggars is a matter of personal choice; however, your money can often be put to better long-term use if donated to a reputable charity. Charities and development organisations always need assistance from volunteers – see p316 for some suggested organisations.

Although around one-third of India's population subsists on less than US$1 per day, the country has an estimated 85,000 (and growing) millionaires (in US$).

India has one of the world's largest Diasporas – over 25 million people in 130 countries – who pumped US$23 billion into India's economy in 2005 alone.

POPULATION

India is tipped to exceed China as the planet's most populous nation by 2035. At the time of the last population census in 2001, India was home to a staggering 1,027,015,247 people. The states of West Bengal, Orissa, Sikkim and the seven Northeast states have a combined population of 155,963,673 – around 15% of the total population of India. Kolkata is India's second-largest city, with 13,216,546 people, but an estimated 75% of the population of the Northeast live in rural areas.

ADIVASIS

India's Adivasis ('original inhabitants' in Sanskrit) are descended from the tribes who lived in India before the rise of the Vedic civilisation. Adivasis make up around 8% of the total population and the Northeast has the largest concentration of tribes in the country – around 90% of the population in Arunachal Pradesh, Meghalaya, Mizoram and Nagaland, and 20% to 30% of the population in Orissa, Assam, Manipur, Sikkim and Tripura.

Although the 'Scheduled Tribes' have political representation thanks to the parliamentary quota system, the vast majority of Adivasis depend on subsistence agriculture. The literacy rate for Adivasis is just 29.6%, less than half the national average. Dispossession and exploitation of Adivasis continues at a shocking rate, often with the connivance of government officials. Development schemes in tribal areas are given the green light with little consideration for how they might affect Adivasi communities and, more importantly, with little compensation for displaced people.

Cultural imperialism is another problem for the tribes of the Northeast. Tribal people are increasingly being coerced into adopting the mainstream culture of the plains. Simultaneously, Western Christian missionaries are spreading the view that traditional customs and beliefs are 'backward' and even sinful. Although tours to Adivasi areas are a popular activity in the Northeast, providing much-needed income for tribal communities, travellers are also playing a part in the erosion of traditional values. To minimise your impact, look for tour companies that employ tribal people as guides and make a direct financial contribution to the communities they visit.

Many tribal communities have turned to armed revolt to protect their culture from assimilation into the Indian mainstream. For more on the complex cultures of the Northeast, see p44.

For more statistics, see the Census of India website at www.censusindia .net and this book's Snapshot chapter (p25). For regional populations, see the Fast Facts boxes at the start of each regional chapter.

RELIGION

Traditional Naga costume is linked to vanished battle rituals. Many Nagas still wear a *yanra* necklace, which once symbolised how many heads the wearer had taken in battle.

Religion suffuses every aspect of life in India, from the morning *puja* (prayers) to the evening call of the *muezzin* (prayer leader) from the local mosque. Every day, people decide to devote their lives to spiritualism, abandoning their possessions to become Buddhist monks and wandering *sadhus* (mendicant Hindu holy men).

Hinduism is practised by approximately 82% of Indians, though the proportion is much lower in most of the Northeast states. Along with Buddhism and Jainism, the Hindu faith originated in India, with roots extending beyond 1000 BC. Today, Hindus are in the majority in West Bengal, Orissa, Sikkim, Assam and Tripura.

Islam was introduced to northern India by invading armies in the 16th and 17th centuries. Immigration from Bangladesh has swelled the Muslim population of West Bengal and Assam to around 25% of the population. In other states, Muslims make up less than 2% of the population.

The Northeast also has significant numbers of Christians – around 85% of the population in Mizoram and Nagaland, 65% of the population in Meghalaya and 30% of the population in Manipur, compared to a national average of just 2.3%.

Buddhism is widely practised in Sikkim (by 30% of the population) and the mountainous west of Arunachal Pradesh (by 13% of the population). Arunachal Pradesh also has a huge population of animists – around 40% of the population – who follow traditional religions such as Donyi-Polo worship. The Northeast also has small populations of Jains, Sikhs and other minority religions.

Communal Conflict

Religious conflict has been a long and bloody part of India's history. The media tends to focus on recent events, but the roots of religious violence in India goes back to the waves of foreign invasion that began in the 11th century.

The main schism – between Hindus and Muslims – is further inflamed by memories of the intercommunal violence that followed Partition (see p35). Much of the animosity is linked to the reversed roles of the two communities in the Mughal era. Muslims regard this period as the peak of their civilisation, while Hindus see it as a time when their culture and religion were under threat.

Since Partition, political and religious leaders from both communities have fanned the flames of intercommunal violence, with Muslims frequently coming out worse from the encounters. Clashes between Sikhs and Hindus followed the assassination of former prime minister, Indira Gandhi (p37) by Sikh separatists in 1984.

Kashmir has been wracked by intercommunal violence ever since Independence, spawning two major wars between India and Pakistan. Most of the conflicts in the Northeast also have a religious dimension. Tribal communities are fighting oppression at the hands of Hindus, Muslims and Christians, and rival faith groups have their own insurgent armies carrying out retaliatory attacks.

Shakunthala Jagannathan's *Hinduism – An Introduction* unravels the basic tenets of Hinduism – if you have no prior knowledge, this book is a terrific starting point.

Hinduism

Hinduism has no founder, central authority or hierarchy, and unlike Judaeo-Christian religions, there is no proselytising agenda. Essentially, Hindus believe in Brahman, who is eternal, uncreated and infinite. The multitude of gods and goddesses are merely manifestations – knowable aspects – of this formless, ageless phenomenon.

Hindus believe that earthly life is cyclical; in the sense that human beings are repeatedly reborn (a process known as samsara) and the quality of each rebirth is dependent upon your karma (conduct or action) in previous lives. It is believed that living a righteous life and fulfilling your dharma (social duty) will enhance your chances of being born into a higher caste and enjoy better circumstances. If bad karma has accumulated, rebirth may take animal form, but ultimately, only humans can gain sufficient self-knowledge to escape the cycle of reincarnation and achieve moksha (liberation).

Numerology and astrology play an important role in Hindu rituals. Horoscopes and sacred numbers are used to predict auspicious dates for weddings and religious rituals. The number seven is particularly revered – the Vedas speak of seven sacred *rishis* (sages) and the Hindu wedding ceremony requires the bride and groom to walk seven times around a sacred fire.

There are around 330 million deities in the Hindu pantheon; those worshipped is a matter of personal choice or tradition.

OM

Pronounced 'aum', the Om is perhaps Hinduism's most venerated symbol. The triform shape symbolises the creation, maintenance and destruction of the universe (and thus the holy Trimurti), while the inverted *chandra* (crescent or half moon) represents the discursive mind and the *bindu* (dot) stands for Brahman. Om is equally venerated by Buddhists – according to Buddhist teachings, the mantra will lead to a state of blissful emptiness if repeated with complete concentration.

HOLY BOOKS

Like all religions, Hinduism has its own sacred texts. Written in Sanskrit between 1500 BC and 1200 BC, the Vedas form the basis of orthodox Hinduism. These sacred texts are divided into four groups: Rig-Veda (hymns), Yajur-Veda (sacrificial prayers), Sama-Veda (chants) and Atharva-Veda (ceremonial knowledge). A second group of texts, the Puranas, tell the legends and parables of the Hindu deities. Further tales of the gods appear in two epic Sanskrit poems – the Ramayana and Mahabharata – see opposite.

Islam draws primarily on the Quran, believed to be the literal word of Allah, as revealed to the prophet Mohammed, and the Hadith, derived from conversations with the Prophet. The Sikhs follow the Guru Granth Sahib, the collected teachings of the Sikh gurus, which were first recorded in the 16th century. The core text of Buddhism is the Tripitaka, a collection of sutras (scriptures) containing the teachings of the Buddha. In Tibetan Buddhism, the sutras are divided into the Kanjur (the literal words of Buddha) and Tanjur (conversations with the Buddha). Jains have their own text, the Kalpa Sutra, telling the story of the 24 Jinas (Jain prophets).

GODS & GODDESSES

As the ultimate godhead, Brahman is formless, eternal and the source of all existence. Brahman is impossible for the human mind to fully conceive, so the godhead is usually represented through the Trimurti – Brahma, Vishnu and Shiva – symbolising creation, preservation and destruction.

Brahma

Brahma was the creator of the universe and the source of humanity. Brahma is generally depicted with four (crowned and bearded) heads, each turned towards a point of the compass. His consort is Saraswati, the goddess of learning, and his vehicle is a swan. He is sometimes shown sitting on a lotus that rises from Vishnu's navel, symbolising the interdependence of the gods.

Brahma was once worshipped across India, but Brahma temples are rare today. One theory is that Brahma's role as creator is finished, and he waits in meditation until he is called upon to re-create the world again. A more likely reason is the legend that Brahma was humiliated by Shiva, coinciding with the rise of Shaivite Hinduism.

Vishnu

The preserver or sustainer, Vishnu protects and sustains all that is good in the world. He is usually depicted with four arms, holding a lotus, a discus, a mace and a conch shell – to be blown like a trumpet, symbolising the cosmic vibration from which all existence emanates. His consort is Lakshmi, the goddess of wealth, and his vehicle is Garuda, half-bird, half-man. The Ganges is said to flow from his feet.

Vishnu has 22 incarnations – the most revered are Rama, the hero of the *Ramayana*, and Krishna, the blue-skinned hero of the *Mahabharata*. Krishna's dalliances with the *gopis* (milkmaids) and his love for Radha have inspired countless paintings and songs.

Some Hindus also worship Buddha as an incarnation of Vishnu.

Shiva

Shiva is the destroyer, but through the cosmic dance, he facilitated creation – many worshippers credit Shiva rather than Brahma with creation of the universe. Shiva's creative role is symbolised by the lingam, a symbolic phallus, marked with three white stripes – the *tripundra*, symbolising knowledge, purity and penance. Sadhus – mendicant followers of Shiva –

Two impressive publications containing English translations of holy Hindu texts are *The Bhagavad Gita* by S Radhakrishnan and *The Valmiki Ramayana* by Romesh Dutt.

Shiva is sometimes characterised as the lord of yoga, a Himalaya-dwelling, ganja-smoking ascetic with matted hair, an ash-smeared body and a third eye symbolising wisdom.

often mark the *tripundra* on their foreheads using ash. Shiva takes many forms, including Pashupati, champion of the animals, and Nataraja, lord of the *tandava* (cosmic dance), who paces out the cosmos' creation and destruction.

Shiva is frequently depicted holding a trident (representative of the Trimurti) and riding Nandi, his loyal bull – a symbol of power, justice and moral order. Shiva's consort, Parvati, is revered as the source of *shakti* – divine female power. The concept of *shakti* is embodied in the mother goddess Devi (mother and destroyer of evil).

In Bengal, the goddess is often worshipped in her fearsome incarnation as Kali, or her warlike incarnation as Durga. *Shakti* worship is frequently linked to animal sacrifice (and human sacrifice, before the British era) harking back to pre-Vedic tribal religions.

Other Prominent Deities

Loved across India, elephant-headed Ganesh is the god of good fortune, remover of obstacles, and patron of scribes. His broken tusk was used to write sections of the Mahabharata and his animal mount is a mouse or rat. According to legend, Ganesh was born to Parvati while Shiva was travelling and grew up without knowing his father. When Shiva returned, the protective Ganesh blocked the doorway and Shiva lopped off his head in rage. When he discovered that he had slaughtered his own son, Shiva vowed to replace Ganesh's head with that of the first creature he came across, which happened to be an elephant.

Hanuman, the king of monkeys, is the hero of the Ramayana and loyal ally of Rama; he embodies the concept of bhakti (devotion). Respect for Hanuman spread across the ancient world – in 16th-century China, he appears as Sun Wukong – hero of *Journey to the West,* the basis for the TV series *Monkey.*

The Mahabharata

Thought to have been composed around the 1st millennium BC, this epic poem focuses on the exploits of Krishna, an incarnation of Vishnu in human form. The story centres on conflict between the heroic gods (Pandavas) and the demons (Kauravas) – two rival dynasties, fighting for control of the kingdom of Hastinapura. Both sides were evenly matched until Krishna acted as charioteer for the Pandava hero Arjuna, leading to triumph for the Pandavas.

The Ramayana

Composed around the 3rd or 2nd century BC, the Ramayana is believed to be mostly the work of the poet Valmiki. Like the Mahabharata, it deals with conflict between the gods and demons.

The story goes that the childless King of Ayodhya called upon the gods to provide him with a son. His wife gave birth to a boy named Rama, but the child was really an incarnation of the god Vishnu. Later in life, Rama won the hand of the princess Sita in a competition and was chosen by his father to inherit the kingdom, but his stepmother intervened and put her son in Rama's place.

Rama, Sita and Rama's brother, Lakshmana, were exiled and went off to the forests, where Rama and Lakshmana battled demons and dark forces. During these adventures Rama spurned the advances of Surpnakha, sister of Ravana, the demon king of Lanka. In revenge, Ravana captured Sita and spirited her away to his palace in Lanka. The rest of the poem describes Rama's quest to rescue Sita, assisted by the loyal monkey god Hanuman and his army of monkeys.

Devout male Hindus often become sadhus, surrendering all their material possessions in pursuit of spirituality through meditation, study of sacred texts, self-mortification and pilgrimage.

Held every three years in one of four locations around India, the Kumbh Mela is the largest human gathering on earth, attracting up to 100 million Hindu devotees.

Rama is almost certainly a real historical king, and the battle against Ravana may refer to a historical battle between the Aryan rulers of India and the Dravidian rulers of neighbouring Sri Lanka.

SACRED ANIMALS & PLANTS

Animals, particularly snakes and cows, have long been worshipped in the subcontinent. The cow represents fertility and nurturing, while snakes (especially cobras) are associated with fertility and welfare. Naga stones (snake stones) serve the dual purpose of protecting humans from snakes and propitiating snake gods.

Plants can also have sacred associations. The banyan tree symbolises the Trimurti, while mango trees are symbolic of love. Meanwhile, the lotus – India's national flower – is believed to have emerged from the primeval waters and is mystically connected to the mythical centre of the earth through its stem.

WORSHIP

Worship and ritual play a paramount role in Hinduism. In most Hindu homes you'll find a dedicated shrine, where members of the family pray daily to the deities of their choice. Beyond the home, temples are the focal point of Hindu worship. The ritual of puja (literally 'respect' or 'adoration') ranges from silent prayer to elaborate ceremonies and animal sacrifices. Devotees leave the temple with a handful of *prasad* (temple-blessed food), which is humbly shared among friends and family. Other forms of worship include *aarti* (the auspicious lighting of lamps or candles) and the playing of soul-soothing bhajans (devotional songs).

The portal website www .islam.com contains information on all aspects of Muslim worship, from Islamic festivals to recommended Muslim baby names.

Islam

Islam was founded in Arabia by the Prophet Mohammed in the 7th century AD. The Arabic term *islam* means to surrender, and believers (Muslims) undertake to surrender to the will of Allah (God). The will of Allah was revealed to Mohammed and recorded in the Quran, which forms a guide for all aspects of Muslim life. Islam is monotheistic and builds on the previous teachings of Christianity and Judaism. However, Islam recognises no religious hierarchy – divine authority comes directly from the Quran.

Following Mohammed's death, a succession dispute split the movement. Most Muslims in India are Sunnis, who follow the dynasty of Abu Bakr, the first Muslim caliph of Arabia. Shiites reject Abu Bakr and follow the direct bloodline of Mohammed. Shias believe that only imams (religious teachers) can reveal the true meaning of the Quran.

All Muslims share a belief in the Five Pillars of Islam:

- Shahadah – the declaration of faith: 'There is no God but Allah; Mohammed is his prophet'.
- Prayer – ideally five times a day; the muezzin (prayer leader) calls the faithful to prayer from the minarets of every mosque.
- Zakat – tax, usually taking the form of a charitable donation.
- Fasting – observing the fasting month of Ramadan; children, the sick, pregnant women, the elderly and travellers are usually exempt.
- Haj – the ritual pilgrimage to Mecca, which every Muslim aspires to do at least once in their lifetime.

Sikhism

Founded by Guru Nanak in the 15th century, Sikhism is a monotheistic religion that incorporates elements of Hinduism and Sufism (Islamic mysticism). Like Muslims, Sikhs believe that the will of God was revealed through human messengers – the 10 Sikh gurus – whose teachings are recorded in the Guru Granth Sahib. Like Hindus and Buddhists, Sikhs believe in rebirth and karma, but the goal of Sikhism is to live in a state of *hukam* (harmony) with the will of God.

Historically persecuted by both Hindus and Muslims, the Sikhs developed a militaristic code of conduct as self-defence. Fundamental to Sikhism is the concept of Khalsa – a chosen race of soldier-saints who abide by strict moral codes (including abstinence from alcohol, tobacco and drugs) and fight for *dharmayudha* (righteousness). There are five *kakkars* (emblems) denoting the Khalsa brotherhood:

- *kesh* – an unshaven beard and uncut hair
- *kangha* – the comb, to maintain ritually uncut hair
- *kaccha* – loose shorts, symbolising modesty
- *kirpan* – the dagger or sword, symbolising power and dignity
- *karra* – the steel bangle, symbolising fearlessness

Many Sikhs take the warrior name Singh, meaning 'Lion', but Sikh religion encourages hospitality, and gurdwaras (Sikh temples) have huge kitchens where meals are provided free to all who attend. The Sikh community in the Northeast is largely made from migrant workers; Sikhs have an India-wide reputation for business acumen.

> For an excellent guide to all things Buddhist, browse the resources on www.dharmanet.org.

Buddhism

A major religion in Sikkim, Arunachal Pradesh and parts of West Bengal, Buddhism was founded on the teachings of Siddhartha Gautama, the historical Buddha, thought to have lived from about 563–483 BC. Born a prince in modern-day Nepal, the Buddha encountered the suffering of ordinary people for the first time aged 29. He abandoned his luxurious life and embarked on a quest for emancipation from the world of suffering. The Buddha finally achieved nirvana (the state of full awareness) at Bodhgaya in Bihar (p269) aged 35.

After his death, the message of Buddhism was spread across Asia by his followers, including the Emperor Ashoka, and Padmasambhava, the Indian monk who introduced Buddhism to Tibet. Most Buddhists in India today follow the Tibetan tradition, reintroduced by monks travelling south over the Himalaya in the 15th century (and more recently, by Tibetan refugees).

The Buddha taught that existence is based on Four Noble Truths – that life is rooted in suffering, that suffering is caused by craving worldly things, that one can find release from suffering by eliminating craving and that the way to eliminate craving is by following the Noble Eightfold Path. This path consists of right understanding, right intention, right speech, right action, right livelihood, right effort, right awareness and right concentration. By successfully complying with these one can attain nirvana.

> For more insights into Tibetan Buddhism, read the teachings of the Dalai Lama – useful introductory texts include *Transforming the Mind* and *The Way to Freedom*, or visit www.dalailama .com.

Christianity

There are two large pockets of Christianity in India – one in the south and another in the Northeast. South Indian Christians trace their conversion (possibly spuriously) to St Thomas the Apostle in AD 52, while the Christians of the Northeast were converted by European missionaries from around the 18th century. Christianity is now the main religion in Nagaland, Meghalaya and Mizoram, and Christians form a significant minority in Manipur and Arunachal Pradesh. The Christians of the Northeast represent a broad sweep of Christian traditions – Catholics, Anglicans, Lutherans, Baptists, Presbyterians, Methodists and Pentecostals.

> Northeast India is one of the last places in the world where Christianity is actually gaining converts – aided by missionaries from 40 different Christian churches.

Followers of the obscure Aghori cult smear themselves with cremation ash, use human bones in rituals and even – it is alleged – consume human flesh to gain spiritual power.

Animism

Although Christianity, Hinduism, Buddhism and Islam have all made inroads, many Northeast tribes follow traditional animist religions, particularly in Arunachal Pradesh. Most tribal religions are based on Donyi-Polo ('Sun-Moon') worship, which emphasises the oneness of all living things. The sun and moon are venerated as symbols of Bo Bomong, the omnipresent supreme force, and devotees believe all life can be traced back to Sedi Melo, a combination of male and female spiritual power.

The Donyi-Polo religion experienced a major revival in the 1990s under the leadership of Talom Rukbo, a community worker who campaigned against the conversion agenda of Christian missionaries. Tribes in eastern Arunachal Pradesh worship deities known as Rangfrah and Rangsanhum, but followers of these religions are deliberately targeted by missionaries and Christian insurgent groups.

Around 7200 people in Mizoram follow Judaism – the Bnei Menashe sect believe that Manmasi, the mythical ancestor of the Mizos, was the son of Joseph in the Old Testament.

Other Religions

Predominantly a west-coast religion, Zoroastrianism is followed by small numbers of traders in the Northeast. This ancient religion was founded by Zoroaster (Zarathustra) in Persia and carried to India by refugees after the rise of Islam in the 10th century. Many elements of later Judeao-Christian religions were derived from Zoroastrian traditions.

Another minority are the Jains, followers of an ancient dharmic philosophy that arose in the 6th century BC as a reaction to the caste restraints of Hinduism. Founded by Mahavira, Jainism teaches that moksha (liberation) can be attained by achieving complete purity of the soul. Nonviolence and

---

KNOW YOUR GOMPAS

The rugged hills of Sikkim, Arunachal Pradesh and West Bengal are dotted with atmospheric gompas (Buddhist monasteries). However, Buddhist mythology is incredibly complicated and you can spend hours exploring a gompa and still understand only a fraction of what is going on. Fortunately, many Buddhist monks speak English and will gladly explain things if you ask.

The focal point of a gompa is the *dukhang* (prayer hall) where monks assemble for the morning puja (prayers from the Buddhist sutras). The walls may be covered in vivid murals or *thangkas* (cloth paintings) of bodhisattvas (enlightened beings) and *dharmapalas* (protector deities) depicted in frightful poses to symbolise the eternal fight against ignorance. By the entrance to the *dukhang* you'll find a mural depicting the wheel of life – a graphic representation of the core elements of Buddhist philosophy (see www.buddhanet.net/wheel1.htm for an interactive description of the wheel of life).

Almost all gompas hold masked *chaam* dances to celebrate the victory of good over evil and of Buddhism over pre-existing religions. Dances to ward off evil feature masks of Mahakala, the Great Protector, a diabolical-looking figure with a headdress of human skulls, while other dances feature wild-eyed stags and sinister masks of human skulls. These characters are often depicted with a third eye in the centre of their foreheads, signifying the need for inner reflection. The main *chaams* take place for Losar (Tibetan New Year) in February/March and Loosong (Sikkimese New Year) in December/January. If you can't visit when a *chaam* is taking place, ask a monk to show you the room where the masks and costumes are stored.

Another unusual activity at Buddhist monasteries is the production of butter sculptures, ornate and slightly psychedelic models made from coloured butter and dough. The sculptures are deliberately built to decay, symbolising the impermanence of human existence. Many gompas also produce exquisite sand mandalas – geometric patterns made from sprinkled coloured sand, then destroyed to symbolise the futility of the physical plane.

The best time to visit any gompa is during the morning puja. The first puja takes place at around 7am – visitors are welcome to watch, but try not to disturb the novices.

MAGNIFICENT MEHNDI

Before auspicious ceremonies such as marriage, Indian women have their hands and feet painted with intricate henna designs known as *mehndi*. Traditional designs incorporate stylised floral patterns and the paisley symbol, thought to represent a mango or the fruit of the cashew tree.

Derived from the leaves of the henna plant, *Lawsonia inermis,* henna paste leaves an orange-brown stain on the skin that can last up to a month. Many henna artists produce versions of popular tattoos for the tourist market. If you're thinking about getting *mehndi* applied, allow at least a couple of hours for the application and drying of the henna paste.

It's always wise to request the artist to do a 'test' spot on your arm before proceeding, as some henna dyes contain additional chemicals that can cause allergies or scarring. If good henna is used, you should not feel any pain during or after the procedure.

---

vegetarianism are core philosophies. Jains follow the teachings of 24 enlightened teachers known as Tirthankars (or Jinas) – equivalent to prophets in other religions.

WOMEN IN INDIA

Women in the Northeast face the same challenges as women in the rest of the country. Indian women are entitled to vote and own property, but Indian society is heavily male dominated and the idea of female emancipation has yet to catch on outside the major cities.

Although the percentage of women in politics has risen over the past decade, women are still underrepresented in the national parliament, accounting for around only 10%. Campaigners continue to fight for the Women's Reservation Bill, which proposes a 33% reservation of seats for women in parliament.

Although the professions are still very much male dominated, women are steadily making inroads, especially in urban centres. For village women it's harder to get ahead, but many international NGOs are backing microfinance schemes that allow women to start small businesses, increasing the power of women within the family.

In low-income families, girls can be regarded as a liability because of the cost of the marriage dowry. For the urban, middle-class woman, life is materially much more comfortable, but pressures still exist – a career and education are fine before marriage, but after the wedding, women are expected to 'fit in' with in-laws and be a homemaker.

In cities as well as villages, women can face dire consequences if they fail to live up to the expectations of their husband or his family – for example, failing to produce a son and heir. Every year, thousands of married woman are beaten or burnt to death, or emotionally harassed to the point of suicide. Fewer than one in 250 cases are reported to the police, and only 10% of reported cases are pursued through the legal system. A similarly depressing situation exists with rape and domestic violence.

In October 2006, the Indian parliament passed a landmark bill (on top of existing legislation) giving increased protection and rights to women suffering domestic abuse. The new law covers any form of physical, sexual (including marital rape), emotional and economic abuse, particularly in relation to dowry demands. Perpetrators face imprisonment and fines, and women are legally permitted to remain in the marital house (in the past many were thrown out and made destitute).

Although the law is a step in the right direction, there are considerable obstacles to enforcement, particularly in rural communities. Few women outside the major cities are educated, so there is only limited awareness of

Many women wear anklets and toe rings as decoration, but these are always made of silver – wearing gold on the feet is taboo.

Sati: A Study of Widow Burning in India by Sakuntala Narasimhan looks at the startling history of *sati* (widow's suicide on her husband's funeral pyre; now banned) on the subcontinent.

For more information on issues affecting women in modern India, visit www .aidwa.org and www .sewa.org.

the new laws, and many women are too frightened to speak out for fear of social stigma and persecution.

Although the constitution allows for divorcées (and widows) to remarry, women who do are frequently considered outcasts from society. A woman who seeks divorce may be rejected by her own family, and in extreme circumstances, the husband's family may resort to murder to restore the family 'honour'. Despite this, divorces are reportedly growing by 15% per annum, with most cases registered in large cities.

Women haven't always had such a low status in Indian society. Before the rise of modern Hinduism and Islam, women played an active role in the priesthood and had much more power in social affairs. Devi (mother goddess) worship is a legacy of this period in Indian history. Several tribes in Arunachal Pradesh and Meghalaya still follow a matrilineal pattern of inheritance (from mother to daughter).

Women travellers should also read p317.

ARTS

India has a rich legacy in the arts. Beauty can be found in the most commonplace and surprising of situations – on hand-painted billboards, in the magnificent paintings on trucks and cycle rickshaws, and the delicate tracery of *mehndi* (henna) on the hands of Indian brides. Then there are the fabulous classical arts of India – music, painting, metalwork, sculpture and the glorious architecture of India's temples.

Dance

Delve into India's vibrant performing-arts scene – especially Indian classical dance – at Art India (www.artindia.net).

Dance is an ancient Indian art form and is traditionally linked to mythology and classical literature. Indian classical dance is based on well-defined traditional principles, and the study of dance often has profound religious overtones. Classical dance in the Northeast got a major boost in 1901 when Rabindranath Tagore set up a dance school at Shantiniketan (p132). Classical forms you may see in the Northeast include:

- Bharata Natyam (also spelt *bharatanatyam*) – a Tamil dance form now embraced throughout India. Dance movements recall the motion of fire, and the celestial dances of the *apsaras* (celestial handmaidens).
- Kathak – with Hindu and Islamic influences, *kathak* was particularly popular with the Mughals. *Kathak* suffered a period of notoriety for its risqué depictions of the Krishna and Radha love story.
- Manipuri – originally from Manipur, this delicate, lyrical dance came to mainstream attention in the 1920s under the influence of Bengali writer Rabindranath Tagore.
- Odissi – claimed to be India's oldest classical dance form, Odissi was performed in Orissa as early as 2200 BC.
- Satriya – classical Assamese dance, first practiced in the satras (Hindu monasteries) of Majuli Island.

Indian Classical Dance by Leela Venkataraman and Avinash Pasricha is a lavishly illustrated book with good descriptions about the various Indian dance forms, including Bharata Natyam, Odissi, Kuchipudi and Kathakali.

India's folk dances are widespread and varied, particularly in tribal areas. In Assam, young men and women come together in April for folk dances known as *bihu* to usher in the Assamese New Year. Naga tribes have similar dances celebrating festivals and the changing seasons, often performed in traditional costume: the *khamba lim* dance is said to mimic the mating ritual of the peacock. Tripuris carry out the *hajgiri* dance to honour Lakshmi and ensure plentiful harvests.

Honouring the female-dominated royal family of Meghalaya, Khasi women perform the slow *nongkrem* dance in October in the village of Smit, near Shillong, to pray for a good harvest – see p217. As well as classical dance,

Manipuris are famous for their folk dances. Holi is marked by the energetic *dhol-cholom* (drum dance), incorporating dramatic leaps and twirls, while the *thang-ta* dance recalls the traditional Manipuri martial art of sword and shield fighting.

In Sikkim and Arunachal Pradesh, dances focus on Buddhist legends. Major Buddhist festivals are celebrated with *chaam* dances, which feature elaborate costumes and wild-eyed masks of Buddhist deities. Orissan folk dances include *chhau,* a dance based on traditional martial arts that draws on themes from the Ramayana and Mahabharata.

Music

Indian classical music traces its roots back to Vedic times, when religious poems chanted by priests were collated in the Rig-Veda (see p50). Over the millennia Indian music has been shaped by many influences – today, Indian classical music can be broadly divided into Carnatic (South Indian, with a focus on singing) and Hindustani (North Indian) styles, but both are played all over the country.

Core features include the raga (the melodic shape of the music) and *tala* (the rhythmic meter characterised by the number of beats). The most common *tala, tintal,* has 16 beats. The audience follows the *tala* by clapping at the appropriate beat, which in *tintal* is at beats one, five and 13. There's no clap at the beat of nine; that's the *khali* (empty section), which is indicated by a wave of the hand.

Significantly, there is no fixed speed for the *tala* – musicians speed up and slow down the cycle throughout the raga to add energy and drama. Musicians use the first beat of the *tala, sam,* as a reference point for improvisation and melodies. In most classical ensembles, the rhythm is provided by drums, most commonly the tabla (a high-pitched tuned wooden drum) and *doogri* (bass tone drum), which are played using the fingertips.

Indian music is melodic rather than harmonic. A drone instrument – typically a *tanpura* (like a fretless sitar, with four strings tuned to the same tone) or a *surpeti* (a hand-pumped harmonium) – plays a single note repeatedly, setting the base tone for the raga. Other instruments then improvise the melody within the tonic framework set by the drone. There is no fixed pitch in Indian music; *swaras* (notes) are defined relative to the drone note, *sa*. However, every raga is based on a fixed scale of notes that form the basis of the melody.

One of the best-known melody instruments is the sitar, a stringed, fretted instrument, with a soundbox made from a dried gourd and a series of 'sympathetic' strings that resonate in harmony with the plucked strings. By far the most famous sitarist is the Bengali musician Ravi Shankar (father of American singer Norah Jones). Numerous Western bands have used sitars to add an 'Indian' feel to their music. Other stringed instruments include the sarod (a lute with a goatskin drum as a soundbox and a similar set of sympathetic strings to the sitar) and the *sarangi* and *esraj* – two stringed instruments with sympathetic strings, played upright using a violin-style bow.

Indian regional folk music is widespread and varied. Wandering musicians, magicians, snake charmers and storytellers often use song to entertain their audiences, drawing on events from the Hindu epics. At Hindu temples, listen out for bhajans – Hindu devotional songs. In Muslim areas, you may come across qawwali (Islamic devotional singing), performed at mosques or at musical concerts.

Sikhs have their own devotional songs, known as *shabad,* and the Buddhists of the Northeast use ritual chanting from the sutras (sacred Buddhist texts) as part of the daily puja (prayer) ceremony, often accompanied by

Fans of Indian music should look no further than www.musicindia online.com, a fantastic music portal with an archive of hundreds of downloadable songs and instrumentals.

cymbals, gongs and Tibetan horns. The tribes of the Northeast have their own unique music, with a focus on singing and drumming. Western-style heavy rock has also taken off in a big way in tribal areas – particularly in Nagaland and Mizoram.

By far the most common music you will hear in India is *filmi* – the scores from Indian films. Most Indian films are actually musicals, and while actors sing the songs onscreen, a whole industry exists behind the scenes, composing and producing the film scores. These days, a lot of *filmi* music consists of rather cheesy pop-techno tunes, not the lyrically poetic and mellow melodies of old times. To ascertain the latest *filmi* favourites, simply ask at any music shop.

Another musical genre you may hear is *bhangra* – a dance and music form that grew out of the traditional harvest celebrations in the Punjab but is now combined with electronic beats to create India's most popular club sound.

Encyclopedia of Indian Cinema by Ashish Rajadhyaksha and Paul Willemen comprehensively chronicles India's cinema history, spanning from 1896 to the 21st century.

Cinema

India's film industry was born in 1897 when the first Indian-made motion picture, *Panorama of Calcutta,* was screened in Calcutta (Kolkata). India's first feature film, *Raja Harishchandra,* was made in Bombay (Mumbai) in 1913, and the first Bengali feature, *Billwamangal,* was produced in Calcutta in 1919.

Today, India's film industry is the biggest in the world. Studios in Bollywood (in Mumbai) produce a staggering 1000 movies per year, compared to the 600 films produced annually in Hollywood, and there are smaller studios in Kolkata, Hyderabad, Bengaluru (Bangalore) and Chennai, producing features in minority languages.

Characterised by big-name stars, exotic foreign locations and extravagant song and dance routines, Bollywood cinema is mainstream and predominantly in Hindu, attracting a worldwide audience of around 3.7 billion. Film purists look to Bengal as the home of Indian art-house cinema. Bengali films have complex plotlines, dialogue in Bengali, and a conspicuous absence of big production song-and-dance numbers.

Mainstream films have plots that resonate with ordinary people – love, war, sport, family conflicts, and the downtrodden overcoming oppression, corruption and poverty. Mid-plot, characters are suddenly transported to London or the Swiss Alps for sequin-covered song-and-dance routines, often featuring hundreds of extras. Kung fu fight sequences crop up in most films as heroes battle love rivals, gangsters and corrupt cops to save the day and win the girl.

Perhaps the most compelling film about the role of women in rural India is Mehboob Khan's *Mother India,* a moving tale of love, loss and the maternal bond.

Reflecting local morality, sex scenes are a complex sequence of suggestions and innuendo. The lack of nudity is compensated for by heroines writhing to music in clinging wet saris. Even kissing is taboo, though smooches are slowly creeping onto the big screen, usually provoking outcry from community leaders. Quite a few films have fallen foul of moral and religious sensibilities in recent years – cinemas have even been bombed for screening movies that deal with contentious issues such as promiscuity, homosexuality and religion.

Hundreds of Bollywood blockbusters are released ever year – most flop, but those that succeed propel their stars, and the singers and musicians behind scenes, to unimaginable fame and glory. Stars such as Shah Rukh Khan, Preity Zinta, Aishwarya Rai, and Amitabh and Abishek Bachchan are some of the world's most recognised people, revered by one in four human beings on the planet.

In the Northeast, cinema is a more contemplative affair, taking the reality of human life as its base. Bengali cinema is defined by dialogue, social commentary and an honest observation of human interaction. Some of the finest films in Indian history have come from Bengali legends like Guru Dutt, Ritwik Ghatak, Aparna Sen, Mrinal Sen and Satyajit Ray. If you see no other Indian art-house films, try to catch Ray's *Apu* trilogy as a heart-rending introduction to the trials of rural life in the Northeast.

For more film recommendations, see the boxed text, p17.

Literature

India has a literary tradition dating back to the days of the great Sanskrit poets, but later works in Hindu, English and regional languages also contributed to this rich tapestry. More than 800 languages are spoken in India and each region has its own specific literary tradition.

Bengalis are credited with producing some of India's most celebrated literature. Social reform and national pride were the rallying cries of the Bengal Renaissance movement, which flourished from the 19th century onwards. Famous Renaissance writers include social reformer Ram Mohan Roy and nationalist hero Bankimchandra Chatterjee, whose poem *Bande Mataram* was used as an anthem by the Indian Independence movement. The person most credited with propelling India's cultural richness to global acclaim is Bengali poet and cultural icon, Rabindranath Tagore – see the boxed text on below.

India boasts an ever-growing number of internationally acclaimed authors who re-create the experience of life on the subcontinent using rich and sensuous language. Many Bengali authors write in Bengali, making their work a little inaccessible to nonspeakers, but several books by Ashutosh Mukherjee and Sharat Chandra Chatterjee are available in English translations – Sharat's legendary novella *Devdas* has been made into eight successive Indian films. UK-born Bengali writer Jhumpa Lahiri won the 2000 Pulitzer Prize for Fiction for *Interpreter of Maladies*, a tremendous collection of short stories, several set in Bengal.

India's latest shining literary star is India-born Kiran Desai, who won the 2006 Man Booker Prize for her superb novel, *The Inheritance of Loss*, set in Kalimpong. The youngest woman to ever win the Booker Prize, Kiran Desai is the daughter of the Bengali-German novelist Anita Desai, who received three Booker Prize nominations herself.

Other Indian authors worth reading for their insights into Indian culture include Kerala-born Arundhati Roy, who won the Booker Prize for *The God*

For details about English-language Indian literature, from historical to contemporary times, check out Indian English Literature (www .indianenglishliterature .com).

For excellent information on Bengali literature, including online translations of work by Bengali authors, see www.para baas.com.

RABINDRANATH TAGORE

India's best-loved poet, writer, painter, patriot and patron of the arts, Rabindranath Tagore (or 'Rabi Babu' as he's known to Bengalis) has had an unparalleled impact on Bengali culture. Born to a wealthy, prominent family in Calcutta (Kolkata) in 1861, he began writing as a young boy and never stopped, dictating his last poem only hours before his death in 1941.

As well as being a champion of Indian Independence, Tagore is credited with introducing India's historical and cultural greatness to the Western world. He won the Nobel Prize for Literature in 1913 with his mystical collection of poems *Gitanjali* (Song Offering), and in his later years, he toured around Asia, America and Europe, spreading a message of human unity and global understanding.

For all his internationalism, Tagore is best remembered as a Bengali patriot, writing the words and music for both the Indian and Bangladeshi national anthems. In 1915 Tagore was awarded a knighthood by the British, but he surrendered it in 1919 as a protest against the Amritsar massacre. For an introduction to Tagore's work, read his *Selected Short Stories*, available around the world.

of Small Things, and Booker- and Nobel-prize winning author VS Naipaul (although born in Trinidad, his book *India: A Million Mutinies Now* has to be one of the most penetrating insights into Indian life). And you can't overlook Mumbai-born Salman Rushdie, who bagged the Booker Prize in 1981 for *Midnight's Children* – a fantastical metaphor for India's modern history, told through the eyes of children born at the exact clock moment of Indian Independence.

For further recommendations of just some of the many brilliant Indian novels available, see p17.

Architecture

For more on the myriad forms and fascinating traditions of Indian temple architecture, visit www .indiantemples.com.

As in Europe, the most striking Indian architecture is reserved for religious buildings. India's temples, mosques, gurdwaras, churches and monasteries come in an incredible variety of forms, with certain styles linked to specific regions and the worship of specific deities.

Hindu temple architecture follows complex rules, based on numerology, astrology, astronomy and religious law, which govern the location, design and building of each temple. Essentially, a Hindu temple is a map of the universe. Images of the temple deity reside in a plain central chamber, the *garbhagriha* (inner shrine or sanctum sanctorum), symbolising the 'womb-cave' from which the universe emerged.

In most temples, the shrine is surmounted by a *sikhara,* a curvilinear tower, usually topped with an ribbed stone disk known as an *amlaka,* and a *khalasa,* shaped like a traditional water pot. Some temples have *mandapas* (temple forechambers) covered by smaller *sikharas.* Some of the most dramatic temple *sikharas* in the Northeast are found in Orissa – the temples of Bhubaneswar (p244) feature amazingly ornate *sikharas,* while the carving-covered Sun Temple at Konark (p256) was built in the shape of a gigantic chariot.

Perhaps the most distinctive style of temple architecture in the Northeast is the 'Bengali hut' style – a square shrine (the perfect shape in Hinduism), surmounted by a rounded dome or *sikhara*-like tower. Famous examples include Kolkata's Dakshineswar Kali Temple (see p112) and the Tripura Sundari Mandir (p223) near Agartala. Migrant workers from the south have built temples in the Dravidian style, reached through soaring pyramidal gateway towers known as *gopurams,* often covered with hundreds of carvings of Hindu deities.

Architecture buffs will appreciate *Masterpieces of Traditional Indian Architecture* by Satish Grover and *The History of Architecture in India* by Christopher Tadgell, both of which include insights into temple architecture.

Jain temples resemble Hindu temples, but interiors are a riot of sculptures and mirrored mosaics. Gurdwaras (Sikh temples) can be identified by their elegant onion domes, typically made from white marble and topped by a *nishan sahib* (flagpole) flying a triangular flag with the Sikh insignia.

The Buddhist architecture of Sikkim, West Bengal and Arunachal Pradesh is defined by gompas (monasteries) and stupas – dome-like ceremonial towers used to enshrine sacred objects or as reliquaries for the remains of revered lamas (Buddhist monks). Buddhist monasteries are built according to strict guidelines, and interiors are frequently covered in vivid murals depicting characters from the Tantric Buddhist mythology. Murals are renewed regularly by local Buddhists as a sign of devotion and to accrue good karma for future incarnations. For more on Buddhist architecture, see p54.

India's Muslim invaders introduced new architectural conventions from Persia and Arabia, including arched cloisters and domes. The Mughals gave India some of its most distinctive buildings in the form of elegant mosques with towering minarets (prayer towers). Islam eschews idolatry or the portrayal of God, but the divine is evoked using elegant calligraphy and decorative designs. All mosques follow a similar design, with a large

---

TEMPLE TANKS

Next to most temples in India, you'll find a large water-filled *kunda* (tank or reservoir), used for ritual bathing and religious ceremonies. Devotees use tanks for swimming and ritual washing – some temple tanks are believed to have extraordinary healing properties or the power to wash away sins. Devotees (as well as travellers) may be required to wash their hands and feet in a temple tank before entering a place of worship. Many tanks are stocked with fish and turtles, which are venerated as symbols of Hindu deities, and which help keep the water free from algae, mosquito larvae and other waterborne pests.

---

communal prayer hall oriented around a mihrab (niche) indicating the direction of Mecca. Running water is provided in front of the mosque for ritual washing.

Churches in India reflect the fashions and trends of European and American ecclesiastical architecture. Kolkata and the hill stations of West Bengal have a number of stately British-era churches, and the modernist churches of various Christian sects can be found all over the Northeast states.

Painting

India has a rich history of painting, from primitive rock art to the exquisite murals that adorned Buddhist and Hindu caves and temples across the subcontinent as early as AD 500. Much of this artistic legacy was destroyed by the Mughals as part of their purge of idolatry, but monasteries in inaccessible mountain areas such as Sikkim and Arunachal Pradesh protected some fine examples of Buddhist monastery art. Today, with help from Tibetan refugees, ancient styles of painting have been revived, with new monasteries providing opportunities for budding temple artists.

The Mughals replaced indigenous arts with their own painting styles, most famously in the form of Mughal miniatures. This delicate style of painting rose to prominence in the time of Akbar (1542–1605), and various styles developed around the country. Most large museums in the Northeast display original Mughal paintings and you can find some impressive re-creations by modern artists.

Modern art was kick-started in the 20th century under the influence of the Bengal School – a reactionary movement led by students of the Calcutta School of Art – which sought to rekindle interest in traditional Indian art. This philosophy inspired many of the paintings of Rabindranath Tagore (p59), Jamini Roy and several other prestigious Bengali artists. Other Indian artists to keep an eye out for include Francis Newton Souza, Tyeb Mehta, Syed Haider Raza, Akbar Padamsee, Ram Kumar and Maqbool Fida Husain.

Modern paintings are exhibited regularly in galleries in larger cities – Kolkata's Centre for International Modern Art (p109) is one of the best places to catch cutting-edge Bengali painting.

Handicrafts

In India, traditional crafts are as respected as fine art. All of the ethnic groups in the Northeast have their own unique crafts and folk arts, many with profound spiritual overtones. Some crafts are the exclusive preserve of women, or reserved for a specific social or religious group. In rural areas, people often have to fashion everything they need from things found in nature, so many crafts fulfil a practical as well as aesthetic function.

Although most crafts are regional, artisans move around the country, ensuring that many handicrafts are found nationwide. Specialities of the

Indian Art by Roy Craven provides a sound overview of India's art history, tracing its early beginnings in the Indus Valley to the development of various forms of Hindu, Islamic and Buddhist art.

Sprinkled with sumptuous colour illustrations, *Traditional Indian Textiles* by John Gillow and Nicholas Barnard explores India's stunning regional textiles.

Northeast include woodcarving, basketware, paintings, metalwork, carpet-weaving and handloom weaving. The patterned fabrics woven by the hill tribes of the Northeast are some of the most striking textiles in India.

For detailed information of the kind of handicrafts on offer, see p307.

SPORT
Cricket

Through scintillating text and pictures, *The Illustrated History of Indian Cricket* by Boria Majumdar adeptly explores this popular sport, from its origins right up to modern times.

Cricket is more than just the national sport – it is the national obsession. Children play in every open space with planks of wood and old tennis balls to honour their heroes in the national team – cricketers like ace batsman Sachin Tendulkar (the 'Little Master'), all-rounder Sourav Ganguly (the 'Bengal Tiger') and Sikh offspin bowler Harbhajan Singh (fondly dubbed the 'turbanator'). The sport has not been without its dark side though, with Indian cricketers named along with players from Pakistan and South Africa in match-fixing scandals in 2000.

India's first recorded first-class cricket match was in 1864. The national cricket team won its first test series in 1952 at Chennai against England, and the team bought home the cricket World Cup in 1983. Local matches are played across the Northeast, and international matches are played at various stadiums from October to April, including Kolkata's Eden Gardens (Ranji) Stadium (p121). Match tickets are usually advertised in the local press a few weeks in advance.

Get up-to-date cricket information at **Cricinfo** (www.cricinfo.com).

Hockey

Field hockey has a loyal following in India. Between 1928 and 1956, India won six consecutive Olympic gold medals, but with the fading influence of the sport, there have been no gold medals since 1980. Nevertheless, it's one of the sports you'll encounter on cable TV – and occasionally live. Two recommended hockey websites are www.indianhockey.com and www .bharatiyahockey.org.

Keeping your finger on the pulse of Indian sporting news is just a click away on Sify Sports (www.sify.com/sports).

Soccer

Many Indians know more about England's Manchester United than the teams playing in the National Football League, but the sport is much more popular in the Northeast, with three Kolkata teams in the Premier Division – Mohun Bagan, East Bengal and Mohammedan Sporting. The president of FIFA (Fédération Internationale de Football Association) visited Kolkata in 2007 to raise the profile of Indian soccer. For more information on the sport, see www.indianfootball.com and www.the-aiff.com.

Polo

One of the oldest team sports on earth, polo was allegedly invented in Manipur, though various other nations also claim the honour. The sport flourished under the Mughals and later the British, who established one of the world's oldest polo clubs in Kolkata in 1862. Interest in polo declined sharply after Independence, but you can catch a few *chukkas* (polo sessions) in Kolkata and more widely in Manipur, where 35 teams compete in the state league. Check local newspapers for details.

Tennis

Tennis is currently big news in India. As doubles partners, Leander Paes and Mahesh Bhupathi were the first Indians to win Wimbledon's prestigious title in 1999, and the two players have since won prestigious titles in Australia and the US. Sania Mirza thrashed US Open champion Svetlana Kuznetsova at the Dubai Open in 2005 and is now ranked 53rd in singles and 25th in doubles in the world rankings.

Held in Kolkata, the annual Sunfeast Open is part of the WTA Tour, Tier III. For information on tournaments, contact the All India Tennis Association (www.aitatennis.com).

Other Sports

Horse racing, held primarily in the cooler winter months, is especially popular in Kolkata (see p121), with huge amounts of money changing hands through legal (and illegal) gambling. The website www.indiarace.com has more details of race meetings.

Another traditional sport that has survived is kabaddi, essentially an elaborate game of tag, where players must catch a member of the opposite team while holding a single breath of air and repeating the word 'kabaddi'. The first ever Asian Kabaddi Championship was held in Kolkata in 1980 – for details of upcoming tournaments, contact the **International Kabaddi Federation** (www.kabaddiikf.com).

MEDIA

Although most newspapers, radio stations and TV channels have political allegiances, the Indian media enjoys extensive freedom of expression. Kolkata has a string of highly respected newspapers – most importantly the *Telegraph* (www.telegraphindia.com) – and the Northeast has numerous local papers, magazines and journals, in a range of languages and dialects. Most major publications have a presence on the web – see www.onlinenewspapers.com/india.htm for a nationwide list. Important English-language dailies and news magazines in the Northeast are listed on p293.

Indian TV was originally dominated by the dreary government-controlled national broadcaster **Doordarshan** (www.ddindia.gov.in). However, recent years have seen an explosion in satellite TV channels, covering everything from news, culture and Bollywood films to bhajans (religious devotional songs). Most providers offer a handful of English-language movie and news channels among the Indian soap operas, gameshows and Hindi blockbusters.

Programmes on the government-controlled All India Radio (AIR; www.allindiaradio.org) include news, interviews, music and sport. There are also mushrooming nationwide private channels that offer music (in an incredible array of forms), news, sport and chat – covering many subjects once considered taboo, such as sexual and marital problems.

Consult local newspapers for TV and radio listings.

For online links to major Indian English-language newspapers, head straight to Samachar (www.samachar.com).

Environment

THE LAND

India has a land area of 3,287,263 sq km, covering some of the most dramatic landscapes on earth – steamy jungles and tropical rainforest, waterlogged marshlands and arid deserts, rising to the soaring peaks of the Himalaya. Most of these landscapes are represented in the Northeast, from the swamps of West Bengal to the jungles of Nagaland and the snow-capped mountains of Sikkim.

The Himalaya

Creating an impregnable boundary between India and its neighbours to the north, the Himalaya are the world's highest mountains, as well as being some of the youngest. This mighty ridge began to rise in the Jurassic era (80 million years ago) when Laurasia, the main landmass in the northern hemisphere, tore away from Gondwanaland in the southern hemisphere. The Indian landmass was pulled across the divide by plate tectonics and thrust against the soft sedimentary crust of Laurasia, buckling the plate upwards to form the Himalaya. Fossils of sea creatures from this time can still be found at 5000m above sea level. This continental collision is an ongoing process and the Himalaya are growing in height by up to 8mm each year.

The peaks of the Himalaya form a natural land border between Northeast India and the Tibetan Plateau, defining the landscape of Sikkim, Western Nepal, Bhutan and Arunachal Pradesh. Mt Khangchendzonga (8598m), located in Sikkim, is the world's third-highest mountain and the highest point in India. The increase in elevation is dramatic – with the summit of Mt Khangchendzonga located just under 100km away from the pan-flat Bengal Plains.

Although it looks like a continuous range on a map, the Himalaya is actually a series of interlocking ridges that are separated by broad valleys. Until the technology was created to construct roads through the Himalaya, many of these valleys existed in complete isolation, preserving a diverse series of mountain cultures, including the Buddhist civilisations of Sikkim and western Arunachal Pradesh. Even today, these areas are disputed by China as part of its questionable claim to all lands formerly controlled by Tibet.

In landscape and culture, most states in the far Northeast are closer to Southeast Asia than the rest of India...

The Northeast Hills

The northeast boundary of India is made up of densely folded hills that spill over into neighbouring Myanmar (Burma), marking the point of impact between the Indian and Eurasian plates. Rising abruptly from the plains, the Naga, Manipur and Chin Hills are drained by dozens of rivers that empty into the Bay of Bengal. The entire region was once densely forested, but deforestation through logging and slash-and-burn agriculture is changing the landscape dramatically.

In landscape and culture, most states in the far Northeast are closer to Southeast Asia than the rest of India; identical tribal groups are found on both sides of the India–Myanmar border. Floating between Assam and Bangladesh is the soaring Meghalaya Plateau, a limestone massif thrust upwards by tectonic forces and eroded into wild shapes by the world's highest annual rainfall – a staggering 12,000mm per year, 10 times the rainfall of most countries in Europe.

The Bengal & Assamese Plains

Covering most of central India, the vast Northern Plains drop just 200m between Delhi and the waterlogged marshlands of Assam and West Bengal. Dotted with small villages, rice paddies and patches of jungle, this vast plain ends abruptly at the Himalaya and the Northeast Hills. Snaking west through the plains of Assam, the Brahmaputra River is the lifeblood of the Northeast, rising as the Yaluzangbu in Tibet and merging with the Ganges before emptying into the Bay of Bengal in Bangladesh.

The people of the Northeast have a love-hate relationship with the Brahmaputra. Every monsoon, the river swells and bursts its banks, destroying villages and roads but flooding the rice paddies with mineral-rich silt. The river can reach 10km wide even in the dry season; in the monsoon, the floodwaters inundate hundreds of square kilometres of farmland, blocking many of the roads through Assam. In recent years, the Indian government has harnessed many of the tributaries of the Brahmaputra to provide hydro-electric power for the Northeast.

The World Wide Fund for Nature (WWF; www.wwf india.org) promotes environmental protection and wildlife conservation in India; see the website for offices around the country.

The Coast

Straddling the border between India and Bangladesh, the salt marshes of the Sunderbans are covered by the largest mangrove forest in the world, sprawling over thousands of swampy islands in the delta of the Hooghly and Brahmaputra rivers. Malaria, man-eating tigers and a lack of fresh water all serve to keep human habitation to a minimum. The Sunderbans National Park in West Bengal contains the largest concentration of wild tigers in the country – see p66.

Heading south from the Sunderbans, the coast becomes drier and the swamps give way to shallow sandy beaches. Most of Orissa is a flat alluvial plain, used for intense rice cultivation, but patches of forest remain on the Chota Nagpur plateau in the north and west of the state. Bird life abounds on the huge Hirakud Reservoir in the western hills and Chilika Lake, on the coast south of Puri.

For an evocative introduction to the Sunderbans, read Amitav Ghosh's *The Hungry Tide*, a thoughtful exploration of the conflict between man and nature.

WILDLIFE

With a staggering 89,451 recorded species of fauna, India has some of the richest biodiversity in the world. Many species that are found nowhere else still cling to the forests of the Northeast, including the one-horned Indian rhinoceros and the iconic Indian hornbill.

Understandably, wildlife watching has become one of the country's prime tourist activities and there are dozens of national parks offering opportunities to spot rare and unusual wildlife. If you're keen on getting close to nature, see the boxed text, p70, detailing where and when to view wildlife.

Animals

Indian wildlife is fascinating and diverse. The jungles of the Northeast hide a host of signature species – elephants, tigers, monkeys, leopards, antelopes and rhinos. Most of these species are severely endangered by human competition for land, water and other resources, particularly in the overpopulated Bengal and Orissan plains. Elephants and buffalo are widely pressed into service as beasts of burden, but dwindling numbers of wild elephants can still be found in the hills of Orissa and remote parts of the Northeast states.

South of Kolkata (Calcutta), the Hooghly River empties into the Bay of Bengal, marking the western boundary of the vast Sunderbans delta – 80,000 sq km of swamps and watercourses that provide a home to tigers (estimated at 274 in 2004), aquatic reptiles, fish, wild boars, sea turtles and snakes. Chitals (spotted deer) have evolved the ability to secrete salt from their glands to cope with this salt-laden environment.

India's national animal is the tiger, its national bird is the peacock and its national flower is the lotus. The national emblem of India is a column topped by three Asiatic lions.

THE STAGGERING SUNDERBANS

Unsurveyed until 1911, the Sunderbans is the world's largest mangrove forest, covering 4143 sq km of islands and sandbars and 1874 sq km of rivers, creeks and inlets, straddling the border between West Bengal and Bangladesh. The forest used to be even bigger, but human expansion has reduced forest cover by 40% over the last century. The main threats are forest clearing for firewood and shrimp farming, which also affects fish stocks in the Bay of Bengal by reducing the nursery grounds available to wild species.

The dominant tree in the Sunderbans is the sundari – a hardy, mangrove species whose wood is much sought-after for boat building and fuel. Sundari trees have evolved special techniques for dealing with the intense salinity of the water – including the ability to excrete salt through their leaves. Animals have developed similar techniques – spotted deer in the Sunderbans secrete excess salt through their glands.

Since 2001 the Sunderbans has been protected as a Unesco International Biosphere Reserve for its incredible biodiversity; at the last count, the mangroves were home to 334 plant species, 120 fish species, 35 types of reptiles, 270 bird species and 42 mammal species, including 30,000 spotted deer and 270 royal Bengal tigers.

The *baghs* (tigers) of the Sunderbans are the most notorious man-eaters in India, killing some 100 humans a year, most of them wood collectors, honey gatherers and fishermen. The tigers have such a fearsome reputation that local villagers wear masks of faces on the back of their heads whenever they enter the forest in order to trick tigers into thinking they are being watched. Officials from the Sunderbans Tiger Reserve – the national park set up to protect the Sunderbans – go one step further, with spiked body armour and neck braces to offset the very real risk of attack.

Visitors can spot tigers from boat tours through the creeks, arranged in Kolkata (Calcutta; p113) or the park headquarters at Sajnekhali (p127).

The website www.sundarbanstigerproject.info is a one-stop shop for information on tiger conservation in the Sunderbans.

The jungles and marshlands of West Bengal, Orissa and the Northeast states provide a home to tigers, leopards, panthers, clouded leopards, Bengal jungle cats, civet cats, sloth bears, and numerous species of deer and antelopes, including sambar, chitals and the threatened *muncjak* (barking deer). Guar and *mithun* (which are both ancestors of the modern water buffalo) range across the Northeast region. *Mithun* horns are still used as decoration on traditional tribal houses in parts of Nagaland and Arunachal Pradesh.

Wild elephants are found in several national parks in Orissa, Assam and West Bengal, and domesticated elephants are still used for forestry in some parts of the northeast. The endangered one-horned Indian rhinoceros (*Rhinoceros unicornis*) is the signature species of Assam's Kaziranga National Park. Smaller numbers of rhinos are also found in nearby Manas National Park and the Jaldhapara Wildlife Sanctuary in West Bengal.

Primates range from the extremely rare hoolock gibbon and slow loris – an adept insect catcher with huge eyes for nocturnal hunting – to species that are so common as to be a pest, most notably the stocky and aggressive rhesus macaque and the elegant grey langur. Perhaps the most striking primate in the northeast is the golden langur, a slender, graceful monkey with golden orange fur and a famously calm temperament.

Cobras are believed to have power over the monsoon and the snakes are worshipped during the Nagapanchami Festival each August – to the despair of animal-rights campaigners – many snakes die from exhaustion and overfeeding!

India has 238 species of snakes, of which 50 are poisonous. The rice paddies and jungles of the Northeast provide cover for various species of cobra, including the legendary king cobra, the world's largest venomous snake, which grows up to 5m (for obvious reasons, snake charmers stick to smaller species!). Other poisonous snakes include the krait, Russel's viper and the saw-scaled viper. Constrictors include the reticulated python and the gigantic Indian python – used as a model for Kaa in the cartoon of the *Jungle Book* –

which can reach 9m in length. Also found here is the remarkable flying snake, which can flatten its body to glide between the treetops.

India's snakes live in the fear of the snake-killing mongoose, which has evolved ingenious techniques for hunting poisonous snakes, tricking the reptiles into striking until they are exhausted and then eating the snakes head first to avoid being bitten. Keep an eye out for mongooses crossing the road while travelling through rural areas across the northeast.

Birds abound in the Northeast. The lakes of Orissa attract hundreds of species of migratory birds, including cranes, herons, ospreys and flamingos. Jungle areas are home to the distinctive great Indian hornbill, the largest of all hornbills. Hornbill beaks are used as ornamentation by many tribes in Nagaland and Arunachal Pradesh. The iridescent monal pheasant is found across the Northeast region, particularly in Sikkim. Other notable birds include storks, parrots, rare francolins and floricans, and the Steppe eagle and griffon vulture, which are both often spotted soaring over the foothills of the Himalaya. Bird-watchers should check out the reserves listed on p75.

The Himalaya harbours its own hardy range of creatures. Yaks (shaggy, horned oxen weighing up to a tonne) are a common beast of burden in northern Arunachal Pradesh and Sikkim. Officially, only males can be called yaks – the proper name for female yaks is *dri*. To make things more complicated, most 'yaks' are actually *dzo* (male) or *dzomo* (female) – a cross between yaks and domestic cattle.

Wild herbivores include *urial* (wild sheep) and *bharal* (blue sheep), *kiang* (Tibetan wild ass), Himalayan ibex (a graceful mountain antelope), Himalayan *tahr* (mountain goat) and the rare *chiru* (Tibetan antelope), threatened by hunting for its soft fur. Perhaps the most endangered herbivore of all is the musk-deer, hunted almost to extinction for the scent produced by glands in its abdomen. Recent attempts at captive breeding in other parts of India are providing some hope for this threatened species.

Predators of the Himalaya include black and brown bears, tigers and the endangered snow leopard, an animal so elusive that many locals claim it can appear and disappear at will. Tiny populations cling on in Sikkim and Arunachal Pradesh but snow leopards are almost never seen, even by the scientists who study them. The rare red panda inhabits the bamboo thickets of the eastern Himalaya, particularly in Sikkim and Bhutan.

Indian mugger crocodiles – the source of the word 'mugger' – are found in many rivers across the Northeast, and sharks hunt offshore in the Bay of Bengal. In past centuries, Hindu zealots threw themselves into the shark-infested waters off Sagar Island (West Bengal) to be consumed as human sacrifices. Rare Gangetic dolphins are still found in the Brahmputra – around 200 are thought to range along the river, hunting by sonar through the turgid, silt-filled waters.

ENDANGERED SPECIES

Despite its amazing biodiversity, Indian wildlife faces a growing challenge from the exploding human population. At last count, India had 459 threatened species, comprising 244 species of plants, 86 species of mammals, 70 species of birds, 25 species of reptiles, three species of amphibians, eight species of fish and 23 species of invertebrates.

In 1972 the Wildlife Protection Act was introduced to stem the abuse of wildlife, followed by a string of similar pieces of legislation with bold ambitions but few teeth with which to enforce them. Launched in 1973 to protect India's big mammals, even this project has been undermined by accusations of wardens being complicit in poaching. The main threats to wildlife continue

Must-have books for bird-watchers include the *Pocket Guide to Birds of the Indian Subcontinent* by Richard Grimmett, Carol Inskipp and Tim Inskipp, *A Birdwatchers' Guide to India* by Krys Kazmierczak and Raj Singh, and *The Book of Indian Birds* by Salim Ali.

A brand-new bird species was discovered in Arunachal Pradesh in 2005. Identified from a handful of sightings, *Bugun liocichla* was the first new bird to be discovered since 1948.

The Wildlife Protection Society of India (www.wpsi-india.org) is a prominent wildlife conservation organisation campaigning for animal welfare through education, lobbying and legal action against poachers.

FAREWELL TIGER?

India's tigers face a growing threat from the trade for Chinese medicine. Spurious health benefits are linked to every part of the tiger, from the teeth to the penis, and a whole tiger carcass can fetch upwards of US$10,000. Estimates from conservationists suggest that the current population may be as low as 1200, with a further 1% of tigers falling every year to poachers. This is already below the threshold for a viable gene pool.

The Chinese enthusiasm for tiger parts might be more understandable if tiger medicines had any provable health benefits. In reality, the entire trade relies on the placebo effect – the basis for using tiger parts in Chinese medicine is the idea that tigers are 'energetic' animals. Chinese officials are now considering allowing tigers to be farmed on a commercial scale, a decision that would massively increase the demand for tiger parts and sign a death warrant for the remaining wild tigers.

---

to be habitat loss due to human encroachment and poaching by tribal people, insurgents and squatter farmers.

Conservation in the Northeast is complicated by the fact that many species roam across international borders. To make things worse, smuggling is rife across the porous borders with Bhutan, Nepal and Tibet. Many tribal groups rely on bush meat for food – often targeting endangered species – and logging has long been a source of income for armed rebel groups, many of which operate out of remote wilderness areas.

China is the main destination for ivory, rhino horn, and skins and body parts from slaughtered bears and tigers – see the boxed text on this page. The Northeast's rhinos are also threatened by poaching – rhino horn is highly valued as an aphrodisiac and as a material for making handles for daggers in the Persian Gulf. Wild elephants are poached for ivory that regularly makes its way into souvenir shops. We implore you not to support this trade by buying ivory souvenirs.

In tribal areas of the Northeast, all sorts of rare animals are killed for food and for body parts used for traditional tribal costumes, from hornbills and wild buffalo to civet cats and rare gibbons. In mountain areas, the *chiru* (Tibetan antelope), is threatened by furriers who weave its fur into wool for expensive *shahtoosh* shawls.

In the water, the freshwater dolphins of the Brahmaputra are in dire straits from pollution and human competition, with gill-net fishing and hydroelectric dams being major threats. The sea turtle population on the Orissa coast also faces problems – see the boxed text, p260.

Plants

India's total forest cover is estimated to be around 20% of the total geographic coverage, despite an optimistic target of 33% set by the Forest Survey of India. The country boasts 49,219 plant species, of which around 5200 are endemic.

Tropical forests occur in the hills of the Northeast states, and large areas of savanna and jungle are found in lowland areas of Assam, West Bengal, Tripura and Orissa. Distinctive trees of the lowlands include the hardwood sal *(Shorea robusta)*, mango and pipal trees, and the Indian banyan (fig), with its dangling aerial roots. All these species face a challenge from introduced species such as the eucalyptus, a water-hungry species introduced by the British to dry out malarial swamps.

By far the biggest threat to forestry in the Northeast is firewood harvesting, particularly by illegal squatters. Since Partition, tens of thousands of landless peasants have flooded across the border from Nepal and Bangladesh, settling

In the early 20th century there were believed to be at least 40,000 wild tigers in India. Current estimates suggest there are fewer than 3500.

India is losing 6% of its forests each year to slash-and-burn agriculture, logging and clearance for development Bengal's Sunderbans has decreased in size by 40% since the 1900s.

in wilderness areas across the Northeast. Traditional slash-and-burn agriculture has also had a devastating effect on forestry, particularly in Nagaland, Mizoram and Arunachal Pradesh. The loss of forest cover has led to a marked increase in erosion and landslides during the monsoon.

The foothills of the Himalaya preserve classic Alpine species, including blue pine and *deodar* (Himalayan cedars), and deciduous forests of apple, chestnut, birch, plum and cinnamon. Hardy plants such as anemones, edelweiss and gentians grow above the snowline, while rare orchids and other wildflowers appear every summer in high mountain meadows.

NATIONAL PARKS & WILDLIFE SANCTUARIES

The Northeast has numerous national parks and wildlife sanctuaries, preserving an amazing variety of ecosystems, from the swamps of the Sunderbans to the snow-covered slopes of Mt Khangchendzonga. In addition to the official parks and reserves, six areas have been designated as biosphere reserves – the Sunderbans in West Bengal, Khangchendzonga in Sikkim, Similipal in Orissa, Nokrek in Meghalaya, and Manas and Dibru-Saikhowa in Assam. These biospheres overlap many of the national parks and sanctuaries, providing safe migration channels for wildlife and allowing scientists to monitor biodiversity.

We strongly recommend visiting at least one national park/sanctuary during your travels – the experience of coming face-to-face with a wild elephant, rhino or tiger will stay with you for a lifetime. Wildlife reserves tend to be off the beaten track and infrastructure can be limited – book transport and accommodation in advance, and check opening times, permit requirements and entry fees before you visit. Many parks close to conduct a census of wildlife in the off season and monsoon rains can make wildlife-viewing tracks inaccessible, particularly in the monsoon-drenched Northeast.

Almost all parks offer jeep/van tours, but you can also search for wildlife on guided treks, boat trips and elephant safaris. For various safari possibilities, see p75.

ENVIRONMENTAL ISSUES

With over one billion people, expanding industrialisation and urbanisation, and chemical-intensive agriculture, India's environment is under threat. An estimated 65% of India's land is degraded in some way, and the government has fallen short on most of its targets for environmental protection. The Northeast is particularly vulnerable because of the fragile political situation – many of the armed rebel groups operating in the Northeast use poaching, smuggling and illegal logging to finance their operations.

Despite dozens of new environmental laws, corruption continues to exacerbate environmental degradation – worst exemplified by the flagrant flouting of environmental rules by companies involved in hydroelectricity, uranium, oil exploration and mining. Typically, the people most affected are low-caste rural farmers and Adivasis (tribal people) who have limited political representation and few resources to fight the commercial ambitions of big business.

Many of the problems experienced today were a direct result of the Green Revolution of the 1960s when a quantum leap in agricultural output was achieved using chemical fertilisers and pesticides. Poverty and conflict have also played a role in the Northeast's environmental problems – economic migrants from Bangladesh and farmers displaced by political violence have settled on the edges of many national parks, poaching for food and clearing the forests for firewood and farmland.

The Foundation for Revitalisation of Local Health Traditions has a search engine for medicinal plants at www.medicinalplants.in. Travellers with a serious interest should pick up CP Khare's *Encyclopedia Of Indian Medicinal Plants*.

See our Indian Safari itinerary on p23 for recommended national parks or pick up a copy of *Indian National Parks & Sanctuaries* by Anand Khati.

Rather than decreeing from on high, some of the most successful environmental schemes have returned power to local communities through the creation of seed banks, micro-loan schemes and water-users cooperatives. Organic and biodynamic farming – based on natural compost and timing farming to natural and lunar cycles – is also gaining ground (see www.biodynamics.in for details). Many fair-trade companies are now sourcing biodynamic tea and other crops from the Northeast.

India's environmental problems are depressingly familiar. Between 11% and 27% of India's agricultural output is lost due to soil degradation through over-farming and loss of tree cover – a particular problem in the Northeast states. Pollution from industry, human habitation and agricultural chemicals is further affecting the health and quality of life for India's rural poor. Assam's economically important oil industry has been accused of dumping polluted waste water into tea gardens and rural farmland.

The human cost is heart-rending – crushing levels of debt and poverty drive hundreds of farmers to suicide every year. Lurking behind all these problems is a basic Malthusian truth: there are simply too many people for India to support at its current level of development. While the Indian government could undoubtedly do more, some share of blame must also fall on Western farm subsidies that artificially reduce the cost of imported produce, undermining prices for Indian farmers. Western agribusiness may also like to take a cynical bow for promoting the use of nonpropagating GM seed stocks.

As anywhere, tourists tread a fine line between providing an incentive for change and making the problem worse. Ecotours are providing an incentive for the preservation of wildlife but also encouraging the development of wilderness areas. Always look for tour operators who try to minimise their effect on the environment – elephant rides and jeep tours run by the national-park authorities are usually formulated with the best interests of wildlife in mind.

Seek out tour companies that employ local people as guides – this transfers money from tourism to the areas that need to be preserved, creating a direct link between conservation and earnings. One particularly innovative scheme

Get the lowdown on Indian environmental issues at Down to Earth (www.downtoearth.org.in), an online magazine that delves into stories overlooked by the mainstream media.

MAJOR NATIONAL PARKS & WILDLIFE SANCTUARIES

Park/Sanctuary	Page	Location	Features	Best time to visit
Bhitarkanika Wildlife Sanctuary	p266	northeast Orissa	estuarine mangrove forests: saltwater crocodiles, water monitors, pythons, wild boars & chitals	Dec-Feb
Chandaka Wildlife Sanctuary	p250	eastern Orissa	upland forest: elephants, leopards, chitals, sambar & crocodiles	Oct-May
Debrigarh Wildlife Sanctuary	p264	near Sambalpur, Orissa	dry deciduous forest: tigers, leopards, deer, boars & sloth bears & bird life	Oct-May
Jaldhapara Wildlife Sanctuary	p137	northern West Bengal	forest & grasslands: Indian one-horned rhinos, deer & elephants	mid-Oct– May
Kaziranga National Park	p208	Assam, Northeast states	dense grasslands & swamp: rhinos, deer, buffaloes, elephants, tigers & bird life	Feb-Mar
Manas National Park	p204	Near Guwahati, Assam	Lowland forest & rivers: tigers, deer, rare birds, langurs, hispid hare & pygmy hog	Feb-Mar
Similipal National Park	p264	Balasore, Orissa	forest & waterfalls: tigers, leopards, elephants, crocodiles & bird life	Nov-Jun
Sunderbans Tiger Reserve	p127	southern West Bengal	mangrove forests: tigers, deer, monkeys & bird life	Oct-Mar

is the ecotourism project run by Manas Maozigendri (MMES), which employs former Bodo insurgents to protect the forest from poachers – see p205.

Always consider your environmental impact while travelling in wilderness areas, including while trekking (see p78). Sikkim and other mountain states have banned plastic bags – help out by refusing plastic bags whenever they are offered. Purifying your own water will always win you a gold star – trekking routes in Sikkim and West Bengal are scarred by thousands of abandoned plastic water bottles.

Air Pollution

Air pollution from industry and vehicle emissions is a major concern in urban areas. Indian diesel reportedly contains around 50 to 200 times more sulphur than European diesel and the ageing engines of Indian vehicles would fail most emissions tests in Europe or the USA. While Delhi and Mumbai (Bombay) have switched their public transport systems to less-polluting Compressed Natural Gas (CNG), Kolkata remains one of the most polluted cities in the world. Around 70% of Kolkata residents suffer from some form of respiratory disease – with most of the blame falling on heavy traffic, impure fuels and polluting industry in populated areas.

Industry remains one of the biggest polluters in the Northeast. Factories share space with residential housing in most large cities and government controls on emissions are almost nonexistent, even after high-profile disasters like the gas leak from the Union Carbide plant in Bhopal in 1984. The massive growth of budget air travel is pumping even more greenhouse gases into the atmosphere – modern ideas such as carbon balancing hold little truck in a nation embracing the freedom of the skies for the first time.

Climate Change

Changing climate patterns, linked to global carbon emissions, have been creating dangerous extremes of weather across the Northeast. India stands far behind the USA, Australia and Europe in the global league of per capita carbon emissions, yet the subcontinent is one of the regions set to suffer most from of the effects of global warming.

Elevated monsoon rainfall is already causing widespread flooding and destruction across the Northeast, with Kolkata and the Assam plains being particularly affected. Hill towns in West Bengal and Sikkim have experienced devastating landslides, while islands in the Sunderbans delta have been inundated by rising sea levels. In coastal areas, rising salinity has damaged farmland and killed off endangered species, and Orissa has been ravaged by a series of devastating cyclones.

Conversely, other areas are experiencing reduced rainfall, causing drought and panic over access to water supplies. Drought has even reached the Khasi Hills of Meghalaya, formerly the wettest place on earth; massive deforestation has altered drainage patterns over the Meghalaya Plateau, causing crops to fail despite the massive rainfall.

Deforestation

Since Independence, some 5.3 million hectares of Indian forests have been cleared for logging and farming or damaged by urban expansion, mining, industrialisation and river dams. A third of the Sunderbans mangrove forests have been cleared since 1960, and the damming of rivers for irrigation and hydroelectric power have reduced the flow of fresh water into the Sunderbans. Rising levels of salinity are now threatening many rare species of plants and animals, and the loss of the mangroves is reducing the nursery grounds for the fish that stock the Indian Ocean and Bay of Bengal.

Air pollution in many Indian cities has been measured at more than double the maximum safe level recommended by the World Health Organization.

Once the wettest place on earth, Cherrapunjee in Meghalaya is now facing droughts because of changing drainage patterns caused by deforestation.

THE LONELY PLANET FOUNDATION

The Lonely Planet Foundation proudly supports nimble nonprofit institutions working for change in the world. Each year the foundation donates 5% of Lonely Planet company profits to projects selected by staff and authors. Our partners range from Kabissa, which provides small nonprofits across Africa with access to technology, to the Foundation for Developing Cambodian Orphans, which supports girls at risk of falling victim to sex traffickers.

Our nonprofit partners are linked by a grass-roots approach to the areas of health, education or sustainable tourism. Many projects we support – such as one with BaAka (Pygmy) children in the forested areas of Central African Republic – choose to focus on women and children as one of the most effective ways to support the whole community.

Sometimes foundation assistance is as simple as helping to preserve a local ruin like the Minaret of Jam in Afghanistan; this incredible monument now draws intrepid tourists to the area and its restoration has greatly improved options for local people.

Just as travel is often about learning to see with new eyes, so many of the groups we work with aim to change the way people see themselves and the future for their children and communities.

India's first Five Year Plan in 1951 recognised the importance of forests for soil conservation, and various policies have been introduced to increase forest cover. Almost all have been flouted by officials, criminals and by ordinary people clearing forests for firewood and allowing grazing in forest areas. Try to minimise the use of wood-burning stoves while you travel – particularly while trekking in the mountains of Sikkim.

Protected for years by the inaccessible topography, the forests of the Northeast are being cleared at a shocking rate for firewood and slash-and-burn agriculture, particularly in Nagaland, Manipur, Meghalaya and Mizoram. Without tree cover to anchor the soil, landslides are becoming increasingly common, and rainfall quickly leeches the nutrients out of exposed soil, driving farmers to clear ever larger areas of forest. There are knock-on effects in the lowlands – with no tree cover to act as a barrier, floods and droughts are becoming increasingly severe.

The problems are particularly acute in Orissa, where marginalised tribal communities are forced to practise shifting agriculture in order to survive. Clearing of woodland for cattle fodder and fuel has led to a massive increase in silt run-off into rivers and estuaries, choking important wetlands such as Chilika Lake. Increased sediment deposits are reducing the volume of drinking water in many reservoirs and altering the salinity of brackish marshland habitats, to the detriment of salt-adapted species.

Denotification, a process allowing states to relax the ban on the commercial exploitation of protected areas, is another factor. Officially, the states are supposed to earmark an equivalent area for afforestation, but enforcement is lacklustre and the land set aside may be unsuitable for forestry. On another front, invasive foreign plant species such as the eucalyptus are swamping indigenous flora.

Numerous charities are working with rural communities to encourage tree planting and many religious leaders have joined the movement, including the Dalai Lama. Oxfam is currently funding the planting of 100,000 mango, papaya, guava, banana, drumstick, neem and subadul saplings in Bihar, Assam and West Bengal to reduce soil erosion and damage from flooding.

Although India has problems with plastic waste, it is nothing compared to Europe – the average Indian uses 2kg of plastic per year, while the average European uses 60kg a year.

Plastic Waste

Ah, plastic! What a wonderful invention. Only a tiny proportion of plastic products can be reused or recycled and plastic rubbish persists in the environment for 1000 years before crumbling into a polluting chemical dust. Across the Northeast, plastic bags and bottles litter streets, streams and beaches; animals choke on the waste and the plastic clogs water courses, increasing the risk of landslides and water-borne diseases like malaria. Campaigners estimate that about 75% of plastics used are discarded within a week and only 15% are recycled.

Travellers may feel that efforts to avoid plastic are futile when locals toss rubbish from every bus window, but Western companies are the driving force behind disposable packaging and the switch from glass to plastic bottles by the Indian soft-drinks industry. However, there are some welcome signs of change. Sikkim banned plastic bags in 1997 after several children died tragically in a landslide caused by a build up of discarded plastic bags. A similar ban in Darjeeling, Kalimpong and Kurseong finally came into force in March 2007.

You can do your bit to help by purifying your own water – see p341 – or carrying a canteen and obtaining refills of boiled or purified water from guesthouses as you travel. Also set a good example by refusing plastic bags (and explaining why!) and insisting on soft drinks in recyclable glass bottles and tea in terracotta cups at train stations.

Noise pollution in major cities has been measured at over 90 decibels – more than one and a half times the recognised 'safe' limit. Bring earplugs!

Water Resources

Arguably the biggest threat to public health in India is inadequate access to clean drinking water and proper sanitation. With the population set to double by 2050, agricultural, industrial and domestic water usage are all expected to spiral, despite government policies designed to control water use.

The Northeast is in the surprising position of suffering from both too much rainfall and droughts. Climate change is bringing elevated levels of monsoon rainfall, causing flooding and landslides, but elevated areas have faced droughts because of increased drainage caused by deforestation. In

INDIA'S HYDROELECTRIC REVOLUTION

Hydroelectricity is India's buzzword for the 21st century. With an ever-increasing human population becoming ever hungrier for electric power, damming the rivers that flow down from the Himalaya has become big business, and nowhere more so than in Arunachal Pradesh. The state has the potential to supply a third of India's electricity needs and dozens of new hydroelectric plants have sprung up in locations along the tributaries of the Brahmaputra, turning falling water into crores of rupees.

Unfortunately Indian hydroelectricity is not quite as green as it sounds. To create the new hydroelectric plants in Arunachal Pradesh, whole valley systems are being flooded, displacing dozens of tribes from their ancestral homelands. The new Subansiri Lower Project (SLP), India's largest dam, is set to displace 5000 people from the Apatani, Nishi and Hill Miri tribes. Ironically, only two villages are being destroyed by the dam itself; the rest will be displaced by a new forest reserve, designed to replace the forests being submerged by the dam.

Unlike the Narmada Valley Development in Eastern India, the SLP has no nationwide campaigns and no celebrities questioning the environmental impact of hydroelectric power. Few of the tribes have the money to take on the combined forces of government and big business in the courts, and the land provided by the state government for relocation is frequently unsuitable for the traditional types of farming and forestry practised by tribal people.

Safety is another concern – most of the 168 proposed dams lie in Seismic Zone 5, the most earthquake-prone region of India, despite warnings from seismic reports. However, with the UN heavily promoting the projects as a tool for flood control, the construction of the dams is almost a foregone conclusion: a sad irony considering the massive areas of forest that will vanish under reservoirs in the next 10 years.

coastal areas, particularly in the Sunderbans, rising sea levels and damming of rivers for irrigation and hydroelectric power have led to a marked increase in water salinity. In Orissa the problem has been exacerbated by a series of tropical cyclones, bringing salt water far inland.

Industry, farming and human habitation also contribute to the pollution of drinking water across the Northeast. The Assamese oil industry has faced particular criticism for pumping contaminated water into lakes and rivers, damaging yields from local tea plantations. Few cities have adequate sewage-processing facilities and raw sewage often finds its way directly into drinking-water supplies, aiding the spread of water-borne diseases.

As well as problems from sedimentation (see the Deforestation section, p71) many parts of West Bengal and Orissa are witnessing falling fish stocks due to overfishing by migrants and landless peasants. This is a particular issue in the Sunderbans, where shrimp farmers use fine-mesh nets, damaging mangrove saplings and wiping out the nursery grounds for many species of sea fish.

Water distribution is another volatile issue. Since 1947 an estimated 35 million people in India have been displaced by major dams, mostly built for hydroelectricity projects to provide energy for this increasingly power-hungry nation. While hydroelectricity is one of the greener power sources, valleys across the Northeast are being sacrificed to create new power plants, and displaced people rarely receive adequate compensation; see the boxed text, p73.

The Subansiri Lower Project (SLP) has the capacity to produce 2000 megawatts of electricity – equivalent to three nuclear power stations.

Activities

The Northeast covers every imaginable terrain, including rainforest and tow-ering mountains. With all this to play with, the opportunities for adventurous activities are endless. Take your pick from trekking, mountaineering, jungle safaris, elephant rides, river boats, yoga…the list goes on and on. It would take a whole book to cover all the options, but some of the most popular activities are covered in the following sections.

CHOOSING A TOUR OPERATOR

Regardless of what you decide to do, you need to exercise a little caution when choosing an operator. We receive regular reports of dodgy companies taking poorly equipped tourists into dangerous situations. Remember that travel agents are only middle-men and the final decisions about safety and equipment come down to the people actually operating the trip. Check out all tour operators, trekking companies and activity providers carefully. Make sure that you know in advance what you are getting, then make sure that what you get matches what you paid for.

Where possible, stick to companies that provide activities themselves, using their own guides and teaching staff. If you go through an agency, look for operators who are accredited by the **Travel Agents Association of India** (www.travelagentsofindia.com), the **Indian Association of Tour Operators** (www.iato .in) or the **Adventure Tour Operators Association of India** (www.indianadventure.com). Note that dodgy operators often change their names to sound like trusted companies – so it's a good idea to consult official tourist offices for lists of government-approved operators and seek first-hand recommendations from fellow travellers.

Always check safety equipment before you set out and make sure you know what is included in the price quoted. If anything is substandard, let the operator know. If they refuse to make the necessary changes, go with another company. For any activity, make sure that you have adequate insur-ance, including cover for any risky activities (see p303).

OUTDOOR ACTIVITIES

All sorts of activities are possible in India's outdoors, such as trekking, moun-taineering, jungle safaris and white-water rafting, along with more relaxing activities such, as elephant rides, boat tours and pony treks.

MEETING THE WILDLIFE

India has some of the most amazing flora and fauna on earth – from lumbering elephants and growling tigers to desert orchids and trailing lianas. Here are some excellent ways to get up close and personal with Indian wildlife.

Bird-Watching

India has some of the world's major bird breeding and feeding grounds. Try the following prime bird-watching sites in the Northeast.
Northeast states Birding tours by raft at Potasali Eco-Camp (p207) near Tezpur in Assam.
Orissa Domestic species and migrating waterbirds – including flamingos – from November to January at Similipal National Park (p264), Bhitarkanika Wildlife Sanctuary (p266) and Chilika Lake (p258).

India Outdoors (www .indiaoutdoors.com) provides information on an incredible range of outdoor activities, from abseiling and rock-climbing to scuba-diving and water skiing.

The Wildlife Protection Society of India (www .wpsi-india.org/tiger) is campaigning to save tigers in the wild – see the website for listings of tiger reserves.

The website www.bird ing.in is a one-stop shop for bird-watchers in India, with listings of bird-watching sites and all the species you are likely to see.

Sikkim Birding tours with Sikkim Tours & Travels (p166) in Gangtok and Khecheopalri Trekkers Hut (p185) at Khecheopalri Lake.

West Bengal Bird-watching tours through Kalimpong's Gurudongma Tours & Travels (p156).

Elephant Safaris

Elephant rides provide an amazing way to get close to Indian wildlife. Many of the Northeast's national parks have their own working elephants, which can be hired for safaris into areas that are inaccessible to jeeps and walkers. You might even find yourself just metres from a rumbling rhino or a snarling Bengal tiger. As well as being a childhood dream for most travellers, elephant rides are much less disturbing to wildlife than noisy jeeps. To find out the best times to visit parks, see regional chapters and the boxed text, p70.

Bihar & Jharkhand Elephant safaris in Jharkhand's Betla (Palamau) National Park (p269).

Northeast states Elephant safaris to spot one-horned Indian rhinos at Kaziranga National Park (p208) and other wildlife and rare species, like the pygmy hog, hispid hare and golden langur at Manas National Park (p204).

West Bengal Jumbo rides around Jaldhapara Wildlife Sanctuary (p137) to spot one-horned Indian rhinos.

Horse Riding

Several hill stations in West Bengal offer pony rides, from gentle ambles through town to more serious pony trails through the forest. As well as these leisure rides, ponies are used as transport on many *yatra* (pilgrimage) trekking routes – see the regional chapters for details. Good places to saddle up include the following:

Northeast states Dibrugarh (Assam; p212)

West Bengal Mirik (p138) and Darjeeling (p147)

Jeep Safaris

The Northeast has numerous jeep safaris visiting national parks, tribal villages, and remote temples and monasteries. You can normally arrange a custom itinerary, either with travel agents or directly with local jeep drivers – see the regional chapters for information. Popular options include:

Bihar & Jharkhand Jeep tours to spot wild beasties in Betla (Palamau) National Park (p269).

Northeast states Jeeps to tribal villages in the Northeast states from Guwahati (p200), and wildlife-spotting tours in Kaziranga National Park (p208) and Manas National Park (p204).

Orissa Animal-focused jeep safaris in Similipal National Park (p264) and Badrama and Debrigarh Wildlife Sanctuaries (p264).

Sikkim Agencies in Gangtok (p166) arrange jeep tours to the Yumthang Valley (p190) and other remote areas in North Sikkim (p190 and p189).

ADVENTURE ACTIVITIES

For a fascinating account of the first trekking forays into Sikkim, read *Among the Himalayas* by Major Laurence Austine Waddell.

The Northeast is paradise for adrenaline junkies and fans of the great outdoors. Trekking is possible throughout the country, including the hills of Orissa and the wind-scoured valleys of the Himalaya. Among other adrenaline-charged activities, it's possible to rock-climb in the hills and go white-water rafting on the mighty rivers that drain from the Himalaya. See the following sections for some suggestions. Remember to take out adequate insurance cover for any adventure activities before you travel (see p303).

Boat Tours

Boat tours are possible all over India – take your pick from slow river rides, nature cruises and trips to fantastic festivals. Here are some options:

Kolkata (Calcutta) Cruises to watch the immersion of the idols during the Durga Puja festival (October) in Kolkata (p113).

Northeast states Steamboat cruises along the Brahmaputra River in Assam with Jungle Travels India (p200) and wildlife-spotting boat safaris at Manas National Park (p204).

Orissa Boat tours to hunt for crocodiles, freshwater dolphins and birds at Bhitarkanika Wildlife Sanctuary (p266) and Chilika Lake (p258).

West Bengal Boat tours to track tigers in the huge Sunderbans Tiger Reserve (p129 and p113).

Cultural Tours

Tours to tribal areas are permitted in several parts of the Northeast, providing a fascinating window onto the traditional way of life of India's Adivasis (see p48 for more on the tribes of the Northeast). Some tours are quite exploitative but better tours employ tribal guides and try to minimise the effect of tourism on tribal people. Reputable tribal tours include the following:

> Adivasis (tribal people) make up 8% of the Indian population, or 45 million people, and 573 scheduled tribes are recognised in the Indian constitution.

Northeast states Travel agencies in Guwahati arrange tours of fascinating tribal districts in the Northeast states (p200), Dibrugarh (p212), Kohima (p226), Aizawl (p239) and Bomdila (p234).

Orissa Tours to visit Orissa's tribal communities – see the boxed text (p262), the Orissa Tourism entry on p243 and the tours for Puri (p254).

Cycling & Motorcycling

There are some sensational organised, motorcycle tours that pass through Sikkim, or you can rent a motorcycle and set your own itinerary. Recommended motorcycle tours are covered on p331 and information on buying or renting a motorcycle in India is provided on p329.

Sikkim is particularly appealing for cyclists – there's hardly any traffic and the quiet mountain roads are surrounded by breathtaking scenery. It's best to bring your own bike if you intend to tackle the hills, though good-quality mountain bikes are available in Kolkata – see p326 for more on cycling in India. For local exploration, bikes can be rented cheaply from guesthouses and shops in Konark (p258) and Puri (p256) in Orissa.

> For a great introduction to cycling around Sikkim, including photos and video clips, see the informative blog on the website www.cycling aroundtheworld .nl/Sikkim.

Kayaking & White-Water Rafting

Across the Northeast, mighty rivers charge down from the hills and mountains, offering some fantastic opportunities for white-water rafting. Things aren't quite as organised as in nearby Nepal, but rivers in West Bengal provide some of the best and most accessible rafting in North India. The main rafting season is from September to November and March to June and the level of rapids varies from modest Grade II to raging Grade IV. Most rafting operators offer multiday rafting safaris as well short thrill rides. Check the safety procedures before joining any rafting trip and make sure that lifejackets are in good working order.

> Rafting is possible on many of the rivers that snake down through the Northeast from the Himalaya – see www .indiarafting.com for popular options.

Rafting on the Rangeet and Teesta Rivers can be arranged through agents in Darjeeling (p147) and Teesta Bazaar (p158). Arunachal Pradesh is said to have the best rafting and kayaking in all of India but so far there are no commercial operators – try contacting travel agents in the Northeast states to see if you can arrange a bespoke trip (see p193).

Rock-Climbing & Mountaineering

The mountains of Sikkim, West Bengal and Arunachal Pradesh offer some dramatic opportunities for mountaineering and the rocky hills of Meghalaya and Assam provide some impressive rock-climbing for climbers with their own gear. The Northeast has everything from frozen waterfalls and alpine routes to big walls and escarpments, but you'll need to bring everything with you from home – including ropes, boots, harnesses, head-torch, chalk and protection. There are no bolted routes so bring a decent rack – plenty of nuts, hexacentrics, cams, quickdraws and slings, some industrial rigging karabiners as disposable anchors and spare rolls of climbing tape for jamming off-width cracks.

The last 10m of India's highest mountain, Khangchendzonga (8598m), is off-limits to climbers as a sign of respect to local Buddhists.

Darjeeling has a number of climbing centres that offer mountaineering and rock-climbing training courses – both indoors and outdoors – from March to December. Courses run on set dates and most of the equipment you need is provided, but bring your own warm-weather clothing. For more information, see p148.

Trekking

The Northeast offers some amazing trekking, particularly in the foothills of the Himalaya, with temples, Buddhist monasteries, remote lakes and mountain passes as popular destinations. Many peaks above 5000m can be summited by trekkers as well as mountaineers. You may also be able to arrange treks

---

RESPONSIBLE TREKKING

To help preserve India's natural beauty, consider the following tips when trekking. Try to choose trekking agencies and tour operators that focus on sustainable, low-impact tourism.

Rubbish

- Carry out all rubbish (including cigarette butts, sanitary napkins, tampons and condoms) and any rubbish you may find. Set a good example as well as reducing pollution.
- Never bury rubbish: digging encourages erosion and buried rubbish may be dug up and consumed by animals (this can be harmful to them).
- Take reusable containers or stuff sacks. Avoid plastic bags and plastic water bottles.
- Carry a canteen and a water filtration or purification system in remote areas. In villages, refill your canteen with boiled water or filtered water provided by local environmental organisations.

Human Waste Disposal

- To prevent the spread of disease, use toilets where provided. If there aren't any, bury your waste. Dig a small hole (15cm) at least 100m from any watercourse (bring a lightweight trowel) and adequately cover it with soil and a rock. Use minimal toilet paper (preferably none). In snow, dig down to the soil.
- If the area is inhabited, ask locals if they have any concerns about your chosen toilet site.
- Ensure that these guidelines are applied to portable toilet tents used by trekking groups. All members (including porters) should use them.

Washing

- Don't use detergents or toothpaste in or near watercourses, even if these products are biodegradable.
- For personal washing, use biodegradable soap and a water container at least 50m away from the watercourse. Disperse the waste water widely so the soil can adequately filter it.
- Wash cooking utensils 50m away from watercourses using a scourer, sand or snow instead of detergent.

Clothing, Fires & Cooking

- Bring proper clothing for the extreme cold of the mountains – research weather conditions in advance and seek professional advice on clothes and equipment. This will reduce the need for fires for warmth.

to tribal areas in Nagaland, Mizoram, Meghalaya and Arunachal Pradesh through travel agents in the Northeast states – see p193 for some recommended companies.

However, the trekking industry is not as well developed as in nearby Nepal. Accommodation is only available on a handful of routes and trekkers must carry everything they need, including food, sleeping bags, emergency equipment and (on some routes) drinking water. Rubbish must be carried out with you when you leave. Acute Mountain Sickness is also a risk on any routes over 3000m, including several routes in Sikkim. Finally you need to consider permits, as many routes pass close to the disputed border between India and Tibet.

Because of this independent trekking can be risky. Most people opt for organised treks with local trekking agencies, though it is sometimes possible to

- Cutting wood causes deforestation – a major problem in India – so avoid open fires and stay in lodgings that don't use wood to cook or heat water where possible.
- Use a lightweight kerosene, alcohol or Shellite (white gas) stove and avoid stoves powered by disposable butane-gas canisters.
- If you must light an open fire, try to use existing fireplaces and only use dead, fallen wood. Be sure to fully extinguish a fire, which can be done by spreading the embers and flooding them with sand or water.

Cultural Sensitivity

- Respect local cultural practices when interacting with communities, including local attitudes to modesty.
- Observe official regulations in areas you visit. Many rules are there to protect the local way of life.
- Do not hand out pens, sweets or money to children; this promotes begging. If you want to give, donate to local schools and community centres.
- Always seek permission from landowners if you intend to enter private property.
- Where possible, trek with a local guide. This way, money from tourism will directly benefit the people it affects.

Flora & Fauna

- Always stick to existing tracks. Blazing new trails will create new watercourses, contributing to erosion. Walk through rather than around mud patches and puddles – walking around the edge increases the area being degraded.
- Don't pick flowers or other plants – covering vegetation plays a vital role in keeping the topsoil in place.
- Avoid disturbing wild or domesticated animals and shut any gates you open.
- Hunting is illegal in India and it adds to the pressure on species already endangered by loss of habitat – don't do it.
- Refrain from feeding wildlife (don't leave food scraps behind either). Wild animals can become dependent on handouts and random feeding can lead to attacks on humans, unbalanced animal populations and disease. Place foodstuffs out of reach while you camp (tie packs to rafters or trees).

MOUNTAINEERING IN INDIA

Mountaineers need permission from the **Indian Mountaineering Federation** (IMF; www.indmount .org) in Delhi to climb most peaks over 6000m, and the expedition royalties are significant – from US$1500 to US$8000 per expedition, depending on the height of the peak. Special rules apply to Khangchendzonga – the peak is worshipped as a deity by the Lepcha people, so mountaineers must stop before the summit as a sign of respect. Many peaks lie in restricted areas near the Chinese border and climbers must pay additional fees for Inner Line– and Restricted Area Permits, plus any national park fees that apply. Discounts are available for groups who make arrangements through approved travel agents inside India. Contact the IMF for more information on any aspect of mountaineering in India.

---

hire your own porters, packhorses and guides through local tourist offices. If you do make your own arrangements, ensure that your guide speaks English and make an emergency plan for evacuation from the route. Tell someone at the trailhead where you are going and when you intend to be back, and never trek alone. On any organised trek, make sure that you have all the equipment you need and ensure that you know exactly what is included in the fee you agree. Proper travel insurance is essential – see p303.

Sikkim is the premier trekking destination in the Northeast. Travel agencies in Gangtok (p166) and Pelling (p174) can arrange treks all over Sikkim, including the popular trek to the 4940m Goecha La (p187). Many people also trek stages of the leisurely 'Monastic Loop' around West Sikkim, which passes a series of monasteries and mountain viewpoints (see p187). More impressive treks are possible near Darjeeling in West Bengal, including the dramatic Singalila Ridge along the Nepali border – see p152.

> Porters are often shoddily treated by trekking companies, so make sure your trek organiser follows the International Porter Protection Group Guidelines at www.ippg .net/guidelines.

Canyoning & Caving

In Meghalaya, **Cherrapunjee Holiday Resort** (p218) offers unusual canyoning trips that utilise surreal 'living bridges' woven from living trees by local tribes.

Millennia of torrential monsoon rains have hollowed out an amazing system of caves underneath the northeastern state of Meghalaya, including the 22km-long Krem Um Im-Liat Prah/Krem Labbit system, India's longest cave. Caving trips can be arranged through tour agents in Shillong (p214). However, this is serious caving and it's best to bring equipment from home.

> Meghalaya has 750 recorded caves, but only 250 have ever been explored.

HOLISTIC & SPIRITUAL ACTIVITIES

Not all activities in the Northeast involve hauling yourself up mountains. Travellers with an interest in spirituality or alternative therapies will find courses and treatments that focus on healing body and mind. After all, this is the country that gave the world meditation, massage and mantras! Meditation, Ayurveda (Indian herbal medicine) and yoga have gained respect even in mainstream circles and there are several places where you can practise to improve your technique in the Northeast.

Yoga & Ashrams

India is famous as the home of yoga – a system of mental and physical exercises designed to train the consciousness for perfect control of mind and body. The most common yoga forms are hatha (following the *shatkarma* system of postures and meditation), ashtanga (following the 'eight limbs' system of postures and meditation), pranayama (controlled yogic breathing) and Iyengar (a variation of ashtanga yoga using physical aids for advanced postures).

Most of the opportunities for yoga practise in the Northeast are in ashrams – places of communal living that are established on the philosophies of a guru (spiritual guide – the word literally means 'dispeller of darkness' or 'heavy with wisdom'). Some ashrams require a minimum time commitment; a donation may be required, and residents may be required to follow strict rules on silence, diet and behaviour. As spiritual communities, most ashrams also have a proselytising agenda – make sure you are happy with the ashram ethos before you commit.

Alternatively, many upmarket hotels have spas offering yoga and alternative therapies without the religious overtones (see below) and there are numerous private yoga centres – readers have recommended the courses run by Art of Living (see p112) in Kolkata.

Laughter yoga – based on the therapeutic effects of group laughter – is also popular; several clubs meet daily in Kolkata's Rabindra Sarovar park (see p110).

The following ashrams in the Northeast accept visitors:

Kolkata Belur Math (Kolkata; p111) The headquarters of the Ramakrishna Mission; branches are found countrywide.

West Bengal International Society for Krishna Consciousness (ISKCON; Mayapura; p132) Global headquarters of the Hare Krishna movement, with branches all over India.

Based on the healing power of laughter, laughter yoga is a growing phenomenon in the Northeast. See www.laughteryoga.org for more on the movement.

Spa Treatments

If you just want to enjoy the effects of India' healing arts, the Northeast has several upmarket spas, and private practitioners of massage and other traditional therapies can be found in larger towns and cities. However, be cautious of one-on-one massages by private operators, particularly in tourist towns. Paying more for an established centre is usually better than a groping by a dodgy masseur.

Recommended spots for indulgence include:

Kolkata Exclusive Banyan Tree spa treatments at the Oberoi Grand (p115).

Orissa Plush resort spas in Bhubaneswar (p248) and Puri (p255).

Most Indian spa treatments are based on Ayurveda (Indian herbal medicine) – read *The Handbook of Ayurveda* by Shantha Godagama for an introduction to the most popular techniques.

Food & Drink

The Northeast is a feast for all the senses, but particularly the sense of taste. As well as treats found all over India, the Northeast has its own unique regional cuisines. Bengalis feast on freshwater fish and seafood, Assamese food is dominated by fermented ingredients and tart flavours, the Himalayan states dine on dumplings and noodle soups, Oriya (Orissan) cooking features subtle spices and sweet desserts, and tribal cooking is a whirl of exotic meats and jungle ingredients.

Indian pepper was so valued in medieval times that it was used in Europe in lieu of money – hence the phrase 'peppercorn rent'.

STAPLES & SPECIALITIES

Spices

The spices used in Indian cooking create a map of medieval trade routes. Christopher Columbus was searching for Indian black peppercorns when he stumbled across America. Coriander has been grown in India for millennia. Curry leaves and green cardamoms are cash crops in the steamy south, while black cardamoms flourish in the foothills of the Himalaya. Cinnamon and ginger came to India through China. Turmeric, nutmeg and cloves were shipped in from Southeast Asia and tamarind arrived from Africa. Saffron was introduced to Kashmir from the Mediterranean and cumin was imported from Egypt. Even the chilli that gives Indian food its famous punch arrived by sea, imported from South America by Portuguese traders in the 16th century.

Monisha Bharadwaj's *The Indian Kitchen* is a beautifully presented cookbook with over 200 traditional recipes. It contains handy tips such as how to best store spices.

There is no such thing as a 'curry' in India – the term comes from the Tamil word *kari,* meaning either 'black pepper' or 'spiced sauce'. Instead, most dishes are defined by their ingredients, cooking style and the masala (spice) mix used in their preparation. Perhaps the most famous masala is garam (hot) masala – built on a foundation of cinnamon, roasted cumin, cloves, nutmeg, chilli and green or black cardamoms.

Rice

Rice is the backbone of Northeast Indian cuisine, served boiled or fried with thalis (plate meals) and 'wet' and 'dry' sauces. Boiled rice and dhal (stewed lentils or pulses) is the staple diet in many rural parts of Bengal, Orissa, Sikkim and Assam. The Assamese are also fond of *chira* – unhusked boiled rice, beaten flat and served with yoghurt and *jaggery* (palm sugar) for breakfast.

India was only introduced to the chilli pepper in the 16th century. Prior to the colonial era, heat was added to food using black peppercorns.

As well as fragrant basmati rice, farmers in the Northeast states cultivate Thai-style glutinous rice, which is baked into *pithas* (rice cakes) and ground down and fermented to make *lau-pani* (rice wine). In tribal areas, glutinous rice is mixed with meat or fish and roasted inside tubes of bamboo or banana leaves.

Pulao (fried rice) was bought to India by the Mughals; unlike in the West, it is served as a main course, not a side dish. Muslim areas serve spiced meat and fried rice as biryani, while Chinese and Tibetan restaurants serve rice fried with chicken, egg, vegetables or meat – livened up with a variety of chilli-based condiments.

Bread & Noodles

The word roti, the generic term for Indian bread, is used interchangeably with chapati to describe the unleavened round bread made with whole-wheat flour and cooked on a *tawa* (hotplate). *Puri,* or *poori,* is deep-fried dough puffed up like a soft, crispy balloon. It's often served with *channa* (chickpea curry). Flaky *paratha* – unleavened bread fried in ghee – is often filled with *aloo* (potato) or *paneer* (unfermented cheese). Thick, tear drop–shaped naan is cooked in a *tandoor* (clay oven) – it comes plain, buttered or filled with garlic, fruit or mince.

In Tibetan influenced areas, such as Sikkim and Arunachal Pradesh, *tsampa* (barley flour dough) is used to make noodles and the wrappings for *momos* – steamed or fried dumplings stuffed with vegetables, cheese or meat. Fat *thenthuk* (pulled noodles) are used in Tibetan soups, while thin yellow noodles are used for chow mein (Chinese-style fried noodles). Many Tibetan restaurants serve *tingmo* (steamed Tibetan bread) – it's often flavoured with garlic but delicious with butter and honey.

Tsampa is the main form of starch in Tibetan Buddhist areas, and throwing tsampa flour in the air at festivals is believed to bring good luck.

Dhal

All of India is united in its love for dhal (lentils or pulses). You may encounter up to 60 different pulses: the most common are *chana,* a slightly sweeter version of the yellow split pea; yellow or green *moong dhal* (mung beans); salmon-coloured *masoor* (red lentils); *tuvar dhal* (yellow lentils; also known as *arhar*); *rajma* (kidney beans); *kabuli chana* (chickpeas); *urad* (black gram or lentils); and *lobhia* (black-eyed peas).

Meat

Goat (known as mutton since the days of the Raj) and lamb crop up in numerous dishes, particularly in the mountains. Chicken appears everywhere and in everything. Religious taboos make beef forbidden to Hindus and pork to Muslims. However, pork is a popular meat for the tribes of the Northeast. Dog meat also appears on tribal menus, along with a host of bush meats, including many endangered species – see p67. The Buddhist tribes of Sikkim and Arunachal Pradesh enjoy buffalo and yak meat, often fried with noodles or rolled into momos.

Mughlai cuisine is dominated by meats – typically chicken and lamb or mutton – served in rich curries, kebabs, koftas (rissoles) and biryanis. Tandoori dishes are a firm Mughal favourite – meat is marinated in spices and yoghurt and roasted in a traditional *tandoor.*

Fish & Seafood

Northeastern cuisine makes extensive use of farmed fish, including carp varieties such as *katla* and *rui* (rohu), *magur* (catfish) and *chingri* (river prawns). *Ilish hilsa,* a small bony fish that migrates into Indian rivers from the sea, is the favourite fish of Bengal. It is particularly delicious when cooked steamed in plantain leaves. *Bhetki* (seabass) is a popular white fish for grills and curries. Also look out for *shukti* – pungent dried and salted sea fish.

Fruit & Vegetables

Sabzi (vegetables) come fried, roasted, curried, stuffed, baked, mashed into koftas or wrapped in batter to make deep-fried *pakora* or *bhajia,* both types of vegetable fritters.

Potatoes are cooked with various masalas, or mashed and fried for the street snack *aloo tikka* (mashed potato patties). Cauliflower is often cooked with potatoes to make *aloo gobi* (potato-and-cauliflower curry), or mixed with other vegetables. Fresh green peas turn up stir-fried with other vegetables in *pulaos* and biryanis and as *mattar paneer* (peas and unfermented cheese in gravy).

Eggplant/aubergine, known locally as *baigan* or *brinjal,* can either be curried or sliced and deep-fried. Many curries make use of *saag,* a generic

India has more than 500 varieties of mangoes, and supplies almost 60% of the world with what is regarded as the king of fruit.

NAMKIN

If you travel by bus or train anywhere in India, you will encounter *namkin* vendors selling a range of savoury snacks. The word *namkin* covers a vast range of salty treats prepared using dried pulses, peanuts, rice flakes, chilli and spices, and noodle-like strands of fried dough made from lentil, potato or chickpea flour. Common varieties of *namkin* include *bhujia* – thin, spicy gram flour noodles – and Bombay Mix, which is a combination of dried green peas, spices, peanuts and *bhujia*.

---

term for leafy greens like mustard, spinach and fenugreek leaves. Bumpy-skinned *karela* (bitter gourd) and *bhindi* (okra) are usually fried dry with spices.

Citrus fruits such as oranges (which are usually yellow-green), tangerines, grapefruits, kumquats and sweet limes, are sold all over India. Apples and pears are grown in the mountains; guavas, grapes, papaya and pineapples are farmed in the plains; and coconuts grow naturally along the coast. The mango originated in Northeast India – fat *fazli* mangoes are the speciality of West Bengal.

Pickles, Chutneys & Relishes

Indians love their condiments. *Chatnis* (chutneys) come in dozens of varieties. Chopped onions and radish are served as a side dish with *pudina chatni* (mint, onion, garlic, chilli, ginger, lemon juice and spices). If you order a thali, you'll usually find a dollop of *achar* (pickles) on the side. Fiery red lime pickle is made from juiced limes mashed with chilli, mustard oil and spices. Other ingredients used in *achar* include mango, lemons, ginger and various garden vegetables.

South Indian meals are served with coconut chutney, a red-hot mix of coconut, chilli, spices and curd. Another popular condiment is *raita* (spiced yogurt, with shredded cucumber, carrot or diced pineapple; served chilled). The typical Chinese or Tibetan sauce rack contains soy sauce, chopped chillies in vinegar, and a pungent red or green paste made from chillies, garlic and vinegar.

The banana is widely used as a vegetable in the Northeast. Orissan cooks serve plantains (green bananas) with vegetables in the popular *dalma* stew, and Bengalis use banana pith *(thor)* and flowers *(mochar)* in all sorts of spicy sauces.

Dairy

Milk makes a staggering contribution to Indian cuisine. *Dahi* (curd/yogurt) is served as a side dish to counter hot spices or stirred into curries, soups and marinades. It is also the main ingredient for *lassi* – a sweet or savoury yoghurt shake. Ghee (clarified butter) is used for frying and flavouring. *Paneer* (Indian soft cheese) is cooked in a similar way to meat – look out for delicious skewers of spiced *paneer,* cooked in the tandoor. Most Indian sweets are also built on a base of milk sweetened with *jaggery* (palm sugar).

Hard cheeses were bought to the mountains of West Bengal by Swiss missionaries in the 1950s. Small cubes of 'Kalimpong cheese' are sold throughout Sikkim and the West Bengal Hills. Close to the Bhutanese border, look out for *ema datsi* – a fiery soup made from chilli and melted cheese.

Sweets

Northeast Indians have a famously sweet tooth, particularly in the state of West Bengal. Sweetshops sell myriad varieties of *mithai* (Indian sweets), many of which are wrapped in edible silver leaf. The main ingredients for *mithai* are milk, sugar (or jaggery), fruit and nuts. Popular types of *mithai*

Each year, at least 13 tonnes of pure silver are converted into edible foil for wrapping Indian sweets.

include *barfi* (a sweet milk-based fudge), *halwa* (an Arabic sweetmeat made with nuts and fruit), *ladoos* (gram flour and semolina sweetmeats) and *jalebis* (orange-coloured whorls of deep-fried batter that are dunked in syrup).

Some sweets are more like desserts. Invented in Kolkata (Calcutta), *rasgulla* is a sweet treat made from balls of *chhana* (unpressed *paneer*) flavoured with rosewater. Another syrupy treat is *gulab jamun* – deep-fried balls of dough soaked in rose-flavoured syrup. Another favourite pudding is *kheer*, a creamy rice pudding flavoured with cardamom, saffron, pistachios, flaked almonds, cashews or dried fruit. *Kulfi* is a firm-textured ice cream made with milk, nuts and fruit. It's best sampled in restaurants – street vendors often melt and re-freeze their ice-creams.

Street vendors sell piles of *peitha* (sweet pumpkin crystallised with sugar syrup), attracting swarms of honey bees. Most markets also have stalls selling raisins, dates, dried apricots and other dried fruit.

Sweet tooths will love *The Book of Indian Sweets* by Satarupa Banerjee, which contains a lip-smacking array of regional recipes, including many treats from Bengali and Orissa.

INDIA-WIDE CUISINE

Some dishes are found all over India, carried across the subcontinent by invading armies and migrant workers. However, popular Indian dishes served in the West rarely appear on menus inside India, partly because most Indian restaurants overseas are actually Bangladeshi or Pakistani restaurants.

North Indian Cuisine

Punjabi cooking crops up frequently on restaurant menus in the Northeast. The charcoal-fired *tandoor* produces piping-hot naan bread and a gamut of kebabs: *sheekh* (spiced lamb or chicken mince on iron skewers), *tangri* (chicken drumsticks), *boti* (spicy bite-sized bits of boneless lamb), tikka (marinated chunks of chicken, fish or *paneer*) and, of course, the ubiquitous tandoori chicken, sold as a 'whole' or 'half' bird with a wedge of lime. Vegetarian Punjabi dishes include *aloo gobi* and *aloo mattar* (a curry made with potatoes and green peas).

For a comprehensive travellers' guide to Indian cuisine, grab Lonely Planet's *World Food India*.

Rajasthani breads like rotis, *puris* and *parathas* are served with curries and sauces. Mughlai dishes like *murg dopiaza* (chicken in a rich onion sauce), *rogan josh* (Kashmiri lamb and tomato curry), *dum aloo* (curried potatoes, often stuffed) and 'Mughlai chicken' (the default chicken curry of the north) crop up so regularly they feel like old friends.

PAAN

Indian meals are often rounded off with *paan*, a fragrant mixture of chopped betel nut (the fruit of the areca palm) with lime paste, spices and flavourings, wrapped in an edible leaf from the *paan* vine. Although *paan* is eaten as a digestive and palate cleanser, betel nut is mildly narcotic, with a similar stimulant effect to nicotine – red-stained teeth are a sure sign of a heavy paan habit.

There are two basic types of *paan* – *mitha* (sweet) and *saadha* (with tobacco) – that are sold by *paan*-wallahs, who are sure to strategically position their stalls in close proximity to busy restaurants. The consumption of *paan* is an artform – the leaf parcel should be chewed slowly until a mild sensation of numbness sets in, then you should spit out the gloopy red juice, preferably into a spittoon.

There have been numerous attempts to ban paan because of the lurid-red spit marks left behind on the streets and the potential health risks – principally tooth decay and mouth cancer from the tobacco in *saadha paan*. However, with hundreds of millions of regular users, there is little risk of a *paan* ban anytime soon.

Balti cooking was
invented as a marketing
ploy by expat Indians
in northern England. in
India, 'balti' is just an
alternative name for
the common wok, also
known as a *kadhai*.

South Indian Cuisine

South Indian dishes crop up everywhere in the Northeast. Food is typically
vegetarian, and almost every dish is served with spicy coconut chutney and
sambar, a peppery sauce flavoured with mustard seed, tamarind, ground
lentils and chilli.

The most common dishes are *idlis,* spongy fermented rice cakes, cooked
in a steamer, and dosas – savoury pancakes made from fermented rice and
lentil flour. Common varieties include the *masala dosa* (stuffed with spiced
potatoes), the *rava dosa* (with a semolina batter) and the Mysore dosa (a
potato-filled dosa with extra garlic and chilli).

Other widely eaten snacks include *vadas* (doughnut-shaped deep-fried
lentil savouries) and *appams* or *uttappams* (crisp-collared rice-flour and
coconut-milk pancakes).

REGIONAL SPECIALITIES
Kolkata & West Bengal

Bengalis are fiercely proud of their cuisine. The flavours of Bengali cooking
come from jaggery, *malaikari* (coconut milk), *shorsher tel* (mustard oil) and
posto (poppy seed). Fish is the foundation of Bengali cooking; perhaps the
definitive Bengali dish is *bhetki paturi* (bhetki fish steamed in banana leaf).
Most dishes are served with dhal (prepared with yellow *chana* lentils) and
rice, or sometimes *luchi* (small puris).

Recommended Bengali
cookbooks include *The
Calcutta Cookbook* by
Minakshie Dasgupta and
*Bengali Cooking: Seasons
and Festivals* by Chitrita
Banerji, which also
explains the customs and
significance of different
Bengali dishes.

Bengali sweets and puddings are legendary. Sweet shops in Bengal stock
dozens of varieties of *mithai* (Indian sweets). Popular treats include *mishti
dhoi* (sweetened curd) and *rasgulla* (cheese balls in rose syrup). See the boxed
text, p117 for more on Bengali cuisine.

Orissa

Oriya (Orissan) cooking is known for its subtle flavours and delicate spices.
Freshwater and saltwater fish are core ingredients, many dishes feature
kankada (crab) and *chungudi* (prawns). Coconut crops up in many Oriya
dishes, and plantains (green bananas), jackfruit and papaya are cooked in
savoury sauces.

Tamarind adds a lovely sour flavour to Oriya cooking and many dishes are
flavoured with *pancha-phutana,* a mix of cumin, mustard, fennel, fenugreek
and *kala zeera* (black *nigella* seeds). Popular Oriya dishes to look out for
include *dalma* (a spiced lentil sauce with vegetables, fruit and plantain) and
ambul (fish cooked with mustard and tangy dried mangoes).

Puddings and sweets are as popular in Orissa as in Bengal. *Kheer* – creamy
Indian rice pudding – was allegedly invented in Orissa two thousand
years ago. It's still prepared daily in the famous Jagannath temple in Puri
(p253).

Sikkim

For recipes online, go to:
www.indiaexpress.com
/cooking
www.recipesindian.com
www.milonee.net/bengali
_recipes

Sikkimese food takes its inspiration from Tibet. Chow mein (fried noodles
with meat, egg or vegetables) can be found everywhere, as can *momos*
(steamed or fried barley-flour dumplings). Soups include *thukpa* (with
Tibetan noodles) and hot-and-sour soup, which is a warming blend of
vegetables, chilli, eggs and vinegar. *Tsampa,* barley-flour dough, is the
default starch.

In rural areas you may find condiments such as *mesu* (a pickle of sour
fermented bamboo shoots) and *sidra ko achar* (pickled fish with tomato and
chilli). The Sikkimese make extensive use of *chhurpi* (local cottage cheese)
and black lentils, served stewed as *khalo dhal.* Another local staple is *kinema* –
fermented soybeans.

Northeast States

The diverse tribal groups of the Northeast states have produced dozens of cuisines and signature dishes.

ARUNACHAL PRADESH

The food of northern Arunachal Pradesh is broadly similar to Tibetan and Sikkimese cooking. *Momos, tsampa* and *thukpa* crop up everywhere. Tribes from the lowlands have a similar diet to the Nagas, and Assamese food is common in larger towns and cities. The local spirit is *apong* – made from fermented millet or rice.

ASSAM

Assamese cooking features strong flavours but few spices – turmeric, mustard and fenugreek are the main flavourings. One uniquely Assamese ingredient is *thekera* – a sour seasoning derived from a plant in the mangosteen family. Traditionally, meals begin with *khar* (an alkaline sauce, prepared using ash from burned plantain fibre) and end with *tenga* (a lime-flavoured fish stew, made from pieces of sweet-tasting *rohu* fish). The Assamese enjoy duck meat and pork, but many Assamese Hindus avoid chicken. Rice is the standard accompaniment – many areas serve up Thai-style glutinous rice as well as basmati-like *joha* rice.

MANIPUR & MIZORAM

Fish is farmed from lakes and ponds all over Manipur and most local dishes are flavoured with *ngari* – fermented fish paste. It's a major ingredient in *iromba,* a pungent vegetable and bamboo-shoot stew. Other distinctive Manipur dishes include *kangsoi* (vegetables stewed with dried fish) and *kobok* (puffed or roasted rice sweetened with molasses).

The cuisine of Mizoram is based on pork, chicken, bamboo shoots and rice. Many dishes are boiled, and flavour is added using *rawt,* a paste of chillies, ginger and onion. Again, rice wine is a popular quaff – in Manipur and Mizoram, it's known as *zu.*

MEGHALAYA

The Khasi people, who make up the ethnic majority of central Meghalaya, make extensive use of pork – commonly served as *jadoh* (red rice cooked with pork) or *jastem* (rice with pork in turmeric gravy). Many dishes feature the pungent flavour of *tungrymbai* (fermented soybeans), and rice flour is used to make *putharo* (rice-batter crepes), *pukhen* (sweet fried rice cakes) and *pusla* (steamed rice cakes wrapped in leaves).

The Garo from western Meghalaya make extensive use of *nakham* (dried fish), normally served in a spicy soup, while the Jaintas of eastern Meghalaya are famous for fermented mushrooms.

NAGALAND

Nagas have a taste for all kinds of fish, as well as pork and bush meat, and dog is also widely consumed. Meat is dried or smoked and many dishes are flavoured with *akhuni* (fermented soybeans). Extensive use is made of glutinous rice, which is often steamed inside banana leaves or roasted in segments of bamboo stem. The Nagas are also fond of *zutho* – rice wine.

TRIPURA

Like Bengalis, Tripurans are passionately fond of fresh and dried fish. *Shidol* (a fermented preserve made of tiny freshwater fish) is a mainstay

Some of the Northeast's most exotic dishes are reserved for festivals – see p301 for listings.

The Assamese *bih-jolokia* (literally 'poison-chilli') has been measured at 1,041,427 Scoville units – four times the heat of Tabasco sauce – see the boxed text, p208.

The Naga love of fish may come from their seafaring origins – according to tribal legends, the Nagas came to the Northeast from the sea in wooden canoes.

of every Tripuran kitchen. Popular fish dishes include *nona ilish paturi* (salted pieces of *hilsa* fish, wrapped in an edible leaf and fried) and *pithali* (dried fish stew). Pork and bamboo shoots are popular ingredients found in tribal areas.

DRINKS
Nonalcoholic Drinks

The highest-quality Darjeeling tea is graded as SFTGFOP, which stands for Special Fine Tippy Golden Flowery Orange Pekoe.

Chai (tea), the national drink, is made with copious amounts of milk and sugar – it's often livened up with spices as *masala chai.* Chai is the perfect antidote to the rigours of the road – the vendor's chant of '*garam* chai, *garam* chai' (hot tea, hot tea) will become one of the most welcome sounds of your trip.

More upmarket restaurants serve European-style tea: just leaves, water and milk or lemon. Darjeeling is famous for its fine teas, normally served without milk. In mountain areas and traveller towns, restaurants offer refreshing lemon tea, spruced up with ginger and honey.

More than 75% of the coffee grown in South India and the Northeast states is immediately exported to Europe and Russia.

In recent years the number of Indian coffee drinkers has skyrocketed, with swanky coffee chains such as Barista and Café Coffee Day appearing across the subcontinent. Most large cities in the Northeast also have 'coffee houses' linked to southern coffee-growing cooperatives.

'Lime soda' is another Indian institution – just soda water, the juice of a small lime and salt or sugar. Salted lemon soda is effectively isotonic and great when you're feeling dehydrated. If spices and sugar are added as well, it's known as *masala soda.* Another popular thirst quencher is *jal jeera,* made from lime juice, cumin, mint and rock salt.

Lassis (yoghurt shakes) can be sweet, salty or fruit flavoured. *Falooda* is a rose-flavoured drink made with milk, cream, nuts and strands of vermicelli, while *badam* milk (served hot or cold) is flavoured with almonds. *Gola,* fruit-flavoured syrup, served over crushed ice, is the local version of the slurpee.

Fresh-juice vendors and drink stands can be found across India, but juice is mixed with water, which may not be clean. If in doubt, stick to packaged juices, such as Maaza (mango juice), Appy (Apple juice) and Frooti (mango again).

For information about safely drinking water in India see the boxed text, p341.

Alcoholic Drinks

People in the Northeast love 'country liquor' – a host of spirits distilled both legally and illegally out of anything lying to hand. All the Northeast states have their own local 'rice wines' made from fermented rice, known variously as *lau-pani, zutho, zu* or *raksi.* Other local versions of hooch include toddy, distilled from fermented palm sugar, and *mahua,* distilled from the fermented flowers of the *mahua* tree. All these spirits are safe to drink when pure, but dodgy vendors have been known to spice them with methyl alcohol and other dangerous additives – talk to locals about safe places to sample these beverages.

TIP FOR BEER DRINKERS

The glycerol used as a preservative in Indian beer can cause headaches. To avoid a thumping cranium, open the bottle and quickly tip it upside down, with the top immersed, into a full glass of water. An oily film (the glycerol) descends into the water – when this stops, pull the bottle out quickly and enjoy a glycerol-free beer.

Beer is widely guzzled around India. Most of the domestic brands are straightforward Pilsners of 5% alcohol by volume; travellers champion Kingfisher, but every state has its own local beers. Drinkers in the Northeast have a preference for 'strong beers' – syrupy concoctions around the 8% alcohol mark. In Sikkim, look out for *tongba* – warm beer prepared from fermented millet and sipped through a bamboo straw from a metal-bound wooden pot.

The wine-producing industry in Maharashtra and Karnataka is growing rapidly. Some of the better restaurants in Kolkata serve very drinkable reds and whites from Chateau Indage, Grover Vineyards and Sula Vineyards.

Indian Made Foreign Liquors (IMFLs) are similar to the overseas versions but made locally with a base of rectified spirit. There are also plenty of local rums, whiskys, brandies and gins, though telling one from the other can be a challenge. Sikkimese liquors have a particularly good reputation. Recent years have also seen a rise in the consumption of imported beers, wines and spirits, particularly in larger cities.

India has the world's biggest whisky market with an annual growth rate of around 10%.

Sikkim is famous for its novelty liquor bottles – Old Monk Rum comes in a monk-shaped bottle, the Old Gold Whisky bottle is shaped like a dagger and the Sikkim Fireball Brandy bottle is a bright red ball.

CELEBRATIONS

Food plays a major role in the festivals of the Northeast, particularly festival sweets. Northeast treats include *pithas* (sweet rice cakes), handed out at the Bhogali Bihu/Makar Sankranti festival in January/February, and boxes of *mithai* (traditional Indian sweets) passed around at Diwali in October/November.

Ramadan is the Islamic month of fasting, when Muslims abstain from eating, drinking or smoking between sunrise and sunset. On the final day of Ramadan, the fast is broken with the Eid al-Fitr feast, marked by meaty biryanis and a huge proliferation of special sweets.

WHERE TO EAT

Northeast India has thousands of restaurants – or 'hotels'. Signboards draw attention to the fact that a restaurant is 'veg' (vegetarian, plus dairy and eggs), 'pure veg' (vegetarian, no eggs) or 'nonveg' (anything goes).

Because of the massive migration of workers inside India, most restaurants serve cuisines from across the country. The best places to find regional food are small local canteens and roadside *dhabas* – the ubiquitous roadside restaurants catering to travellers along India's highways, known in some areas as *bhojanalayas*.

Indian sweets, cheap dosas and other South Indian vegetarian snacks are sold at 'fast food' restaurants, also known as *misthan bhandars*. Almost all hotels have restaurants and there are thousands of sit-down restaurants serving all sorts of food at all sorts of prices – see the Eating sections of the regional chapters for recommendations.

Restaurants rarely have children's menus; however, there are plenty of dishes that don't have a spicy kick – see p295 for tips on travelling with children.

Street Food

From dawn till the last customers slip away at night, the streets of the Northeast are crowded with vendors. There is always something frying, boiling, roasting, peeling, juicing, simmering, mixing or baking, and it's usually delicious. The golden rule is to eat where the locals eat – busy food stalls almost always serve fresh and hygienic food.

Popular street snacks include *chaat* (Indian-style spiced salad) and vegetables fried up as *pakora* or *bhajia* (vegetable fritters) in spicy gram-flour

Street Foods of India by Vimla and Deb Kumar Mukerji gives recipes of some of the subcontinent's favourite munchies, from samosas and *bhelpuri* to *jalebis* and *kulfi*.

STREET FOOD DOS AND DON'TS

Most street stalls serve delicious, healthy food, but there's a fair bit of dodgy cooking around. To stay safe from stomach bugs, observe the following rules:

- Always follow the crowd – if the locals are avoiding a particular vendor, you should too.
- Look at the profile of the customers – any place frequented by families is normally a safe bet.
- Check where the vendor is cleaning the utensils, and how food is stored. Dirty surfaces and buzzing flies are a warning sign to go elsewhere.
- Don't be surprised if snacks are refried before serving – it heats them up and kills germs.
- Unless a place is reputable (and busy), it's best to avoid eating meat from the street.
- Juices are usually safe if the vendor presses the juice in front of you, but never drink anything that has been standing in a jug.
- Be wary of glistening presliced melon, pineapple and other fruit. It keeps its luscious veneer with a regular dousing of (often unfiltered) water.

---

batters. Fried samosas – pyramid-shaped pastries filled with spiced vegetables or (occasionally) meat – are a perfect snack food for long train and bus journeys.

Meat is more of a gamble, but you can find street stalls serving tasty lamb and chicken kebabs in Muslim areas. Again, following the golden rule should keep you safe. Street food needn't be unfamiliar – omelettes, slammed between two slices of white bread, are sold everywhere.

Platform Food

Most trains in India have a dining car, but every train platform in the country has its own frenetic catering in the form of food carts, snack stalls and roving vendors shouting out the merits of their wares. It is a culinary circus, as giant woks sizzle with fresh pakora and samosas, peanuts are flash-roasted in pans of hot sand, dosas swirl on hotplates, puris pop and omlettes bubble on hand-pumped gas stoves. At stops in larger stations, there is often time to jump off and grab a snack, but don't get left behind.

Vegetarians & Vegans

India produces some of the best vegetarian food you'll find anywhere on the planet. However, there's little understanding of veganism (the term 'pure vegetarian' means without eggs), and animal products such as milk, butter, ghee and curd are included in most Indian dishes. Chefs can prepare vegan food on demand if you can make yourself understood. For tips, see www .vegansworldnetwork.org – click on the Directory link, then on India.

WHERE TO DRINK

Sonf – the traditional Indian palate cleanser – is served as tiny coloured candies or loose green seeds with sugar crystals on the side. Pop a few seeds in your mouth after eating for cool, fresh breath.

Alcohol is widely consumed in West Bengal, Orissa and Sikkim but many of the Northeast states are officially dry. Mizoram, Manipur and Tripura are all difficult places to find a drink, except in tribal areas. Several states also have regular dry days when the sale of alcohol from liquor shops is banned. Your best chance of finding an alcoholic drink in a 'dry' area is to visit the bar at a top-end hotel.

Bars and pubs are only found in larger cities, usually at hotels. Elsewhere, people drink at restaurants. Note that Indian bars are often seedy, male-dominated affairs – not really the kind of place thirsty female travellers would want to venture into alone. For recommendations, see the Drinking sections of this book's regional chapters.

HABITS & CUSTOMS

Three main meals a day is the norm in India. Breakfast favourites include roti/chapattis with curried pulses, hot *parathas,* dhal and rice, and *idli sambar* – steamed South Indian rice-flour patties with a hot, sour dipping sauce. In areas frequented by backpackers, you can find Western staples like cornflakes, muesli, porridge and pancakes, usually topped with fruit.

Lunches tend to consist of dishes that can be eaten quickly – thalis, rice with sauces and snack meals at street stands. Dinner is usually the main meal of the day – curried vegetables or meat are served with rice or Indian breads, various side condiments and dhal, all served together with papad (or pappadams – fried or roast lentil-flour wafers) on the side. Bengalis and Orissans love desserts at any time of day, not just with meals.

City restaurants stay open till 10pm or later, but in rural areas, everything can shut down for the night as soon as it gets dark.

Food & Religion

Eating in India can be influenced by all sorts of religious taboos. Hindus avoid foods that are thought to inhibit physical and spiritual development – the taboo on eating beef (the cow is holy to Hindus) is the most rigid restriction.

Devout Hindus (and Jains) also avoid alcohol and foods such as garlic and onions, which are thought to heat the blood and arouse sexual desire. Ashrams may also ban stimulating foods and drinks such as chocolate, tea, coffee and fizzy soft drinks.

Pork is taboo for Muslims and stimulants such as alcohol, coffee and tea are avoided by the devout. Halal is the term for all permitted foods, and haram for those prohibited. Fasting is considered an opportunity to earn the approval of Allah, to wipe the sin slate clean and to understand the suffering of the poor.

Jainism's central tenet is strict vegetarianism, and rigid restrictions are in place to avoid even potential injury to any living creature – Jains abstain from eating vegetables that grow underground because of the potential to harm insects during cultivation. Buddhists are more pragmatic – vegetarianism is common, but not a requirement.

India's Sikh, Christian and Parsi communities have few or no restrictions on what they can eat, but tribal communities in the Northeast have their own complicated eating taboos, with proscriptions on pork, beef, poultry and eggs in some areas.

Hindus offer ritual food known as *prasad* to the gods whenever they visit temples – priests hand out a palm-full of prasad to all visitors, but you should be careful of stomach upsets from contaminated offerings.

Legend says that Buddha, after falling asleep during meditation, decided to cut his eyelids off in an act of penance. The lids grew into the tea plant, which, when brewed, banished sleep.

EATING INDIAN STYLE

Most Indians eat with their right hand as the left is reserved for toilet duties. You can use your left hand for holding drinks and serving yourself from a communal bowl, but it shouldn't be used for bringing food to your mouth. Before and after a meal, it's good manners to wash your hands – most restaurants have a sink in the dining room expressly for this purpose. If you're worried about hygiene, carry a small bar of soap in your day pack.

Once your meal is served, mix the food with your fingertips. If you are having dhal and *sabzi,* mix the dhal into your rice and have the *sabzi* in small scoops with each mouthful. If you are having fish or meat curry, mix the gravy into your rice and take the flesh off the bones from the side of your plate. Scoop up lumps of the mix with your fingertips and use your thumb to shovel the food into your mouth.

COOKING COURSES

You might find yourself so inspired by Indian food that you want to take home a little Indian kitchen know-how – cooking courses are cropping up all over the country, though there are only a few so far in the Northeast. As well as the following listings, you could always try asking at your hotel to see if it can arrange a private class.

Hot Stimulating Café (p148; Darjeeling, West Bengal)
Kali Travel Home (p112; Kolkata, West Bengal)

EAT YOUR WORDS
Useful Phrases
BENGALI

What would you recommend?	*aapni ki kete bohlen*
I'm vegetarian.	*aami vejiterian*
I'd like the ..., please.	*aami ... chai pleez*
Please bring a/the...	*... aanen pleez*
bill	*bilta*
fork	*akta kata*
glass	*akta glash*
a glass of wine	*ak glash wain*
knife	*akta churi*
menu	*menuta*
mineral water	*mineral watar*
plate	*plet*
spoon	*akta chamuch*
I don't eat ...	*aami ... kai na*
Could you prepare a meal without ...?	*aapni ki ... chara kabar tohiri kohrte paaren*
beef	*gohrur mangshoh*
fish	*maach*
meat	*maangshoh*
meat stock	*mangsher stok*
pork	*shuohrer mangshoh*
poultry	*hash murgi*
red meat (goat)	*khashir mangsho*
I'm allergic to ...	*aamar ... e alarji aache*
nuts	*baadam*
seafood	*maach*
shellfish	*chingri maach*
That was delicious.	*kub moja chiloh*

HINDI

What would you recommend?	*aap ke kyaal meng kyaa achchaa hogaa?*
I'm (a) vegetarian.	*main hoong shaakaahaaree*
I'd like the ..., please.	*muje ... chaahiye*
Please bring a/the ...	*... laaiye*
bill	*bil*
fork	*kaangtaa*
glass	*glaas*
glass of wine	*sharaab kee kaa glaas*

knife	*chaakoo*
menu	*menyoo*
mineral water	*minral vaatar*
plate	*plet*
spoon	*chammach*

I don't eat ...	*maing ... naheeng kaataa/kaatee* (m/f)
Could you prepare a meal	*kyaa aap ... ke binaa kaanaa taiyaar kar*
without ...?	*sakte/saktee haing?* (m/f)
beef	*gaay ke gosht*
fish	*machlee*
meat stock	*gosht ke staak*
pork	*suar ke gosht*
poultry	*murgee*
red meat (goat)	*bakree ka gosht*

I'm allergic to ...	*muje ... kee elarjee hai*
nuts	*meve*
seafood	*machlee*
shellfish	*shelfish*

That was delicious.	*kub moja chiloh*

Food & Drink Glossary

achar – pickle

aloo – potato; also *alu*

aloo tikka – mashed potato patty

appam – South Indian rice pancake

badam – nuts, usually almond

baigan – eggplant/aubergine; also known as *brinjal*

barfi – fudge-like sweet made from milk

bhajia – vegetable fritter

bhindi – okra

biryani – fragrant spiced steamed rice with meat or vegetables

chaat – Indian-style spiced salad, often prepared with *namkin*

chai – tea

channa – spiced chickpeas

chapati – round unleavened Indian-style bread; also known as *roti*

chatni – chutney

chawal – rice

dahi – curd/yogurt

dhal – curried lentil dish; a staple food of India

dhansak – Parsi sauce with curried lentils and rice

dopiaza – a rich curry sauce with double *(do)* onions *(piaza)*.

dosa – South Indian lentil-flour pancake

falooda – rose-flavoured drink made with milk, cream, nuts and noodles

faluda – long chickpea-flour noodles

farsan – savoury nibbles

ghee – clarified butter

gosht – lamb or mutton, sometimes called 'josh'

gobi – cauliflower

gulab jamun – deep-fried balls of dough soaked in rose-flavoured syrup

halwa – soft sweetmeat made with nuts and fruit

idli – South Indian spongy, round, fermented rice cake

jaggery – hard, brown, sugarlike sweetener made from palm sap

jalebi – orange-coloured whorls of deep-fried batter dunked in sugar syrup

jal jeera – a salted lemon juice drink with cumin

karela – bitter gourd

keema – spiced minced meat

kheer – creamy rice pudding

kofta – balls of minced vegetables or meat

korma – a creamy sauce with curd and ground nuts

kulfi – flavoured (often with pistachio) firm-textured ice cream

ladoo – sweetmeat ball made with gram flour and semolina; also *ladu*

lassi – refreshing yogurt-and-iced-water drink

maachli – fish

methi – fenugreek

misthi dhoi – Bengali sweet; curd sweetened with jaggery

mithai – Indian sweets

momo – Tibetan steamed or fried dumpling stuffed with vegetables or meat

Mughlai – used for any number of meat sauces from the central plains

murg – chicken; also *murgi*

murli – white radish

naan – tandoor-cooked flat bread

namak – salt

namkeen – savoury nibbles

pakora – fried-batter vegetable

paneer – soft, unfermented cheese made from milk curd

pani – water

pappadam – thin, crispy pulse-flour crisps; also *papad*

paratha – Indian-style flaky fried bread

pilaf – see *pulao*

pulao – rice cooked in stock and flavoured with spices; also *pulau* or *pilaf*

puri – flat savoury dough that puffs up when deep fried; also *poori*

raita – mildly spiced yoghurt with fruit or vegetables

rasam – dhal-based broth flavoured with tamarind

rasgulla – sweet little balls of cream cheese flavoured with rose water

rogan josh – rich, spicy lamb curry

saag – leafy greens

sabzi – vegetables

sambar – soupy South Indian mustard and tamarind sauce

samosa – deep-fried pastry triangles filled with spiced vegetables/meat

sonf/saunf – fennel seeds, used as a digestive and mouth freshener after meals

tandoor – clay oven

tawa – flat hotplate/iron griddle

thali – all-you-can-eat plate meals, served on a compartmentalised plate

thukpa – Tibetan noodle soup

tiffin – snack; also refers to meal container often made of stainless steel

tikka – spiced, marinated, chunks of chicken, *paneer* etc

toddy – alcoholic drink, tapped from palm trees

tsampa – Tibetan staple of roast barley flour

uttapam – South Indian rice pancake with onion, chilli, coriander and coconut

vada – South Indian deep-fried lentil ring-donut

Kolkata (Calcutta)

Simultaneously noble and squalid, cultured and desperate, Kolkata is a daily festival of human existence. And it's all played out before your very eyes on teeming streets where not an inch of space is wasted. By its old spelling, Calcutta, India's second-biggest city conjures up images of human suffering to most Westerners. But Bengalis have long been infuriated by one-sided depictions of their vibrant capital. Kolkata is locally regarded as the intellectual and cultural capital of the nation. Several of India's great 19th- and 20th-century heroes were Kolkatans, including guru-philosopher Ramakrishna, Nobel Prize–winning poet Rabindranath Tagore and celebrated film director Satyajit Ray. Dozens of venues showcase Bengali dance, poetry, art, music, film and theatre. And while poverty certainly remains in-your-face, the dapper Bengali gentry continue to frequent grand old gentlemen's clubs, back horses at the Calcutta Racetrack and play soothing rounds of golf at some of India's finest courses.

As the former capital of British India, Kolkata retains a feast of dramatic colonial architecture, with more than a few fine buildings in photogenic states of semi-collapse. The city still has many slums but is also developing dynamic new-town suburbs, a rash of air-conditioned shopping malls and some of the best restaurants in India. This is a fabulous place to sample the mild, fruity tang of Bengali cuisine and share the city's passion for sweets.

Friendlier than India's other mega-cities, Kolkata is really a city you 'feel' more than just visit. But don't come between May and September unless you're prepared for a very serious drenching.

HIGHLIGHTS

- Be awed by the magnificent colonial folly that is the **Victoria Memorial** (p102)

- Enjoy bizarre random encounters while strolling between the faded colonial buildings and assorted religious monuments around **BBD Bagh** (p107)

- Savour lipsmackingly authentic Bengali cuisine at modest **Bhojohari Manna** (p117) or cosily homey **Kewpies** (p117)

- Contrast the urbane universalism on display at **Tagore's House** (p111) and the **Ramakrishna Centre** (p111) with the gruesome sensual fascination of **Kali Temple** (p109)

- Consider **volunteering** (p112) to help the destitute after a humbling visit to the rubbish-heap 'homes' around former **Chinatown** (p108)

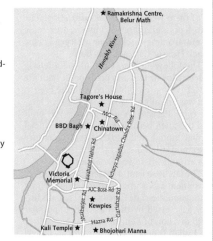

HISTORY

In the Hindu epics, the God Shiva was understandably dismayed to happen upon the charred corpse of Sati, his newly wed wife (an incarnation of Kali). However, his decision to destroy the world in retribution was considered somewhat of an over-reaction by fellow deities. Vishnu interceded to stop Shiva's 'dance of destruction', but in so doing dismembered Sati's cadaver into 51 pieces. These gory chunks landed at widely disbursed points across India. One of her toes fell at Kalikata (now Kalighat, p109), where the site became honoured by a much revered temple.

Famed as Kalikata/Kalighat might have been, the place was still a fairly typical rural backwater when British merchant Job Charnock showed up in 1686. Charnock reckoned the Hooghly River bend would make an ideal settlement, and by 1698 the villages of Sutanuti, Gobindapur and Kalikata had been formally signed over to the British East India Company. The British thereupon created a miniature version of London-on-Hooghly, with stately buildings, wide boulevards, English churches and grand formal gardens. The grand illusion vanished abruptly at Calcutta's frayed edges where Indians servicing the Raj lived in cramped, overcrowded bastis (slums).

The most notable hiccup in the city's meteoric rise came in 1756, when Siraj-ud-Daula, the nawab of nearby Murshidabad, recaptured the city. Dozens of members of the colonial aristocracy were imprisoned in a cramped room beneath Fort William. By morning, around 40 of them were dead from suffocation. The British press exaggerated numbers, drumming up moral outrage back home: the legend of the 'Black Hole of Calcutta' was born.

The following year, Clive of India retook Calcutta for Britain and made peace with the nawab, who promptly sided with the French and was soundly defeated at the Battle of Plassey (now Palashi). A stronger fort was built and the town became British India's official capital, though well into the late 18th century one could still hunt tigers in the bamboo forests around where Sudder St lies today.

The late 19th century Bengali Renaissance movement saw a great cultural reawakening among middle-class Calcuttans. This was further galvanised by the massively unpopular 1905 division of Bengal, sowing the seeds of the Indian Independence movement. Bengal was reunited in 1911, but the British promptly transferred their colonial capital to less troublesome Delhi.

Initially loss of political power had little effect on Calcutta's economic status. However, the impact of partition was devastating. While West Pakistan and Punjab saw a fairly equal (if bloody) exchange of populations, migration in Bengal was almost entirely one way. Around four million Hindu refugees from East Bengal arrived, choking Calcutta's already overpopulated bustees. For a period, people really were dying of hunger in the streets, creating Calcutta's abiding image of abject poverty. No sooner had these refugees been absorbed than a second vast wave arrived during the 1971 India–Pakistan War.

After India's partition the port of Calcutta was hit very hard by the loss of its main natural hinterland, now behind closed Pakistan–Bangladesh borders. Labour unrest spiralled out of control, while the city's dominant party (Communist Party of India) spent most of its efforts attacking the feudal system of land ownership. Attempts to set strict rent controls and residents' rights were well intentioned but have since backfired. Kolkata rents remain amongst the lowest in India but when tenants pay as little as Rs 1 a month, landlords have zero interest in maintaining or upgrading properties. The sad result is that many fine old buildings are literally crumbling before one's eyes.

Since 2001 Calcutta has officially adopted the more phonetic spelling, Kolkata. Around the same time the city administration implemented a new business-friendly attitude that is now encouraging a very noticeable economic resurgence.

ORIENTATION

Kolkata sprawls outwards from the holy chocolate-sludge that is the Hooghly River. Apart from the gigantic Howrah (Haora) train station, most points of interest lie on the east bank.

Administrative Kolkata takes up several blocks of colonial-era buildings around BBD Bagh. North of here lanes are narrow and intriguingly vibrant. Well south in Alipore and Gariahat are the wealthiest districts of the Bengali upper classes. Long-distance bus stations are around the top of a vast park called the Maidan. Budget travellers head for the nearby Sudder St area, Kolkata's equivalent of Bangkok's Khao San Rd. Here you'll find backpacker cafés, moneychangers, helpful travel agencies and Kolkata's savviest beggars. Upmarket dining and boutiques are most prevalent around Park, Camac and Elgin Sts. The central business district is around Shakespeare Sarani but corporate offices are increasingly relocating to Sector 5 of Salt Lake City, a new-town area that starts around several kilometres northeast of the centre.

Maps

Hawkers sell various city maps. None are perfect but the TTK *Road Guide to Kolkata* (Rs 75) is clearer than the IMS version. **Catchcal** (www.catchcal.com/map/map.html) has a searchable online map. The **Geographical Survey of India** (Map p104; ☎ 22475731; 13 Wood St; 🕓 10.30am-1pm & 2.30-5pm Mon-Fri) sells Rs 12 city maps. Very bureaucratic procedure.

INFORMATION
Bookshops

Secondhand books are sold from street stalls lining College St between MG and Coolootola Rds (mostly academic) and from several small bookshops (p104) around the junction of Sudder and Mirza Ghalib Sts (traveller oriented), such as **Bookland** (Sudder St).

Other top bookshops:

Classic Books/Earthcare Books (Map p104; ☎ 22296551; www.earthcarebooks.com; 10 Middleton St) Charming family publisher-bookshop with strengths in environmentalism, politics, spirituality and women's issues. Behind Drive-Inn

Crossword (Map p110; ☎ 22836502; www.crossword bookstores.com; 8 Elgin Rd; 🕓 10.30am-8.30pm) Large chain bookshop with café. Sells *Times Food Guide*.

Oxford Book Shop (Map p104; ☎ 22297662; www .oxfordbookstore.com; 17 Park St; 🕓 10am-9pm Mon-Sat, 11am-8pm Sun; 🖳) Excellent bookshop with browse-seating and café (coffee Rs 40 to 60). Appealing line-sketch postcards. Stocks Lonely Planet guides.

Seagull Bookstore (Map pp98-9; ☎ 24765865; www .seagullindia.com; 31A SP Mukherjee Rd) Academic bookshop with particular strengths on regional politics. Enter from the lane leading to Indira cinema.

Internet Access

Internet centres all over town mostly offer excellent connection speeds for as little as Rs 10 per hour. Reliable choices:

Cyberia (Map p104; 8 Kyd St; per hr Rs 10; 🕓 8.30am-10pm) Hourly minimum fee.

DirecWay (Map p106; 3 Khetra Das Rd; per 90 min Rs 30; 🕓 11am-8pm) Cramped.

Hotline/Saree Palace (Map p104; 7 Sudder St; per hr Rs 15; 🕓 8.30am-midnight) Helpful, pleasant environment and long hours, with travel services available and fabrics for sale.

I-way (Map p104; 59B Park St; per hr Rs 30; 🕓 10.30am-9.30pm) Spacious, with super-fast connections and high powered AC.

Junction 96 (Map p110; Sarat Bose Rd; per hr Rs 15)

Netfreaks (Map p104; 2/1 Sudder St; per hr Rs 20; 🕓 9.30am-9pm Mon-Sat, 10am-5pm Sun)

Internet Resources

Some useful websites on Kolkata include www.catchcal.com, www.kolkata-india.com, www.kolkatahub.com, www.kolkatainform ation.com and www.calcuttaweb.com.

FESTIVALS IN KOLKATA

Dover Lane Music Conference (late Jan) Indian classical music at Nazrul Mancha in Rabindra Sarovar park.
Kolkata Boi Mela (www.kolkatabookfaironline.com; late Jan/early Feb) Asia's biggest book fair.
Saraswati Puja (early Feb) Prayers for educational success, all dressed in yellow.
Rath Yatra (Jun/Jul) Major Krishna chariot festival similar to the Puri equivalent (p251).
Durga Puja (www.durgapujas.com; Oct) Kolkata's biggest festival. Gaudily painted idols of the 10-armed goddess Durga and entourage (see p111) are displayed in fabulously ornate pavilions (*pandals*) for five days of veneration. Then they're thrown into the Hooghly River amid singing, water throwing, fireworks and indescribable traffic congestion. Afterwards half the city goes on holiday.
Lakshmi Puja (Oct) and **Kali Puja** (Diwali, Nov) feature more idol dunking.
Kolkata Film Festival (www.calfilmfestival.org; 2nd week of Nov) Week-long festival of Bengali and international movies, with lectures, discussions and special screenings, notably at the Nandan Complex (p121).

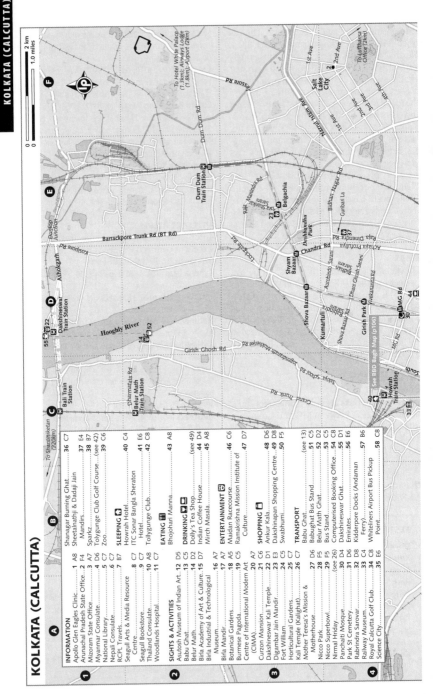

KOLKATA (CALCUTTA)

INFORMATION
Apollo Glen Eagles Clinic..............	1 A8
Arunachal Pradesh State Office......	2 F4
Mizoram State Office.....................	3 A7
Myanmar Consulate.......................	4 D6
National Library.............................	5 C7
Nepali Consulate...........................	6 C7
RCPL Travels.................................	7 B7
Seagull Arts & Media Resource	
Centre..	8 C7
Seagull Bookstore..........................	9 C7
Thailand Consulate........................	10 A8
Woodlands Hospital.......................	11 C7

SIGHTS & ACTIVITIES
Asutosh Museum of Indian Art.12	D5
Babu Ghat...................................	13 C5
Belur Math...................................	14 D2
Birla Academy of Art & Culture..15	D7
Birla Industrial & Technological	
Museum......................................	16 A7
Birla Mandir.................................	17 A7
Botanical Gardens........................	18 A5
Burmese Pagoda..........................	19 C5
Centre of International Modern Art	
(CIMA)..	20 A7
Curzon Mansion..........................	21 C6
Dakshineswar Kali Temple...........	22 D1
Digambar Jain Mandir..................	23 E3
Fort William................................	24 C5
Horticultural Gardens...................	25 C7
Kali Temple (Kalighat)..................	26 C7
Mother Teresa's Mission &	
Motherhouse.............................	27 D6
Nicco Park....................................	28 F5
Nicco Superbowl..........................	29 F5
Nirmal Hriday...............................	(see 26)
Panchati Mosque..........................	30 D4
Park St Cemetery.........................	31 D6
Rabindra Sarovar.........................	32 D8
Railway Museum..........................	33 C4
Royal Calcutta Golf Club..............	34 C8
Science City.................................	35 E6

Shanagar Burning Ghat.................	36 C7
Sheetalnathji & Dadaji Jain	
Mandirs......................................	37 E4
Sparkz...	38 B7
Tollygunge Club Golf Course......(see 42)	
Zoo..	39 C6

SLEEPING 🛏
Howrah Hotel...............................	40 C4
ITC Sonar Bangla Sheraton	
Hotel..	41 E6
Tollygunge Club...........................	42 C8

EATING 🍴
Bhojohari Manna...........................	43 A8

DRINKING 🍷 🍸
Dolly's Tea Shop..........................(see 49)	
Indian Coffee House.....................	44 D4
Mirch Masala................................	45 A8

ENTERTAINMENT 🎭
Maidan Racecourse......................	46 C6
Ramakrishna Mission Institute of	
Culture.......................................	47 D7

SHOPPING 🛍
Ankur Kala....................................	48 D6
Dakshinapan Shopping Centre.......	49 D8
Swabhumi.....................................	50 F5

TRANSPORT
Babu Ghat...................................(see 13)	
Babughat Bus Stand......................	51 C5
Belur Math Ghat...........................	52 D2
Bus Stand.....................................	53 C5
Computerised Booking Office.........	54 C8
Dakshineswar Ghat.......................	55 D1
Emirates.......................................	56 E6
Kidderpore Docks (Andaman	
Ferry)...	57 B6
Whiteliners Airport Bus Pickup	
Point...	58 C8

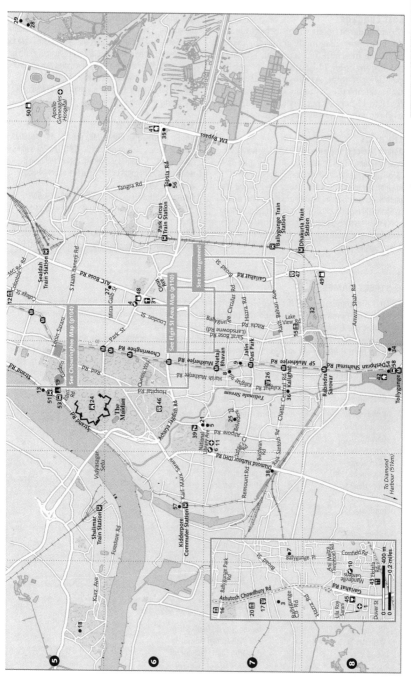

Left Luggage

Most Sudder St hotels will store bags for a fee. At the airport, diagonally across the carpark from the international terminal, is a useful cloakroom open 24 hours that charges Rs 5 per day per item. At Howrah and Sealdah train stations the 24-hour cloakrooms charge Rs 10 to 15 per bag per day and require users to show valid long-distance train tickets.

Libraries

Asiatic Society (Map p104; ☎ 22290779; www.asiatic societycal.com; 1 Park St; admission free; ⏲ 10am-5pm Mon-Fri) Priceless collection of ancient books and illuminated manuscripts. A few of these are displayed in a mothballed one-room museum, including a letter signed by Shah Jahan and a 250 BC Ashokan inscription. Getting to see them involves a hilariously bureaucratic procedure involving five separate sign-ins on four different floors. Bring your passport.

National Library (Map pp98-9; ☎ 24791381; www .nlindia.org; 5 Alipore Rd; ⏲ 9am-8pm Mon-Fri, 9.30am-6pm Sat & Sun) The largest collection in India. Books are too numerous for open shelving, so are accessed from vaults by request slip. Membership is free but requires two photos.

Seagull Arts & Media Centre (Map pp98-9; ☎ 24556942; www.seagullindia.com; 36C SP Mukherjee Rd; day membership Rs 50) Arts bias, cultural events.

Medical Services

Apollo Gleneagles Clinic (Map pp98-9; ☎ 24618028; www.apollohospitals.com/Kolkata; 48/1F Lila Roy Sarani, Gariahat Rd; ⏲ 8am-8pm) Health checks and dental work; its sister hospital in Salt Lake City offers 24-hour ambulance service.

Bellevue Clinic (Map p104; ☎ 22872321; www .bellevueclinic.com; 9 Loudon St) Hospital with 24-hour pharmacy.

SRL Ranbaxy Path Lab (Map p104; ☎ 22271315; 30B Chowringhee Rd; ⏲ 7.30am-7.30pm Mon-Sat) Does

---

STREET NAMES

After Independence, the Indian government changed any street name that had Raj-era connotations. The Communists continued the process. Humorously they chose to rename Harrington St so that the US consulate found itself on Ho Chi Minh Sarani.

Today most major Kolkata streets have two or even three names. Citizens and taxis still tend to go by the British-era names. But confusingly most maps, street signs and business cards use the new names (or sometimes both). This text uses what we found, quite unscientifically, to be the most commonly employed variant, *italicised* in the list below:

Old name	New name
Ballygunge Rd	Ashutosh Chowdhury Ave *(AC Rd)*
Brabourne Rd	Biplabi Trailokya Maharaja Rd
Camac St	Abinindranath Tagore St
Central Ave	*Chittaranjan (CR) Ave*
Chitpore Rd	*Rabindra Sarani*
Chowringhee Rd	Jawaharlal Nehru Rd
Free School St	*Mirza Ghalib St*
Harrington St	*Ho Chi Minh Sarani*
Harrison Rd	Mahatma Gandhi *(MG)* Rd
Kyd St	Dr M Ishaque Rd
Lansdowne Rd	*Sarat Bose Rd*
Loudon St	Dr UM Bramhchari St
Lower Circular Rd	*AJC Bose Rd*
Old Court House St	Hemant Basu Sarani
Park St	Mother Theresa Sarani
Rowden St	Sarojini Naidu Sarani
Theatre Rd	*Shakespeare Sarani*
Victoria Terrace	*Gorky Terrace*
Waterloo St	Nawab Siraj-ud-Daula Sarani
Wellesley St	*RAK* (Rafi Ahmed Kidwai) *Rd*
Wood St	Dr Martin Luther King Sarani

KOLKATA IN...

Two Days

From the north of the **Maidan** (p107), stroll at random through the crumbling colonial wonderland of **BBD Bagh** (p108). Collect a Marble Palace permit at West Bengal tourism (for tomorrow) then brace yourself for **Chinatown** (p108). Recover with a meal or coffee on **Park St** (p508) and tour the **Indian Museum** (p105). Reach the grandiose **Victoria Memorial** (p102) by 7.15pm for the sound-and-light show. Next day see the colourful **Mullik Ghat flower market** (p108) and head for **Belur Math** (p111) and **Dakshineswar** (p112), spiritual centres of the Ramakrishna movement. On the way back into town, stop off at the bizarre **Marble Palace** (p110). In the evening, fit in a cultural show at the **Nandan Complex** (p121).

Two Weeks

Kolkata's astounding contrasts aren't necessarily best appreciated by ticking off sights in standard touristic fashion. Consider approaching the city thematically.

- **Traditional Kolkata** – hand-drawn rickshaws (p124), effigy makers in Kumartuli (p111), sunset at Babu Ghat (p109), Mullik Ghat flower market (p109), sheep sacrifices at Kali Temple (p109)
- **Colonial Kolkata** – Victoria Memorial (p102), the main post office (p102), golf at the Tollygunge Club (p112), a flutter at the Maidan racecourse (p121), a drink at the Fairlawn Hotel (p120)
- **Modern Kolkata** – dancing at Tantra nightclub (p120), coffee at Barista (p120), simulator rides at Science City (p112), cocktails at Roxy (p120), browsing at Oxford Book Shop (p97)
- **Squalid Kolkata** – street kids on Howrah train station (p109), rubbish-pile homes in Chinatown (p108), volunteering (p112) to help the destitute
- **Multicultural Kolkata** – synagogues, mosques and churches of BBD Bagh (p107), Belur Math (p111), meditation evenings (p112), reading Tagore (p59), laughing-yoga at Rabindra Sarovar (p110)

---

same-day tests for dengue (Rs 1400) and Chikungunia (Rs 500).

Wockhardt Medical Centre (Map p104; ☎ 24754320/24754096; www.wockhardhospitals.net; 2/7 Sarat Bose Rd; consultation Rs 300; ☺ doctor available 9am-1pm) Good first stop for a doctor's consultation.

Woodlands Hospital (Map pp98-9; ☎ 24567075-89; 8/5 Alipore Rd)

For more extensive listings check www.kolkatainformation.com/diagnostic.html

Money

Most banks have ATMs accepting major international cards. There's a Camara Bank ATM on Kyd St, close to Sudder St. For foreign exchange, private moneychangers are much better than banks. Many will exchange travellers cheques but nobody seems to want Bangladesh Takas. There are dozens more booths around Sudder St. Shop around for rates.

Globe Forex (Map p104; ☎ 22828780; 11 Ho Chi Minh Sarani; ☺ 9.30am-6.30pm Mon-Fri, 9.30am-2.30pm Sat)

LKP Forex (Map p104; Hilson Hotel, Sudder St; ☺ 9am-9pm) Great rates and long hours in the foyer of a back-packer guest house.

Permits

FOREIGNERS' REGIONAL REGISTRATION OFFICE

You can get permits for Sikkim (free) in one working day at the **Foreigners' Regional Registration Office** (FRRO; Map p104; ☎ 22473301; 237A AJC Bose Rd; ☺ 10am-5pm Mon-Fri). For Manipur (Imphal only), Arunachal Pradesh (not Tawang) and Nagaland (Mon, Phek), FRRO has started offering limited-area permits for groups of four applicants, issued in 24 hours and for free. This sounds almost too good to be true. If it really works, please let us know! Each permit application requires one photo and a passport photocopy.

STATE OFFICES

The following can issue state-specific Inner Line permits to Indian nationals. However, except at Sikkim House, foreigners shouldn't expect any permit help whatsoever.

Arunachal Pradesh (Map pp98-9; ☎ 23341243; Arunachal Bhawan, Block CE 109, Sector 1, Salt Lake City)

Manipur (Map pp98-9; ☎ 24758163; Manipur Bhawan, 26 Rowland Rd)

Mizoram (Map pp98-9; ☎ 24757887; Mizoram Bhawan, 24 Old Ballygunge Rd) Take the lane beside 23 AC Rd for 100m. Enter to left through unmarked black gates.

Nagaland (Map p104; ☎ 22825247; Nagaland House, 1st fl, 11 Shakespeare Sarani)

Sikkim (Map p104; ☎ 22815328; Sikkim House, 4/1 Middleton St) Permits issued within 24 hours if the issuing officer is in town. Bring your passport, a passport photo, and photocopies of your passport's identity pages and Indian visa.

Photography

Electro Photo-Lab (Map p104; ☎ 22498743; 14 Sudder St; ◷ 10am-10pm) Offers instant passport photos (Rs 60 for six mugshots), film developing and digi-prints.

Harico Electronics (Map p106; ☎ 22281345; 3B Chowringhee Rd) Stocks print- and slide-film, including Sensia 100 (Rs 220).

Post

Kolkata's imposing **main post office** (GPO; Map p106; Netaji Subhash Rd, BBD Bagh; ◷ 8am-8pm Mon-Sat) is an attraction in itself, a statue of a traditional Bengali mail-runner standing beneath its vast central cupola. There's poste-restante service (passport required), a philatelic bureau and even a loveable little **postal museum** (☎ 22437331; Koilaghat St; ◷ 11am-4pm Mon-Sat).

Convenient branch post offices include Park St (Map p104) and Mirza Ghalib St (Map p104).

Courier services:

DHL (Map p104; ☎ 22813132; 21 Camac St; ◷ 24hr)

FedEx (☎ 22834325; Crescent Tower, AJC Bose Rd)

Telephone

The **Central Telegraph Office** (Map p106; Red Cross Pl; ◷ 24hr) has phone and fax services, but calls are just as cheap from ubiquitous PCO/STD/ISD booths throughout the city. Electro Photo-Lab (see above) sells SIM cards for mobile phones.

Tourist Information

Cultural happenings are announced in the *Telegraph* newspaper's *Metro* section or buy a copy of the very useful *Cal Calling* (Rs 30) from the entranceway desk of West Bengal Tourism. **CityInfo** (www.explocity.com) is an advertisement-led listings pamphlet available free from better hotels.

India Tourism (Map p104; ☎ 22825813/22827731; 4 Shakespeare Sarani; ◷ 10am-6pm Mon-Fri, 10am-1pm Sat) Gives away reasonably good Kolkata maps.

West Bengal Tourism (Map p106; ☎ 22488271; www.westbengaltourism.com; 3/2 BBD Bagh; ◷ 10am-5.30pm Mon-Fri, 10am-1pm Sat) Somewhat chaotic, primarily selling tours.

Travel Agencies

There are dozens of travel agencies around Sudder St alone. Elsewhere useful addresses

RCPL Travels (Map pp98-9; ☎ 24400665; travelcal@vsnl.net; www.kingdomofbhutan.info; 5/4 Ballygunge Pl) Bhutan specialists.

Travel People (Map p104; ☎ 22892291; www.travelppl.com; 227/2 AJC Bose Rd; ◷ 9am-5pm) Professional and obliging.

Visa Extension

In an absolutely dire emergency, the FRRO (see Permits, p101) just might extend your Indian tourist visa by a few days. Don't count on it.

DANGERS & ANNOYANCES

Kolkata feels remarkably unthreatening. There's a fair share of beggar-hassle around the tourist ghetto of Sudder St and some tourists have got into trouble there by accepting late-night invitations to sample drugs or girls – a dangerous idea in any city.

A more day-to-day worry is crossing the road: the mad traffic takes no prisoners. Pickpockets sometimes cruise public transport. *Bandhs* (strikes) occur with monotonous regularity, closing shops and stopping all land transport (excluding planes but including taxis to the airport). Monsoon-season flooding is highly inconvenient but rickshaw-wallahs somehow manage to ferry passengers through knee-deep, waterlogged streets.

SIGHTS

Most attractions that don't charge for photography forbid it.

Chowringhee Area

All of the sites in this area appear on Map p104, except where otherwise noted.

VICTORIA MEMORIAL

Had it been built for a beautiful Indian princess rather than a dead colonial queen, the incredible **Victoria Memorial** (VM; ☎ 22235142; admission to grounds Rs 4, to interior Indian/foreigner Rs 20/150; ◷ 10am-5pm Tue-Sun) would surely rate as one of India's greatest buildings. It's a vast, beautifully proportioned confection of white marble domes set in attractive, well-tended parkland. Think US Capitol meets Taj Mahal.

Built to commemorate Queen Victoria's 1901 diamond jubilee, the structure was finally finished nearly 20 years after her death. It's most photogenic viewed at sunset across the reflecting ponds from the northeast. But the many interior galleries are worth seeing, especially the Kolkata Gallery, which traces an impressively even-handed history of the city, including the experience of Indians living under British rule. Some colonial statues offer a chuckle. Before the north door a sleepy Victoria seems to be nodding off on her throne. In the main entranceway King George V faces his wife Mary but looks more the queen himself in his camp posing britches. No wonder interior photography is forbidden.

By day, enter from north or south gates (though you can exit to the east). For the informative English-language **sound-and-light show** (Indian/foreigner Rs 10/20; ✆ 7.15pm Tue-Sun) enter from the east gate.

AROUND THE VM
In the evenings around the VM's north gate, local couples surreptitiously fondle (and more) in the surrounding gardens, take **horse carriage rides** along Queens Way or watch the sweetly gaudy play of **musical fountains**.

Loosely styled on the Buddhist stupa at Sarnath, the nearby **Birla Planetarium** (✆ 22231516; Chowringhee Rd) is one of the world's largest and looks impressive when floodlit. Its outer circle forms a small but well-presented, tomb-like gallery featuring astronomer busts and planetary pictures. But the **star shows** (admission Rs 20; ✆ 1.30pm & 6.30pm in English) are slow moving and rather stilted.

Whitewashed with a central crenellated tower, the 1847 **St Paul's Cathedral** (✆ 22230127; Cathedral Rd; ✆ 9am-noon & 3-6pm) would look quite at home in Cambridgeshire. Inside, its extraordinarily broad, unbutressed nave twitters with birdsong and retains the original hardwood pews. Don't miss the stained-glass west window by pre-Raphaelite maestro Sir Edward Burne-Jones.

The bright, ground-floor galley of the **Academy of Fine Arts** (✆ 22234302; 2 Cathedral Rd) has changing **exhibitions** (admission free; ✆ 3-8pm) featuring local contemporary artists. The dusty upstairs **museum** (admission Rs 5; ✆ noon-6.30pm Tue-Sun) has a room each of Mughal miniatures, old textiles, antique carpets and 20th-century paintings. There's also a special, air-conditioned shrine-like room displaying several watercolours by Bengali-Renaissance superstar Rabindranath Tagore (see also p111).

THE MAIDAN
After the 'Black Hole' fiasco, a moated 'second' **Fort William** (Map pp98–9; closed to public) was constructed in octagonal, Vaubanesque form (1758). The whole village of Gobindapur was flattened to give the new fort's cannons a clear line of fire. Though sad for then-residents, this created the **Maidan** (pronounced moi-dan), a

---

MOTHER TERESA
For many people, Mother Teresa (1910–97), was the living image of human sacrifice. Born Agnes Gonxha Bojaxhiu to Albanian parents in Uskup (now Skopje, Macedonia), she joined the Irish Order of Loreto nuns and worked for over a decade teaching in Calcutta's **St Mary's High School** (✆ 2298451; 92 Ripon St). Horrified by the city's spiralling poverty she established a new order, the Missionaries of Charity and, in 1952, opened Nirmal Hriday (Sacred Heart; see p109). This was the first of many refuges offering free shelter and a little human dignity to the destitute and dying. Although the order expanded into an international charity, Mother Teresa herself continued to live in absolute simplicity. She was awarded the Nobel Peace Prize in 1979 and beatified by the Vatican in October 2003, the first official step towards being made a saint.

But this 'Saint of the Gutters' is not universally beloved. For some Kolkatans it's slightly galling to find their cultured, predominantly Hindu city popularly linked in the world's mind with a Catholic heroine whose work underlined the city's least appealing facet. Meanwhile Germaine Greer has accused Mother Teresa of religious imperialism, while Christopher Hitchens' book, *The Missionary Position*, decries the donations from dictators and corrupt tycoons. Many have questioned the Missionaries of Charity's minimal medical background and Teresa's staunchly Catholic position against contraception, which seems particularly untenable given Kolkata's growing AIDS and hepatitis epidemic. Of course, the organisation was never primarily focused on saving lives, simply offering a little love to the dying. Before Mother Teresa, even that was an unknown luxury for the truly destitute. But today, for the critics, it's not quite enough.

CHOWRINGHEE

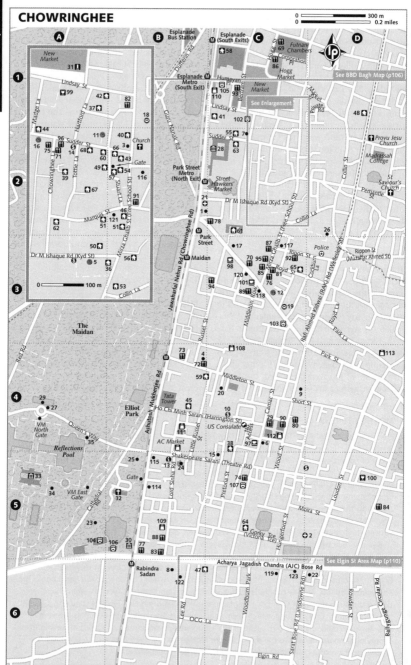

0   300 m
0   0.2 miles

See BBD Bagh Map (p106)

New Market

Esplanade
Bus Station

Esplanade
(South Exits)

Esplanade Metro
(South Exit)

See Enlargement

New
Market

Lindsay St

Sudder St

Park Street
Metro
(North Exit)

Street
Hawkers'
Market

Dr M Ishaque Rd (Kyd St)

Provu Jesu
Church

Madrassah
College

St
Saviour's
Church

Park
Street

Maidan

Police

Rippon St
(Muzaffar Ahmed St)

The
Maidan

Park St

Middleton St

Elliot
Park

Short St

VM
North
Gate

Queen's
Way

Tata
Tower

Ho Chi Minh Sarani (Harrington St)

US Consulate

Reflections
Pool

AC Market

Shakespeare Sarani (Theatre Rd)

VM East
Gate

Gorky
(Victoria

See Elgin St Area Map (p110)

Rabindra
Sadan

Acharya Jagadish Chandra (AJC) Bose Rd

Elgin Rd

vast 3km-long park that is today as fundamental to Kolkata as Central Park is to New York City. Fort William remains hidden within a walled military zone, but for an amusingly far-fetched tale of someone who managed to get in, read *Simon Winchester's Calcutta*.

INDIAN MUSEUM

Around central lawns, Kolkata's main **museum** (☎ 22499979; www.indianmuseum-Calcutta.org; Chowringhee Rd; Indian/foreigner/camera Rs 10/150/50; ☯ 10am-4.30pm

Tue-Sun) fills a glorious colonnaded palace with aging glass-and-hardwood display cabinets that are almost attractions in themselves. Exhibits range from fabulous Hindu bronzes to whole elephant skeletons. Notice the 2000-year-old eyeliner pencils, gag at the human embryos in formaldehyde and don't miss the impressive life-size reproduction of the 2nd-century BC Barhut Gateway. Before 1875, many exhibits were originally displayed by the Asiatic Society (see p100) in one of Asia's earliest museums.

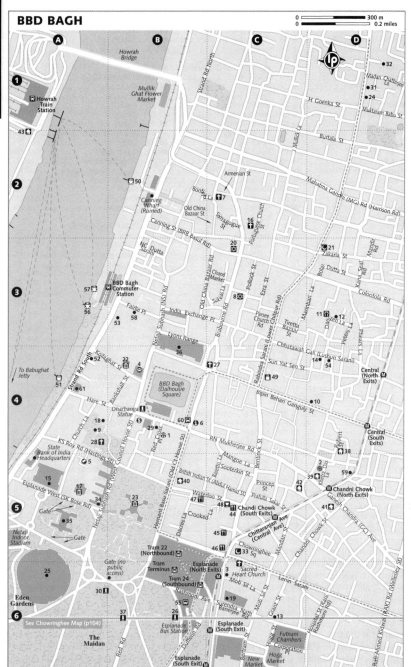

BBD BAGH

0 — 300 m
0 — 0.2 miles

Howrah Bridge

Mullik Ghat Flower Market

Howrah Train Station

Canning Wharf (Ruined)

BBD Bagh Commuter Station

Fairlie Pl

To Babughat Jetty

BBD Bagh (Dalhousie Square)

Dharbanga Statue

State Bank of India Headquarters

Eden Gardens

Netaji Indoor Stadium

Gate

Gate

Gate (no public access)

Tram 22 (Northbound)

Tram Terminus

Tram 24 (Southbound)

The Maidan

See Chowringhee Map (p104)

Esplanade Bus Station

Esplanade (South Exit)

New Market

Hogg Market

Futnani Chambers Corporation

Sacred Heart Church

Esplanade (North Exits)

Esplanade (South Exit)

Chandni Chowk (South Exits)

Chandi Chowk (North Exits)

Central (South Exits)

Central (North Exits)

Chittaranjan (Central Ave)

PARK STREET CEMETERY

Today Park St is one of Kolkata's top commercial avenues. But when it was constructed in the 1760s, it was a simple causeway across uninhabited marshlands built for mourners to access the then-new **Park Street Cemetery** (Map pp98-9; cnr Park St & AJC Bose Rd; ☾ 7.30am-4.30pm). Today that cemetery remains a wonderful oasis of calm with mossy Raj-era graves – from rotundas to soaring pyramids – jostling for space in a lightly manicured jungle. Buying the guide booklet (Rs 100) supports its maintenance.

MOTHER TERESA'S MISSION

Many visitors pay respects at Mother Teresa's large, sober tomb within the Sisters of Charity's **Motherhouse** (Map pp98-9; ☎ 2452277; 54a AJC Bose Rd; ☾ visits 8am-noon & 3-6pm Fri-Wed, prayers 4.30pm Fri, volunteer briefings 3pm Mon, Wed & Fri). There's a small **museum** displaying Teresa's worn sandals and battered enamel dinner-bowl. Upstairs, **'Mother's room'** is preserved in all its simplicity with a crown-of-thorns above her modest camp bed.

Enter opposite The Web internet café in the first alley north of Ripon St.

BBD Bagh Area

All of the sites in this area appear on Map p106, except where otherwise noted.

NORTH OF THE MAIDAN

Curiosities around New Market (see p121) include the fascinatingly crumbling **Futani Chambers**, the perfect '50s-style façade of **Elite Cinema**, the brilliant colonial-era **Metropolitan Building** and the fanciful **Tippu Sultan's Mosque**. On an elegant palm-shaded courtyard tucked unexpectedly behind a barrier of hawkers' stalls, the luxurious **Oberoi Grand** (see p115) hotel offers blissfully elegant respite from the surrounding commotion.

Across Esplanade bus station, the north end of the Maidan is dotted with monuments. Circus performers, political firebrands and dealers in mystic medicines frequently entertain crowds around the **Sahid Minar**, a 48m-tall round-topped obelisk originally celebrating a British military leader. Beyond is a sombre **WWI cenotaph** and a **statue of LBG Tilak**, who disdains the perfectly framed (if gated) view of the grand 1799 **Raj Bhavan** (http://rajbhavankolkata .nic.in/main.asp; closed to public). Though designed to resemble Lord Curzon's English country house, the Raj Bahvan actually looks more like the US White House. It's now the highly guarded official residence of the West Bengal governor.

The vast **Ranji Stadium** in Eden Gardens hosts international cricket matches. Behind is a lake and picturesque **Burmese pagoda**, but they're currently out-of-bounds due to an arcane political squabble. Instead, walk past the western end of the low-domed **West Bengal Assembly building** for the most impressive view of the resplendent **High Court** building, a wonderful architectural mongrel halfway between Oxford college and Venetian opera set. In slightly more restrained style is the grand **treasury building**, whose arched cloisters are comically stacked with decades worth of dusty paperwork bundles that bureaucrats never need yet don't dare to throw away. Between the two is the imposing colonnaded cube of the **former Calcutta Town Hall Building** (4 Esplanade West). Here **Kolkata Panorama** (☎ 22131098; guided tour Indian/foreigner Rs 10/100; ❤ 11am-6pm Tue-Sun) introduces the city's heritage through a lively collection of working models and interactive exhibits. It's well designed, though historically selective, and many foreigners will struggle to appreciate fully the detailed sections on Bengali popular culture.

Yet more colonnades buttress the stone-spired 1787 **St John's Church** (☎ 22436098; K Sankar Roy Rd; admission Rs 10; ❤ 8am-5pm). In its somewhat overgrown grounds are two curious octagonal monuments, the **mausoleum of Job Charnock**, Kolkata's disputed 'founder', and a 1902 **Black Hole Memorial** that was hidden away here in 1940.

AROUND BBD BAGH
Arranged around BBD Bagh is much of Kolkata's finest colonial architecture. Originally called Tank Sq, its palm-lined central reservoir-lake ('tank') once supplied the young city's water. Some locals still use its later-colonial name **Dalhousie Sq**, commemorating British Lieutenant-Governor Lord Dalhousie. But with delicious irony, the square is now re-renamed after the nationalists who tried to assassinate him. In fact the BBD trio (Binoy, Badal and Dinesh) bungled their 1930 raid, killing instead an unlucky prisons inspector. Nonetheless the attack was a highly symbolic moment in the self-determination struggle. The assassination took place within the photogenic 1780 **Writers' Building**, whose glorious south façade looks something like a French provincial city hall. Originally built for clerks ('writers') of the East India Company, it's still a haven of pen-pushing bureaucracy.

There are many more imposing colonial edifices. The red-brick **Standard Buildings** (32 BBD Bagh) have carved nymphs and wonderful wrought-iron balconies at the rear. The former **Standard Chartered Building** (Netaji Subhash Rd) has a vaguely Moorish feel, while **St Andrews Church** has a fine Wren-style spire. The grandly domed, 1866 **General Post Office** (see p102) was built on the ruins of the original Fort William, site of the infamous 'Black Hole of Calcutta' (see p96).

BARABAZAAR & CHINATOWN
Scattered north and northeast of BBD Bagh lies an unexpected wealth of religious buildings. Alone none warrants a special trip, but weaving between them is a great excuse to explore some of Kolkata's most vibrantly chaotic alleys. Looking like a tall-spired church, **Moghan David Synagogue** (Canning St) is somewhat more impressive than **BethEl Synagogue** (Pollock St). The 1797 Portuguese-Catholic **Holy Rosary Cathedral** (Brabourne Rd; ❤ 6am-11am) has eye-catching crown-topped side towers. Hidden away amid the bustle of Old China Bazaar St, the 1707 **Armenian Church** (Armenian St; ❤ 9am-11am Sun) is claimed to be Kolkata's oldest place of Christian worship. It has a low but finely proportioned, whitewashed spire that's best spied from Bonfield Lane. To the east the 1926 red-sandstone **Nakhoda Mosque** (1 Zakaria St) rises impressively above the bustling shop fronts of ever-fascinating Rabindra Sarani. Its roof, bristling with domes and minarets, was modelled on Akbar's tomb at Sikandra. Less than 500m south lie the scanty remnants of Kolkata's ragged little **Chinatown**. Most Chinese have since moved away, and at first glance the area looks pretty unappealing. But if you wander up Damzen Lane you'll find two **Chinese Temples** (one now used as a local school) and a somewhat decrepit **gateway** (10 Damzen Lane) – built big enough for the family's domestic elephants. Just off the main road Chhatawali Gali (Lushun Sarani), notice the sad ruins of the once-grand 1924 **Nangking Restaurant**. To get a closer look you'll pass an extensive shoulder-high **garbage heap**. But it's more than garbage. At closer inspection you'll see that Kolkata streetfolk have burrowed homes right into it. Very humbling.

Hooghly Riverbank
The Hooghly might look unappealingly murky, but it's holy to Hindu Kolkatans whose main festivals often involve plunging divine *puja* images into its waters (see p97). The riverside **ghats** are interesting any morning or evening when die-hard devotees

bathe and make offerings. A photogenic if distinctly seedy vantage point is **Babu Ghat** (Map pp98-9), hidden behind a grubby, pseudo-Greek gateway near Eden Gardens. Here the votive floating candles simply add to the spectacle of colourful sunsets viewed through the impressively elegant **Vidyasagar Setu** suspension bridge. Crossing that bridge takes you (eventually) to the **Botanical Gardens** (Map pp98-9; ☎ 26685357; ☺ 7am-5pm) that were founded in 1786 to develop a then newly discovered herbal bush called 'tea'. The gardens' 200-year-old **banyan tree** is claimed to have the second-largest canopy in the world.

HOWRAH (HAORA)

Howrah bridge (Rabindra Setu; Map pp98-9), Kolkata's 700m-long architectural icon, is a vibrating abstraction of steel cantilevers, traffic fumes and sweat. Although over 60 years old, it probably remains the world's busiest bridge. Beneath the east end, **Mullik Ghat flower market** is a sensory overload of sights and smells that's very photogenic. But beware that photography of the bridge itself is strictly prohibited. Nonetheless you might be able to sneak a discreet shot from one of the various river-ferries that ply across the Hooghly to the vast **Howrah train station**. This 1906 edifice has clusters of towers topped in terracotta tiles giving it a look reminiscent of a Spanish desert citadel. The station serves millions daily, emptying trains picked clean by legions of destitute street children who are the subject of much charity work and plenty of moving prose.

Some 500m south, the new open-air **Railway Museum** (admission Rs 5; ☺ 1-8pm Fri-Wed) has a two-storey model of Howrah train station, several 19th-century steam locos and a toy-train **ride** (adult/child Rs 20/10).

South Kolkata

KALIGHAT

Between Kalighat and Jatin Das Park Metro stations, Kalighat's **Kali Temple** (Map pp98-9; ☎ 22231516; ☺ 5am-2pm & 4-10pm) is Kolkata's holiest spot. The current structure, painted silver-grey with rainbow highlights, dates from 1809. Of course the site is many, many centuries older (see p96) and possibly the source of Kolkata's name. Inside, pilgrims jostle to present hibiscus offerings to the three-eyed Kali image whose crown can occasionally be glimpsed through the throng from the bell-pavilion. Priests loitering around the temple

might whisk you to the front of the queue for an obligatory 'donation' (around Rs 50 per person). Behind the Mandir, goats are ritually beheaded to honour the ever-demanding goddess.

The temple is entered from the west along a narrow alley. Right next door is Mother Teresa's world famous, if surprisingly small, **Nirmal Hriday** (251 Kalighat Rd) home for the dying (see boxed text, p103), with neo-Mughal mini-domes pimpling the roof corners.

Surrounding alleys are full of **market stalls** selling votive flowers, brassware, religious artefacts and Kali pictures. Off **Kalighat Rd** you may spot pot-painter artisans at work.

A short walk away on the putrid Tolisnala Stream, **Shanagar Burning Ghat** hosts an impressive gaggle of monuments to celebrities cremated there.

ALIPORE

Kolkata's 16-hectare **zoo** (Map pp98-9; ☎ 24791152; Alipore Rd; admission Rs 10; ☺ 9am-5pm Fri-Wed) first opened in 1875. The spacious lawns and lakeside promenades are very popular with weekend picnickers and although some big-cat cages are rather confining, it rates as one of India's best zoos. Until he died in March 2006 the oldest resident had been Adwaita, an approximately 200-year-old giant tortoise, once the pet of controversial colonialist Robert Clive (see p33). Take bus 230 from Rabindra Sadan.

Directly south of the zoo's entrance, the access road to the National Library loops around the very regal **Curzon Mansion**, once the colonial Viceroy's residence. It's not (yet) a museum.

Around 1km southeast on Belvedere Rd are the delightfully tranquil **Horticultural Gardens** (Map pp98-9; admission Rs 10; ☺ 6-10am & 1-5pm).

ELGIN ROAD & GARIAHAT

Opposite the modern Forum Mall, **Netaji Bhawan** (Map p110; ☎ 24756139; www.netaji.org; 38/2 Elgin Rd; admission Rs 5; ☺ 11am-4pm Tue-Sun) is the former family home of Subhas Chandra Bose (p111), displaying personal effects of the iconic Independence fighter.

Further east **CIMA** (Centre for International Modern Art; Map pp98-9; ☎ 24858509; Sunny Towers, 2nd fl, 43 Ashutosh Chowdhury Rd; admission free; ☺ 11am-7pm Tue-Sat, 3-7pm Mon) is one of the best places in Kolkata to see cutting-edge contemporary Bengali art, though the exhibition space is not enormous.

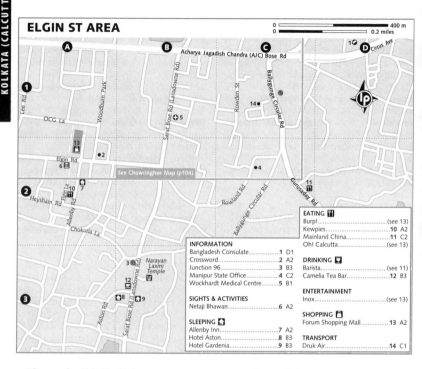

ELGIN ST AREA

0 — 400 m
0 — 0.2 miles

INFORMATION	
Bangladesh Consulate	1 D1
Crossword	2 A2
Junction 96	3 B3
Manipur State Office	4 C2
Wockhardt Medical Centre	5 B1

SIGHTS & ACTIVITIES	
Netaji Bhawan	6 A2

SLEEPING	
Allenby Inn	7 A2
Hotel Aston	8 B3
Hotel Gardenia	9 B3

EATING	
Burp!	(see 13)
Kewpies	10 A2
Mainland China	11 C2
Oh! Calcutta	(see 13)

DRINKING	
Barista	(see 11)
Camelia Tea Bar	12 B3

ENTERTAINMENT	
Inox	(see 13)

SHOPPING	
Forum Shopping Mall	13 A2

TRANSPORT	
Druk Air	14 C1

The nearby **Birla Mandir** (Map pp98-9; Gariahat Rd; ☼ 6-11.30am & 4.30-9pm) is a large Lakshmi Narayan temple complex in cream-coloured sandstone whose three classically corn-cob shaped towers are more impressive for their size than their carvings. The temple was built between 1970 and 1996 by one of India's wealthiest clans.

RABINDRA SAROVAR

Scenic in the dawn haze, **Rabrindra Sarovar** (Map pp98–9) is a lake ringed by parkland where Kolkatans gather for early-morning yoga, meditation and group exercises. These include ho-ho ha-ha-ha group laugh-ins. At such informal **Laughing Clubs** (☼ 6am-7am), engagingly described by Tony Hawks in *The Weekenders: Adventures in Calcutta*, a good (even if forced) giggle can be refreshingly therapeutic.

Facing the park further east, the **Birla Academy of Art & Culture** (Map pp98-9; ☎ 24666802; 109 Southern Ave; admission Rs 2; ☼ 4-7pm Tue-Sun) has lively temporary exhibitions and an impressive three-storey Dakatkali statue in its grounds, visible through the gates: passers-by pay quiet homage.

Northeast of the lake, the **Gariahat** area is one of Kolkata's most popular local shopping areas.

North Kolkata
KOLKATA UNIVERSITY AREA

College St is the heartland of Kolkata's vibrant academic universe. The **Asutosh Museum of Indian Art** (Map pp98-9; ☎ 22410071; www.caluniv.ac.in; Centenary Bldg, 87/1 College St; admission Rs 10; ☼ 11.30am-4.30pm Mon-Fri) has priceless if slightly dry displays of fabulous antique Indian sculpture, brasswork and Bengali terracotta, with some more light-hearted toys and 20th-century folk art upstairs. The museum is down the first lane off College St as you walk north from Coolootola Rd. It's within **Kolkata University**, facing some grand, older collegiate buildings. Nearby is the mythic Indian Coffee House (p119).

MARBLE PALACE

This extraordinarily grand 1853 **mansion** (Map pp98-9; ☎ 22393310; 46 Muktaram Babu St; ☼ 10am-4pm Tue-Wed & Fri-Sun) is indulgently overstuffed with statues and lavishly floored with marble inlay.

Yet its fine paintings droop in their dusty frames and the antique furniture is haphazardly draped in torn old dust sheets. It would make a great horror-movie set.

Although admission is technically free, guards, 'guides' and even the toilet monitor are expectant of tips. Importantly, before visiting you need to get a permission note from either West Bengal Tourism or India Tourism (see p102). However, some travellers report bribing their way in without.

To find the site from MG Rd metro station, walk two blocks north – away from the striking modernist **Panchaiti Mosque** (Chittaranjan Ave) – turning west between sari shops at 171 and 173 Chittaranjan Ave.

To continue to Tagore's House, walk west down Muktaram Babu St, turn right on Rabindra Sarani, and walk north for two blocks passing the wonderful olde-worlde **Ram Prasad apothecary shop** (204 Rabindra Sarani) and some interesting **stone-carving workshops**.

TAGORE'S HOUSE

Within Rabindra Bharati University, Rabindranath Tagore's comfortable 1784 family mansion has become a shrine-like **museum** (Rabindra Bharati Museum; Map pp98-9; ☎ 22695242; 246D Rabindra Sarani; Indian/foreigner Rs 10/50, student Rs 5/25; ⊙ 10.30am-4.30pm Tue-Sun) to India's greatest modern poet. Even if his personal effects don't inspire you, some of the well-chosen quotations might spark an interest in Tagore's deeply universalist philosophy. There's also a decent gallery of paintings by his family and contemporaries. The photo of Tagore with Einstein could win a 'World's Wildest Hair' competition.

JAIN TEMPLES

Several eye-catching Jain temples are grouped together on Badridas Temple St. The best known is 1867 **Sheetalnathji Jain Mandir** (Map pp98-9; donation appropriate; ⊙ 6am-11.30am & 3-7pm), a dazzling pastiche of colourful mosaics, spires, columns and slivered figurines. Directly opposite, the more sedate 1810 **Dadaji Jain Mandir** has a central marble tomb-temple patterned with silver studs. The temples are 1.6km from Shyam Bazar metro, two blocks south of Aurobindo Sarani via Raja Dinendra Rd.

In bird-filled gardens 250km west of Belgachia Metro, the **Digambar Jain Mandir** (Map pp98-9; ⊙ 6am-noon & 5-7pm), has a tall lighthouse style tower. On closer examination the tower's 'lamp' actually contains a meditating ministatuette.

KUMARTULI

This fascinating district is named for the *kumar* (sculptors) who fashion giant **puja effigies** of the gods, eventually to be ritually immersed in the holy Hooghly. Different workshops in lanes off Rabindra Sarani specialise in certain body parts, creating the straw frames, adding clay coatings or painting the divine features with brilliant colours. Kumar workshops are busiest for the two months before the October/November Durga Puja festival (see p97).

BELUR MATH

Amid palms and manicured lawns, this extensive, peaceful **religious centre** (Map pp98-9; ☎ 26545892; www.sriramakrishna.org/belur.htm; Grand Trunk

---

SUBHAS CHANDRA BOSE

In the early 1940s the two most prominent figures in the Indian anticolonial campaign were Gandhi (who favoured nonviolence) and Subhas Chandra Bose (who certainly didn't). Eminently intelligent, Cambridge-educated Bose managed to become Chief Executive of Calcutta despite periods in jail after accusations of assault and terrorism. During WWII he fled first to Germany, then Japan. He formed the Indian National Army (INA) mostly by recruiting Indian soldiers from Japanese POW camps. The INA then marched with Japan's invading force towards northeastern India, getting bogged down, and eventually defeated in Manipur and Nagaland. Bose fled but later died in a mysterious plane crash.

Today his image is somewhat ambivalent in much of India. But in Bengal, Bose remains a hero nicknamed Netaji (revered leader). Patriotic songs are intoned before his many statues and Kolkata's airport is named for him.

In 2005 Shyam Benegal's biographical film *Netaji Subhas Chandra Bose: The Forgotten Hero* was taken to court by radical Bose supporters for suggesting that the Bengali hero secretly married a non-Indian.

Rd; ⏱ 6.30am-noon & 3.30-8.30pm) is the headquarters of the Ramakrishna Mission. Its centrepiece is the huge 1938 **Ramakrishna Mandir** (⏱ 6.30am-12.30 & 3.30-8pm), which somehow manages to look like a cathedral, Indian palace and Istanbul's Aya Sofya all at the same time. That's deliberate and perfectly in keeping with the message of 19th-century Indian sage **Ramakrishna Paramahamsa** who preached the unity of all religions.

Within the compound on the Hooghly riverbank, several smaller **shrines** (⏱ 6.30am-11.30 & 3.30-5.15pm) include the **Sri Sarada Devi Temple** entombing the guru's wife. Larger yet essentially similar in design, the 1924 **Swami Vivekananda Temple** marks the cremation spot of the mission's founder and Ramakrishna's most famous disciple. **Swami Vivekananda's room** is also preserved.

Accessed from the car park is an interesting **museum** (admission Rs 3; ⏱ 8.30-11.30am & 3.30-5.30pm Tue-Sun) that charts the life and times of Ramakrishna and associates.

Take minibus 10 from the Esplanade or bus 56 from Howrah train station. Continue your Ramakrishna experience with a boat across the Hooghly to Dakshineswar.

DAKSHINESWAR KALI TEMPLE

Shaped like an Indian Sacré Coeur, this 1847 **Kali Temple** (Map pp98-9; ☎ 25645222; ⏱ 6.30am-noon & 3.30-9pm) was where Ramakrishna started his remarkable spiritual journey. Decorated with sepia photos, Ramakrishna's small room is now a place of special meditative reverence. Find it in the outer northwest corner of the temple precinct.

Taxis from Shyam Bazar metro cost Rs 85. However, arriving by (uncovered) river boat from Belur Math Ghat (Rs 7, 20 minutes) is an integral part of the Dakshineswar experience.

ACTIVITIES
Bowling

Several modern bowing alleys charge Rs 80 to 90 per game plus Rs 30 entry. Try **Megabowl** (Map p104; ☎ 22881311; 3rd fl, Metro Shopping Centre; ⏱ 11am-9pm), **Sparkz** (Map pp98-9; ☎ 24481744; Diamond Harbour Rd, Alipore) beneath Majerhat Bridge or **Nicco Superbowl** (Map pp98-9; ⏱ noon-10pm) beside Nicco Park (opposite).

Golf

The beautiful golf course at the **Tollygunge Club** (Map pp98-9; ☎ 24732316 ext 142; SP Mukherjee Rd) charges US$40 green fees for visitors but only

Rs 150 if you're staying here. Renting clubs ranges Rs 100 to 300.

The magnificent **Royal Calcutta Golf Club** (Map pp98-9; ☎ 24731288; rcgc2vsnl.net; 18 Golf Club Rd) was established in 1829, making it the oldest golf club in the world outside Britain. Foreign guests unaccompanied by a member pay US$50 for an 18-hole round, but will need their own clubs.

Volunteering

Several organisations welcome foreign volunteers (see p317).

COURSES
Cooking

Kali Travel Home (opposite) can arrange highly recommended three-hour Bengali cooking courses (US$14) led by local housewives in their homes. Three-days advance notice is usually required.

Meditation & Dance

The peaceful **Aurobindo Bhawan** (Map p104; ☎ 22822162; 8 Shakespeare Sarani) offers free, half-hour **meditation sessions** (⏱ 7pm Thu & Sun) and various **classical Indian dance lessons** (Rs 100-150; ⏱ 4pm): Orissan (Monday), Bharatnatyam (Thursday), Kathak (Friday and Saturday).

Yoga

Five-day yoga courses are organised by the **Art of Living** (☎ 24631018; aolkol@vsnl.net) at varying locations. Call well ahead for details.

KOLKATA FOR CHILDREN

Kolkata has two excellent hands-on places to really experience practical science. The **Birla Industrial & Technological Museum** (Map pp98-9; ☎ 22477241; 18A Gurusaday Rd; admission Rs 15; ⏱ 10am-5.30pm) has loads of buttons to press and levers to pull, though some older galleries need repairing. The more dramatic **Science City** (Map pp98-9; ☎ 23434343; EM Bypass; admission Rs 20, rides Rs 10-40; ⏱ 9am-9pm) is arranged like a theme park. Spherical, spiral and up-turned hemispherical buildings create a uniquely futuristic skyline around a thought-provoking physics garden. Twice hourly the Time Machine (Rs 10) gives short, sci-fi themed simulator rides, the Mirror-Maze is brilliantly disorientating and Evolution Park (Rs 10) walks you past animatronic dinosaurs in the eerie half dark.

The little **Nehru Children's Museum** (Map p104; ☎ 22483517; 94/1 Chowringhee Rd; adult/child Rs 5/3;

11am-7pm Wed-Sun, 3-7pm Tue) displays 400 dolls from 37 countries and has colourful dioramas retelling the Hindu epics. **Nicco Park** (☎ 23578101-4; Block BN, Sector 5, Salt Lake City; admission Rs 50, rides Rs 15-40; 11am-8pm) is a colourful theme park with a roller-coaster, a log flume and various fairground rides attractively arranged around a central lake. Last entry 7pm. Take bus 201 from Belgachia metro.

TOURS

West Bengal Tourism (Map p106; ☎ 22485917; www .westbengaltourism.com; BBD Bagh) operates a full-day city sightseeing tour (Rs 150; hdeparts 7.30am daily) that includes Belur Math, Dakshineswar temple and Eden Gardens. It arranges Hooghly River charter boats and runs special cruises during the Durga Puja festival (p97) to see the immersion of the idols. Two-day/one-night trips to the Sunderbans Tiger Reserve (p127) cost Rs 1200 to 3600 per head, including permits.

Enthusiastic expats at **Kali Travel Home** (☎ / fax 25587980; www.traveleastindia.com) offer accompanied city walks and longer customised tours around Bengal, Darjeeling and Sikkim.

SLEEPING

The great majority of foreigner-accepting budget accommodation is around the Sudder St traveller area. Standards vary wildly, but that area also offers some perfectly decent midrange hotels for around half the cost of equivalent standards elsewhere in Kolkata. Business travellers generally prefer southern Chowringhee or outer Kolkata.

Looks can be deceptive. Some bright façades mask lacklustre crash pads. Other great places are hidden within buildings that look like crumbling wrecks. Décor degrades fast in this climate, so the best choice is generally whichever was most recently renovated.

In summer you can get big off-season discounts, but AC will be virtually essential. In winter fan rooms are fine but demand is high, so you might just have to take whatever's available. Top-end hotels often cost less than half the rack-rate when booked through internet discounters. Taxes and service charges vary so widely (0% to 25%) that for fairness these have been included in our listed prices.

Most cheaper places lock their gates around 11pm so if planning to be late, forewarn the staff. Check-out time is 10am at several budget hotels.

Sudder & Park St Areas

The following places appear on Map p104.

BUDGET

If all our suggestions are full, there are dozens more similarly priced places within a stone's throw.

Salvation Army Red Shield Guest House (☎ 225 20599; 2 Sudder St; dm Rs 70, d with shared/private bathroom from Rs 150/250) Popular rooms and dingy, sex-segregated dorms are made much more palatable by the relaxing upstairs lounge area.

Centrepoint Guest House (☎ 22528184; ian_ra shid@yahoo.com; 20 Mirza Ghalib St; dm Rs 80, s/d from Rs 200/250) The whole 4th floor is a sprawling bunk-bed dormitory that's brighter than most. Good for early risers.

Times Guest House (☎ 22521796; 3 Sudder St; s/d Rs 100/250) First impressions are highly off-putting but the double rooms are actually decent value with bathroom and natural light. Singles are basic with shared toilets. Above the Zurich Café,

Tourist Inn (☎ 22523134; 1st fl, 4/1 Sudder St; s/d with shared bathroom Rs 120/240, q with bathroom Rs 500, d with AC Rs 800-1200;) In a creaky old house, this comparatively inviting cheapie also has two AC rooms with excellent bathrooms, mosaic floors and fully renovated interiors that bring out their colonial-era appeal.

Paragon Hotel (☎ 22522445; 2 Stuart Lane; dm Rs 80, s/d with shared bathroom from Rs 130/180, s/d with private bathroom from Rs 260/300) The narrow courtyard and open roof areas are such good places to meet fellow travellers that few seem to mind the jam-packed dorms or grotty, minuscule rooms. Bring your own padlock.

Modern Lodge (☎ 22524960; 1 Stuart Lane; r with shared/private bathroom from Rs 150/250) Not modern at all, but remarkably good value. The unusually well-kept, simple rooms have high ceilings, but fans and lamps share a single switch in cheaper rooms. No in-room plugs for battery charging.

Continental Guesthouse (☎ 22520663; Sudder St; s/d Rs 150/200, with toilet Rs 300/350) Good tiling but some peeling paint in the better rooms and the lower ceilings upstairs. Hot water by bucket.

Hotel Maria (☎ 22520860, 22224444; 5/1 Sudder St; s/d with shared bathroom Rs 150, s with private bathroom Rs 220, d with private bathroom Rs 250-300;) Somewhat mouldering but pleasantly set in a green courtyard. On-site Internet room available.

Timestar Hotel (☎ 22528028; 2 Tottie Lane; s/d from Rs 175/300) This crumbling colonial mansion house has grubby walls but newly tiled floors in the bathrooms.

Hotel Neelam (☎ 22269198; 11 Kyd St; s/d from Rs 200/350) Another once-grand colonial mansion that was recently repainted but not remodelled. Huge, creaky rooms have shared basic bathrooms.

Milan Guest House (☎ 30228621; 1st fl, 33/3 Mirza Ghalib; s/d Rs 200/300; ✷) Of many lacklustre budget places crammed into the same uninspiring side alley, the Milan is marginally the best value. Rooms are windowless and tend to overheat but are unusually well tended for the price. Optional AC costs Rs 300 extra.

Capital Guest House (☎ 22520598; 11B Chowringhee Lane; s with shared bathroom Rs 250-290, d with private bathroom from Rs 350-390; ✷) As charming as a prison, but with so many rooms that there's hope of a vacancy when other places are full.

MIDRANGE

Hotel VIP InterContinental (☎ 22520150; fax 22293715; 44 Mirza Ghalib St; fan s/d Rs 400/550, with AC from Rs 800/1000; ✷) Of three close-by 'VIP' hotels, the friendly little InterContinental has the best-value rooms, attractive with new moulded ceilings, marble floors and smart, small bathrooms. It's virtually unsigned beside a piano-rental shop.

Pioneer International (☎ 222520057; 1st fl, 1 Marquis St; d without/with AC Rs 450/650) The aged house is rotting and the wobbly wooden stairway unappetizing, but within, the hotel's six rooms are remarkably neat with new tiled floors. Reasonable value.

our pick Sunflower Guest House (☎ 22299401; 4th fl, 7 Royd St; s/d with fan Rs 600/650, d with AC Rs 850) One of Kolkata's best-kept accommodation secrets hides unexpectedly excellent rooms whose freshly tiled bathrooms have new geysers. It's within the archaic-looking 1865 Solomon Mansions building. Ride up in a wonderfully original if grimy 1940s lift with 2006 workings. The urbane owner might invite you to his private rooftop garden.

Hotel Gulshan Palace (☎ 22521009; www.gulshan group.com; 42B Mirza Ghalib St; AC s/d from Rs 660/780; ✷) Decent value despite rather offish management. Deluxe rooms have two-tone wooden furniture and pleasant curtains.

Jaapon Guest House (☎ 22520657; jaapon_001@ yahoo.com; 30F Mirza Ghalib St; s/d from Rs 660/880; ✷) This very friendly, all-AC mini-hotel is tucked away in a small alley. Some walls are slightly scuffed and lower rooms a little dark, but

upper-floor deluxe rooms (s/d Rs 1100/1300) are a good choice.

Super Guest House (☎ 22520995; super_guest house@hotmail.com; 30A Mirza Ghalib St; d 660-990; ✷) Good, brightly decorated rooms with AC are dotted about three separate but very close-by locations.

Chowringhee YMCA (☎ 22521017; fax 22492234; 25 Chowringhee Rd; s/d Rs 700/1000 plus Rs 50 'membership'; ✷) Surely Kolkata's strangest accommodation, the YMCA has large, beautifully redecorated rooms with optional AC (Rs 250 extra). But reaching them takes you through a nightmarishly run-down Victorian building that would make an ideal setting for a cop-movie shoot-out scene. No reception, per se. Weird.

CKT Inn (☎ 22520130; fax 22520665; 3rd fl, 12/1 Lindsay St; s/d Rs 825/1100; ✷) In an office building with central AC and a lift, CKT furniture's has some slight '50s-style quirks and the water is usually hot. A pleasantly calm choice despite slightly rucked carpets.

Hotel Presidency Inn (☎ 22520057; www.hotelpresi dencyinn.com; 2/1 Marquis St; s/d from Rs 900/1020; ✷ ▣) A blue-glass exterior conceals decent rooms with marble floors, pseudo antique flourishes and a fresh flower on arrival. The pricier rooms (Rs 1620) are larger but not significantly better.

Hotel Majestic International (☎ 22442266; 12/1 RAK Rd; d Rs 960-1440; ✷) This reworked old cinema has 40 quiet, comically over-ornate, marble-floored rooms, but many are small and opening the lift doors requires a crowbar!

Ashreen Guest House (☎ 22520889; ashreen_guest house@yahoo.com; 2 Cowie Lane; d Rs 395-495, d with AC Rs 720; ✷) Possibly Kolkata's best value mini-hotel, the rooms are sparkling clean with some playful interior touches. Rooms from Rs 440 have geysers and 'double ventilation' (ie corner windows) but Rs 395 ones tend to overheat. Service is remarkably proactive and helpful. The associated **Aafreen Tower** (☎ 22293280; aafreen_tower@yahoo.co.in; 9A Kyd St; d Rs 500, d with AC Rs 770; ✷) is similar but larger with glass elevators.

TOP END

Fairlawn Hotel (☎ 22521510; www.fairlawnhotel.com; 13A Sudder St; s/d US$52.20/63.80; ✷) Taking guests since 1936, the Fairlawn is a Raj-era home (built 1783) set behind an attractive garden-café. The hotel's unique sitting room is jammed full of family mementos and photos, but most rooms, while impeccably clean, are only relatively basic, midrange standard.

Housez 43 (☎ 22276020; housez43@gmail.com; 43 Mirza Ghalib St; s/d from Rs 2750/3300; ☒) This handily central boutique hotel has gone overboard with bright colours and the sake-pot lamps are fun. Rooms are trendy and appealing… at least now that they're new.

Lytton Hotel (☎ 22491872/3; www.lyttonhotelindia .com; 14 Sudder St; standard s/d Rs 2860/3300, deluxe Rs 3080/3850; ☒) This relaxing three-storey hotel has two good restaurants and corridor-décor enlivened by panels of Tiffany-style stained-glass. The fresh deluxe rooms have understated pseudo-period furniture and possibly the cleanest bathtubs in India. Professional, low-key service.

Park Hotel (☎ 22499000; www.theparkhotels.com; 17 Park St; d deluxe/luxury US$270/303; ☒ ▣ ▨) If you'd choose the Hard Rock Hotel in Las Vegas, in Kolkata you'll love the Park. Pick the stylishly modern 'luxury' rooms with goldfish-bowl wash basins, pine floors and in-set lighting panels. The lobby is buffeted with live music from Someplace Else pub, while Kolkata's svelte chic-clique sip cocktails at the Aqua bar around a sizeable yet hard-to-find swimming pool.

our pick Oberoi Grand (☎ 22492323; www .oberoikolkata.com; 15 Chowringhee Rd; s/d from US$303/330; ☒ ▣ ▨) A marvellous oasis of genteel calm, the Oberoi offers five-star perfection in a magnificent columned palace. Staff anticipate your needs, a sumptuous Banyan Tree spa massages away your problems and trickling fountains welcome you home.

Southern Chowringhee

Southern Chowringhee hotels tend to be pricey, but are very handy for the business district. The following options all appear on Map p104.

Sikkim House (☎ 22815328; 4/1 Middleton St; d/ste Rs 770/1160; ☒) Large, clean but lacking panache, the functional all-AC rooms are especially good value for this pricey part of town.

Old Kenilworth Hotel (Purdey's Inn; ☎ 22825325; 7 Little Russel St; d without/with AC Rs 1800/2475; ☒) Run by the same Anglo-Armenian family since 1948, this is more of a spacious homestay than a hotel. Recently repainted rooms are very large if not overly luxurious. Many have dining areas, sparse '50s-style furniture and unique Heath Robinson–style rope-drag fans on the high ceilings. There's a private lawn, but no restaurant.

The Astor (☎ 22491872/3; http://astorkolkata.com; 15 Shakespeare Sarani; s Rs 3080-3520, d/ste Rs 3850/4400; ☒) Built in 1905, the exterior has the stolid grandeur of an Edwardian nursing home, while stairways display some period furniture and original wrought-iron banisters. Most rooms are comfortable but avoid the cheapest, windowless singles.

Senator Hotel (☎ 22893000; www.thesenatorhotel .com; 15 Camac St; s/d from US$127/138; ☒) Mid-sized, well-located business hotel with several stylish flourishes. The wood-and-leather bed boards are fashionable, but bathtubs are rather small. Elite rooms (6th floor, US$195) are brighter with pistachio walls and flat-screen TVs.

Worth considering if seriously discounted online:

Golden Park (Map p104; ☎ 228833939; 13 Ho Chi Minh Sarani; s/d/ste Rs 7150/7590/10890; ☒) The central atrium has a big 3-D Persian-style mural.

Hotel Hindusthan International (☎ 22802323; www.hindusthan.com; 235/1 AJC Bose Rd; d US$275-440; ☒ ▨) Vast 1960s concrete hotel totally remodelled with parquet floors and sumptuous mattresses. Swimming pool could be cleaner. North-facing rooms somewhat noisy.

Elgin St Area

This area is a good, untouristy base for shopping and dining. All options appear on Map p110.

Hotel Aston (☎ 24863145; hotelaston@gmail.com; 3 Aston Rd; s/d Rs 1200/1440) In a quiet street behind the Samilton Hotel, the Aston's small but vaguely stylish new rooms have excellent marbled bathrooms.

Hotel Gardenia (☎ 24863249; palmantu@hotmail.com; 42/1B Sarat Bose Rd; s/d Rs 960/1320, executive Rs 1320/1560) Beside the colourful Lakshmi Narayan temple, the Gardenia's larger executive rooms are reasonable value and have a low-key sense of modernist style.

Allenby Inn (☎ 24855984; allenbyinn@vsnl.net; 1st fl, 1/2 Allenby St; s/d Rs 3300/3850; ☒) Just 50m southeast of the Forum Mall, this stylishly upmarket guest house has dark-brown décor, green-tiled floors and plenty of abstract art. Some rooms are very large, though towels could be softer.

BBD Bagh Area

Total renovation should majestically revive the iconic 1840s **Great Eastern Hotel** (www.thegrandhotels .net; BBD Bagh) by the time you read this. Others options listed are handy for Chandni Chowk metro. The following are on Map p106.

Bengal Buddhist Association (Bauddha Dharmankur Sabha; ☎ 22117138; Robert St; tw Rs 200) Although intended for Buddhist students, tourists are welcome to rent these very clean, simple rooms with fan, mosquito nets and spotless shared bathrooms (cold water). Quiet location off a small courtyard.

Broadway Hotel (☎ 22363930; http://business.vsnl .com/broadway; 27A Ganesh Chandra Ave; s/d/t Rs 445/545/700) Well-preserved old furniture gives the lovingly cleaned rooms a vaguely 1950s feel veering unintendedly towards the retro-trendy.

Hotel Embassy (☎ 22379040; ssa@cal.vsnl.net.in; 27 Princep St; s/d Rs 660/880, renovated s/d Rs 990/1320; 🔀) In Kolkata's answer to New York's Flatiron Building, the Embassy has sad, sick-green corridors leading to rather better rooms. Choose the well-maintained, un-renovated ones whose old-yet-appealing feel is similar to equivalents at Hotel Broadway but with added AC. Slicker renovated rooms have less character and some damp patches.

Gypsy Inn (☎ 22126650; 2nd fl, 2 Chandni Chowk St; d non-AC/AC Rs 400/660; 🔀) Brightly whitewashed new rooms have geysers if little style. Enter via the stairway behind that of similar **Esplanade Chambers** (☎ 22127101; s/d from Rs 660/880; 🔀).

Howrah Train Station Area

Within a five-minute walk of the station there are numerous budget and lower midrange options. Chaotic traffic means that most suffer from deafening road noise, but there are two relatively peaceful budget exceptions. Both appear on Map pp98–9.

our pick **Howrah Hotel** (☎ 26413878; www.thehow rahhotel.com; 1 Mukhram Kanoria Rd; s/tr/q with shared bathroom Rs 125/270/380, d with shared bathroom Rs 205, s/tr/q with private bathroom Rs 215/370/485, d with private bathroom Rs 255-430) Luxury it ain't but this 1890 mansion has loads of character for such an ultra-budget place. The brilliantly antiquated reception has featured in three movies and the inner courtyard is an unexpected oasis of birdsong. Rooms are rather tatty but basically clean, many retaining original tile work, Italian chequer-board marble floors and high ceilings. The hotel is five minutes' walk from Howrath train station. Enter around the corner from the less appealing Hotel Bhimsain, which shares the same building.

Yatri Niwas (☎ 26601742; Howrah Train Station extension; dm Rs 100, d/tr Rs 350/400, d with AC Rs 500; 🔀) An Esheresque convent-style façade hides a more Soviet interior. Expect a melee at reception

where potential guests must show valid long-distance train tickets. Howrah train station is a five-minute walk. Maximum stay is one night, with check-out by 9am.

Outer Kolkata

All the following options appear on Map pp98–9.

our pick **Tollygunge Club** (☎ 24732316; www.tolly gungeclub.org; d/ste Rs 3030/3704; 🏊) Set in idyllic calm amongst mature trees and golf greens, this otherwise-exclusive colonial-era club rents good, motel-standard guest rooms. Guests get temporary club membership allowing access to the wonderful Raj-era Wills Lounge bar and (except Monday) use of many sporting facilities, including especially reasonable rates for using the golf course. Book ahead.

ITC Sonar Bangla Sheraton Hotel (☎ 23454545; www.itcwelcomgroup.in; EM Bypass; s/d from US$250/275; 🔀 🖥 🏊) Proudly eco-friendly, the rectilinear buildings of this 2003 'seven-star resort' are arranged around attractive lily ponds that naturally filter and recycle liquid waste. Luxurious rooms have a slightly Japanese vibe. With excellent restaurants, faultless service and a three-hole minigolf course, the hotel inspired a whole chapter in the paperback *The Weekenders: Adventures in Calcutta*. It's inconveniently far from the centre but close to Science City.

Airport Area

Although classier options exist further down VIP Rd, the following are walkably close to the terminals (around 1km): well placed if there's a strike.

Airways Lodge (☎ 25127280; Jessore Rd; s/d from Rs 220/330, with AC Rs 550/660; 🔀) One of several cheapies around Airport Gate 2, the fan rooms are sweltering claustrophobic boxes but the AC rooms are refreshingly cool, with very slight hints of style in the wrought-iron furniture. Covered rooftop restaurant.

Hotel White Palace (☎ 25117402; 28/1 Italgacha Rd; s/d from Rs 770/880; 🔀) This comparatively smart new place is 200m west of Airport Gate 1. Turn off Jessore Rd at a tiny mosque, then walk down the lane opposite the ultra-budget Om Lodge. AC costs Rs 200 extra.

EATING
Traveller Cafés

The Sudder St area has several backpacker-friendly places offering comfortably familiar standbys – from banana pancakes (around

Rs 20) to burgers, milkshakes and toasted sandwiches complimented with fresh fruit juices, plus a range of good-value, if slightly unrefined, Indian dishes. These options can be found on Map p104.

Zurich Restaurant (3 Sudder St; mains Rs 14-65; 6.30am-10.30pm) Convivially comfortable diner atmosphere with good-value thalis (from Rs 35) and explanations of Indian menu items for the uninitiated.

Blue Sky Cafe (Chowringhee Lane; mains Rs 20-140; 6.30am-10pm;) Stylish high-backed zinc chairs at long glass tables encourages conversation amongst fellow travellers.

Fresh & Juicy (Chowringhee Lane; mains Rs 25-60; 6.30am-10pm) Five-table café lacking any décor but offering great value, with good food and excellent banana lassis.

Restaurants

The *Times Food Guide* (Rs 75) lists hundreds of restaurants, though reviews are suspiciously uncritical. Most restaurants levy a 12.5% tax and some posher places add a further 10% 'service charge'. Tips are welcome at cheaper places and expected at most expensive restaurants.

BENGALI

Bengali cuisine is a wonderful discovery, with a whole new vocabulary of names and flavours (see the boxed text, below). Portion sizes are typically small, so order two or three dishes, along with rice and sweet tomato-*khejur* (date palm) chutney.

Radhuni (Map p104; 17G Mirza Ghalib St; dishes Rs 15-80, rice Rs 8; 7.30am-11pm) Cheap, unpretentious place for local breakfasts and surprisingly creditable Bengali food.

our pick Bhojohari Manna (Map pp98-9; ☎ 24401933; www.bhojohorimanna.org; 9/18 Ekdalia Rd aka PC Sorcan Sarani; dishes Rs 15-170; noon-9pm;) Already an urban legend, this tiny restaurant-cum-takeaway serves absolutely sublime Bengali food at prices so reasonable you can just keep tasting. The *mochar ghonto* (Rs 25) is pure perfection. Gently spicy *chingri malaikari* (Rs 130) contains a prawn so big it speaks lobster. Sketches on the walls are by celebrated film-director Satyajit Roy's dad. Get near on tram 24 from Kalighat metro to Gariahat Rd.

Rupasi Bangla (Map p104; 1/1C Ripon St; dishes Rs 20-125, lunch thali Rs 55; noon-11pm) Cane, glass and wrought-iron furniture create a low-key but gently stylish ambiance in which to savour a great range of genuine Bengali cuisine. Friendly management can help you decipher unfamiliar menu terms.

Kewpies (Map p110; ☎ 24759880; 2 Elgin Lane; dishes Rs 50-170, thalis Rs 155-285; 12.30-3pm & 7.30-11pm Tue-Sun) Dining at Kewpies is almost like being invited to a dinner party in the chef's eclectic, gently old-fashioned home. First-rate Bengali food comes in small but fairly priced portions (minimum charge Rs 200 per person). Find it down the tiny alley beside Netaji Bhawan.

CHINESE

South of Sudder St, several places on Mirza Ghalib St serve Chinese food, including cheap-if-bland Hong Kong, midrange Golden Dragon and very swish Tung Fong.

Song Hay (Map p106; ☎ 22480974; 3 Waterloo St; lunch mains Rs 25-70, dinner mains Rs 44-150; 9am-10.30pm;) This modest, family restaurant looks pretty dowdy but serves prize-winning real Chinese food at very reasonable prices.

Mainland China (Map p110; ☎ 22837964; 3A Guru-saday Rd; mains Rs 150-600, rice Rs 90; 12.30-3.30pm & 7-11.30pm) World-class Chinese food in gently sophisticated surroundings. Has superb

---

BENGALI CUISINE

Fruity and mildly spiced, Bengali food favours the sweet, rich notes of jaggary (palm sugar), *daab* (young coconut), *malaikari* (coconut milk) and *posto* (poppy seed). *Chingri* (river prawns) and excellent fish (particularly *bhekti* and *ilish*) are more characteristic than meat. Mustard fans will savour *bhekti paturi* (fish steamed in banana leaf). Excellent vegetarian choices include *mochar ghonto* (mashed banana-flower, potato and coconut) and *doi begun* (brinjal mini-eggplants in creamy sauce). Rice or sometimes *luchi* (small puris) are the usual accompaniment. A traditional soft drink is *aampora shorbat* made from cooked green mangoes with added lime zing.

Bengali desserts and sweets are legendary. Most characteristic is *mishti dhoi* (curd sweetened with jaggary), best when the crust dries to a fudge texture leaving the remainder lusciously moist.

A vast selection of recipes and a very handy five-page Bengali menu decoder can be found at http://milonee.net/bengali_recipes/list.html.

lobster-lemongrass soup (Rs 120), acceptable dim-sum (Rs 110 to 130) and unusually drinkable Indian wines, notably the Sula Sauvignon Blanc (Rs 190 per glass). Reservations advised, enter behind Barista Coffee.

THAI
Many restaurants serve pseudo-Thai food, but for the real thing visit the calm **Dynasty Restaurant** (1st fl, Lytton Hotel, 14 Sutton St; mains Rs 85-260) or splurge at the world-class **Baan Thai** (Oberoi Grand, 15 Chowringhee Rd; mains Rs 250-600).

MULTICUISINE
Eating your way along Park St's many fine dining options could take weeks. Several restaurants are fashionably hip but the old faithfuls often turn out more reliable fare.

Peter Cat (Map p104; ☎ 22298841; Middleton Row; mains Rs 75-140, beers Rs 80-100; ☙ 11am-11.30pm; ☒) Opposite KFC, this phenomenally popular Kolkata institution offers top-quality Indian cuisine, fizzing sizzlers, great chelo-kebabs and beers quaffed from pewter tankards. Waiters wear Rajasthani costumes in an atmosphere redolent of a mood-lit 1970s steakhouse.

Mocambo (Map p104; ☎ 22175372; Mirza Ghalib St; mains Rs 80-200; ☙ 11.30am-11.30pm) Although somewhat old-fashioned, reliable kebabs and European dishes like creamy Chicken Tetrazini ensure a very loyal following.

Bar-B-Q (Map p104; ☎ 22299078; 43 Park St; mains Rs 85-140, rice Rs 70, beers Rs 80; ☙ noon-4.30pm & 7-11pm) This enduring family favourite offers truly delicious Indian and Chinese food in separate nearby sections. Genteel head waiters are sharp-witted but obliging and décor is comfortably unpretentious.

On Track (Map p104; ☎ 22273955; Mirza Ghalib St; mains Rs 90-180; ☙ 11am-3pm & 7-11pm) An almost full-sized steam train heads straight for the window offering parents a unique, upmarket dining experience in leather-seated Pullman carriages while the kids play in the locomotive. Over-keen waiters flock like vultures, but food standards vary.

Oh! Calcutta (Map p110; ☎ 22837161; 4th fl, Forum Shopping Mall, Elgin Rd; mains Rs 150-650, rice Rs 75; ☙ 12.30-3pm & 7.15-11pm) High-class Bengali, Mughlai and continental cuisine in a suave pseudo-colonial atmosphere that's a delightfully calm contrast to the brash modernity of the surrounding mall.

Amber/Essence (Map p106; ☎ 22483477; 1st & 2nd fl, 11 Waterloo St; mains Rs 120-200; ☙ 1.30pm-11pm) The reliable Indian and continental food is the same on different floors but the slightly pricier 2nd-floor dining room has the nicer décor, being upmarket yet relaxed, with trendy grey-and-orange back-lit panelling.

Ivory (Map p104; ☎ 22811313; www.ivorykitchen.com/kol/; 5th fl, Block D, 22 Camac St; mains Rs 215-285, prawn mains Rs 400-500; ☙ noon-3pm & 7-11pm; ☒) Fashionably suave Indian, Chinese and continental dining with some of the most original curries in town, originally dreamt up by India's leading celebrity chef. Excellent lunch buffets Rs 390 to 455.

INDIAN REGIONAL
Aminia (Map p106; Hogg St; mains Rs 25-55; ☙ 10.30am-10.30pm) This bright but old-fashioned budget eatery has high ceilings and more under-employed staff than there are menu items. Curries are tasty if greasy. Tandoori chicken costs just Rs 25 per quarter.

Drive Inn (Map p104; 10 Middleton St; mains Rs 30-60; ☙ 1-10pm) Plate-lickingly good Indian vegetarian food served in a modest open-air 'garden' with simple fan-pavilion tables. Try the stuffed capsicum.

Only Parathas (Map p104; ☎ 30588841; Lord Sinha Rd; mains Rs 36-150; ☙ noon-11pm; ☒) Calm and relatively stylish, this new restaurant offers high-quality Punjabi vegetarian food, including (but not limited to) 133 types of *paratha* (bread).

Chennai Kitchen (Map p106; ☎ 22488509; P15/1 Chowringhee Sq; dosas Rs 25-55, thali Rs 69; ☙ noon-10pm Tue-Sun) Remarkably good South Indian food served in a stylishly retro-modernist diner-style atmosphere with glass waterfall, designer steel servingware and glass tables inlaid with spice designs.

our pick Teej (Map p104; ☎ 22170730; 2 Russel St; mains Rs 110-250, thalis Rs 150-250, house thali Rs 250; ☙ noon-3.30pm & 7-10.45pm; ☒) Above a good sweet shop and Dominos pizzeria, this wonderfully atmospheric place has been superbly painted with Mughlai-style designs to look like a Rajasthani *haveli* (merchant's house). The excellent, 100% vegetarian food is predominantly Rajasthani, too. Superb Paneer Sartaj.

ITALIAN & TEX-MEX
Jalapenos (Map p104; 10 Wood St; mains Rs 85-185; ☙ 11.30am-10.15pm; ☒) Approximations of Mexican food along with some pseudo Lebanese and Italian offerings in a pleasant if unremarkable interior.

Pizza Hut (Map p104; ☎ 22814343; 22 Camac St; pizzas Rs 90-415; ⏲ 11am-11pm) Popular with travellers seeking a taste of home.

Fire and Ice (Map p104; ☎ 22884057; Kanak Bldg, Middleton St; mains Rs 160-300, beers Rs 100; ⏲ 11am-11pm; 🏷) Modern Italian restaurant offering real pastas and pricey fresh-ground Italian coffee. Red designer ducting runs along high ceilings, while self-consciously handsome wait-staff sport black shirts, white aprons and bandanas.

Quick Eats

Snacks stalls (Map p104; Bertram St & Humayan Pl; snacks Rs 10-45; ⏲ 10am-9pm) abound around New Market with puris on Bertram St, pastries round the corner outside CitiMart, espressos and pizza within the New Empire cinema, and great dosas, fresh juices and *momos* directly opposite across Humayan Pl. For baked potatoes, cheap biriyanis, chow mein and Rs 30 curry roti, look down nearby Madge Lane or further east around the Collin St/Ripon St junction triangle.

Türkish Çörner (Map p104; Mirza Ghalib St 43; kebabs Rs 25-40; ⏲ 10am-10pm) Takeaway kebabs, falafels and small but delicious shwarmas along with fascinating stories of the chef's escape from Iraq.

ROLL HOUSES

Bengal's trademark fast food is the *kati roll*. No, that's nothing like a bread roll. Take a paratha roti, fry it with a one-sided coating of egg then fill with sliced onions, chilli and your choice of stuffing – typically curried chicken, grilled meat or *paneer* (unfermented cheese). Roll it up in a twist of paper and it's ready to eat, generally on the street. Roll houses are usually just hole-in-the-wall serveries, like revered **Hot Kati Rolls** (Map p104; 1/1 Park St; rolls Rs 15-35; ⏲ 11am-10.30pm). But the classic, recently relaunched 1932 roll house **Nizams** (Map p106; 23/24 Hogg St; rolls Rs 15-60, kebabs Rs 55-80; ⏲ noon-11pm) has seating along with faintly *Tintin*-esque cartoon décor.

SWEETS, CAKES & PASTRIES

Ubiquitous Bengali sweet shops often also serve snack meals.

KC Das (Map p106; Lenin Sarani; sweets from Rs 10; ⏲ 7.30am-9.30pm) This historic, if not especially atmospheric, Bengali sweet shop invented *rasgulla* (syrupy sponge balls) in 1868.

Jarokha/Gupta Brothers (Map p104; www.guptabros .com; Park Mansion, Mirza Ghalib St; sweets Rs 3-10; mains Rs 70-100; ⏲ 7.30am-10.30pm) A wooden spiral stairway leads up to a haveli-style vegetarian dining room above this celebrated Bengali sweet shop.

Kookie Jar (Map p104; Rowden St; cakes from Rs 10; ⏲ 8am-10pm) Kolkata's most heavenly cakes and brownies along with great pizza slices. No seating, but there are cafés next door.

Kathleen Confectioners (Map p104; 12 Mirza Ghalib St; snacks Rs 5-25; ⏲ 8am-8pm) Appealing stand-and-eat chain bakery serving delicious savoury pastries and sickly sweet cake slices. There are many other branches, including one on AJC Bose Rd.

FOOD PLAZAS

Several comfortable outlets – organised fast-food-style – serve wide varieties of cuisines including regional Indian, continental and Chinese:

Burp! (Map p110; 5th fl, Forum Shopping Mall, Elgin Rd; Rs 20-70; ⏲ 10.30am-10pm) Twelve-unit food court cooking up almost anything. Use a prepaid cashcard (refundable deposit Rs 20)

Food First (Map p104; 5 Camac St; ⏲ 7.30am-11pm) Options include Nachos and Roesti.

Haldirans (Map p104; Chowringhee Rd; Rs 30-85; ⏲ 10.30am-9.30pm) Great thalis and Bengalis sweets.

Ridhi Sidhi (Map p104; Emami Shopping Centre, 3 Lord Sinha Rd; mains Rs 20-40; ⏲ 9.30am-10pm) *Momos*, dosas, chow mein.

DRINKING
Coffee & Tea Shops
COFFEE

Flury's (Map p104; Park St; coffees Rs 30-55, cakes Rs 45-115; ⏲ 7.30am-9.45pm; 🏷) This wonderfully enticing Art Deco palace-café serves unusual, semi-sweet Belgian Mocha coffee and offers all-day breakfasts (Rs 100 to 200), but sandwiches and croissants aren't always fresh.

Ashalayam (Map p104; www.ashalayam.org; 1st fl, 44 Mirza Ghalib St; coffee Rs 6; ⏲ 10.30am-7pm Mon-Fri, 10.30am-2pm Sat; 🏷) Calm, bright little charity craft-shop café serving cheap machine-frothed Nescafé (see p121).

Indian Coffee House (Map pp98-9; upper floors, 15 Bankim Chatterjee St; coffee Rs 7; ⏲ 9am-9pm Mon-Sat) Once a meeting place of freedom fighters, bohemians and revolutionaries, this legendary place has crusty high ceilings, archaic fans and grimy walls ringing with deafening student conversation. It's perversely fascinating despite bland chow meins (Rs 25) and dishwater coffee.

Increasingly ubiquitous, the Starbucks-style chains **Barista** (Map p104; Humayan Pl; coffees Rs 24-50; 9am-10pm;) and **Cafe Coffee Day** (Map p104; 18K Park St; coffees Rs 20-50; 10.30am-11pm;) are reliably youthful places to linger in air-conditioned comfort. Both have numerous alternative branches (see maps).

TEA
our pick Dolly's Tea Shop (Map pp98-9; 24224650; Unit G62, Dakshinapan Shopping Centre, 2 Gariahat Rd; teas Rs 10-30, snacks Rs 15-50; 10.30am-7.30pm Mon-Fri, 10.30am-2.30pm Sat) If shopping at Dakshinapan, don't miss this characterful teahouse offering 24 different infusions and as many iced flavours. Regal matriarch Dolly is a tea writer-researcher whose magnetic presence attracts a wonderfully eclectic clientele.

Camellia Tea Bar (Map p110; 1st fl, Samilton Hotel, 37 Sarat Bose Rd; teas Rs 18-30; 6.30am-11.30pm) Multifarious teas served cocktail-style on a roofgarden. Try spicy Thai-chai or curious Irish Tea with ice-cream float.

Bars
Kolkata has an increasingly cutting-edge cocktail bar scene for those with thick wallets, but cheaper places are usually dingy and almost inevitably attract a 100% male clientele. Places in all ranges have a penchant for over-loud music.

Broadway Bar (Map p106; Broadway Hotel, 27A GC Ave; beers Rs 60; 11am-10.15pm) Back-street Paris? Chicago 1930s? Prague 1980s? This cavernous, unpretentious old pub defies easy parallels but has a compulsive left-bank fascination. Cheap booze, 20 ceiling fans, grimy walls, marble floors and, thankfully, no music. Clientele 100% male.

Fairlawn Hotel (Map p104; 13A Sudder St; beers Rs 80; 12.45-2pm & 7.30-9.30pm) Waving palms and an ideal location make the historic Fairlawn's calm garden café the perfect travellers place for a cold brew (no spirits).

Mirch Masala (Map pp98-9; 24618900; 49/2 Gariahat Rd; mains Rs 80-140, beers Rs 90; noon-3pm & 7am-10.30pm) Drinks and North Indian food served in a striking environment that's feels like a Bollywood Tex-Mex joint. Half a taxi-chassis has been added for good measure. Enter beneath Hotel Park Palace on Garcha 1st Lane, behind Pantaloons department store.

Blue & Beyond Restaurant (Map p104; 10th fl, Lindsay Hotel, Lindsay St; beers Rs 95, mains Rs 70-275; 12.30-10.30pm) Come for the fabulous views over New Market from the open-air rooftop terrace. Views are even better from the 9th-floor elevator landing.

Copper Chimney Lounge (Map p104; 22834161; 31 Shakespeare Sarani; beers Rs 110; noon-11pm;) Chic 21st-century neo-Ottoman bar with hookah water pipes (Rs 150), shimmering string-curtain dividers and mesmerising lighting effects. It's above a highly rated eponymous restaurant, behind HSCB bank. DJ on weekends.

Chowringhee Bar (Map p104; Oberoi Grand Hotel; beers Rs 120;) Not quite the colonial delight one might hope, but there's pleasant lighting, pool tables and soft live jazz some evenings. The next-door coffee shop stays open 24 hours.

Rocks (Map p106; 9 Waterloo St; beers Rs 120; 11am-midnight;) Three floors of bars guarded by snarling bouncers. The top has the most inviting décor, its wavy ceiling inset with 'stars'. The live Bengali music is high quality but has an even higher decibel level. Predominantly male clientele.

Roxy (Map p104; Park Hotel; small beer Rs 120; 6-11pm;) With a *Clockwork Orange* retro-futuristic atmosphere, Roxy is the best (and most expensive) of several fun pub-bars around and within the Park Hotel, including Someplace Else and Aqua Bar.

ENTERTAINMENT
Nightclubs
Kolkata's high-voltage nightclubs are mostly within top hotels. Variable cover charges range Rs 300 to 1000 per couple, commonly redeemable for drinks of the same value. Single women often go free but single men (known as 'stags') are generally excluded unless a guest at the hotel.

Tantra (Map p104; Park Hotel; 7pm-4am Wed & Fri, 7am-midnight Thu, 4pm-4am Sat & Sun;) The city's top spot. The relatively small but throbbing dance floor faces an alluring if not-so-quiet chill-out zone across the large central island of bar.

Marrakech (Map p104; Cinnamon Restaurant, 1st fl, 24 Park St; cover Rs 500, beers Rs 135; 6pm-midnight Mon-Thu, 6pm-2am Fri-Sun;) Appealingly Moroccan-themed club-bar with small dance floor. DJs crank up the volume after 10pm.

For 'stags' the best hope is **Venom** (Map p104; 8th fl, Fort Knox, 6 Camac St; 6pm-2am). If you don't get in, right beside it is DJ-bar **Little High** (Map p104; 8th fl, Fort Knox, 6 Camac St; no cover, beer Rs 100, hookah Rs 200; 7pm-midnight;), which lacks a dance floor but spins similar contemporary sounds.

Cultural Programmes

Kolkata's famous poetry, music, art, film and dance are regularly showcased at the Nandan Complex (AJC Bose Rd) comprising the **Rabindra Sadan** (Map p104; ☎ 22239936) and **Sisir Mancha** (Map p104; ☎ 22235317) theatre halls and an art-house cinema. Tourist Information offices and pamphlets (p102) give extensive listings of events here and at many other venues.

Cinemas

Cinemas are ubiquitous with at least nine around New Market alone.

Globe (Map p104; ☎ 22495636; Madge Lane) Great art-deco façade

Inox (Map p110; ☎ 23584499; 4th fl, Forum Shopping Mall, 10/3 Elgin Rd; tickets Rs 140-230) Modern multiplex.

Nandan Cinema (Map p104; ☎ 22231210; 1/1A AJC Bose Rd) For more intellectual, art-house films.

New Empire Cinema (Map p104; ☎ 22491299; 1-2 Humayan Pl)

Spectator Sports

Kolkata is sports mad. Dozens of clubs on the Maidan practise everything from cricket to kabaddi, especially at weekends. Even if you don't know Ganguly from a googly, the electric atmosphere of an international **cricket** match at Ranji Stadium in Eden Gardens is an unforgettable experience.

Arguably India's best place to watch **horse racing** is from the 19th-century grandstands at **Maidan racecourse** (☎ 22291104; www.rctconline.com; 12.30-3.20pm Nov–mid-Apr), the Victoria Memorial providing a beautiful backdrop. Over 40 meets annually; days vary. Enter from Acharya Jagdish Rd for the **main stands** (admission Rs 14).

SHOPPING

New Market has a grand colonial clocktower, but by day it's a pestilential nest of handicraft touts. Come before 8am, while touts are sleeping, to calmly appreciate the adjacent Hogg Market (fresh food and live chickens). Traditional, ultra-crowded shopping alleys spread in confusing profusion north of BBD Bagh, progress being slightly more manageable along Rabindra Sarani, which offers intriguing thematic groupings of trades at different points. Many Kolkatans prefer to shop in the southerly Gariahat district.

For more Western-style retail therapy, the five-storey **Forum Shopping Mall** (Map p110; Elgin Rd) is as good (or as bad) as small American equivalents. **Metro Shopping Centre** (Map p104;

Ho Chi Minh Sarani) is similar, **22 Camac** (Map p104; 22 Camac St) is snobbier, while **Emami Shoppers' City** (Map p104; 3 Lord Sinha Rd) is unthreateningly suburban.

Crafts & Souvenirs

GOVERNMENTAL EMPORIA

For good-quality souvenirs at decent fixed prices, head to the state-government emporia. A large number are gathered at **Dakshinapan Shopping Centre** (Map pp98-9; Gariahat Rd; 11am-7pm Mon-Fri, to 2pm Sat), which, along with Dolly's Tea Shop (opposite), just about justifies the long trek to this soul-crushing monstrosity of 1970s architecture. The fabrics are particularly good value and the Tripura Emporium has great deals on bamboo- and cane-ware.

Similar if dustier cane-ware is available more centrally at **Assam Craft Emporium** (Map p104; ☎ 22298331; Assam House, 8 Russel St; 10am-6pm Mon-Fri, 10am-2.30pm Sat). **Nagaland Emporium** (11 Shakespeare Sarani; 10am-6pm Mon-Fri, 10am-2pm Sat) sells Naga crafts, including traditional shawls. (Rs 300 to 1500) and double-face bronze 'trophy' necklaces for wannabe head-hunters.

Several more government emporia can be found along Chowringhee Rd, including the impressive if comparatively pricey **Central Cottage Industries Emporium** (Map p106; www.cottageemporiumindia.com; Metropolitan Bldg, 7 Chowringhee Rd; 10am-7pm Mon-Fri, to 2pm Sat) showcasing handicrafts from right across India.

Towards Salt Lake City, **Swabhumi** (Map pp98-9; www.swabhumi.com; admission Rs 20; noon-10pm) is a shopping centre-cum-cultural park with dozens of well-stocked craft stalls and boutiques plus rather dubious 'cultural performances'.

CHARITY COOPERATIVES

Buy gifts and support great causes:

Ankur Kala (Map pp98-9; ☎ 22478476; www.ankurkala.org; 76 Park St) Handicrafts from a cooperative training centre, empowering women from the slums.

Ashalayam (Map p104; www.ashalayam.org) Super greetings cards, handmade paper and fabrics funding the (ex)street kids who made them (see p119).

Women's Friendly Society (Map p104; 29 Park Lane; 8am-5pm Mon-Fri, 8am-1pm Sat) Hand-embroidered tableware, fabrics and children's clothes from another cooperative society for destitute women (founded 1886).

Clothing

Kolkata is great value for tailored or off-the-peg clothing, with smart shirts at just Rs 100 from Chowringhee Rd Hawkers Market. The choice around Newmarket is endless.

Music

Peddlers sell Bengali pop CDs on street corners, but for a vast selection of genres visit the flashy, AC chain shops **Music World** (Map p104; cnr Park St & Middleton Row; 10am-9pm) or **Planet M** (Map p104; Block B, 22 Camac St; 10.30am-8.30pm).

Musical Instruments

Shops and workshops along Rabindra Sarani sell a great range of musical instruments. For tablas and other percussion try numbers 248, 264 and 268B near Tagore's House (p111). For stringed instruments from *esraj* to sitar to violin, shops around number 8 are better. Family run since the 1850s, **Mondal & Sons** (Map p106; 8 Rabindra Sarani; 10am-6pm) counts Yehudi Menuhin among its satisfied customers.

GETTING THERE & AWAY

See also p323 for international destinations.

Air

Kolkata's **Netaji Subhash Bose International Airport** (NSBIA; ☎ 25118787) offers handy connections to Europe (London, Frankfurt) and several Asian cities. Arrive very early for international flights as security checks can take hours. On strike days (remarkably common) all road transport, including taxis, stops completely between 6am and 6pm, so consider sleeping within walking distance of the terminal before an important flight (see p116). Airline offices are generally open from 9.30am to 1pm and 2pm to 5pm Monday to Friday, give or take 15 minutes. A few also open on Saturday.

INTERNATIONAL

International airlines flying out of Kolkata:
Air India (Map p104; ☎ 22822356/59; 50 Chowringhee Rd)
Biman Bangladesh Airlines (Map p104; ☎ 22276001; 55B Mirza Ghalib St)
British Airways (☎ 9831377470)
Cosmic Air (Map p106; ☎ 21121344/39538660; www .cosmicair.com; Room 207/208, 2nd Fl, 25 Black Burn Lane)
Druk Air (Map p110; ☎ 22902429; 3rd fl, block B Tivoli Court, 1A Ballygunge Circular Rd) Thrice-weekly flights to Bhutan and Bangkok. Tickets from RCPL Travels (p102).
Emirates (Map pp98-9; ☎ 40099555, 1-800-2332030; Trinity Tower, 83 Topsia Rd South)
GMG Airlines (Map p104; ☎ 30283030; 12 Park St) Flies to Chittagong and Dhaka, Bangladesh.

Gulf Air (Map p104; ☎ 22837996; Chitrakoot Bldg, 230A AJC Bose Rd)
Lufthansa (☎ 22299365; 8th fl, IBM Tower, Information Technology Park, DN62, Sector 5, Salt Lake City)
Singapore Airlines (Map p104; ☎ 22809898; 2nd fl, 1 Lee Rd)
Thai Airways International (Map p104; ☎ 22838865; 8th fl, Crescent Towers, 229 AJC Bose Rd)

DOMESTIC

Domestic airlines flying out of Kolkata:
Air Sahara (S2; Map p104; ☎ 22826118; 2A Shakespeare Sarani)
Indian Airlines (IC; Map p106; ☎ 22114433; 39 Chittaranjan Ave)
IndiGo (6E; http://book.goindigo.in)
Jet Airways (9W; Map p104; ☎ 22292227; www .jetairways.com; 18D Park St)
Kingfisher (IT; www.flykingfisher.com)
spiceJet (SG; http://book.spiceJet.com)

Boat

Ten days before departure, ferry tickets for Port Blair (Andaman Islands) go on sale at the **Shipping Corporation of India** (Map p106; ☎ info 22482354, ticketing 22482141; Hare Rd; 10.30am-1pm). The ferries depart from **Kidderpore Docks** (Map pp98-9; Karl Marx Sarani), 3km southwest of the centre. Enter at Gate 3, right opposite Kidderpore commuter train station.

Bus

Esplanade bus stand (Map p106) is the departure point for destinations within West Bengal. Buses to Malda (Rs 400, nine hours) leave at 9.30am, 8.30pm and 10pm. For Darjeeling or Sikkim take one of many night buses to Siliguri (Rs 400 to 650, 12 hours), departing between 6pm and 8pm.

From Babughat bus stand (Map pp98–9) beside Eden Gardens commuter train station, many overnight services run to Ranchi, Puri and Bhubaneswar (all from Rs 160, 12 hours) departing between 5pm and 8pm. **Whiteliners** (☎ 24444444) has aircon buses (Rs 450).

For Dhaka (Bangladesh) direct buses depart Tuesdays, Thursdays and Saturdays from Karunamoyee, Salt Lake City, operated by **Bangladesh Road Transport Corporation** (BRTC; Map p104; 21/A Mirza Ghalib St). Various private services, including **Shyamoli Paribahan** (Map p104; ☎ 22520802; 6/1 Marquis St), run daily (Rs 550, 13 hours), but involve changing vehicles at the Benapol border.

Train

Check carefully whether your train departs from Howrah (Haora; HWH, Map pp98–9) or Sealdah stations (SDAH, Map pp98–9). Both have trains to Delhi and Guwahati, though most longer distance services use Howrah.

Buying tickets is usually easier by internet, through Sudder St agencies or from city-centre booking offices. Indian Railways' **Foreign Tourist Bureau** (Map p106; ☎ 22224206; 6 Fairlie Pl; ⏰ 10am-5pm Mon-Sat, 10am-2pm Sun) has a tourist quota for most trains ex-Kolkata, but there's usually a queue and you must show foreign-exchange receipts or else pay US dollars, British pounds or euros. Next door and also one block south there are

computerised booking offices (Map p106; ☎ 22227282; 14 Strand Rd South & 6 Fairlie Pl; ⏰ 8am-8pm Mon-Sat, 8am-2pm Sun) offering tickets on the wider train network, but you can't access the tourist quota here. Plan ahead. Other **computerised booking offices** (Map pp98-9; ⏰ 8am-2pm Mon-Sat) include one just north of Tollygunge Metro station

GETTING AROUND
To/From the Airport

NSBIA Airport is in the northeastern suburbs, some 5km east of Dum Dum metro station. Oddly, trains on the new suburban Airport Line only operate twice daily to Sealdah (Rs 10) at 7am and 9.40pm. Whiteliner Express

DOMESTIC FLIGHTS FROM KOLKATA

Destination	Airline/Frequency	Duration
Agartala	IC twice daily, DN & 9W daily	50min
	IT MonWedFri via Guwahati	3hr
Ahmedabad	IT MoTuWeFrSun	2¾hr
Aizawl	DN & IC daily	1hr
Bagdogra (Siliguri)	DN & 9W daily, IC TueSat	55min
Bangalore	DN, IC, SG & 9W daily	2¼hr
Bhubaneswar	DN, IC & S2 daily	55min
Chennai	9W twice daily, DN, SG & IC daily	2hr
Delhi	DN, IC, IT, SG, S2, 6E & 9W daily+	2hr
Dibrugarh	IC TuWeThSaSu	1½hr
	IT TuThSa via Guwahati	3hr
	DN MoWeFrSu via Guwahati	3hr
Dimapur	IC daily, usually indirect	1-2hr
Gaya	IC Wed	1hr
Guwahati	DN, IC & 9W twice daily	
	6E, SG, S2 & IT daily	1½hr
Hyderabad	DN, IT, S2 & 9W daily, IC MoWeFr	2hr
Imphal	DN & IC daily	1¼hr
	9W MoTuWeFrSa via Guwahati	2¾
Jaipur	6E daily, IC MoTuThSa, IT ThuSat	2½hr
Johrat	9W WedFri	1½hr
	9W ThuSun via Guwahati	2¾hr
	IC TueSat via Tezpur	2¼hr
Lilabari (North Lakhimpur)	DN TuThSa via Guwahati	3hr
Lucknow	S2 daily	2½hr
Mumbai	DN, IC, IT, S2 & 9W twice daily	2½hr
Nagpur	6E daily	1½
Patna	DN & S2 daily	1hr
Port Blair	DN & S2 daily, IC TuThSaSu	2hr
Raipur	DN daily	2½hr
Ranchi	DN twice daily	1hr
Shillong	IC Mon, Wed	1¾hr
Silchar	DN & IC daily	1½hr
Tezpur	IC TueSun	1¼hr

buses from Tollygunge Metro (Rs 25 to 35, 80 minutes) run up to four times hourly between 8.20am and 8.30pm via Gariahat and Salt Lake City. Fixed-price taxis cost Rs 130/210 to Dum Dum metro/Sudder St.

Cheap but crowded options include minibus 151 from Airport Gate 1 (1.2km from the terminals) to BBD Bagh or frequent bus 30B from Airport Gate 2. The latter eventually grinds all the way to Babughat bus stand, but we'd suggest hopping off at Dum Dum station (Rs 5, 25 minutes) and continuing by metro (Rs 6, 20 minutes) to central Kolkata. (Dum Dum road passes Kolkata's original 1848 ordinance factory responsible for infamous hollow-tipped Dum-Dum bullets, internationally banned in 1899.)

Note that Airport Gate 2 is just a pedestrian-sized gateway in the perimeter wall opposite Oasis Lodge (Jessore Rd). From the airport's domestic terminal walk under the elevated railway and continue for around 10 minutes through the discouraging ruins of a derelict school-complex. Just when you think you must be wrong, you reach the outer perimeter road. Across that, beyond a huddle of rickshaws, there's a gap in the wall leading into busy Jessore Rd.

Bus

Local buses are passenger-crammed mechanical monsters hurtling along at frighten-ing speeds wherever the chronic congestion abates. Routes can be a little confusing (eg 30B isn't the same as 30B/1) but at least Western-script numbers are used. Some buses even have signboards in English. Conductors somehow fight through the crowds to collect fares (Rs 2 to 10).

Ferry

The fastest way from central Kolkata to Howrah train station is generally by river ferry (tickets Rs 4, 8am to 8pm Monday to Saturday). These depart every 15 minutes from Armenian, Fairlie, Bishe June and Babu Ghats. Private and public ferries cost the same. They're packed at rush hour.

Metro

It's as crowded as any underground system at rush hour, but Kolkata's one-line Metro (tickets Rs 4 to 8; 7am to 9.45pm Monday to Saturday, 3pm to 9.45pm Sunday) remains the city's most stress-free form of public transport. Men beware not to sit in assigned 'Ladies' seats. For BBD Bagh use Central or Chandni Chowk stations, for Sudder St area use Esplanade or Park St.

Rickshaw

Kolkata is the last bastion of human-powered 'tana rickshaws', with the greatest concentra-

MAJOR TRAINS FROM KOLKATA

Destination	Train no & name	Fares (Rs)	Duration (hr)	Departures
Bhubaneswar	2073 *Shatabdi Exp*	CC 147	7	1.35pm Mon-Sat (H)
Chennai	6003 *Chennai Mail*	2AC/3AC/SL 1973/1264/469	30	9.55pm daily (H)
Delhi	2381 *Poorva Exp*	2AC/3AC/SL 1811/1163/433	23	9.05am or 9.20am daily (H)
Delhi	2329 *Kranti Exp*	3AC/SL 1128/419	23	1pm Mon, Fri (S)
Guwahati	5657 *Kanchenjunga Exp*	2AC/SL 1457/341	22	6.45am daily (S)
Guwahati	*Saraighat Exp*	2AC/SL 1482/347	18	15.45 Mon, Wed, Thu, Fri, Sun (H)
Mumbai CST	2810 *Mumbai Mail*	2AC/3AC/SL 2189/1399/517	33	7.55pm daily (H)
New Jalpaiguri	2343 *Darjeeling Mail*	2AC/3AC/SL 1027/661/245	10	10.05pm daily (S)
New Jalpaiguri	3147/3149 *Cooch Behar Exp*	2AC/3AC/SL 1027/661/245	12	7.35pm daily (S)
Patna	2023 *Lal Quila Exp*	2AC/SL 981/235	11	8.10pm daily (S)
Puri	2837 *Puri Exp*	2AC/3AC/SL 946/611/227	9	10.35 daily (H)
Varanasi	3005 *Amritsar Mail*	2AC/3AC/SL 1251/801/295	15	7.10pm daily (H)
Varanasi	3133 *Sealdah-Varanasi Exp*	SL 289	25	8.55pm daily (S)

CC – AC chair-car, 2AC – AC two-tier, 3AC – AC three-tier, SL – non-AC sleeper, H – ex-Haora, S – ex-Sealdah

---

BANNING RICKSHAWS?

Is it morally unacceptable to have a bare-footed man pulling you around the un-sanitary, flooded streets by the sweat of his brow? Some believe so. No new *tana*-rickshaw licenses have been issued for years, and since 2003 the West Bengal adminis-tration has pondered outlawing them alto-gether. But others fear that impoverished rickshaw-wallahs (1800 licensed, many more unofficial) could be pushed into star-vation if their business is banned. And are the less-practical cycle-rickshaws really so much kinder?

---

tion around New Market. During the mon-soon the high-wheeled rickshaws can be the only transport able to get through the worst-flooded streets. Although rickshaw pullers sometimes charge foreigners disproportionate fares, many are virtually destitute, sleeping on the pavements beneath their rented chariots at night. Tips are heartily appreciated.

Outside the centre and in Howrah you'll find cycle-rickshaws.

Autorickshaws are not generally for hire but act as share taxis on fixed routes (Rs 4.50 per short hop).

Taxi

Kolkata's ubiquitous yellow Ambassador taxis are surprisingly cheap (from Rs 20 for a shorter trip). But be warned that the fare you pay will be roughly double the reading on the digital meter (or around 3.5 times the reading on now-rare old-style mechanical meters). This is official and not a scam. Exact rates for longer trips are calculated using conversion charts that every driver carries, but handing over twice the meter reading usually works without a fuss. Just make sure the meter's switched on.

A problem of taxi travel is the one-way sys-tem. Complex to start with, around 2pm the direction of traffic flow reverses on many roads. Not surprisingly many drivers are reluctant to make journeys around this chaotic time.

Prepaid taxis from a booth in front of How-rah station cost Rs 65 to Sudder St, Rs 190 to the airport.

Tram

Trams cost just Rs 3.50 per hop. The challenge is getting on, as stops aren't marked or set. Route 24 and 29 head from Esplanade to Ali-pore and Kalighat; the 29 continuing south to Tollygunge, the 24 usefully cutting across town to Gariahat market. Route 22 heads north up Rabindra Sarani. Route 14 heads east from BBD Bagh along Bipin Behan Ganguly St.

West Bengal

Emerging from the tempestuous Bay of Bengal in a maze of primeval mangroves, West Bengal stretches across the vast Ganges plain before abruptly rising towards the mighty ramparts of the Himalaya. This long, narrow state is India's most densely populated and straddles a breadth of society and geography unmatched in the country. As the cradle of the Indian Renaissance and national freedom movement, erstwhile Bengal has long been considered the country's cultural heartland, famous for its eminent writers, poets, artists, spiritualists and revolutionaries. Overshadowed perhaps by the reputation of its capital Kolkata (Calcutta), it is nonetheless surprising that this rich and diverse state receives so few foreign tourists.

In the World Heritage–listed Sunderbans, the Ganges delta hosts not only the world's most extensive mangrove forest, but also the greatest population of the elusive Royal Bengal tiger. On the Ganges plains a calm ocean of green paddies surrounds bustling trading towns, mud-and-thatch villages, and vestiges of Bengal's glorious and remarkable past: ornate, terracotta-tiled Hindu temples and monumental ruins of the Muslim nawabs (ruling princes).

As the ground starts to rise, the famous Darjeeling Himalayan Railway begins its ascent to the cooler climes of former British hill stations. The train switches back and loops its way to Darjeeling, still a summer retreat and a quintessential remnant of the Raj. Here, amid Himalayan giants and renowned tea estates, lies a network of mountain trails. Along with the quiet, orchid-growing haven of nearby Kalimpong, once part of Bhutan, these mountain retreats offer a glimpse into the Himalayan cultures of Sikkim, Bhutan, Nepal and Tibet.

HIGHLIGHTS

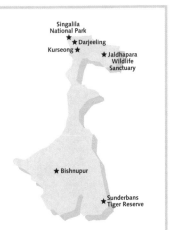

- Rise early to witness morning's first light on the sacred peaks of Khangchendzonga from the colonial hill station of **Darjeeling** (p140)

- Step aboard the toy train on the **Darjeeling Himalayan Railway** (p145) as it steams to the tea town of Kurseong

- Trace the footsteps of traders along rhododendron-lined trails in **Singalila National Park** (p152)

- Capture a wild rhinoceros with your camera from the back of an elephant in the jungles of **Jaldhapara Wildlife Sanctuary** (p137)

- Savour the warmth and glow of the ancient terracotta temples in **Bishnupur** (p131) under a setting orange sun

- Take a river-boat journey through the mysterious **Sunderbans Tiger Reserve** (opposite), with the prospect of sighting royalty (in the form of a tiger)

History

Referred to as Vanga in the Mahabharata, this region has a long history predating the Aryan invasions of India. It was part of the Mauryan empire in the 3rd century BC before being overrun by the Guptas. For three centuries from around the 9th century AD, the Pala dynasty controlled a large area based in Bengal and including parts of Orissa, Bihar and modern Bangladesh.

Bengal was brought under Muslim control by Qutb-ud-din, first of the sultans of Delhi, at the end of the 12th century. Following the death of Aurangzeb in 1707, Bengal became an independent Muslim state.

The British established a trading post in Kolkata in 1698, which quickly prospered. Sensing rich pickings, Siraj-ud-daula, the nawab of Bengal, came down from his capital at Murshidabad and easily took Kolkata in 1756. Robert Clive defeated him the following year at the Battle of Plassey, helped by the treachery of Siraj-ud-daula's uncle, Mir Jafar, who commanded the greater part of the nawab's army. He was rewarded by succeeding his nephew as nawab, but after the Battle of Buxar in 1764 the British took full control of Bengal.

In 1947 Indian independence from Britain and the subsequent partition of the country saw the state of Bengal divided on religious grounds, causing the upheaval of millions of Bengalis (see p35).

Climate

The monsoon deluges West Bengal from mid-June until late September and the resulting flooding wreaks havoc with the roads and railways from the plains to the hills.

Information

Useful websites include those of the **state government** (www.wbgov.com) and the **tourist department** (www.wbtourism.com).

Activities
TREKKING

While pleasant walks along pine-scented trails are possible in all West Bengal's hill stations, the best multiday treks are organised from Kalimpong (see p156) and Darjeeling (see p152).

RAFTING

Adrenaline-pumping white-water rafting trips are held on the mighty Teesta and Rangeet

Rivers from the tiny riverside town of Teesta Bazaar (p158), and can be organised in Darjeeling (see p147).

Getting There & Around

The vast majority who enter West Bengal arrive in Kolkata. Siliguri's Bagdogra airport has services to Kolkata, Delhi and Guwahati, as well as daily helicopter flights to Gangtok.

Most arriving by land do so on Indian Railways, which has main lines running south to Bhubaneswar and Chennai (Madras), and west to Gaya, Varanasi and Delhi. Other rail lines connect the state to Assam in the northeast and to Jharkhand in the southwest. There are also numerous long-distance buses that connect surrounding states.

Most cities and towns within West Bengal are connected by rail and bus, while overcrowded share jeeps ply the winding roads of the West Bengal Hills.

SOUTH OF KOLKATA

SUNDERBANS TIGER RESERVE

Home to one of the largest concentrations of tigers on the planet, this 2585-sq-km **reserve** (☎ 03218-55280; admission per day Rs 15) is a network of channels and semi-submerged mangroves that is part of the world's largest river delta. Royal Bengal tigers (officially estimated to number 274) not only lurk in the impenetrable depths of the mangrove forests, but also swim the delta's innumerable channels. Although they're known to have an appetite for humans (see the boxed text, p130), tigers are typically shy and sightings are a very rare exception. Nevertheless, a trip to this watery World Heritage site is rewarding with or without a glimpse of the big cats. Cruising the broad waterways through the world's biggest mangrove forest

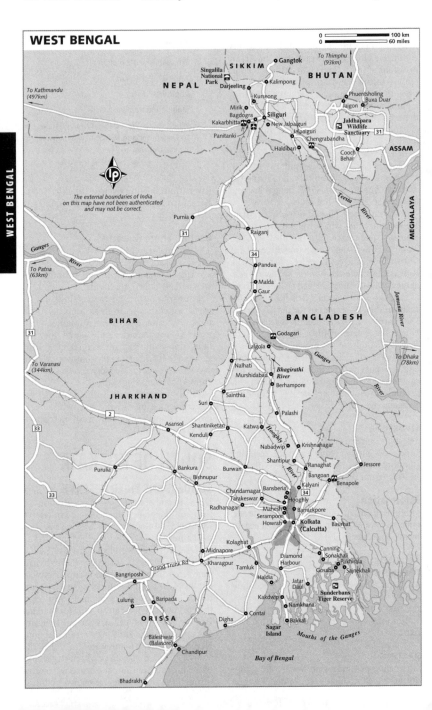

WEST BENGAL

0 — 100 km
0 — 60 miles

To Thimphu
(93km)

SIKKIM

Gangtok

BHUTAN

NEPAL

Singalila
National
Park

Darjeeling

Kalimpong

Kurseong

Phuentsholing
Buxa Duar

To Kathmandu
(497km)

Mirik

Jaigon

Bagdogra

Siliguri

Kakarbhitta

New Jalpaiguri

Jaldhapara
Wildlife
Sanctuary

31

Panitanki

Jalpaiguri

Chengrabandha

ASSAM

Haldibari

Cooch
Behar

The external boundaries of India
on this map have not been authenticated
and may not be correct.

Teesta River

MEGHALAYA

Purnia

Raiganj

31

Ganges

To Patna
(63km)

River

34

Pandua

Malda

Gaur

BIHAR

BANGLADESH

Jamuna River

31

Godagari

Lalgola

To Varanasi
(344km)

Nalhati

Bhagirathi
River

Murshidabad

Ganges

To Dhaka
(78km)

Berhampore

River

JHARKHAND

Suri

Sainthia

2

Palashi

33

Asansol

Shantiniketan

Katwa

Hooghly

Kenduli

Nabadwip

Krishnanagar

Shantipur

Ranaghat

Jessore

Purulia

Bankura

Burwan

River

Bangoan

Bishnupur

Chandarnagar

Bansberia

Kalyani

Benapole

33

Tarakeswar

Hooghly

Radhanagar

Mahesh

Barrackpore

Serampore

Kolkata
(Calcutta)

Basirhat

Howrah

Kolaghat

Canning

Sonakhali

Midnapore

Diamond
Harbour

Pakhirala

Bangripashi

Kharagpur

Tamluk

Gosaba

Sajnekhali

Grand Trunk Rd

Haldia

Jatar
Dault

Sunderbans
Tiger Reserve

Lulung

Baripada

Kakdwip

Namkhana

Baleshwar
(Balasore)

Digha

Contai

Bakkali

ORISSA

Sagar
Island

Mouths of the Ganges

Chandipur

Bhadrakh

Bay of Bengal

WEST BENGAL

FESTIVALS IN WEST BENGAL

Lepcha & Bhutia New Year (Jan; West Bengal Hills, p133) Colourful fairs and traditional dances in and around Darjeeling.

Gangasagar Mela (mid-Jan; Sagar Island, p130) The most intense West Bengal festival; hundreds of thousands of Hindu pilgrims converge where the Ganges meets the sea, to bathe en masse.

Magh Mela (6-8 Feb; Shantiniketan, p132) Crafts take centre stage at this festival.

Bengali New Year (Naba Barsha; mid-Apr; statewide) A statewide holiday celebrates the first day in the Bangla Calendar.

Rath Yatra (Car Festival; Jun/Jul; Mahesh) Celebrated by pulling Lord Jagannath's chariot in Mahesh, 3km from Serampore (p131).

Jhapan Festival (mid-Aug; Bishnupur, p131) Draws snake charmers to honour the goddess Manasa, the central figure of snake worship.

Fulpati (Sep-Oct; Darjeeling, p140) Linked to Durga Puja, this predominantly Nepali festival is also celebrated by Lepchas and others with processions and dancing from Ghoom to Darjeeling.

Durga Puja (Oct; statewide, p131) Across the state, especially in Kolkata, temporary castles *(pandals)* are raised and intense celebrations take place to worship Durga. After four colourful days, beautiful images of the 10-armed goddess are immersed in the rivers.

Darjeeling Carnival (7-16 Nov; Darjeeling, p140) Celebrating the region's unity with cultural shows, activities, children's festivals, jazz music and even a *momo* (Tibetan dumpling) –eating contest.

Jagaddhatri Puja (Nov; Chandannagar, p131) Honours the goddess Jagaddhatri.

Rash Mela (Nov; Cooch Behar & the Sunderbans) Immortalises the union of Lord Krishna and Radha.

Teesta Tea & Tourism Festival (Nov; West Bengal Hills, p133) Features cultural events.

Paush Mela (Dec; Shantiniketan, p132) Folk music, dance, theatre and Baul songs radiate over town.

Bishnupur Festival (late Dec; Bishnupur, p131) Highlights handicrafts and local music.

---

and watching wildlife, whether it be a spotted deer, 2m-long water monitor or luminescent kingfisher, is sublime and a world away from Kolkata's chaos.

The best time to visit the tiger reserve is between October and March. Visiting independently is difficult, with permits and tricky transport connections to organise, and it's not cheap; you'll have to bear the cost of boat rentals alone. Organised tours (see right) are the easy and comfortable alternative.

At Sajnekhali, the official gateway into the reserve, you'll find the **Mangrove Interpretation Centre** (admission Rs 2; ⏱ 8.30am-5pm), with a small turtle and crocodile hatchery, displays on local conservation issues and a collection of pickled wildlife.

Boats are available for hire at Sajnekhali, costing Rs 400 for a three-hour island trip to Rs 1200 for a full day. You'll also need a guide (fixed rate is Rs 200 per day) and a boat permit (Rs 50 per day).

Permits

Foreigners need a permit to visit the Sunderbans Tiger Reserve. Free permits are issued at the **West Bengal Tourism Centre** (☎ 22488271; www .wbtourism.com; 3/2 BBD Bagh; ⏱ 10.30am-4pm Mon-Fri, to 1pm Sat) in Kolkata. The process may take up to an hour and you'll need your passport.

Tours

Tours vary widely in prices, so it is worth shopping around. Tours typically include return transport from Kolkata, as well as all the fees and necessary permits, but do check what is and isn't included in your deal.

The **West Bengal Tourism Centre** (☎ 22488271; www.wbtourism.com; 3/2 BBD Bagh, Kolkata; ⏱ 10.30am-4pm Mon-Fri, to 1pm Sat) organises weekly boat cruises during the high season (September to January), costing from Rs 1350 per person for one night and two half-days, including food and onboard accommodation. Trips with a worthwhile extra day start from Rs 2050.

A better option, especially if you want to sleep on dry land, is **Sunderban Tiger Camp** (☎ 033-32935749; www.sunderbantigercamp.com; ⏱ year-round; 🛏). It provides expert guides and quality accommodation, with good food and even a bar. Tiger-spotting excursions are onboard comfortable river boats with ample shade, and there are sufficient tiger stories and glasses of tea to keep you awake. Traditional entertainment and walks to a local village are arranged for the evenings. All-inclusive prices range

WEST BENGAL

LIVING AMONG TIGERS

For those who live and work in the Sunderbans, tigers are an everyday part of life. Muslims and Hindus alike revere the tiger-god Dakshin Roy and the forest saviour Bonobibi, who protects them from the man-eaters. Wives of men working in the Sunderbans have even taken to living their days as widows; only when their husbands return do they don their marital ornamentation.

Since tigers are less likely to attack if they suspect they're being watched, honey collectors and woodcutters wear masks painted with human faces on the backs of their heads. The tigers' extraordinary swimming prowess mean fishermen are not immune; at night tigers have been known to climb aboard fishing boats, which are anchored midstream, and abscond with not-so-happy prey.

Thanks to strategic perimeter fencing near villages, the numbers of human deaths attributed to tigers has dropped from an estimated 200 a year to about 30, despite an (official) increasing tiger population.

---

from Rs 2150/3440 per person for one-/two-night trips staying in comfortable tents to Rs 3400/6280 for more luxurious cottages.

Sleeping & Eating

Choices for the independent traveller are either overpriced or inconveniently located.

Kamal Kamini (☎ 03128-236035; d with shared bathroom Rs 80-200) Located far away in Gosaba's bazaar, this dingy, bottom-end option is the only choice if you're determined to see the Sunderbans as an independent traveller.

Sajnekhali Tourist Lodge (☎ 03218-214960; dm/d incl 1 meal & breakfast Rs 220/550) While perfectly located in Sajnekhali, its rooms are dark and dank. Some private tour operators use this accommodation option, so bookings are essential. Dorms can't be booked in advance.

Getting There & Away

From Kolkata (Babu Ghat) it's quickest to get a bus to Sonakhali (Rs 45, three hours); aim for the first departure at 6.30am. Then go by boat to Gosaba (Rs 11, 1½ hours, hourly), where there are shared cycle-rickshaws to Pakhirala (Rs 8, 45 minutes). From there, take another boat to Sajnekhali (Rs 4, 10 minutes). The last Kolkata bus leaves Sonakhali at 4.30pm.

DIAMOND HARBOUR

☎ 03174 / pop 37,238

Diamond Harbour, once the main port of the East India Company, rests 51km south of Kolkata, where the Hooghly turns south and flows into open sea. While it's a popular picnic spot, there isn't much to see besides a ruined Portuguese fort. However, it's a good staging area for points in the south.

Diamond Harbour Tourist Centre (Sagarika Tourist Lodge; ☎ /fax 255246; dm Rs 80, d from Rs 300, with AC from Rs 700; ❄) is a satisfactory overnight stop. The better rooms have their back to the ocean.

Buses from Kolkata (Rs 24, 1½ hours) come and go every 30 minutes.

SAGAR ISLAND

☎ 03210 / pop 185,301

According to legend, after the sage Kapil reduced King Sagar's 60,000 sons to ashes, it was at Sagar Island that the Ganges revived their souls by flowing over their dusty remains. Each year the **Gangasagar Mela** (p129) is held here, near the Kapil Muni Temple, honouring the legend.

Within sight of the temple, **Larica Sagar Vihar** (☎ 240226; dm Rs 100, d Rs 360-600) has large, clean rooms with mosquito nets and a decent restaurant (mains Rs 20 to 80). Other choices include a rather dark, dank youth hostel and various ashrams. Note that prices soar during the mela.

From Diamond Harbour, take a bus to Hardwood Point (Rs 20, one hour), where a ferry (Rs 6, 25 minutes) crosses the Hooghly to Sagar Island. Buses run the 30km from the ferry landing to the temple (Rs 25, 45 minutes).

BAKKALI

☎ 03210

Bakkali is a beach town located 132km south of Kolkata. The white-sand **beach** is rather desolate and exposed, but OK for a stroll. An hour north is the colourful fishing village of **Namkhana**.

A few minutes' walk from Bakkali's beach is the **Bakkali Tourist Lodge** (☎ 225260; dm/d Rs 80/400). It's rather run-down, but comfortable for a night or two.

A government bus departs from Kolkata's Esplanade for Bakkali daily at 7am (Rs 69, four hours).

DIGHA

☎ 03220

Digha, the 'Brighton of the East', is located on the Bay of Bengal, 185km southwest of Kolkata. While it's a nice escape from the city, this is not a spot for a surf. A less crowded seaside hideaway can be found 14km north at Shankarpur.

The bright, balconied **Digha Tourist Lodge** (☎ 266255; fax 266256; d from Rs 300, with AC Rs 700; 🔁) offers the best value, but look at a few rooms as they vary widely.

Several buses run daily from Kolkata's Esplanade (Rs 75, five hours).

NORTH OF KOLKATA

UP THE HOOGHLY

On the Hooghly River, 25km north of Kolkata, Serampore was a Danish trading centre until Denmark's holdings in India were transferred to the East India Company in 1845. At **Serampore College** there are impressive colonial buildings and a remarkable cast-iron gate donated by the Danish king. Further upriver is the former French outpost of **Chandarnagar**, where you can visit the Eglise du Sacre Coeur and the 18th-century mansion now housing the **Cultural Institut de Chandarnagar** (admission free; 🔁 11am-5.30pm, closed Thu & Sat), with collections documenting this colonial outpost.

In 1537 the Portuguese set up a factory in **Hooghly**, 41km north of Kolkata, which became an important trading port long before Kolkata rose to prominence. After a lengthy siege, the Portuguese were expelled from Hooghly in 1632 by Shah Jahan, but were allowed to return a year later. Climb the lofty minarets of the **Imambara** (admission Rs 4; 🔁 8am-5.30pm), where the view will take your breath away. The building was constructed in 1836 to host the Shiite procession of Muharram. Only 1km south of Hooghly, **Chinsura** was exchanged by the Dutch for the British possessions on the (Indonesian) island of Sumatra in 1825. There is a fort and a Dutch cemetery, 1km to the west.

About 6km north of Hooghly, **Bansberia** has two interesting temples. The 13 *sikharas* (spires) at **Hansewari** look like something you'd expect to see in St Petersburg, while the ornate

DURGA'S BATH

Since Durga is the goddess of all things and beings, it shouldn't come as a surprise that the list of ingredients required for rituals during the Durga Puja (p129) is a long and strange one. For instance, the goddess' daily bath requires no less than 75 items. These range from extracts of bitter fruit and dew collected off lotus pollens to soil from beneath a prostitute's door. Yes, from beneath a prostitute's door! It's believed that men leave their virtues behind when entering such an establishment, thus making the doorstep's soil a potent one. It's also thought that this ingredient symbolises the festival's inclusion of all levels of Bengali society. Fascinatingly, instead of bathing Durga's clay image itself, the bath is given to a mirror holding her reflection.

terracotta tiles covering the **Vasudev Temple** resemble those seen in Bishnupur.

BISHNUPUR

☎ 03244 / pop 61,943

Known for its beautiful terracotta temples, Bishnupur flourished as the capital of the Malla kings from the 16th to the early 19th centuries. The architecture of these intriguing **temples** (Indian/foreigner Rs 5/100; 🔁 dawn to dusk) is a bold mix of Bengali, Islamic and Orissan styles. Intricately detailed façades of numerous temples play out scenes of the Hindu epics Ramayana and Mahabharata. The most striking temples are the Jor Bangla, Madan Mohan, the multi-arched Ras Mancha and the elaborate Shyam Rai. Cycle-rickshaw-wallahs offer tours (the best way to negotiate the labyrinth of lanes) for Rs 100. There's a small **museum** (admission Rs 10; 🔁 11am-7pm Tue-Sun) that's worth a look for its painted manuscript covers, stone friezes, musical instruments and folk-art gallery.

Bishnupur is in Bankura district, famous for its **pottery**, particularly the stylised Bankura horse, and Baluchari silk saris.

Bishnupur Tourist Lodge (☎ 252013; dm Rs 80, d from Rs 300, with AC Rs 650; 🔁) is a typically sleepy government-run hotel with adequate, unremarkable rooms. It's close to the museum and a Rs 20 rickshaw ride from the train station.

Regular buses run to Kolkata (Rs 60, five hours) and to Shantiniketan (Rs 65, five hours). Three daily trains run to Kolkata (2nd class/chair Rs 84/278, four hours); the quickest depart at 7.30am and 5.30pm.

SHANTINIKETAN

☎ 03463

Shantiniketan is the epitome of its Bengali name, which means peaceful *(shanti)* abode *(niketan)*. Rabindranath Tagore (see the boxed text, p59) founded a school here in 1901, which later developed into the Visva-Bharati University, with an emphasis on humanity's relationship with nature.

Spread through the leafy university grounds are eclectic statues, the celebrated **Shantiniketan Murals** and the **Tagore Prayer Hall**. Oddly, Tagore's car, a black Humber, sits silently behind a glass-walled garage, its fate sealed by the fact that it was used by him. The **museum and art gallery** (admission Rs 5; ☺ 10.30am-1pm & 2-4.30pm Thu-Mon, 10.30am-1pm Tue) in the Uttarayan complex are worth a peek if you're an aficionado of Tagore. The bookshop at the main gate has plenty of Tagore's titles (Rs 80 to Rs 250) in English.

Sleeping & Eating

There are several options in the quiet leafy streets of Bhubandanga and Jamboni.

Shantiniketan Tourist Lodge (☎ 252699; fax 252398; Bhubandanga; dm/d/d with AC Rs 80/350/850; ☒) This government-run hotel is central, simple and clean enough, though the staff are indifferent and the restaurant has a very limited range of lack lustre dishes (mains Rs 40 to 100).

Hotel Santiniketan (☎ 254434; Bhubandanga; s/d/d with AC Rs 250/300/700; ☒) This bold and balconied hotel has the best and cleanest rooms around. The ground-floor rooms are pleasantly cool, and there's a garden for relaxing and wishing you could order a beer. The restaurant (mains Rs 35 to 80) dishes up tasty curries, including a few South Indian dishes.

Chhuti Holiday Resort (☎ 252692; Jamboni; d from Rs 800, with AC Rs 1400; ☒) This cluster of cottages looks great from the outside but the stone-floored cottages are small and can be damp. Its restaurant (mains Rs 50 to 100) is a cut above the others though, with a good range of Indian, Chinese and continental dishes.

About the only place to get a cold beer is the dimly lit bar down the side of the **Hotel Embika** (Bhubandanga).

Getting There & Away

Several trains ply between Bolpur station, 2km south of the university, and Kolkata daily. The best are 2337/8 (2nd class/chair Rs 72/235, 2½ hours) departing at 10.10am from Howrah and 1.10pm from Bolpur. To New Jalpaiguri choose between 5657 (sleeper/3AC Rs 190/505, eight hours) departing at 9.30am or 2503 (2nd class/ chair Rs 126/425) departing at 11.28am. Numerous buses go to Murshidabad (Rs 45, four hours) and Bishnupur (Rs 65, five hours).

NABADWIP & MAYAPUR

☎ 03472 / pop 115,036

Nabadwip, 114km northwest of Kolkata, is an important Krishna pilgrimage centre, attracting throngs of devotees, and is an ancient centre of Sanskrit culture. The last Hindu king of Bengal, Lakshman Sen, moved his capital here from Gaur.

Across the river from Nabadwip, Mayapur is a centre for the Iskcon (Hare Krishna) movement. There's a large temple and the **Iskcon Guest House** (☎ 245620; d/q Rs 100/350), which runs a private bus to/from Kolkata (Rs 135, five hours; ring for details).

MURSHIDABAD & BERHAMPORE

☎ 03482 / pop 36,894

In Murshidabad, rural Bengali life and 18th-century architecture meld on the verdant shores of the Bhagirathi River. When Siraj-ud-daula was nawab of Bengal, Murshidabad was his capital, and he was assassinated here after the defeat at Plassey (now Palashi). The Bhagirathi River flows south to the Hooghly and was once the major trading route between inland India and the port of Kolkata, 221km south.

Hazarduari (Indian/foreigner Rs 5/100; ☺ 10am-5pm Sat-Thu), a palace famous for its 1000 doors (real and false), was built here for the nawabs in 1837. It now houses an astonishing collection of antiquities from the 18th and 19th centuries, including historical paintings such as Marshall's celebrated *Burial of Sir John Moore*. Beneath the lofty dome of Durbar Hall hangs a vast chandelier, rumoured to have been a gift from Queen Victoria. In the Archive Gallery rests a lustrous Arabic manuscript from the 13th century. The dilapidated **Great Imambara** stands on the palace grounds; its renovated interior deserves a look.

Murshid Quli Khan, who moved the capital here in 1705, is buried in a different section of town, beneath the stairs at the impressive ruins of the **Katra Mosque**. Siraj-ud-daula was assassinated at the **Nimak Haram Deohri** (Traitor's Gate). Within the **Kathgola Gardens** (admission Rs 7; ⏰ 6.30am-5.30pm) is an interesting Jain Parswanath Temple and a museum.

Berhampore is 11km south of Murshidabad and acts as its bus and railway hub.

Sleeping & Eating

The few hotels here have private bathrooms with bucket hot water.

Hotel Samrat (☎ 251147; NH-34 Panchanantala; s/d from Rs 150/200, d with AC from Rs 600; 🏠) This is the best place to stay in Berhampore, with a range of satisfactory rooms and a basic restaurant (mains Rs 20 to 120).

Hotel Manjusha (☎ 270321; d Rs 300-400) This hotel in Murshidabad sits gloriously on the bank of the Bhagirathi, behind the Great Imambara. Downstairs rooms are cheapest, while rooms 201 to 203 have river and Hazarduari views.

Getting There & Around

There's a daily express train 3103/4 to/from Kolkata (2nd class/chair Rs 71/236, four hours), departing from Sealdah station (Kolkata) at 6.25pm and Berhampore at 6.24am. Regular buses leave for Kolkata (Rs 56, six hours) and Malda (Rs 45, five hours).

Shared autorickshaws (Rs 10) whizz between Murshidabad and Berhampore. Cyclerickshaw-wallahs offer guided half-day tours to see the spread-out sites for Rs 100.

MALDA

☎ 03512 / pop 161,448

Malda, 347km north of Kolkata, is a convenient base for visiting the ruins of Bengal's former capitals in nearby Gaur and Pandua. Malda is also famed for its Fajli mangoes ripening in summer.

Hotels are scattered along the highway and around the bus and train stations.

Continental Lodge (☎ 252388; fax 251505; 22 KJ Sanyal Rd; s/d Rs 150/250, d with AC from Rs 500; 🏠) is a friendly lodge almost directly opposite the bus station; it offers bright, clean rooms for every budget.

Hotel Pratapaditya (☎ 268104; Station Rd; s/d from Rs 160/225, d with AC Rs 650-1200; 🏠) is the quietest option and is just off the highway, only 500m from the train station (Rs 4 by rickshaw). It offers a wide variety of rooms, has helpful staff, and a good Indian and continental restaurant (mains Rs 35 to 75).

Hotel Purbanchal (☎ 266183; NH-34; s/d from Rs 250/300, with AC Rs 500/575; 🏠) has standard rooms that are rather small, but you can pay extra for a TV and more space.

The best train from Kolkata (Sealdah station) is 2503 (2nd class/chair Rs 111/372, six hours), departing 9.05am Tuesday, Thursday and Sunday. Train 2503 continues to New Jalpaiguri (Rs 91/301, four hours), departing at 3.05pm. If returning to Kolkata, take the 2066 to Howrah (Rs 122/390, seven hours), departing 6am Monday to Saturday. Buses depart regularly for Siliguri (Rs 110, six hours), Berhampore/Murshidabad (Rs 53, five hours) and Kolkata (from Rs 120, 10 hours).

GAUR & PANDUA

Rising from the flooded paddy fields of Gaur (16km south of Malda) are mosques and other vestiges of the 13th- to 16th-century capital of the Muslim nawabs. Little remains from the 7th- to 12th-century pre-Muslim period, when Gaur was the capital of the successive Buddhist Pala and Hindu Sena dynasties.

Wander through the ruins of the impressive **Baradwari Mosque** and the intact arcaded aisle of its corridor, or beneath the fortress-like gateway of **Dakhil Darwaza** (1425). The **Qadam Rasul Mosque** enshrines the flat footprint of the Prophet Mohammed. The adjacent **tomb of Fath Khan** (1707) startlingly informs you that he 'vomited blood and died on this spot'. Lotus-flower motifs grace the terracotta façade of the **Tantipara Mosque** (1480), while remnants of colourful enamel cling to the **Lattan** and **Chamkati mosques**.

North of Pandua (18km north of Malda) are the vast ruins of the 14th-century **Adina Masjid**, once India's largest mosque. Within an intact section of arched and domed bays sits the tomb of Sikander Shah (1364–79), the builder of this mosque. About 2km away is the **Eklakhi mausoleum**, so-called because it cost Rs 1 lakh (Rs 100,000) to build.

The monuments are spread throughout Gaur and Pandua along some of the worst roads in India; it's worth hiring a taxi from Malda for half a day (Rs 500).

WEST BENGAL HILLS

SILIGURI & NEW JALPAIGURI

☎ 0353 / pop 655,935 / elev 119m

The vibrant, crowded trading hub encompassing the twin towns of Siliguri and New Jalpaiguri (NJP) is the jumping-off point for Darjeeling, Kalimpong, Sikkim, the northeast states, eastern Nepal and Bhutan. For most

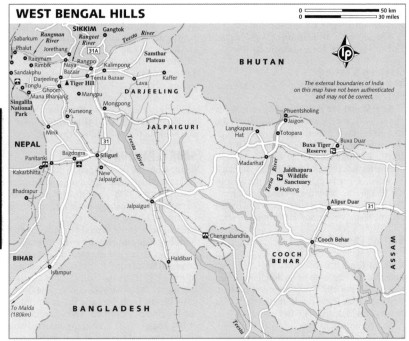

travellers, Siliguri is an overnight transit point where there are good meals, great shopping and a glimpse of snowy peaks.

Orientation

Most of Siliguri's hotels, restaurants and services are spread along Tenzing Norgay Rd, better known by its old moniker, Hill Cart Rd. NJP Station Rd leads southward to NJP station, while branching eastward off Hill Cart Rd are Siliguri's other main streets, Sevoke and Bidhan Rds, which bound the bustling Hong Kong Market area.

Information

INTERNET ACCESS

Beauty Dot Com (Hotel Empees, Bidhan Rd; per hr Rs 20; ☺ 9am-10pm) Cool and fast.

Cyber Space (Hotel Vinayak, Hill Cart Rd; per hr Rs 30; ☺ 10am-8.30pm) Digital-camera friendly.

Net-India (Sify iway; 22 Hill Cart Rd; per hr Rs 30; ☺ 9am-10pm)

Net-N-Net (Hill Cart Rd; per hr Rs 25; ☺ 9.30am-9.30pm)

MEDICAL SERVICES

Sadar Hospital (☎ 2436526, 2585224; Hospital Rd)

MONEY

Delhi Hotel (☎ 2516918; Hill Cart Rd; ☺ 7am-9.30pm) Currency and travellers cheques exchanged.

State Bank of India (☎ 2431364; Hill Cart Rd; ☺ 10am-3.30pm Mon-Fri, till 1pm Sat) Currency and travellers cheques (only American Express and Thomas Cook) exchanged. ATMs on Bidhan and Hill Cart Rds (hidden just north of the bank).

UBI Bank ATM (Hill Cart Rd)

PHOTOGRAPHY

Photo labs are abundant on Hill Cart Rd.

Cyber Space (Hotel Vinayak, Hill Cart Rd; ☺ 10am-8.30pm) USB connection and CD burning (Rs 50).

POST

General post office (☎ 2538850; Hospital Rd; ☺ 7am-7pm Mon-Sat, 10am-3pm Sun)

TOURIST INFORMATION

Darjeeling Gorkha Hill Council Tourist Office (DGHC; ☎ 2518680; Hill Cart Rd; ☺ 10am-4.15pm Mon-Fri) A friendly office with useful (if dated) brochures on Darjeeling, Kalimpong, Kurseong and Mirik.

Government of Assam Tourist Office (Pradhan Nagar Rd; ☺ 10am-4.15pm Mon-Fri) A desk, no phone, two men, three chairs and five pamphlets.

Sikkim Tourist Office (☎ 2512646; SNT Terminal, Hill Cart Rd; ☺ 10am-4pm Mon-Sat) Issues permits for Sikkim (see p151). If you apply in the morning, your permit will typically be ready by the afternoon; bring your passport and one passport-sized photo.

West Bengal Tourist Office (☎ 2511979; slg_omntdc@sancharnet.in; Hill Cart Rd; ☺ 10am-5pm Mon-Fri) Helpful staff (if prodded), who can also book accommodation for the Jaldhapara Wildlife Sanctuary (p137) between 11am and 4pm. Less helpful information desks are also at the airport and NJP train station.

Sleeping

Dozens of budget and midrange hotels are along Hill Cart Rd, with most congregated near the Tenzing Norgay central bus terminal.

BUDGET

Most budget options have rooms with attached bathrooms and a choice of toilet design. Hot water usually comes in buckets, though several hotels have geysers (hot-water heaters).

Hotel Chancellor (☎ 2432372; cnr Sevoke & Hill Cart Rds; s/d from Rs 125/250, new block s/d 370/400) This is a no-frills but friendly Tibetan-run place. Ask for a room in the newer section, with its brighter, quieter rooms. The older section cops a fair bit of traffic noise. A TV costs Rs 50 per night.

Hotel Apsara (☎ 2514252; 18 Patel Rd; s/d Rs 150/200) A block behind busy Hill Cart Rd is this clean, simple, inexpensive and quiet option (most bathrooms have squat toilets).

Hotel Hill View (☎ 2519951; Hill Cart Rd; s/d from Rs 150/250) A rarity in Siliguri – a budget hotel with some charm. This vintage 1951 accommodation comes complete with a friendly and helpful manager, and the handful of basic rooms (one has a private bathroom) are spacious and clean.

Hotel Breeze (☎ 2691136; NJP Station Rd; d from Rs 180) Less than a 10-minute walk (Rs 7 rickshaw ride) north from NJP station, this hotel has a range of rooms from the simple, bare-bones type to those with a little more comfort. All rooms are doubles, but solo travellers should ask for a discount.

Conclave Lodge (☎ 2514102; Hill Cart Rd; s/d from Rs 200/350) Tucked away behind the more visible Hotel Conclave, this lodge has spotless, quiet rooms with private bathrooms.

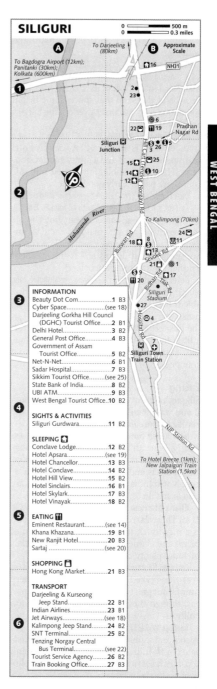

SILIGURI

0 ___ 500 m
0 ___ 0.3 miles

Approximate Scale

To Darjeeling (80km)
To Bagdogra Airport (12km); Panitanki (30km); Kolkata (600km)
NH31
Pradhan Nagar Rd
Siliguri Junction
Hill Cart (Tenzing Norgay) Rd
To Kalimpong (70km)
Mohananda River
Buxwan Rd
Sevoke Rd
Bidhan Rd
Tilak Rd
Hospital Rd
Siliguri Stadium
Siliguri Town Train Station
NJP Station Rd
To Hotel Breeze (1km); New Jalpaiguri Train Station (1.5km)

WEST BENGAL

WEST BENGAL

MIDRANGE & TOP END

All rooms boast a TV and a private bathroom with a geyser.

Hotel Skylark (☎ 2535388; fax 2537641; 1 Tilak Rd; s/d Rs 400/500, with AC Rs 700/800; ✷) Just off Bidhan Rd, Hotel Skylark is a clean and tidy, firm-bedded option that sports some bright rooms and leafy balconies overlooking Siliguri Stadium.

Hotel Vinayak (☎ 2431130; fax 2531067; Hill Cart Rd; d Rs 400-700, with AC Rs 900-3200; ✷) A friendly hotel with spotless rooms and a pretty good restaurant. The comfortable, fan-cooled non-AC rooms are particularly good value.

Hotel Conclave (☎ 2516144; www.hotelconclave.com; Hill Cart Rd; s from Rs 500/600, with AC from Rs 750/900; ✷) This sparkling, contemporary hotel boasts fine woodwork, quality mattresses and an unexpected external glass elevator. The rooms are spotless and downstairs is the excellent Eminent Restaurant (see below).

Hotel Sinclairs (☎ 2517674; www.sinclairshotels.com; off NH31; s/d from Rs 1870/2310; ✷ ▨) This comfortable three-star hotel languishes far from the noise of Hill Cart Rd, about 2km north of the bus terminal. The rooms are spacious, if a little tired, but there's an excellent restaurant-cum-bar and the chance to dive into a cool pool.

Eating

Siliguri has plenty of good restaurants, though if you want a cold beer with your curry, the choice is more limited.

New Ranjit Hotel (☎ 2431785; Hill Cart Rd, mains Rs 25-70) Beneath Sartaj (see below), this busy vegetarian restaurant is the place to find wonderful dosas and other South Indian delicacies. North Indian and Chinese veg dishes are also available.

Khana Khazana (☎ 2517516; Hill Cart Rd; mains Rs 35-85) This relaxed restaurant's secluded patio is a nice lunch spot. The extensive menu of pizzas and Chinese and South Indian specials includes plenty of vegetarian options.

Eminent Restaurant (Hotel Conclave, Hill Cart Rd, mains Rs 45-110; ☯ 7am-11pm; ✷) This stylish eatery pumps out great tandoori delicacies and pizzas, though the AC can make it a little too chilly.

Sartaj (☎ 2431759; Hill Cart Rd, mains Rs 75-140; ✷) A cool and sophisticated restaurant with first-rate North Indian tandooris and curries and top-notch service. There's a bar, and alcohol is served to your table.

Shopping

There are numerous markets here, from the bright and traditional hawkers' market near NJP station to the high-rise Hong Kong Market in Siliguri where you will find imported goods at smugglers' prices. Siliguri is also known for its cane-ware, and you will find everything from letter racks to lounge suites spread along Hill Cart Rd.

Getting There & Away

AIR

Bagdogra airport is 12km west of Siliguri. **Indian Airlines** (☎ 2511495; www.indianairlines.in; Hill Cart Rd; ☯ 10am-1pm & 1.45-4.30pm Mon-Sat) has three flights a week to Kolkata (US$138, one hour), five to Delhi (US$268, four hours) and three to Guwahati (US$103, 50 minutes). **Jet Airways** (☎ 2538001; www.jetairways.com; Hill Cart Rd; ☯ 9am-5.30pm Mon-Sat) has similar fares to Kolkata (daily), Delhi (daily) and Guwahati (four per week). **Air Deccan** (☎ 39008888; www.airdeccan.net) has daily flights to Kolkata (Rs 1974) and Delhi (Rs 3974), and three flights a week to Guwahati (Rs 1474).

Daily helicopter flights (Rs 2000, 30 minutes, 10kg luggage limit) go from Bagdogra to Gangtok at 1.30pm (Tuesday, Thursday, Saturday, Sunday) and 2pm (Monday, Friday, Wednesday). You can buy tickets from **Tourist Service Agency** (TSA; ☎ 2531959; tsaslg@sancharnet.in; Pradhan Nagar Rd), close to the Delhi Hotel.

BUS

Most North Bengal State Transport Corporation (NBSTC) buses leave from **Tenzing Norgay central bus terminal** (Hill Cart Rd), as do many private buses plying the same routes. NBSTC bus services include those listed opposite.

Sikkim Nationalised Transport (SNT) buses to Gangtok (Rs 70, 4½ hours) leave at 8.30am, 10am and 1.30pm from the **SNT terminal** (Hill Cart Rd). There are also deluxe buses (Rs 90) departing here at 7am and 12.30pm. If travelling to Sikkim, you'll require a permit available in Siliguri at the adjacent Sikkim Tourist Information Centre (p135).

JEEP

A faster and more comfortable way of getting around the hills is by share jeep. There are a number of jeep stands: for Darjeeling (Rs 80, 2½ hours) and Kurseong (Rs 50, 1½ hours), look around and opposite the bus terminal; for Kalimpong (Rs 70, 2½ hours) there's a

NBSTC BUSES FROM SILIGURI			
Destination	Fare (Rs)	Duration (hr)	Frequency
Berhampore	167	9	6.45am, 8pm & 9pm
Darjeeling	60	3½	every 30min
Guwahati	277	12	5pm
Kalimpong	50	3	hourly
Kolkata	220-250	12-16	6-8pm
Kurseong	40	2	every 30min
Madarihat	60	3	hourly
Malda	112	6½	hourly
Mirik	45	2½	hourly
Patna	245	14	5pm

stand on Sevoke Rd; and for Gangtok (Rs 120, four hours) jeeps leave from next to the SNT terminal.

Chartering a jeep privately costs roughly 10 times that of a shared ticket. An option for XL-sized Westerners is to pay for and occupy all the front three seats next to the driver.

TRAIN
The fastest of the four daily services to Kolkata is the *Darjeeling Mail* 2344 (sleeper/3AC Rs 263/684, 11 hours, departs 8pm), which stops in Malda (Rs 154/375, four hours). A better option for Malda is the *New Jalpaiguri Sealdah Express* 2504 (2nd class/chair Rs 111/372, four hours, departing 9.45am Monday, Wednesday and Saturday). The *North East Express* 2505 is the fastest to Delhi (sleeper/3AC Rs 441/1185, 27 hours, departs 4.35pm), travelling via Patna (Rs 235/604, 11 hours). Eastward, train 2506 reaches Guwahati (sleeper/3AC Rs 214/544, eight hours, departs 9am).

There's a **train booking office** (☎ 2537333; cnr Hospital & Bidhan Rds; ☽ 8-11.30am & noon-8pm Mon-Sat, to 2pm Sun).

Toy Train
The diesel toy train (p145) climbs the 80km from New Jalpaiguri to Darjeeling in nine long hours (2nd/1st class Rs 42/247, departs 9am). It's wise to make reservations (booking fee 2nd/1st class Rs 15/30) two to three days in advance at NJP station or the train booking office. If steam is your passion, you can catch the steam version to Darjeeling from Kurseong (p140).

Getting Around
From the bus terminal to NJP train station a taxi/autorickshaw costs Rs 200/90, while cycle-rickshaws charge Rs 50 for the 35-minute trip. Taxis between Bagdogra airport and Siliguri cost Rs 300.

JALDHAPARA WILDLIFE SANCTUARY
☎ 03563 / elev 61m
This rarely visited **sanctuary** (☎ 262239; Indian/foreigner Rs 25/100; ☽ mid-Sep–mid-Jul) protects 114 sq km of forests and grasslands along the Torsa River and is a refuge for over 50 Indian one-horned rhinoceros *(Rhinoceros unicornis)*.

The best time to visit is mid-October to May, particularly in March and April when wild elephants, deer and tigers (rarely seen) are attracted by new grass growth. Your best chance of spotting a rhino is aboard an elephant (Indian/foreigner Rs 120/200 per hour); these lumbering safaris are booked by the tourist lodges (see below). If staying elsewhere, you'll be last in line for elephant rides.

The West Bengal Tourist Office in Siliguri (p135) organises overnight **tours** (per person Rs 2050; ☽ departs 10am Sat) to Jaldhapara, which include an elephant ride, transport, accommodation and all meals.

Sleeping & Eating
Lodges should be booked well in advance through the West Bengal Tourist Office in Siliguri, Darjeeling or Kolkata.

Hotel Relax (☎ 262304; d Rs 300) A very basic option opposite the Jaldhapara Tourist Lodge, with OK beds, cement floors and squat toilets.

Jaldhapara Tourist Lodge (☎ 262230; dm Rs 300, cottage Rs 650, d Rs 1000) This West Bengal Tourism Development Corporation (WBTDC) hotel is outside the park precincts near Madarihat. All meals are included in the room rates. Rooms in the characterless newer wing are the better option. The old wing has musty, dark rooms.

Hollong Forest Tourist Lodge (☎ 262228; d Rs 1000, plus compulsory Rs 180 per person for breakfast & dinner) This is the most comfortable option and is located within the park itself. Lunch is available for an additional Rs 75.

Getting There & Away
Jaldhapara is 124km east of Siliguri. Buses frequent the route from Siliguri to Madarihat (Rs 60, three hours, hourly 6am to 4pm), 9km from Jaldhapara. A taxi from Madarihat to Hollong inside the park is Rs 150.

WEST BENGAL

CROSSING INTO BANGLADESH, BHUTAN & NEPAL

To/From Bangladesh

At the time of research there was no direct bus from Siliguri to the border at Chengrabandha. Take a private bus from outside the Tenzing Norgay central bus terminal to Jalpaiguri (Rs 40) and change there for Chengrabandha. The border post is open from 8am to 6pm daily. From near the border post you can catch buses on to Rangpur, Bogra and Dhaka. Visas for Bangladesh can be obtained in Kolkata and New Delhi (see p323).

To/From Bhutan

Bhutan Transport Services has a counter inside Tenzing Norgay central bus terminal. Four buses leave daily for Phuentsholling (Rs 65, departures 7.30am, noon, 2pm, 3pm). Indian immigration is in Jaigon, next to **Hotel Kasturi** (☎ 03566-363035; fax 263254; NS Rd; s Rs 300, d Rs 375-1000). Non-Indian nationals need a valid visa authority from a Bhutanese tour operator to enter Bhutan. See www.tourism.gov.bt and Lonely Planet's *Bhutan* for details.

To/From Nepal

For Nepal, local buses pass the Tenzing Norgay central bus terminal every 15 minutes for the border town of Panitanki (Rs 20, one hour). More comfortable buses (Rs 35) leave from outside the bus terminal. Share Jeeps to Kakarbhitta (Rs 50) are readily available in Siliguri. The Indian border post in Panitanki is officially open 24 hours and the Nepal post in Kakarbhitta is open from 6am to 7pm. See p152 for information on buses from Darjeeling to Kathmandu. Foreign exchange is available at a **Nepal Bank counter** (🕒 7am-5pm) close to the border. Onward from Kakarbhitta there are numerous buses to Kathmandu (NRs 530) and other destinations. Bhadrapur airport, 23km southwest of Kakarbhitta, has regular flights to Kathmandu. For onward air transport and connection to Bhadrapur contact **Jhapa Travel Agency** (☎ 98320221020; jhapatravels@hotmail .com) in Kakarbhitta. Visas for Nepal can be obtained at the border, or in Kolkata or New Delhi (see p324).

MIRIK

☎ 0354 / pop 9179 / elev 1767m

Nestled near the Nepal border, halfway between Siliguri and Darjeeling, is this low-profile hill station and honeymoon destination. Mirik is surrounded by an undulating carpet of tea estates, orange orchards, cardamom plantations and forests of tall, dark Japanese cedars. It is a quiet retreat that remains off most visitors' radars. Some of Mirik's higher hilltops offer wonderful views of morning's first light striking Khangchendzonga (8598m).

Check email at **Krishnanagar Cyber Café** (Main Rd, Krishnanagar; per hr Rs 30). There are no money-changing facilities in Mirik.

Sights & Activities

Mirik is centred on the artificial **Sumendu Lake** and there's a walk around its 3.5km circumference. On the west side of the lake, climb the steps to the diminutive **Hindu Devi Sthan temple complex**, set among moss-covered evergreens, banana trees and stands of bamboo. Perched high above Mirik, the richly painted **Bokar Gompa** gazes over the town.

Pedal boats (per 30min Rs 60) can be hired near the bridge and **pony rides** (half/full round-the-lake trips Rs 80/160) are offered for various trips around Mirik.

Sleeping & Eating

Most hotels crowd the main road of Krishnanagar, the compact area to the south of the lake. All rooms mentioned have a private bathroom. Prices stated are for the high season (October to November and March to May); these drop by up to 50% in the low season.

Lodge Ashirvad (☎ 2243272; dm Rs 75, s/d Rs 150/250, d with geyser Rs 350) A very friendly and clean budget hotel down a small lane opposite Samden Restaurant. The rooms are spotless and there's a great rooftop terrace. Hot-water buckets cost Rs 10.

Hotel Ratnagiri (☎ 2243243; s/d with geyser Rs 400/600) Ratnagiri has some warm, wood-panelled doubles upstairs plus larger family suites. Some rooms have balconies and views of Sumendu Lake; all have TV and geyser. There's a garden restaurant out the back (mains Rs 30 to 90).

Hotel Jagjeet (☎ 2243231; www.jagjeethotel.com; d from Rs 750, mains Rs 30-115; ☐) This is the best hotel in Krishnanagar with a variety of rooms, most with balconies, and attentive service. The streetfront restaurant is deservedly popular, serving excellent Indian, Chinese and continental dishes.

Mirik Orange County Retreat (☎ 2243612; cottages incl tax Rs 1300-1800) These luxury, two-storey cottages afford glorious views of the township and surrounding countryside, including Khangchendzonga. To ensure a room it is advisable to book through **Glenary's** (☎ 0354-2257554; fax 2257556) in Darjeeling. Prices are based on double occupancy; additional guests cost Rs 300.

Samden Restaurant (☎ 2243295; mains Rs 10-16; 5.30am-9pm) A great 'local', next to the Jagjeet, drawing monks and those in love with *momos* and noodle soups (*thukpas* and *thanthuks*).

Getting There & Away
Buses leave for Darjeeling (Rs 45, three hours) and Siliguri (Rs 45, three hours). Share jeeps depart regularly to Darjeeling and Siliguri (Rs 50, 2½ hours) and Kurseong (Rs 60, three hours). Tickets can be purchased from the lakeside shack at the base of the main road.

KURSEONG
☎ 0354 / pop 40,067 / elev 1458m
Kurseong, 32km south of Darjeeling, is the little sister of the Queen of the Hills further up the track. It is a great stopover for those looking for a quiet alternative to the jostling crowds of Darjeeling. Kurseong – its name derived from the Lepcha word *kurson-rip,* a reference to the small white orchid prolific in this area – is also home to several churches and is surrounded by renowned tea estates. It is the southern terminus for the steam-powered toy trains of the **Darjeeling Himalayan Railway**.

Hill Cart Rd (Tenzing Norgay Rd) – the main thoroughfare from Siliguri to Darjeeling – and its close shadow, the railway line, wind through town passing tea and paneer sellers and tiny cubicles where 'suitings and shirtings' are sewn on chattering machines. Here you will struggle to find a souvenir shop.

There are numerous good walks in the area, including one to **Eagle's Crag** (2km return) that

affords splendid views down the Teesta and the plains to the south. Along Pankhabari Rd, the graveyard at St Andrews has poignant reminders of the tea-planter era, while the organic **Makaibari Tea Estates** (☎ 2330181; Tue-Sat) welcomes visitors to its aromatic factory. Old colonial buildings abound on the ridge above town, and the **Forestry Museum**, **St Mary's Grotto**, and the **Kunsamnamdoling Gompa** run by *ani* (Buddhist nuns) are well worth visiting.

You can check your email at **Kashyup Computers & Systems** (Hill Cart Rd; per hr Rs 30) and **Cyberzone** (Hotel Delhi Darbar, Hill Cart Rd; per hr Rs 25).

Sleeping & Eating
Hotel Delhi Darbar (☎ 2345862; Hill Cart Rd; d Rs 300, mains Rs 25-50; ☐) This budget option is found just uphill from the train station. It's friendly and passably clean (if only they would ditch the carpet), hot water comes by the bucket and some bathrooms have sit-down, flush loos.

Kurseong Tourist Lodge (☎ 2344409; d Rs 800, with balcony Rs 900, mains Rs 30-80) This lodge exudes character with warm, wood-lined rooms that smell of polish and feature stunning views. The toy train whistles past the café where you can snack on *momos,* or you can enjoy a cold beer, a refreshing cuppa and a fine Indian, Chinese or continental meal at its scenic restaurant.

ourpick **Cochrane Place** (☎ 2330703; www.imperialchai.com; 132 Pankhabari Rd; s/d from Rs 1750/2000, mains Rs 40-120) This exceptional boutique hotel surrounded by tea plantations and overlooking the twinkling lights of Siliguri is a destination in its own right. This much-extended colonial chalet is full of antique furniture and individually decorated rooms. Trainspotters will be beside themselves in Pandim (each room is named after a Himalayan peak). The owners are rightly proud of their kitchen, which re-creates tastes of the Raj and all meals are available either as set menus, part of the tariff or à la carte. The hotel is wheelchair friendly, provides airport (Bagdogra) and train station pick-up, and has a wealth of local knowledge to point you towards trails and sights in the region.

Glenary's Junction (Kurseong Train Station; snacks Rs 10-25; 8am-7pm) Tucked into the cute station is a branch of Darjeeling's favourite cake shop. Sit down for biscuits, brownies, cakes, tea, coffee and assorted hot snacks, or browse the great photos of the Darjeeling Himalayan Railway's glory days.

WEST BENGAL

Getting There & Away

Numerous share jeeps run to Darjeeling (Rs 40, 1½ hours), Siliguri (Rs 50, 1½ hours), Kalimpong (Rs 100, 3½ to four hours) and Mirik (Rs 60, 2½ hours). Buses leave from near the train station for Darjeeling (Rs 25, two hours) and Siliguri (Rs 40, 2½ hours).

The Darjeeling Himalayan Railway's steam toy train (p145) for Darjeeling (2nd/1st class Rs 25/144, four hours) leaves at 6am, weather permitting, while the diesel version (originating at New Jalpaiguri) departs around 1.17pm. A diesel train (originating in Darjeeling) to Siliguri (2nd/1st class Rs 30/166, four hours) departs at 11.55pm.

DARJEELING

☎ 0354 / pop 109,160 / elev 2134m

Draped over a steep mountain ridge, surrounded by tea plantations and backed by a splendid Himalayan panorama, the archetypal hill station of Darjeeling is rightly West Bengal's premier drawcard. When you aren't gazing at Khangchendzonga (8598m), you can explore colonial mansions and churches, Buddhist and Hindu temples, botanical gardens and a zoo for Himalayan fauna. The steep narrow streets are crowded with colourful souvenir and handicraft shops, and a good steaming brew and excellent Indian and Tibetan fare are never far away. For the adventurous there are superb treks which trace ancient trade routes and provide magnificent viewpoints.

Most tourists visit after the monsoon (October and November) and during spring (mid-March to the end of May) when skies are dry, panoramas are clear and temperatures are pleasant.

History

This area belonged to the Buddhist chogyals (kings) of Sikkim until 1780, when it was annexed by the invading Gurkhas from Nepal. The Gurkhas' aggressive territorial expansion led to growing conflicts with the British and, after several battles, the East India Company gained control of the region in 1816. The company then returned most of the lands back to Sikkim in exchange for British control over any future border disputes.

During one such dispute in 1828, two British officers stumbled across the Dorje Ling monastery, on a tranquil forested ridge, and passed word to Calcutta that it would be a perfect site for a sanatorium; they were sure to have also mentioned its strategic military importance in the region. The Chogyal of Sikkim (still grateful for the return of his kingdom) happily leased the uninhabited land to the East India Company in 1835 and a hill station was born.

Forest gradually made way for colonial houses and tea plantations, and by 1857 the population of Darjeeling reached 10,000, mainly because of a massive influx of Gurkha labourers from Nepal.

After Independence, the Gurkhas became the main political force in Darjeeling and friction with the state government led to calls for a separate state of Gorkhaland in the 1980s. In 1986, violence and riots orchestrated by the Gurkha National Liberation Front (GNLF) brought Darjeeling to a standstill. A compromise was hammered out in late 1988, which granted the newly formed Darjeeling Gorkha Hill Council (DGHC) a large measure of autonomy from the state government.

Although this appeased some Gurkhas, the breakaway Gorkhaland Liberation Organisation (GLO) and its armed wing, the Gorkha Volunteers' Cell (GVC), have continued to call for full secession. Since 2001 both the GVC and DGHC have been accused of political killings. Meanwhile the DGHC's internal wranglings over its relationship with Kolkata and Delhi have seen the introduction and dropping of 'Autonomous' in its name (and an 'A' in its acronym), and the proposal of a new council: Gorkha Hill Council, Darjeeling (GHCD).

Orientation

Darjeeling sprawls over a west-facing slope in a web of interconnecting roads and steep flights of steps. Near the top of town is the atmospheric and open square known as Chowrasta, the focal point of Victorian Darjeeling. North of Chowrasta is the forested Observatory Hill and skirting the hill is Bhanu Bhakta Sarani, from where there are stupendous views of Khangchendzonga. The zoo lies to the northwest, reached from Chowrasta on foot via HD Lama Rd.

Hill Cart Rd (aka Tenzing Norgay Rd), which runs the length of town, is Darjeeling's major vehicle thoroughfare. From the chaotic Chowk Bazaar it leads north towards the zoo and Himalayan Mountaineering Institute, and heads south past the train station en route to Ghoom. Nehru Rd (aka the Mall), the main shopping street, heads south from

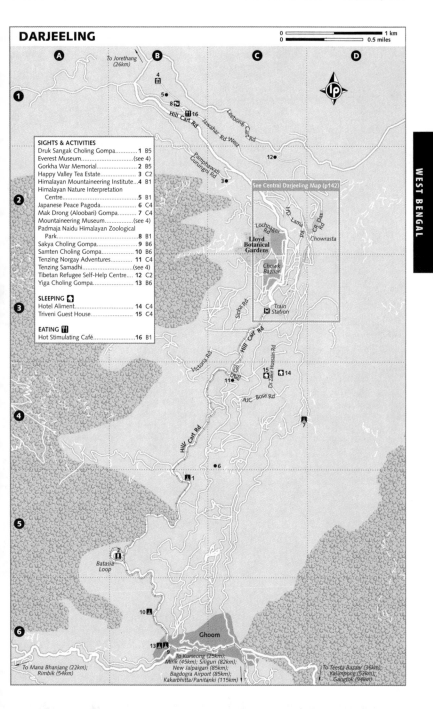

DARJEELING

SIGHTS & ACTIVITIES
Druk Sangak Choling Gompa..............1 B5
Everest Museum...........................(see 4)
Gorkha War Memorial......................2 B5
Happy Valley Tea Estate...................3 C2
Himalayan Mountaineering Institute..4 B1
Himalayan Nature Interpretation
  Centre....................................5 B1
Japanese Peace Pagoda...................6 C4
Mak Drong (Aloobari) Gompa...........7 C4
Mountaineering Museum................(see 4)
Padmaja Naidu Himalayan Zoological
  Park.......................................8 B1
Sakya Choling Gompa.....................9 B6
Samten Choling Gompa..................10 B6
Tenzing Norgay Adventures.............11 C4
Tenzing Samadhi..........................(see 4)
Tibetan Refugee Self-Help Centre....12 C2
Yiga Choling Gompa......................13 B6

SLEEPING
Hotel Aliment..............................14 C4
Triveni Guest House.......................15 C4

EATING
Hot Stimulating Café......................16 B1

CENTRAL DARJEELING

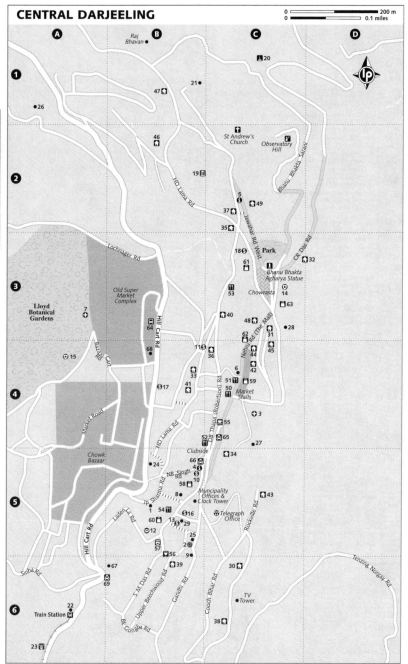

WEST BENGAL

0   200 m
0   0.1 miles

Ⓐ **Ⓑ** **Ⓒ** **Ⓓ**

❶

Raj
Bhavan

●26

47

21●

❷

46

St Andrew's
Church

Observatory
Hill

HD Lama Rd

19

Bhanu Bhakta Sarani

5
37
49

35

Jawahar Rd West

Park

❸

Lochnager Rd

Old Super
Market
Complex

18

Lloyd
Botanical
Gardens

7

64

Hill Cart Rd

53

61

Chowrasta

Bhanu Bhakta
Acharya Statue

14

63

CR Das Rd

32

40

48

28

❹

15

Bazar Cart Rd

68

11
36

33

62
31

Nehru Rd (The Mall)

44
45
42

6

Market Road

41
17

BB Thapa (Robertson) Rd

51
50

59

Market
Stalls

3

55

52
65

❺

Chowk
Bazaar

●24

HD Lama Rd

Clubside
66

NB Singh
Rd

4
10

58

27

34

JP Sharma Rd

8

Muncipality
Offices &
Clock Tower

43

Rockville Rd

1
54

16

Telegraph
Office

60
13
29

Laden La Rd

12

25

2@

57
56
39
9

30

❻

67

Sinha Rd

69

S M Das Rd

Upper Beechwood Rd

Gandhi Rd

Cooch Bihar Rd

TV
Tower

Tenzing Norgay Rd

38

Train Station

22

23

Chowrasta, meeting Laden La Rd (which leads to Hill Cart Rd) and Gandhi Rd (which accesses many cheap hotels) at a junction called Clubside.

Information
BOOKSHOPS
Oxford Book & Stationery Company (Map p142; ☎ 2254325; Chowrasta; 9.30am-7.30pm, closed Sun in low season) Unquestionably the best bookshop in Darjeeling, selling a vast selection of books and maps on Tibet, Nepal, Sikkim, Bhutan and the Himalaya.

EMERGENCY
Police assistance booth (Map p142; Chowrasta)
Sadar Police Station (Map p142; ☎ 2254422; Market Rd)

INTERNET ACCESS
Bellevue Cyber Café (Map p142; Chowrasta Rd; per hr Rs 30; 9am-8pm)
Compuset Centre (Map p142; Gandhi Rd; per hr Rs 30; 8am-8pm) Digital-camera friendly.

Digital Doughnuts (Map p142; Nehru Rd; per hr Rs 30; 7.30am-8pm) Found within Glenary's (p150).

MEDICAL SERVICES
D&DMA Nursing Home (Map p142; ☎ 2254327; Nehru Rd) For serious medical problems, this is the best private hospital.
District Hospital Darjeeling (Map p142; ☎ 2254218; Bazaar Cart Rd; 24hr) Public hospital and emergency department.
Tibetan Medical & Astro Institute (Map p142; ☎ 2256035; HD Lama Rd; 9am-5pm Mon-Fri, 9am-1pm Sat) Traditional medicine – located within Hotel Seven Seventeen.

MONEY
Hotel Seven Seventeen (Map p142; ☎ 2255099; 26 HD Lama Rd) Exchanges most currencies and travellers cheques (Amex and Thomas Cook).
ICICI Bank ATM (Map p142; Laden La Rd) Accepts most international bank and credit cards. There's another ATM on HD Lama Rd (Map p142).

Poddar's (Map p142; Laden La Rd; ⏰ 9am-9pm) Matches the State Bank's rate and changes most currencies and travellers cheques. It accepts credit cards and is a Western Union money transfer agent.

State Bank of India (Map p142; Laden La Rd; ⏰ 10am-4pm Mon-Fri, to 2.30pm Sat) Changes only US dollars and pounds sterling, and travellers cheques issued by Amex (in US dollars) and Thomas Cook (in US dollars and pounds sterling). The commission rate is Rs 100 per transaction. It has an adjacent ATM and another in Chowrasta (Map p142) that accept Visa cards.

PHOTOGRAPHY
Compuset Centre (Map p142; Gandhi Rd; ⏰ 8am-8pm) Memory card reader and CD burning for Rs 50.
Das Studios (Map p142; ☎ 2254004; Nehru Rd; ⏰ 9am-6pm Mon-Sat) Film and printing.

POST
Main post office (Map p142; ☎ 2252076; Laden La Rd; ⏰ 9am-5pm) Reliable parcel service and poste restante.

TOURIST INFORMATION
Darjeeling Gorkha Hill Council Tourist Reception Centre (DGHC; Map p142; ☎ 2255351; Jawahar Rd West; ⏰ 9am-7pm Mon-Sat, 10am-1pm Sun high season, 10am-4.30pm Mon-Sat low season) The staff are friendly, well-organised and the best source of information in Darjeeling. The centre also has counters at the train station and the Mall.
West Bengal Tourist Bureau (Map p142; ☎ 2254102; Chowrasta; ⏰ 10.30am-4.30pm Mon-Fri) Little useful information but sells a basic map of town (Rs 3) and can book accommodation at government lodges, including those at Jaldhapara Wildlife Sanctuary (p137).

TRAVEL AGENCIES
Most travel agencies here can arrange local tours (and some can also arrange treks, rafting trips and other activities). Reliable agencies and their specialities include the following:
Clubside Tours & Travels (Map p142; ☎ 2254646; www.clubside.in; JP Sharma Rd; ⏰ 8.30am-6pm) Arranges treks and tours in West Bengal, Sikkim and Assam, and wildlife tours in Kaziringa, Manas and Jaldhapara National Parks. It's also a Jet Airways agent.
DGHC Tourist Reception Centre (see Tourist Information above) Offers various organised tours and rafting trips at Teesta Bazaar near Kalimpong.
Diamond Tours & Travels (Map p142; ☎ 9832094275; Old Super Market Complex; ⏰ 8am-7pm) Books buses to various destinations from Siliguri.
Himalayan Travels (Map p142; ☎ 2256956; kkgurung@cal.vsnl.net.in; 18 Gandhi Rd; ⏰ 8.30am-7pm) Experienced company arranging treks and mountaineering expeditions in Darjeeling and Sikkim.

Kasturi Tours & Travels (Map p142; ☎ 2254430; Old Super Market Complex; ⏰ 8am-7pm) Sells bus tickets to various destinations from Siliguri.
Samsara Tours, Travels & Treks (Map p142; ☎ 2252874; samsara1@sancharnet.in; Laden La Rd) Helpful and knowledgeable agency offering rafting and trekking trips.

Sights & Activities
See p152 for information on trekking around Darjeeling.

MOUNTAIN VIEWS
As with other hill stations, Himalayan views are a big attraction in Darjeeling. The skyline is dominated by Khangchendzonga, India's highest peak and the world's third-highest mountain. The name 'Khangchendzonga' is derived from the Tibetan words for 'big five-peaked snow fortress'. Views from **lookouts** along Bhanu Bhakta Sarani, which runs from Chowrasta around the north side of Observatory Hill, can be stunning in clear weather.

TIGER HILL
To set your eyes on a spectacular 250km stretch of Himalayan horizon, including Everest (8848m), Lhotse (8501m), Makalu (8475m), Khangchendzonga, Kabru (6691m) and Janu (7710m), rise early and get to **Tiger Hill** (Map p141; 2590m), 11km south of Darjeeling, above Ghoom.

The sunrise over the Himalaya from here is truly spectacular and has become a major tourist attraction, with convoys of jeeps leaving Darjeeling for Tiger Hill every morning during the high season around 4.30am. At the summit, you can either pay Rs 5 to stand in the pavilion grounds, or buy a ticket for one of the heated lounges in the pavilion (Rs 20 to 40, including a cup of chai).

Organised sunrise trips (usually with a detour to Batasia Loop on the way back) can be booked through a travel agency (left) or directly with jeep drivers at the Clubside taxi stand. It's also possible to jump on a jeep going to Tiger Hill from along Gandhi or Laden La Rds between 4am and 4.30am, allowing you to check whether skies are clear before you go. Return trips cost around Rs 65/450 per person/jeep.

Some people take the jeep one way to Tiger Hill and then spend their day wandering back to Darjeeling, visiting the gompas in Ghoom along the way.

TOY TRAIN

The **Darjeeling Himalayan Railway** (Map p142), known affectionately as the Toy Train, made its first journey along its precipice-topping, 2ft-wide tracks in September 1881 and is one of the few hill railways still operating in India. It's even listed as a World Heritage site. Besides its regular diesel service to/from New Jalpaiguri and steam service to/from Kurseong (p152), there are joy rides (Rs 240) during the high season that leave Darjeeling at 10am and 12.50pm for a two-hour steam-powered return trip to Ghoom. It's wise to book at least a day ahead at the **train station** (Hill Cart Rd).

TEA PLANTATIONS

Happy Valley Tea Estate (Map p141; Pamphawati Gu-rungni Rd; ☯ 8am-4pm Mon-Sat), below Hill Cart Rd, is worth visiting when the plucking and processing are in progress. March to May is the busiest time, but occasional plucking also occurs from June to November. An employee will whisk you through the aromatic factory and its various processes before politely de-manding a tip – Rs 20 from each visitor is ap-propriate. Take the turn-off 500m northwest of the Office of the District Magistrate, or take Lochnager Rd from Chowk Bazaar.

See the boxed text, below, for more about Darjeeling tea.

OBSERVATORY HILL

Sacred to both Buddhists and Hindus, this hill was the site of the Dorje Ling monas-tery, the gompa that gave the city its name. Today, devotees of both religions come to a **temple** (Map p141) in a small cave, below the crest of the hill, to honour Mahakala, a Bud-dhist deity and an angry form of the Hindu god Shiva. The summit is marked by several shrines, a flurry of colourful prayer flags and the notes from numerous devotional bells. A path leading up to the hill through giant Japa-nese cedars starts about 300m along Bhanu Bhakta Sarani from Chowrasta. Be careful of the marauding monkeys.

GOMPAS & PAGODAS

Together, Darjeeling and Ghoom are home to a number of fascinating Buddhist monaster-ies. Probably the most scenic is **Bhutia Busty Gompa** (Map p142), with Khangchendzonga providing a spectacular backdrop. The shrine originally stood on Observatory Hill, but was rebuilt in its present location by the chogyals of Sikkim in the 19th century. The gompa houses a fine gold-accented mural and the original copy of the Tibetan Book of the Dead, but permission is required to see it. To get here, follow CR Das Rd downhill for 400m from Chowrasta and take the right fork where the road branches.

WEST BENGAL

ANYONE FOR TEA?

The tea bush was first brought to Darjeeling from Assam by British planters looking for a way to break China's monopoly over the tea trade. Credit for the discovery of tea as it's drunk in the Western world should really go to the Khamti and Singpho tribes of Assam, who first introduced British explorers to the healing powers of fermented tea leaves brewed in hot water.

Darjeeling produces around 25% of India's tea, including some of the world's finest brews, but there's more to tea than just plucking and drying. After picking, the leaves are placed in a 'withering trough', where high-speed fans reduce the moisture content to around 30%, before they're rolled with heavy rollers to force the remaining water onto the surface. The rolled leaves are then fermented in a high-humidity chamber to produce their distinctive flavour; this is a fine art and too little or too much fermentation can spoil the entire batch. Fermentation is stopped by passing the leaves through a dry air chamber, which reduces the moisture to just 3%. With all this hot air flowing around, the smell of tea permeates every corner of the tea factory.

The finished tea is sorted into grades – unbroken leaves are set aside for Golden Flowery Or-ange Pekoe teas, while broken leaves end up as Golden Broken Orange Pekoe, Orange Fannings and Dust – and then graded by expert tasters, who march up and down long lines of teacups, sampling every crop and grading it according to colour, taste and fragrance. Low-grade leaves are blended into household teas, while the best leaves are sold to international tea traders. Teas from estates around Darjeeling and Kurseong (also marketed as Darjeeling tea) regularly and justifiably achieve the world's highest prices. To buy a brew, see p151.

Yiga Choling Gompa (Map p141; camera per photo Rs 10), the region's most famous monastery, exudes a feeling of warmth that is not lost on most who visit here. First built in 1850, it enshrines a 5m-high statue of the Maitreya Buddha (Future Buddha) along with 300 of the most beautifully bound Tibetan texts. It's just west of Ghoom, about a 10-minute walk off Hill Cart Rd. Other gompas of interest in this area include the fortresslike **Sakya Choling Gompa** (Map p141) and the **Samten Choling Gompa** (Map p141), with the protector Garuda atop its ornate Buddha backdrop. These gompas are both on Hill Cart Rd and can be reached by share jeep from Darjeeling (Rs 10).

About halfway between Ghoom and Darjeeling is the vast **Druk Sangak Choling Gompa** (Map p141), inaugurated by the Dalai Lama in 1993. Known for its vibrant frescoes, it houses 300 Himalayan monks who study philosophy, literature, astronomy, meditation, dance and music.

On the opposite side of the ridge is the welcoming **Mak Drong Gompa** (Map p141). It's also known as Aloobari Gompa and is a pleasant walk (45 minutes) from town.

Perched on a hillside at the end of AJC Bose Rd is the gleaming white **Japanese Peace Pagoda** (Map p141; ✆ pujas 4.30–6am & 4.30–6.30pm), one of more than 70 pagodas built by the Japanese Buddhist Nipponzan Myohoji organisation around the world. Drumming resonates through the forested grounds during their daily *pujas* (prayers). It's about a 35-minute walk from Clubside along Gandhi and AJC Bose Rds.

PADMAJA NAIDU HIMALAYAN ZOOLOGICAL PARK
This **zoo** (Map p141; admission incl Himalayan Mountaineering Institute Indian/foreigner Rs 20/100; ✆ 8.30am–4.30pm Fri-Wed, ticket counter closes 4pm) was established in 1958 to study, conserve and preserve Himalayan fauna. This is one of India's better zoos and the animals are cared for by dedicated keepers. Housed within the rocky and forested environment is India's only collection of Siberian tigers, as well as Himalayan black bears, red pandas, snow leopards and Tibetan wolves. The **Himalayan Nature Interpretation Centre** (admission Rs 5; ✆ 2.30–4pm) in the middle of the zoo has tacky wildlife dioramas featuring the snow leopard and clouded leopard.

The zoo is a pleasant 30-minute walk down from Chowrasta along Jawahar Rd West; alternatively, take a share jeep from the Chowk Bazaar bus/jeep station (Rs 10, about 10 minutes) or a private taxi (Rs 50).

HIMALAYAN MOUNTAINEERING INSTITUTE
Tucked away within the grounds of the zoological park, this prestigious **mountaineering institute** (Map p141; HMI; ✆ 2254087; www.exploredarjeeling.com/hmidarj.htm; admission incl zoo Indian/foreigner Rs 20/100; ✆ 8.30am–4.30pm Fri-Wed) was founded in 1954 and has provided training for some of India's leading mountaineers. Within the complex is the fascinating **Everest Museum**, which traces the history of attempts on the world's highest peak. Next door is the **Mountaineering Museum**, with a relief model of the Himalaya, dusty specimens of Himalayan fauna and more historic mountaineering equipment.

On a nearby hilltop, where Tenzing Norgay was cremated, stands the **Tenzing Samadhi statue**. The intrepid mountaineer lived in Darjeeling for most of his life and was the director of the institute for many years.

Various mountaineering courses are offered here (see p148).

TIBETAN REFUGEE SELF-HELP CENTRE
Established in 1959, this **refugee centre** (Map p141; Lebong Cart Rd; ✆ dawn–dusk Mon-Sat) comprises a home for the aged, school, orphanage, clinic, **gompa** and **craft workshops** that produce carpets, woodcarvings, leatherwork and woollen items. There's also an interesting **photographic exhibition** portraying the establishment and workings of the centre.

The refugees are welcoming, so wander through the workshops; the spinning wheels are a testament to their improvisational genius. The handicrafts are for sale in the **showroom** (✆ 2252552), which doesn't have as many knick-knacks as the souvenir shops in town, but the proceeds go straight back into the Tibetan community. See p151 for details regarding Tibetan rugs, and p317 if you're interested in volunteering.

Share jeeps from the Chowk Bazaar bus/jeep station run along Lebong Cart Rd and pass the turn-off to the centre (Rs 10, about 20 minutes). You can also walk here from Chowrasta along CR Das Rd. It's easy to get lost, so ask for directions along the way. A chartered taxi costs around Rs 200 return.

LLOYD BOTANICAL GARDENS

These pleasant **gardens** (Map p142; ☎ 2252358; admission free; ☺ 8am-4.30pm) contain an impressive collection of Himalayan plants, most famously orchids and rhododendrons, as well as temperate trees from around the world. It's a lovely respite from the bustle of central Darjeeling. Look for the magnificent wisterias planted in 1878, now escaping from their glasshouse. Follow the signs along Lochnager Rd from the Chowk Bazaar bus/jeep station. A map and guide (Rs 5) is available from the park office.

OTHER ATTRACTIONS

The most conspicuous Hindu temple in Darjeeling, **Dhirdham Mandir** (Map p142), is a replica of the famous Pashupatinath Temple in Kathmandu. It's easy to find – just below the Darjeeling train station. There's a great view over Darjeeling from its grounds.

If you're travelling on the Toy Train, or walking back from Tiger Hill, look out for the scenic and sobering **Gorkha war memorial** (Map p141; admission Rs 5; ☺ dawn-dusk) where the train makes its famous **Batasia Loop**.

The **Bengal Natural History Museum** (Map p142; Bishop Eric Benjamin Rd; adult/child Rs 5/2; ☺ 10am-4pm), established in 1903, houses a mildewed and moth-eaten collection of Himalayan and Bengali species – try not to laugh at the stuffed crocodile. The museum is hidden away in a compound just off Bishop Eric Benjamin Rd.

WHITE-WATER RAFTING

Darjeeling is the easiest place to organise white-water rafting trips along the Rangeet and Teesta Rivers. Rafting trips leave from Teesta Bazaar (p158), along the road to Kalimpong. The rapids are graded from Grade II to Grade IV, and the best times for rafting are September to November and March to June.

The **DGHC** (Map p142; ☎ 2255351; Jawahar Rd West; ☺ 9am-7pm daily high season, 10am-4.30pm Mon-Sat, 10am-1pm Sun low season; moderate rapids 11/18/25km trip Rs 350/450/700, challenging rapids Rs 500/600/800) runs trips for minimums of four to six people and can also arrange transport to Teesta Bazaar (Rs 350) and accommodation at its Chitrey Wayside Inn (p158). Private companies, such as **Samsara Tours, Travels & Treks** (Map p142; ☎ 2252874; samsara1@sancharnet.in; Laden La Rd; tours Rs 1200-1700), offer similar routes, for a minimum of four people, and its prices include lunch and transport.

OTHER ACTIVITIES

The **Darjeeling Gymkhana Club** (Map p141; ☎ 2254341; Jawahar Rd West; membership per day/week Rs 50/250)

DARJEELING, EVEREST & TENZING

There's a statue in Siliguri and one in Darjeeling, and the road linking the two is named after him. Tenzing Norgay looms large in Darjeeling, where his son, Jamling, himself an Everest summitteer, lives in the family house from where he leads mountaineering and trekking expeditions.

Tenzing Norgay was just 18 years old in 1932 when he left his village of Thame, in the Khumbu region of Nepal, to seek adventure and income with the new trend: European-led mountaineering expeditions. Lining up for work with other hopeful sherpas at the Planters' Club in Darjeeling each season, Tenzing would eventually get his first tilt at Everest with Eric Shipton in 1935. These early expeditions approached Everest from the north (Tibet), after weeks of walking from Darjeeling via Kalimpong, Jelepla and Tibet's Chumbi Valley.

After several attempts on Everest and numerous successful climbs on other peaks over the next two decades, Tenzing Norgay joined John Hunt's British Everest expedition of 1953 and made history with the rangy bee keeper from New Zealand, Edmund Hillary. Tenzing became a world figure much in demand, but remained in Darjeeling to be with his family and to develop the Himalayan Mountaineering Institute.

British, Nepali and Indian nationalism ensured a spectacular and occasionally contentious celebration of the great climb. The 'who reached there first?' question was quickly elevated from innocent curiosity to nationalist politics by a sensationalist media. It is still the question at the top of the list when Jamling gives motivational speeches in the West. As detailed in *Touching My Father's Soul*, Jamling admits also asking this of his father, mentor and inspiration, 12 months prior to Tenzing's death. As for Jamling's own response to this impertinent question under a typically wet and grey Darjeeling sky: 'It doesn't matter, the peak is a dome that can support several climbers simultaneously.'

offers tennis, squash, badminton, roller-skating and table tennis; call to check the schedules.

Be an aristocrat for the day and join the **Planters' Club Darjeeling** (Map p142; ☎ 2254348; per day Rs 100). Lounge in style or rack them up in the billiards room (Rs 100 per person per hour) and pray the power doesn't cut out.

From Chowrasta, children can take a **pony ride** around Observatory Hill for Rs 40, or through tea estates to visit a monastery for Rs 80 per hour.

Courses

LANGUAGE
Beginner and advanced lessons in written and spoken Tibetan are offered at the **Manjushree Centre of Tibetan Culture** (Map p142; ☎ 2256714; www .manjushree-culture.org; 12 Ghandi Rd; 3-/6-/9-month courses Rs 9030/13,760/18,490 plus Rs 1350 registration; ⏲ Mar-Dec). It also supplies discounted guesthouse accommodation for students.

MOUNTAINEERING
The **Himalayan Mountaineering Institute** (p146) runs 15-day adventure courses (US$325), including climbing, jungle survival and canoeing, and 28-day basic and advanced mountaineering courses (US$650), between March and December. Foreigners should apply directly to the centre at least three months in advance.

Tenzing Norgay Climbing Club (Map p141; ☎ 2258045; DB Giri Rd; per day Rs 300) runs indoor/outdoor climbing courses using modern equipment and techniques.

COOKING
The owner at **Hot Stimulating Café** (Map p141; Jawahar Rd West; lessons Rs 600) offers informal *momo*-making lessons.

Tours
During the high season the DGHC and other travel agencies offer a variety of tours around Darjeeling. The half-day 'seven-point tour' (Rs 75 per person) includes the zoo, Himalayan Mountaineering Institute, Tibetan Refugee Self-Help Centre and several viewpoints. See p144 for Tiger Hill sunrise-tour information.

Taxis can be hired for custom tours for around Rs 600 per half-day.

Sleeping
Darjeeling has an ever-increasing number of hotels crowding the ridge and only a small selection is mentioned here. Prices given are for the high season (October to early December and mid-March to June), when it is wise to book ahead. In the low season prices can drop by 50%; however, feel free to negotiate at any time. Most midrange hotels occupy the centre of town, while the top-end choices opt for the leafy havens north of Chowrasta. The nicest budget options stand atop the ridge, and reward travellers with vistas and exercise.

BUDGET
All choices below have private bathrooms and free hot water (either geyser or bucket), unless stated otherwise. Most hotels have both squat and sit-down flush toilets available.

Triveni Guest House (Map p141; ☎ 2253878; Dr Zakir Hussain Rd; dm Rs 60, s with shared bathroom Rs 80, d Rs 160-200) This is a simple lodge – the dorm has only three beds – but it's popular and very friendly. Rooms are spartan but clean and some have nice views, as does the inexpensive restaurant. Bucket hot water is Rs 10.

Hotel Long Island (Map p142; ☎ 2252043; Dr Zakir Hussain Rd; s Rs 150, d Rs 200-250) A basic option with simple rooms that have views. Toilets are attached but hot-water showers are shared.

Hotel Aliment (Map p141; ☎ 2255068; aliment web@sify.com; Dr Zakir Hussain Rd; d Rs 250-400; 💻) A travellers favourite with good food (and cold beer), a library, rooftop patio, helpful owners and cosy wood-lined rooms. The upstairs rooms have a TV and valley views. All rooms have geysers, but they only operate for 1½ hours in the evening.

Andy's (Map p142; ☎ 2253125; Dr Zakir Hussain Rd; s/d from Rs 250/300) This simple, spotless, stone-walled place is a friendly option that has airy, carpeted rooms and a rooftop terrace with a great view. It asks for a 50% payment upfront.

Hotel Pagoda (Map p142; ☎ 2253498; Upper Beechwood Rd; d Rs 250, with shared bathroom Rs 200) Though lacking views, this is a conveniently located budget option offering small, clean rooms. It's tucked away on an alley off some steps above the post office on Laden La Rd.

Maple Tourist Lodge (Map p142; ☎ 2252813; Old Kuchery Rd; s/d Rs 360/475, with shared bathroom Rs 240/315) This option is housed in an old colonial house below Observatory Hill. Ground-floor rooms are a bit damp, though others are better. Room and meal packages are available.

MIDRANGE
The following all have TV and private bathrooms with geysers, unless stated otherwise.

Hotel Alice Villa (Map p142; ☎ 2254181; hotelalice villa@yahoo.com; 41 HD Lama Rd; d from Rs 700) This small hotel occupies a charming old bungalow close to Chowrasta and provides inexpensive heritage accommodation. The rooms are spacious and well cared for with plenty of character and cosy open fireplaces.

Pineridge Hotel (Map p142; ☎ 2254074; pineridge hotel@yahoo.com; Nehru Rd; s/d from Rs 750/850) Pity the Pineridge. So much restoration potential and a great location, but the reality is drafty, dilapidated standard rooms and only slightly better deluxe rooms. There's still some Raj charm, and with a bucket of coal (Rs 150) glowing in the fireplace maybe you can forget the broken window.

Dekeling Hotel (Map p142; ☎ 2254159; www.dekeling .com; Clubside; d Rs 850-1050) A warm, friendly welcome is guaranteed at this spotless, Tibetan-run hotel. Most of the comfortable rooms have views (and are priced accordingly) and there are great, cosy, common areas and a scenic loft. Breakfast (Rs 250) is served upstairs, while the hotel's excellent restaurant, Dekevas (p150), is on the ground floor. For those looking for a quiet getaway, talk to the owners about their out-of-town Hawk's Nest Resort.

Bellevue Hotel (Map p142; ☎ 2254075; www.darjeeling -bellevuehotel.com; Chowrasta; d Rs 900-1500) This rambling complex comprises a variety of wood-panelled rooms. Most are spacious with grass-mat floors, a wood-burning *bukhari* (heater) and a conspicuously absent TV. The affable staff, communal breakfast/lounge area and the outlook over Chowrasta towards Khangchendzonga all make this a popular choice.

Main Olde Bellevue Hotel (Map p142; ☎ 2254178; www.darjeelinghotel.com; Nehru Rd; d Rs 1000-1500) This welcoming hotel comprises two buildings, the lower one more modern, with a huge lounge and terrace, but ordinary rooms, and the other a Raj place too derelict to be called charming and too rustic to be comfortable, but apparently due for renovation.

Hotel Seven Seventeen (Map p142; ☎ 2252017; www .hotel717.com; 26 HD Lama Rd; s/d/tr Rs 1000/1300/1600) An inviting Tibetan-themed place with exceptionally friendly service and clean, though small, rooms. Don't confuse it with the other, older Hotel Seven Seventeen, which is up the street and closer to the Chowk Bazaar bus/jeep station.

Classic Guesthouse (Map p142; ☎ 2257025; rajn_das sic@hotmail.com; CR Das Rd; d Rs 1200) This small hotel, just below Chowrasta, has just five rooms all boasting valley views and vertigo-inducing balconies. The hosts are friendly and an electric heater (in winter) makes for a cosy stay.

Hotel Shangrila (Map p142; ☎ 2254149; 5 Nehru Rd; d Rs 1500) Cute, clean and full of charm describes this very appealing boutique hotel and restaurant on the Mall. There are only four double rooms, each with bay windows, double beds, fireplaces and views.

Other recommendations:

Crystal Palace Hotel (Map p142; ☎ 2253317; 29/30 HD Lama Rd; s/d Rs 500/600) Clean, almost budget category, and convenient to bus station.

Hotel Valentino (Map p142; ☎ 2252228; Rockville Rd; d incl breakfast Rs 800-1000) Has a restaurant and bar downstairs.

Hotel Polynia (Map p142; ☎ 2254127; fax 2254129; 12/1 DB Thapa Rd; d from Rs 1500) Some large rooms with views over town.

TOP END

These hotels offer rooms on the so-called 'American Plan', with breakfast, lunch and dinner included; taxes and service charges usually add 15% to 20% to the bill.

ourpick Elgin (Map p142; ☎ 2257226; elgin@elgin hotels.com; HD Lama Rd; s/d Rs 4100/4400) This delightful, grand yet friendly heritage hotel is brimming with colonial ambience. The spacious bedrooms combine enough originality to keep them interesting and enough renovation to ensure comfort. Most of the elegantly furnished rooms have separate sitting areas, open fireplaces and marble bathrooms. The restaurant is pukka and the lovely gardens are the perfect place to relax and enjoy high tea.

Mayfair Hill Resort (Map p142; ☎ 2256376; www .mayfairhotels.com; Jawahar Rd West; s/d from Rs 5000/6000) Originally a maharaja's summer palace, and soon to be renamed Mayfair Darjeeling, this plush and genteel choice sits among lovingly manicured gardens and sculptures near the Raj Bhavan. Soft carpets, sumptuous leather, coal fires and fine art add to the warm welcome. When you have finished watching DVDs in your palatial room, head to the Library Bar or take a brisk shuffle around Observatory Hill.

Windamere Hotel (Map p142; ☎ 2254041; www.win damerehotel.com; Jawahar Rd West; s/d from Rs 5200/6600) This rambling relic of the Raj on Observatory Hill attracts an eclectic crowd, and though its rooms are getting a little tired, they are comfortable, clean and spacious. One for the true Raj aficionado – the gins are pink, the liveried staff are genuinely friendly and you won't leave hungry.

WEST BENGAL

Other recommendations:

Fortune Resort Central (Map p142; ☎ 2258721; www.fortuneparkhotels.com; 12/1 DB Thapa Rd; s/d incl taxes Rs 4628/5550) Comprising the erstwhile Hotel Central. Century-old polished wood, thick rugs, open fires and room to swing two cats.

Eating

Darjeeling has a great choice of restaurants dishing up Indian, Chinese, Tibetan and some good international fare, but the availability of ingredients is much more seasonal than found on the plains. Note that most restaurants close their doors by 8pm or 9pm.

Hot Stimulating Café (Map p141; Jawahar Rd West; meals Rs 20-40) This tiny café, on the road to the zoo, offers beautiful views and serves up simple, cheap meals and chai.

Frank Ross Café (Map p142; ☎ 2258194; Nehru Rd; mains Rs 20-105) This option is strictly vegetarian and offers a global menu, including pizzas, burgers, South Indian snacks, and even enchiladas, tacos and nachos.

Hotel Lunar (Map p142; Ghandi Rd, mains Rs 25-75) Lunar is one of the best vegetarian restaurants in Darjeeling where you also can enjoy a great view and wonderful service. It's squeezed beneath Hotel Dekeling and above Dekevas.

Hotel Chanakya (Map p142; ☎ 2257495; DB Thapa Rd; mains Rs 30-70) An authentic Bengali diner where you can fill up with veg and nonveg thalis and be confident the chilli isn't toned down for Western tastes.

Kunga Restaurant (Map p142; ☎ 2253971; 51 Ghandi Rd, mains Rs 35-70) Kunga's Tibetan cuisine is tasteful simplicity. Its steamed *momos* are legendary as are its *thugpas* (noodle soups; *gyathuk*, *thenthuk* and *bhagthuk*). For a filling breakfast, try its muesli and fruit curd.

Park Restaurant (Map p142; ☎ 2255270; Laden La Rd; mains Rs 30-140) The Park is popular with local tourists and fills up quickly. Savour North Indian curries or select from the fish- and chicken-dominated Thai Lemon Grass menu – all satisfactorily executed. There's no alcohol licence but it's worth asking for a beer.

La Casse Croute (Map p142; ☎ 2257594; HD Lama Rd; mains Rs 35-120) A one-table pizza joint that satisfies those looking for a change of taste: excellent pizzas, paninis, salads and sandwiches. Also serves breakfast, pancakes and good coffee.

Dekevas Restaurant (Map p142; ☎ 2254159; mains Rs 40-80) Cosy Dekevas is known for great Tibetan fare of *momos* and noodle soups, and pizzas, but not legroom.

our pick **Glenary's** (Map p142; Nehru Rd; dishes Rs 50-120; ⏱ 11.30am-9pm) This elegant restaurant atop the famous bakery and café (see below) delights patrons with good food, grand views, cold beer and superior service. The continental sizzlers (veg and nonveg), Chinese dishes, curries and tandoori specials are excellent, though we'd like to see a greater selection of Indian cuisine. The chicken *rashmi kebab* (chicken marinated in spiced yogurt before being baked tandoori style) is divine.

SELF-CATERING

Frank Ross Pharmacy (Map p142; ☎ 2258194; Nehru Rd) As well as pharmaceuticals you can stock up on general groceries and imported foods, such as excellent Druk marmalade from Bhutan to replace the fluorescent substance that your hotel provides.

Drinking

Where in the world is a better place to sip a cup of Darjeeling tea? If a cool pint is your idea of drinking, there are a couple of good choices.

TEA

Glenary's (Map p142; Nehru Rd; small pot Rs 22; ⏱ 7.30am-8pm, till 9pm in high season) Below the restaurant, this café is home to massive windows and grand views – order your tea, select a cake, grab your book and sink into some wicker.

Goodricke, the House of Tea (Map p142; Nehru Rd) Sit and sip up to nine varieties of brewed tea from local estates – cup and cookies Rs 20 – before purchasing packaged tea.

Elgin (Map p142; ☎ 2257226; HD Lama Rd; high tea Rs 150; ⏱ 4.30-5pm) Take high tea with cakes, sandwiches and shortbread in the sunroom or out in the gardens.

Windamere Hotel (Map p142; ☎ 2254041; Jawahar Rd West; high tea Rs 240; ⏱ 4.30-6pm) High tea with biscuits and all.

BARS

Joey's Pub (Map p142; SM Das Rd; beer Rs 80; ⏱ 1-10pm) This friendly pub, near the post office, is the most atmospheric choice and it's also a great place to meet other travellers. It has European footy on TV, warm rum and cold beer.

Buzz (Map p142; ⏱ 6-10.30pm) This kitsch Hollywood bar is in the basement at Glenary's. It has live bands Saturday and Sunday at 6.30pm.

Also recommended:

Windamere Hotel (Map p142; ☎ 2254041; Jawahar Rd West; ⏱ 1-8pm) Sofas, slippers, pink gin and cold beer.

Entertainment

Inox Theatre (Map p142; ☎ 2257226; www.inoxmovies
.com; Rink Mall, cnr Laden La & SM Das Rds; tickets Rs 60-130)
Three cinemas and several classes of seating.

Shopping

DARJEELING TEA

This is some of the finest tea in the world and
is a very popular and portable souvenir. The
best supplier here, with over 50 varieties, is
Nathmull's Tea Rooms (Map p142; www.nathmulltea.com;
Laden La Rd). Expect to pay Rs 50 per 100g for a
decent tea and up to Rs 1000 per 100g for the
finest brews. Try before you buy at **Goodricke,
The House of Tea** (Map p142; Nehru Rd).

Cheaper tea is available in Chowk Bazaar,
but the packaging isn't particularly sturdy.
Avoid the tea in fancy boxes, because it's usually blended and packaged in Kolkata.

TIBETAN CARPETS

Tibetan Refugee Self-Help Centre (Map p141; Lebong Cart
Rd; ☼ dawn-dusk Mon-Sat) Gorgeous carpets made
to order and shipped to your home address.
Hayden Hall (Map p142; ☎ 2253228; Laden La Rd; ☼ 9am-
6pm Mon-Sat) Closer to Chowrasta, this place sells
carpets as part of its charitable work (Rs 3600
to 4000 for a 3ft x 6ft carpet).

TREKKING GEAR

The **Trekking Shop** (Map p141; Singalila Market, Nehru Rd)
sells satisfactory Nepali counterfeit clothing,
and waterproofs and jackets, as well as Chinese-
and Russian-made boots (larger sizes are rare).

OTHER SOUVENIRS

There are numerous souvenir shops at Chowrasta and along Gandhi and Nehru Rds sell-

---

> **PERMITS FOR SIKKIM**
>
> Forms for Sikkim permits (p162) are avail-
> able at the **Office of the District Magistrate**
> (Map p142; ☎ 2254233; Hill Cart Rd; ☼ 11am-
> 1pm & 2.30-4pm Mon-Fri), downhill from the
> Chowk Bazaar bus/jeep station. They must
> be filled out and stamped here, and then
> taken to the **Foreigners' Regional Registra-
> tion Office** (Map p142; ☎ 2254278; Laden La
> Rd; ☼ 9.30am-5pm), which also stamps your
> form. Then go back to the magistrate's of-
> fice, which issues the permit while you wait.
> The whole process takes about 1½ hours
> and there's no fee – bring your passport.

---

ing Nepali woodcarvings (including masks),
thangkas (Tibetan cloth paintings), religious
objects and jewellery.

Das Studios (Map p142; ☎ 2254004; Nehru Rd;
☼ 9am-6pm Mon-Sat) Sells photographic prints
of Khangchendzonga and other places around
Darjeeling.

Chowk Bazaar is a crowded, noisy and fascinating place to buy tea, spices and incense.
There are several so-called Buddha shops at
Chowk Bazaar and on NB Singh Rd, selling
prayer flags, *thangkas* and prayer wheels.

Getting There & Away

AIR

The nearest airport is 90km away at Bagdogra,
about 12km from Siliguri. See p136 for details
about flights to/from Bagdogra.

Indian Airlines (Map p142; ☎ 2254230; ☼ 10am-5pm
Mon-Sat) is at Chowrasta. **Clubside Tours & Travels**
(Map p142; ☎ 2254646; clubside@satyam.net.in; JP Sharma
Rd; ☼ 8.30am-6pm) and **Pineridge Travels** (Map p142;
☎ 2253912; pineridge@dte.vsnl.net.in; ☼ 10am-5pm Mon-
Sat) are Jet Airways agents.

BUS

From the Chowk Bazaar bus/jeep station (Map
p142), regular buses depart for Mirik (Rs 40,
three hours) and Siliguri (Rs 60, three hours).
Tickets can be bought from the ground-floor
counter at the Old Super Market Complex
(Map p142) that backs on to the station.

Kasturi Tours & Travels (Map p142; ☎ 2254430; Old
Super Market Complex; ☼ 8am-7pm) and **Diamond Treks,
Tours & Travels** (Map p142; ☎ 2258961; Old Super Mar-
ket Complex; ☼ 8am-7pm) can book 'luxury' buses
from Siliguri to destinations such as Kolkata
(Rs 380, 12 hours). **Samsara Tours, Travels & Treks**
(Map p142; ☎ 2257194; samsara1@sancharnet.in; Laden La
Rd) offers similar services. These tickets don't
include transfers to Siliguri.

JEEP & TAXI

Numerous share jeeps and taxis leave the
crowded south end of the Chowk Bazaar bus/
jeep station for Siliguri (Rs 80, 2½ hours) and
Kurseong (Rs 40, 1½ hours). Jeeps leave for
Mirik (Rs 50, 2½ hours) about every 1½ hours.
Ticket offices on the ground floor of the Old
Super Market Complex sell advance tickets for
the frequent jeeps to Kalimpong (Rs 90, two
hours) and Gangtok (Rs 130, four hours).

At the northern end of the station, three to
four jeeps a day leave for Jorenthang (Rs 80,
two hours), where it's easy to get a connection

to anywhere in northern or West Sikkim. You must already have a permit to enter Sikkim (see p151) via this route.

Darjeeling Transport Corporation (Map p142; ☎ 9832081338, 2258967; Laden La Rd) has jeeps to Gangtok (share/charter Rs 130/1300, four hours, share jeeps depart 8.30am and 1pm) and Siliguri (share/charter Rs 80/800, 2½ hours, hourly).

To New Jalpaiguri or Bagdogra, get a connection in Siliguri, or charter a jeep or taxi from Darjeeling (Rs 1000).

TRAIN

The nearest major train station is at New Jalpaiguri (NJP), near Siliguri. Tickets can be bought for major services out of NJP at the Darjeeling train station's **computerised reservations counter** (Map p142; ☎ 2252555; ⊙ 8am-2pm).

Darjeeling Himalayan Railway

The diesel toy train leaves Darjeeling at 9.15am for NJP (2nd/1st class Rs 45/247, seven hours), stopping at Ghoom (Rs 20/96, 50 minutes), Kurseong (Rs 26/144, three hours) and Siliguri (Rs 38/217, 6½ hours). It's an exhausting haul to NJP, so if you simply want to experience the train, take the steam train to/from Kurseong or the joy ride (p145).

TO/FROM NEPAL

Foreigners can only cross the border into Nepal at Kakarbhitta/Panitanki (not at Pasupati).

Diamond Treks, Tours & Travels (Map p142; ☎ 2258961; Old Super Market Complex) and **Kasturi Tours & Travels** (Map p142; ☎ 225 4430; Old Super Market Complex) sell tickets for buses from Darjeeling to Kathmandu (Rs 600). These are not direct buses and involve transfers in Siliguri and at the border – leaving a lot of room for problems. However, it's not difficult to do this yourself and you'll save some money. See p138 for Siliguri–Panitanki transport, as well as border and Nepali bus details.

Getting Around

Share jeeps to anywhere north of the city centre, eg North Point (Rs 5), leave from the northern end of the Chowk Bazaar bus/jeep station. To Ghoom, get a share jeep (Rs 12) from the Hill Cart Rd jeep stand at Chowk Bazaar (Map p142).

There are several taxi stands around town, but rates are absurd for short hops. You can hire a porter to carry your bags up to Chowrasta from Chowk Bazaar for around Rs 50.

TREKKING AROUND DARJEELING

A number of rewarding and picturesque treks are accessible from Darjeeling. October and November's clear skies and warm temperatures make it an ideal time to trek, as do the long days and rhododendron blooms of May and early June. The **DGHC** (Map p142; ☎ 2255351; Jawahar Rd West; ⊙ 9am-7pm daily high season, 10am-4.30pm Mon-Sat, 10am-1pm Sun low season) produces the excellent *Himalayan Treks* leaflet, which includes a map and descriptions of major trekking routes.

Most popular is the **Singalila Ridge Trek** from Sandakphu to Phalut; it passes through scenic **Singalila National Park** (admission Rs 100, camera fee Rs 50) and offers Himalayan views. Guides (about Rs 350 per day) are mandatory and can be hired privately through travel agencies or at the trek's starting point in Mana Bhanjang, 26km from Darjeeling. Mana Bhanjang is served by morning buses from Darjeeling's Chowk Bazaar bus/jeep station (Rs 20, two hours). The usual trekking itinerary is described on below.

From Rimbik, there are connecting morning buses to Darjeeling (Rs 80, five hours). If you don't have five days, there are short cuts available at Sandakphu and Sabarkum. There are basic **trekkers' huts** (dm/d/tr Rs 100/400/500) at Mana Bhanjang, Tonglu, Garibas, Sandakphu, Phalut, Rammam, Srikhola and Rimbik – book through **Glenary's** (Map p142; Nehru Rd; ⊙ 11.30am-9pm). You can organise meals at the huts for Rs 20 to 45. Other (better maintained) private accommodation options are available for similar prices along the route. All-inclusive guided treks on this route, including porters, meals and accommodation, are offered by Darjeeling travel agencies (p144) for Rs 1200 to 2000 per day depending on the level of service.

SINGALILA RIDGE TREK		
Day	**Route**	**Distance (km)**
1	Mana Bhanjang (2130m) to Tonglu (3100m) via Meghma Gompa	14
2	Tonglu to Sandakphu (3636m) via Kalipokhri & Garibas	17
3	Sandakphu to Phalut (3600m) via Sabarkum	17
4	Phalut to Rammam (2530m) via Gorkey	16
5	Rammam to Rimbik (2290m) via Srikhola	19

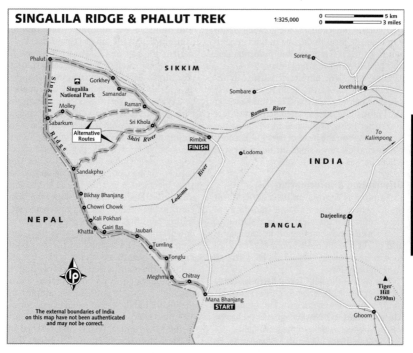

SINGALILA RIDGE & PHALUT TREK

1:325,000

WEST BENGAL

Nearer to Kalimpong is the great **Rochela Trek**, which gives you a taste of the stunning Samthar Plateau (p159). You can trek for four to eight days through dense forests, visiting remote villages and crossing a pass at 3000m. Note that it takes four days, with camping, to reach the highpoint of Rochela from Kalimpong.

Recommended trekking agencies:

DGHC Tourist Reception Centre (Darjeeling, p144; Kalimpong, p154) Charges about Rs 2000 per day (all-inclusive) for Singalila Ridge and organises guides/porters (Rs 350 per day) for Rochela.

Gurudongma Tours & Travels (☎ 255204; www .gurudongma.com; Hilltop, Rinkingpong Rd, Kalimpong) Offering customised all-inclusive treks in this region, with knowledgeable guides and accommodation.

Samsara Tours, Travels & Treks (Map p142; ☎ 2252874; samsara1@sancharnet.in; Laden La Rd) Experienced agency offering reasonably priced rafting and trekking trips.

Tenzing Norgay Adventures (Map p141; ☎ 2253718; www.tenzing-norgay.com; DB Giri Rd) Professional outfit offering treks in Darjeeling, Sikkim, Tibet and Bhutan.

Trek Mate (Map p142; ☎ 2256611; chagpori@satyam .net.in; Nehru Rd) Readers have recommended the treks (Rs 1400 per person per day), while the rental gear is clean and well maintained.

If you need clothing or gear (and you should carry your own sleeping bag even if relying on huts), it can be rented from Trek Mate (sleeping bag Rs 30, down jacket Rs 20, boots Rs 30, rain gear Rs 15 per day). The Trekking Shop (p151) stocks clothing and boots. The DGHC in Kalimpong has a few tents for rent.

KALIMPONG
☎ 03552 / pop 42,980 / elev 1250m

This bustling bazaar town sprawls along a ridge overlooking the roaring Teesta River and within sight of Mt Khangchendzonga. Kalimpong lacks Darjeeling's crowds and commercialism, yet it boasts Himalayan views, tranquil retreats, Buddha shops, temples and churches, and a fascinating nursery industry.

Kalimpong's early development as a trading centre focused on the wool trade with Tibet, across the Jelepla Pass. Like Darjeeling, Kalimpong once belonged to the chogyals of Sikkim, but it fell into the hands of the Bhutanese in the 18th century and later passed to the British, before becoming part of

India at Independence. Scottish missionaries, particularly the Jesuits, made great efforts to win over the local Buddhists in the late 19th century and Dr Graham's famous orphanage and school is still running today.

The Gorkhaland movement is active in Kalimpong, so it's worth checking the security situation before you arrive. The Gurkha leader CK Pradhan was assassinated here in October 2002 after being implicated in an assassination attempt on the head of the GNLF, and is commemorated by a small shrine on the spot where he was gunned down.

Orientation & Information

Kalimpong is centred on its chaotic Motor Stand, where people mill and transport options come and go. Nearby are restaurants, cheap hotels and shopping, while most sights and quality accommodation are a few kilometres from town, accessed via DB Giri and Rinkingpong Rds.

The staff at the **DGHC Tourist Reception Centre** (☎ 257992; DB Giri Rd; ◷ 9.30am-5pm) are very helpful, as is the private website www.kalimpong.org. The **post office** (☎ 255990; Rinkingpong Rd; ◷ 9am-5pm Mon-Fri, till 4pm Sat) is next to the town hall.

The **Central Bank** (SDB Giri Rd; ◷ 10am-3pm Mon-Fri, till noon Sat) and **Soni Emporium** (☎ 255030; DB Giri Rd; ◷ 8am-8pm) exchange various currencies and travellers cheques for a small commission. **Net Hut** (per hr Rs 35; ◷ 9am-8pm), near the Motor Stand, is a tight squeeze but the best internet option.

There is nowhere in Kalimpong to obtain permits for Sikkim, but free 15-day permits are available at the border at Rangpo (see p162). You need to present three passport photos.

Sights
GOMPAS

Built in 1926, the **Tharpa Choling Gompa**, off KD Pradhan Rd, contains statues of the Bhaisajya, Sakyamuni and Maitreya Buddhas (past, present and future, respectively). Garuda protects each Buddha from above, his mouth devouring hatred and anger (the snake), while his feet hold down symbols of ignorance and worldly attachment. Interestingly, the controversial Dorje Shugden and other wrathful deities are kept in a locked room adjacent to the gompa. The small room is painted with images of flayed animals and humans. The controversy over the Dalai Lama's edict to not worship Shugden has split the local Tibetan community. It's a 30-minute walk (uphill) from town, past the top of Tripai Rd.

Near the top of RC Mintri Rd, past JP Lodge, is the ancient **Thongsa Gompa** (Bhutanese Monastery). The monastery was founded in 1692, but the present building, surrounded by 219 small prayer wheels, was built in the 19th century after the Gurkhas rampaged across Sikkim. Its old murals downstairs are fading, and upstairs you will find bright new frescoes.

Kalimpong's largest monastery, Zong Dog Palri Fo-Brang Gompa, aka **Durpin Gompa**, sits atop spectacular Durpin Hill (1372m) and was consecrated after its opening by the Dalai Lama in 1976. There are impressive wall and ceiling paintings in the main prayer room downstairs (photography is permitted), and interesting 3-D mandalas on the 2nd floor. Primarily Nyingpa, the monastery is a compilation of the many different sects of refugees who cooperated in its construction. From the highest storey you can see Siliguri on the plains and the top of Khangchendzonga. The monastery is located about 5km south of the town centre, and is best reached by chartered jeep (Rs 80 return). The **Jelepla Viewpoint**, about 300m below the gompa, looks out to the Himalaya and over the Relli and Teesta Rivers.

ST TERESA'S CHURCH

A fascinating missionary church built in 1929 by Swiss Jesuits and designed to gain acceptance from the locals, St Teresa's construction mimics a Bhutanese gompa. The carved apostles look like Buddhist monks, and the carvings on the doors resemble *tashi tagye*, the eight auspicious symbols of Himalayan Buddhism. The church is found off 9th Mile Rd, about 2km from town. Take a taxi or walk and ask for directions.

MANGAL DHAM

This ungainly modern **temple** (Relli Rd; ◷ 6am-7pm) is sacred to Krishna. In its ballroomlike prayer hall there are eight vibrant, life-size dioramas from the Krishna Leela. The temple is dedicated to Guruji Shri Mangaldasji, who's commemorated in a shrine below the prayer hall. The temple is about 500m downhill from Thongsa Gompa, or you can walk from the centre along Relli Rd and turn left by the Roman Catholic church.

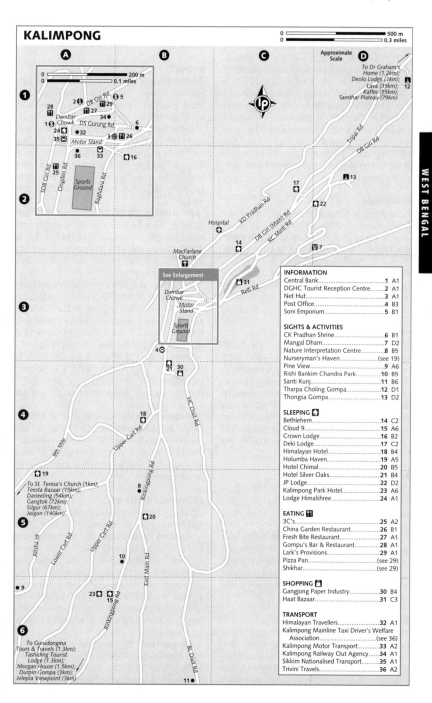

KALIMPONG

WEST BENGAL

WEST BENGAL

DR GRAHAM'S HOME

This working **orphanage and school** was built in 1900 by Dr JA Graham, a Scottish missionary, to educate the children of tea-estate workers, and now has more than 1300 students. There's a small **museum** (admission free; ☿ 9am-3.30pm Mon-Fri) that commemorates the founder and his wife Katherine. The 1925 **chapel** above the school features fine stained-glass windows. The gate is 4km up the steep KD Pradhan Rd and the buildings are 650m from there. Many people charter a taxi to get here (Rs 80) and then walk back to town.

NURSERIES

Kalimpong is a major flower exporter and produces about 80% of India's gladioli, as well as many orchid varieties. Visit **Nurseryman's Haven** (☎ 256936; 9th Mile) to have a look at orchids; **Santi Kunj** (BL Dixit Rd; ☿ 8.30am-noon & 1.30-4pm Sun-Fri) to see anthuriums and the bird of paradise flower; and **Pine View** (www.pineviewcactus.com; Atisha Rd; admission Rs 5) to gaze at its eminently photographable cactus collection.

OTHER ATTRACTIONS

The **Nature Interpretation Centre** (Rinkingpong Rd; admission free; ☿ 10.30am-4pm Fri-Wed) has what must be the world's most educational badminton court. Around the court are a number of well-organised dioramas depicting the effects of human activity on the environment. It's an easy walk from the town centre. About 450m further up the hill is the small but serene **Rishi Bankim Chandra Park** (also known as Kalimpong Park).

Activities

The **DGHC Tourist Reception Centre** (☎ 257992; DB Giri Rd; ☿ 9.30am-5pm) can arrange treks (see p152) and the same rafting trips as the Darjeeling DGHC (see p147).

Gurudongma Tours & Travels (☎ 255204; www.gurudongma.com; Hilltop, Rinkingpong Rd) organises interesting tours, which include trekking, rafting, mountain biking, bird-watching and fishing, around Kalimpong, Darjeeling and Sikkim.

Sleeping

The most memorable (and expensive) places to stay are well outside Kalimpong's busy core. You'll find cheaper options within walking distance of the Motor Stand. High-season rates (October to early December and mid-March to early June) are given below; prices can drop by 50% in the low season.

BUDGET

All hotels have private bathrooms and free bucket hot water, unless specified otherwise. Most give you the option of sit-down flush or squat toilets.

Lodge Himalshree (☎ 255070; Ongden Rd; s/d with shared bathroom Rs 100/150) This is a friendly but very basic little place located on the top floor of a tall building right in the busiest part of town. The stairs are steep and the rooms are plain and clean. Hot-water buckets cost Rs 10.

Hotel Chimal (☎ 255776; Rinkingpong Rd; s/d from Rs 250/350) Hotel Chimal is set in lovely terraced gardens about 1km south of the Motor Stand. The rooms with private bathroom are basic affairs, but very clean, and the hosts are friendly and helpful.

Deki Lodge (☎ 255095; www.geocities.com/dekilodge; Tripai Rd; s/d/tr Rs 250/550/900) This older-style, Tibetan-owned lodge is close to the Thongsa and Tharpa Choling monasteries and still handy to town. It's a friendly place, with a pleasant café and rooftop viewing area.

Crown Lodge (☎ 255846; off Baghdara Rd; s/d Rs 350/600) The large rooms with TV, private bathrooms with geyser, and some comfortable furnishings with character make the Crown Lodge a good choice.

JP Lodge (☎ 257457; www.jplodge.com; RC Mintri Rd; d Rs 650, with shared bathroom Rs 450) The hosts here are very friendly and the smallish rooms are clean and bright, and most have views. There's an interesting wood-lined attic with views to lounge about in.

MIDRANGE & TOP END

All places listed here have private bathrooms and running hot water; most also have TVs.

Tashiding Tourist Lodge (☎ 255929; Rinkingpong Rd; s Rs 400-750, d Rs 800-1000) Set in overgrown gardens, with the feel of an abandoned Raj summer cottage, this rustic stone lodge looks charming from the outside but is very neglected inside. Furnishings are rudimentary and the bathrooms are of questionable functionality. For this price it is advised to check your room first.

Morgan House (☎ 255384; Rinkingpong Rd; s Rs 500-1500, d Rs 1100-2000) This is the upscale version of the nearby Tashiding Tourist Lodge – both government-managed heritage properties –

and does not it show. Boasting a glorious setting and outward appearance, the uninterested staff and dog-eared rooms nevertheless disappoint.

Cloud 9 (☎ 259554; cloud9kpg@yahoo.com; Rinkingpong Rd; d Rs 700-800) A very friendly place, with wood-panelled rooms, a cosy TV lounge and a good restaurant and bar, serving Bhutanese, Tibetan and Chinese food, downstairs.

ourpick Holumba Haven (☎ 256936; www.holumba.com; 9th Mile; s/d from Rs 850/1050) This welcoming guesthouse is situated in a splendid orchid nursery, Nurseryman's Haven, just 1km out of town. The spotless rooms are arranged in cottages secreted around the lush landscaped garden and springwater is piped directly into the rooms. Some cottages have attached kitchens, but excellent home-style meals are available in the dining room. The owners are an open encyclopaedia on Kalimpong's history and attractions.

Kalimpong Park Hotel (☎ 255304; www.indiamart.com/kalimpongparkhotel; s/d from Rs 1300/1800) This hotel, located off Rinkingpong Rd, was the former home of the maharaja of Dinajpur and has oodles of Raj-era charm. Wicker chairs and flowers line the veranda, and there's a delightful bar and restaurant. The rooms in the new wing lack the charm of the old house.

Deolo Lodge (☎ 274452; Deolo Hill; d Rs 1500) Commanding outstanding views (when not lost in the cloud), this DGHC hotel sits atop Deolo Hill, high above and several kilometres from town. The spacious rooms are clean and the staff friendly; there's a multicuisine restaurant and ample clean mountain air.

Himalayan Hotel (☎ 254043; www.himalayanhotel.co.in; Upper Cart Rd; s/d Rs 1600/2500, with 3 meals Rs 2400/4100) This hotel was opened by the revered David MacDonald, an interpreter from Francis Younghusband's mission to Lhasa in 1904 and one of those who helped the 13th Dalai Lama escape Tibet in 1910. Now run by his grandson, the original rooms have loads of Raj appeal beneath high Himalayan-oak ceilings and the balcony is a great place to socialise or curl up with a book. The new suites mesh old-world charm with modern comfort; their terraces gaze upon Khangchendzonga.

Hotel Silver Oaks (☎ 255296; silveroaks@elginhotels.com; Rinkingpong Rd; s/d Rs 3800/4100) This Raj-era homestead has been delightfully renovated into a modern and very comfortable hotel.

The rooms here are spacious, beautifully furnished and offer grand views down the valley. The tariff includes all meals in the excellent restaurant and there is also a sociable bar.

Eating
RESTAURANTS
Besides the options below, most midrange and top-end hotels have quality restaurants.

Shikhar (☎ 255966; DB Giri Rd; mains Rs 8-20) This hugely popular vegetarian restaurant with Tibetan and Indian snacks and meals is tucked under the Pizza Pan restaurant. Ultra-cheap *momos* and filling chow mein are the most popular orders.

Fresh Bite Restaurant (☎ 274042; DB Giri Rd; mains Rs 30-60) A menu covering everything from miso soup to buff steak spaghetti draws in locals and travellers. The food is quite good and the owner has a country retreat, which he will no doubt mention. The restaurant is situated upstairs, located across from the DGHC.

China Garden Restaurant (☎ 257456; Lal Gulli; mains Rs 35-90) In the China Garden Hotel near the Motor Stand, this is Kalimpong's best Chinese restaurant. The authentic soups, noodles and the spicy ginger chicken attract aficionados, though several Indian curries have snuck onto the menu.

Gompu's Bar & Restaurant (☎ 257456; off SDB Giri Rd; mains Rs 40-90) Gompu's is famous for its massive *momos* (pork, chicken and veg), and has been pleasing locals and travellers with Tibetan, Bhutanese, Indian, Chinese and continental fare for ages. It's found within the hotel of the same name.

Pizza Pan (☎ 258650; DB Giri Rd; mains Rs 80-120) The 'acceptable pizzas for Kalimpong', as one local quipped, come in two sizes with a variety of veg and non-veg toppings, and are indeed acceptable, as is the coffee.

QUICK EATS
Kalimpong cheese has been produced in Kalimpong since the Jesuits established a dairy here in the 19th century. Kalimpong lollipops share a history with the cheese; they are made at the dairy from milk, sugar and butter.

Lark's Provisions (DB Giri Rd) The best place to pick up Kalimpong cheese (per kg Rs 150) and a packet of Kalimpong lollipops (Rs 25). Also sells groceries and crackers.

WEST BENGAL

3C's (SDB Giri Rd; cakes & snacks Rs 5-30) A popular bakery and restaurant offering various pastries and cakes.

Shopping

As you wander around you will notice lots of Buddha shops. These are wholesale shops selling to retailers and distributors from all over India and worth a look for a bargain. Along RC Mintri Rd there's a profusion of fabric shops selling Tibetan cloth and Indian or Chinese silk brocade – both higher in quality and lower in cost than that seen in Darjeeling.

Gangjong Paper Industry (Primtam Rd; ⊙ 10am-6pm) This small place, hiding below Hotel Silver Oaks, is a bit whiffy: apparently the fibre from the bark of the daphne tree that goes into this paper is resistant to all sorts of attack and decay. There's a small showroom selling attractive notebooks, greeting cards, lanterns etc coloured with natural dyes.

Haat Bazaar (btwn Relli & RC Mintri Rds) On Wednesday and Saturday, this normally quiet bazaar roars to life, attracting nearby villagers who can buy anything from flip-flops to aromatic spices.

Getting There & Away

All the bus and jeep options, and their offices mentioned here, are found at the chaotic Motor Stand.

BUS & JEEP

Bengal government buses run regularly to Siliguri (Rs 50, 2½ hours), and there's also a single Sikkim Nationalised Transport (SNT; Rs 70, 3½ hours) bus to Gangtok at 1pm.

Trivini Travels (☎ 257311) and **Himalayan Travellers** (☎ 9434166498) run minibuses or share jeeps to Gangtok (Rs 80, three hours, departs 7.30am and 1.30pm), Lava (Rs 50, 1½ hours, departs 8am and 1.45pm) and Kaffer (Rs 80, three hours, departs 8am and 1.45pm).

Kalimpong Mainline Taxi Driver's Welfare Association (KMTDWA; ☎ 257979) has regular share jeeps to Siliguri (Rs 70, 2½ hours), Gangtok (Rs 80, 2½ hours), Lava (Rs 40, 1½ hours), Kaffer (Rs 60, 2½ hours) and Jorenthang (Rs 60, two hours, departs 7.15am). **KS & AH Taxi Driver's Welfare Association** (☎ 259544) has a jeep to Ravangla in Sikkim (Rs 100, 3½ hours, departs 2pm). **Kalimpong Motor Transport** (☎ 255719) has a regular share-jeep service to Darjeeling (Rs 70, 2½ hours).

Jeeps can also be chartered heading to Darjeeling (Rs 800), Siliguri (Rs 800) and Gangtok (Rs 850).

TRAIN

The **Kalimpong Railway Out Agency** (☎ 259954; Mani Rd; ⊙ 10am-4pm Mon-Sat, till 1pm Sun) sells a small quota (mostly sleeper class) of tickets from New Jalpaiguri train station.

TO/FROM BHUTAN & NEPAL

Trivini Travels (☎ 257311) has one bus to the Bhutanese border, Jaigon (Rs 100, 5½ hours, departs 2.15pm). The government bus makes the same trip (Rs 95) at 8.40am. Border information can be found on p138.

Kalimpong Mainline Taxi Driver's Welfare Association (KMTDWA; ☎ 257979) has regular jeeps to the Nepal border at Panitanki (Rs 90, three hours). See p138 for crossing details.

Getting Around

Taxis can be chartered for local trips from along SDB Giri Rd. A half-day rental to see most of the sights should cost Rs 600.

AROUND KALIMPONG
Teesta Bazaar

About 16km west of Kalimpong, Teesta Bazaar is an important centre for white-water rafting. Most people book in Darjeeling (see p147 for details) or at the DGHC office in Kalimpong, but you can also book here with the **DGHC** (☎ 03552-268261; Chitrey Wayside Inn, NH-31A), about 1.5km from Teesta Bazaar along the road to Kalimpong.

The friendly **Chitrey Wayside Inn** (dm Rs 100, d with private bathroom & geyser Rs 450) boasts a bar, restaurant and balcony overlooking the jungle banks of the Teesta River. The spacious rooms are clean, if spartan, and meals are good.

Teesta Bazaar is situated about 30 minutes by road from Kalimpong; you can take any bus or share jeep (Rs 25) in the direction of Darjeeling.

Lava & Kaffer

About 35km east of Kalimpong, Lava (2353m) is a small village with a Kagyupa **gompa** and a bustling **market** on Tuesday. The summit of Khangchendzonga can be seen from **Kaffer** (1555m), also known as Lolaygaon, about 30km further east. Both villages see few tourists and make peaceful and scenic getaways.

The picturesque drive from Kalimpong passes through mist and moss-laden old-growth forests.

Daffey Munal Tourist Lodge (☎ 03552-277218; dm Rs 100, d with private bathroom & geyser Rs 600) has huge, clean rooms with fireplaces. It's a rambling old place in Kaffer run by the DGHC.

Jeeps and a daily bus serve Kalimpong from both Lava (Rs 40, 1½ hours) and Kaffer (Rs 60, 2½ hours).

Samthar Plateau

This remote and beautiful plateau offers awesome views of Bhutan's Himalayan range and a chance to visit traditional villages. For trekking information, see p152. **Gurudongma Tours & Travels** (☎ 255204; www.gurudongma.com; Hilltop, Rinkingpong Rd, Kalimpong; s/d from Rs 2115/2820) runs the cosy Farm House at Samthar, which has accommodation in cottages, rooms or tents. It'll arrange transport for its customers from Kalimpong.

WEST BENGAL

Sikkim

If you're feeling jaded by the heat and hassles of India, Sikkim is the perfect antidote. It's clean (plastic bags are banned) and the mountain air is fresh. Best of all the people are among India's most friendly, with a charming manner that's unobtrusive and slightly shy. To really savour some true Sikkimese atmosphere, visit a village tongba-bar for some local millet beer: it's a bit like warm Japanese sake. Plunging mountain valleys are lushly forested, interspersed occasionally with rice terraces and groves of flowering rhododendrons. Tibetan-style Buddhist monasteries (gompas) add splashes of vermilion to the green ridgetops and are approached through atmospheric avenues of colourful prayer flags set on long bamboo poles.

Straddling the Sikkim–Nepal border is Khangchendzonga (Kanchenjunga; 8598m), the world's third-highest mountain. Khangchendzonga's guardian spirit is worshipped in a series of spectacular autumn festivals and its magnificent multiple white peaks can be spied from many points around the state.

An independent kingdom until 1975, Sikkim has long been considered one of the last Himalayan Shangri Las. But hurry. In the last few years a tourist boom has seen ever multiplying numbers of visitors, mostly middle-class Bengalis escaping the Kolkata heat. Every year more concrete hotels protrude from once-idyllic villagescapes and most towns are already architecturally lacklustre huddles of multistorey box-homes.

Fortunately, although Sikkim is tiny, its crazy contours make road construction very tough. So for now, finding the 'real' Sikkim is just a matter of hiking away from the metalled roads. Just watch out for those infamous leeches.

HIGHLIGHTS

- Hike between the endearing Buddhist gompa villages of **Yuksom** (p185) and **Tashiding** (p188)
- Get that *Sound of Music* feeling in the Alpine **Yumthang Valley** (p190)
- See two gigantic religious statues face-off at **Namchi** (p171)
- Gaze awestruck at India's highest mountain, Khangchendzonga, from the comfort of a café in **Pelling** (p174) or the strenuous trek to **Goecha La** (p187)
- Sup millet beer from antiquated tongba-tubs in end-of-the-world hamlets like **Thanggu** (p190)

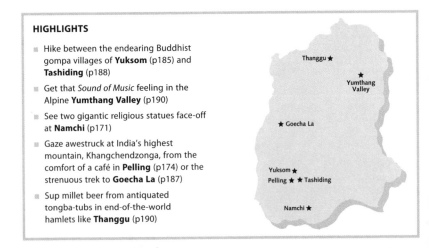

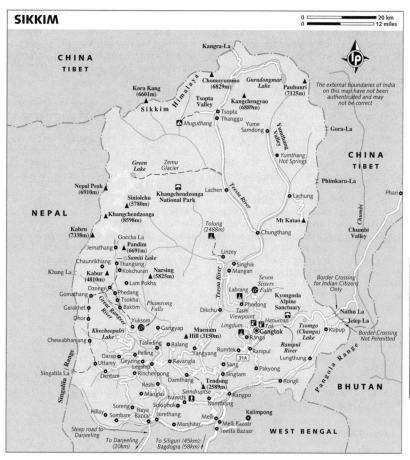

SIKKIM

History

Lepchas, the 'original' Sikkimese, migrated here from Assam or Myanmar (Burma) in the 13th century, followed by Bhutias (Khambas) who fled from religious strife in Tibet during the 15th century. The Nyingmapa form of Mahayana Buddhism arrived with three refugee Tibetan lamas who bumped into each other at the site of modern-day Yuksom. Here in 1641 they crowned Phuntsog Namgyal as first chogyal (king) of Sikkim. The capital later moved to Rabdentse (near Pelling), then to Tumlong (now hidden ruins behind Phodong) before finally settling in Gangtok.

At their most powerful the chogyals' rule encompassed eastern Nepal, upper Bengal and Darjeeling. However, much territory was later lost during wars with Bhutan and Nepal, and throughout the 19th century large numbers of Hindu Nepali migrants arrived, eventually coming to form a majority of Sikkim's population.

In 1835 the British bribed Sikkim's chogyal to cede Darjeeling to the East India Company.

FAST FACTS

▪ Population: 540,490

▪ Area: 7096 sq km

▪ Main language: Nepali

▪ When to go: late September to mid-November; April and May

Tibet, which regarded Sikkim as a vassal state, raised strong objections. In 1849, amid rising tensions, the British annexed the entire area between the present Sikkim border and the Ganges plains, repulsing a counterinvasion by Tibet in 1886. In 1903-04, Britain's real-life James Bond character Francis Younghusband twice trekked up to the Sikkim–Tibet border. There, armed with little more than derring-do, he deliberately set about inciting a fracas that would 'justify' his astonishing single-handed invasion of Tibet.

Sikkim's last chogyal ruled from 1963 to 1975, when he was deposed by the Indian government after a revolt by Sikkim's Nepali population. China has never officially recognised India's claim to Sikkim, so to bolster pro-Delhi sentiment the Indian government has made Sikkim a tax-free zone, pouring crores of rupees into road building, electricity, water supplies and local industry – including liquor production. As a result Sikkim is surprisingly affluent by Himalayan standards – and rates of alcoholism are the highest in the country. Meanwhile the Sikkim Democratic Front (SDF) state government has earned a reputation as the most environmentally aware in India, banning plastic bags and fining people who pollute streams.

Climate

When visiting Sikkim timing is crucial. Summer's monsoon rains hide the main attraction, those soaring mountains. The Yumthang and Tsopta Valleys are already very cold by October and will scare brass monkeys between December and February. Overall Sikkim's best season is late September to mid-November plus April and May.

Information

October and May are high seasons for Bengali tourists: prices double and normally serene monasteries get overrun. Crowd pressure is worst directly after the Durga Puja celebrations (early October). However, immediately before Durga Puja, things are contrastingly very quiet. Those few days can make a truly vast difference.

PERMITS
Standard Permits

Entering Sikkim requires a permit. Happily these are free and a mere formality, although you might need photos and passport photocopies to apply. Permits are most easily obtainable at the following:

- Indian Embassies abroad when getting your Indian visa (the best solution)
- the Rangpo border post on arrival (but not at Melli or Jorethang)
- Sikkim House in Kolkata (p101)
- Sikkim Tourism in Siliguri (p135)
- Major Foreigners' Regional Registration Offices (FRROs), including those in Kolkata (Calcutta; p101) or Darjeeling (p151)

FESTIVALS IN SIKKIM

Sikkim has dozens of festivals, many explained on www.sikkiminfo.net/fairs&festivals.htm. The most characteristic festivals feature colourful masked dances known as *chaams*, retelling stories from Buddhist mythology. Exact dates generally follow the Tibetan lunar calendar, handily listed under 'Government Holiday' on www.sikkim.gov.in.

Bumchu (Jan/Feb; Tashiding Gompa, p188)

Losar (Feb/Mar; Pemayangtse, p176, Rumtek, p169) Sikkim's biggest *chaam* dances take place just before Tibetan New Year.

Khachoedpalri Mela (Mar/Apr; Khecheopalri Lake, p185) Butter candles float across the lake.

Drupchen (May/Jun; Rumtek, p169) *Chaam* dances form part of the annual group-meditation ceremony, with Tse Chu dances every second year honouring Padmasambhava.

Saga Dawa (May/Jun; all monastery towns) Buddhist scriptures paraded through the streets.

Phang Lhabsol (Aug/Sep; Ralang, p173) Masked dances honouring Khangchendzonga.

Diwali (Oct/Nov; widespread) Firework time for the Nepali community.

Mahakala Dance (Nov; Ralang, p173)

Teesta-Tea-Tourism Festival (Dec; Gangtok & Rumtek, p170) Music, dancing, floral displays, archery and a river-rafting competition.

Losoong (Dec/Jan; widespread incl Old Rumtek, p170, Lingdum, p170, Phodong, p188) Sikkimese New Year, preceded by *chaam* dances in many locations.

Extensions

Standard permits are valid 15 days. Two days before expiry you can extend the permit for a further 15 days (free). This is possible up to three times, so 60 days is the maximum allowed in Sikkim. For the extension go to:

- Gangtok Foreigner Registration Office (p165)
- Tikjuk police station (p174) 5km from Pelling
- Superintendent of Police (SP) offices at Mangan or Namchi (a less-reliable option).

Once you leave Sikkim you must wait three months before you can reapply for another permit. However, if you're on Sikkim-to-Sikkim public transport cutting through a corner of West Bengal (between Rangpo and Melli), your permit remains valid.

Permit Validity

The standard permit is valid for visits to the following:

- Gangtok, Rumtek and Lingdum
- South Sikkim
- anywhere on the Gangtok–Singhik road
- most of West Sikkim to which paved roads extend.

However, for more remote areas you'll need additional special permits. For foreigners, areas nearest to the Chinese border are out of bounds entirely.

Special Permits

High-altitude treks, including the main Goecha La and Singalila Ridge routes, require trekking permits valid up to 15 days and organised by trekking agents.

Restricted area permits for Tsomgo (Changu) Lake (day trips) and visits anywhere north of Singhik (maximum of five days/four nights) are issued locally through approved tour agencies. You'll have to join the agent's 'tour', but such 'tours' simply mean a rental jeep, guide and agreed itinerary. Virtually any Gangtok agency can arrange this within 24 hours. You'll usually need a minimum group size of two (sometimes four), so single travellers have every excuse to make friends.

Dangers & Annoyances

Sikkim is generally a very safe place, but some locals' alcoholic tendencies can add a certain unpredictability.

Sikkim's famous little leeches aren't dangerous but they're ubiquitous in damp grass. Stick to dry, wide paths. If trekking through leechy terrain, letting them suck a little blood is often easier than endless stops to remove the morph-magician rascals.

Activities

Sikkim offers considerable **trekking** potential. Day hikes between villages follow age-old footpaths and normally don't require extra permits: the best-known options are along the Monastery Loop, notably between Yuksam and Tashiding (p187). Nepal-style, multiday group treks head into the really high mountains towards Goecha La at the base of Khangchendzonga. For this, permits and guides are required and although there are variants, most groups tend to follow pretty much the same route (p187). Tour agencies are striving to open new trekking areas, notably the fabulous route across Zemu Glacier to Green Lake in Khangchendzonga National Park. However, the permits remain very expensive and take months to arrange, while several other tempting routes are close to sensitive borders so remain off limits, at least for now.

EAST SIKKIM

GANGTOK

☎ 03592 / pop 31,100 / elev 1400-1700m

Sikkim's capital is mostly a functional sprawl of multistorey concrete boxes. But true to its name (meaning 'hill top') these are steeply layered along a sharp mountain ridge. When clouds clear (typically at dawn), views are inspiring, with Khangchendzonga poking its pointy white nose above the western horizon. Gangtok's manmade attractions are minor, but it's not a bad place to wait out a day or two while organising trekking permits or trips to the north.

Orientation

Gangtok's crooked spine is none other than the Rangpo–Mangan road, National Highway 31A, though commonly it's written cryptically as 31ANHWay. The tourist office, banks and many shops line central Mahatma Gandhi (MG) Marg. Nearby Tibet Rd is the nearest Gangtok gets to a travellers' enclave.

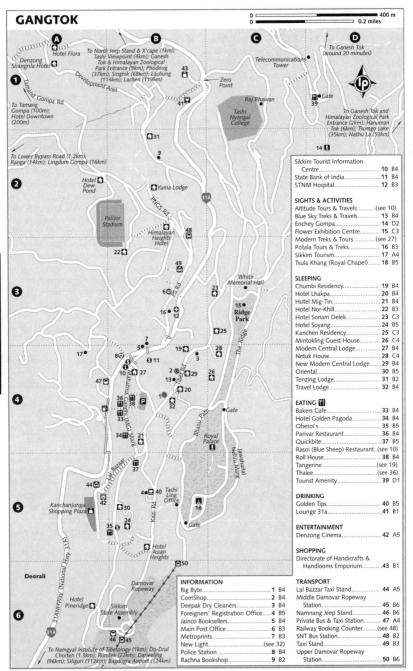

GANGTOK

To North Jeep Stand & X'cape (1km);
Tashi Viewpoint (4km); Ganesh
Tok & Himalayan Zoological
Park Entrance (9km); Phodong
(37km); Singhik (68km); Lachung
(114km); Lachen (119km)

To Ganesh Tok
(around 20 minutes)

Telecommunications
Tower

To Tamang
Gompa (100m);
Hotel Downtown
(200m)

To Ganesh Tok and
Himalayan Zoological Park
Entrance (2km); Hanuman
Tok (6km); Tsomgo Lake
(35km); Nathu La (53km)

To Lower Bypass Road (1.2km);
Ranga (14km); Lingdum Gompa (16km)

White
Memorial Hall

Ridge
Park

Royal
Palace

Kanchanjunga
Shopping Plaza

Tashi
Ling
Office

Hotel
Asian
Heights

Deorali

Damovar
Ropeway

Sikkim
State Assembly

To Namgyal Institute of Tibetology (1km); Do-Drul
Chorten (1.3km); Rumtek (22km); Darjeeling
(96km); Siliguri (112km); Bagdogra Airport (124km)

Sikkim Tourist Information Centre	10 B4
State Bank of India	11 B4
STNM Hospital	12 B3

SIGHTS & ACTIVITIES
Altitude Tours & Travels	(see 10)
Blue Sky Treks & Travels	13 B4
Enchey Gompa	14 D2
Flower Exhibition Centre	15 C3
Modern Treks & Tours	(see 27)
Potala Tours & Treks	16 B3
Sikkim Tourism	17 A4
Tsula Khang (Royal Chapel)	18 B5

SLEEPING
Chumbi Residency	19 B4
Hotel Lhakpa	20 B4
Hotel Mig-Tin	21 B4
Hotel Nor-Khill	22 B3
Hotel Sonam Delek	23 C3
Hotel Soyang	24 B5
Kanchen Residency	25 C3
Mintokling Guest House	26 C4
Modern Central Lodge	27 B4
Netuk House	28 C4
New Modern Central Lodge	29 B4
Oriental	30 B5
Tenzing Lodge	31 B2
Travel Lodge	32 B4

EATING
Bakers Cafe	33 B4
Hotel Golden Pagoda	34 B4
Oberoi's	35 B5
Parivar Restaurant	36 B4
Quickbite	37 B5
Rasoi (Blue Sheep) Restaurant	(see 10)
Roll House	38 B4
Tangerine	(see 19)
Thalee	(see 36)
Tourist Amenity	39 D1

DRINKING
Golden Tips	40 B5
Lounge 31a	41 B1

ENTERTAINMENT
Denzong Cinema	42 A5

SHOPPING
Directorate of Handicrafts & Handlooms Emporium	43 B1

TRANSPORT
Lal Bazzar Taxi Stand	44 A5
Middle Damovar Ropeway Station	45 B6
Namnang Jeep Stand	46 B6
Private Bus & Taxi Station	47 A4
Railway Booking Counter	(see 48)
SNT Bus Station	48 B2
Taxi Stand	49 B2
Upper Damovar Ropeway Station	50 B6

INFORMATION
Big Byte	1 B4
ComShop	2 B4
Deepak Dry Cleaners	3 B4
Foreigners' Registration Office	4 B5
Jainco Booksellers	5 B4
Main Post Office	6 B3
Metroprints	7 B3
New Light	(see 32)
Police Station	8 B4
Rachna Bookshop	9 B2

Information

BOOKSHOPS

Jainco Booksellers (31ANHWay) Small but very central.

Metroprints (31ANHWay) A little photocopy stall selling the excellent artist's-view map-guide, *Gangtok, in a Nutshell* (Rs 50).

Rachna Bookshop (☎ 204336; www.rachnabooks .com; Development Area) Gangtok's best-stocked and most convivial bookshop. A mini film-club and jazz café are planned upstairs. Gentle live guitar music sometimes serenades you while you browse.

EMERGENCY

Police station (☎ 222033; 31ANHWay)
STNM hospital (☎ 222944; 31ANHWay)

INTERNET ACCESS

Big Byte (Tibet Rd; per hr Rs 25; ⏰ 8.30am-8pm) Slow but cheap.

ComShop (Tibet Rd; per hr Rs 30; ⏰ 9am-8pm)

New Light (Tibet Rd; per hr Rs 30; ⏰ 9am-7pm) Decent if variable connection at the back of a general store. Good Skype-phone option.

LAUNDRY

Deepak Dry Cleaners (☎ 227073; Tibet Rd; ⏰ 7am-8pm Fri-Tue) Next-day laundry service.

MONEY

Stock up with rupees in Gangtok: exchange is virtually impossible elsewhere in Sikkim. ATMs accepting foreign cards include UTI Bank and HDFC, both on MG Marg.

State Bank of India (MG Marg; ⏰ 10am-2pm & 3-4pm Mon-Fri, 10am-1pm Sat) Changes cash and major travellers cheques.

PERMIT EXTENSION

Foreigners' Registration Office (Kazi Rd; ⏰ 10am-4pm, 10am-noon on 'holidays') In the alley beside Indian Overseas Bank. Takes under an hour.

POST

Main post office (PS Rd) Has a poste-restante service.

TOURIST INFORMATION

Bookshops overflow with listings pamphlets and guidebooks on Sikkim, but few offer useful, critical appraisals. Maps approach pure fiction.

Sikkim Tourist Information Centre (☎ 221634; www.sik kimtourism.com; MG Marg; ⏰ 10am-4pm, to 7pm high season) has some useful free booklets, sells helicopter tours and can advise on the latest permit requirements. Other queries will likely be passed to commission-paying travel agents.

Sights

NAMGYAL INSTITUTE OF TIBETOLOGY

Housed in traditionally styled Tibetan architecture, this unique **institute** (☎ 281642; www .tibetology.com; admission Rs 5; ⏰ 10am-4pm Mon-Sat, closed 2nd Sat of month) was established in 1958 to promote research into Mahayana Buddhism and Tibetan culture. It contains one of the world's largest collections of Buddhist books and manuscripts, plus statuettes, *thangkas* (Tibetan cloth paintings) and sacred objects, such as a *kapali* (sacred bowl made from a human skull). Further along the same road, the **Do-Drul Chorten** is a large white Tibetan pagoda surrounded by dormitories for young monks.

The institute sits in an **Orchid Sanctuary**, and is conveniently close to the lower station of **Damovar Ropeway** (per person Rs 50; ⏰ 9.30am-5.30pm), a new cable car running from just below the Tashi Ling offices on the ridge. Views are stupendous. Alternatively pay Rs 10 by share taxi from central Gangtok along 31ANHWay.

THE RIDGE

With views east and west, it's very pleasant to stroll through shady parks and gardens on the city's central ridgetop. Sadly its focal points, the **Royal Palace** and **Raj Bhawan,** are out of bounds for visitors. When the orchids bloom (March) it's worth peeping inside the **Flower Exhibition Centre** (admission Rs 5; ⏰ 8.30am-5.30pm), a modestly sized tropical greenhouse full of bonsai and exotic plants. The once-grand 1932 **White Memorial Hall** (Nehru Marg) opposite is now a dilapidated childrens' sports hall.

ENCHEY GOMPA & VIEWPOINTS

Approached through gently rustling conifers high above Gangtok, this **monastery** (⏰ 6am-4pm Mon-Sat), dating back to 1909, is Gangtok's most attractive, with some decent murals and statues of Tantric deities. It comes alive for the colourful **Detor Chaam** (December/January) masked dances.

From the gompa, follow the access road northeast around the base of an unmissable **telecommunications tower**. An initially obvious path scrambles up in around 15 minutes to **Ganesh Tok viewpoint**. Festooned in colourful prayer flags, Ganesh Tok offers superb city views and its minicafé serves hot teas. Across the road, a lane leads into the **Himalayan Zoological Park** (☎ 223191; admission Rs 10, vehicles Rs 25, video Rs 500; ⏰ 8am-4pm). Red pandas, Himalayan bears

SIKKIM

and snow leopards roam around in extensive wooded enclosures so large that you'll really value a car to shuttle between them.

Hanuman Tok, another impressive viewpoint, sits on a hilltop around 4km drive beyond Ganesh Tok, though there are short cuts for walkers.

Perhaps Gangtok's best view of Khangchendzonga is from the **Tashi viewpoint** at the northwest edge of town beside the main route to Phodong.

Activities
SCENIC FLIGHTS
For eagle-eye mountain views, **Sikkim Tourism** (☎ 281372; stdcsikkim@yahoo.co.in) arranges scenic helicopter flights. Book at least three days ahead. Prices are for up to five passengers (four for Khangchendzonga ridge):

- brief (approximately 20 minutes) buzz over Gangtok (Rs 6900)
- circuit of West Sikkim (Rs 46,750, one hour)
- Yumthang Valley (Rs 55,250, 70 minutes)
- Khangchendzonga ridge (Rs 63,750, 1½ hours)

Tours
Classic 'three-point tours' show you Ganesh Tok, Hanuman Tok and Tashi viewpoints (Rs 350). Almost any travel agent, hotel or taxi driver offers variants, including a 'five-point tour' adding Enchey Gompa and Namgyal Institute (Rs 400), or 'seven-point tours' tacking on either old-and-new Rumtek (Rs 650) or Rumtek plus Lingdum (Rs 900). All prices are per vehicle holding three or four passengers.

TOUR AGENCIES
For high-altitude treks, visits to Tsomgo Lake or tours to Northern Sikkim you'll need a travel agency. We've been very happy with **Altitude Tours & Travels** (☎ 9832370501; www.trekkinginsikkim.com; Tourism Bldg, MG Marg) and **Modern Treks & Tours** (☎ 224670; www.modernhospitality.com; Modern Central Lodge, MG Marg). However, as there are over 120 agencies available, the best idea is to check with fellow travellers for the latest recommendations. Other well-known if less recently tested agencies include:

Blue Sky Treks & Travels (☎ 205113; blueskytourism@yahoo.com; Tourism Bldg, MG Marg)

Potala Tours & Treks (☎ 200043; www.sikkimhimalayas.com; PS Rd)

Sikkim Tours & Travels (☎ 202188; www.sikkimtours.com; Church Rd)

Sleeping
Accommodation rates typically drop 15% to 30% low season, much more if demand is very low and you're good at bargaining.

BUDGET
Many cheaper hotels quote walk-in rates of around Rs 500. Some are worth it. Others are just waiting for you to bargain them to Rs 200. Check rooms carefully as standards can vary widely even within the same hotel. Foreigners generally flock around central Tibet Rd, the only area where a Rs 150 room is likely to be approximately inhabitable.

New Modern Central Lodge (☎ 201361; newmoderncentral@hotmail.com; Tibet Rd; dm Rs 50-70, d Rs 150-250, d with private bathroom Rs 300) It's been the traveller favourite for so long that people still come here despite somewhat ill-kept rooms and the complacent albeit friendly new management. With plenty of cheap rooms and a useful meeting-point café, it will probably remain the backpacker standby.

Modern Central Lodge (☎ 204670; info@modernhospitality.com; 31ANHWay; d from Rs 200) Former managers of what is now the New Modern Central Lodge have taken their reliable services to this handy but noisy new location. All rooms have private bathroom. Although standards aren't luxurious, the price is right. Great home-cooked food on the roof garden.

Hotel Lhakpa (☎ 201175; Tibet Rd; d from Rs 200) Very gloomy, cheap box rooms with rarely functioning geysers lurk above an unrepentantly local Tibetan café.

Travel Lodge (☎ 203858; Tibet Rd; d Rs 250-600) Unusually good-value rooms have BBC World TV and well-heated showers with towels and soap provided, though the ground-floor cheapies have thin walls and upstairs a few suffer from damp. Price depends heavily on season and bargaining.

Hotel Mig-Tin (☎ 204101; Tibet Rd; d Rs 250-600) Above a lobby with naïve Tibetan-style murals and a great little meet-up café, the best rooms are slightly worn but excellent value out of season, assuming you bargain a little. Avoid the cheapest rooms that are damp and airless.

Tenzing Lodge (☎ 204036; Development Area; d Rs 300-600) Of over 40 similar hotels in Development Area, Tenzing is comparatively inexpensive, with clean, simple rooms off misleadingly plush marble stairways. Some private bathrooms lack toilet seats. Eerily empty low season.

MIDRANGE & TOP END
All places listed here have cable TV and private bathroom with hot showers. Most add 10% tax.

Kanchen Residency (☎ 9732072614; kanchenresidency@indiatimes.com; Tibet Rd; d back/side/front Rs 450/600/700) Above the dismal (unrelated) Hotel Prince, this sparklingly airy discovery is spacious, light and well run. Front rooms have great views.

Mintokling Guest House (☎ 224226; www.mintokling.com; Bhanu Path; s/d from Rs 450/650) Set on a lawn within in a secluded garden, this expanded family home is a real oasis with Bhutanese fabrics, timber ceilings and some local design features. Very friendly.

Hotel Downtown (☎ 284219; Tamang Gompa Rd, Upper Sichey; d Rs 550/650) Certainly not downtown, but this new, out-of-centre minihotel is neat, clean and great value.

Hotel Sonam Delek (☎ 222566; slg_hsdelek@sancharnet.in; Tibet Rd; d Rs 600-1000) This longstanding favourite has good service, reliable food, and the best-value 'deluxe' rooms (Rs 700 to 880) have real mattresses, Tibetan motif bedheads and decent views. Bigger 'super deluxe' rooms have better views, but the cheapest 'standard' rooms are a very noticeable step down – in the basement.

Hotel Soyang (☎ 229219; www.sunflower-hotels.com/soyang.html; d Rs 850-1500) The outlandish pseudo-Chinese lobby décor is simultaneously cheesy yet atmospheric. Rooms are old fashioned, but the cheapest ones are excellent value with very clean, white-tiled bathrooms. The Soyang is the third of four hotels along a quiet, winding, easy-to-miss back lane off MG Marg signed for the Hotel Ben.

Oriental (☎ 221180/1; www.orientalsikkim.com; MG Marg; s/d/ste Rs 1200/1600/1800) This cosy boutique hotel has Sanderson-style fabrics, a hint of canopy over beds, and an appealing little 1st-floor lounge area decorated with aspidistra and Tibetan ornaments.

Netuk House (☎ 202374; slg_netuk@sancharnet.in; Tibet Rd; s/d Rs 1450/2200) Perfectly central yet unsigned and easy to miss amid endless flowers, the Netuk has 10 rooms in three very different styles. The newest have colourful Tibetan-style façades, local rugs and shared

sitting terraces. There's a delightful communal sitting lounge.

Chumbi Residency (☎ 226618; www.chumbiresidency.com; Tibet Rd; s/d from Rs 1550/1950) This wonderfully central, three-star hotel has comfortable if somewhat cramped rooms with fresh white walls and green marble tables. A few have views. Service is professional and the relaxed Tangerine bar-restaurant is firmly recommended (see below).

Hotel Nor-Khill (☎ 205637; norkhill@elginhotels.com; PS Rd; d Rs 5865) Oozing 1930s elegance, this sumptuous 'house of jewels' was originally the King of Sikkim's royal guesthouse. Historical photos and artwork feature throughout, and the piano-lounge lobby features antique furniture and imperial-sized mirrors. The spaciously luxurious old-building rooms attract film stars and Dalai Lamas.

Eating
RESTAURANTS & CAFES
Most budget hotels have cheap café-restaurants serving standard Chinese/Tibetan dishes, basic Indian meals and Western breakfasts. For good-value South Indian vegetarian food, try **Parivar Restaurant** (dishes Rs 25-50) and **Thalee** (mains Rs 25-50), next to each near the Gandhi statue (MG Marg). Beside Enchey Gompa, the misleadingly named **Tourist Amenity** (snacks Rs 8-20) is a cheap, basic teahouse serving great veg momos (dumplings) for a giveaway Rs 12, including complimentary soup.

Hotel Golden Pagoda (MG Marg; curries Rs 35-100 plus rice Rs 350; ☺ 10am-3pm & 7-9.30pm) The licensed restaurant on the top floor of this midrange hotel serves tasty Indian vegetarian food at reasonable prices.

Bakers Cafe (MG Marg; mains Rs 30-100; ☺ 8.30am-8.30pm) The perfect breakfast escape, this cosy Western-style café has great Viennese coffee (Rs 35) and excellent pastries.

Our pick Tangerine (Ground fl, Chumbi Residency, Tibet Rd; mains Rs 50-100) Descend five floors of stairs for sublime cuisine, tasty Western snacks or cocktails at the brilliant Japanese-style floor-cushioned bar area. Try the paneer makahani (Indian cheese in a creamy, garlic-tomato-ginger sauce) or sample Sikkimese specialities, like pork gyaree (with ginger and garlic) or sochhya (stew with nettle shoots). Stylishly relaxed décor.

Rasoi (Blue Sheep) Restaurant (MG Marg; buffet adult/child Rs 90/50; ☺ noon-3.30pm & 6-11pm) Brand new and thus super clean, the buffet offers

SIKKIM

four excellent vegetarian choices plus breads, rice and dessert. No alcohol.

QUICK EATS

Roll House (MG Marg; rolls Rs 10-25; ☺ 8am-8pm) In an alley just off MG Marg this hole-in-the-wall serves delicious *kati* rolls (see p119) that upstage even the Kolkata originals.

Quickbite (MG Marg; snacks Rs 20-40; ☺ 8am-8pm) Takeaway snacks from dosas to pizzas to Indian sweets.

Oberoi's (MG Marg; snacks Rs 25-60; ☺ 7.30am-8.30pm) *Momos*, chowmein, sandwiches, Indian snacks and pizzas.

Drinking

Lounge 31a (Zero Point; beers Rs 59, snacks Rs 40-130, waterpipes Rs 99; ☺ 11.30am-9pm) Swooping glass architecture offers light-suffused sunset views and a hip sense of modernist style.

Square (PS Rd; meals from Rs 135, beers Rs 60) This stylish little restaurant-bar has big view windows that are great for a cosy beer, but the pseudo-Thai food is overpriced.

Golden Tips (www.goldentipstea.com/Showrooms.asp; Kazi Rd; teas from Rs 25; ☺ 12.30-9.30pm) An inviting tea showroom with a wide selection of blends to buy and taste.

Entertainment

Denzong Cinema (☎ 202692; Lal Bazar; tickets from Rs 15) Screens the latest Bollywood blockbusters in Hindi.

X'cape (☎ 228636; Vajra Cinema Hall; entry Rs 400; ☺ from 7pm Sat) Gangtok's leading nightclub.

Shopping

Directorate of Handicrafts & Handloom Emporium (☎ 222926; Zero Point; ☺ 10am-4pm Mon-Sat,

daily Jul-Mar) This emporium sells a range of excellent-value gifts, including purses (Rs 25), handwoven carpets (from Rs 2110), handmade paper and ornately carved *choktse* (Sikkimese low wooden tables, from Rs 1500).

Several souvenir shops on MG Marg and PS Rd sell pricier Tibetan and Sikkimese handicrafts. Bustling Lal Bazaar has several stalls selling wooden tongba pots, prayer flags and Nepali-style knives.

A few Sikkimese liquors come in novelty souvenir containers. Opening a 1L monk-shaped bottle of Old Monk Rum (Rs 210) means screwing off the monk's head! Fireball comes in a bowling ball–style red sphere.

Getting There & Away

Landslides and route changes mean road journeys can take vastly longer than expected. If flying out of Bagdogra, play safe by making the Gangtok–Siliguri trip a full day ahead.

AIR

The nearest airport to Sikkim is Bagdogra near Siliguri (p136), with flights to Kolkata, Delhi and Guwahati. **TSA Helicopters** (☎ 0353-2531959; www.mountainflightindia.com) shuttle from Gangtok to Bagdogra (Rs 2000, 30 minutes) supposedly departing at 10am daily, returning around 1.30pm. However, service is weather dependent and might also be cancelled if bookings are insufficient. In Gangtok, **Sikkim Tourism** (☎ 221634) sells the tickets. See p326 for information on helicopter safety in India.

Bagdogra is 124km from Gangtok. If you don't want to bother going into Siliguri (12km away) for public transport, fixed-price taxis cost Rs 1450 direct Gangtok–Bagdogra. You

---

SIKKIM SIPS

In much of India, drinking alcohol seems a slightly shameful activity, boozers often huddle in half-dark bars as though embarrassed to be seen. Not so in Sikkim. Here every second café serves beer (Hit and Dansberg are local brews) and the state is famous for its liquors. But although quality is pretty good, telling between Sikkimese rum, whisky and brandy isn't always easy on a blind tasting. Locals tend to slurp 'pegs' (60ml measures) at a prodigious speed. As a result it's not uncommon to see unconscious figures sprawled face down on the streets, left snoring where they fell.

In Sikkimese villages, don't miss a chance to try tongba. You'll receive a girded wooden tub of fermented millet seeds onto which you pour boiling water. Suck the resultant liquid through a bamboo straw. It tastes a little like Japanese sake. Regular sipping and topping up prevents the drink getting too strong.

Note that on full-moon and new-moon days, selling alcohol is prohibited so bars stay closed.

might get slightly better prices from jeeps in the carpark: look for Sikkim (SK) number plates.

BUS
See the table, below, for buses from the governmental **SNT bus station** (PS Rd).

SHARE JEEPS & MINIBUSES
From the hectic but relatively well-organised **private bus and taxi station** (31ANHWay), share jeeps/minibuses depart until mid afternoon to Darjeeling (Rs 125/90, five hours), Kalimpong (Rs 87/60, three hours) and Siliguri (Rs 130/80, four hours), some continuing to New Jalpaiguri train station (Rs 135/100, 4½ hours). There are one-off jeeps to Kakarbhitta (Rs 160, 4½ hours) on the Nepali border and Phuentsholing (Bhutan border, Rs 200, six hours, 8am). Prepurchase tickets.

West Sikkim sumos depart when full from **Namnang jeep stand**. That's roughly hourly for Geyzing (Rs 120, 4½ hours), Ravangla (Rs 70, three hours), Namchi (Rs 92, three hours) and Jorethang (Rs 98 to 112, three hours). Last service is around 3pm. Jeeps for Yuksom, Tashiding and Pelling (Rs 130 to 150, five hours) depart around 7am and again around 12.30pm, but services to Pelling multiply in the high season. With a small group, consider chartering for 10 times the one-way fare, thereby allowing photo stops en route.

Sumos to North Sikkim use the **north jeep stand** (31ANHWay), about 3km north of the centre.

TRAIN
The nearest major train station is over 120km away at New Jalpaiguri (NJP). There's a computerised **railway booking counter** (☎ 222016; ⏰ 8am-1pm Mon-Sat, to noon Sun) at the SNT Bus Stand.

BUSES FROM GANGTOK (SNT BUS STATION)

Destination	Cost (Rs)	Duration (hr)	Departures
Jorethang	55	4	7am
Kalimpong	60	4	7.15am
Namchi	55	3	7am, 2pm
Pelling	85	5½	7am
Ravangla	44	3	7am
Siliguri (via Rangpo)	75-100	5	hourly, 6am-1.30pm

Getting Around
Share taxis (Rs 10 per hop) run along 31AN-HWay stopping at designated 'Taxi Stops'. Fixed-rate service (chartered) taxis loiter on MG Marg.

AROUND GANGTOK
Rumtek and Lingdum Gompa are most easily visited on a 'seven-point tour' (see p166). Viewing the temples takes perhaps half an hour each, but the infinitely winding county lane that links them is a big part of the attraction, curving through mossy forests high above river valleys and artistically terraced rice-slopes.

Rumtek
☎ 03592 / elev 1690m
Facing Gangtok distantly across a vast green valley, Rumtek village is entirely dominated by its very extensive gompa complex. Spiritually the monastery is hugely significant as the surrogate home of Buddhism's Kagyu (Black Hat) sect (see the boxed text, p170). However, visually it is not Sikkim's most spectacular and by day it can get annoyingly crowded in the high season. To experience Rumtek at its most serene, stay the night and hike around the delightful nearby hilltops at dawn.

SIGHTS
Rumtek Gompa Complex
This rambling, walled **complex** (☎ 252329; www.rumtek.org; admission free) is a whole village within a village containing religious buildings, schools and several small lodge-hotels. To enter, foreigners must show both passport and Sikkim permit.

Within, the main **monastery building** (admission Rs 5; ⏰ 6am-5pm) was constructed between 1961 and 1966 to replace the Tsurphu Monastery in Tibet, which had been destroyed during China's Cultural Revolution. The giant throne within awaits the crowning of Kagyu's current spiritual leader, the (disputed) **17th Karmapa** (Ogyen Trinley Dorje; www.kagyuoffice.org). This young lama fled from Tibet in 2000 but currently remains based at Dharamsala: Indian authorities have prevented him officially taking up his Rumtek seat for fear of upsetting Chinese government sensibilities.

Rear stairs lead up to the **Golden Stupa**. It's not really a stupa at all, just a smallish concrete room, but it holds the ashes of the 16th Karmapa in a jewel-studded reliquary to which

SIKKIM

FLYING BLACK HATS

The Black Hat sect is so named because of the priceless ruby-topped headgear used to crown the Karmapa (spiritual leader) during key ceremonies. Being woven from the hair of angels, the hat must be kept locked in a box to prevent it from flying back to heaven. But maybe that's just what it has done. Nobody has seen it since 1993 when the 16th Karmapa died. Only when the 17th Karmapa is finally crowned, will anyone dare to unlock the box and check.

pilgrims pay their deepest respects. If locked, someone from the colourful **Karma Shri Naland Institute of Buddhist Studies** opposite can usually open it for you.

Rumtek holds impressive masked *chaam* dances during the annual **Drupchen** (group meditation) in May/June, and two days before Losar (Tibetan New Year) when you might also catch traditional *lhamo* (Tibetan opera) performances.

Old Rumtek Gompa

About 1.5km beyond the gompa towards Sang, a long avenue of white prayer flags leads attractively down to powder-blue **Old Rumtek Gompa** (admission free). Despite the name, the attractive main prayer hall has been so thoroughly renovated that it looks virtually new. However, the interior is a riotous festival of colour and the lonely location is idyllic with some wonderful west-facing views. Two days before Losoong (Sikkimese New Year), Old Rumtek holds the celebrated **Kagyed Chaam** dance.

SLEEPING & EATING

Options within the gompa complex include **Sungay Guesthouse** (☎ 252221; dechenb@dte.vsnl.net.in; d/tr Rs 400/200) whose comfortable if rather Spartan rooms have varnished wood-veneer walls and private bathrooms with geyser. Doubles have great balcony views, hence the higher price. Further up where the monastery access road bends, **Sangay Hotel** (☎ 252238; s/d with shared bathroom per person Rs 100/150) is a typically Sikkimese half-timbered house offering tiny cell rooms above a rustic restaurant.

Outside the gompa walls and 300m back towards Gangtok, the friendly **Shambhala Mountain Resort** (☎ 252240; resort_shamhala@sify.com;

d Rs 2500) has attractive gardens and an appealing lobby, but the once-pleasant rooms have some scuffing and the bathtubs are somewhat stained. Rooms 201 to 204 have balconies at no extra charge.

Several new, quietly upmarket resorts are springing up along the Ranipul–Rumtek road.

Lingdum Gompa

Only completed in 1998, peaceful Lingdum Gompa is more visually exciting than Rumtek. Its structure grows out of the forest in grand layers with photogenic side towers, though the exterior paintings are not especially accomplished. The extensively muralled main prayer hall enshrines a large Sakyamuni Buddha wreathed in an expansive gilded aura. Frenetic chanting adds to the magical atmosphere. The isolated gompa complex has a café but its pilgrims' rooms no longer accept general tourists.

Getting There & Away

Rumtek is 26km from Gangtok by a very winding road. Lingdum Gompa is a 2km walk from Ranka village, reached by rough backlanes from Gangtok. Relatively sporadic share jeeps run to either from Gangtok's Lal Bazaar (Rs 22, one hour), but return transport fizzles out by 1pm. Linking the two sites requires private transport or a tour.

TOWARDS TIBET
Tsomgo (Changu, Tsangu) Lake
elev 3780m

Pronounced Changu, this scenic lake is an established tour stop for Indian visitors, but permits are necessary. To get one sign up for a 'tour' by 2pm and most Gangtok agents can get the permit for next-day departure (two photos required). Tours (ie guided shared taxis) typically cost Rs 700/450 per person for groups of two/three. Individual travellers usually can't get the permit.

At the lakeside, food stalls sell hot chai, chow mein and *momos,* while short **yak rides** (about Rs 80) potter along the shore. If you can muster the puff, the main attraction is clambering up a nearby hilltop for inspiring views.

Nathu La

Four days a week, Indian citizens (but not foreigners) are permitted to continue 18km along the spectacular road from Tsomgo Lake to the 4130m **Nathu La** (Listening Ears Pass). Here the border post to southeastern Tibet 'opened' with much fanfare in 2006. As yet only local villagers are eligible to cross, and only to travel 8km to the first Tibetan market. But keep asking. Maybe one day it will be possible to reach Yatung (52km) in Tibet's fabled **Chumbi Valley**, where the Sikkimese kings once had their summer palace. From there, the road towards Lhasa (525km) winds up onto the Tibetan plateau via the old fortress town of **Phari**, one of the world's highest settlements.

A few kilometres southeast of Nathu La, better-known **Jelep La** was the pass used by Francis Younghusband in the British Great Game era attack on Tibet (1904). Until 1962 Jelep La was the main trade route between Kalimpong and Lhasa, but it shows no signs whatsoever of reopening.

SOUTH SIKKIM

The main sights in South Sikkim are Namchi's gigantic statues. The region has plenty of other great viewpoints, too, but visitors generally hurry straight through en route to Pelling leaving much of the region comparatively untourist. Ravangla (p173) falls administratively within South Sikkim, but we cover it in the Gangtok to Pelling section (see p580) where it fits more logically.

NAMCHI
☎ 03595 / elev 1524m
Soon, two utterly vast statues will be facing off from opposite hillsides across this quietly prosperous market town. The Buddhist one at Samdruptse is already finished, the Hindu one at Solophok is still under construction.

Sights
SAMDRUPTSE
Painted in shimmering copper and bronze tones, the impressively vast 45m **Padmasambhava statue** (Indian adult/child Rs 10/5, foreigner Rs 50/10; ☺ 7am-5pm) stops just short of kitsch. Completed in 2004 on a foundation stone laid by the Dalai Lama, it's visible from miles around, shining like a golden cone amid the forests of Samdruptse hill. The site is 7km from Namchi, 2km off the Damthang road.

Taxis want around Rs 250 return. Alternatively you could walk back to Namchi,

short-cutting via steps down to and through a **rock garden** (admission Rs 10). Or more interestingly follow the nose of the Samdruptse hill down to **Ngadak Gompa**. Ngadak's ruined **old dzong**, dating back to 1717, is delightfully 'real' despite the unsightly steel buttressing that stops it from falling down. Its unpainted stone exterior incorporates ancient carved door pillars and upstairs intriguing but very decrepit fragments of painting remain on the peeling old cloth wallpaper.

SOLOPHOK
As if one gigantic statue weren't enough, work is proceeding at a prodigious rate to raise a new 33m (108ft) **Shiva statue** on Solophok hilltop. Due for completion in mid 2008, the site is expected to become a major pilgrimage point. A surrounding complex of temples and visitor pavilions is already partly built. Solophok is 6km from central Namchi. The access road passes the hospital and stadium, winds around the base of the interesting **Dec-chen Gompa**, then continues up past Dungmali Guesthouse.

Sleeping & Eating
our pick **Dungmali Guest House** (☎ 263272; Solophok Rd, 4th km; d Rs 200-350) For now, this family homestay offers just three rooms, the best having a private bathroom and a fabulous view window and sitting room. But in the next two years, inspired owner Bimuka Dungmali plans to add traditional Sikkimese hut-bungalows and create a more upmarket ecoresort with spa, and yoga-meditation hall. She already grows her own organic veg, offers bird-watching walks in 2.4 hectares of private jungle and can take you to meet a traditional healer.

Hotel Samdruptse (☎ 264708; Jorethang Rd; d Rs 400-800) The Samdruptse has its share of scuffed paint and damp patches but the best rooms have great balconies with superb views. It's above Namchi's finest restaurant, 300m west of the centre facing the Solophok-bound road junction.

Above the main square's taxi stand, between **Padma Shova Lodge** (☎ 263144), under reconstruction, and the neat **Hotel Zimkhang** (☎ 263625), climb two floors to find internet access at the Bon Pizzeria.

Getting There & Around
Taxis gather in the central stand. Around 200m east in descending layers off the Rangpo

BUSES FROM NAMCHI

Destination	Cost (Rs)	Duration	Departures
Gangtok via Damthang	55	3hr	2pm
Jorethang	13	70 min	9am, 11.30am, 4.30pm
Ravangla	17	1½ hr	11.30am, 2pm, 4.30pm

road are the main market, the jeep stand and the **SNT bus stand** (☎ 263847). See above for details of SNT services.

Share jeeps leave when full to Jorethang (Rs 25, one hour) and Ravangla (Rs 30, one hour) plus, till lunchtime only, to Gangtok (Rs 92, 3½ hours) and Siliguri (Rs 100 via Melli, four hours). For Geyzing (Rs 90, three hours), a single jeep leaves around 12.30pm: otherwise change in Jorethang.

JORETHANG

☎ 03595 / elev 518m

This useful transport hub between West Sikkim, Namchi and Darjeeling/Siliguri could make a launching point for visits to interesting but lesser-known Sikkimese villages like **Rinchenpong** (country getaways) or **Reishi** (hot springs and holy cave).

At its westernmost edge, Jorethang's most striking feature is the **Akar Suspension Bridge**, 400m north of which are the passingly photogenic roadside Shiva niches of **Sisne Mandir** (Legship Rd).

The brightest, friendliest accommodation option remains **Hotel Namgyal** (☎ 276852; d Rs 350), on the main drag 70m east of the bridge

BUSES FROM JORETHANG

Destination	Cost (Rs)	Duration (hr)	Departure
Gangtok	55	4	7.30am
Namchi	13	1	8.30am, 4pm
Pelling (via Geyzing)	45	3	3pm
Ravangla (via Namchi)	30	2½	noon
Siliguri	56	3½	9.30am

just before the SNT bus station. Across the road beside the Darjeeling jeep stand there's a particularly helpful tourist office and several other hotels. One longish block further east, turn right to find the main market and several cheap eateries, including **Sanjay Hotel** (snack meals Rs 10). Had you turned left instead, you'd have found the bustling main jeep stand hiding one short block north of the main road.

Getting There & Away

Useful services from the SNT bus station are listed on left.

From the main jeep stand, sumos leave regularly to Namchi (Rs 25, one hour), Geyzing (Rs 52, two hours), and Siliguri (Rs 94, three hours). For Gangtok jeeps cost Rs 98 via Melli, Rs 112 via Namchi. A couple of sumos leave around noon for Tashiding (Rs 47, 1½ hours) and Yuksom (Rs 96, three hours). There are also morning jeeps to Kakarbhitta (Rs 133, four hours). Buy tickets before boarding.

Jeeps to Darjeeling (Rs 90, two hours) leave until about 3pm from opposite the SNT bus stand.

WEST SIKKIM

Sikkim's greatest tourist draw is simply staring at Khangchendzonga, white-peaked magnificence from Pelling. Most visitors then add excursions to nearby waterfalls and monasteries, plus perhaps a spot of walking. Some lovely one-day hikes start from the charming village of Yuksom. That's also the trailhead for serious multiday group-trek expeditions to Dzongri (group trekking permits required).

GANGTOK TO PELLING

There are three main routes from the capital to Sikkim's main tourist hub. The longest and least interesting loops a long way south to Rongphu, then back via Melli, Jorethang and Legship. Fortunately this is normally only used by public sumos when landslides block the two possible routes via Singtam and Ravangla. Both of these are highly attractive, especially the longer, little-used route via Yangang (hired jeep only), which approaches Ravangla along an extremely dramatic cliff-edge drive around the precipitous base of Maenam Hill.

Ravangla (opposite) makes a good tea stop. Better still, if you have a chartered vehicle, have lunch 3km west of Ravangla at the lonely

PADMASAMBHAVA

Known as Guru Rinpoche in Tibetan, Sibaji in Nepali/Hindi or Padmasambhava in Sanskrit, this 8th-century 'second Buddha' is credited with introducing Tantric Buddhism to Tibet. Padmasambhava statues and murals are common throughout Sikkim. In his most classic form, he's usually shown sitting cross-legged with wild, staring eyes and a *tirsul* rod tucked into the folds of his left sleeve. This spears a trio of heads in progressive stages of decomposition representing the three *kayas* (aspects of enlightenment) . Meanwhile notice Padmasambhava's right hand surreptitiously giving a two-fingered Aloha greeting from behind a *dorje* (mini sceptre).

Padmasambhava has seven other alternative manifestations. The most striking of these, Dorje Bhurpa Vajrakila, shows him with three frightful heads and a lusty wench gyrating on his groin.

Mt Narsing Resort (☎ 9733084105; mains Rs 30-75), a rustic bungalow place with fabulous tree-framed views towards the mountains. You could also sleep here in simple bungalows (s/d Rs 550/850) with shared amenities or more luxurious cottages (Rs 1600/3100)

Don't miss the charming little **Bon Monastery** (right) before reaching Kewzing where the road starts its descent on seemingly endless hairpins to Legship (p174), only to climb all the way back up the other side again to Geyzing (p174).

Ravangla (Rabongla)

☎ 03595 / elev 2009m

Rapidly expanding Ravangla is spectacularly perched overlooking a wide sweep of western Sikkim, the gompas of Old Ralang, Tashiding, Pemayangtse and Sangacholing, all distantly visible against a horizon that's sawtoothed with snow-capped peaks.

The town itself is a modern creation of little aesthetic distinction, but useful as a hub to visit Ralang. Around the main road junction is a concentration of shops, small eateries and plentiful hotels, including **Hotel 10-Zing** (☎ 260705; d from Rs 300), a slightly eccentric place whose best room (Rs 450) has a new bathroom, gingham-wrapped TV and comes complete with Ozzy Ozbourne poster.

Hotel Snow-White (☎ 9836089533; s/d/tr Rs 300/400/700) has small but clean new rooms sharing very neat bathrooms. There are good if partially obscured views from the rear.

Several more hotels, many with views, line the Kewzing road for about a kilometre.

GETTING THERE & AWAY

Transport gathers in front of Hotel 10-Zing. Buses leave around 9.30am for Gangtok (Rs 44, three hours), and at 9am and 1pm for Namchi (Rs 17, 1½ hours). Until around 2pm, share jeeps leave when full to Namchi (Rs 30, one hour) and Geyzing (Rs 60, two hours) via Legship (Rs 32). **Mainamla Travels** (☎ 260688) runs several morning jeeps to Gangtok (Rs 74, three hours).

Around Ravangla

RALANG

At Ralang 13km below Ravangla, the splendid 1995 **Palchen Choeling Monastic Institute** (New Ralang Gompa) is home to about 200 Kagyu-order monks. Arrive early morning or around 3pm to hear them chanting in mesmerising unison. There's a 9m-high golden statue of the historical Buddha in the main hall, and locally the gompa is famous for elaborate butter sculptures. At November's very impressive **Mahakala Dance** the dancers wear masks representing the Great Protector and chase away negative energy. Ask to peek inside the room where the amazing costumes are stored.

About 1.5km downhill on the same road is peaceful **Old Ralang Gompa**, established in 1768.

A chartered taxi to Ralang costs around Rs 350 from Ravangla (return with two hours' wait).

BON MONASTERY

Beside the main Legship road, 5.5km from central Ravangla, small but fascinating **Yung Drung Kundrak Lingbon** is the only Bon monastery in Sikkim. The Bon faith, ('Mahayana with more laughs') preceded Buddhism in Tibet. It's relevance and impact on Buddhist philosophy is brought superbly alive by the impeccable explanations of the monastery's joyful English teacher, Lama Yungdrung Tenzing.

MAENAM HILL

A steep three- to four-hour hiking trail leads from the Ravangla–Ralang road to the top of **Maenam Hill** through the rhododendrons and magnolia blooms of the **Maenam Wildlife**

SIKKIM

Sanctuary. The views are wonderful and you just might see rare red pandas and monal pheasants (Sikkim's state bird). A guide is useful to avoid getting lost in the forest on return. Longer treks continue to **Borong** village.

GEYZING, TIKJUK & LEGSHIP
☎ 03595

Geyzing is West Sikkim's capital, but for permit extensions you need Tikjuk, half way to Pelling.

Tikjuk

Sikkim Permits can be extended at Tikjuk's **Police Station** (☎ 250844; ☷ 10am-4pm Mon-Sat) beside the main Pelling Rd, 4km from Geyzing. Nearby the **District Secretariat** (☷ 10am-4pm Mon-Fri) offers internet access in its **Community Information Centre** (per hr Rs 20).

Geyzing (Gyashaling)
elev 1552m

Apart from its vaguely interesting Sunday market, Geyzing is most useful as West Sikkim's transport hub. However, for a pleasantly peaceful accommodation alternative, go 2.3km towards Sakyong (itself a village with considerable potential). Here the **Tashigang Resort** (☎ 250340; www.tashigangresort.com; s Rs 900-1300, d Rs 1150-1560, plus tax 20%) offers magnificently wide views from almost all except the cheapest 'deluxe rooms'. Curious roof lawns top the slightly frumpy red-brick building offering more chances for mountain contemplation.

GETTING THERE & AWAY
Useful SNT bus services are listed below.

Share jeeps to Pelling (Rs 20, 20 minutes) and Legship (Rs 25, 30 minutes) leave when full, roughly every half-hour. Taxis cost Rs 150 to 200.

Jorethang-bound jeeps (Rs 52, 1½ hours) leave regularly throughout the day. There are several morning jeeps to Siliguri (Rs 125, four hours) and Gangtok (Rs 120, five hours) via Ravangla (Rs 60, two hours). Services to Tashiding (Rs 50, 1½ hours), Khecheopalri Lake (Rs 60, two hours) and Yuksom (Rs 70, 2½ hours) depart around 11am.

Legship

When no other transport is available, especially to or from Tashiding, try connecting here. Should you get stranded, **Hotel Trishna** (☎ 259887; d with shared/private bathroom from Rs 200/300) is simple but has plenty of greenery and a rooftop terrace.

PELLING
☎ 03595 / elev 2083m

Pelling's raison d'etre is its jaw-dropping dawn view of Khangchendzonga. It's not so much a town as a 2km string of tourist hotels, but don't be put off. The view *is* worth it. Despite hordes of visitors, locals remain surprisingly unjaded, and the best budget hotels are great for meeting fellow travellers. Don't miss strolling up to the **helipad** for even more panoramic views.

Orientation & Information

Pelling is nominally divided into Upper, Middle and Lower areas, though these effectively merge. A focal point of Upper Pelling is a small roundabout where the main road from Geyzing turns 180 degrees in front of Hotel Garuda. At the same point, minor roads branch south to Dentem and southwest to the helipad and **tourist office** (☷ 10am-4pm Mon-Sat).

Until Pelling's new telephone exchange is finished, the nearest internet access is in Tikjuk (left)

Tours

Hotel Garuda (opposite) and **Simvo Tour & Travels** (☎ 258549; per person/jeep Rs 175/1600) plus several other agencies offer one-day tours. A popular choice visits Yuksom via Khecheopalri Lake and three waterfalls. Several agents can arrange treks and permits for groups of four or more.

Sleeping

Unless otherwise stated all places listed have private bathrooms with hot water. Note that many hotels build new floors whenever they can afford to do so. That means that top storey rooms are usually the freshest. However, sometimes prices overreflect that fact.

BUSES FROM GEYZING (GYASHALING)			
Destination	Cost (Rs)	Duration	Departure
Gangtok	75	4½hR	8am
Jorethang	30	2hr	8am, 1pm
Pelling	10	30min	2pm
Siliguri	95	5hr	8am
Tashiding	30	3hr	2pm

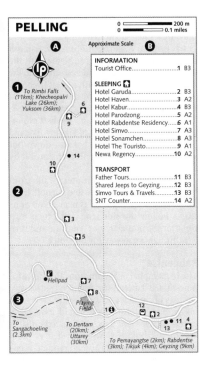

PELLING

Approximate Scale

To Rimbi Falls (11km); Khecheopalri Lake (26km); Yuksom (36km)

Helipad

Playing Field

To Sangachoeling (2.3km)

To Dentam (20km); Uttarey (30km)

To Pemayangtse (2km); Rabdentse (3km); Tikjuk (4km); Geyzing (9km)

Budget
The Garuda and Kabur are backpacker specialists. Others are just cheap local hotels.

Hotel Garuda (☎ 258319; dm Rs 60, d with shared bathroom Rs 150, d with private bathroom Rs 250-400) Pelling's backpacker favourite has clean, unsophisticated rooms, unbeatable Khangchendzonga views from the roof and a cosy Tibetan-style bar-restaurant ideal for meeting other travellers. Tours are good value and guests receive a handy schematic guide map.

Hotel Kabur (☎ 258504; r Rs 150-600) The Kabur's delightful staff fall over themselves to help. Great-value rooms have cute wicker lamps, towels and toilet paper, though a few have sticking locks and broken switches. Viewed from the charming café and open terrace, Khangchendzonga preens itself above the trees. A small rental car is available.

Hotel Parodzong (☎ 9733084348; d back/front Rs 250/300) No nonsense good-value rooms have clean squat toilets and water heaters. From those facing north you can see Khangchendzonga from your bed, albeit across a communal walkway terrace.

Hotel Haven (☎ 258238; d Rs 400-700) Choose view rooms 501 or 502, which are big, very clean and not cursed with carpets. Other rooms costing the same aren't nearly as good.

Midrange & Top End
The vast majority of Pelling's hotels are midrangers catering primarily to Bengali families. Rates typically drop 30% low season (before bargaining) and are highly negotiable whenever occupancy is down. With over 100 hotels and counting, the best place is often whichever has just been finished, probably blocking the view of the place behind it. Views tend to be best from Upper Pelling hotels, especially those near the old-helipad playing field but prices are accordingly higher there. Back-facing, viewless rooms should be cheaper.

Hotel The Touristo (☎ 258206; s Rs 350-700, d Rs 475-900) The best rooms have good Khangchendzonga views and pink marble floors in the neat, clean bathrooms. Cheaper options are viewless and rather small.

Hotel Simvo (☎ 258347; d Rs 600-1200) Down steps beside the Hotel Sonamchen and with similar fine views, the Simvo's upper rooms are its best but vastly more expensive than the acceptable cheapies on the bottom floors, which aren't as dingy as the corridors might suggest.

Hotel Rabdentse Residency (☎ 258612; rabdentse .pelling@yahoo.co.in; standard s/d/tr Rs 750/850/950) Hidden away down stairs behind the Touristo, this is an excellent midrange find with unusually obliging staff and a great attention to detail. A few rooms without views rooms go for just Rs 350. The idiosyncratic, bottom-floor restaurant cooks up really excellent Indian food, but doesn't serve beer.

Hotel Sonamchen (☎ 258346; d Rs 1000-2500) A big dragon design on the ceiling welcomes you in but sadly the rooms aren't anywhere near as atmospheric. Nonetheless, most – even on the cheapest bottom floor – have truly superb Khangchendzonga views, but the upstairs rooms are overpriced.

Newa Regency (☎ 258245; www.newaregency.com; s/d Rs 1450/1800) Pelling's most stylish choice is a triangular slice of modern architecture softened within by some delightful Sikkimese touches, notably in the charming 1st-floor sitting room. Some views are often partly obscured and oblique, but the service is impeccable.

SIKKIM

Eating
Pelling's best dining is in the hotels. The Kabur and Rabdentse Residency serve particularly good food, while the Garuda's great place for a beer and a travel chat. There aren't really any grocery shops, just a handful of kiosks.

Getting There & Away
At 7am SNT buses leave Pelling for both Gangtok (Rs 85, 5½ hours) via Ravangla and Siliguri (Rs 105, 4½ hours) via Jorethang (Rs 35, 2½ hours). Booking ahead is advised at the **SNT counter** (☎ 250707; Hotel Pelling; ☼ 6am-7pm) in Lower Pelling.

The frequency of shared jeeps increases as the season progresses but year-round rides depart early morning and around noon to Gangtok (Rs 150, five hours) and at 8am to Siliguri (Rs 150, 4½ hours). **Simvo Tours & Travels** (☎ 258549) also offers high-season sumos to Darjeeling (Rs 175, five hours, 8am). **Father Tours** (☎ 258219) has jeeps to Kalimpong (Rs 120, four hours, 6.15am). If nothing is available ex-Pelling, change in Geyzing. Share jeeps to Geyzing (Rs 20, 20 minutes) leave when full (around twice an hour) from near Hotel Garuda. They pass close to Pemayangtse, Rabdentse and Tikjuk police station. For Khecheopalri Lake (Rs 60) or Yuksom (Rs 60) jeeps originate from Geyzing and although booking ex-Pelling is sometimes possible, it's often easier simply to join a day-trip tour and throw away the return ticket.

AROUND PELLING
Pemayangtse Gompa
elev 2105m
Literally translated as 'Perfect Sublime Lotus', 1705 **Pemayangtse** (donation appropriate) is one of Sikkim's oldest and most significant Nyingmapa gompas. Magnificently set on a hilltop overlooking the Rabdentse ruins, the atmospheric compound is ringed by gardens and traditional monks' cottages walled in unpainted stone. The contrastingly colourful prayer hall is beautifully proportioned, its doors and windows painted with Tibetan motifs. Its interior has been renovated many times, the most recent incarnation featuring murals, including multiple images of Guru Padmasambhava's three-headed form, overlaid into infinity as though for a 'Bohemian Rhapsody' video. Upstairs, fierce-looking statues depict all eight of Padmasambhava's incarnations (see p173). On the top floor, **Zandog Palri** is an astounding seven-tiered model of Padmasambhava's

heavenly abode, hand made over five laborious years by a single dedicated lama.

In February/March impressive *chaam* dances celebrating Losar culminate with the unfurling of a giant embroidered scroll and the zapping of evil demons with a great fireball.

A 10-minute stroll from the gompa, **Hotel Elgin Mount Pandim** (☎ 250756; mtpandim@elginhotels.com; s/d Rs 3350/4280) has arguably the best mountainscape viewpoint in all of Sikkim. The old hotel had become somewhat run-down but a total, rebuild should totally transform it by the time you visit.

Pemayangtse is 25 minutes' walk from Upper Pelling. The signposted turnoff from the Pelling–Geyzing road is near an obvious stupa. Follow the side lane (left), then turn right for the monastery or continue and turn left through a gateway for the hotel.

Rabdentse
The royal capital of Sikkim from 1670 to 1814, now-ruined **Rabdentse** (admission free; ☼ dawn-dusk) consists of chunky wall-stubs with a few inset inscription stones. These would look fairly unremarkable were they not situated on such an utterly fabulous viewpoint ridge. A small almost-finished **museum** building should eventually house local archaeological finds. The entrance to the site is around 3km from Upper Pelling, 1km closer to Geyzing than the Pemayangtse turn-off. From the site's ornate yellow gateway, the ruins are a further 15 minutes' hike around a pond then across a forested hill.

Sangachoeling Gompa
The second-oldest gompa in Sikkim, **Sangachoeling** has some beautiful murals and a magnificent ridgetop setting. It's a steep 3km walk from Pelling starting along the track that veers left where the asphalted road rises to Pelling's new helipad.

A jungle trek continues 10km beyond Sangachoeling to **Rani Dhunga** (Queen's Rock), supposedly the scene of an epic Ramayana battle between Rama and 10-headed demon king Ravana. Take a guide.

Darap
For a relaxing day trip from Pelling, walk down to gently pleasant **Darap village** using the web of village footpaths through small rural hamlets. Khangchendzonga should be visible

(Continued on page 185)

Spirituality permeates the air at the
Kali Temple (p109) in Kalighat, Kolkata
(Calcutta)

The ever-colourful and fragrant Mullik Ghat flower
market (p109), Kolkata

Working hard, but still smiling – one of the last of the rickshaw pullers, Kolkata (p124)

178

Picturesque Darjeeling (p140), complete with Himalayan backdrop, West Bengal

The grandeur of British India on display, Victoria Memorial (p102), Kolkata

Lamas of the Gelukpa order blow traditional horns during a ceremony at Sakya Choling Gompa (p146), Darjeeling, West Bengal

MARTIN HUGHES

Verdant tea plantations (p145) – home to Darjeeling's most famous export, West Bengal

The World Heritage–listed Toy Train (p145) provides
a scenic and romantic journey into Darjeeling, West Bengal

CHRIS BEALL

Enjoy mountain-fresh air while trekking (p163) along trails of attractive forested hills, Sikkim

RICHARD I'ANSON

Khangchendzonga (8598m), India's highest peak, from the meadows of Dzongri (p187), Sikkim

Buddhist prayer flags fly in
Rumtek (p169), Sikkim

Monks share a joke, Rumtek Gompa (p169), Sikkim

Colourful 300-year-old prayer hall, Pemayangtse Gompa
(p176), near Pelling, Sikkim

Local women in colourful saris ascend the steps to the rock-carved Udayagiri caves (p245), Bhubaneswar, Orissa

MARK DAFFEY

Erotic statuettes decorate the Sun Temple (p257), Konark, Orissa

TONY WHEELER

Not even former prime minister Indira Gandhi was permitted entry here: Lingaraj Mandir (p244), Bhubaneswar, Orissa

JOHN MOCK

See elephants in their natural habitat at
Kaziranga National Park (p208), Assam

Visit the tea estates surrounding Jorhat (p209),
which make a relaxing getaway, Assam

Fishermen arrive back ashore on the popular Puri beach (p251), Orissa

GREG ELMS

Fishing nets hang to dry, as fisherman take it easy along the banks of the Brahmaputra River (p197), Assam

Spectacular drop at Nohkalikai Falls (p218), Cherrapunjee, Meghalaya

JOE BINDLOSS

SARA-JANE CLELAND

Greetings from the Northeast – local man outside the Tripura Sundari Mandir (p223), Udaipur, Tripura

Monks performing *puja* (prayers) at the Mahabodhi Temple (p272), located adjacent to the site where Buddha attained enlightenment, Bodhgaya

The Varanasi ghats (p279) – a truly mystical place to experience at dawn

There's no shortage of activity going on at Sadarghat (p289), Dhaka, Bangladesh

Looking out towards the spectacular Annapurna mountain range (p287) from Pokhara, Nepal

(Continued from page 176)

to your right most of the way, at least if clouds are magnanimous. Hotel Garuda offers guided walks with a ride home afterwards.

THE MONASTERY LOOP
☎ 03595

The three-day 'Monastic Trek' from Pelling to Tashiding via Khecheopalri Lake remains possible; however, improvements to the Pelling–Yuksom road means dust clouds get stirred up by ever-more frequent tourist jeeps, diminishing the appeal of hiking the trek's on-road sections. Consider catching a ride to wonderful Yuksom (via Khecheopalri Lake using tour jeeps) and hiking from there to Tashiding (one day, no permit required). Even if you don't trek further than the Yak Restaurant, Yuksom is a delightful place to unwind.

Pelling to Yuksom

Tourist jeeps stop at several relatively lacklustre time-filler sites. **Rimbi** and **Khangchendzonga Falls** are forgettable but **Phamrong Falls** are impressive. Although it's several kilometres up a dead-end spur road, virtually all Yuksom-bound tours visit **Khecheopalri**, dropping you for about half an hour at a car park that's a five-minute stroll from the little lake.

KHECHEOPALRI LAKE
elev 1951m

Pronounced 'catch-a-perry', this holy lake is highly revered by Sikkimese Buddhists who believe that birds assiduously remove any leaves that fall onto its surface. During **Khachoedpalri Mela** held in March/April, butter lamps rather than leaves are floated out across the lake. The birds aren't fooled. Prayer wheels line the lake's jetty, which is backed by fluttering prayerflags and Tibetan inscriptions, but the setting, ringed with forested hills, isn't really dramatic. To sense its reputed serenity you could try staying overnight and visiting once the constant trail of tourists has petered out.

Khecheopalri Trekkers Hut (☎ 9733076995; dm/tw Rs 50/150) is an isolated pale-green house-hotel about 300m back down the access road from the car park. Rooms are modest but clean and share several bathrooms. You can get tongba and filling meals, and the owners are helpful with trekking information, sometimes offering bird-watching or culturally themed guided

hikes. If sleeping over, you'll have time to trek up to **Khecheopalri Gompa** above the lake.

Around the car park is a Buddhist nunnery (behind a shrine-style gateway), a small shop, and the very basic Jigme Restaurant serving tea, *momos* and chow mein. There's no village.

Share jeeps to Geyzing (Rs 60, two hours) leave the lake at about 6am travelling via Pelling (23km).

The trail to Yuksom (9km) descends to the main road, emerging near the Khangchendzonga Falls. After a suspension bridge, follow the short-cut trail uphill to meet the Yuksom road, about 2km below Yuksom village. Ask at the Trekkers Hut for detailed directions.

Yuksom (Yuksam)
elev 1780m

Loveable Yuksom is historic and charming. It's the main trailhead for the Khangchendzonga Trek (p187), but, lacking direct views of the high mountains, has thus far been spared the rapacious development that's overwhelming Pelling. The **Community Information Centre** (per hr Rs 50; ☘ 10am-1pm & 3-5pm) offers internet connection in an unlikely hut near Kathok Lake.

SIGHTS

The word Yuksom means 'meeting place of the three lamas', referring to the trio of Tibetan holy men who crowned the first chogyal of Sikkim here in 1641. The site is now **Norbugang Park**, which contains a prayer house, chorten and the supposedly original **Coronation Throne** (Norbugang). Standing beneath a vast cryptomeria pine it looks something like an ancient Olympic medal podium made of whitewashed stone. Just in front is a spooky footprint fused into the stone. This was supposedly left by one of the crowning lamas: lift the little wooden guard-plank to see it.

Walking to Norbugang Park from Hotel Tashi Gang you'll pass murky **Kathok Lake**, from which anointing waters were taken for the original coronation.

When Yuksom was Sikkim's capital, a royal palace complex known as **Tashi Tenka** sat on a slight ridge to the south with superb almost 360-degree views. Today barely a stone remains but the views are still superb. To find the site take the small path marked by two crumbling little whitewashed stupas near the village school. The site is less than five minutes' walk away through tiny **Gupha Dara**, a sub-hamlet of around a dozen semi-traditional houses.

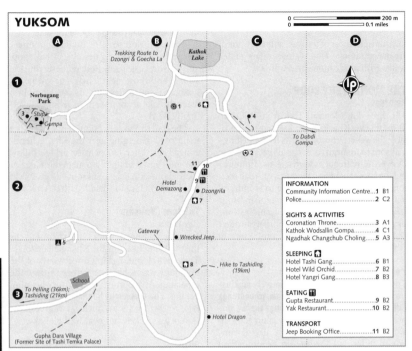

High above Yuksom, **Dubdi Gompa** is set in beautifully tended gardens behind three photogenic, coarsely hewn stupas. Established in 1701, it's touted as Sikkim's oldest monastery but the cubic prayer house looks vastly newer. There's no resident monk so if you want to look inside, locate the caretaker before you start the steep 45-minute climb from Yuksom's village clinic. The way rises through thickets of trumpet lilies and some lovely mature forest.

Yuksom has two photogenic new gompas. **Kathok Wodsallin Gompa** near Hotel Tashi Gang exudes a wonderful Chinatown kitsch and enshrines a big gilded Padmasambhava statue. Similarly colourful is **Ngadhak Changchub Choling**, accessed through an ornate gateway opposite Hotel Yangri Gang.

The trail to Dzongri and Goecha La heads uphill beyond the Hotel Tashi Gang, passing a police post where trekking permits are carefully checked.

SLEEPING & EATING

Many small hotels are dotted all along the meandering main street, especially towards the entrance of the village.

Hotel Wild Orchid (☎ 241212; tw/tr Rs 150/225) This neat, clean half-timbered house is slightly ragged but the most charming budget option. Bathrooms are shared.

Hotel Yangri Gang (☎ 241217; tw without/with bathroom Rs 150/200, deluxe s/d from Rs 300/400) Basement rooms are functional concrete cubes, but deluxe options are airy with wooden half-panelling and good hot showers.

Hotel Tashi Gang (☎ 241202; d Rs 1100, deluxe Rs 1300) Yuksom's most appealing option is tastefully designed to resemble a Sikkimese monastery. The décor of some rooms is a little too monastic, but deluxe versions have local fabrics, a *thangka* on the wall and most enjoy fine views.

Beers, chow mein and *thukpa* are cheaply available from a pair of atmospheric restaurants, Yak and Gupta, side by side at the bus/jeep stand. Both have an attractive thatched rotunda with one round table at which diners are effectively forced to get friendly. Eat early as everything closes for Yuksom's 8pm curfew.

GETTING THERE & AWAY

Between 5.30am and 6.30am, several shared jeeps leave for Jorethang (Rs 80, four hours), via Tashiding (Rs 45, 1½ hours) from in front of Yak Restaurant. Given enough demand, jeeps for Gangtok (Rs 160, six hours) and for Geyzing via Pelling (Rs 60, approximately 2½ hours) leave at 6.30am.

Dzongri & Goecha La – The Khangchendzonga Trek

For guided groups with permits, Yuksom is the starting point of Sikkim's classic trek to Goecha La, a 4940m pass with quite fabulous views of Khangchendzonga.

Taking seven to 10 days, trek costs start at US$30 to US$50 per person per day (assuming a group of four), including food, guides, porters and yaks.

Trekking agencies will sort out the permits. Paperwork must be done in Gangtok, but given two or three days, agents in Pelling or Yuksom can organise things by sending a fixer to the capital for you.

Don't underestimate the rigours of the trek. Don't hike too high too quickly: altitude sickness usually strikes those who are fittest and fastest (see p341). Starting at dawn makes sense as rain is common in the afternoons, spoiling views and making trail sections annoyingly muddy.

ROUTE NOTES

The route initially follows the Rathong Valley through unspoilt forests then ascends steeply to **Bakhim** (2740m) and the rustic village of **Tsokha** (3050m), where spending two nights helps with acclimatisation.

The next stage climbs to pleasant meadows around **Dzongri** (4025m). Consider another acclimatisation day here spent strolling up to **Dablakang** or **Dzongri La** (4550m, four-hour round trip) for fabulous views of Mt Pandim (6691m).

From Dzongri, the trail drops steeply to **Kokchuran** then follows the river to **Thangsing** (3840m). From huts here or at **Samiti Lake** (4200m), an early morning assault takes you to head-spinning **Goecha La** (4940m) for those incredible views of Khangchendzonga. Readers have recommended an alternative viewpoint reached by climbing an hour up from the left side of Samiti Lake.

The return is by essentially the same route but with short cuts that are sometimes a little overgrown. Alternatively at Dzongri you could cut south for about a week following the **Singalila Ridge** along the Nepal–Sikkim border

to emerge at **Uttarey**, from where public transport runs to Jorethang.

Stage	Route	Duration (hr)
1	Yuksom to Tsokha, via Bakhim	6-7
2	Acclimatisation day at Tsokha,	2-3
3	Tsokha to Dzongri	4-5
4	Acclimatisation day at Dzongri, or continue to Kokchuran	1
5	Dzongri (or Kokchuran) to Samiti Lake, via Thangsing	7 (or 6)
6	Samiti Lake to Goecha La, then down to Thangsing	8-9
7	Thangsing to Tsokha	6-7
8	Tsokha to Yuksom	5-6

SLEEPING

There are trekkers' huts at Bakhim, Tsokha, Dzongri, Kokchuran, Thangsing and Samiti Lake (very run-down). Most have neither furniture nor mattresses, you just cuddle up with fellow trekkers on the floor. Bring a mat and good sleeping bag. Huts sometimes get booked-out during high trekking season, so some camping might be involved.

EATING

You (or your porter) will need to carry supplies, but limited food (and tongba) is available at Dzongri.

Yuksom to Tashiding trek

For this long but highly rewarding one-day trek, starting in Yuksom is easier than coming the other way. No trekking permits are required.

Start down the pathway between hotels Yangri Gang and Penathang. The most attractive but longest route leads around behind the **Phamrong Falls** (heard but not seen) then rises to **Tsong**, where **Susan Chetri** (☎ 9832352756; su_zee2000@yahoo.co.in) plans a homestay at her family's typical half-timbered house. From the terrace there are terrific views. Look for the blue-framed home towards the eastern end of the village: it's on the right side of the main trail when heading for Tashiding.

Beyond Tsong the trail divides. The upper route leads up fairly steeply to lonely **Hongri Gompa**, a small, unusually unpainted ancient monastery building with a superlative ridgetop location. Local folklore claims the gompa was moved here from a higher location where monks kept being ravaged by yeti.

Till this point the route is relatively easy to follow, with recently laid stone grips. But descending from Hongri there are slippery patches with lurking leeches. At **Nessa** hamlet, finding the way can be mildly confusing. A few minutes beyond in attractive **Pokhari Dara** (where a tourist lodge is mooted beside the sweet little pond), the trail divides again beside the village shop. Descending takes you the more direct way to Tashiding. Continuing high along the ridge brings you to **Sinon Gompa** very high above Tashiding. The final approach to that monastery has some fascinating, ancient *mani* walls but the descent to Tashiding is long and steep by the short-cut paths or almost 10km of long switchbacks by road.

Tashiding
elev 1490m

Little Tashiding is just a single, sloping spur-street forking north off the Yuksom–Legship road, but its south-facing views are wide and impressive. Walking 400m south from the junction towards Legship takes you down past a series of atmospheric **mani walls** and brightly photogenic **Tibetan inscriptions** to a colourful **gateway** at the Km 14 post. From here an obvious if sometimes slippery moss-stone footpath leads somewhat steeply up to the ancient **Tashiding Gompa** in around 40 minutes. Founded in 1641 by one of the three Yuksom lamas (see p185), the monastery's five colourful religious buildings are strung out between more functional monks' quarters. Notice the giant-sized prayer wheel with Tibetan script picked out in gilt. Beautifully proportioned, the four-storey **main prayer hall** has a delicate filigree top knot and looks great from a distance. On closer inspection most of the exterior décor is rather coarse, but wonderfully wide views from here across a semi–wild flower garden encompass the whole valley towards Ravangla.

Beyond the last monastic building, a curious compound contains over a dozen white chortens, including the **Thong-Wa-Rang-Dol**, said to wash away the sins of anyone who gazes upon it. Smaller but more visually exciting is the golden **Kench Chorgi Lorde** stupa.

In January or February, the monastery celebrates the **Bumchu** festival during which lamas gingerly open a sacred pot. Then, judging from the level of holy water within, they make all-important predictions about the coming year.

Tashiding village's three basic, friendly hotels all have shared bathrooms. **Hotel Blue Bird** (☎ 243563; dm/s/d Rs 100) serves good-value food and, like the slightly neater **Mt Siniolchu Guest House** (☎ 243211, 9733092480; d/tr Rs 100/150) further up, has very helpful owners. **New Tashiding Lodge** (☎ 243249; Legship Rd; tr Rs 200), 300m south of the market, has fine views from Rooms 3, 4 and 5 and even better ones from the shared bathroom.

Share jeeps to Geyzing (Rs 50, 1½ hours) or Jorethang (Rs 60, two hours) via Legship (Rs 25, one hour) pass the main junction, mostly between 6.30am and 8am. A few jeeps to Yuksom pass through during early afternoon.

NORTH SIKKIM

☎ 03592

The biggest attractions in North Sikkim are the idyllic Yumthang and Tsopta Valleys. Reaching them and anywhere north of Singhik currently requires a special permit but that's easy to obtain (see p163) unless you're travelling alone. It's perfectly possible to visit Phodong and Mangan/Singhik independently using public jeeps. However, they can be conveniently seen during brief stops on any Yumthang tour and at no extra cost.

GANGTOK TO SINGHIK

The narrow but mostly well paved 31ANHWay clings to steep wooded slopes high above the Teesta River, occasionally descending long coils of hairpins to a bridge, photogenically draped in prayer flags, only to coil right back up again on the other side. If driving, consider brief stops at **Tashi Viewpoint** (p166) and the **Seven Sisters Waterfall** at Km 30. The latter's a multi-stage cascade cutting a chasm above a roadside cardamon grove.

Phodong
elev 1814m

A little strip of roadside restaurants at Phodong make a popular lunch stop. Simple rooms are available, too, notably the **Hotel Dzhambala** (☎ 9434136873; d Rs 150-250), where English is spoken. Around 1km southeast near the Km 39 post, a 15-minute walk along a very degraded former road leads to the **Phodong Gompa** (established in 1740). The potentially beautiful two-storey prayer hall is somewhat marred by metal gratings but contains extensive murals and a large statue of the 9th Karmapa.

Walk on another 30 minutes to the much more atmospheric and peaceful **Labrang Gompa** (established in 1884). Its prayerhall murals repeat the same Padmasambhava pose 1022 times. Upstairs a fearsome deity sports a necklace of severed heads. *Chaam* dances take place in early December.

Phodong to Singhik

North Sikkim's district headquarters, **Mangan** (Km 67 post) proudly declares itself to be the 'Large Cardamon Capital of the World'. Some 1.5km beyond, weather-blackened stupas on a sharp bend mark a small footpath; a three-minute descent leads to a panoramic **viewpoint**.

Singhik has two decent accommodation choices both with more great views. Set in a roadside flower garden, **Friendship Guest House** (☎ 234278; s/d Rs 200/400) has rooms with shared bathrooms within the home of an adorable Sikkimese family (who speak no English).

Singhik Tourist Lodge (☎ 234287; Km 71; d Rs 550) is a clean if slightly musty hotel where rooms have heaters and private bathrooms with geysers. There's a restaurant, too, but it's usually only open when groups are prebooked (through the tourist office in Gangtok).

Singhik is a Rs 50 taxi ride from Mangan, which is served by regular jeeps from Gangtok (Rs 90, three hours).

BEYOND SINGHIK

With relevant permits (and a tour jeep for foreigners) you can continue north of Singhik. Accommodation is available in Lachung and Lachen, with two more basic options in Thanggu. We have listed a few favourites but normally your tour agencies will preselect for you. Some family places stay open on the off chance of passing Indian tourists, but many better lodges close up when there's no pre-booked group due.

Cheaper hotels tend to have a mixed bag of rooms whose prices are the same whether or not the room has geyser, shower, heating, window or balcony. Some do, some don't. It's pot luck, so try to see a few different rooms even if you can't choose your hotel.

Lachen and Lachung are both Lepcha villages with a unique form of local democracy in which the *pipon* (headman) is elected every year.

Upper Teesta Valley
LACHEN

Till recently Lachen was an untouched, traditional Lepcha village. That's changing fast with pretty roadside houses being progressively replaced by concrete house-hotels. Nonetheless, alleyways remain sprinkled with old wooden homes on sturdy stone bases and Tibetan-style constructions with colourful, faceted window frames. Logs are stacked everywhere for winter fuel.

Around 15 minutes' walk above town, **Lachen Gompa** is an attractive two-storey monastery with engrossing, superbly coloured murals.

Lachen is the trailhead for expedition treks to **Green Lake** along the Yeti-infested Zemu Glacier towards Khangchendzonga's northeast face. These require long advance planning and very expensive permits.

NORTH SIKKIM TOUR TIPS

- A group size of four or five people strikes the ideal to balance cost spreading and space in the jeep.
- To find jeep-share partners, try hanging out in the café at New Modern Central Lodge (Gangtok) between 6pm and 6.30pm a few days before you plan to travel. There's no fixed system, just ask other travellers.
- Less than four days is too rushed to comfortably visit both Yumthang/Lachung and Lachen. Three-night/four-day tours start at Rs 2500 per person for groups of five depending on accommodation standards.
- Leave Gangtok early on the first day: it's a shame to arrive in the dark.
- Your (obligatory) 'guide' is actually more of a translator. Don't assume he'll stop at all potential points of interest without prodding.
- Bring a torch for inevitable power cuts.
- Don't miss tasting tongba (tiny extra cost).

SIKKIM

If you can choose your accommodation, a great budget option is super-friendly **Bayul Lodge** (tw Rs 250), hose upper façade is colourfully carved with Tibetan motifs. It's above the tiny video-cinema, beside the post office.

Hotel Sonam Palgey (www.sonampalgey.com; d Rs 3000) is considered the most comfortable in town.

THANGGU & TSOPTA

Beyond a sprawling army camp 32km north of Lachen, **Thanggu** has an appealing end-of-the-world feel. Misleadingly named, **Thanggu Resort** (tw Rs 300; ☺ May-Nov) is an outwardly ordinary family house incorporating a very traditionally styled kitchen, dining area and tongba-drinking den (tongba Rs 10). Rooms are simple but two have attached squat toilet and views of the river.

A boulder-strewn moorland stream leads on 2km to tiny **Tsopta**. Indian visitors can continue 30km north to **Gurudongmar Lake**, but for foreigners the only option (if the guide allows) is veering left up the lovely **Tsopta Valley**. Just above the tree line, the scenery feels rather like Glencoe (Scotland) but the valley's western horizon has the added drama of a glacier-toothed mountain wall. Zo-yaks and donkey convoys wander through on missions to supply some of the Indian military's more far-flung outposts way beyond.

Lachung

Soaring rock-pinnacled valley walls embroidered with long ribbons of waterfall surround amorphous little Lachung. To appreciate the full drama of its setting, take the metal cantilever bridge across the wild Yumthang River to the Sanchok side then climb 1.5km along the Katao road for great views from the **Lachung Gompa** (established 1880). The gompa's refined murals include one section of original paintings (inner left wall as you enter) and its twin giant prayer wheels chime periodically.

Mt Katao, nearly 30km beyond, is popular with Bengali tourists who drive up to the top to play in the snow. However, it remains off limits to foreign tourists.

SLEEPING

Hotels are dotted about a very wide area with the most convenient concentration around Faka Bazaar where the Lachung village road turns off the main Yumthang road. Rates start at Rs 250 for the most basic, but prices double in high season. Many outwardly modern places maintain traditional Tibetan-style wood-fire stoves and can churn salt-butter tea for you in a traditional *sudah* plunger device.

Sila Inn Lodge (☎ 214808; s Rs 250 d Rs 350-400) Open year-round, the family-run Sila has a typically mixed bag of rooms above a friendly hostelry-restaurant, best on the top floor.

Nearby hotels **Le Coxy** (www.nivalink.com/lecoxy resort) and **Sonam Palgey** (www.sonampalgey.com) are more upmarket.

Modern Residency (Taagsing Retreat; ☎ 214888; Singring Village; d Rs 2500) In a side lane around 3km south of Lachung, this brilliantly colourful flight of fancy rises like a fairytale Tibetan monastery. Staying here is one great advantage of taking a tour with Modern Treks & Tours (p166). Rooms have local design features and are comfortable, though walk-in prices are very steep. Even if you don't stay, the building is well worth visiting. One upper floor has a veritable minimuseum and the top-floor roof, above the prayer room, offers magnificent views across the valley, marred only by the disgracefully tasteless pink concrete of the Marco Polo Hotel, 500m directly below.

Yumthang

The main point of coming to Lachung is continuing 23km further north to admire the majestic Yumthang Valley. Guides will doubtless enthuse about the highly overrated 'holy' **hot springs**, a grimy, unlit 2 sq metre pool in an unlit, rubbish-ringed hut. However, the real drama starts about 1km north of there. After driving that 1km, walk about five minutes gently downhill to the riverbank. Now, weather permitting, you should have 360-degree views of an utterly magnificent Alpine scene: glaciers, spiky peaks and a veritable candelabra of jagged mountains rising towards Tibet.

Northeast States

India's 1947 Partition left the Northeastern states dangling like a crooked cartographic handle, way out on the edge of the national map and consciousness. Yet the great Brahmaputra valley was a Vedic heartland and the backdrop to many a Krishna tale. And Assam's beautiful tea plantations remain India's most productive. The surrounding states are home to a fascinatingly fragmented jigsaw of Tibeto-Burman 'tribal' peoples. Each ethnolinguistic group has jostled – often violently – to assert itself in the face of immigration and neglect.

But once you're past the hurdle of the infuriating permits (not required for Assam, Meghalaya or Tripura), you'll find the region disarmingly friendly. In Christian 'tribal' states like Mizoram and Nagaland you're likely to find some of India's best-spoken English, with former 'head-hunter tribes' now more interested in penning rap songs about their love of Jesus. Arunachal Pradesh offers a particularly phenomenal patchwork of hilltribe cultures. Its spectacular forested mountains crest in a series of gorgeous Tibetan-Buddhist valleys dotted with colourful monasteries, including India's largest at wonderful Tawang.

Yet despite some stunning mountain scenery, fabulous rice-and-tea plantation vistas and a selection of magnificent national parks, the area's lack of a truly iconic attraction means that few travellers ever venture Northeast. What a missed opportunity.

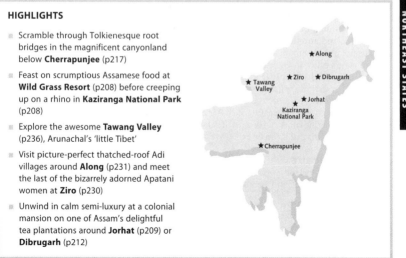

HIGHLIGHTS

- Scramble through Tolkienesque root bridges in the magnificent canyonland below **Cherrapunjee** (p217)

- Feast on scrumptious Assamese food at **Wild Grass Resort** (p208) before creeping up on a rhino in **Kaziranga National Park** (p208)

- Explore the awesome **Tawang Valley** (p236), Arunachal's 'little Tibet'

- Visit picture-perfect thatched-roof Adi villages around **Along** (p231) and meet the last of the bizarrely adorned Apatani women at **Ziro** (p230)

- Unwind in calm semi-luxury at a colonial mansion on one of Assam's delightful tea plantations around **Jorhat** (p209) or **Dibrugarh** (p212)

FAST FACTS

Arunachal Pradesh

- Population: 1.1 million (64% ST*)
  Area: 83,743 sq km
- Capital: Itanagar
- Main languages: dozens

Assam

- Population: 26.6 million (13% ST*)
- Area: 78,438 sq km
- Capital: Dispur
- Main languages: Assamese, Bengali, Bodo

Manipur

- Population: 2.4 million (35% ST*)
- Area: 22,327 sq km
- Capital: Imphal
- Main languages: Manipuri (Meitei), Assamese, Bengali

Meghalaya

- Population: 2.3 million (86% ST*)
- Area: 22,429 sq km
- Capital: Shillong

- Main languages: Khasi, Garo, Assamese, Bengali

Mizoram

- Population: 895,000 (95% ST*)
- Area: 21,081 sq km
- Capital: Aizawl
- Main languages: Mizo and English

Nagaland

- Population: 2 million (88% ST*)
- Area: 16,579 sq km
- Capital: Kohima
- Main languages: Nagamese, various Naga languages, English, Hindi

Tripura

- Population: 3.2 million (31% ST*)
- Area: 10,486 sq km
- Capital: Agartala
- Main languages: Bengali and Kokborok

*ST = percentage of 'scheduled' tribal peoples.

Permits

Permits are essential for Nagaland, Arunachal Pradesh, Mizoram and Manipur. Entering without one would be considered a very serious matter. Indian citizens need an Inner Line Permit, issued without much fuss at each relevant state's office in Guwahati (addresses p198), Kolkata (Calcutta; p101) or elsewhere. The rest of this section applies only to foreigners who require either a Restricted Area Permit (RAP) or an effectively identical Protected Area Permit (PAP). Getting either can be a real headache. And for Arunachal it can be expensive.

MINIMUM GROUP SIZE

As a general rule, permit applicants need a minimum group size of four people. Exceptions:

- Nagaland – for a legally married couple with a marriage certificate.
- Arunachal Pradesh – smaller groups allowed if you pay the full four-person fee (US$200), through travel agencies only.

Once you arrive, authorities will be very unimpressed if some people listed on your permit are 'missing', especially in Nagaland where the group must also stick together for crossing district boundaries. However in Mizoram things seem much more flexible, so should the other three people on your four-person Mizoram permit become inexplicably incapacitated, you'll probably be allowed to continue alone (hint).

VALIDITY & REGISTRATION

Permits are usually valid for up to 10 days from an exact starting date that you must specify. The permit *might* be extendable but only in state capitals at the Secretariat, Home Department. In Arunachal permit extensions cost another US$200 for up to four people. When applying you must specify exactly where you plan to visit and your permits will be valid for those districts. Foreigner permits for Manipur allow only fly-in, fly-out visits to Imphal, but even getting one of those is a minor miracle.

Be sure to make plenty of photocopies of the permit. You will need at least one for every checkpoint, and for police registration. Registration is compulsory both on arrival and every night that you stay in a new location. Travelling on a tour, your guide will do this for you. Travelling without a guide or 'guardian' can confuse authorities in Nagaland and Arunachal and might result in you being refused entry even with a valid permit. However, on the ground realities seem very variable between individual checkposts and officers.

WHERE TO APPLY

State offices tell you to apply through the Ministry of Home Affairs in Delhi. But that takes months and can end in frustration.

If it works, by far the quickest option is the new system operated at Kolkata's FRRO (see p101). A relatively reliable way to get permits is by prebooking a tailor-made tour through a reputable agency:

Agency	Based in	est for
Himalayan Holiday (p234)	Bomdila	all areas, notably Arunachal
Jungle Travels (p200)	Guwahati	all areas
Omega (p239)	Aizawl	Mizoram
Purvi Discovery (p212)	Dibrugarh	Arunachal, Nagaland
Rhino (p200)	Guwahati	all areas
Tribal Discovery (p226)	Kohima	Nagaland

Start the application process at least six weeks ahead.

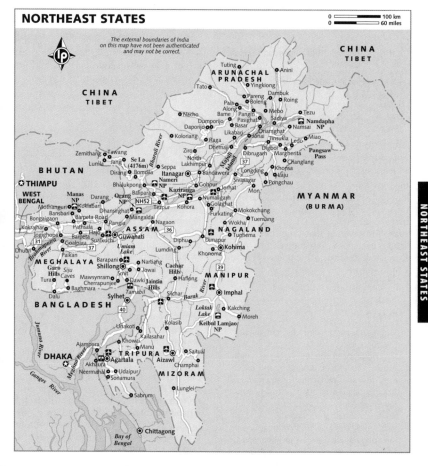

NORTHEAST STATES

The external boundaries of India on this map have not been authenticated and may not be correct.

TRAVELLING SAFELY IN THE NORTHEAST STATES

A wide variety of insurgent groups are active in the Northeast. Some want independence from India, others want linguistic autonomy, yet more are effectively fighting clan or turf wars. Although many Western governments currently advise against travel in Manipur, Tripura, Nagaland and Assam (an announcement that might affect your insurance), it's worth noting that not all of these states are equally affected. Generally Manipur really is too risky to contemplate. However, the most accessible tourist areas of Tripura and Nagaland are usually OK, and within the huge state of Assam, pockets of rebel activity are mostly limited to the Cachar Hills and remote patches of the far east. The problem is that trouble can flare up suddenly and unpredictably. One-off bombings have hit the normally safe cities of Guwahati and Dimapur just as they have struck London and Madrid, so the level of danger to travellers is hard to quantify. A flare up of attacks by ULFA (an Assamese independence outfit) in late 2006 made headlines but most locals see these as a last gasp from a discredited organisation rather than a popular uprising. Still it's wise to keep abreast of the latest news with the *Assam Tribune* (www.assamtribune.com). Mizoram, Meghalaya and the vast majority of Arunachal Pradesh are considered safe.

Some areas including Manas National Park have a relatively high malaria risk.

COSTS

Costs per person:

State	Through FRRO Kolkata	Through agency
Arunachal Pradesh	free (not Tawang)	US$50 + commission
Manipur	free	Rs 1500 + commission
Mizoram	not possible	commission (Rs 400)
Nagaland	free but limited	commission only

Climate

The Northeastern state's tourist season is October to April. Assam's beautiful rice plains look best in October. Most national parks only open from November and you'll see many more of the big animals if you wait till February. However, at that time the Assamese scenery becomes a comparatively drab brown. Don't underestimate the temperature swings. Until October you'll really need decent air-conditioning anywhere that's not well up a

TOURS

Visiting the permit states by tour smooths the bureaucracy, but travel is still comparatively slow and rugged. Agencies simply supply a sumo jeep, translator and driver-cum-mechanic, plus a tent for emergencies. Accommodation is often relatively basic, meals are haphazard and delays commonplace. It's all part of the experience and still vastly more comfortable than travelling by rare, packed-full, over-fast local transport.

mountain. But by December even sweaty Guwahati can feel chilly at night. Warm clothes will be useful at any time in Tawang, which can get cut off by snowdrifts from December (usually cleared within a day or two), and where temperatures can dip to -15°C in January.

ASSAM

Fascinating Assam (officially known as Asom, and sometimes written as Axom) straddles the fertile Brahmaputra valley, making it the most accessible core of India's Northeast. The archetypal Assamese landscape offers mesmerising autumnal vistas over seemingly endless gold-green rice fields patched with palm and bamboo groves, and distantly hemmed with hazy blue mountain horizons. In between are equally endless, equally gorgeous manicured plantations producing some 60% of India's tea. Unlike the stereotype tea hills of Sri Lanka or Darjeeling, Assamese tea estates are virtually flat and take their particular scenic splendour from the dappled shade of interplanted acacia trees that shield sensitive tea leaves from the blazing sun.

To a casual observer, the Assamese people look 'Indian', in great contrast to the Tibeto-Burman features of most other Northeasterners. But don't be misled. Assamese culture is proudly distinct: the Neo-Vaishnavite faith is virtually a 'national' religion and the *gamosa* (a red-and-white embroidered scarf worn for prayer by most Assamese men) is a subtle mark of 'national' costume. Despite the relative similarities of the Bengali and Assamese alphabets, Assam is vehemently NOT Bengal. Indeed the influx of Bengali migrants to the state remains one of Assam's hottest political issues. The Assamese have long bemoaned a perceived neglect and imperial attitude from Delhi for failing to stem that tide of immigration.

Meanwhile, by no means all of Assam is ethnically Assamese. Before the 13th–15th century Ahom invasions, much of today's Assam was ruled from Dimapur (ironically now appended to Nagaland) by a Kachari-Dimasa dynasty, while the Chutiaya (Deori-Bodo) kingdom was an important force further west. While this might seem a note of minor historical interest, the Dimasa and Bodo peoples didn't just conveniently disappear. During the 20th century, increasing ethnic consciousness led their descendents to resent the Assamese in much the same way as the Assamese have resented Bengal and greater India. The result was a major Bodo insurgency that was only settled in 2004–05 with the creation of the BTC ('Bodoland'; see boxed text, p205). And in the Cachar Hills around Haflong, the Dimasas continue a violent campaign for autonomy.

Don't let that put you off. Assam is a delightful, hospitable and deeply civilised place that you can easily grow to love. Its national parks protect a remarkable range of wildlife. And don't miss the delicious Assamese food: fruity, mild and finely pH-balanced using a unique banana-alkaline extract called *khar*.

For more information, visit www.assam tourism.org.

History

The Brahmaputra Valley had a dazzling golden era as the Kamarupa kingdom in the 4th to 9th centuries; its dynasties founded splendid cities and its Asura 'demon' kings fought epic battles with Krishna & Sons. By the 12th century a Kachari kingdom controlled the east, and Chutiyas the west, all to be eventually subjugated by the Ahoms who invaded from Southeast Asia and fought ongoing battles with Mughal India for centuries. Ahom (locally spelt Asom hence Assam) rule was fatally undermined by fearsome Burmese attacks in 1817, which decimated the population and carted off many of the survivors as slaves leaving the Assam's fertile valleys tragically sparsely populated. This proved a

FESTIVALS IN THE NORTHEAST

Tribal dances linked to the crop cycle take place throughout the year.

Brahmaputra Beach Festival (Jan; Guwahati, p197) Elephant races and adventure sports.
Kaziranga Elephant Festival (late Jan; Kaziranga, p208) New tourist tempter.
Torgya (Jan) and **Losar** (Feb/Mar) Tibetan-Buddhist *chaam* masked dances held most spectacularly at Tawang Gompa, (p237)
Chapchar Kut (Mar; Mizoram statewide; http://mizotourism.nic.in/festival.htm) Annual forest clearance dances.
Ashokastami Mela (Mar/Apr; Unakoti, p224) Shivaite pilgrims bathe amid Tripura's greatest ancient sculptures.
Rongali Bihu (late Apr; Assam statewide) Assamese new year.
Ambubachi Mela (Jun; Kamakhya Mandir, Guwahati, p198) Tantric rituals and even more animal sacrifices than usual.
Behdienkhlam (Jul; Jowai, Meghalaya, p218) Jaintia cultural festival.
Kang (Rath Yatra; Jul; Manipur & Assam, statewide) Chariot-fest for Krishna's birthday.
Durga Puja (Oct; all Hindu areas, p97) The region's biggest festival.
Nongkrem dance (Oct; Smit, p217) Five-day Khasi royal festival.
Buddha Mahotsava (variable; Tawang p236; http://tawang.nic.in/tawangbm/main.html) Government-sponsored Buddhist cultural festival.
Diwali (Oct/Nov; all Hindu areas) Lamps lit on banana-stem posts outside homes, Kali images dunked in rivers, general good humour.
Wangala (Oct/Nov; Asanang, p219) Four-day Garo harvest festival.
Ras Mahotsav Festival (third week of November; Majuli Island, p210) Major Vaishnavite festival with plenty of Krishna-epic recitations and dance-theatre.
Pawl Kut (Nov/Dec; Mizoram statewide) Mizoram's harvest festival.
Hornbill Festival (Dec; Kohima, p226) Nagaland's biggest event with wildly costumed dance performances by all main Naga tribes.

NATIONAL PARKS

Assam's top attractions are its national parks, the bigger ones subdivided into autonomous 'ranges'. Undoubtedly the most popular is Kaziranga (p208), where your chance of seeing wild rhinos (albeit often at a considerable distance) is very high at least in the central range. But Kaziranga is also the busiest park and the hordes of other tourists can be off-putting during peak season. For peace and scenery it's hard to beat Nameri (p207), but you won't see bigger animals there. The great attraction at both Manas (p204) and the less interesting Orang (p205) is sleeping within the parks' lodges to watch the jungle awakening at dawn. But you'll need to book way ahead (via Barpeta Road, p204).

Each national park operates fundamentally similar pricing structures. To **entrance fees** (Indian/foreigner Rs 20/250 per day) add Rs 500/50 for a camera or Rs 1000/500 for a video. Whether you bring your own jeep or rent locally, there's also a **vehicle toll fee** (Rs 200-300), including the services of an armed escort (who is customarily tipped an additional Rs 50). Visiting by jeep is not like going on safari in East Africa: to avoid the many marshy areas, routes are confined to set tracks. That can cause frustrating 'traffic jams' in peak season and parks only open once the tracks have been hand cleared of overgrowth (usually in late October).

Many park ranges offer dawn **elephant rides** (Indian/foreigner Rs 120/750) before opening to traffic (book the night before). These are typically better than jeeps for getting close to bigger animals, but only last an hour so you don't travel very far. Even an hour seems quite long if there are four people crushed on one elephant.

A bonus attraction are the unusually delightful places to stay close to Kaziranga (Wild Grass, p208), Nameri (Eco-Camp, p207) and Manas (Bansbari Lodge, p204), all managed by enthralling, larger-than-life characters.

National Park Overview

Park	Elephant rides?	Open jeeps?	Season	Main appeal
Kaziranga (p208)	yes	easy to rent	Nov-Apr	rhinos, elephants, easy access
Manas (p204)	some	limited rental	Oct-Mar	park lodges, Bengal Floricans, Bodo community involvement
Nameri (p207)	no	no (walk)	Nov-Apr	hikes, scenery, birds, rafting
Orang (p205)	yes	bring your own	Nov-Apr	peace, park lodge

windfall to the colonial Brits who arrived to fill the power vacuum. They nabbed much of the best land to experiment with a newfangled Chinese shrub they called tea. With few local labourers available to work the new plantations, the Brits imported Adivasi workers from Jharkand and beyond. These workers never intermarried with local people and their 'tea-tribe' descendents, remarkably, still form the vast majority of estate tea pickers (while Assamese have taken over the snooty desk jobs of the colonial planters).

During the colonial era, Assam was much larger, covering most of the Northeast. It was here that India's first commercial oil wells were developed, making Assam among the richest areas in British India. But independence proved an economic disaster. Assam was initially slated to join East Bengal in what would eventually become Bangladesh. How-

ever, frantic last minute negotiations reversed the decision. Assam finally joined India, albeit without Muslim Sylhet, which decided by referendum to go to East Pakistan. Partition meant that Assam's oil and tea exports could no longer take the sensible, direct rail line to the nearest port (Chittagong) but now had to wind right through northern Bengal. Like Calcutta (Kolkata), Assam was suddenly flooded with millions of Hindu Bengalis preferring not to live in Pakistan. This created enormous and ever-growing ethnic tensions, made all the worse after 1970 when a second wave of Muslim Bengalis started fleeing the war in proto-Bangladesh.

Providing the bulk of India's oil, but gaining few of the benefits, Assam felt economically cheated by India. This sentiment bubbled over into widespread rebellion after India's pitifully meek response to the brief 1962

Chinese invasion (which approached close to Tezpur at one stage). Assamese student groups turned militant and the United Liberation Front of Asom (ULFA) started its violent demands for Assamese independence. At the same time tensions were simmering in the hill areas where local tribal people were in turn offended by the condescendingly 'colonial' attitude of their Assamese overlords. Greater Assam was eventually split into today's seven sisters states, but not before decades of separatist conflicts.

Dangers & Annoyances

In the far east of Assam, ULFA insurgents continue fighting for an independent Assam and the ejection of Bangladeshi immigrants. Their operations are mostly limited to relatively small, isolated areas, notably the Pengri Forest Reserve east of Digboi, but they do organise occasional one-day bandhs (strikes) that can bring transport to a halt as far afield as Ledo, Tinsukia and Dibrugarh. Western Assam's long-standing conflict over a Bodo tribal homeland was largely settled in 2005 (see p205) and central parts of Assam are generally safe. However, parts of south Assam are unstable, so it's not currently advisable to visit Haflong.

Some pockets of rural Assam, including Manas National Park, suffer a relatively high malaria risk.

GUWAHATI

☎ 0361 / pop 964,000

Sprawling almost 20km along the Brahmaputra's southern riverbank, the Northeast's main gateway city is a major business centre servicing the tea and oil industries. Although not that attractive overall, green hillocks rise curiously above Guwahati's noisy smog and the city's water tanks and riverbanks are patchily pleasant. Come here to arrange tours to other Northeast states, see a few of the fascinating temples and then move swiftly on.

History

Guwahati is considered the site of Pragjyotishpura, a semi-mythical town founded by Asura King Naraka who was later killed by Lord Krishna for a pair of magical earrings. The Kamakhya temple (p198) has long been one of tantric Hinduism's great shrines. Scores of beautiful carvings found beneath the dowdy 1970s Reserve Bank of India (Station Rd, Ambari) show that the city had reached an artistic peak in the 14th century. In the 17th century, Guwahati was the theatre of intense Ahom-Mughal fighting, the city changing hands eight times in 50 years before the Ahom's final victory in 1681. Guwahati became the last capital of the Ahoms in their declining years after King Rudra Singh's conversion to Hinduism and the loss of their former capital Rangpur (now in Bangladesh). The 19th-century British administrative outpost here was wiped out along with most of the old city by a huge 1897 earthquake, followed by a series of devastating floods.

The city became capital of Assam in 1972 and the Asom State Government is now ensconced in a Disneyesque new secretariat complex, 6km south of the train station in the Dispur district.

Orientation

Hectic commercial bustle animates the central Fancy- and Pan-Bazaar areas and stretches 10km southeast down GS road from Paltan

BRAHMAPUTRA EXPERIENCES

The Brahmaputra is one of India's greatest rivers. It's known as the Tsangpo in Tibet and the Siang in its gushing Arunachal reaches, where powerful rapids around Tuting (p231) and Karko will one day surely rate among the world's top rafting challenges. By the time it reaches Assam the river is truly vast, cutting the state in two with mile upon mile of sandbanks and flood plains. You might even spot blind, Gangetic dolphins (January is the best time). Cheap ways to experience this entrancing, flat enormity include public ferry rides to the world's biggest river island (Majuli, p210) or on the longer Dibrugarhroute (p213). Rhino Travels' Mou Chapori (p210) lets you sleep on an otherwise uninhabited Brahmaputra sandbank-islet, Wild Grass (p208) can organise four-person, three-day boat-and-camp trips around Dibrugarh or Kaziranga (Rs 48,000 to 68,000, all inclusive), while **Assam-Bengal Navigation** (www.assambengalnavigation.com) run a variety of comparatively luxurious cruises in restored former mail steamers (US$245 per person per day including tours and food) bookable through Jungle Travels (p200).

Bazaar (the bus station area). Things are marginally quieter in the older Ambari-Jorpulkuri area with oases of peace in lake-gardens and small riverside parks.

Information
EMERGENCY
Police station (☎ 2540138; HB Rd)

INTERNET ACCESS
i-way (Lamb La; per hr Rs 20; ✆ 9am-last customer)
KB Infosys (☎ 2734031; GNB Rd; per hr Rs 15;
✆ 10am-8pm Mon-Sat) Hidden above a silk shop on the corner of Lamb La.
Web-Net (NCB Rd, Panbazar; per hr Rs 20; ✆ 9am-10pm; ✆) Cramped but good connection and decent air-con.

MEDICAL SERVICES
Downtown Hospital (☎ 2331003; GS Rd, Dispur) The area's best.

MONEY
Make sure to stock up on rupees: beyond Guwahati the Northeast's currency-exchange facilities are very limited.
LPK Forex (☎ 2664450; www.lkpforex.com; Jayant Commercial Complex, J Borooah Rd; ✆ 10am-5pm Mon-Sat) Top rates for cash and travellers cheques in a booth behind Jet Airways.
State Bank of India (MG Rd; ✆ 10am-2pm & 3-4pm Mon-Fri) Changes major currencies and travellers cheques. Has an ATM.
Standard Chartered Bank (GNB Rd) 24-hr ATM but no currency exchange.

PERMITS
Indian citizens can pick up Inner Line Permits at the relevant state offices. Foreigners might get a cursory tourist brochure but shouldn't expect even the tiniest morsel of permit help. See p192.
Arunachal House (☎ 2452859) Heading south from the GNB flyover, take the first left off RG Baruah Rd, then turn right up an unmarked dead-end lane. Like a scene from Kafka, three bored, pan-chewing bureaucrats sit beneath a slowly whirring fan staring at their watches till it's time to go home.
Manipur Bhawan (☎ 2540707; Rajgarh Rd)
Mizoram House (☎ 2529411; GS Rd, Christian Basti)
Nagaland House (☎ 2332158; Sachel Rd, Sixth Mile, Khanapara) New office at the southeast city limits.

POST
Main post office (ARB Rd; ✆ 9.30am-4pm) Chaotic.

TOURIST LODGES
Many states have government tourist lodges. But, unusually, throughout Assam these are very often the best-value cheap or lower midrange options in town. Consider booking ahead as most are small. Tourist lodges usually have an information office or resident tourist officer, though these folks tend to take remarkably long lunch breaks.

TOURIST INFORMATION
Assam Tourism (☎ 2547102; www.assamtourism.org; Station Rd) Operates an informal desk within the Tourist Lodge and a tour agency booth just outside.

Sights
KAMAKHYA MANDIR
Hindus believe that when Shiva carried away the corpse of his first wife, Sati (see p96), her body disintegrated and her yoni (female genitalia) fell here. **Kamakhya Mandir** thus became an important centre for sensual tantric worship of female spiritual power (Shakti). Goats, doves and buffaloes are ritually beheaded in a gory pavilion and the hot, dark inner sanctum is sticky with sacrificial blood. Kamakhya hosts the huge **Ambubachi Mela** in June/July celebrating the end of the mother goddess' menstrual cycle with even more blood.

Nine other nearby mandirs represent incarnations of Shakti.

The complex is 7km west of central Guwahati, 3km off the airport road by a spiralling side road. Occasional buses from Guwahati's Kachari bus stand (Rs 5, 20 minutes) run all the way up. Continue 1km further towards a minor hill-top temple, **Bhubneswari Mandir**, for sweeping Brahmaputra viewpoints.

RIVERSIDE GUWAHATI
Some tourists pay a fortune to spot rare golden langurs in Bhutan's national parks. Yet at **Umananda Mandir** these loveable monkeys often loiter at the gates, politely soliciting snacks from devotees. This Shiva temple complex sits on a prettily forested river-island, accessed by 36-seater **cruise boats** (Rs 10 return; ✆ 9.30-4pm). The boats depart when full (roughly half-hourly) from **Kachari Ghat**, which itself offers attractive afternoon riverviews.

Sukreswar Devalaya comprises three mostly modern-looking temples, including one where

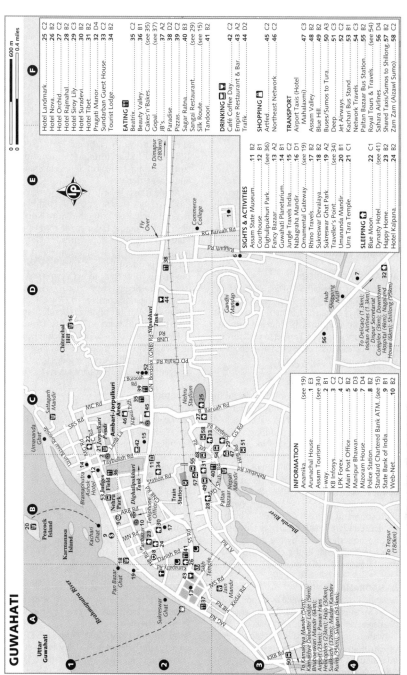

GUWAHATI

0   600 m
0   0.4 miles

NORTHEAST STATES

INFORMATION
Anamika............................(see 19)
Arunachal House...........................1 E3
Assam Tourism.....................(see 34)
i-way................................2 B1
KB Infosys...........................3 C2
LPK Forex............................4 C2
Main Post Office....................5 B2
Manipur Bhawan....................6 D3
Mizoram House.....................7 D4
Police Station.......................8 B2
Standard Chartered Bank ATM..9 B1
State Bank of India................10 B2
Web-Net..............................11 B2

SIGHTS & ACTIVITIES
Assam State Museum..............12 B1
Courthouse......................(see 36)
Dighulipukhuri Park..............13 A2
Fancy Bazaar.....................14 B1
Guwahati Planetarium...........15 C2
Jungle Travels India............16 D1
Nabagraha Mandir..............(see 19)
Ornamental Gateway............17 B2
Rhino Travels....................18 B2
Sukreswar Devalaya............19 A2
Sukreswar Ghat Park..........(see 34)
Traveller's Point.................20 B1
Umananda Mandir..............21 C1
Urra Tara Temple................

SLEEPING
Blue Moon........................22 C1
Dynasty Hotel..................(see 41)
Happy Home......................23 B2
Hotel Kalpana...................24 B2
Hotel Landmark..................25 C2
Hotel Nova........................26 B2
Hotel Orchid......................27 C2
Hotel Rajmahal..................28 B2
Hotel Siroy Lily..................29 C3
Hotel Suradevi...................30 B2
Hotel Tibet.......................31 B2
Pragati Manor...................32 D4
Sundarban Guest House.......33 C2
Tourist Lodge.....................34 B2

EATING
Beatrix............................35 C2
Beauty Valley....................36 B1
Cakes 'n Bakes...............(see 35)
Gopal.............................(see 37)
JB's................................37 A2
Paradise..........................38 D2
Pizzas.............................39 C2
Sagar Ratna......................40 B3
Sangai Restaurant.............(see 29)
Silk Route.......................(see 15)
Tandoori.........................41 B2

DRINKING
Café Coffee Day.................42 C2
Empire Restaurant & Bar......43 A2
Trafik.............................44 D2

SHOPPING
Artfed............................45 C2
Northeast Network.............46 C2

TRANSPORT
Airport Taxis (Hotel Mahalaxmi)...47 C3
Assam Valley....................48 B2
Blue Hill.........................49 B2
Buses/Sumos to Tura........50 A3
Deep.............................51 C3
Jet Airways.....................52 B1
Kachari Bus Stand............53 B1
Network Travels...............54 C3
Paltan Bazaar Bus Station...55 B2
Royal Tours & Travels........56 D4
Sahara Airlines................57 B2
Shared Taxis/Sumos to Shillong....58 C2
Zam Zam (Aizawl Sumo)....

holy water dribbles continuously over a Shiva lingam from a suspended bell-metal amphora. Almost adjacent, little **Sukreswar Ghat Park** (MG Rd; adult/child/camera Rs 5/2/5; ☺ 9am-9pm) contains a playful, multi-arched **ornamental gateway** built by the British. Two of its eight missile-shaped spires are leaning precariously, perhaps due to the devastating 1897 earthquake that destroyed virtually every other building in Guwahati.

FANCY BAZAAR

Guwahati's commercial centre around Fancy Bazaar is chaotically fascinating with minarets, a silver-spired church and a Sikh temple dome all rising like lighthouses above the stacked signboards and shop fronts. At night, Guwahati's homeless curl up here while the nouveau riche nibble Rs 47 cones of Baskin Robbins ice cream.

ASSAM STATE MUSEUM

This excellent **museum** (☎ 2540651; GNB Rd; adult/camera/video Rs 5/10/250; ☺ 10am-4.15pm Tue-Sun) displays tribal artefacts, ancient Assamese coins, fabrics and fabulous sculptures that hint at Guwahati's 14th-century grandeur. You get to walk through reconstructed tribal homes, and upstairs there's an engrossing reference library.

OLD GUWAHATI

There's a vaguely sweet naivety to strolling amid the floodlit statues, balloon sellers and bubble blowers of **Nehru Park** (HB Rd; adult/child Rs 10/5; ☺ 10am-9pm Fri-Wed) or paddling a boat on the water tank of **Dighulipukhuri Park** (HB Rd; admission Rs 2, boats per adult/child Rs 15/10; ☺ 9.30am-8pm). Above the latter rises the distinctive beehive dome of the **Courthouse** (MG Rd). Nearby, the **Guwahati planetarium** (☎ 2548962; MG Rd; star shows Rs 15; ☺ noon & 4pm) looks somewhere between a mosque and a grounded UFO. The half-hidden **Urra Tara Temple** (Lamb La) is Guwahati's second holiest, backed by the gently attractive **Jorpulkuri ponds** in the city centre's most prestigious residential quarter.

NABAGRAHA MANDIR

Several hill tops are crowned by minor curiosities. One such is **Nabagraha Mandir** (Temple of the Nine Planets; admission Rs 80-100), northeast of Central Guwahati by autorickshaw, famed as a centre of astrology. Beyond its aggressive monkey guardians, a darkly atmospheric inner sanctum holds nine ancient stone Shiva lingams.

Tours

Traveller's Point (☎ 2604018; www.assamtourism.org; Tourist Lodge, Station Rd) Assam Tourism's commercial booth offers various good-value Northeast packages for minimum-sized groups of three (sometimes five) people. This includes city tours (Rs 225/300/450 per person in groups of six/four/two), day excursions to Hajo and Sualkuchi (adult/child Rs 450/375, minimum five people) and two-day all-inclusive packages to Kaziranga National Park (from Rs 1280/2280 Indian/foreigner), including accommodation, transport, food, elephant ride and tea-garden visit.

Jungle Travels India (☎ 2660890; www.jungletravelsindia.com; 1st fl, Mandovi Apt, GNB Rd) Highly experienced agency covering the entire Northeast with wide-ranging tailor-made tour options. Planned fixed-date departures for Nagaland and Arunachal Pradesh will make it easier for independent foreign travellers to form the groups necessary to get permits. Agents for Assam–Bengal river cruises (www.assambengalnavigation.com, see p197) and Bansbari Lodge (p204). The building is beside Standard Chartered Bank marked 'Not Just Dosaz'.

Rhino Travels (☎ 2540666; MN Rd) Helpful, professional agency with a similarly wide range of tour possibilities and its own river lodge (p210). Also an agent for Manas elephant safaris (p204).

Sleeping

BUDGET

Sundarban Guest House (☎ 2730722; ME Rd, first side lane; s Rs150-600, d Rs 300-800; ☒) At this well-kept, friendly if unfinished hotel, the bargain top-floor options (s/d Rs 150/300 with shared bathroom) are possibly the cleanest rock-bottom rooms in town. Many nastier cheap hotels line the surrounding lanes.

Tourist Lodge (☎ 2544475; Station Rd; s/d Rs 275/330, d with AC Rs 633; ☒) Convenient for the train station, the fresh, clean rooms have fan, geyser and balcony. It's a genuine bargain, though be prepared for some train noise and climbing up to five-storeys of stairs.

Other cheap possibilities:

Hotel Kalpana (☎ 2545686; CK Rd; dm/s/q Rs 55/60/210) Slightly forbidding old mansion whose rock-bottom, shared bucket-bath rooms aren't quite as awful as the price would imply.

Hotel Suradevi (☎ 2545050; MN Rd; dm Rs 85, s/d with shared bathroom Rs 100/170, with private bathroom Rs 150/230) Well-organised warren of spartan rooms.

Hotel Tibet (☎ 2639600; AT Rd; s/d/tr from Rs 150/250/350) Perfectly survivable bed factory, very handy for the bus station.

Happy Home (☎ 2730759; Jasawanta Rd; d/tr with shared bathroom Rs 250/350 , s/d with private bathroom Rs200/400) Nine-room family hotel with surprisingly acceptable rooms above a cheap restaurant.

Kamakhya Debutter Lodge (☎ 2734099; Kamakhya Temple Complex; tw Rs 200-300, q Rs 500) Simple and very clean with a unique location, the upper terrace facing Kamakhya Mandir.

MIDRANGE & TOP END

All the hotels listed here offer cable TV and private bathrooms with hot water. Many add 25% tax/service charge.

Hotel Siroy Lily (☎ 2608492; Solapara Rd; s/d Rs 550/750, with AC Rs 850/1050; 🍴) A professionally run, well-maintained hotel with a lift, a pleasantly air-conditioned foyer and complimentary newspapers delivered to your door. Try the Manipuri food in its modest restaurant (see Sangai Restaurant, right).

Hotel Nova (☎ 2523464; SS Rd; s/d from Rs 680/890, with AC Rs 890/1090 plus 25%; 🍴) In the buzzing Fancy Bazaar area, this 15-room hotel is immaculately well kept and has a striking 1960s feel. Beneath the ceiling fans of the recommended restaurant (mains Rs 50 to 120) one could imagine stoned Vietnam War journalists scribbling reports between slices of cold turkey.

Hotel Rajmahal (☎ 2549141; www.rajmahalhotel .com; AT Rd; s/d with fan from Rs 1200/1800, with AC from Rs1900/2500 plus 25%; 🍴 🛗) If you pick this 10-storey semi-international tower hotel, pay the extra Rs 100 and upgrade to the attractively re-modelled super-deluxe rooms (Rs2000/2600). The rooftop swimming pool would be a great attraction if it was cleaned more regularly.

Pragati Manor (☎ 2341261; pragatimanor@lycos.com; GS Rd; s/d from Rs 1800/2100; 🍴) Were it nearer the centre, Pragati Manor would be Guwahati's undisputed upmarket pick. A costumed door-man ushers you into this 47-room oasis where modern architecture is softened with Indian art. Back rooms look out over palm-swathed hillocks and there's a glass-pod elevator.

Dynasty Hotel (☎ 2516021-5; dynasty_hotel@sify .com; SS Rd; s/d from Rs 2800/3000; 🍴) The dynasty's very classy foyer and wonderful restaurants seem discordantly civilised amid the melee of Fancy Bazaar. However, the musty rooms and damp-patched corridors are somewhat disappointing.

Other possibilities:

Hotel Orchid (☎ 2523471; B Baruah Rd; s/d from Rs 300/425, with AC Rs 700/1000; 🍴) Neat clean rooms leading off less appealing corridors. Slightly inconvenient location.

Blue Moon (☎ 2540059; bluemoon@hotmail.com; Bhubon Rd; s/d Rs 650/800; 🍴) Clean, decent-sized rooms in a somewhat soulless hotel near the planetarium.

Hotel Landmark (☎ 2455248; B Baruah Rd; s/d from Rs 1549/1849; 🍴 🖥) Although the décor lacks a real upmarket touch, the Rs 3500 suites are ultrapopular during cricket matches thanks to perfect views across the cricket ground.

Eating
RESTAURANTS

As well as the restaurants reviewed below there are many floating boat-restaurants moored between Kachari and Sukreswar Ghats, with the Kamakazi boat offering a disco, too. Be prepared for mosquitos. Many of Guwahati's more upmarket restaurants are often in hotels or sprinkled inconveniently widely down GS and GNB Rds.

Silk Route (☎ 2608024; GNB Rd; mains Rs 25-80; 🍴) Reasonably priced *momos* (Tibetan dumpling), Chinese and Thai food are served in a cosy, slightly atmospheric two-storey place, with cheaper Indian food available in friendly, simpler places nearby.

JB's (MG Rd; mains Rs 30-95; 🍴) All-in-one complex with bakery, ice-cream parlour, somewhat Mexican-styled snack bar and (upstairs via the sweet counter) a restaurant serving world-class Indian vegetarian food.

Gopal (☎ 2510364; Kamrup Chamber Rd; mains Rs 45-70; 🍴) Just around the corner from JB's, Gopal is another decent veggie option whose stylish décor has an appealing, low-key modern vibe.

Sangai Restaurant (☎ 2608492; Hotel Siroy Lily; dishes Rs 20-70; 🍴) The dining room doesn't look special but ask for the 'local' menu and choose from Guwahati's best selection of Manipuri specialities. Try *erongba* (jackfruit-kernel chutney) with *nga-thongba* (fish and ginger curry) on *chakhao* (black Manipuri rice).

Delicacy (☎ 2233402; junction of GS & RGB Rds, Ganeshguri; dishes Rs 20-100; 🕑 9am-4pm & 8-11pm; 🍴) Tucked beneath a repulsive overpass junction, the odd location is far from central but worth the trek for Guwahati's very best selection of northeastern cuisine styles. There are almost a dozen types of rice alone. Take bus 1, 2, 3 or 21 from near the museum.

Sagar Ratna (☎ 9954097416; MD Shah Rd; mains from Rs 45, coffee Rs 26; 🕑 8am-11pm; 🍴) This sparkling,

NORTHEAST STATES

modern chain restaurant specialises in vegetarian Indian food. Big windows, wickedly delicious coconut dosas (lentil-flour pancake) and good air-con justify slightly elevated prices.

Paradise (☎ 2666904; GNB Rd; thalis Rs 60-240; ☒) Famous if overrated place for Assamese cuisine in comfortable surroundings. Upstairs is air-conditioned and more attractive.

Tandoori (☎ 2516021-5; Dynasty Hotel, SS Rd; mains Rs 100-300; ☽ noon-3pm & 7-11pm) Majestic North Indian cuisine is served at stylish low tables by waiters in Mughal uniforms. A fountain tinkles in the background accompanying gentle live tabla music.

QUICK EATS
MC Rd offers several tastefully appointed fast-food joints. Choose **Pizzas** (☎ 2663329; pizzas Rs 40-285) for tasty if bready pizzas, cartoon-walled **Beatrix** (Rs 30-70) for burgers and **Cakes'n'Bakes** (mains Rs 15-25) for delicious fresh pastries (from Rs 6).

Beauty Valley (Dighulipukhuri Park; fast-food meals Rs 35-80; ☽ 11.30am-9.30pm) Romance on a budget illuminated by fairy lights on an open balcony overlooking the Dighulipukhuri tank. Decent chicken rolls.

Anamika (Sukreswar Ghat Park; mains Rs 25-70) Inexpensive al-fresco dining amid the palm trees.

Drinking
Café Coffee Day (Taybullah Rd; espresso Rs 23; ☽ 10am-11pm; ☒) Guwahati's most central answer to Starbucks pumps out contemporary music and attracts the city's gilded youth with perfect (if very slow) macchiatos.

Empire Restaurant and Bar (☎ 2514305; HB Rd; mains Rs 60-110, beers Rs 60; ☽ 10am-10pm) This cheesy, comic-book caricature of a 1970s *Cheers* bar, is more time warp than retro but it's fun for a quick Rs 20 'peg' of Old Monk rum. Live music on weekend nights is amusingly dreadful.

Trafik (☎ 2661275; GNB Rd; beers Rs 60; ☽ 10am-10pm) Trafik is a hip if predictably under-lit bar that rolls out a vast screen to show key cricket matches.

Shopping
Northeast Network (☎ 2603833; www.northeastnetwork.org; JN Borooah Lane; ☽ 9.30am-5.30pm Mon-Fri) This worthy, nonprofit NGO seeds self-help projects in rural villages, including several handloom weaving cooperatives. Buying beautiful (and good-value) cotton work here

supports this fine work and allows you to peep inside one of old Guwahati's few remaining colonial-era mansions.

Artfed (☎ 2548987; GNB Rd; ☽ 10am-8pm) Well stocked with bargain bamboo crafts, wicker work and many a carved rhino. Several nearby shops specialise in Assam's famous *muga* and *pat* golden-toned silks, though you might find prices somewhat cheaper in Sualkuchi (see opposite) where it's woven.

Getting There & Away
AIR
Guwahati's pleasantly orderly Lok-Priya Gopinath Bordoloi International Airport is 'international' thanks to Indian Airlines' Wednesday flight to Bangkok. However, there's considerable competition between domestic carriers:

Air Deccan (DN; ☎ 1-800 4257008; www.airdeccan.net)
Indian Airlines (IC & CD; ☎ 2264425; Ganeshguri)
IndiGo (6E; ☎ 9910383838; http://book.goindigo.in)
Jet Airways (9W; ☎ 2668255; GNB Rd)
Kingfisher (IT; ☎ 1-800 1800101; www.flyingkingfisher.com)
Sahara Airlines (S2; ☎ 2548676; GS Rd)
spiceJet (SG; ☎ 1-800 1803333; http://book.spiceJet.com)

Flights include the following:

Destination	Duration	Airline/Frequency
Agartala	40min	DN & IC/daily; 9W/Mon, Tue, Sat, Sun; IT/Mon, Fri, Sun
Aizawl	1hr	IC/Wed, Sun
Bagdogra	50min	IC/Tue, Thu, Sat; 9W/Mon, Wed, Fri; DN/Mon, Wed, Fri, Sun
Bangkok	2½hr	IC/Wed
Delhi	2¼hr	9W/twice daily; IC, 6E, DN & S2/daily
Dibrugarh	55min	DN/Mon, Wed, Fri, Sun; IT/Tue, Thu, Sat
Gaya	70min	IC/Wed
Imphal	50min	6E & DN/daily; 9W/Mon, Tue, Wed, Fri, Sat; IC/Wed, Sun
Jorhat	50min	9W/Thu,Sun
Kolkata	50-70min	DN, IC & 9W/twice daily; 6E, SG, S2 & IT/daily
Lilabari	1hr	IC/Tue, Sat; DN/Tue, Thu, Sat
Silchar	40min	IC/daily

BUS & SUMO
Most long-haul buses leave in the early morning or run overnight, so timed as to arrive around dawn. Buses for the various state gov-

ernments, including Assam State Transport Company (ASTC), leave from the **Paltan Bazaar bus station** (☎ 2730410; AT Rd). As if the multifarious ticket desks here weren't enough, there are also dozens of private operators strewn along surrounding roads and lanes. Prices might be somewhat higher but services are often more comfortable, including '2+1' coaches with only three seats to each row. Companies with particularly extensive networks include **Network Travels** (☎ 2522007; GS Rd), **Assam Valley** (☎ 2631843; GS Rd), **Royal Tours & Travels** (☎ 2519094; GS Rd) and **Blue Hill** (☎ 2607145; HPB Rd). **Deep** (☎ 2152937; HPB Rd) has a useful Siliguri service.

Destination	Fare (Rs)	Duration (hr)
Agartala (Tripura)	355-500	24-26
Dibrugarh	265-320	12
Dimapur via Numaligarh	218-250	10
Imphal (Manipur) via Mao	500	18-20
Jorhat	210-250	8
Kaziranga	150-210	6
Kohima (Nagaland)	310	13
Rangia	20	1½
Shillong (Meghalaya)	64	3½
Silchar	310	12-15
Siliguri (West Bengal)	330	13
Sivasagar	240	9½
Tezpur	110	5

For Shillong shared taxis/sumos (Rs 110/150) leave from outside Hotel Tibet. For Aizawl (Mizoram), **Zam Zam** (☎ 2639617; ME Rd, second side lane) runs several daily sumos (Rs 650, 16 hours) via Silchar (Rs 350, 11 hours).

Buses/sumos to Tura (Rs 175/230, six/10 hours) in western Meghalaya depart from KRB Rd.

HELICOPTER
Pawan Hans Helicopters (☎ 2416720) shuttle twice daily to Shillong (Rs 725, 30 minutes) and thrice weekly to Tura in Meghalaya. For Arunachal, choppers fly daily, except Sunday, to Naharlagun near Itanagar (Rs 3000, 1¼ hours). On Monday and Wednesday they serve Lumla (Rs 3000) for Tawang. Phone your booking then pay at the airport if the service actually decides to fly.

TRAIN
Trains to Kolkata take around 24 hours, so to arrive early morning take the 7.15am *Kamrup Express* to Howrah (sleeper/2AC Rs 299/1212).

For Darjeeling or Sikkim take the 10.30pm *Kanchenjunga Express* to New Jalpaiguri (sleeper/2AC Rs 164/663) arriving 7.35am. For Jorhat (6½ hours, depart 6.30am except Sunday) via Dimapur (four hours) the train is much faster than buses. Trains to Jorhat, Dibrugarh and Tinsukia cut through Nagaland, but you don't need a Nagaland permit as long as you stay on the train (though that's not true for buses). Until gauge conversion is complete, trains to Tezpur, North Lakhimpur and beyond start from Rangia (p204).

Getting Around
Shared taxis to the airport (Rs100/400 per person/car, 23km) leave from the driveway of Hotel Mahalaxmi (GS Rd) between 6am and 5pm. Avoid shifty freelancers nearby who might scam you en route.

There's a wide, if sometimes confusing, network of city buses. A useful hub is the Kachari bus stand, with services to Kamakhya Mandir (Rs 5, 15 minutes), Hajo (bus 25; Rs 15, one hour) and Sualkuchi (bus 22; Rs 15, 1¼ hours). Autorickshaws charge Rs 20 to 50 for shorter hops.

AROUND GUWAHATI
Hajo & Sualkuchi
Around 30km from Guwahati, **Hajo** attracts Hindu and Buddhists pilgrims with few ancient temples topping assorted little hillocks. Best known is the 1583 **Hayagriba-Madhava Mandir** with a silver-eyed, horse-headed Vishnu image in its haunting sanctum. Access (barefoot) is by a long stone stairway from the village centre, where bus 25 from Guwahati terminates. Muslims also swarm to Hajo for the hill-top **Poa Mecca mosque**, where an 800-year-old Tabrizi king-cum-saint's tomb was restored by the son of Shah Jahan. For non-Muslims the wide views and simple whitewashed architecture don't necessarily justify walking the sweaty 4.2km spiral road from central Hajo. If you're driving on to Manas, there's a well-surfaced, attractively winding Hajolink road.

Day tours from Guwahati combine Hajo with the dreary silk-weaving town of **Sualkuchi**, 7km further south by unsurfaced road. Bus 22 runs to Sualkuchi

Madan Kamdev & Baihata Chariali
From this busy NH31 crossroads at **Baihata Chariali** (30km north of Guwahati) it's easy to find bus connections to virtually anywhere

in northern Assam. Just 2km east then 3.5km south by asphalted road (Rs 150 return by autorikshaw) are the **Madan Kamdev** ruins. Here on a gentle hill behind what is possibly the world's cheapest **museum** (admission Rs 1; 🕙 10am-4pm Tue-Sun) lies a curiously haphazard jumble of 11th-century carved fragments, including Khajuraho-style scenes with lions mounting cows and horses humping young maidens. Madan Kamdev probably isn't worth a special trip but makes a pleasant tea stop if you're driving by. Beware that food ordered from the site's **Prashanti Restaurant** (tea Rs 5) can take several lifetimes to arrive.

Rangia
☎ 3621

Though Rangia is certainly not an attraction itself, all trains to Tezpur (8.30am) and Margung (ie Jonai) via North Lakhimpur and Dhemaji (6pm overnight sleeper) depart from **Rangia Junction**, at least until the railway's gauge has been standardised with the Guwahati mainline. Access from Guwahati is easiest by road. Get off passing buses at the unpromising junction near NH31's Km 1082 and take a Rs 5 rickshaw (1.2km) to the train station.

If driving by on the NH31, a great lunch stop is **New Highway Chef Dhaba** (☎ 242728; NH31 Murara; mains Rs 15-60) with funky dining platforms and possibly the best fish *tenga* in Assam.

NORTHWESTERN ASSAM (BODOLAND)
Manas National Park
☎ 03666

Straddling the Bhutanese border, the key attractions of Bodoland's **Manas National Park** (www .manas100.com; 🕙 Oct-Mar) are its genuine sense of community involvement, unique, comfortable lodges at Bansbari (comfort) and Mothanguri (landscape views), and the chance to spot a rare Bengal Florican. This Unesco World Heritage site suffered severe poaching during the Bodo conflicts so tigers are no longer the common sight that they were back in the early-1980s, though their awesomely large territorial claw markings are clearly visible on forest trees.

Exciting to ponder, though potentially bottom-breaking in reality, are unique multiday GPS-guided elephant-back safaris (US$425 to US$600 per person including food) sold through Rhino Travels (p200)

The park's two main ranges are entered from **Bansbari** (access from Barpeta Road) and **Koklabari**. You can connect between the two either by skirting the park boundary or on safari through the park (easier westbound) with a highly recommended stop at **Mothanguri**.

BARPETA ROAD

Not to be confused with Barpeta (a celebrated neo-Vaishnavite centre), dusty **Barpeta Road** is the main hub town for Manas. The **Manas Field Director's Office** (☎ 261413; www.manasassam.org; Main Rd) is 1km south of the rail tracks. Book here for Mothanguri (see opposite) and Satsimolo (see opposite) lodges. Covered jeep rental costs from Rs 1400 per day.

Barpeta Road has superb value budget accommodation at the unusually clean and friendly **Manas Guest House** (☎ 260935; Durgabari Rd; s/d with shared bathroom 60/100, s/d with private bathroom from Rs 150/250, d with AC Rs 850; 🔀), two blocks east of Main Rd behind the sprawling Municipal Market.

Howly, 8km south, holds a vast **Raash Mela festival** in November with up to 150,000 neo-Vaishnavite devotees arriving for enactments of the Krishna scriptures.

Barpeta Road's ASTC bus station is near the market but most other long-distance services (eg for Siliguri, Cooch Behar or Guwahati) depart from Simlaguri Junction, 3km south where Main Rd meets the NH31. Buses to Bansbari (Rs 10, 1½ hours) leave twice hourly till around 4pm from a point directly across the rail tracks from Main Rd's north end.

Trains run to Guwahati (three hours) at 9.40am and 1.10pm, and overnight to New Jalpaiguri at 11.15pm.

BANSBARI

Manas permits for the main range are organised at the range office in this quiet tea-growing village. Just before the park gate, 500m further north, is the wonderfully comfortable and welcoming **Bansbari Lodge** (www.assambengalnavigation .com/bansbari.htm; d Rs 1250). Bookings (100% essential) are handled by Jungle Travels in Guwahati (p200). The lodge will arrange all park formalities and provides guests with the only reliable source of open-top rental jeeps (Rs 1000) in the area. Before the December burn off, these are virtually essential to pass through high grasses in the park. At quoted rates, the lodge is great value, but annoyingly foreigners are sometimes 'forced' to take a full jungle plan (including all meals, elephant ride, jeep safari and guides). Indian guests are allowed to pick and mix the services they want.

MOTHANGURI

Within the park, 20km north of Bansbari, two loveably dated **lodges** (d Rs 500) sit just 10 minutes' walk from the unguarded **Bhutan border crossing**. The better, seven-room **upper lodge** has enchanting views across the Beki River backed by attractively layered hill ridges. Rooms are slightly aging but perfectly acceptable with mosquito nets and showers. The generator works if you bring your own diesel fuel. You should bring food, too, but staff will cook it for you while you laze in the sitting room stroking the stuffed man-eating tiger. Book months ahead through the **Field Director's Office** (☎ 261413; abhijitrabha@hotmail.com; Barpeta Road).

KOKLABARI

Manas' eastern **Bhunyapara Range** is separately managed by **MMES** (Manas Maozigendri; ☎ 268052, 261413; mahammes4_U@yahoo.com, abhijitrabha@hotmail.com; Barpeta Road). Usual national park fees apply (p196) and jeeps are available to rent (Rs 1000 per day plus petrol). MMES is a truly community-based organisation that has managed to recruit former Bodo insurgents and poachers as park guardians with remarkable success. At the village of **Koklabari**, at the park entrance, there is a fascinating little **museum** (Rs 30) displaying handmade guns, traps and other poaching weapons that they have impounded. Off the village market, a **handicraft workshop** makes and sells traditional bags, waistcoats and *aronai* scarves.

Within the range lives an estimated 80% of the world's population of Bengal Floricans. These bustard-like birds are easiest to observe from January to March.

The range office has three neat **guest rooms** (d/tw Rs 400/400) with mosquito nets and shared sit-down flush toilet. Nearing completion at the park gate is the **Jhobgang Jungle Camp** (d Rs 600) offering accommodation in traditionally styled Bodo bamboo cottages with attached bathrooms. Village homestays are also planned.

From Pathsala on the NH31, Koklabari is 30km up a wide but rough road. There's a single daily bus at 2pm, returning to Pathsala at 6am (Rs 15, two hours). Taxis cost Rs 800. Using 'jeepable' back lanes it's 34km from Koklabari to Bansbari through Betabari, Rupahi, Salbari and Barengabari villages.

GUWAHATI TO TEZPUR

If you're driving, consider a tea stop at Madan Kamdev (see p203), 35km out of Guwahati.

Orang National Park

The main attraction within this newly decreed **national park** (☎ 9954177677; Nov-Apr) is the chance to sleep at the relatively basic two-room **Satsimolo Lodge** (tw Rs 500). Book via Barpeta Road, opposite). It overlooks a waterhole where Orang's comparatively limited population of big animals often come for a dawn wallow. Elephant-back excursions are available but for a jeep tour (and even to reach Satsimolo) you'll need your own vehicle. There's much less chance of seeing rhinos here than at Kaziranga, but with very few other visitors, the experience is altogether calmer. See p196 for entry fees. There's a brand-new **Tourist Lodge** (☎ 9854165351; Indian/foreigner Rs 300/500) just outside the park gate.

BODOLAND

Linguistically related to the Garos of Meghalaya, the Bodo (pronounced Boro) plains people consist of around 16% of Assam's population. Their often-violent two-decade struggle for a Bodo homeland was initially led by the All Bodo Students Union (ABSU). In 1993 the ABSU legitimised themselves and created an autonomous council whose decrees included a demand that all Bodo women should wear *dokhona* (bright-coloured traditional Bodo costume). However, splits in the leadership caused a resumption of hostilities by the breakaway Bodoland Liberation Tigers Force (BLTF) faction. Peace was finally achieved after the BLTF signed up to a territorial council (BTC, www.bodolandcouncil.org) in 2004 and was rewarded with partial authority over a large Bodo autonomous district (BTAD), nicknamed 'Bodoland'. With a 'capital' at Kokrajhar, Bodoland consists of a long, narrow strip of northwestern Assam stretching as far as Orang. A rival Bodo group, the pro-independence National Democratic Front of Bodoland (NDFB) still seeks to gain its own piece of the pie, but its trouble-making power was undercut when in late 2004 it was ejected from its guerrilla bases in southeastern Bhutan, attacked by over half of Bhutan's entire armed forces.

In Bodo language, 'thank you' is *gwjwnthwng* (pronounced 'g'jn-tng').

The park is 125km from Guwahati, 70km from Tezpur and 15km off the NH52 by a smooth but unasphalted road that turns south at Dhansirghat. Dhansirghat is 7km west of Orang village, where informally renting a jeep to the park gates costs around Rs 800 (or Rs 1200 return with park excursion, excluding toll and entry fees). Guwahati-Tezpur buses pass regularly through Orang village.

TEZPUR

☎ 03712 / pop 59,000

Banasura, the thousand-armed demon king, was so overprotective of his beautiful daughter (Usha) that he had her locked into an impregnable 'fire fortress' (Agrigarh). But the ploy failed to keep away unwanted suitors. Through surreptitious magic, a dashing prince called Aniruddha managed to slip in and secretly marry her. Banasura was not a happy demon. He pondered feeding Aniruddha to his pet snakes as punishment. But the lad turned out to be none other than Lord Krishna's grandson. Krishna sent in his troops and an almighty battle ensued. The resulting carnage was so appalling that the site has been known ever since as Tezpur (or Sonitpur), the City of Blood.

That gory name gives entirely the wrong impression. Tezpur is probably Assam's most attractive city thanks to a series of beautifully kept parks, several lakes and various enchanting views of the mighty Brahmaputra River as it boldly caresses the town's central underbelly.

Internet access is available at **Softec Point** (NB Rd; per hr Rs 20; ☼ 9am-10pm), half a block north of the Baliram Building restaurants.

Sights

One block west then north of the main bus station, **Padun Pukhuri Lake** (adult/child Rs 5/2; ☼ 9am-7pm) has a bridge-linked island that becomes lover's lane at dusk. Two blocks nearer the river is the very appealing **Chitralekha Udyan** (Cole Park; Jenkins Rd; adult/child/camera Rs 10/5/20; ☼ 9am-8pm), where a U-shaped pond wraps around manicured lawns set with pretty trees and dotted with fine ancient sculptures gathered from various local ruins. The bearded chap wearing Mesopotamian-style costume is Banasura. For kids there's a **waterslide** (admission Rs 100; ☼ Apr-Oct). Tickets are sold in the southeast corner near the Tourist Lodge, but the entrance is from the south side.

A block east (passing Don Bosco School) then south is the small **Ganeshgarh temple**. Opposite, a ghat leads down to the sandy Brahmaputra banks and a floating restaurant. Continue nearly 1km east along the narrow, winding riverside lane to find **Agrigarh Hill** (Padma Park; adult/child Rs 10/5; ☼ 8am-7.30pm). Naturally this can't be proven to be Banasura's fire fortress site, but river views are lovely and there's plenty of not-quite-tacky statuary vividly illustrating the Usha legend.

Set among a chaos of boulders on the other side of town, **Oguri Hill** (adult/child Rs 5/2; ☼ 11am-4pm) has the best views of all, both towards the Brahmaputra and north to the crinkly, white-toothed Himalayan horizon. However, the views are only really clear at dawn when the park is technically closed. Ask nicely and the folks at the next-door Seismology Observatory might let you look from there instead. Access is off Da-Parbatia Rd, via a 1.5km spur of lane road that's the second left turning just after crossing the rail tracks.

Some 5km west, the ruined 6th-century **Da-Parbatia Mandir** (pronounced do-par-*bu*-tiya) has a celebrated Gupta-style carved door frame but is otherwise simply a stone platform in a field that nonspecialists might find underwhelming.

East of Tezpur, **Bharali Mukh**, the junction of the Bharali (Kameng) and Brahmaputra Rivers, is reputedly the best place in Assam to spot rare, blind **Gangetic dolphins** (☼ Nov-Jan), but finding a boatman to see them is hit and miss.

Sleeping

Youth Hostel (☎ 231021; dm/s Rs 50/100) Just north of the Da-Parbatia Rd, 400m west of the rail tracks, the hostel has peeling paint but decent-enough beds and mosquito nets. Bookings and IYHA card required.

Hotel Durba (☎ 224276; KK Rd; s/d Rs 250/400) Around 400m north of the bus station, Durba's clean, windowless rooms have sit-down flush toilets and geysers in tiled attached bathrooms.

Tourist Lodge (☎ 221016; Jenkins Rd; r without/with AC Rs 330/550; ✷) Facing Chitralekha Udyan, two blocks south of the bus station, the Tourist Lodge offers excellent-value, spacious rooms with bathrooms and mosquito nets.

Hotel Luit (☎ 222083; Ranu Singh Rd; s/d 'old wing' Rs 200/300, 'new wing' Rs 600/700, with AC Rs 1000/1200) Close to the bus station the Luit is on a small lane linking KK/Jenkins Rd and Main Rd. The smartest hotel in Tezpur, the reception is professional and budget rooms are remarkably reasonable, but the air-con rooms have aging bathtubs and require a sweaty climb to the 5th floor (unless the lift is mended). Taxes 25%.

Eating

Baliram Building (☎ 232726; cnr NB & NC/SC Rds) is a modern glass tower containing several floors of good dining. The ground-floor **dosa house** (☸ 6am-9pm) serves South Indian fare and cheap breakfasts. Semi-smart **China Villa** (☸ 10am-10.30pm) offers Indian and Chinese food in air-conditioned comfort, while the rooftop **Chat House** (☸ 8am-9.30pm) is an open-sided snack bar with city views.

Tiger Hill (☎ 9435081018; Fire Station Rd; mains Rs 30-80; ☸ 6am-9pm) On balmy evenings when the breeze keeps mosquitoes away, Tiger Hill is a gently pleasant place to dine al fresco on the lawns at the foot of Oguri Hill (visible but no direct access from here). Unusually for Assam, the food is highly spiced: that *bih-jolokia* perhaps? (see the boxed text, p208).

Getting There & Away

Near the Tourist Lodge, **Anand Travels** (☎ 220083/231657; Jenkins Rd) is the Indian Airlines agent. Direct flights to Kolkata (US$94, 1¼ hours) operate on Wednesdays, when you could arrive from Shillong. On Tuesdays and Sundays Kolkata flights ($170, 3¼ hours) go via Jorhat (US$64, 40 minutes). The airport is an intimidating military affair ringed with razor-wired fences. Its guarded gates are 10km up the NH52 (along which Balipara-bound buses pass regularly), then 600m east. Regular Balipara-bound buses pass nearby.

The busy **bus station** (KK/Jenkins Rd) has regular departures for Guwahati (Rs 110, five hours) via Orang village (1½ hours) and Jorhat (Rs 90, four hours) via Kaziranga (Rs 50, two hours). Private buses for the same destinations have booths just outside. APST buses for Dirang (Rs 205, 7½ hours) via Bomdila leave at 6.30am.

Sumos (shared jeeps) for Ziro, Along, Bomdila, Dirang and Tawang have their booking counters around the Hotel Durga.

Buses to Bhalukpong (Rs 28, 1½ hrs) via Balipara and Potasali junction leave roughly twice hourly from the northwest corner of Padun Pukhuri.

The one daily passenger train to Rangia (Rs 50, 6¼ hours) departs at 6.15am. The train station is southwest of Chitralekha Udyan, and has a computerised booking counter for connecting services.

TOWARDS TAWANG

One of the Northeast's most appealing excursions is the beautiful, very varied drive to Tawang in Arunachal Pradesh's 'Little Tibet' (see p236). Without a permit you must stop at Bhalukpong.

If they create a tea-tasting café as mooted, drivers might consider a short detour to the **Addabarie Tea Estate** (☎ 03714234354), 3km east of Balipara along the NH52 then 2km north. The estate also maintains the appealing but extraordinarily overpriced **Wild Mahseer Lodge** (www.oldassam.com/wildmahseer/default.html; d Rs 5000-18,000).

Nameri National Park

Whether or not you visit the park, it's well worth coming to **Potasali** en route to Tawang to sleep at the delightful **Eco-Camp** (☎ 9435250052; dm/d Rs 100/1150 plus Rs 60 per person membership). Colourful fabrics, private toilets and thatched over-shelters make the luxurious 'tent' experience feel far removed from camping. From your heavy bamboo bed, you can hear all the magical sounds of the jungle provided thoughtless fellow tourists don't decide to crank up their beat-boxes. There are also some excellent bird-watching opportunities in the area. In a bigger thatched-roof construction, dorm beds are great value and there's an atmospheric open-sided restaurant serving decent buffet dinners.

At dawn next morning, walk 1.3km to the riverbank for a good chance of seeing white-topped mountains rising above layers of forested Arunachal foothills across an idyllic Bharali River bend. The **Nameri National Park** (☸ Nov-Apr) begins on the far riverbank. Eco-Camp can arrange a canoe crossing and guide but you explore on foot. Usual park fees apply (p196). The Eco-Camp can also organise raft trips down the river (Rs 955 per boat for a two hour, 15km run). That includes two boatmen but assumes you'll transport the raft to the start point. If you can't, it's usually possible to rent a suitable jeep with roof rack (Rs 350).

By public transport, get off twice-hourly Tezpur buses at a tiny, signed junction 12km north of Balipara. Eco-Camp is a 2km walk east.

Bhalukpong

☎ 03782

Little Bhalukpong is a market village straddling the Assam border. There's a petrol station and several cheap dives on the Arunachal

N O R T H E A S T   S T A T E S

side but the best accommodation (handy if the Nameri Eco-Camp is full) is **Bhalukpong Tourist Lodge** (☎ 234037; cottage Rs 550-650) on the Assam side. It offers appealing cottages ranged around a raised grassy area overlooking a sweep of the Bharali/Kameng River, just 300m east of Bhalukpong's busy market.

KAZIRANGA NATIONAL PARK
☎ 03776

Assam's must-do attraction is a rhinoceros-spotting safari in the expansive flat grasslands of **Kaziranga National Park** (☼ Nov-Apr, elephant rides 5.30am & 6.30am, jeep access 7.30-10.30am & 2.30-5pm). Kaziranga's population of around 1800 Indian one-horned rhinos (up from just 200 in 1904) represents over two-thirds of the world's total. There are several 'ranges', but Kaziranga's central range generally offers the best viewing chances for rhinos, elephants and swamp deer along with plenty of bird life, including greater adjutant storks (take binoculars). One-hour **elephant rides** (Indian/foreigner Rs 120/750 plus park fees) are especially satisfying when a 'team' of several elephants makes a pincer movement to surround rhinos without frightening them off.

Information
For Kaziranga's central range, everything is close to Kohora village. That's marked by an obvious Rhino Gate near the Km 378 marker on the NH37 highway. Don't head for the park entrance (2km north) till you've paid relevant fees (p196) at the **range office** (☎ 262428; ☼ 24 hr), located within the Kaziranga Tourist Complex, 800m south of the Rhino Gate. Jeep rental (from Rs 550) is available across the complex's grassy central square, just east of

---

SOME LIKE IT HOT

How hot is a chilli pepper? Incredibly there is a whole science to measuring spiciness. A grading system assesses peppers in Scoville Units of pungency. Pimento scores 500, Tabasco sauce tops 2500 and Jalapeño peppers go up to 8000. But that's nothing compared to Tezpur's *bih-jolokia* (translating to poison chilli), which has been recorded at a phenomenal 1,041,427. That made it the world's hottest chilli. At least until March 2006 when it was out-hotted by a Dorset Naga chilli grown in unexotic rural England.

---

which is the **elephant-ride booking office** (☼ 6-7pm). A taxi ride to and from the elephant-ride departure point costs Rs 150 extra.

Better hotels can organise all bookings, paperwork and jeep rentals for you at minimal extra cost.

WHEN TO GO
Elephant rides start from November, but at that time grass is elephant-high so the ride can feel like sailing mysteriously on a green sea. The grass burns off in December or January improving visibility, and by February new sprouts and cooler temperatures tempt more larger animals to venture into the open. In especially dry years the park opens for jeep safaris from mid-October.

Sleeping & Eating
Several hotels add 15% tax. When Kaziranga is closed (May to mid-October) prices drop at least 30%.

TOURIST COMPLEX
All of the following are within a five-minute walk of the range office. Booking ahead is wise, but advance payment is often required.

Kunjaban Lodge (☎ 262423; dm without/with linen Rs 25/50) Offers perfectly passable three- and 12-bed dorms.

Bonoshree Lodge (☎ 262423; s/d Rs 210/260) Has aging but well-renovated rooms with tiled-floor bathrooms in a long, green bungalow.

Bonani Lodge (☎ 262423; s/d ground fl Rs 320/380, 2nd fl Rs 350-410) Spacious, whitewashed rooms in a two-storey building with wicker furniture.

Prashanti Cottage (☎ 262429; d Rs 690) This excellent option has six modernist split-level units.

Aranya Lodge (☎ 262429; s/d Rs 630/690, with AC 750/860; ❄) Is a could-be-anywhere concrete hotel, but better rooms have air-con and there's a restaurant and bar.

Network Travels Motel (☎ 262699; d Rs 450) Serves up cafeteria meals (Rs 30 to 50), mostly for transiting bus passengers.

AROUND THE COMPLEX
Uninspired Rs 500 house-hotels are sprinkled along 2km of the NH37 east of Rhino Gate. None are great value, nor as good as equivalents in the Tourist Complex. However, there are two much better options.

ourpick **Wild Grass Resort** (☎ 262085; www.old assam.com; d high season/off season Rs 1600/900; ⬛) This delightful, ecofriendly resort is so justifiably popular that it doesn't even bother with a sign. Raja-inspired room décor makes you feel like you're on safari, the atmospheric dining room serves fabulous Assamese food and there's a jungle-edged, summer-only swimming pool. Accomplished Krishna dances are performed nightly in the garden folly. Wild Grass is 600m off the NH37, south of Km 373 (ie 4km east of Kohora). In season, bookings are essential.

Bonhabi Resort (☎ 262675; www.bonhabiresort.com; s/d Rs 1200/1400; 🏊) Suave modern rooms, some with air-con, are highly comfortable but the experience is somewhat marred by all-night generator noise.

Getting There & Away

Buses between Guwahati (Rs 150 to 210, six hours) or Tezpur and Jorhat (Rs 60, two hours) or Dimapur all pass through Kohora on the NH37. Many Network buses even divert the 800m up to the Tourist Complex for a lunch stop. A small public call office (PCO) directly west of Rhino Gate can book bus seats. If stranded, you could increase your chances of a ride by taking the twice-hourly local bus to Bokakhat (Rs 10), 20km east. Overnight tours to Kaziranga run regularly from Guwahati (see p200).

UPPER ASSAM
Jorhat
☎ 0376 / pop 70,000

En route to Majuli Island, Jorhat offers few sights but you could take a tea-estate retreat or play a round of golf at the 1876 **Gymkhana Club** (☎ 2311303; Club Rd; green fees Rs 100) – though it might need a few days' notice to rustle up a set of rentable clubs.

Jorhat's commercial street (Gar-Ali) meets the main east thoroughfare (AT Rd) in front of the lively **central market** area, where you will see giant hornets buzzing around golden-brown piles of jaggary. Head 400m west along AT Rd then south to find the small **museum** (Postgraduate Training College, MG Rd; admission free; 🕙 10am-4.30pm Tue-Sun) and nearby **Assam Tourism** (☎ 2321579) in the good-value Tourist Lodge (see right).

SLEEPING & EATING

Around 1km west of the market, immediately before the well-ordered ASTC bus station (AT Rd), little Solicitor Rd (aka Biman Barua Rd) hosts nearly a dozen hotels. Price and quality varies within properties as much

as between them, so look carefully. For budget fan-rooms with a little soul pick **Hotel Janata Paradise** (☎ 2320610; Solicitor Rd; d Rs 200-400), whose spacious lobby-restaurant (🕙 noon-4pm & 8-9pm) serves an excellent value 10-dish Assamese thali for just Rs 35. **Tourist Lodge** (☎ 2321579; MG Rd; s/d Rs 210/330) is another budget accommodation option.

Hotel Dilip (☎ 2321610; s/d/tr from Rs 300/350/500; 🏊) is good for compact, quick-cooling air-con singles (Rs 450) with hot shower. **Hotel Dipti** (☎ 2326910; Solicitor Rd; s/d from Rs 250/500; 🏊) has sad standard rooms but excellent deluxe air-con rooms on its upper floors (Rs 500 to 1000). **Hotel Heritage** (☎ 2321719; Solicitor Rd; d fan/ AC Rs 425/950; 🏊) is a reliable midrange choice, a modern tower despite the name.

Hotel GK Palace (☎ 2309972; Gar-Ali; d fan/AC from Rs 650/1100; 🏊), located just 200m east of the train station, is a smart new business hotel with obliging staff, a 'Chill Bar' and acres of marble.

GETTING THERE & AWAY

Jet Airways (☎ 2325652) serves both Kolkata (US$141, 1½ hours) and Guwahati (US$81, 50 minutes) twice weekly. **Indian Airlines** (☎ 2320011) flies to (but not from) Kolkata. Both airlines are based within the fading Hotel Paradise (Solicitor Rd) beside Hotel Heritage. The airport, 6km east of town, is prone to severe fog in winter.

From the **ASTC bus station** (AT Rd), buses leave several times hourly to Sivasagar (Rs 25, 1½ hours) and Bokakhat (Rs 60, 1¾ hours), from where it's 20km by local bus to Kaziranga. It's simpler to just use one of the many Tezpur or Guwahati buses (Rs 200, eight hours).

On Monday to Saturday the Guwahati–Jorhat express train (2nd class/AC-chair Rs 127/420, seven hours) departs at 6am and returns at 1.45pm.

Around Jorhat
TEA ESTATE GETAWAYS

Jorhat is surrounded by tea estates. At a few, colonial-era planters' bungalows are now available as relaxing, do-nothing heritage-style getaways. But don't turn up without prebooking.

Dating from the 1870s, **Sangsua** (☎ 2385075, bookings 9954451548; www.heritagetourismindia.com/sang sua.html; d Rs 1500-1800) has wonderful lawns and verandas. There's some antique furniture but standards are homly rather than lavish. Ghatoonga Bungalow on the same estate is being prepared for hotel service. Tours of the tea plantation (Rs 250) are possible if prebooked. The site is 7km down rural tracks from Km 442 on the NH37 (Jorhat–Deragaon road). Furkating-bound local trains leaving Jorhat at 7am and 5pm daily stop at nearby Moabondha station (Rs 7, 45 minutes).

With its classical portico and wide, cowmown lawns, **Thengal Manor** (☎ 2339519, bookings 9954451548; Jalukanburi; s/d/tw Rs 2000/2500/2000 plus 15%) looks incredibly grand. Old photos, wind-up gramophone and medal certificates from King George VI add atmosphere, rooms have four-poster beds and there's a selection of rare, locally relevant books to read. However, the effect is slightly marred by patches of wall damp and hot-water issues. The cheaper twin is smaller and windowless. Opinions on the Rs 360 set dinners vary wildly. Thengal is 15km south of Jorhat on the MG Rd extension towards Titabor.

DHEKIAKHOWA

This major neo-Vaishnavite **pilgrimage site** was the home-temple of Madhavdev (Mahavadeva), Sankardev's major disciple and convert. There's plenty of *kritan* chanting and singing, especially between 10am and noon, and at any time during **Bhadra** (17 August to 18 September). You're likely to be given a very generous welcome, but the temple complex itself isn't really photogenic. It's 12km east of Jorhat, then 3km north off the NH37 at Km 471 passing some typical Assamese houses of mud-plastered bamboo en route.

NIMATIGHAT

A windswept sandbank at Nimatighat is the departure point for photogenically overcrowded ferries to Majuli Island (see right). On an otherwise deserted river island reached from here by private launch (Rs 50), **Mou Chapori River Resort** (☎ 9435357171; hornbill121@rediff.com; furnished tent/bamboo hut/luxury cottage d Rs 600/1200/2000) is due to open at the time of publication. Its traditionally styled hut accommodation should be idyllically peaceful, and regular one-day group tours by private boat (Rs 800 per person) promise to offer a particularly convivial way to get a taste for Majuli Island. Book via Rhino Travels (p200).

Nimatighat is a very potholed 12km from Jorhat by shared auto (Rs10, 40 minutes) or very rare, overcrowded buses (Rs 8).

Majuli Island

☎ 03775

In the midst of the great grey Brahmaputra River, an ever-shifting puzzle of sandbanks includes **Majuli**, the world's largest river island. A few days here allows you to gently contemplate mesmerising landscapes of rice fields, water meadows and fish traps, meet the local Mising people and learn about neo-Vaishnavite philosophy at one of Majuli's 22 ancient *satras* (see boxed text, opposite).

Ferries arrive 3km south of **Kamalabari**, from where the main village **Garamur** is a further 5km. For a brief visit, the most interesting but accessible *satras* are the large, beautifully peaceful **Uttar Kamalabari** (1km north then 600m east of Kamalabari) and **Auniati** (5km west of Kamalabari) where monks are keen to show you their little museum of Ahom royal artefacts. The best chances of observing chanting, dances or drama recitations are around dawn and dusk or during the big **Ras Mahotsav Festival**, held in the third week of November.

SLEEPING & EATING

All accommodation is very basic – bring a sleeping bag. If actively interested in neo-Vaishnavite philosophy you can usually arrange space at a *satra* guesthouse.

La Maison de Ananda (☎ 274768; dm Rs 150), hidden away in a green Garamur back lane, this is a new but traditionally styled thatched house on bamboo stilts with three bamboo beds and locally made fabrics. It's run by local guide and fixer Danny Gam (☎ 9435205539).

At the central crossroads in Garamur, **Hotel Island** (☎ 274712; s/d/tr Rs 120/240/350) is a less-than-exciting dive.

Cheap eateries in central Kamalabari and Garamur serve simple Indian food.

GETTING THERE & AWAY

Overcrowded little public ferries from Nimatighat depart at 10.30am and 3pm (adult/jeep Rs 12/450, 2½ hours) returning at 7.15am and 2pm. Most ferries can only carry two vehicles. The timetable makes day trips pointless as you'd get barely one hour on the island. An alternative is chartering your own ferry (Rs 4000), ask the **harbour manager** (☎ 9435203421).

GETTING AROUND

Buses meet arriving ferries and leave once full to Garamur (Rs 10) via Kamalabari, where three-wheelers are easier to rent.

Sivasagar (Sibsagar)

☎ 03772 / pop 64,000

This oil-service town was once the capital of the Ahom dynasty that ruled Assam for over 600 years. Sivasagar takes its name ('waters of Shiva') from its graceful central feature, an attractive rectangular reservoir dug in 1734 by Ahom queen Ambika. Rising proudly above the tank's partly wooded southern banks are the finest extant trio of typical Ahom **temple-towers**. The central 33m-high **Shivadol Mandir** is the tallest Shiva temple in India. Its uppermost trident balances upon an egg-shaped feature whose golden covering the British reputedly tried (but failed) to pilfer in 1823. Several sadhus sit along the temple approach path and its interior is atmospherically eerie, lit only by a few votive mustard-oil lamps. Dominating the tank's western side, the red-painted **Assam Tai Museum** normally displays exhibits on Ahom history but was under renovation at the time of research. Two minutes' walk away at the tank's southwest corner, **Assam Tourism** (☎ 2222394) is located within the great-value **Tourist Lodge** (☎ 2222394; s/d Rs 210/260), whose six large rooms have clean tiled floors. Around 500m from Shivadol (south then east on Hospital Rd) are a gaggle of hotels along AT Rd close to the ASTC bus station. The most appealing of these is the surprisingly swish **Hotel Shiva Palace** (☎ 222629; fax 225184; s/d economy Rs 480/576, with AC & hot water from Rs 875/1000) incorporating a decent, air-conditioned restaurant.

SATRAS

A *satra* is a monastery of neo-Vaishnavism, Assam's distinctive form of everyman Hinduism. Formulated by 15th-century Assamese philosopher Sankardev, the faith eschews the caste system and idol worship, focussing on Vishnu as God, especially in his Krishna incarnation. Much worship is based around the dance and melodramatic play acting of scenes from the holy Bhagavad Gita. The heart of any *satra* is its *namghar*, a large, simple, prayer hall often usually open sided and shaped like an oil tanker sailing west. Beneath the eastern end is the inner sanctum hosting an eternal flame, the Gita and possibly a horde of instructive (but not divine) images. *Satras* are highly spiritual but don't expect anything enormously photogenic.

From the ASTC bus station several buses leave each daytime hour to Jorhat (Rs 26, 1½ hours) and Dibrugarh (Rs 38, 2¼ hours). For Guwahati (Rs 240, 9½ hours) government buses depart between 7am and 9.15am, plus at 8pm and 9.30pm, with many private services from offices on nearby AT Rd.

For Kareng Garh, use Gargaon buses (Rs 10, 45 minutes), which depart from an unmarked stop on BG Rd: walk 300m north up AT Rd from the bus station, then turn right.

Simaluguri Junction train station, 16km southeast, is on the Tinsukia Dimapur mainline.

Around Sivasagar

Dotted around Sivasagar are many lemon-squeezer-shaped temples and ochre-brick ruins built by the Ahom monarchs during their 17th- and 18th-century heydays.

TALATALGARH

Though not enormously dramatic, the most-famous Ahom ruin complex is around 4km west down AT Rd. You'll pass a WWII-era metal lift-bridge across the Dikhaw River. Some 2km later at the roadside, **Rang Garh** (Indian/foreigner Rs 5/100; ☺ 8am-5pm) is a two-storey oval-shaped pavilion from which Ahom monarchs would watch buffalo and elephant fights. Just beyond here turn left, passing the Golaghar (Ahom ammunition store) to reach the extensive, two-storey palace ruins, **Talatalgarh** (Indian/foreigner Rs 5/100; ☺ 8am-5pm). Like Rang Garh, the lumpy brick structure and its beautifully tended gardens are most attractive when viewed at a distance from the entrance gate.

KARENG GARH

This dramatic, if largely unadorned, brick **palace** (Indian/foreigner Rs 5/100; ☺ 8am-5pm) is a unique four-storey structure shaped like a sharpened, stepped pyramid. Dating from 1752 it's the last remnant of the Ahom capital that preceded Sivasagar. Its forest-and-paddy setting is potentially delightful but marred by a nearby electrical transformer substation. It's 900m north of the Sivasagar–Sonali road: turn just before Gargaon (14km).

Diehard Ahom fans driving on to Mon (Nagaland) might consider diverting around 4km off the main road to see **Charaideo Maidam** (28km from Sivasagar), the burial mounds of many Ahom monarchs, looted in the 19th century but now restored.

GAURISAGAR

Like a practise run for Sivasagar, Gaurisagar has an attractive tank behind which lies a trio of distinctive temples built in the 1720s by the 'dancing girl queen' Phuleswari. Most impressive is the **Devidol** (admission free; ☼ 24hr). It's not as tall as Sivasagar's Shivadol but sports finer stone carvings, albeit many significantly eroded. The site is just 50m off the main NH37 Sivasagar–Jorhat road at Km 501.5.

Dibrugarh

☎ 0373 / pop 122,000

Totally rebuilt after a devastating 1950 earthquake, 'tea-city' Dibrugarh offers few sites but is a logical launching point for closing a loop between Kaziranga and the Ziro–Along–Pasighat route.

ORIENTATION & INFORMATION

From Dibrugarh town train station, RKB Path follows the railway tracks northeast passing HS Rd (which leads to AT Rd via the market area). After 800m RKB Path meets Mancotta Rd close to the small east Arunachal bus station and fast-connection internet café, **Ajmera** (Sachit Studio, Mancotta Rd; per hr Rs 20; ☼ 10am-9pm). Across the railway tracks, 1km south on Mancotta Rd then 300m right on Convoy/TRP Rd, is the main bus station.

Unmarked behind a modernist **Radha-Krishna temple**, the 3km east of centre, local tour agency **Purvi Discovery** (☎ 2301120; www.purviweb.com; Medical College Rd, Jalan Nagar) organises vehicle rental (from Rs 1500 per day plus petrol) and two-hour **tea tours** (admission Rs 400; ☼ Tue-Sat Apr-Nov) at Dibrugarh's relatively traditional Ethelwold Estate given three day's notice. It also organises **horse-riding trips** (around Rs 7000 per day incl meals, set date departures, ☼ Oct-Apr).

SLEEPING

There's a knot of hotels around the junction of HS and AT Rds.

Asha Lodge (☎ 2320053; AT Rd; s/d with shared toilet Rs 60/120) The only ultra budget option in town.

East End Hotel (☎ 2322698; New Market; s/d from Rs 230/345) Located just off HS Rd, is a handily central option with tired, basic but clean good-value budget rooms with attached cold shower.

Hotel Indsuriya (☎ 2326322; RKB Path; s/d with fan Rs 345/564, with AC from Rs 805/1035; ⌘) Near the train station, is an upper midrange option with bright, modern corridors, a children's play area, some local furniture motifs and a

Princess Diana plate among the Assam textiles of the lobby display.

Hotel Devika (☎ 2325956; HS Rd extension; s/d with fan Rs 563/813, d with AC Rs 1313-1988; ⌘) Outwardly upmarket hotel, whose attractively decorated corridors belie disappointingly bare rooms.

Dibrugarh area's two most charming accommodation options are old tea-planters' houses operated through Purvi Discovery (see left):

Jalannagar South Bungalow (Convoy Rd; s/d upstairs Rs 1500/2600, r downstairs Rs 1600) Has upstairs rooms with polished floorboards, Gujarati bedspreads and settees around an attractive tiled fireplace. Downstairs rooms lack atmosphere having been added as an afterthought between what were once supporting stilts. It's located 700m from the main bus station.

Mancotta Chang Bungalow (Mancotta Rd; s/d main Bldg Rs 2000/3600, s 'executive' Rs 1000) This truly delightful 1849 building is 4km from the ASTC bus station set in tree-shaded lawns with acres of polished hardwood floors on the upper, veranda floor. The slightly smaller downstairs rooms are also delightful, if with a slightly less heritage feel. The misleadingly named 'executive' rooms are much more basic in a small, nondescript brick house with simple, shared 1940s-style lounge.

EATING & DRINKING

Flavours (☎ 2326438; Mancotta Rd; mains Rs 60-; ☼ 10am-10pm) Behind a small colourful ice-cream/fast-food dispensary, this upbeat little restaurant has a clean, Western atmosphere and serves bready pizzas as well as masala dosas (till 7pm). Just north of the railway tracks.

H20 (Mancotta Rd; mains Rs 50-110, beers Rs55) This fun upstairs bar-restaurant located nearly opposite the east Arunachal bus station has elements of spaceship décor and serves lemon chicken that's delicious if more garlic than lemony.

Hotel Mona Lisa (Mancotta Rd South; fresh juice Rs 65) Has a juice-bar in its lanterned courtyard.

El Dorado (☎ 2326805; City Regency Hotel, RKB Path; beers Rs 90, pegs from Rs 30) Suave if exaggeratedly under-lit international-style bar with bottle-spinning barman and Indian trance music.

GETTING THERE & AWAY

Indian Airlines (☎ 2300114; Circuit House Rd) flies to Kolkata (US$100, one hour) daily except Mondays. **Kingfisher** (☎ 1-800 1800101; www.fly kingfisher.com) flies to Guwahati thrice weekly. **Air Deccan** (www.airdeccan.com) flies daily to both, and is generally much cheaper. Mohanbari airport is 16km northeast of Dibrugarh, 4km off the Tinsukia road. Shared three-wheelers (Rs 10) operate from AT Rd to Mohanbari market. To find Mohanbari market, walk out of the airport, turn right and continue 500m.

From the **main bus station** (TRP Rd), ASTC buses run three times hourly to Sivasagar (Rs 38, 2¼ hours), Jorhat (Rs 68 to 90, four hours) and Tinsukia (Rs 23, 1½ hours) until 5pm, and to Digboi (Rs 35 to 40, 2½ hours) at 7.30am, 1.15pm and 2.30pm. Various services to Guwahati (Rs 265 to 320, 12 hours) leave around 7am. More leave at around 9.30pm both from here, from outside the train station and from the east Arunachal bus station, where you'll also find 6am buses to Khonsa and Changlang (Rs 85, six hours).

A new bus station is being developed at Murlidhar Jalan at the Tinsukia edge of town.

The best-timed overnight train for Guwahati (3AC/2AC Rs 865/1275, 14½ hours) is the 4pm *Kamrup express*, bound eventually for Kolkata-Howrah (38½ hours). For Dimapur take the 10.45pm Delhi-bound *Brahmaputra Mail* arriving around 6am. Weekly trains run all the way to Amritsar (Tuesday morning) and Chennai (Sunday night).

Dibrugarh to Pasighat

Until the controversial Bogibeel road-rail bridge is finished (estimated 2010), crossing the Brahmaputra River from Dibrugarh will remain an all-day affair. Buses to the north bank loop all the way round via Tezpur. Don't trust maps that show roads to Pasighat via Sadiya or Tezu: such routes could take days with several tough sections and river crossings en route. An interesting alternative is the rough-and-ready **DKO Ferry** (passenger/bicycle/motorbike/vehicle/elephant Rs 67/44/199/1500-3087/4190) to Oriamghat near **Pasighat** (Arunachal Pradesh, see p230) carrying passengers and two jeeps (booking not possible). It departs daily at 8am in both directions taking eight hours upstream, 5½ hours return. Brief stops en route give scenic glimpses of isolated riverside hamlets like **Berachapuri** and **Tinmil**, where fishing canoes sport domed central sun shelters.

Departure points vary according to the river's water level; usually Maijan (5km from Dibrugarh) or Nagaghuli (12km). Bring an umbrella, sunscreen or both. Dibrugarh's **Kusum Hotel** (☎ 2320143; Talkiehouse Rd) and

Pasighat's Hotel Siang offer a jeep-ferry-jeep combination ticket (Rs 250), though it's somewhat cheaper to reach the ferry by taxi than cram aboard the waiting bus on arrival.

SOUTH ASSAM

Arguably south Assam's most attractive area is the **Cachar Hills**, but the region is currently suffering serious insurgency from the DHD (Dimasa separatists), whose poetically named subfactions (like 'Black Widow', led by Jewel Gorlosa) are also embroiled in a bloody turf war. That means visits to **Haflong**, once a popular hill station, are not advised. However, further south, the predominantly Bengali city of Silchar is contrastingly safe.

Silchar

☎ 03842 / pop 155,000

Flat, sprawling and without any real tourist attractions, Silchar is nonetheless a useful transport hub for breaking journeys between Shillong and Mizoram or Tripura. Club, Central and Park Rds converge at a small roundabout near the main bus station and Deroot Cinema. There's patchy internet access at **CyberMagic** (☎ 261837; Park Rd; ⏰ 8am-10pm). Hotels are remarkably good value.

The budget rooms at **Hotel Geetanjali** (☎ 231738; Club Rd; s/d from Rs150/265, d with AC Rs 550) are much better than its gloomy foyer suggests. Located four minutes' walk from the bus station, down a narrow passageway before Indian Airlines,

Although not quite as plush as its lobby suggests, **Hotel Kalpataru** (☎ 245672; s/d from Rs170/290, d with AC Rs 550; ❄) is a neat, new hotel that is handily located right beside the bus station.

The six-storey **Hotel Kanishka** (☎ 246764; Narsingtola; s/d from Rs 290/520; ❄) has super new rooms with some fun touches like Art Deco designs on doors and a grandfather clock in the little lobby. It's cheaper and more stylish than the better-known Hotel Borail View. It's on the first paved link street between Park and Central Rds.

Silchar's **airport** (☎ 282311) is at Kumbeergram, 30km from Silchar. Shared Ambassador taxis (per person/car Rs 70/350) depart from outside **Indian Airlines** (☎ 245649; Club Rd; ⏰ 10am-5pm), which provides daily flights to Kolkata (Rs 5675), Guwahati (Rs 3855) and Imphal (Rs 2810, 30 minutes), and three services weekly to Agartala (Rs 3855, 35 minutes). Air Deccan has daily budget flights to Kolkata.

Buy bus and sumo tickets from various counters around the bus station.

To	Bus fare (Rs)	Sumo fare (Rs)	Departures	Duration (hr)
Agartala	220	250	6.30am	11+
Guwahati	310	375	7.30am, 7pm	12-15
Jowai	205 (ASTC)	325	6.45, 7, 7.45am	6-9
Shillong	250	325	7am, 5.30pm	8-11

To Jowai you'll usually pay the full Shillong fare, except on slow ASTC buses. For Agartala, buses run some sections in military convoys making progress appallingly slow: consider breaking the trip at Kailasahar (for Unakoti, p224)

MEGHALAYA

Carved out of Assam in 1972, hilly Meghalaya (the Abode of Clouds) is a cool, pine-fresh contrast to the sweaty Assam plains. Set on dramatic horseshoes of rocky cliff above the Bengal plains, Cherrapunjee and Mawsynram are statistically the wettest places on earth. Most of this precipitation falls April to September (and mostly at night) creating some very impressive waterfalls and carving out some of Asia's longest caves. Meghalaya was dubbed the 'Scotland of the East' by 19th-century Brits, and made Shillong the capital of colonial Assam.

Eastern and central Meghalaya are mainly populated by the closely related Jaintia, Pnar and Khasi peoples (see the boxed text, opposite), originally migrants from Southeast Asia. Western Meghalaya is home to the unrelated Garo tribe (see p220). Despite their different ethnic backgrounds, these two groups both use a matrilineal system of inheritance, children taking the mother's family name and babies often carried on the father's back.

SHILLONG

☎ 0364 / pop 268,000
From 1874 until 1972, this sprawling hill station was the capital of British Assam. Since Independence it has developed into a fairly typical modern Indian town, but it still retains elements of charm and the air is refreshingly cool, if you don't mind a good chance of rain.

Information
INTERNET ACCESS
None are fast, all charge Rs 20 per hour.
CyberTech (Thana Rd; ☼ 9am-9pm) Central, but cramped.

Enter-The-Web (Malki Point; ☼ 10am-7pm)
Mookherjee's Cyber Café (☎ 2306031; Keating Rd; ☼ 9am-8pm)
Techweb (☎ 2306102; Zara's Arcade, Keating Rd; ☼ 9am-8.30pm) Bright and relatively comfy.

MONEY
Cash and travellers cheques of many currencies can be exchanged. But not Bangladesh Taka.
Indian Overseas Bank (Excise Lane, Kacheri Rd; ☼ 10am-3pm Mon-Fri)
State Bank of India (Kacheri Rd; ☼ 10am-4pm Mon-Fri, 10am-1pm Sat) Exchange upstairs.

POST
Post office (Kacheri Rd; ☼ 10am-5pm Mon-Sat)

TOURIST INFORMATION
Cultural Pursuits Adventures (MTDF; ☎ 062066552; www.culturalpursuits.com; Basement, Hotel Pegasus Crown, Ward's Lake Rd; ☼ by arrangement) Experienced agency for caving and visits to rural Meghalaya.
Government of India tourist office (☎ 2225632; GS Rd; ☼ 9.30am-5.30pm Mon-Fri, 10am-2pm Sat) Free, basic maps.
Meghalaya Tourism (☎ 2226220; http://meghalaya .nic.in/tourism; Jail Rd; ☼ 6.15am-7.30pm) Mostly interested in selling (good-value) tours.
Survey of India (☎ 2223932; Malki Point; ☼ 9am-4pm) Sells the best (if still flawed) Shillong maps available (Rs 17) and various district maps (Rs 25). Entering the St Trinians–style half-timbered complex requires passport and sign in before a military guard escorts you to the extraordinarily dusty map-sales vault.

Sights & Activities
COLONIAL SHILLONG
Colonial Shillong was ranged around the ever-attractive **Ward's Lake** (admission Rs 5, camera Rs 10; ☼ 5.30am-5.30pm Wed-Mon) with its photogenic ornamental bridge. The city's once-famous half-timbered architecture has been rather swamped by drab Indian concrete, but areas like Oakland retain many older houses, and even in the centre a few gems remain. The 1902 **All Saints' Cathedral** (Kachari Rd) would look perfect on a biscuit tin. Peek in at its fine hardwood beams when students of the attached school have band practise mid-afternoon. Nearby, the turreted **Das-Roy House** (closed to public) lurks behind a traffic circle that harbours five forgotten **Khasi monoliths** and a mini Soviet-style **globe monument**. The **Pinewood Hotel**, a 1920s tea-growers retreat, is particularly iconic and looks great at night (at least from the outside).

KHASI CULTURE

Across much of the region you'll see timeless stone monoliths that were erected as memorials for tribal chieftains. Indeed local Khasi 'monarchies' are still nominally ruled by a *syiem* (traditional ruler). Although they might lack political power, the Syiem of Mylliem remains a considerable economic force, effectively controlling Shillong's vast Iew Duh market while the Syiem of Khrim is elaborately fêted at Smit's annual Nongkrem festival p217).

Many Khasi women wear a *jaiñnkyrsha* pinafore in gingham-checked cotton, fastened on one shoulder and overlaid with a tartan shawl. Most Khasis consider *kwai* (betel) chewing a semi-religious habit. Although nominally Christian, it's still customary to sacrifice chickens and goats at an annual festival to ensure the return of the sun. Khasi markets work on an eight-day rotation and some village fairs feature *yaturmasi* (bull versus bull fights). Thank you in Khasi is *kublei*.

St Anthony's School (Hopkinson Rd) has a fine two-storey arcaded wooden façade.

MUSEUMS

The very professional **Don Bosco Museum of Indigenous Cultures** (www.dbcic.org; Sacred Heart Theological College; Indian/foreigner Rs 90/150, student Rs 30/50; ⊗ 9.30am-3.30pm) displays a truly vast, very well laid-out collection of tribal artefacts interspersed just occasionally with gratuitous galleries on Christian missionary work. The hexagonal museum building is an impressive symbolic tower, seven storeys high for the seven states of the Northeast. Tours (compulsory) last over an hour departing on the half-hour. For an extra Rs 50 you can see a 16-minute video explanation of the famous Khasi Nongkrem festival (p217) or choose from various alternatives.

The memorably named **Wankhar Entomology Museum** (☎ 2544473; Riatsamthiah; admission Rs 25; ⊗ 11am-4pm Mon-Fri or by arrangement) is a remarkable one-room display of pinned butterflies, gruesome Rhinoceros beetles and incredible stick insects located in the home of the original collector.

IEW DUH

This vast **market** at Bara Bazaar is one of the most animated in the Northeast. Thousands of Khasi tribespeople flock in from their villages selling everything from tribal baskets to fish traps to edible frogs. Except, of course, on Sunday when everyone goes to church.

SIAT KHNAM

All around Shillong gambling windows offer 'forecast' odds on Siat Khnam. This is a unique 'sport': a semicircle of photogenic old Khasi men firing hundreds of arrows at a straw-trussed target. Those that stick are counted and winning bets predict the last two digits of this total. It's effectively a lottery but the shooting is a gently fascinating spectacle. Shoots are usually at 3.30pm and 4.30pm daily, except Sunday when a different version is played. Timings can vary somewhat by season.

The easy to miss Siat Khnam site is a small grassy area approximately opposite the big Nehru Stadium on the south river bank. To drive there head east past the Mizo Church, fork left up Bampfyled Rd, then after crossing the hill and descending to the river, turn left: the ground is almost immediately on your right. If walking, take the footpath down to Ginger Restaurant/Polo Towers Hotel. Continue just beyond to Polo Market, then turn right. Walk in front of the Matri Mandir (north side) and along the riverside road for about 1km. The ground is almost opposite the entrance to an army officers' housing area.

Tours

Meghalaya Tourism's city tours (opposite; Rs120) take unsuspecting tourists to a viewpoint at **Shillong Peak** (1960m) and the picnic spot at **Elephant Falls** (adult/child/camera Rs 5/3/10; ⊗ 9.30am-4pm). While pretty enough, neither are exactly mindblowing.

Sleeping

Tariffs are seasonal, and highly negotiable off season. During peak periods hotels fill fast, but there are dozens of choices around the Police Bazaar area so just keep looking.

Hotel Shantiniketan (☎ 2500747; Thana Lane; s/d Rs 50/100) Shoebox bed spaces are squeezed into a sagging old wooden house that could use fumigation and fire escapes. What did you expect for Rs 50? No English spoken.

Baba Tourist Lodge (☎ 2211285; GS Rd; s with shared bathroom Rs 125, with private bathroom s Rs 250-300, d Rs 400-475) Aging but clean and popular with backpackers, Baba hides behind a deceptively small PCO shop. The best rooms have windows and views onto the rear cherry blossoms. It has bucket showers.

Hotel Embassy (☎ 2223164; boulevard@yahoo.co.in; AC Lane; s/d from Rs 200/300) Central yet quiet, bright and very clean compared to the many other cheapies nearby. Beware of hefty 'taxes' (30%) and 'compulsory' meals.

Earle Holiday Home (☎ 2228614; Oakland Rd; d from Rs 350) The cheapest rooms are original half-timbered affairs within a classic 1920 Shillong hill-house that has little turrets and looks sweet when decked with fairy lights at night. Pricier rooms are less atmospheric, if more comfortable, in a new concrete annexe. Also has a great, inexpensive restaurant (opposite).

Hotel Rainbow (☎ 2222534; GS Rd; d Rs 550-650, tr Rs 750) Nine new, pleasantly styled rooms with sauna-style décor (but no geyser) are managed by a super-friendly man called Vicky. The best is room 103 with a little balcony.

our pick Hotel Boulevard (☎ 2229823; boulevard@ yahoo.co.in; Thana Rd; s/d from Rs 820/948) Among dozens of similarly priced hotels, the Boulevard stands out for its unintimidating modernist chic and unusually luxurious standards, even in the cheapest rooms. Don't miss the view from the stylish top-floor bar-café.

Hotel Tripura Castle (☎ 2501111; www.tripuraroyal heritage.com; Cleve Colony; s/d from Rs 1680/2160) Tucked away on a wooded hillside is the distinctively turreted summer villa of the former Tripura maharajas. It's this private 'castle' that features

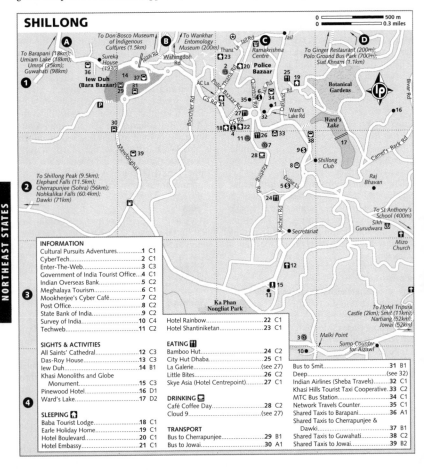

in hotel brochures, but accommodation is actually in a mostly new, if heritage-effect building behind. Pine-framed rooms have a gently stylish, slightly Balinese vibe with some period furniture and a level of service that's hard to beat.

Eating & Drinking

Cheap street stalls abound around Police Bazaar, with many dreary but inexpensive eateries along Thana Rd. Brighter for microwaved snacks is **Little Bites** (Keating Rd; dishes Rs 10-25), while just beyond there's real coffee and good cakes at **Café Coffee Day** (Hotel Mi Casa, Keating Rd; ⏰ 10am-10.30pm).

City Hut Dhaba (☎ 2220386; Oakland Rd; mains Rs 40-110; ⏰ 11am-9.30pm) Tucked behind Earle Holiday Home, modestly priced City Hut claims to serve 'Shillong's best food' and actually delivers. Seating is in attractive, flower-decked pavilions, but they're open sided so bring a coat for winter evenings.

Skye Asia (☎ 2225210; Hotel Centrepoint; mains Rs 70-180; ⏰ 1-9.30pm) With wood and rattan chairs and great views, this top-floor lounge-restaurant serves dainty Thai dishes and cocktails, morphing later into the Cloud 9 bar-disco.

La Galerie (1st fl, Hotel Centrepoint; mains Rs 50-130) Located downstairs from Skye Asia, it's less atmospheric but offers excellent Indian food.

Bamboo Hut (☎ 2501542; Rap's Mansion, MG Rd; mains Rs 35-100) Away from Shillong's commercial centre, this mainly Chinese restaurant has a calm interior that would be pleasant but for those endless Chris de Burgh songs. The menu includes several partly successful Thai options.

Ginger Restaurant (☎ 2222341; www.hotelpolotowers.com; Hotel Polo Towers, Polo Bazaar; mains Rs 90-200; ⏰ 11am-10pm) Sink into designer cream-leather chairs at Shillong's suavest restaurant. Continental dishes include crepes, cannelloni and stroganoff. Attached is the futuristic, metal-panelled bar Platinum (beers Rs 120).

Getting There & Away

Indian Airlines (☎ 2223015; Sheba Travels, Ward's Lake Rd) flies from Kolkata to Shillong (Rs 6030) returning via either Jorhat (Monday) or Tezpur (Wednesday). The airstrip is at Umroi, 35km north of Shillong (Rs 600 by taxi).

From an air-force base 8km towards Cherrapunjee, **Meghalaya Transport Corporation** (☎ 2223129) offers helicopter flights to Guwahati (Rs 725, 30 minutes, twice daily except Sunday) and Tura (Rs 1525, 1½ hours, thrice weekly). Book at the **MTC bus station** (Jail Rd), which also

has a computerised railway-reservation counter (nearest train station is Guwahati), hourly minibuses to Guwahati (Rs 64, 3½ hours), and overnight buses to Silchar (Rs 151, 10 hours) and Tura (Rs 202, 12 hours via Guwahati).

More comfortable private buses for Siliguri (Rs 350, 18 hours), Agartala (Rs 450, 21 hours), Silchar, Dimapur and Aizawl depart from the Polo Ground; book tickets from counters around Police Bazaar, including **Network Travels** (☎ 2222747; Shop 44, MUDA Complex, Police Bazaar) and **Deep** (☎ 9836047198; Ward's Lake Rd).

From a Kacheri Rd parking area, shared taxis/sumos leave frequently to Guwahati (Rs 125/90, 3½ hours). Some shared taxis continue to Guwahati airport (Rs 170).

For most destinations within Meghalaya buses are infrequent and appallingly antiquated. Faster and much more frequent, shared jeeps leave when full from various points around Bara Bazaar, including to Cherrapunjee (Sohra; Rs 40, 1½ hours), Dawki (Rs 70, two hours), Jowai (Rs 50, 1¾ hours) and Barapani (Rs 20, 40 minutes).

Getting Around

Shared black-and-yellow taxis run fixed routes (Rs 7 to 10 per hop) but if empty might ask Rs 50 for a one-way trip within town. For longer hires, contract a van from the **Khasi Hills Tourist Taxi Cooperative** (☎ 2223895; Kachari Rd).

AROUND SHILLONG
Smit

Framing itself as a Khasi cultural centre, Smit is the centre for the major five-day **Nongkrem Festival** in October. This features animal sacrifices and a curious slow-motion shuffling dance performed in full costume in front of the thatched bamboo 'palace' of the local *syiem* (monarch). Smit is 11km from Shillong (Rs 8 by chuntering local bus), 4km off the Jowai road.

Umiam Lake

Accessed from **Barapani**, 17km north of Shillong, Umiam Lake is a hydroelectric reservoir that's popular for watersports and picnics and has a couple of resort hotels.

Cherrapunjee (Sohra)
☎ 03637

Although straggling for several kilometres, **Cherrapunjee** (known locally as Sohra) has a compact centre with its simple two-room **Sohra Plaza Hotel** (☎ 235762; s/d Rs 350/450), sumo stand and one-computer internet shop all huddled near the marketplace. Rolling grassy moors around town start to justify Meghalaya's overplayed 'Scotland of the East' soubriquet. The moors are dotted with Khasi monoliths but heavily scarred by quarrying. What's much more impressive is the series of 'grand canyon' style valleys that plummet away into deep lush bowls of tropical forest sprayed by a succession of seasonally inspiring waterfalls. The **Nohkalikai Falls** (4.4km southwest of Sohra market) are particularly dramatic and you can see them easily enough without quite entering the official **viewpoint** (admission/camera Rs 3/10). Tour buses of Bengali sightseers are whisked on to a minimal museum at Cherrapunjee's **Ramakrishna Mission** (admission free; 9am-2pm) and prodded through the sad, soot-blackened ex-stalagmites of the mildly claustrophobic, 150m-long **Mawsmai Cave** (minimum fee per group Rs 60; 9am-4.30pm). In fact Mawsmai's row of tall roadside **monoliths** are much more impressive than the actual cave.

Better than any of this is descending the narrow road to **Mawshamok** (14km) for views back up to the falls and cliffs. Few places in the Northeast are more scenic, and joyously it's possible to stay at an ecofriendly lodge just 3km further along the ridge in Laitkynsew. The six-room **Cherrapunjee Holiday Resort** (03637264218; www.cherrapunjee.com; d Rs 720-840) is run by truly delightful hosts who offer a selection of hikes, either self-orientated (using their hand-drawn maps) or with a local guide (Rs 70 to 150). The most exciting of these is to seek out three absolutely incredible Tolkienesque **'root-bridges'**, living *ficus elastica* tree-roots that ingenious Khasi villagers have trained across streams to form natural pathways. Three of these root-bridges, including an amazing 'double decker', are near **Nongriat**. Access requires at least a 1½-hour's steep trek down from **Tyrna**, a pretty, palm-clad village 5km from the resort, 2km from Mawshamok. Beware that even for the fittest walker, this hike is highly strenuous and en route there's a truly hair-raising wire bridge to cross. But the scenery is magnificent.

The Cherrapunjee Holiday Resort also encourages summer 'monsoon tourists' to come and experience first-hand the full drama of the world's rainiest place; its unforgettable thunder and dramatic brewing storms.

Dawki
pop 5500

You'll probably only go to Dawki for the Bangladeshi border crossing, but the journey is attractive. South of **Laitlyngkot**, a 10km section of the NH40 Shillong–Dawki road runs dramatically along the lip of the vast green **Pamshutia Canyon**. It then descends through mildly picturesque Khasi villages like **Pongtung** (Km 142) and **Mawsun** (Km 146) amid waving betel-nut palms, finally crossing a suspension bridge over the surreally blue-green **Umngot Creek**, where waters are dotted with flimsy local fishing boats. A colourful boat race is held here every February.

All public sumos from Dawki to Shillong (Rs 70, 2½ hours) depart by 11am (except market days, 3pm), mostly returning early afternoon. That means if coming northbound from Bangladesh you should sleep in Sylhet and start very early as the **Inspection Bungalow** (d Rs100), Dawki's only accommodation, usually refuses tourists. Doing the Shillong–Dawki–Sylhet route is considerably easier southbound.

JAINTIA HILLS
03562

Set in pretty, rolling countryside (think Sussex with rice), **Nartiang** (population 6000) is famous for its **'forest' of monoliths**, a scatterbrained Stonehenge wannabe tucked behind the village football pitch. Raised to honour the Jaintia kings, the highest stone is almost 8m tall. Around 1km away, a famous but heavily over-renovated **Durga temple** was once used for human sacrifices. You can still see the 'endless' hole into which the severed heads were once tipped.

Nartiang probably doesn't justify a special trip from Shillong (56km), but if you're travelling the Silcharroute, it offers blessed respite from the endless coal trucks. Nartiang's 12km off the main road: turn northeast at Ummulong. By public transport it's easier to go via **Jowai** (population 27,300), the district centre of eastern Meghalaya's Jaintia Hills. Although architecturally drab, Jowai's vibrant market is full of *kwai*-chewing, traditionally dressed local women. The town gets particularly lively during the July **Behdienkhlam Festival** when towers of cloth and wood are erected to the accompaniment of music, dancing and archery competitions.

Astoundingly overfilled Jowai–Nartiang share-taxis (Rs 10, 35 minutes) leave from the central market. The last one back departs from Nartiang around 3pm. That makes it just about possible to arrive in Jowai on the 7am Silchar–Shillong bus, see Nartiang, and continue to Shillong the same evening. Jowai–Shillong sumos (Rs 50, 1½ hours) leave when full till around 5.30pm from just beyond Jowai's sorry **Hotel New Broadway** (☎ 212714; Shillong Rd; s/d Rs 150/300).

GARO HILLS

Although administratively part of Meghalaya state, the lush green Garo Hills are easier to visit from Guwahati (Assam) than from Shillong. The landscape's undulations vary from charming patchworks of rice fields, cassava-patch and orange orchard to sad slash-and-burn hillsides of depleted jungle choked with gourd creepers and bamboo thickets. Towns aren't visually distinctive, but cottages in small hamlets remain traditionally fashioned from bamboo-weave matting and neatly cropped palm thatch (increasingly replaced by corrugated metal). Specific sights are limited, but the cuisine and delightfully friendly Garo people make this region a charming, little-known detour between Guwahati and Siliguri (p133).

Tura

☎ 03651 / pop 58,400

Sprawling beneath the wooded dome of Tura Peak, Tura is barely visible amid the thick-pile carpeting of its verdant bamboo groves and waving palm trees. The town is West Garo Hills' regional centre and an unhurried transport hub. Most key facilities are within two minutes' walk of the central market area around which Circular Rd makes a convoluted one-way loop. However, the **Tourist Office** (☎ 242394; ⏲ 10am-5pm Mon-Fri) is 4km away towards Nazing Bazaar. Friendly staff there offer brochures and sketchy maps and can arrange guides for the three-day hike to **Nokrek Biosphere Reserve**. There it's possible to watch for Hoolock Gibbons from a traditional style *borang* (Garo tree house). By road the reserve is around 50km from Tura, 10km off the Williamnagar road via Orag'tok village.

SLEEPING & EATING

Rikman Hotel (☎ 220744; s/d from Rs 390/500, executive ste Rs 1200/1375) Central Tura's most obvious building, just seconds walk from the central market and transport booths. Although some cheaper rooms are small and rather worn, the executive

suites have huge windows, bathtubs with hot water and air-conditioning. A 20% discount is common with gentle bargaining. Rikman's restaurant is probably the best place anywhere to sample Garo cuisine and the lobby offers internet connection (per hour, Rs 50 per hour).

Orchid Lodge (☎ 242394; dm Rs 100, s/d from Rs 450/550) Right beside the inconveniently located tourist office, it has peaceful but spartan rooms. Only the Rs 772 double has a water heater. The kitchen cooks up whatever it happens to have in stock.

GETTING THERE AND AWAY

On Monday, Wednesday and Friday, triangular **helicopter flights** (☎ 0364-2223206) run to Guwahati

Booths selling bus and sumo tickets are dotted around the central market area. For Guwahati, most sumos (Rs 230, six hours) depart at 6.30am and 2pm. They're vastly faster than buses (Rs 175, nine to 11 hours), which mostly leave at 7pm. Buses to Shillong (Rs 230, around 12 hours) depart at 8pm and passing close to Guwahati airport. **Dura Travels** (cnr HK & Circular Rds) offers a 6am shared sumo (Rs100, four to five hours) to Baghmara. **Aashirwad** (☎ 222217) runs handy if grindingly slow night buses to Siliguri (Rs 280, 15 to 17 hours) at 5pm crossing the mighty Brahmaputra on the 2.3km **Naranarayan Setu** road-rail bridge between Jogighopa and Goalpara.

TO/FROM BANGLADESH

The **Bangladesh border post** (⏲ 6am-5pm) is 1.7km from Dawki market at Tamabil. That's Rs 30 by taxi southbound. But northbound expect to walk, as there's usually nothing but massed coal trucks at the checkpoint. There's no official exchange booth but ask at the Bangladesh customs office and a freelance moneychanger can usually be found offering a poor but bearable Rs 1=Tk 1.35 rate. Northbound beware that Tamabil has no Sonali bank so pay your Tk 300 Bangladesh departure tax in Sylhet (55km) or Jaintiapura (17km) from where frequent minibuses run from a triangular junction 350m beyond the checkposts: walk through the black moonscape of coal piles. Trains from Sylhet to Dhaka via Srimangal and Ajampur leave at 7.30am.

THE GARO PEOPLE

Garo facial features range from Burmese to almost African. Traditionally animist *jhum* (slash-and-burn) farmers, the matrilineal Garo were among the first northeastern targets for Christian missionary work, possibly because the Garo language is so relatively simple. Now an estimated 80% of Garos are Christian. Nonetheless 'witch doctors' are still active and superstitious *jhum* villages still practise Wangala dances before the harvest. These dances have been formalised into a four-day '100-Drum' cultural festival, held at Asanang (Asananggri), 18km north of Tura in early November. Check exact dates with Tura's tourist office.

Not surprisingly given the flora, a mainstay of Garo cuisine is *me'a* (bamboo-shoot), often fermented as *me'a mesing*. *Na'tok* (fish) is often cooked in fresh bamboo tubes giving a distinctive flavour. Like in Assam, *khar* (an alkaline banana-extract) and *na'kham* (dried fish) are almost ubiquitous ingredients in Garo recipes, most classic of which is *kap'a*, a delicious ginger-chilli concoction usually incorporating *do'o* (boiled chicken) or *wak* (fatty pork). *Pura* adds rice flour for thickening.

The standard Garo greeting is '*Nameng-a ma?*' And reply '*Nameng-a*'. In Garo 'thank you' is *m'tela*, '(very)' beautiful' is *(bilong'en) si'la* and to appreciate Garo food say '*to-jok*'.

Small public buses run fairly regularly to Asanang via Rongram. To reach the tourist office costs Rs 50/15 by chartered/shared autorickshaw from outside Dura Travels, a minute's walk straight down from Rikman Hotel.

Baghmara & Siju
☎ 03639

Almost on the Bangladesh border, **Baghmara** is the South Garo Hills' district centre. Sitting above the town is a **Tourist Lodge** (☎ 222141; dm Rs 100). From here you can organise jeep hire to visit the **Balpakhram National Park** (entrance 45km away). Traditionally considered by Garo people as the 'abode of souls', the park is reportedly thick with wild flowers and butterflies in spring. Its little 'grand canyon' separates the Garo and Khasi Hills. Speleologists might enjoy **Siju (Sizu) Cave** (34km from Baghmara) once they get beyond the bat-stinking entrance. It's reputedly the third-longest cave in the Indian subcontinent, but you'll have plenty of splashing through the labyrinth of underground streams before reaching much in the way of stalagmites. Bring all your own equipment.

TRIPURA

Tripura is culturally and politically fascinating and the state's royal palaces and temples now draw a growing flow of domestic tourists from Kolkata. However, if you're expecting the exotic grandeur of Rajasthani castles, Tripura might seem a long detour for relatively little.

History

Before joining India in 1949, Tripura (Twipra) was ruled for centuries by its own Hindu royal family (the Manikyas) based first at Udaipur, then Old Agartala (Kayerpur) and finally Agartala. In the 1880s, Tripura's maharajah became a major sponsor of the Bengali-renaissance poet-philosopher Rabindranath Tagore. Indian Partition proved disastrous for Tripura, cut off from its natural trading partners and flooded with Bengali refugees so that the local Borok-Tripuri people were left as a minority in their own state. Resultant tensions have spawned dozens of armed groups fighting for – and against – the creation of an independent tribal state.

Dangers & Annoyances

The Agartala, Udaipur and Kailasahar areas are generally safe. However, there is serious instability in north-central Tripura. All vehicles must travel in armed convoys through two sections of the Agartala–Kailasahar road, and while attacks are rare, they do happen.

Compared to the shy greetings and surreptitious glances elsewhere in the Northeast, Tripura's more forthright stares and slightly forced hospitality can seem a little invasive.

AGARTALA
☎ 0381 / pop 189,330

Tripura's low-key capital is centred on the imposing Ujjayanta Palace. The town feels refreshingly organised and manageable if you're arriving from Bangladesh, whose border is just 3km east of the centre.

Information

BOOKSHOP
Jnan Bichitra Bookzone (☎ 2323781; JB Rd; ☺ 9am-9pm; ⌨) Welcoming, well stocked, sells local postcards.

INTERNET ACCESS
Bluesky (Santipara; per hr Rs 20; ☺ 9am-9pm)
Netzone (6 Sakuntala Rd; per hr Rs 20; ☺ 7am-10pm; ⌨) Best of several closely grouped options.

MONEY
SBI ATM (Palace Compound West) Rs 15,000 limit
State Bank of India (HGB Rd; ☎ 10am-4pm Mon-Sat, 10am-1pm Sat) Counter 31 (top floor) changes cash and travellers cheques, but allow at least an hour.
UTI ATM (Welcome Palace Hotel, HGB Rd) Rs 20,000 limit. Visa only.

TOURIST INFORMATION
TripuraInfo (☎ 2380566; www.tripurainfo.com) Useful news and tourism website.
Tripura Tourism (☎ 2225930; www.tripura.nic.in /ttourism1.htm; 1st fl, Swet Mahal, Palace Complex; ☺ 10am-5pm Mon-Fri, 3-5pm Sat & Sun) Helpful and enthusiastic; with sufficient numbers satff will organise many great-value tours.

Sights

Agartala's indisputable centrepiece is the striking, dome-capped **Ujjayanta Palace**. Flanked by two large reflecting ponds, the whitewashed 1901 edifice was built by Tripura's 182nd Maharaja. The palace looks particularly impressive when floodlit at night. Strollers can enjoy the spectacle for just one hour daily, entering from the relatively grand **Sorth Gate** (admission Rs 3; ☺ 5.30-6.30pm). Access to the palace's comparatively unspectacular interior (now the Tripura state assembly chamber) is very limited: sign in between 2.30pm and 3pm on weekdays (admission free), then report to the caretaker. Of four Hindu temples around the palace compound, the most fanciful is **Jagannath Mandir**.

The small **Tripura Government Museum** (☎ 232 6444; http://tripura.nic.in/museum/welcome.html; Post Office Circle; admission Rs2; ☺ 10am-5pm Mon-Fri) has interesting artefacts recovered from excavations around Tripura. The upstairs gallery shows maharajah portraits, including one with Tagore.

Several **royal mausoleums** are decaying quietly behind Batala market.

The curious, mosaic-fronted **Gedumian Mosque** (Masjid Rd) looks like a mini Brighton Pavilion.

OLD AGARTALA
Nothing much remains of Tripura's second capital, **Old Agartala**, 7km east down AA Rd (the NH44) at Kayerpur, though the small, pointy **Chaturdasha Devata Mandir** (Temple of Fourteen Deities) hosts a big seven-day **Kharchi Puja festival** in July. It's across the river by a bridge that was broken at the time of research.

Sleeping

Vivekananda Hotel (☎ 2380619; Masjid Rd; s/d Rs 50/100) This ultra-basic crash-pad hotel has hard-board-walled box rooms, mosquito nets and tie-dye sheets. The shared squat is cleanish.

All other places listed here offer rooms with private bathroom. Air-con rooms generally have geysers.

Hotel Chandana Guest House (☎ 2311216; Palace Compound Lane; s/d/tr Rs 95/210/285) Lacklustre but cheap and quite bearable, the Chandana's simple rooms have mosquito nets and cold showers. Peaceful yet central.

Galaxy Inn (☎ 2325227; 46 Gangail Rd; s/d from Rs 200/375; ⌨) In a relatively quiet (and dark) street towards the south bus station, the cheaper rooms are good value and nicer than the gloomy corridors might suggest.

Hotel Welcome Palace (☎ 2384940; bantob@san charnet.in; HGB Rd; s/d with fan from Rs 220/330, with AC Rs 550/660; ⌨) This hard-to-beat option has helpful English-speaking staff, zealous room service and superb food. Rooms are neat if not huge with scalding hot showers and multi-channel TV.

Radha International (☎ 2384530; 54 Central Rd; s/d with fan from Rs 375/500, with AC from Rs 500/750; ⌨) This new hotel's great-value air-con rooms are neatly tiled, and doubles have a little sitting area. However, some bathrooms already have damp patches.

Executive Inn (☎ 2325047; 9 Mantri Bari Rd; old Bldg s Rs 275-385, d Rs 495; new Bldg s/d from Rs 660/880; ⌨) The new building has stylishly understated modern rooms with air-con and enough space to relax, but the old building's fan rooms are overpriced.

Other suggestions:
Hotel City Centre (☎ 2385099; jaininn_pvtltd@yahoo .co.in; s/d from Rs 385/495, d with AC from Rs 720; ⌨) New and youthful, with 25 rooms in 10 categories.
Hotel Rajdhani (☎ 2223387; www.hotelrajdhani.co .in; BK Rd; s/d with fan from Rs 290/400, with AC from Rs 590/750; ⌨) High-service hotel with plenty of spoken English. Fan rooms are slightly worn.

NORTHEAST STATES

Eating

Restaurant Rajdhani (☎ 2208635; Top fl, Hotel Rajdhani, BK Rd; mains Rs 35-120; ✗) Playful fake-forest décor and a bird's-eye view on the palace add to the pleasure of fine Indian and Chinese cuisine. The chicken *dopiaza* includes half a hen.

Restaurant Kurry Klub (☎ 2384940; Hotel Welcome Palace, HGB Rd; mains Rs 40-150; ✗ 10am-10pm) Scrumptious tandoori chicken and gingery 'Thai' soup served in a small dining room whose décor would be rather striking if only the lighting was strong enough to see it.

Abhishek Restaurant (☎ 2328296; Durga Bari Rd; mains Rs 60-100; ✗ 11am-10pm; ✗) Reliable Indian-Chinese-Thai food served either on an inviting outdoor terrace or a well air-conditioned marine-themed dining room.

Getting There & Around

Indian Airlines (☎ 2325470; VIP Rd; ✗ 9am-1pm & 2-4pm), **Air Deccan** (www.airdeccan.com), **Jet Airways** (☎ 2341400) and **Kingfisher** (www.flykingfisher.com) all fly to Kolkata and Guwahati. Indian Airlines also flies on Monday, Wednesday and Friday to Silchar (US$90). Agartala's airport is 12km north, Rs 90 by autorickshaw. Arrive early: before being allowed into the check-in area you'll need to get tickets endorsed at airline counters outside the terminal, then visit the immigration desk across the arrivals hall (yes, for domestic departures). Local buses to Narsingarh pass the airport gates.

Private buses can be reserved from various booking offices clustered on Durga Bari Rd, including **Sagar Travels/Network Travels**

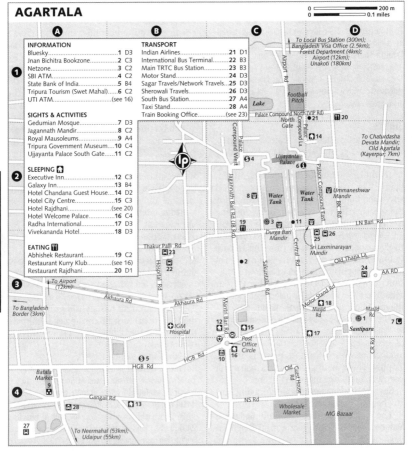

AGARTALA

INFORMATION		
Bluesky	1	D3
Jnan Bichitra Bookzone	2	C3
Netzone	3	C2
SBI ATM	4	C2
State Bank of India	5	B4
Tripura Tourism (Swet Mahal)	6	C2
UTI ATM	(see 16)	

SIGHTS & ACTIVITIES		
Gedumian Mosque	7	D3
Jagannath Mandir	8	C2
Royal Mausoleums	9	A4
Tripura Government Museum	10	C4
Ujjayanta Palace South Gate	11	C2

SLEEPING		
Executive Inn	12	C3
Galaxy Inn	13	B4
Hotel Chandana Guest House	14	D2
Hotel City Centre	15	C3
Hotel Rajdhani	(see 20)	
Hotel Welcome Palace	16	C4
Radha International	17	D3
Vivekananda Hotel	18	D3

EATING		
Abhishek Restaurant	19	C2
Restaurant Kurry Klub	(see 20)	
Restaurant Rajdhani	20	D1

TRANSPORT		
Indian Airlines	21	D1
International Bus Terminal	22	B3
Main TRTC Bus Station	23	B3
Motor Stand	24	D3
Sagar Travels/Network Travels	25	D3
Sherowali Travels	26	D3
South Bus Station	27	A4
Taxi Stand	28	A4
Train Booking Office	(see 23)	

To Local Bus Station (300m);
Bangladesh Visa Office (2.5km);
Forest Department (4km);
Airport (12km);
Unakoti (180km)

To Chaturdasha
Devata Mandir;
Old Agartala
(Kayerpur, 7km)

To Airport (12km)

To Bangladesh Border (3km)

To Neermahal (53km);
Udaipur (55km)

(☎ 2222013) and **Sherowali Travels** (☎ 2310398). However, most leave from the **main (TRTC) bus station** (☎ 2325685; Thakur Palli Rd). Tickets are sold at counter 1 for 6am and noon buses to Guwahati (Rs 355 to 500, around 24 hours) via Shillong (Rs 355 to 500, 21 hours) and 6am buses to Silchar (Rs 190 to 220, 14 hours). TRTC state-run buses (counter 4) are somewhat cheaper and also serve Kailasahar (Rs 68, seven hours) via Manu (Rs 40, five hours), also at 6am. For now BRTC's daily bus to Dhaka (Rs 232, 1pm) still uses the TRTC bus station but a gleaming new International Bus Terminal is nearing completion opposite.

Northbound sumos use the busy **Motor Stand** (Motor Stand Rd).

For Udaipur (Rs 20, 1¾ hours) and Melagarh (for Neermahal; Rs 20, 1½ hours) take a minibus or sumo from the south bus station. Both run several times hourly, but are often outrageously overfull. There's a local bus station on Airport Rd.

Some hotels can organise sightseeing charter taxis (Rs 500 per day plus Rs 5 per km).

Although officially slated to operate from 2007, the planned new railway linking Agartala to Assam has yet to progress beyond Manu. Construction continues, plagued by extortion and attacks from insurgent groups. There's a computerised **train booking office** (⏱ 8am-7.30pm Mon-Fri, 8am-11.30am Sun) at Agartala's main TRTC bus station.

AROUND AGARTALA
Southern Tripura's best-known sights could be combined into a long day trip from Agartala, though sleeping at Neermahal is a better idea. All transport passes the gates of the little **Sepahijala Wildlife Sanctuary** (NH44 extension, Km 23; ⏱ 8am-5pm Sat-Thu), a local picnic- and boating-spot famous for its **spectacled monkeys**.

Udaipur
☎ 03821
South Tripura's regional centre, **Udaipur**, was the historic capital of the Hindu Tripura kingdom for centuries until it moved to Old Agartala. The town remains dotted with ancient temples and a patchwork of tanks (artificial lakes). Ruined but still comparatively massive, **Jagannath Mandir** is the most curious temple, overgrown with creepers Angkor Wat style. It sits at the southwest corner of huge **Jagannath Digthi tank**, around 1km from Udaipur bus stand, and once held the famous Jagannath

statue of Puri. You'll pass three more ancient temple complexes en route to the flimsy Badashaheb bamboo bridge (concrete replacement under construction), which crosses the Gomati River. From here turn left and walk 10 minutes uphill to find the **Bhuveneswari Temple** (small but celebrated in Tagore's writings) just beyond the lumpy brick ruins of the **Rajbari**, hardly recognisable as a 17th-century palace.

At Udaipur bus stand is the friendly **Sarada Guest House** (☎ 225737; d without/with AC Rs 200/400; 🖭), where rooms are windowless but well kept and manager Guru Prasad is extremely helpful with local tips. The restaurant's chicken-egg rolls are delicious.

In central Udaipur, **Gouri Hotel** (☎ 222419; Central Rd; s/d from Rs 150/250; 🖭) is also clean and the two Rs 600 air-con rooms are relatively smart.

MATABARI
When Sati's yoni fell on Guwahati (see p198), her divine right leg dropped on Matabari. This gruesome myth is piously celebrated at the **Tripura Sundari Mandir**, a Kali temple built in 1501, where a steady stream of pilgrims make almost endless animal sacrifices that leave the grounds as bloody as the temple's vivid red *vihara* (resting place, part of monastery). Even more people come here at the big **Diwali festival** (October/November) to bathe in the fish-filled tank, over which the two-storey concrete **Gonabati Yatri Niwas Lodge** (dm/d Rs 66/165) offers views from simple rooms. Book through Tripura Tourism (☎ 0381-2225930).

The temple is 100m east of the NH44, 4km south of Udaipur,.

Neermahal & Melagarh
☎ 0381
Tripura's most iconic building is **Neermahal** (admission Rs 3; ⏱ 9am-4pm), a long red-and-white water palace shimmering on its own boggy island in Rudra Sagar Lake near Melagarh. The delightful waterborne approach (per boat hand rowed/motorised Rs 75/150) is the most enjoyable part of visiting this royal folly whose interior is bare and could use a lick of paint. When there are enough overnight visitors, the palace organises a sound-and-light show.

Boats leave from near the remarkably decent **Sagarmahal Tourist Lodge** (☎ 0381-2544418; dm Rs 66, d without AC Rs 165, d with AC Rs 330-440; 🖭), where most rooms have lake-facing balconies and there's a good restaurant. Bookings are possible through Tripura Tourism (p221) in Agartala.

TO/FROM BANGLADESH

The Northeast's only **Bangladesh visa office** (☎ 2324807; Kunjaban; 🕑 visa applications 9am-1pm, visa collection 4pm) hides in a small lane, about 2km north of Agartala's Ujjayanta Palace. Turn right off Airport Rd beside Barnali giftshop, around 400m beyond the pretty little Vanuvana Vihara temple. The office is 30m ahead on your left. It offers same-day service.

The **Bangladesh border post** (🕑 6am-5pm) is 3km west of central Agartala along Akhaura Rd (Rs 15 by rickshaw). Formalities are slow but friendly. Changing money is hit and miss – ask other (local) travellers or inquire with customs officers. The nearest Bangladesh town with a Sonali bank (to pay your Tk 300 Bangladesh departure tax) is Akhaura, 9km away. Locals pay Tk 50 (around Rs 30) by 'baby taxi' (autorickshaw), but as supply is thin, drivers often ask up to Tk300. Akhaura train station is on the Dhaka–Comilla line. But for Dhaka–Sylhet trains continue 3km further north to Ajampur station. Trains to Sylhet (Tk 130, five hours) depart at 9.20am and 4.40pm.

The lodge is 1km off the Agartala–Sonamura road, 1.3km from Melagarh bus stand.

Getting There & Away

Frequent ever-stopping buses, notably those bound for Belonia or Sapbrum, stop at Udaipur bus stand and Matabari. From Udaipur to Melagarh, minibuses (Rs 13, 50 minutes) leave Udaipur bus stand at 7.30am, 10.30am, 11.30am and 3.10pm, supplemented by occasional sumos departing when full from a roundabout 300m further south. Chartered vans cost Rs 450 (25 minutes) direct to Neermahal.

The last sumos back from Melagarh to Agartala (Rs 20, 1½ hours) leave around 4pm.

NORTH TRIPURA

☎ 03824

Around 180km from Agartala, North Tripura's regional centre is **Kailasahar**, where the excellent new **Unakoti Tourist Lodge** (☎ 223635; d without/with AC Rs 165/330) is a real bargain. **Unakoti** itself, around 10km away, is an ancient pilgrimage centre, famous for its 8th-century bas-relief rock carvings, including a 10m-high representation of Shiva. The **Ashokastami Mela festival** is held here in March/April. Beware that getting to Kailasahar from Agartala requires transiting the most sensitive (insurgency) area of Tripura. Foreign tourists are very rare and will turn heads.

NAGALAND

The Naga people originated in Southeast Asia and are distributed all along the India/Myanmar border. However, in Nagaland they form a majority everywhere except Dimapur – that's historically a Kachari-Bodo city and now

Nagaland's dull but useful main transport hub. Historically Nagas are great warriors. For centuries the 20-plus Naga tribes valiantly fought off any intruders and, in between, kept themselves busy by fighting each other. The antagonistic tribes developed mutually unintelligible languages, so today to communicate with each other Nagas speak a 'neutral' lingua franca called Nagamese (a sort of market Assamese), or use English. Major Naga groups include the developed Angami and Rengma of Kohima district, the Lotha of Wokha district (famed for their cooking) and the Konyak of Mon district, who have the most exotic traditional costumes and architecture. For festivals, Naga women wear a handwoven shawl that's distinctive for each subtribe, while the men dust off their old warrior-wear, loin cloth and all.

It's these colourful festivals that most tourists imagine when booking a Nagaland tour. And the best one, Kohima's December Hornbill Festival, is well worth the trip. At other times (except perhaps in rural Mon district), some find the contrasting lack of spectacle – both culturally and scenically – a disappointment. But if you lower your expectations from those *National Geographic* images, there's still lots of interest in meeting a people whose culture, in the words of one Indian journalist, has been through '1000 years in a lifetime'.

See the website www.nagalandtourism.com for local information. For permit information, see p192.

History

The Nagas were once feared headhunters. Never fully conquered, the various Naga tribes finally came to an uneasy coexistence with British India after the second battle of Khonoma (p227) in 1879. The Brits decided the Naga Hills were too much trouble to colonise, so largely left them alone. However, they encouraged missionaries whose Christianity was much more effective than force at subduing the Naga temperament. Christianity started to give rise to a pan-Naga identity. After fierce WWII battles that devastated many Naga settlements, this Naga sentiment was fanned by charismatic separatist leader AZ Phizo. When India declared independence in 1947, Phizo's Naga National Congress (NNC) declared Independence for Nagaland too. India didn't agree, considering the Naga Hills to be part of Assam. Brutal military actions in the mid-1950s strengthened public support for the NNC, stoking what was to become one of the most brutal and long-lasting insurgencies in the whole Northeast. Tensions were calmed somewhat when Nagaland achieved statehood in 1963 and with the 1980 signing of the Shillong Accords. However, since then the NNC has been superseded by the Maoist National Socialist Council of Nagaland (NSCN), which has fought on, though now split into two mutually antagonistic factions. Both effectively control and tax certain remote rural areas leading to continued instability especially around the Burmese and Manipur borders.

Dangers & Annoyances

The main rebel factions are the puritanical, predominantly Tangkhul-Naga NSCN (IM) based across the Manipur border, and the NSCN (K). The latter, suspected of major narcotics interests, are led by Konyaks and cause trouble notably in Tuensang District. Most major Nagaland towns are stable, but can't be considered totally safe: dozens were killed in 2004 during attacks on the market and train station in normally peaceful Dimapur.

Note that even in Kohima virtually everything closes by 7pm and travel by night is highly discouraged.

Even with a permit, you're not generally expected to wander into villages unaccompanied. You should ask permission from the local headman and, even if you have a guide, will possibly be expected to employ another local guide for each specific district. Guides can be twitchy about taking back roads, not just because of jeep-eating potholes, but also for fear of armed bandits charging hefty 'tolls'.

DIMAPUR

☎ 03862 / pop 308,000 / elev 260m

Nagaland's flat, largely uninspiring commercial centre was once the capital of a big Kachari kingdom that ruled much of Assam before the Ahoms showed up. All that remains are some curious, strangely phallic pillars dotted about scraggy **Rajbari Park** (admission free), site of the former palace complex. It's entered through a disconnected brick portal just 100m behind Dimapur's atmospheric **daily market**, with locals selling their wares beneath bamboo-thatch canopies, about 1km east of the bus station on Kohima road.

There's an ATM at UTI Bank on Circular Rd, 300m west then north of the Plaza restaurant just before **City Tower**, Dimapur's mini Eiffel equivalent.

The pleasant **Circuit House** (s/d Rs 100/200) is directly opposite Rajbari Park, but pre-paying the bill requires an annoying 3km taxi ride to the **District Commissioner's Office** (☎ 226530).

Right beside the NST bus station, the **Tourist Lodge** (☎ 226355; Kohima Rd; dm/s/d Rs 40/150/200) is a basic but acceptable budget option: even the dorm beds have mosquito nets.

Hotel Avilyn (☎ 230245; Kohima Rd; s/d Rs 500/700, with AC from Rs 700/945; 🖳) is a trendy, friendly and super-clean option located halfway between the bus station and Rajbari Park. The best, 'DX' rooms are super stylish, using different colour woods and original (if impractical) designer lamps. Across the road is a decent handicrafts shop.

Plaza Restaurant (☎ 230245; Kohima Rd; s/d Rs 500/700, with AC from Rs 700/945; 🖳), located across the rail tracks in the main commercial centre, looks a bit like a cheap suburban Greek restaurant would anywhere in Europe. But the food is fine, there's an ice-cream parlour next door, and an internet café and snooker hall across the road.

For Naga food, try the restaurant within **Hotel Saramati** (☎ 234761; Supermarket Arcade, Kohima Rd)

Indian (Alliance) Airlines (☎ 229366, 242441) flies in daily from Kolkata (US$130, 1¼ hours). The airport is 400m off the Kohima road, 3km out of town.

NST has hourly buses to Kohima (normal/super Rs 55/64, three hours), daily services to all Nagaland divisional headquarter towns, plus Shillong (Rs 284, 12½ hours) and Guwahati (Rs 218, 10 hours). Private buses for routes within Nagaland use a stand hidden behind the Supermarket Arcade building on

Kohima Road. Private buses for Guwahati and Imphal mostly use an area tucked under the distinctive S-shaped bridge that crosses the railway tracks from the NST bus stand.

Dimapur's train station is directly behind the NST bus stand. Useful overnight expresses run to Guwahati at 9pm (seven hours) and Dibrugarh at 10.20pm (eight hours).

KOHIMA
☎ 0370 / pop 96,000 / elev 1444m
Nagaland's agreeable capital is painted across a series of forested ridges and hill tops like spangled topping on a vast pistachio sundae.

Information
Secretariat, Home Department (☎ 227072; Secretariat Bldg) To extend or add areas to permits.
Tourism department (☎ 2222124; cnr HE & Imphal Rds)
Tribal Discovery (☎ 2228751; yiese_neitho@ rediffmail.com; Science College Rd) Private tour agency. Can arrange permits if given weeks of advanced notice. Neithonuo Yeise ('Nitono') is an eloquent guide to local sites.
UTI Bank (Stadium Approach) Has an ATM.

Orientation
The central commercial area's one-way system means that only northbound traffic passes the NST bus station (and nearby hotels), while southbound traffic passes Stadium Approach for the market. To the south these roads rejoin at the State Legislature building near the Hotel Pine. About 300m further south the Dimapur road branches west, above which is the War Cemetery. Continue 1km towards Imphal and there's a secondary hub around the roundabout facing a grandiose new police headquarters.

Some 400m north of the NST bus station the traffic-clogged Mokokchung road leads north from Chinatown Restaurant, passing the access lane to T-Khel shortly after then continuing 1km to the museum turn-off.

Sights & Activities
Kohima was the scene of an intense 64-day WWII battle. An immaculate **War Cemetery** contains graves of 1200 British and Indian soldiers killed fighting the Japanese here. Farcically, the fighting reached its climax on the deputy commissioner's tennis court (still marked) with seven full days of incredibly short-range grenade lobbing across the net. Deuce!

At the fascinating, if tiny, **central market** (Stadium Approach; ☾ 6am-4pm) tribal people sell 'ed-

ible' delicacies such as wriggling hornet grubs (*borol*). The unusually well-presented **State Museum** (☎ 2220749; admission Rs 5; ☾ 10am-3.30pm Tue-Sun), 2km north of the NST bus station, displays a wealth of interesting Naga-related artefacts: an elephant-jaw chair, colourfully flourished spears, Konyak brass figures and prosperity stones ('wealth without effort'). There's a guide to tribal shawl designs and plenty of mannequin-in-action scenes depicting traditional Naga lifestyles.

The original site of Kohima is **T-Khel** (aka Tsütuonuomia Khel, Kohima Village or Bara Basti). Although practically all older homes here have been demolished and redeveloped, the village *karu* gate remains impressive with two old door panels visible beside and behind it. Eight **monoliths** are obvious on your right as you climb the stairway beside ancient-looking mossy stone walls.

During the big traditional **Hornbill Festival** (December; see opposite), Kohima also hosts a play-off **rock festival** (www.hornbillmusic .com).

Sleeping
BUS STATION AREA
Capital Hotel (☎ 2224365; Main Rd; s/d from Rs 100/150) One of several cheapies across from the NST bus station, rooms are unusually clean for the price and views are fabulous from the shared rear balcony.

Hotel Pine (☎ 2243129; s/d from Rs 330/400) Relaxed budget option with neat wooden floors. It's down a side alley just after Link Cybercafé as you walk away from the state legislature building.

POLICE STATION JUNCTION
Viewpoint Lodge (☎ 2241826; 3rd fl, Keditsu Bldg, PR Hill; s/d Rs 700/1000) Sparkling clean, tiled-floor rooms above two handy internet cafés. Doubles have good views. Curfew at 9pm.

Hotel Japfü (☎ 2240211; hoteljapfu@yahoo.co.in; PR Hill; s/d Rs 900/1200) On the small hill above Viewpoint Lodge, this higher-service option is popular with tour groups thanks to its private parking and good restaurant where some Naga specialities are available. Rooms are comfortable with glassed-in balconies, hot showers and only slightly worn décor.

Eating
Popular Bakery (PR Hill; ☾ 5.30am-8.30pm) Has delicious breakfast pastries (Rs 10) and curious

semi-sweet 'pizzas' (Rs 20). It's 150m downhill from Viewpoint Lodge.

Dream Café (☎ 2290756; instant coffee Rs 10; ❤ 10am-6pm) Is Kohima's youth meeting point, with fashionable primary-coloured walls, twice-monthly live mini gigs and CDs of Naga music for sale from hip-hop to choral to heavy rock. It's where the Dimapur and Imphal roads divide, beneath UCO Bank in the same complex as the cheery Buzz Restaurant (mains Rs 35-65; ❤ 9am-6pm) and AmizOne Internet.

Getting There & Away

There's no airport, but **Super Travels** (☎ 2244781; super_travels02@yahoo.co.in; Hotel Japfü) sells air tickets ex-Dimapur and Guwahati.

The NST bus station offers many Nagaland services, including regular shuttles to Dimapur (normal/super Rs 55/64, three hours). Private buses to Guwahati (Rs 330 to 375, 13 to 15 hours) depart around 2.30pm from Old Minister Hill, some 200m east of police station junction.

From police station junction, frequent minibuses battle through the traffic to the New Secretariat or pass close to the museum. Taxis to Khonoma want Rs 400/700 one way/return.

AROUND KOHIMA
Kisama Heritage Village

This **open-air museum** (adult/child/car/bus Rs 5/5/5/10; ❤ 8am-6pm summer, 8am-4.30pm winter) has rebuilt traditional Naga buildings to display a representative selection of tribal styles, including traditional *morungs* (an active if visually unexciting pre-Christian educational dormitory room) and a full-size log drum. The setting would be very pretty but for all the powerlines. Nagaland's biggest annual festival, the **Hornbill Festival** (1st-7th December) is held here with various Naga tribes converging for a week-long cultural, dance and sporting celebration, much of it in full warrior costume. Kisama is 10km from central Kohima along the well-surfaced Imphal road.

AROUND KISAMA

Kigwema village, 3km south of Kisama, has a few lived-in Angami-Naga homes with traditional-style *kikeh* crossed-horn gables. However, the overall effect isn't especially impressive. Some houses are still roofed with corrugated metal sheets donated by the British army after the village was burnt out in a WWII battle.

A roadside sign 3km north of Kisama points to a hiking trail and invites you to trek to the world's tallest rhododendron bush (supposedly 20m) somewhere in the floral **Dhüku Valley**.

Khonoma

It's well worth the painful 18km of potholes to visit this historic **Angami-Naga village**, site of two major British-Angami siege battles in 1847 and 1879. Built on an easily defended ridge (very necessary back in headhunting days), Khonoma feels comparatively traditional despite having being ravaged by Indian security forces during the long insurgency war. Amid flowers and pomelo trees, squash gourd vines and megaliths, the houses range from corrugated shacks to sturdy concrete homes still decorated with *mithun* skulls (denoting hunting prowess/wealth). Basket weavers work quietly at their open doors, public rubbish-bins are regularly emptied and graves are dotted everywhere along the neatly laid stone stairways that form the main thoroughfares, all overlooked by two domineering churches. Notice the *dahu* circles. These are another show-off symbol of family wealth: building one requires the preamble of funding a feast for the whole village.

There are several *karu* stone gateways with stylised pictogram doors. Through one of these, steps lead up to the '**fort**' passing a *morung*. From the fort there are panoramic views of splendid rice terraces nestled in an arc of surrounding forested mountains.

A small sanctuary near Khonoma is one of the few places where ornithologists have a good chance of spotting a wild **Blyth's Tragopan** (a rare type of pheasant).

Of three simple homestay-guesthouses the best option is **Via Meru's House** (per person Rs 200). The three wooden-floored twin rooms are well kept and share a remarkably acceptable tiled bathroom and toilet. One room has a delightful balcony from where the top section of the village is perfectly framed. It's the unmarked brick cottage in the first flower garden to the left as you walk past the ugly Baptist Church from the village parking area.

Tuophema
☎ 0370

If you're driving between Kohima and Mokokchung, an intriguing overnight option is Tuophema. The village surveys wave upon wave of attractive forested ridges culminating on the southern horizon with Mt Japfü, Kohima appearing to crouch at its feet. Architecturally the village is no more thrilling than any other in the region, but the **karu gate** is finely carved with severed-head motifs. A harder-to-find **tsa-bo tree** gateway grows across a rear stone stairway. On the village's flattened top, above the whiter of Tuophema's two concrete churches, are the *kiputsie* '**glory stones**', whose legends have very varied interpretations.

The main attraction is **Tuophema Tourist Village** (☎ 2270786; s/d/tr Rs 800/1200/1200) where you sleep in comfortable but traditionally styled Naga thatched-roof bungalows set in a delightful flower garden with great sunset views. Rooms have modern bathrooms but traditional bamboo-pole door fasteners and even a little fire hearth in the entranceway. Don't be put off by the name. It's very much a local community project not a bustling holiday camp. The **restaurant** (breakfast Rs 60, lunch Rs 30-70, dinner Rs 140) serves good, genuine Naga food, and the **cultural programme** is unusually atmospheric and well thought-out. Groups of costumed village ladies chant their haunting two-toned songs around a wood fire while 'performing' various household weaving skills. Regardless of audience size, shows cost Rs 800 per troupe (usually three troupes).

Tuophema is 4.5km from Botsa off the Kohima–Mokokchung road.

AROUND TUOPHEMA

The main problem for Tuophema, as with so much of Nagaland, is that there's not a lot to see or do within easy reach. Typical excursions show you Rengma-Naga villages but though these sport photogenic rice barns, they're not enormously atmospheric. Around 9km beyond Tseminyu (the Rengma 'capital', 14km from Tuophema), Tesophenyu is marginally the best of the bunch with a 24-head wooden totem pole and one last remaining thatched, round-ended traditional house – at least while its wizened 98-year-old residents survive. To go much further north you'll require permits for Wokha district.

NORTHERN NAGALAND

To find semi traditional Naga villages that are at all accessible by road, your best bet is exploring the area of the **Konyak tribe** around Mon. The town of **Mon** itself is not especially an attraction but it does have a small tribal **museum** and some basic accommodation. Nearby **Shangnyu** village has a **totem pole** depicting warriors with giant phalluses. **Langmeang** has a relatively high proportion of traditional Naga houses (around 60%) and a log drum. Effectively the only way you're likely to get to these places is on a tour (see p194 for agencies). Note that reaching Mon is much quicker from Sivasagar (Assam, p211) than attempting to take the long, winding

---

THE NAGAS – MYTH AND REALITY

Many visitors have the anachronistic idea that the Naga people are half-naked cannibals who dress in weird and wonderful outfits. In fact, most modern Nagas are Christians who only wear their fancy costumes for festivals and photographers. But the culture remains fascinating.

Naga villages are perched defensively on top of impregnable ridge tops. Although often appearing essentially modern, many are still subdivided into *khels* guarded by ceremonial karu gates. The most interesting gates retain their massively heavy, strikingly carved wooden or stone doors. Although exact designs vary considerably, the central motif is usually a Naga warrior between the horns of a *mithun* (distinctive local bovine), with sun, moon, breasts (for fertility) and weaponry all depicted. A sign of wealth, *mithun* skulls also once adorned traditional Naga houses whose designs typically had rounded or Torajan-shaped prow-fronts. However, these are now rare except in museums or the most remote Konyak villages of Mon district. There you could also still find vast hollow tree-trunk 'drums'. In villages that are not 100% Christian you might still find a *morung* (bachelor dormitory) in which non-Christian young men live communally while learning traditional skills.

Headhunting was officially outlawed in 1935, with the last recorded occurrence in 1963. Nonetheless, severed heads are still an archetypal artistic motif found notably on *yanra* pendants that originally denoted the number of human heads a warrior had taken. Some intervillage wars continued into the 1980s, and a curious feature of many outwardly modern church-crowned settlements are their recently inscribed 'treaty stones' recording peace settlements between neighbouring communities.

road from Kohima via Mokokchung. Indeed, Dimapur–Mon buses drive via Assam.

ARUNACHAL PRADESH

Literally translated as 'Land of Dawn-lit Mountains', Arunachal Pradesh grips northern Assam in an embrace of densely forested ridges. These rise to some fabulous snow-capped peaks along the Chinese border. In Arunachal's deep-cut foothill valleys live at least 65 different tribal groups (101 by some counts), with bucolic cultures and photogenic bamboo-house settlements. High in the beautiful Tawang Valley are several splendid Tibetan-Buddhist monastery villages.

The region was known as Northeast Frontier Agency (NEFA) under the British who mostly left it alone. After Independence, Arunachal Pradesh was administered by Assam until 1972. It only became a fully fledged state in 1987. China has never formally recognised Indian sovereignty here, and it took a surprise Chinese invasion in 1962 before Delhi really started funding significant roads or infrastructure in the state. The Chinese voluntarily withdrew, though the dispute continues. Now the main border passes are heavily guarded by Indian military forces however the overall atmosphere is extremely calm. Arunachal doesn't suffer any real insurgency problems though permits are still required. These are comparatively easy to obtain (see p192) but annoying and expensive enough to deter most potential foreign visitors. Some areas are out of bounds or will require further permission from district headquarters.

Arunachal Tourism (www.arunachaltourism.com) offers more information.

ITANAGAR

☎ 0360 / pop 38,000

Established in 1972 and still growing, Arunachal's tailor-made capital sprawls pleasantly enough across still-green hills. But the only reason to visit is for transport connections. There are two main 'centres', both on the main Naharlagun Rd. One is a 300m stretch between two roundabouts called Zero-Point and (oddly) Bank Tinali. The other centre, marked by an obvious clocktower 3km beyond, is the Ganga Market and APST bus station where **Himalayan Holidays** (☎ 2218534) has a commercial tourist information centre.

Some mysterious **Ita Fort ruins** comprise Itanagar's only historical site, but that's really not saying much. The fort's **western gate** (Bank Tinali) is almost unidentifiable rubble. Better defined but harder to find (in a hill-top park nearly 2km uphill from Bank Tinali), the **south gate** (9am-5pm Sun-Fri) comprises four chunks of restored brickwork reaching 2.5m to 4m high that are visible even when the park is 'closed'.

A 400m stroll from Zero-Point, the **State Museum** (☎ 2222518; admission Rs 50; 9.30am-5pm Tue-Sat) has exhibits on Arunachal's tribes. On the gentle hill above, **Sidhartha Vihara** (☎ sunrise-sunset) is an attractive Tibetan-Buddhist temple draped in colourful prayer flags that makes a very pleasant dawn walk if you're staying nearby.

Sleeping & Eating

Itafort Hotel (☎ 2212590; s/d Rs 250/400, with AC Rs 500/600) Cheaper rooms are windowless boxes with cold water and fan but they're clean and well kept. Better ones have shared road-facing balconies with neat tiled floors, new paintwork and geysers. There's an airy little top-floor restaurant (mains Rs 40 to 80). The hotel is just below Bank Tinali in a small street parallel to the main road.

Hotel Arun Subansiri (☎ 2212806; s/d Rs 700/900) A virtually empty, oversized foyer leads up over-wide stairs to vast unutilised landing areas. Rooms are big, clean and similarly unadorned with high ceilings, hot water and a peculiar toilet mechanism that seems designed to moisten unwary derrières. It's just off Zero-Point towards the Tibetan Temple.

Hotel Donyi Polo (☎ 2212626; hoteldonyi@sancharnet .in; Thana Rd; s/d/ste Rs 1890/2100/2625) Lovely gardens and the quiet hill-top location (750m above Bank Tinali) raise one's expectations too high. Though pleasant enough, the rooms have slightly ragged curtains and the suite's carpets have grubby patches that one doesn't really expect at this price.

Hotel Aane (Bank Tinali; meals Rs 35-90) Pleasant dining room with limited views towards the Tibetan Temple.

Getting There & Away

Helicopter tickets are only sold at the **Helipad** (☎ 2243262; 7.30am-4pm Mon-Sat) located in Naharlagun, 16km east of Itanagar's Zero-Point. Flights run daily (except Sunday) to Guwahati (Rs 3000) and weekly to many destinations, including Along (Rs 3300), Ziro (Rs 1200),

NORTHEAST STATES

Tuting (Rs 4400), Daporijo (Rs 1550) and Pasighat (Rs 2200).

The nearest airport is 67km away at Lilabari near North Lakhimpur (see below).

From the **APST bus station** (Ganga Market) buses leave to Along (5.30am except Tuesday, and 2.30pm daily), Tezpur (Rs 110), Ziro (Rs 125, 5.30am except Wednesday), and Pasighat (Rs 160) via North Lakhimpur (Rs 42). The noon bus to Daporijo goes via Basar, not Ziro.

For shared jeeps and private buses there are several handy ticket counters around Arne Hotel (Bank Tinali). **Sahara** (☎ 2291284) has sumos to Pasighat (Rs 300, 5.30am), Along (Rs 350, 5.30am and 5pm) and Ziro (Rs 300, 5.30am and 11.30am), plus buses to Tezpur (Rs 160, 6am and 1.40pm). **Babu/Green Valley** (☎ 2218530) runs a sumo to Bomdila.

Cranky old minibuses pass Naharlagun (Rs 10), shuttling between Itanagar and Bandawera (Rs 20), the main Arunachal border point on the NH52. At Bandawera you can pick up many through buses to destinations across the Northeast.

AROUND ITANAGAR
North Lakhimpur
☎ 03752

Although it's actually in Assam, North Lakhimpur can make a useful stop in transit to central Arunachal. In some seasons it's also possible, if adventurous and unreliable, to take muddy back roads from here down to Majuli Island (p210) using multiple river crossings.

Passably intriguing are two amusingly kitschy **temples** on the NH52. One (6km west) is shaped like a road bowed by mice. The other at the western local bus stand (2km west) sports a Mexican-hat tower, around which is coiled a vast concrete cobra.

If you're stuck overnight, the **Hotel Asha** (☎ 243922; s/d from Rs180/380, ste Rs 550) sits right beside the private bus station. Don't be put off by its unappealing façade. Rooms are vastly better than you'd guess, set behind an imposing Shiva hallway. Even the cheapest have nicely tiled bathrooms, while the suite has a big double bed, dining table and choice of toilets. Cold showers.

Lilabari airport is 8km northeast of town, Rs 150 by taxi. Air Deccan flies thrice weekly to Kolkata, **Indian Airlines** (☎ 223722) twice weekly to Guwahati

The small private bus station just east of centre, on the main road towards Guwahati, has Network buses for Tezpur (130 Rs, 3½ hours) at 6am and 7pm. Facing here, the **Punjab Hotel** (☎ 222172) can organise the 4pm APST bus to Along (Rs 250) and Pasighat-bound sumos (Rs 350, 6am or 7.30pm), which should ideally be booked at least 24 hours ahead. The ASTC bus station, one block west then north, has eight daily buses to Itanagar, but most leave before 7am.

Several morning sumos leave for Ziro (Rs 140) from **M/M Travels** (☎ 244531) in the easily missed Shreeram Hotel, a small restaurant 350m east of the cobra temple tower.

CENTRAL ARUNACHAL PRADESH

A narrow, peaceful lane winds on and on through tribal villages linking Pasighat, Along, Daporijo and the Ziro Valley. Highlights are Ziro's Apatani faces, the shaggy thatch of traditional Adi homes and the seemingly endless forest landscapes. If everything was closer together, this might be one of the Northeast's most popular tourist trails. However, done as a loop from Itanagar, the trip will normally take a minimum of five exhausting days, by which time the area's gentle delights can start to wear a little thin.

Pasighat
☎ 0368

This useful little transit town and Adi cultural centre nestles in front of a curtain of luxuriantly forested foothills that beckons any traveller to head for the mountains. **Adi Banekebang** (☎ 2104075; taringtabi@rediffmail.com) is a local society that publishes Adi books and is making a movie about Adi history. Pasighat's **Solung Festival** (held from 1st-5th September) attracts traditional Adi dancers from across the region, though the showground is on a rather uninspired schoolyard.

SLEEPING & EATING
Sumo counters and the three cheapest of Pasighat's five hotels are ranged around the extensive central market.

Hotel Oman (☎ 2224464; s/d Rs 300/450) Slightly set back off Gandhi Circle, this is a better, friendlier choice. Set above a small shopping centre, rooms are well kept with mosquito nets and simple bathrooms. Meals are available (Rs 35 to 60) given two-hours' advanced order.

Hotel Aane (☎ 2223333; tw/d Rs 600/1000, d with AC Rs 1500) Smart and brand-new this is Pasighat's only hotel with hot-water showers. Bathrooms are freshly tiled and rooms have balconies (but no mosquito nets). There's an appealing rooftop terrace with bamboo parasols at which you can dine on Indian, Tibetan or Adi specialities (mains Rs 50 to 100).

GETTING THERE & AWAY

Pasighat Aerodrome (☎ 2222088; ☒ 8am-noon Mon-Sat), 3km northeast of central Pasighat, has helicopter flights to Naharlagun (Itanagar) via Mohanbari (Dibrugarh) on Monday, Wednesday and Friday, to Guwahati via Naharlagun on Tuesdays and to Tuting via Along (and back) on Friday.

The strangely inconvenient **APST bus station** (☒ advance bookings 8am-2pm Mon-Fri, 8am-noon Sat) is on the northernmost edge of town. A bus runs to Along (Rs 100, five to six hours, 7am daily except Wednesday) and to Itanagar (Rs 170, at 6am daily except Monday). Beware that easterly sections of the NH52 tend to get washed away during the monsoon, so timings vary enormously.

Sumos run to Along (Rs 200, 5½ hours) at 6am. **Hotel Siang** (☎ 2224559) organises jeep-boat-jeep combination rides (Rs 250, eight hours) to Dibrugarh via Oriamghat (see below)

Around Pasighat

ORIAMGHAT

A daily ferry to Dibrugarh (p213) departs from **Oriamghat** (Assam), a lonely sandbank 30km from Pasighat in an area of very picturesque traditional villages, including simple but typical Mising marshland hamlets around **Kemi**, the lonely Arunachal border post. Particularly photogenic is the wonderful thatched Adi village of **Sille** set in wide rice fields 20km from Pasighat (NH52, Km 523). Tour groups often rush straight past these places assuming (often falsely) that remoter villages will be more 'exotic'.

Oriamghat is 7km down a dead-end lane from Oyam on the NH52.

JONAI

The nearest train station to Pasighat is Margungat Jonai (35km west), with a cheap, overnight service to Rangia (p204).

Along (Aalo)

☎ 03783 / pop 20,000 / elev 302m

This friendly if somewhat nondescript market town is the logical hub for visiting numerous traditional Adi villages in the vicinity.

There's an **Internet Café** (☎ 224597; Abu-Tani Centre, Nehru Chowk; per hr Rs 40; ☒ 6.30am-7pm) opposite the APST bus station. Amid government offices 300m east is the informative little **District Museum** (☎ 222214; admission free; ☒ 9am-4.30pm Mon-Fri) selling some rare, relevant books and tribal-language guides. Walk north then east past the helipad to find the extensive central market selling what look like round pebbles but are actually a kind of yeast for fermenting *apong* (Adi rice beer), or leaf-wrapped square bundles in which is prefermented rice (just add water to make the *apong*).

A guide is useful for some hikes. Although not 'professional', a good choice is English-speaking local farmer **Taje Komut** (☎ 224653; from Rs 1500 per day) who knows most of the trails and is a mine of interesting information.

The best accommodation choice is **Hotel Holiday Cottage** (☎ 222463; Hospital Hill; s/d Rs 250/400) southwest of the helipad. Rooms are fresh and clean with private squat toilet and a reasonable restaurant. The hotel's savvy owner can organise Adi dance shows and traditional feasts (with plenty of *apong*) in a traditional home. **Hotel Yombow** (☎ 224641; Sipu Colony Rd; dm/s/tw/d Rs 125/150/250/300) is a much more basic fallback should Holiday Cottage be full.

If you were really in a hurry, you could fly in from Naharlagun (Itanagar) on the Friday helicopter, race up to Paia, then jump back on the helicopter out again three hours later.

APST buses run to Daporijo (Rs 150, eight hours) at 7am except Monday, and to Itanagar (Rs 230, 12 hours) daily at 6am or 5pm. The latter passes through Likabari (Rs 130) near the Malinithan Ruins (http://aruna chalpradesh.nic.in/malinithan.htm). Timings vary for the Pasighat service (Rs 95, five hours).

Shared jeeps are bookable from various sumo counters opposite the main market. Almost all leave at 5.30am, but there are none to Daporijo unless you charter (Rs 3500).

Around Along

The whole point of coming this far is to visit the area's attractive Gallong-Adi villages. For a balance between accessibility and a relatively unspoilt vibe, a great choice is **Paia**. To get there drive 8km west of Along, 1km beyond **Podbi**, then walk across the metal-plate suspension foot bridge. Paia climbs the hill above and, apart from the school, most buildings

CENTRAL ARUNACHAL'S TRIBAL GROUPS

The various tribes of central Arunachal Pradesh consider themselves very self-consciously different from one another but in reality most are related. Virtually all come from Tibeto-Burman stock and before the very recent arrival of Christianity, most practised Donyi-Polo (sun and moon) worship. A few traditional-minded old men still wear their hair long, tied around to form a top knot above their foreheads. For ceremonial occasions, village chiefs typically wear scarlet shawls and a bamboo-wicker hat spiked with a porcupine quill or hornbill feather. Women favour hand-woven wraparounds like Southeast-Asian sarongs.

Major tribes you're likely to encounter are:

Adi

Divided into five major subgroups, notably Gallong and Minyong, the Adi tribes live mostly between Pasighat and Daporijo. Historically they were often called 'Abor', meaning non-submissive. Much more so than the Nagas, Adi villages (but not towns) still retain a high proportion of beautifully built traditional homes, many still luxuriantly roofed with thick palmyra-leaf thatch. Stilted Adi granaries are ingeniously designed with 'mushroom stones' to prevent rats from reaching the crops. Some men still wear bright green or purple waistcoats with a line or two of embroidery and in the rainy season some still wear boat-shaped basketware hats, known as a *bolup*.

Nishi, Tagin and Hill Miri

To an outsider these three tribes are somewhat hard to differentiate, all living in bamboo stilt houses that are much simpler and less photogenic than those of the Adi. Famously warlike, the Nishi are renowned for their short tempers.

Apatani

Although famous as local traders, the Apatani homeland is confined to the comparatively tiny Ziro Valley plateau (see opposite). Historically Apatani women were considered the region's most beautiful and were prone to kidnapping by lusty, warlike Nishi tribesmen whose territory surrounds Ziro. As a 'defence', Apatani women received facial tattoos and extraordinary nose plugs known as *dat;* blue-black disks sometimes the size of US quarters inserted into holes made in their upper nostrils. Peace with the Nishis in the 1960s meant the end to that brutal practise, so only women in their 50s and above are now so defaced. Meeting these women is undoubtedly a fascinating glimpse of tribal history. But photography is a sensitive issue: snapping a woman because of her imposed ugliness is pretty distasteful and some Apatani women have had cosmetic surgery to remove their tattoos.

are made of bamboo and thatch. Some village youths speak English.

When returning you can stroll 3km along the river bank then cross back over an alternative bridge to **Kabu**. This bridge is a lot more picturesque, being mostly formed of cane with narrow bamboo slat-planks. As many bamboo planks are missing, crossing can be a little too 'exciting' for some tastes. Kabu village is interesting if less photogenic than Paia. Both Kabu and Podbi are on the road from Along towards Tato in the fabled Mechuka valley, home of the Tibetan-Buddhist Memba people.

Readers have recommended a more strenuous hike (with steep sections) starting and finishing at Patum Bridge, 6km east of Along and climbing to the ridge villages of Jomlo Mobuk and Mori. A guide is required.

There are many picturesque Adi villages en route to Pasighat, notably **Lokpeng** (17km) and **Koreng** (88km, 2km before Pangin town). Just 2km before Koreng the road divides, the left fork heading north via **Boleng** to **Yingkiong** and (eventually) **Tuting**. In this region the Siang River canyon offers some phenomenal world-class grade V+ **rafting** challenges, but special permits are required and no local facilities are available – expeditions only.

Pareng is a truly idyllic, little-visited Minyong-Adi village 14km from Boleng up a dead-end country lane.

Daporijo

☎ 03792 / pop 14,000 / elev 699m

Sprawling but attractively set 'Dapo' fills a triangular river junction with a sea of tin roofs amid otherwise green foliage and Adi thatched-roof cottages. If you're driving the 'scenic route' from Along to Ziro; you'll virtually have to sleep here. Try to get one of the four rooms at the **Circuit House** (☎ 223250; d Rs 300), which is scenically plonked on a hill top, overlooking town through a bamboo veil. Otherwise the best market-area option is **Hotel Santanu** (☎ 223531; New Market; s/d from Rs 200/300), with faulty plumbing but decent beds, mosquito nets and surprisingly good local delicacies in the cheerless restaurant (try *papuk* – chicken in banana-flower broth; Rs 60). The Santanu is easy to spot from afar, although its entrance is hidden amid the market stalls.

Between prison-quality Hotels Greenview and Darjeeling are several sumo counters offering early morning jeeps to Itanagar (Rs 380, 11 hours) via Ziro. Contrastingly APST buses to Itanagar (Rs 240, 2pm Friday to Wednesday) run via Basar and Likabari (not via Ziro). APST buses offer the only public transport to Along, departing at 6.30am Tuesday to Sunday.

AROUND DAPORIJO

The wooded mountain scenery is attractive if not world beating. While several Nishi and Hill Miri villages around Daporijo are made of traditional bamboo-and-thatch, few have anything like the grace of Adi equivalents near Along or Pasighat. Nonetheless, it's worth watching out for curious bamboo **totem poles** erected at the roadside to commemorate the recently deceased. They are strung with cane and bamboo-thread loops and often topped, surreally, with an umbrella. Notice the basket near the top of such constructions, which, for a few days after the pole's erection, would have held a chicken. The bird is later set free symbolising the release of the commemorated person's spirit.

If driving to Ziro, the best lunch stop is a new tourist department restaurant perched high above the Komla River (Km post 58), about 11km beyond **Raga**.

Ziro Valley

☎ 03788

This small, highland plateau of rice fields and fenced bamboo groves is cupped by gentle pine-clad hills and dotted with the tight-packed, intriguing villages of the **Apatani tribe**. Tall *babo* poles topped with crosspieces and dangling balls are raised during the Nyakom festival. The number of *babo* outside a house signifies the number of sons in the family. *Lapang* platforms for (male only) community gatherings include some made from impressively vast planks of ancient timber. But the real (if slightly voyeuristic) attraction is the people themselves. Elders have wild hair wound up in a topknot, sometimes with a quill through it. Most notably, older women sport alarming facial tattoos and bizarre nose plugs (see boxed text, opposite, for explanation).

The main if least-interesting towns are **Ziro** (with the helipad) and sprawling **Hapoli** (aka New Ziro, starting 7km further south), which has all the hotels, road transport and main markets. The most authentic Apatani villages are **Hong** (biggest and best known), **Dutta** (atmospheric and easier to reach), **Hari**, **Bamin** and **Hijo**. People watching is often best just before dusk when everyone is walking home from the rice fields.

SLEEPING

Racho Rest House (☎ 225336; SSB Gate; r per day/month Rs 30/400) Even given the barn smells, zero-bedding (bring your own) and shared outdoor well (with toilet hole), you just can't beat the price. The location, 150m towards Hong off the Ziro–Hapoli road, is great for interacting with villagers.

Highland Hotel (☎ 225238; MG Rd, s/d/deluxe Rs 170/300/400) In the market area, this conspicuous yellow building has sit-down flush toilets in its 'deluxe' rooms.

Hotel Blue Pine (☎ 224812; s/d Rs 300/450) Wooden-clad walls, a friendly welcome and a very creditable restaurant balance the slightly long walk from town (unlit at night). Hot water by bucket. It's at the southwest edge of town, 300m off the Itanagar Rd.

Hotel Valley View (☎ 225398; JN Complex, MG Rd; s/d Rs 400/500) Very friendly, with neat, new rooms (most still nearing completion) above a restaurant set back from the main market area.

GETTING THERE & AWAY

Helicopter flights operate on Saturdays to Naharlagun (Itanagar; Rs 1200), Daporijo and Koloriang from what was once the WWII back-up airport supporting the Stilwell Rd and the allies' cross-the-hump airlift to Kunming.

NORTHEAST STATES

Various sumos depart for Itanagar (Rs 200, 6½ hrs) and North Lakhimpur (Rs 144, 4½ hours) around 5.15am and 10.30am. Counters are in Hapoli's main market area notably by the Hotel Centrepoint. Sumos to Daporijo (Rs 200) depart around 11am from an un-marked shop (☎ 225100, worth calling to double-check departure times) beside Pearl Cafe (Hapoli–Ziro road). The easy to use APST bus stop is at Para Bazaar, but it offers few routes of interest to tourists. If it runs, the bus to Itanagar costs Rs 125.

Ziro to the NH52

This section is one of the most beautiful drives in Arunachal. If driving the route southbound, it's worth starting the trip with breakfast at **Viewpoint Cafeteria** (☎ 224462; meals from Rs 40; ☺ 6am-6pm), 5km out of Ziro, which really does have a great view if staff bother to open the curtains. The road then winds down multiple hairpins from 1754m **Joram Top** into attractive forest dotted with small rice terraces and pretty Nishi hamlets. At contrast-ingly ugly **Yazali** town you reach the Ronganadi River, which cascades photogenically down through a boulder-strewn canyon. This is now partly dammed and requires a detour, but the road returns to the valley gorge later passing through some inspiringly pristine stands of steep, mature forest (unless you take the bone-shakingly rough shortcut road to Itanagar from Potin junction).

WESTERN ARUNACHAL PRADESH

Culturally magical, politically fascinating and scenically spectacular, a mountain-hopping journey to Tawang's 'little Tibet' is one of the Northeast's greatest attractions. But allow plenty of time. You could technically go either way in an utterly exhausting day. However, you'd be better to budget on at least five days return from Guwahati (or Tezpur), includ-ing two nights in Tawang and an overnight break each way at Dirang (or less interest-ingly Bomdila). Traveller's Point in Guwahati (p200) offers such a five-day tour (adult/child Rs 5500/5000, minimum group size six), and claims that it can get Arunachal Pradesh per-mits (considerable extra fees) within 48 hours, even for foreigners. This seems unlikely but we didn't test it.

Adding an extra day to visit Nameri Eco-Camp en route is worthwhile. Be prepared for the intense cold in winter.

Bhalukpong to Bomdila

After permit checks in Bhalukpong (p207), the Tawang road passes an **orchidarium** (☎ 03782-23444718; admission free; ☺ 9am-noon & 2-4pm Mon-Sat) at **Tipi** after 6km, then winds steadily up through lush stands of mature forest for around 60km. The trees start thinning after the big roadside **Nag Mandir** temple, but what was once a charm-ing glade has now been transformed into a long strip of army camps that mar the scenery for the next 30km.

Bracketed by military bases, **Tenga** (78km from Bhalukpong) is the turn-off for **Eagles' Nest** (25km west), a unique bird-watching hot-spot for hardcore twitchers to spy the *Bugun Liocichla*. That's a colourful babbler of which only 14 individuals have ever been recorded. Contact Indi Glow at the **Bugun Welfare Society** (☎ 03782-273359) to arrange **lodging** (per person Rs 250) and permits (Indian/foreigner Rs 100/500 per day). Tenga's best accommodation is **Hotel Aphet** (☎ 03782-273506; s/d/tr Rs 300/450/600).

Around 16km before Bomdila, a 2km de-tour takes you into **Rupa**. Above this otherwise scrappy village, there's an ancient Sherdukpen **gompa** (Buddhist monastery) with *mani* (stone carved with the Tibetan- Buddhist mantra) wall and a few obviously old houses.

The road then cranks up to mountain-top Bomdila, a town whose only real recommenda-tion is what seems to be an end-of-the world location. In fact the world continues just across the pass behind.

Bomdila

☎ 03782 / elev 2682m

The provincial town of **Bomdila** snakes 3km down a steep, south-facing mountain slope. Of anywhere between Tezpur and Tawang, Bomdila offers the widest choice of transport connections, but accommodation is pricier than in Dirang and the town has none of Old Dirang's charm despite several **gompas** and a fairly interesting **museum** (admission free; ☺ 10am-4pm Mon-Fri), located close to Hotel La.

Himalayan Holiday (☎ 222017; www.himalayan -holidays.com; ABC Bldg, Main Market) is a well-connected ecotravel agency that offers basic tourist infor-mation and runs sumos from the main bazaar.

SLEEPING & EATING

Potala Lodge (☎ 222248; s/d Rs 250/400) Around 400m east of the market, most rooms have shared bathroom and many are windowless, but rooms 1 and 4 have fairly attractive sunrise views.

The following are close together, 1km above the market near the museum.

Tourist Lodge (☎ 222349; d Rs 150-400) This wooden structure is arranged around a gently attractive fountain pond. The slightly tatty rooms have private bathrooms and geysers.

Hotel La (☎ 222958; s/d Rs 200/300) Most rooms are small, no-nonsense affairs with wooden floors and clean shared bathrooms. A few newly painted rooms upstairs (Rs 800) have geysers but nasty green carpeting.

Hotel Singiyang Phong (☎ 222286; s/d from Rs 715/1210) Behind its upmarket management style and smart foyer, this overpriced hotel is hamstrung by some idiotic internal architecture creating unnecessarily cramped rooms with balconies that can only be accessed by crawling through the windows. The restaurant (mains Rs 40 to 130) also serves 'pizzas' from Rs 90.

GETTING THERE & AWAY

By road, the APST bus station is 2km below the market. Southbound buses supposedly loop round town picking up passengers but in reality don't always bother. Services include Tezpur (Rs 120, 8am ex-Dirang) via Bhalukpong (Rs 90), Itanagar (6.15am but not Fridays), Guwahati (Rs 200, 6am except Wednesdays) and Tawang (Rs 250, 6.30am alternate days) via Dirang (Rs 60, 1½ hours).

Several sumos leave from the market area at 6am and 11am to Tezpur (Rs 180, 162km,

six hours) and at 6.30am to Tawang (Rs 250, 181km, 9½ hours).

Dirang

☎ 03780 / elev 1621m

Fabulous **Old Dirang** is an almost picture-perfect Tibetan-Monpa stone village marred only by the brutal slash of main road that cuts straight through its heart. Even that's softened by day when villagers lay out their millet seed to dry on the smooth concrete surface. Above the picturesque stone houses rises a steep rocky hill topped with Old Dirang's gompa and several *mani* walls. Across the main road a section of village forms a fortified mini-citadel containing what looks like the bailey of a recently part-restored fortress, though it contains only drying hay.

All commercial services are in **New Dirang**, 5.5km further north. It's a contrastingly ordinary valley town, but it's not unpleasant and there's a small huddle of cheap hotels, eateries and sumo counters around the central crossroads beside Hotel Raj.

SLEEPING

With a local guide it might be possible to talk your way into one of Dirang's four governmental bungalows, each offering perfectly survivable rooms for around Rs 100. Otherwise private options include the following:

Hotel Dreamland (☎ 242296; Main Rd; d/tr Rs 200/300) Three-room cottage with just-bearable rooms sharing a grotty toilet amid flower tubs at the rear.

Hotel Moon (☎ 242438; Main Rd; s/d/tr/q Rs 200/300/600/800) Plain rooms with very hard beds. Only the top-floor quad has a private bathroom.

Dirang Resort (☎ 242352; IB Rd; d Rs 650-700) This friendly, family hotel occupies an old-style hill-house, with walls like Battenburg cake, old timber floorboards and a wooden wraparound balcony terrace. Each of the four rooms has a little sitting area, 26-channel TV, and modern tiled bathrooms with hot water and sit-down flush toilet. It's located 300m off the main road where IB Rd curves sharply beyond the Inspection Bungalow.

Hotel Pemaling (☎ 242615; d standard/deluxe/ste Rs 700/1500/2000) On the hillside overlooking New Dirang, 1km south of the centre, this friendly place is Dirang's most comfortable option. The suites have (over) colourful Tibetan box tables and twin-seated balconies with views towards the Sela Pass. Even standard doubles have sparkling clean bathrooms and tiled floors. There's just one claustrophobic single (Rs 450).

EATING

Hotel Samaroah (meals Rs 20-30) Located in a mini shopping centre beside the Hotel Maa Laxmi, this downmarket restaurant offers simple chowmein and *dhal-bhat* (dhal and rice) but is one of very few places where lights stay on during inevitable evening power cuts.

GETTING THERE & AWAY

For Tezpur, **Eastland** (☎ 242446; Hotel Dreamland) has sumos (Rs 270, 7½ hours) at 5.30am and 7pm, and there's an APST bus (Rs 205) at 6am. If heading north, the APST Bomdila–Tawang bus passes through around 8am (alternate days only) or try hitching a ride down to Old Dirang just after dawn (when it's at its most photogenic) and picking up the Tawang bus from there.

Dirang to Tawang

After a few attractive, rural hamlets and a couple more army posts, the road begins a seemingly endless coil of switchbacks that look especially attractive driving south. Eventually you reach the 4176m Sela Pass at Km 240. There can be snow here as early as October. One tiny little shack at the top serves tea. The bare rocky peaks and tundra-fringed lakes are an enormous contrast to the forested foothills. Yet on the other side, the road rapidly descends to another unexpectedly verdant valley system. Sumos usually stop for tea at **Jaswantgarh**, where a lonely war memorial complex commemorates three Indian soldiers who skirmished bravely, if ultimately unsuccessfully, against the advancing Chinese in November 1962. Just above are fragments of gun emplacements and there's a viewpoint with a mountain-spotter guide to the jaw-droppingly beautiful panorama– the enormous Tawang Valley.

THE TAWANG VALLEY

Calling the Tawang Valley a valley just doesn't do justice to its incredible scale. This is a vast sweep of field-patched sloping plateaus dotted with Buddhist monasteries, prayerwheels and archetypal Tibetan-style villages. Yet it's all brushed green with a most un-Tibetan fertility. Above rises an enormous bowl of soaring, sharpened peaks, several reaching over 5000m. Way beneath, the Tawang River cuts a very deep 'V' as it froths its way towards Bhutan. Crossing this or other rivers often means an interminable descent: two villages that appear close on a map might be hours apart in reality.

Indeed just descending from Jaswantgarh to partially attractive **Jang** takes nearly an hour. Another 5km below are the impressive **Jang Falls** (1km detour), where the Narangan River tumbles almost 80m into the Tawang River. Once across the river, the road wiggles back up for the last 30km to Tawang town. Of all the attractive villages en route, the most inspiring is **Rhou**, 18km before Tawang. Rhou's roadside section is photogenic enough. But hidden away above the road, the old village core has a series of brilliantly timeless tower-houses scattered up narrow stone stairways and paths. Access is up some initially unpromising concrete steps 200m east of Km 297.

Tawang

☎ 03794 / elev 3048m

Tawang is the valley's transport hub and accommodation base. Many enchanting **gompas** ring the town (see opposite) and the area's Buddhist pedigree is impeccable. The 6th Dalai Lama was from Tawang, the 13th holed up here in 1911 avoiding Chinese attacks on Lhasa and the present (14th) Dalai Lama fled this way in April 1959. At that time there were no roads to the outside world and it took him four days to walk to Bomdila. China retaliated in 1962 by launching a surprise invasion. Although they later withdrew, the status of Tawang remains a stumbling block in Sino-Indian *rapprochement*. Above Tawang town the hillside is dominated with Indian military camps designed to deter any future attack.

Tawang's setting is more beautiful than the town itself, but the central old-market area has a photogenic bank of colourful **prayer wheels** turned by apple-cheeked Monpa pilgrims sporting woolly black *gurden* skullcaps. Just 50m east is **Monyul Cyber Café** (per hr Rs 50; ☘ 8.30am-8pm). Further west near Snowland restaurant, **PL Traders** (☎ 222987) sell handicrafts including embroidered shoulder bags (Rs 100). Another unmarked shop slightly further along sells a variety of Buddhist pilgrimware including beautiful Tibetan copper prayer-turners.

The bizarrely hard-to-find police station (for compulsory registration) is 2km away near the new hospital. Take a taxi.

SLEEPING

Tawang has roughly 20 small hotels. Many are comparatively pricey as the tourist season is short and heating is expensive.

Tourist Lodge (☎ 222359; tw Rs 200) Slightly tatty but very good value with hot showers and renovations underway, the Tourist Lodge is 150m up a spur of side lane from the main drag.

Hotel Gourichan (☎ 224151; s Rs 350, d Rs 600-900) This smart, pseudo-Tibetan building dominates the upper old-market area, and although rooms aren't as plush as the exterior suggests, all have private bathroom with geyser.

Hotel Dungphoo (☎ 223765; d/tr with shared bathroom Rs 350/400, d with private bathroom Rs 600) Tucked behind the better-value Hotel Gourichan, the rooms are neat and not as outrageously over-priced as other nearby options.

our pick Tenzing Guesthouse (☎ 222893; s/d Rs 450/750, tr Rs 850-1000) This comfortable, idyllically quiet six-room homestay appears to be in the middle of nowhere, 6km down the main road from central Tawang. In fact, on foot, you're just 45 minutes' walk from the gompa (visible directly above), 10 minutes' from Urgelling and a skip away from the new Sanyalling monastery. Owner, Prem, speaks faultless English and can help you choose interesting hikes, and plans to develop some guest cottages in traditional Monpa style.

Tawang Inn (☎ 224096; d/ste from Rs 880/1650) Entered from a back lane 400m southeast of the market, this is central Tawang's most polished choice, with comfy modern rooms and partial views towards the gompa from some suites and from the relatively simple dining room.

EATING

The market area has many cheap but rough-edged eateries.

Snowland (mains Rs 20-90) Serves the same standard range of *momos,* chowmein, *thukpa* and curries, but in a nicer environment with Chinese lamps and glass-top tables. The high-volume 50-Cent music doesn't fit so well. Located a short walk west of the market.

GETTING THERE & AWAY

From Guwahati, helicopters (Rs 3000, two hours) fly on Mondays and Wednesdays to Lumla, 42km from Tawang via the Zemithang road. The APST bus to Bomdila (Rs 170, eight hours) runs via Dirang (Rs 130, 6½ hours) on alternate days. **Himalayan** (☎ 223151) and several other sumo agents run 5.30am shared jeeps to Tezpur (Rs 350, 14 hours), though it's much nicer to stop one night in Dirang en route. Minivans shuttle when full from the market area to Tawang Gompa (Rs 30) or can be hired for excursions.

Around Tawang
TAWANG GOMPA

For most visitors, seeing magical **Tawang Gompa** (☎ 222243; admission free; ☺ sunrise-sunset) is the whole point of their trip. Founded in 1681, this self-contained medieval citadel is reputedly the world's second-largest Buddhist monastery complex after the Potala Palace in Lhasa (Tibet). The 3km upper approach road from Tawang town offers several wonderful vantage points from which the gompa is brilliantly framed with a backdrop of spiky, snow-speckled mountains.

Within the fortified walls, narrow alleys divide three whitewashed-stone rows of monks' dwellings leading up to a central square dominated by the hulking, colourful **prayerhouse**, which was heavily restored between 1992–7. Across the square is a small but interesting **museum** (admission/camera/video Rs 20/20/100; ☺ 7am-sunset) that monks will generally open for you on request. Its curious displays include 700-year-old statuettes, colourful butter sculptures and ornaments that belonged to the 6th Dalai Lama's mother.

All alone around 300m downhill from the gompa's southern ramparts lies the two-room Dron Khung Guesthouse on a valley-view perch that's phenomenally beautiful. Sadly the guesthouse now takes only official dignitaries, though it's always worth asking and even if you're refused, you can still enjoy the view while you're there.

NUNNERIES

Clearly visible on a mountain shoulder above Tawang Gompa is **Gyangong Anigompa**, which is home to a small order of Buddhist nuns. Walking there directly is impeded by a deep, intervening valley, but you could trek first to **Thukje Chueling Anigompa**, a modest but colourful nunnery built in 2002 on the site of the 1595 Bramadungchung Anigompa. By road you willl need to first backtrack almost to Tawang town, then continue past a sign temptingly marked 'Lhasa 508km'. No you can't! Indeed even reaching the nunneries takes you through a military area, so make sure you carry a passport and explain where you're going if asked.

URGELLING GOMPA

The birthplace of the 6th Dalai Lama, ancient **Urgelling Gompa** has a modest (and usually locked) prayerhouse and a row of covered *chortens* (stupas) behind prayer wheels. Its supposed holy 'footprint' looks like a trio of cartoon tadpoles. But the peaceful setting and views up towards Tawang Gompa are highly appealing.

By road it's 6km from Tawang town, 500m off the main Bomdila road: turn down a tiny lane by the Maruti Service Centre. On foot there are short cuts.

There are over a dozen more gompas scattered around Tawang that make for great hiking.

MIZORAM

Seen from the sky, Mizoram seems to have been ploughed by a forgetful god who then left the deep north–south furrows to green over with a fuzz of bamboo. Mizoram is civilised, tidy and almost entirely Christian. You'll see very few Indian faces among the local Thai-Chinese features. People are surreally but uninvasively friendly. Don't be surprised if you're warmly thanked by total strangers for bothering to visit their state.

Mizoram runs entirely to its own rhythm. Most businesses are long shut by 6pm, and virtually everything closes tight on Sundays. Forget breakfast-lunch-dinner, Mizos traditionally have two main meals, *zingchaw*

AW DEAR

Traditionally each Mizo clan has their own language, but there's a widely used Mizo lingua franca that's now taught in schools along with English or Hindi. It's written in Latin script using a system devised by Welsh missionaries that, confusingly for English speakers, spells the long, soft 'oh' sound as 'aw'. A typical Mizo greeting is *chibai*. Thank you is *kalawmeh* (kal-oh may).

(am-meal, 9am to 10am) and *tlaichaw* (pm-meal, 4pm to 6pm). Both feature rice with a selection of boiled leaves, boiled veg and boiled fatty smoked pork. Flavour is added using *rawt*, a salsa of diced chillies, ginger and onion. Express appreciation by saying *dui (lutuk)* – (very) delicious. On paper Mizoram is a dry state, though friendly, wobbling drunks are surprisingly common.

Mizo culture has no real caste distinctions and women seem pretty liberated; in Aizawl girls smoke openly, wear jeans and hang out in unchaperoned posses meeting up with their beaus at rock concerts on the central field. Musical tastes favour gospel, Megadeath and Avril Lavigne, preferably all combined (yes, they try!). Similarly curious are the Aizawl Thunders, Mizoram's local biker gang, who despite their leathers and growling Enfields are determinedly democratic.

History

Every 50 years Mizoram's endless bamboo forests flower for three seasons, producing millions of egg-shaped fruits. Although inedible to humans, these fruits are adored by rats, which multiply rapidly to enjoy the free feast. But after the third year the bamboo stops fruiting. Suddenly hungry, the rats swarm onto anything else edible, notably human crops. This last happened in 1959 causing a serious famine. The Indian government's inept response left Mizos feeling entirely abandoned. The Mizo Famine Front (MFF) later developed into the Mizo National Front (MNF) insurgents. In 1966 they launched a stunning surprise raid, briefly capturing Mizoram's then-tiny capital Aizawl. India's appallingly heavy-handed response was the infamous 'grouping' policy. The entire rural population was coralled into virtual concentration camps. The old *jhumming* hamlets were then destroyed to deprive insurgents of resources (so don't look for ancient 'traditional' homes in Mizoram). Obviously such tactics backfired massively, creating a huge wave of support for the rebels. However, after two decades of fighting, the 1986 ceasefire led to a lasting peace settlement. Today the MNF holds a majority in the democratically elected state government and Mizoram is proud of being the safest Northeast state. Although Mizos remain somewhat bemused as to how their 'country' got lumped in with India, everyone is happy that at least they didn't end up thrown in with Mynamar (Burma), where, it's claimed, the local Mizo population lives on the verge of starvation.

In late 2006 the bamboo forests started flowering again. Let's hope that everyone will be better prepared for the inevitable in 2009.

Permits

Agencies, notably Omega Travels (below), can arrange paperwork and fax you a permit copy. This gets you through arrival formalities, but once in Aizawl collect the original and take it to SP-CID for registration. Officially permits limit you to Aizawl district but with an un-official nod from SP-CID you might be OK travelling further afield.

AIZAWL

☎ 0389 / pop 275,000

Balanced precariously on a razor-sharp ridge, Aizawl (eye-*zole*) could well be the world's steepest capital. Homes at road level might be held there with rear stilts three times higher than their roofs. In comparison, San Francisco seems as flat as Florida.

Addresses refer to areas and junctions ('points' or 'squares'). The unnamed spaghetti of roads and steep linking stairways is confusing, but the central ridge road is reasonably flat linking Zodin Sq (old bus station), Upper Bazaar (shops), Zarkawt (hotels and long-distance sumos) and Chandmari (east Mizoram sumos). This section is walkable, although appalling rush-hour traffic creates suffocating fumes.

Information

Dazzlechips Cyber Cafe (☎ 2342326; Zarkawt; per hr Rs 30; ◷ 10am-10pm) Slow connection, 200m beyond David's Kitchen.

Directorate of Tourism (☎ 2333475; http://mizo tourism.nic.in/; Chandmari)

Newslink (http://newslink .in/) Mizoram's English-language newspaper.

Omega Travels (☎ 2323548; omegatravel89@yahoo .co.in; Zodin Sq; ◷ 9am-5pm Mon-Fri, 9am-3pm Sat) Can arrange tourist permits (Rs 400 for up to eight people). Zova (☎ 9436142938) speaks good English.

SP-CID (☎ 2334082, 2243697; Khatla Maubawk; ◷ 10am-4pm Mon-Fri) Compulsory police registration.

Sights

Mizoram State Museum (☎ 2340936; Zarkawt; admission Rs 5; ◷ 11am-3.30pm Mon-Fri) has interesting exhibits on Mizo culture. It's located up a steep lane from Sumkuma Point past Aizawl's most

distinctive **church**, whose modernist bell-tower spire is pierced by arched 'windows'.

The **Salvation Army 'Temple'** (Zodin Sq) has bell chimes that are endearingly complex.

KV Paradise (Durtlang; admission Rs 5; ◷ 10am-9pm Mon-Sat, noon-9pm Sun). 'V' is for Varte who died in a 2001 motor accident. 'K' is for her husband Khawlhring who has since lavished his entire savings and energy creating a three-storey mausoleum complex to her memory. The marble fountain-patio has wonderful panoramic views. Inside an odd collection displays Varte's wardrobe and shoe collection. Locals call it Mizoram's Taj Mahal, but being a school principal not a Mughal emperor, Khawlhring's Christian taj isn't quite Agrasized. The site is 8km from Zarkawt, 1km off the Aizawl–Silchar road via an improbably narrow mud lane.

Sleeping & Eating

Chawlhna Hotel (☎ 2346418; Main Rd, Zarkawt; s/d with shared bath Rs 100/200, s with private Rs 170-300, d Rs 260-600) is very popular, but **Hotel Chief** (☎ 2346418; Main Rd, Zarkawt; s Rs 480-540, d Rs 540-650) is somewhat more polished with neat tiled floors and almost-hot geysers. The better doubles of **Hotel Tropicana** (☎ 2346156; hoteltropicana@rediffmail.com; s Rs 170-250, d Rs 450-550) are rather cosy with fitted curtains, ethnic table stand and balcony. High above Zemabawk (11km east), the **Tourist Home** (☎ 2352067; Mizoram Science Centre, Zemabawk; d Rs 350-500) offers peace and great new rooms. The best viewpoint in Aizawl is a 10-minute stroll up the hillock in front. Cottage rooms are older.

At **David's Kitchen** (☎ 2341263; mains Rs 65-210; ◷ 10am-10pm Mon-Sat), fine Indian, Chinese and

---

YMA NOT YMCA

Wherever you look in Mizoram you'll see red, white and black tricolours. No that's not the Egyptian flag but the colours of the ubiquitous Young Mizo Association (YMA). This is a community-based volunteer charity to which virtually every local under 45 years of age belongs. It helps the poor at times of need but also runs many day-to-day local services, including rubbish collection. The YMA notably organises free Christian burials: the idea of paying commercial undertakers for coffins and funerals seems a shocking commercialisation of death to most Mizos.

Continental food, mocktails, friendly staff and pleasant décor are undermined by the playing of incessant Kenny G.

On Sundays, hotels are your only hope for sustenance.

Getting There & Away

Indian Airlines (☎ 344733) and **Air Deccan** (www .airdeccan.com) fly to Aizawl (one hour) daily. Indian Airlines also serves Guwahati (US$91, one hour) most days and Imphal (US$61, 30 minutes) thrice weekly. Efficient little Lengpui airport is 35km west. Taxis charge Rs 500. A 9am **airport minibus service** (☎ 2573384; Rs 100) runs from Hotel Ritz (Upper Bazaar) returning around 2pm once the Air Deccan flight has arrived. Obliging minibus-organiser **Malsoma** (☎ 9436374454) also rents a new sumo jeep (Rs 15 per km, Rs 2000 per day minimum).

Counters for long-distance sumos are conveniently clustered around Zarkawt's Sumkuma Point. For Saitual the most central are **RKV** (☎ 2305452) and Nazareth in Chandmari.

Destination	Cost (Rs)	Duration (hr)	Departure time/point
Guwahati	530	14-18	4pm
Saitual	70	3	1pm, 3pm
Shillong	430	15	4pm
Silchar	230	5½	6.30am, 10am, 1pm

Getting Around

Frequent city buses run Zodin Sq–Upper Bazaar–Zarkawt–Chandmari–Lower Chatlang–Zasanga Point then either climb to Durtlang or curl right round past the new Chunga bus station (6km) to Zemabawk. Maruti–Suzuki taxis are ubiquitous and reasonably priced.

RURAL MIZORAM

Mizoram's pretty, green hills get higher as you head east. **Champhai** is widely considered the most attractive district but foreigner permits don't normally allow visits there. For an accessible taste of small-town Mizo life, **Saitual** offers views and a delightful, incredibly good-value **Tourist Lodge** (☎ 2562109; d Rs 150), set in a hill-top garden, 700m north of Saitual market. There's little to do but meet the locals and

find some biscuits for dinner. However, a very bumpy 10km side trip to **Tamdil Lake** is mildly memorable. This local beauty spot is ringed by lush mountains, patches of poinsettia and a few musty if pleasantly situated **cottages** (d Rs 300). There are paddle boats to rent (Rs 10), but no café.

MANIPUR

This 'Jewelled Land' is home to Naga, Kuki, Chin and many other tribal peoples, but the main grouping is the predominantly neo-Vaishnavite Meitei who are battling to have Meitei script used in local schools. Manipuris are famed for traditional dances, spicy multi-dish thalis and the sport of polo that they claim to have invented. Manipur's forested hills provide cover for rare birds, drug traffickers and dozens of guerrilla armies making it by far the Northeast's most dangerous state. Foreigners who miraculously manage to get a permit are required to fly in and out via the capital, **Imphal**, but even there safety can not be assured as was seen with the November 2006 bombing.

Imphal has a **tourist office** (☎ 224603; http://manipur.nic.in/tourism.htm), State Museum and what's supposedly the **world's tallest topiary bush** (http://imphalwest.nic.in/sambanlei.html). The **Shri Govindajee Mandir** has two rather suggestive domes.

Lokpaching battlefield (Red Hill), 16km south of Imphal, has WWII graves and a Japanese memorial. Beyond is picturesque **Bishnupur** with its stone carvers and 15th-century Vishnu temple. **Loktak Lake**, known for floating 'islands' of thick matted weeds, is reportedly home to rare Sangai 'dancing deer'.

Moirang's **INA Museum** (45km) celebrates the town's small but symbolic role in the Indian Independence movement: it was here on 14 April 1944 that the anticolonial Indian National Army (INA) first unfurled India's tricolour while advancing against Japanese WWII forces against British-held Imphal.

Manipuris feel rich when popping across the Myanmar border at **Moreh** (110km from Imphal) for cheap shopping in Namphanglong. Foreign overlanders can only dream of crossing this frontier.

Orissa

Orissa is a captivating state with diverse, vibrant living cultures and an unrivalled architectural legacy. It's where mighty temple chariots carrying powerful deities are pulled through city streets by a heaving throng of devotees, where serene stone carvings of exceptional beauty continue to be excavated from early Buddhist sites and where Adivasis (tribal people) maintain remarkable traditions that predate many of the great empires of the subcontinent.

Orissa is also celebrated for its natural heritage: elephants and tigers crash and prowl through the Eastern Ghats at Similipal National Park, a key tiger reserve. Chilika Lake, Asia's largest lagoon, hosts the rare Irrawaddy dolphin as well as millions of migratory birds, including pink flamingos. Bhitarkanika Wildlife Sanctuary has dolphins, a surfeit of birdlife and monster crocodiles. In January masses of olive ridley turtles pull themselves up onto Orissa's long beaches to lay their eggs; two months later, thousands of tiny hatchlings crawl to the sea.

Ancient civilisations and tradition resonate through contemporary Orissa. Witness the grand Sun Temple of Konark, a dream of genius adorned with a storyboard of Orissan life. Modern artistry is no less adept with stone carving, painting, silverwork and textiles in abundance.

Many of Orissa's attractions are clustered along the coast where weary travellers can also find inexpensive seaside retreats. Inland there's a different India, where tribes live precariously on the edge of mainstream society, yet manage to retain their colourful, fascinating traditions.

HIGHLIGHTS

- Exercise the eyes viewing exquisite carvings of the everyday, the exotic and the erotic at the renowned **Sun Temple** (p257) in Konark
- Mind your mandirs as you explore the myriad **carved stone temples** (p244) in old Bhubaneswar
- Follow Lord Jagannath's mighty car through Puri in the **Rath Yatra** (p253), one of India's most spectacular festivals
- Spy on wild elephants and just maybe an elusive tiger in the jungles of **Similipal National Park** (p264)
- Spot rare Irrawaddy dolphins, crocodiles, lizards, flashy kingfishers and herons as your boat chugs through the mangroves of **Bhitarkanika Wildlife Sanctuary** (p266)
- Rest your weary limbs and indulge in a surplus of seafood in laid-back **Puri** (p251)
- Explore Orissa's **tribal areas** (p262) to witness the distinctive Adivasi culture and barter for hand-beaten metal jewellery and tribal cloth

Similpal National Park ★
Bhitarkanika Wildlife Sanctuary ★
Bhubaneswar ★
★ ★ Konark
Puri
★ Tribal Areas
★ Tribal Areas

ORISSA

History

Despite having been a formidable maritime empire, with trading routes down into Indonesia, the history of Orissa (formerly Kalinga) is hazy until the demise of the Kalinga dynasty in 260 BC at the hands of the great emperor Ashoka. Appalled at the carnage he had caused, Ashoka forswore violence and converted to Buddhism.

Around the 1st century BC Buddhism declined and Jainism was restored as the faith of the people. During this period the monastery caves of Udayagiri and Khandagiri (p245) were excavated as important Jain centres.

By the 7th century AD, Hinduism had supplanted Jainism. Under the Kesari and Ganga kings, trade and commerce increased and

> **FAST FACTS**
>
> - Population: 36.7 million
> - Area: 155,707 sq km
> - Capital: Bhubaneswar
> - Main language: Oriya
> - When to go: November to March

Orissan culture flourished – countless temples from that classical period still stand. The Orissans defied the Muslim rulers in Delhi until finally falling to the Mughals during the 16th century, when many of Bhubaneswar's temples were destroyed.

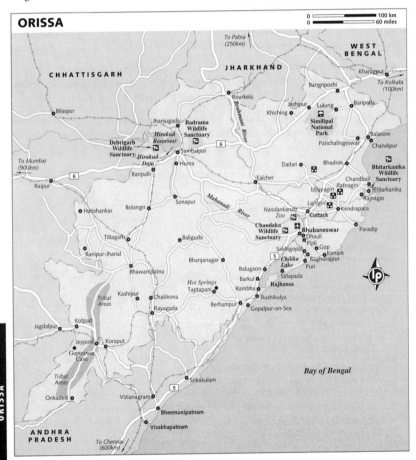

Until Independence, Orissa was ruled by Afghans, Marathas and the British.

At the end of the 1990s a Hindu fundamentalist group, Bajrang Dal, undertook a violent campaign against Christians in Orissa in response to missionary activity. Squeezed in the middle are the tribal people, targeted because they are 'easy souls', without power, and illiterate.

The creation of the neighbouring states of Jharkhand and Chhattisgarh has prompted calls for the formation of a separate, tribal-oriented state, Koshal, in the northwest of Orissa, with Sambalpur as the capital.

Climate

Monsoon time is July to October, when cyclones are likely. Cyclones and severe monsoonal rains can have substantial impacts on road and rail transport. A particularly devastating cyclone struck Orissa in 1999 causing significant damage and the loss of thousands of lives.

National Parks

In 2005 the admission fee for Orissa's wonderful national parks and wildlife sanctuaries was dramatically raised for foreigners to Rs 1000 per day. Because this fee increase is discouraging visits, it is being actively protested by Orissa's private tour companies and may change in the near future.

Information

Orissa Tourism (www.orissatourism.gov.in) has a presence in cities and most tours, with its office being a one-stop shop for information and tour/hotel booking. It also maintains a list of approved guides for tribal-area visits. **Orissa Tourism Development Corporation** (OTDC; www.panthani vas.com), the commercial arm of Orissa Tourism, runs tours and hotels throughout the state.

Dangers & Annoyances

Mosquitoes here have a record of being dengue and malaria carriers. Load yourself up with pills (see p339), repellents and bring a mosquito net in case your hotel doesn't provide one.

Getting There & Away

Air routes connect Bhubaneswar with Delhi, Mumbai (Bombay), Chennai (Madras) and Kolkata (Calcutta). Major road and rail routes between Kolkata and Chennai pass through coastal Orissa and Bhubaneswar with spur connections to Puri. Road and rail connect Sambalpur with Kolkata, Chhattisgarh and Madhya Pradesh.

Getting Around

Public transport in the coastal region is good with ample long-distance buses and trains. For touring around the interior hiring a car is the best option.

FESTIVALS IN ORISSA

Makar Mela (2nd week of Jan; Kalijai Island, Chilika Lake, p258) Celebrates the sun entering the orbit of Capricorn. Surya, the sun god, is the attention of worship.

Adivasi Mela (26-31 Jan; Bhubaneswar, p244) Features art, dance and handicrafts of Orissa's tribal groups.

Magha Mela (Jan/Feb; Konark, p256) Sun festival, with pilgrims bathing en masse at the beach before sunrise then worshipping at the temple.

Maha Shivaratri (Feb/Mar; Bhubaneswar, p244) Devotees fast and perform *pujas* (prayers or offerings) throughout the night ready to witness the priest placing a sacred lamp on the top of Lingaraj Mandir.

Ashokastami (Apr/May; Bhubaneswar, p244) The idol of Lord Lingaraj is taken by chariot to Bindu Sagar for ritual bathing and then to Rameswaram Temple for a four-day stay.

Rath Yatra (Jun/Jul; Puri, p251) Immense chariots containing Lord Jagannath, brother Balbhadra and sister Subhadra are hauled from Jagannath Temple to Gundicha Mandir.

Beach Festival (Nov; Puri, p251) Song, dance, food and cultural activities, including sand artists, on the beach.

Tribal Festival (16-18 Nov; location varies) An exposition of Orissan tribal dances and music. Contact Orissa Tourism as the location changes yearly.

Baliyatra (Nov/Dec; Cuttack, p265) Four days commemorating past trading links with Indonesia. A huge fair is held on the river bank.

Konark Festival (1-5 Dec; Konark, p256) Features traditional music and dance and a seductive temple ritual. Festivities are in the open-air auditorium with the Sun Temple as the backdrop.

BHUBANESWAR

☎ 0674 / pop 647,310

Bhubaneswar's rapid expansion has been tempered by the construction of wide avenues and the green belts; nevertheless a typically hectic, noisy, congested city centre greets the traveller. The old city's spiritual centre is around Bindu Sagar where, from the thousands that once stood here, 50-odd stone temples remain, survivors from the heyday of Orissan medieval temple architecture.

The city is also a base for day trips to Dhauli (p250), Konark (p256), Nandankanan Zoological Park (p250) and Cuttack (p265).

Orientation

Most lodgings, restaurants, banks and transport are within an area bounded by Cuttack Rd, Rajpath, Sachivajaya Marg and the train station.

Information

BOOKSHOPS

Modern Book Depot (☎ 2502373; Station Sq; ⏰ 9.30am-2pm & 4.30-9pm) Maps, English-language novels, coffee-table books and books on Orissa.

EMERGENCY

Police (☎ 2533732; Capitol Police Station, Rajpath)

INTERNET ACCESS

9inetinn (Lewis Rd; per hr Rs 15; ⏰ 9am-11pm)
Cyber World (cnr Janpath & Rajpath; per hr Rs 15; ⏰ 7am-11.30pm)
Info Matrix (74-P Ashok Nagar, Janpath; per hr Rs 15; ⏰ 9am-11pm)
Sify Iway (74-P cnr Janpath & Rajpath; per hr Rs 20; ⏰ 9am-10pm)

LEFT LUGGAGE

Train station (per piece per day Rs 10; ⏰ 24hr)

MEDICAL SERVICES

Capital Hospital (☎ 2401983, ambulance 2400688; Sachivajaya Marg) Pharmacy (24hr) onsite.

MONEY

Centurion Bank (Janpath) MasterCard and Visa ATM.
State Bank of India (☎ 2533671; Rajpath; ⏰ 10am-4pm Mon-Fri, 10am-2pm Sat, closed 2nd Sat in month) Cashes travellers cheques and exchanges foreign currency on the 1st floor.
Thomas Cook (☎ 2535222; 130 Ashok Nagar, Janpath; ⏰ 10am-2pm Sat, closed 2nd Sat in month) Cashes travellers cheques, including Amex, and exchanges foreign currency.

POST

Post office main office (☎ 2402132; cnr Mahatma Gandhi & Sachivajaya Margs; ⏰ 9am-7pm Mon-Sat); Market Bldg (**Rajpath**; ⏰ 9am-5pm Mon-Sat)

TOURIST INFORMATION

Government of India tourist office (☎ /fax 2432203; BJB Nagar; ⏰ 9am-6pm Mon-Fri, 9am-1pm Sat) India-wide information.
Orissa Tourism main office (☎ 2431299; www.orissa tourism.gov.in; behind Panthanivas Bhubaneswar, Lewis Rd; ⏰ 10am-5pm Mon-Sat, closed 2nd Sat in month); airport (☎ 2534006); train station (☎ 2530715; ⏰ 24hr) Tourist information, maps and lists of recommended guides.
Orissa Tourism Development Corporation (OTDC; ☎ 2432382; behind Panthanivas Bhubaneswar, Lewis Rd; ⏰ 10am-5pm Mon-Sat) Commercial arm of Orissa Tourism. Books sightseeing tours, hotels and airline tickets.

Sights

BINDU SAGAR

Also known as Ocean Drop Tank, **Bindu Sagar** reputedly contains water from every holy stream, pool and tank in India – obviously a good place to wash away sin. During the Ashokastami festival (p243), the Lingaraj Mandir's deity is brought here for ritual bathing.

TEMPLES

Lingaraj Mandir and the other temples scattered around Bindu Sagar may suffice for many temple watchers, but for more, amble along to the cluster of temples by Lewis Rd. To see all the major temples, charter an autorickshaw for two to three hours (about Rs 300).

Lingaraj Mandir excludes non-Hindus and Raja Rani charges an entrance fee. Priests expect a donation; Rs 10 is reasonable. Consider it a guiding fee as undoubtedly the priest will reveal something about his temple.

Lingaraj Mandir

The 54m-high **Lingaraj Mandir** is dedicated to Tribhuvaneswar (Lord of Three Worlds). The temple dates from 1090 to 1104, although parts are over 1400 years old, and is surrounded by more than 50 smaller temples and shrines. The granite block, representing Tribhuvaneswar, is bathed daily with water, milk and bhang (marijuana). In the northeastern corner, there's an attractive temple to Parvati and a chamber where 51 beggars and 51 priests eat the daily food offerings that are purportedly consumed by Parvati. The main gate, guarded by two moustachioed yellow lions, is a spectacle in itself as lines of pilgrims approach, *prasad* (temple-blessed food offering) in hand.

Because the temple is surrounded by a wall, and closed to non-Hindus (Indira Gandhi wasn't allowed in, as her husband was a Parsi), foreigners can see it only from a viewing platform. Face the main entrance, walk around to the right and find the viewing platform down a short laneway to the left. You might be asked for a 'donation'; again, Rs 10 is enough. On the way you should see a couple of gigantic wheels used in the Ashokastami festival.

Vaital Mandir

This 8th-century **temple**, with a double-storey 'wagon roof' influenced by Buddhist cave architecture, was a centre of Tantric worship, eroticism and bloody sacrifice. Look closely and you'll see some very early erotic carvings on the walls. The grotesque Chamunda (Durga), representing old age and death, can be seen in the dingy interior, although her necklace of skulls and her bed of corpses are usually hidden beneath her temple robes.

Parsurameswar Mandir

Just west of Lewis Rd lies a cluster of about 20 smaller but important temples. Best preserved is **Parsurameswar Mandir**, an ornate Shiva temple built around AD 650. It has lively bas-reliefs of elephant and horse processions, and Shiva images.

Mukteswar, Siddheswar & Kedargauri Mandirs

Not far from Parsurameswar is the small, 10th-century **Mukteswar Mandir**, one of the most ornate temples in Bhubaneswar. Intricate carvings show a mixture of Buddhist, Jain and Hindu styles. The ceiling carvings and stone arch are particularly striking, as is the beautiful arched *torana* (architrave) in front, clearly showing Buddhist influence.

Siddheswar Mandir, in the same compound, is a later but plainer temple with a fine red-painted Ganesh.

Over the road is **Kedargauri Mandir**, one of the oldest temples in Bhubaneswar, although it has been substantially rebuilt.

Raja Rani Mandir

This **temple** (Indian/foreigner Rs 5/100, video Rs 25; dawn-dusk) is an Archaeological Survey of India (ASI) monument, hence the admission fee. Built around 1100 and surrounded by manicured gardens, it's famous for its ornate *deul* (temple sanctuary) and tower. Around the compass points are pairs of statues representing eight *dikpalas* (guardians) who protect the temple. Between them, nymphs, embracing couples, elephants and lions peer from niches and decorate the pillars.

Brahmeswar Mandir

Standing in well-kept gardens, flanked on its plinth by four smaller structures, this 9th-century **temple** is a smaller version of Lingaraj Mandir. It's notable for its finely detailed sculptures with erotic elements.

STATE MUSEUM

This **museum** (☎ 2431797; Lewis Rd; Indian/foreigner Rs 5/50; 10am-4.30pm Tue-Sun) boasts Orissa's best collection of rare palm-leaf manuscripts, traditional and folk musical instruments, Bronze Age tools, an armoury and a fascinating display of Orissan tribal anthropology.

The magnificent collection of Buddhist and Jain sculptures, which is displayed in chronological order, constitutes the most important antiquities in the museum.

MUSEUM OF TRIBAL ARTS & ARTEFACTS

For anyone considering a visit to the tribal areas, this **museum** (☎ 2563649; admission free; 10am-5pm, closed 2nd Sat in month), off National Hwy (NH) 5, is recommended. Dress, ornaments, weapons, household implements and musical instruments are displayed in well-lit and captioned galleries. Behind the galleries are five representative village houses furnished to illustrate traditional life.

ORISSA MODERN ART GALLERY

Housing a high standard of contemporary art by local artists, this small **gallery** (☎ 2595765; 132 Forest Park; admission free; 11am-1.30pm & 4-8pm Mon-Sat, 4-8pm Sun) also has prints and originals for sale.

UDAYAGIRI & KHANDAGIRI CAVES

Six kilometres west of the city centre are two hills riddled with **rock-cut shelters** (admission to both sites Indian/foreigner Rs 55/100, video Rs 25, guides one side/both sides Rs 150/250; dawn-dusk). Many are ornately

ORISSA

BHUBANESWAR

0 _____ 3 km
0 _____ 2 miles

INFORMATION

9inetinn......................................1 C5
Capital Hospital..........................2 B5
Centurion Bank...........................3 A5
Cyber World................................4 A6
Government of India Tourist Office...5 B6
Info Matrix..................................6 A5
Left Luggage...............................7 B5
Main Post Office..........................8 C4
Modern Book Depot....................9 A5
Orissa Tourism...........................10 C5
Orissa Tourism Development Corporation
   (OTDC)..............................(see 10)
Orissa Tourism........................(see 7)
Post Office............................(see 46)
Sify Iway..................................11 A6
State Bank of India....................12 A5
Thomas Cook.............................13 A5

SIGHTS & ACTIVITIES

Brahmeswar Mandir....................14 D6
Discover Tours...........................15 C5
Former Capital Bus Stand............16 C4
Kedargauri Mandir..................(see 24)

Lingaraj Mandir..........................17 C6
Mukteswar Mandir..................(see 24)
Museum of Tribal Arts & Artefacts...18 A4
Orissa Modern Art Gallery............19 B5
Orissa Tourism Development Corporation
   (OTDC)..............................(see 10)
Orissa Tourism.......................(see 10)
Parsurameswar Mandir................20 C6
Pathani Samanta Planetarium.......21 C6
Raja Rani Mandir........................22 C6
Regional Science Centre.............23 C3
Siddheswar Mandir....................24 C6
State Museum...........................25 A6
Swosti Travels..........................26 A5
Travel Club...............................27 B5
Udayagiri & Khandagiri Caves......28 A5
Vaital Mandir............................29 C5

SLEEPING

Bhubaneswar Hotel....................30 A5
Ginger......................................31 B3
Hotel Bhagwat Niwas.............(see 34)
Hotel Deepali International..........32 A6
Hotel Keshari............................33 A5

Hotel Padma..............................34 A6
Hotel Pushpak......................(see 34)
Hotel Richi................................35 A5
Hotel Sishmo.............................36 A6
Mayfair Lagoon.........................37 B3
New Marrion...............................38 C4
Panthanivas Bhubaneswar...........39 C5

EATING

Café Coffee Day.....................(see 38)
Deep Down South...................(see 38)
Khana Khazana......................(see 34)
Maurya Gardens.....................(see 35)
Mithai Shop and AC Restaurant...40 A6
Park Inn Bar & Restaurant...........41 A6
Zaika......................................42 C5

ENTERTAINMENT

Rabindra Mandeep.....................43 C4
Soochana Bhawan.....................44 C4

SHOPPING

Ekamra Haat..............................45 C4
Market Building..........................46 A5
Orissa State Handloom Cooperative
   (Utkalika)..........................(see 46)

TRANSPORT

Air Sahara................................47 A5
Baramunda Bus Station...............48 A4
Bus Stop for Cuttack & Puri..........49 A6
City Bus Stand..........................50 A5
Indian Airlines...........................51 C4

Ekamra Kanan
Botanical Gardens

To Chandaka
Wildlife Reserve (20km);
Nandankanan
Zoological Park (25km);
NH5

JL Nehru Marg

Sachivalaya Marg

National Hwy 5

CRP
Square

Maharishi College Rd

To Cuttack (36km);
Kolkata (438km)

Patel Marg

Madhusudan Marg

Azad Marg

Bidut Marg

Gopabandhu Marg

Janpath

Bhubaneswar Rd

Daya Canal

See Enlargement

Market
Area

Train
Station

To Berhampur
(160km)

Ekamra Marg

Udyan Marg

Police
Station

Reparth

Lewis Rd

Cuttack Rd

Daya Canal

Gangua Nala

Mahatma Gandhi Marg

Station
Square

Market
Area

Train
Station

Janpath

Cuttack Rd

Biju Patnaik
Airport

Tankapani Rd

To Hirapur Yogini
Temple (11km)

Bindu
Sagar

Garage
Chowk

Kalpana
Square

0 _____ 500 m
0 _____ 0.3 miles

To Chennai
(1232km)

To Dhauli (5km);
Hirapur Yogini
Temple (13km);
Pipli (16km);
Puri (60km);
Konark (64km)

carved and thought to have been chiselled out for Jain ascetics in the 1st century BC.

Udayagiri (Sunrise Hill) on the northern side has the more interesting caves. Ascend the ramp, noting **Swargapuri** (Cave 9) to the right with its devotional figures. **Hathi Gumpha** (Cave 14) at the top is plain, but a 117-line inscription relates the exploits of its builder, King Kharavela of Kalinga, who ruled from 168 to 153 BC.

Clamber up around to the left where you'll see **Bagh Gumpha** (Tiger Cave; Cave 12), with its entrance carved as a tiger mouth. Nearby are **Pavana Gumpha** (Cave of Purification) and small **Sarpa Gumpha** (Serpent Cave), where the tiny door is surmounted by a three-headed cobra. On the summit are the remains of a defensive position. As you descend around to the southeast you'll come to the single-storey elephant-guarded **Ganesh Gumpha** (Cave 10), almost directly above the two-storey **Rani ka Naur** (Queen's Palace Cave; Cave 1). This is the largest and most interesting of the caves and is carved with Jain symbols and battle scenes.

Continue back to the entrance via **Chota Hathi Gumpha** (Cave 3), with its carvings of elephants, and the double-storey **Jaya Vijaya Cave** (Cave 5) with a bodhi tree carved in the central compartment.

Across the road, Khandagiri offers fine views over Bhubaneswar from its summit. The steep path splits about one-third of the way up the hill. The right path goes to **Ananta Cave** (Cave 3), with its carved figures of athletes, women, elephants and geese carrying flowers. Further along is a series of **Jain temples**; at the top is another (18th-century) Jain temple.

Buses don't go to the caves, but plenty pass nearby on NH5, or take an autorickshaw (about Rs 60 one way).

REGIONAL SCIENCE CENTRE
Dinosaur-infatuated kiddies will love this parkland **museum** (☎ 2542795; Sachivajaya Marg; admission Rs 7; ☼ 10.30am-7pm Tue-Sun, 10am-5.30pm Mon) with its prehistoric beasties. Included in the admission is a 30-minute movie screened hourly. Other treats are hands-on demonstrations of the laws of physics and displays on astronomy and insects.

PATHANI SAMANTA PLANETARIUM
This interesting **planetarium** (☎ 2581613; JL Nehru Marg; admission Rs 12; ☼ 2-6pm Tue-Sun, show in English 4pm) features hour-long 'out-of-this-world' shows.

Tours
Orissa Tourism (☎ 2431299; www.orissatourism.gov.in; behind Panthanivas Bhubaneswar, Lewis Rd; ☼ 10am-5pm Mon-Sat, closed 2nd Sat in month) offers a free guided tour of Bhubaneswar's temples at 8am on the last Sunday of the month. The tour, starting and finishing points are different each time, so contact Orissa Tourism for details.

A city tour offered by **OTDC** (☎ 2432382; www.panthanivas.com; behind Panthanivas Bhubaneswar, Lewis Rd; Rs 180; ☼ 10am-5pm Mon-Sat) covers the Nandankanan Zoo, Dhauli, the Lingaraj and Mukteswar temples, the State Museum, and Udayagiri and Khandagiri Caves. Another tour goes to Pipli, Konark and Puri. Both tours require a minimum of five people and leave from the Panthanivas Bhubaneswar hotel.

The private tour operators below organise customised tours into Orissa's tribal areas; these can also include visits to handicraft villages, and Similipal National Park and Bhitarkanika Wildlife Sanctuary. Prices will depend on number of people, transport (non-AC/AC) and hotel standards, but expect to pay US$50 to US$100 per person per day for tours that include transport, accommodation and a professional guide. Tribal tours usually start on a Sunday or Monday to synchronise with village markets.

Discover Tours (☎ 2430477; www.orissadiscover.com; 463 Lewis Rd) A recommended agency specialising in tribal and textile village tours, as well as Bhitarkanika and Similipal.

Swosti Travels (☎ 2535773; www.swosti.com; Hotel Swosti, Janpath) Apart from hotel bookings and car rental, it runs tours to the tribal areas and national parks.

Travel Club (☎ 2341115; www.travelclubindia.com; Room 5 BDA Market Complex, Palaspalli) Operates tribal and wildlife tours.

Sleeping
Bhubaneswar has plenty of accommodation, but no great traveller dens. Rates drop substantially during the monsoon season, June to September. Many places have 24-hour checkout, which means you check out 24 hours after you check in.

BUDGET
Hotel Padma (☎ 2313330; fax 2310904; Kalpana Sq; s with shared bathroom Rs 70, d Rs 200-250) Hotel Padma is cheap and not very cheerful. Its lowest priced singles masquerade as prison cells. Slightly more comfort comes with paying

more: an extra Rs 50 brings a TV and phone. Car rental can be organised here.

Hotel Bhagwat Niwas (☎ 2313708; Kalpana Sq; s/d from Rs 160/250, d with AC Rs 750; ✸) Hiding behind the Padma and signed down a small lane, the much friendlier Bhagwat has decent rooms with a TV around a courtyard, some boasting a balcony. Checkout is 24 hours.

Bhubaneswar Hotel (☎ /fax 2313245; Cuttack Rd; s/d from Rs 175/235, with AC Rs 600/700; ✸) The Bhubaneswar is another welcoming hotel with rooms that are nothing special. The hierarchy of room rates is determined by your TV choice. Non-TV viewers will be quite happy in cheaper rooms, which are the better option. Checkout is 24 hours.

Hotel Richi (☎ 2534619; fax 2539418; 122A Station Sq; s/d from Rs 250/400, d with AC from Rs 700; ✸) Proximity to the train station makes this a (very) popular haven for weary travellers. Booking ahead is advised. Rates include bed, tea and breakfast, there's 24-hour checkout and a 24-hour coffee shop to while away ungodly hours.

Hotel Deepali International (☎ 5560678; 54 Buddhanagar, Kalpana Sq; s/d Rs 300/350, with AC Rs 700/750; ✸) Probably the best hotel on Cuttack Rd, and certainly the friendliest, this tidy and well-cared-for hotel is partially hidden behind a rank of small stalls. The rooms are clean and comfortable and there's a choice of toilets types; checkout is 24 hours.

MIDRANGE & TOP END

Panthanivas Bhubaneswar (☎ 2432314; Lewis Rd; r Rs 490, with AC Rs 790; ✸) The Panthanivas is well located, quiet and the closest hotel to the temples. The spacious rooms are a little tired and musty but perfectly comfortable. Checkout is at an inconvenient 8am.

Hotel Pushpak (☎ 2310185; Kalpana Sq; s/d Rs 500/550, with AC Rs 700/750; ✸) All rooms are comfortable and have a private bathroom, and while the cheaper rooms are rather threadbare, the AC rooms are good. Checkout is 24 hours; there's a restaurant and bar.

Hotel Keshari (☎ 2534994; 113 Station Sq; s/d from Rs 675/775, with AC Rs 1300/1450; ✸) Five minutes' walk from the train station, Keshari has a decent restaurant and noon checkout. Inspection is essential as some of the cheaper rooms are to be avoided but the AC rooms are OK. The hotel asks you carry US dollars but you can argue to pay in rupees.

ourpick Ginger (☎ 2303933; www.gingerhotels.com; Jayadev Vihar, Nayapalli; s/d Rs 999/1199; ✸ ▣) This is one of a chain of progressive hotels that has set new standards for midrange accommodation in India. It may look a bit corporate and sterile at first glance, but the young friendly staff and clean modern lines will win you over. The spotless rooms have LCD TVs, wi-fi access, tea and coffee, minifridge, and opening windows so you can regulate the central AC with fresh air. Meals are served buffet style in the restaurant – there's no room service (hence the sparkling clean rooms). There's a gym to use and a Rs 50 discount if you book on the net.

New Marrion (☎ 2380850; marrion@sancharnet.in; 6 Janpath; s/d from Rs 1950/2650; ✸ ☎ ▣) The New Marrion is a large, conveniently located hotel with clean, spacious rooms where you can negotiate the price. A real bonus of this place is the proximity to Foodville, a court of restaurants, including Deep Down South (opposite), a Chinese restaurant, and a café with real coffee.

Hotel Sishmo (☎ 2433600; www.hotelsishmo.com; 86 Gautam Nagar; s/d Rs 2700/3500; ✸ ☎ ▣) A well-appointed place with friendly staff and some pleasant rooms; the better ones have views of the pool (which nonguests can use for Rs 150) and distant temples. There's a relaxing bar and a very good restaurant. The tariff includes bed, tea and breakfast, and discounts are a possibility.

Mayfair Lagoon (☎ 2360101; www.mayfairhotels.com; Jaydev Vihar; standard/deluxe cottages Rs 5000/10,000, villas Rs 20,000; ✸ ☎ ▣) This five-star hotel has the feel of an adventure movie set. In the jungly grounds you'll find static tigers, deer and herons, and even a twin-prop 1942 aircraft. The luxurious cottages are scattered around a lagoon, and facilities run to a complimentary breakfast, a British-style pub, and oriental and Indian restaurants. Of course there's a spa and gym. A discount is possible.

Eating & Drinking

ourpick Khana Khazana (Outside Hotel Padma, Kalpana Sq; mains Rs 35-70) This is an amazingly popular street stall morphing into a restaurant. Alfresco diners savour tandoori chicken or, more likely, the stall's famous and filling chicken biryani. Otherwise you are stuck with large serves of delicious chow mein featuring chicken, vegetables and prawns. Feeding starts at 5.30pm and finishes when the food runs out – which it does by about 9.30pm.

Mithai Shop & AC Restaurant (Rajpath; mains Rs 25-75) In addition to its range of North and South Indian curries, this place is Jagannath's gift to thali lovers and connoisseurs of Indian sweets and ice cream. Cyclone-force fans make it difficult to hold the menu but are most refreshing when the heat strikes.

Maurya Gardens (☎ 2534619; Hotel Richi, Station Sq; mains Rs 65-100) The Maurya restaurant is so dimly lit you may have trouble reading the menu of Indian, Chinese and continental dishes. The curries are nice and hot, though if you want a beer with your meal you have to eat (same menu) in the bar next door. Nearest to the train station, it's suitable for pre- or post-travel drinks.

Deep Down South (☎ 2380850; New Marrion, Janpath; mains Rs 30-50) Here you'll find all the South Indian culprits expertly executed. First have a lassi, and then go for a *masala dosa* (curried vegetables inside a crisp pancake) served on a plastic banana leaf, backed with an all-you-can-eat sambar. Room left over? There's a sweet shop attached.

Zaika (☎ 5539738; Lewis Rd; mains Rs 30-70) A clean, modern oasis on busy, dusty Lewis Rd. As well as excellent curries and tandoori there is an extensive Chinese menu but alas no beer. Fresh prawns and pomfret are ritually tandooried on Wednesday and Sunday.

Park Inn Bar & Restaurant (Rajpath; meals Rs 40-100; 10am-11pm) A cinema-dark bar with attentive waiters always ready to suggest another cold beer. Lots of nice cooking smells from the kitchen make you hungry for chicken, fish or prawn dishes.

Café Coffee Day (New Marrion, Janpath; drinks Rs 20-80) Yes it's a chain, but you'll appreciate the real coffee beans, the refreshing iced drinks and the chilly AC on any typically sweltering day.

Entertainment

Rabindra Mandeep (☎ 2417677; Sachivajaya Marg) and **Soochana Bhawan** (☎ 2530794; Sachivajaya Marg) are concert venues periodically used for music or dance performances. Phone the venues to find out what's coming up.

Shopping

A wide-ranging exposition of Orissan handicrafts can be found at **Ekamra Haat** (☎ 2403169; Madhusudan Marg; 10am-9pm), a permanent market in a large garden space.

Orissan textiles, including appliqué and *ikat* (a technique involving tie-dyeing the thread before it's woven) works, can be bought around **Market Building** (Rajpath) or the **Orissa State Handloom Cooperative** (Utkalika; Eastern Tower, Market Bldg; 10am-1.30pm & 4.30-9pm Mon-Sat).

Both sides of Rajpath, between Janpath and Sachivajaya Marg, are given over to day and night sell-almost-anything markets. You'll be able to buy a mosquito net here (Rs 250, check the seals first) for a visit to the coast.

Getting There & Away
AIR

Indian Airlines (☎ 2530544; www.indianairlines.in; Rajpath; 10am-5pm Mon-Sat), or its subsidiary Alliance Air, flies daily to Delhi (US$315, 2.30pm), Mumbai (US$335, 2.25pm), Chennai (US$250, 3.55pm) and Kolkata (US$130, 12.55am).

Air Sahara (☎ 2535729; www.airsahara.net; airport; 10am-5.30pm) flies to Delhi, Hyderabad, Bengaluru (Bangalore) and Kolkata. Check the website for schedules and latest fares.

BUS

Baramunda bus station (☎ 2400540; NH5) has frequent buses to Cuttack (Rs 12, one hour), Puri (Rs 25, 1¼ hours) and Konark (Rs 25,

ORISSA

two hours), and hourly buses to Berhampur (Rs 98, five hours).

Several services go to Kolkata (Rs 200 to 525, 12 hours), where price relates to comfort, Sambalpur (Rs 180, nine hours) and infrequent services to Baripada (Rs 120, seven hours).

Cuttack buses also go from the city bus stand, just off Station Sq, and the bus stop at the top end of Lewis Rd, from where buses also go to Puri.

TRAIN

The *Coromandal Express* No 2841 travels daily to Chennai (non-AC sleeper/3AC sleeper/2AC sleeper Rs 397/1061/1502, 20 hours, 9.40pm). The *Purushotlam Express* No 2801 goes to Delhi (Rs 489/1320/1876, 31 hours, 9.48pm) and the *Konark Express* No 1020 to Mumbai (Rs 493/1358/1943, 37 hours, 3.15pm). Howrah is connected to Bhubaneswar by the *Jan Shatabdi* No 2074 (2nd class/chair Rs 142/460, seven hours, 6am daily except Sunday) and the *Howrah Dhauli Express* No 2822 (Rs 130/439, seven hours, 1.15pm). To Sambalpur, the *Bhubaneswar-Sambalpur Express* No 2893 (chair Rs 356, five hours, 6.40am) is quick, comfortable and convenient.

Getting Around

No buses go to the airport; a taxi costs about Rs 100 from the centre. An autorickshaw to the airport costs about Rs 50, but you'll have to walk the last 500m from the airport entrance. Prepaid taxis from the airport to central Bhubaneswar cost Rs 100, and Puri or Konark Rs 600. There are ever-willing cycle- and autorickshaws to take you around.

AROUND BHUBANESWAR
Nandankanan Zoological Park
Famous for its blue-eyed white tigers, the **zoo** (☎ 246 6075; Indian/foreigner Rs 5/40, car Rs 35, optional guide Rs 45, camera/video Rs 5/500; ☼ 8am-5pm Tue-Sun) also boasts rare Asiatic lions, rhinoceroses, copious reptiles, monkeys and deer. Just inside the gate, the small Nature Interpretation Centre has some displays about Orissa's major national parks.

Undoubtedly the highlight is the **lion and tiger safari** (Rs 30), which leaves on the hour from 10am to noon and 2pm to 4pm) in an electric bus. Other attractions include a toy train and boat rides. A **cable car** (Rs 25; ☼ 8am-4pm) crosses a lake, allowing passengers to get

off halfway and walk down (300m) to the **State Botanical Garden**.

OTDC has a **café** (mains Rs 25; ☼ 8am-4.30pm) selling basic food but unfortunately it can't be counted on for having cold drinks.

OTDC tours stop here for only an (insufficient) hour or so. From Bhubaneswar, frequent public buses (Rs 6, one hour) leave from Kalpana Sq (near Padma Hotel) and outside the former Capital bus stand for Nandankanan village, about 400m from the entrance to the zoo. They may state 'Nandankanan' or 'Patia' as their destination. By taxi, a one-way trip costs about Rs 300.

Dhauli
After slaughtering members of his family to gain power, and then hundreds of thousands of people on the battlefield, Ashoka penitently converted to Buddhism. In about 260 BC one of his famous edicts was carved onto a large rock at Dhauli, 8km south of Bhubaneswar. The rock is now protected by a grill-fronted building and above, on top of a hillock, is a carved elephant. Ashoka's edicts are detailed on several noticeboards at the base.

On a nearby hill is the huge, white **Shanti Stupa** (Peace Pagoda), built by the Japanese in 1972. Older Buddhist reliefs are set into the modern structure.

The turn-off to Dhauli is along the Bhubaneswar–Puri road, accessible by any Puri or Konark bus (Rs 7). From the turn-off, it's a flat 3km walk to the rock, and then a short, steep walk to the stupa. By autorickshaw/taxi, a one-way trip costs about Rs 100/250.

Chandaka
Also known as the City Sanctuary because of its proximity, **Chandaka Wildlife Sanctuary** (Indian/foreigner Rs 10/1000, car Rs 20, guide Rs 150, camera/video Rs 25/200; ☼ 8am-5pm Tue-Sun) was declared primarily to preserve wild elephants and elephant habitat. If you are lucky, you can also see leopard, deer, mugger crocodiles and over 100 species of birds.

Chandaka's 200 sq km represents a remnant of the forest that once covered the northeastern Ghats. Facilities include five watchtowers, two of which contain rest houses for overnight stays. Before you visit you must pay for and collect an entry permit, gain permission for photography and reserve a rest house, all at the office of the **Divisional Forest Officer** (☎ 2472040; Chandaka Wildlife Division, SFTRI campus,

Ghatika). Chandaka is about 20km by road from Bhubaneswar, and visits and transport are best organised through a travel agent in Bhubaneswar.

Hirapur

Among iridescent-green paddies, 15km from Bhubaneswar, is a small village with an important **Yogini Temple**, one of only four in India. The low, circular structure, open to the sky, has 64 niches within, each with a black chlorite goddess. Getting here requires hired transport or coming on OTDC's tours.

Pipli

This town, 16km southeast of Bhubaneswar, is notable for its brilliant appliqué craft, which incorporates primary colours and small mirrors and is used for door and wall hangings, and the more traditional canopies hang over Lord Jagannath and family during festival time. Lampshades and parasols are the main tourist item, and hung outside the shops they turn the main road into an avenue of rainbow colours. Pipli is easily accessible by any bus between Bhubaneswar and Puri or Konark.

SOUTHEASTERN ORISSA

PURI

☎ 06752 / pop 157,610

Attracted by spiritual or earthly pleasures, three types of visitors come to Puri: Hindu pilgrims, Indian holidaymakers and foreign travellers, and each group sets up camp in different parts of town. For Hindus, Puri is one of the holiest pilgrimage places in India, with religious life revolving around the great Jagannath Mandir and its famous Rath Yatra (Car Festival).

Puri's other attraction is its long, sandy beach and esplanade – an Indian version of an English seaside. Backing this, in Marine Pde, is a long ribbon of old hotels, flashy resorts and company holiday homes that become instantly full when Kolkata rejoices in a holiday.

In the 1970s Puri became a scene on the hippie trail wending its way through Southeast Asia, attracted here by the sea and bhang, legal in Shiva's Puri. Travellers now come just to hang out, gorge on good food and recharge their backpacking spirit.

Orientation

The action is along a few kilometres of coast, with the backpacker village clustered around Chakra Tirtha (CT) Rd to the east, busy Marine Pde to the west and resorts in the middle. A few blocks inland is the holy quarter's chaotic jumble of streets. Buses and trains arrive in the centre of town.

Information
BOOKSHOPS
Loknath Bookshop (CT Rd; ☼ 9am-noon & 3-9pm) Sells and exchanges secondhand books.

EMERGENCY
Police (☎ 222025; CT Rd)

INTERNET ACCESS
Halla Gulla.com (CT Rd; per hr Rs 30; ☼ 8am-10pm; 🖳) CD burning from digital camera costs Rs 40 to 55 per CD.
Nanako.com (CT Rd; per hr Rs 25; ☼ 7am-11pm; 🖳) CD burning costs Rs 30 to 50.

LEFT LUGGAGE
Train station (per piece per day Rs 10; ☼ 24hr)

MEDICAL SERVICES
Headquarters Hospital (☎ 223742; Grand Rd)

MONEY
ICICI Bank (1 Naya Plaza, Grand Rd) MasterCard and Visa ATM.
Samikshya Forex (☎ 2225369; CT Rd; ☼ 6am-10pm) Cashes travellers cheques and foreign currencies.
State Bank of India (☎ 223682; CT Rd; ☼ 10.30am-4pm Mon-Fri, 10.30am-1pm Sat) Cashes travellers cheques and foreign currency; also a MasterCard and Visa ATM.

POST
Post office (☎ 222051; cnr Kutchery & Temple Rds; ☼ 10.30am-5.30pm)

TOURIST INFORMATION
Orissa Tourism CT Rd (☎ 222664; CT Rd; ☼ 10am-5pm Mon-Sat); train station (☎ 223536; ☼ 7am-9pm) Tourist information, hotel, vehicle and tour booking.
OTDC (☎ 223526; Marine Pde; ☼ 6am-10pm) Booking office and start/finish point for day tours.

TRAVEL AGENCIES
There are numerous travel agencies within and around the hotels on CT Rd that can arrange air, bus and train tickets and car hire.
Gandhara International (☎ 2224623; www.hotel gandhara.com; Hotel Gandhara, CT Rd)

ORISSA

PURI

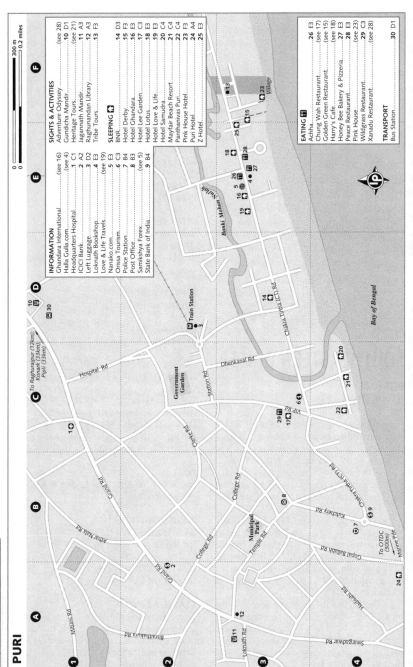

INFORMATION

Ghandara International........................(see 16)
Halla Gulla.com.................................(see 4)
Headquarters Hospital.............................1 C1
ICICI Bank..2 A2
Left Luggage...3 D2
Loknath Bookshop..................................4 E3
Love & Life Travels............................(see 19)
Nanako.com...5 E3
Orissa Tourism.......................................6 C3
Police Station...7 B4
Post Office..8 B3
Samikshya Forex...............................(see 5)
State Bank of India................................9 B4

SIGHTS & ACTIVITIES

Adventure Odyssey............................(see 28)
Gundicha Mandir...............................10 D1
Heritage Tours.................................(see 21)
Jagannath Mandir...............................11 A3
Raghunandan Library...........................12 A3
Tribe Tours..13 F3

SLEEPING

BNR..14 D3
Hotel Derby...15 F3
Hotel Ghandara...................................16 E3
Hotel Lee Garden.................................17 C3
Hotel Lotus...18 E3
Hotel Love & Life.................................19 E3
Hotel Samudra....................................20 C4
Mayfair Beach Resort...........................21 C4
Panthanivas Puri..................................22 C4
Pink House Hotel.................................23 F3
Puri Hotel...24 A4
Z Hotel...25 E3

EATING

Achha...26 E3
Chung Wah Restaurant.......................(see 17)
Golden Green Restaurant....................(see 15)
Harry's Cafe.......................................(see 18)
Honey Bee Bakery & Pizzeria................27 E3
Peace Restaurant.................................28 E3
Pink House......................................(see 23)
Wildgrass Restaurant............................29 C3
Xanadu Restaurant............................(see 28)

TRANSPORT

Bus Station...30 D1

0   300 m
0   0.2 miles

ORISSA

To Raghurajpur (12km);
Konark (33km);
Pipli (33km)

To OTDC (300m)

Bay of Bengal

Village

Train Station

Government Garden

Municipal Park

RATH YATRA – THE CAR FESTIVAL

One of India's greatest annual events, **Rath Yatra**, takes place each June or July (second day of the bright half of Asadha month) in Puri (and elsewhere across Orissa), when a fantastic procession spills forth from Jagannath Mandir. Rath Yatra commemorates Krishna's journey from Gokul to Mathura. Jagannath, brother Balbhadra and sister Subhadra are dragged along Grand Rd in three huge 'cars', known as *ratha*, to Gundicha Mandir.

The main car of Jagannath (origin of 'juggernaut') stands 14m high. It rides on 16 wheels, each over 2m in diameter – in centuries past, devotees threw themselves beneath the wheels to die gloriously within the god's sight. Four-thousand professional temple employees haul the cars, which take enormous effort to pull and are virtually impossible to turn or stop. In Baripada a woman-only team pulls Subhadra. Hundreds of thousands of pilgrims (and tourists) swarm to witness this stupendous scene, which can take place in temperatures over 40°C.

The gods take a week-long 'summer break' at Gundicha Mandir before being hauled back to Jagannath Mandir, in a repeat of the previous procession. After the festival, the cars are broken up and used for firewood in the temple's communal kitchens, or for funeral-pyre fuel. New cars are constructed each year.

Periodically, according to astrological dictates, the gods themselves are disposed of and new images made. The old ones are buried in a graveyard inside of the northern gate of Jagannath Mandir.

Orissa Tourism's *Puri Shree Jagannath Dham* (Rs 60) reveals the annual cycle of festivities associated with Lord Jagannath.

Love & Life Travels (☎ 224433; Hotel Love & Life, CT Rd; ⏳ 7am-10pm)
Samikshya Forex (☎ 2225369; CT Rd; ⏳ 6am-10pm)

Dangers & Annoyances

Ocean currents can be treacherous in Puri, so don't venture out of your depth. Watch the locals or ask one of the curiously outfitted *nolias* (fishermen/lifeguards), with their white-painted, cone-shaped wicker hats, for the best spots.

Muggings and attacks on women have been reported along isolated stretches of beach, even during the day, so take care.

Sights

JAGANNATH MANDIR

This mighty **temple** belongs to Jagannath, Lord of the Universe and incarnation of Vishnu. The jet-black deity with large, round, white eyes is hugely popular across Orissa. Built in its present form in 1198, the temple (closed to non-Hindus) is surrounded by two walls; its 58m-high *sikhara* (spire) is topped by the flag and wheel of Vishnu.

Guarded by two stone lions and a pillar crowned by the Garuda that once stood at the Sun Temple at Konark, the eastern entrance, or Lion Gate, is the passageway for the chariot procession of Rath Yatra. The southern, western and northern gates are guarded by statues of men on horseback, tigers and elephants, respectively.

Jagannath, brother Balbhadra and sister Subhadra reside supreme in the central *jagamohan* (assembly hall). The brothers have arms but no hands, while smaller Subhadra, sitting in between, has neither. Priests continually garland and dress the three throughout the day for different ceremonies. Incredibly, the temple employs about 6000 men to perform the complicated rituals involved in caring for the gods. An estimated 20,000 people – divided into 36 orders and 97 classes – are dependent on Jagannath for their livelihood. The kitchen, with 400 cooks, is reportedly the largest in the world.

Non-Hindus can spy from the roof of **Raghunandan Library** (cnr Temple Rd & Swargadwar Rd; ⏳ 9am-1pm & 4-7pm Mon-Sat) opposite. Ask permission; a 'donation' is compulsory (about Rs 10) and your amount is entered in a book. On Sunday a nearby hotel takes over the scam and demands Rs 50 – easily negotiated down to Rs 20.

BEACH

Puri is no palm-fringed paradise – the **beach** is wide, shelves quickly with a nasty shore break and is shadeless; but it is the seaside. To the east it's a public toilet for the fishing village. Between Pink House Hotel and Hotel Shankar International, the beach improves, but keep away from the fetid drain oozing into the sea.

By Marine Pde the beach is healthier and often crowded with energetic holidaymakers, especially at night. Look out for artists constructing **sand sculptures**, a local art form.

It's worth getting up before sunrise to watch the fishermen head out through the surf and, for a little financial motivation, they might take you along.

Tours

OTDC (☎ 223526; Marine Pde; tour No 1 Rs 130, tour No 2 Rs 110) runs day trips. Tour No 1 skips through Konark, Dhauli, Bhubaneswar's temples, Udayagiri and Khandagiri Caves plus Nandankanan Zoo. Tour No 2 goes for a boat jaunt on Chilika Lake.

Several tour operators organise tours into Orissa's tribal areas that can include visits to handicraft villages plus Similipal National Park and Bhitarkanika Wildlife Sanctuary. Tribal tours have to be approached cautiously as not all agencies have experienced guides and the necessary local contacts to conduct a suitable and responsible tour. For more recommended options in Bhubaneswar, see p247, and for more details see the boxed text, p262.

Adventure Odyssey (☎ 2226642; travelpack _orissa@hotmail.com; CT Rd) Runs a Chilika Lake tour for two people for a combined US$100. Includes a night camp on Rajhansa beach.

Heritage Tours (☎ 2236656; www.heritagetourorissa .com; Mayfair Beach Resort Hotel, off CT Rd) Organises customised tours of tribal villages and markets for US$60 per person (based on twin share) per day.

Tribe Tours (☎ /fax 2224323; CT Rd; ⏱ 7.30am-9pm) Organises a Chilika Lake day tour for two people for Rs 650 plus Rs 550 per hour for the boat.

Festivals

A four-year calendar of festivals and events can be consulted at www.orissatourism.gov .in. Highlights of the festival-packed year include the celebrated festival of **Rath Yatra** (see p253) and the **Puri Beach Festival** (23–27 November) featuring magnificent sand art, food stalls, traditional dance and other cultural programmes.

Sleeping

For Rath Yatra, Durga Puja (Dussehra), Diwali or the end of December and New Year, book well in advance. For foreigners, Z Hotel and Hotel Ghandara (which only take foreign

tourists) may offer the best chance of finding a bed.

Prices below are for October to February. Significant discounts can be negotiated during the monsoon, while prices can triple during a festival. Annoyingly, many hotels have early checkout times owing to the early arrivals of overnight trains bringing fresh holidaymakers.

BUDGET

These places are mostly in a strip along the eastern end of CT Rd. The Z and Ghandara have dorms suitable for solo women travellers.

Hotel Love & Life (☎ 224433; fax 226093; CT Rd; dm Rs 30, s/d with shared bathroom Rs 80/100, s/d with private bathroom from Rs 125/250, cottages Rs 250, with AC Rs 750; ✷) The dorms and rooms in the three-storey building are simple but adequate, while the cottages at the rear are more comfortable. The hosts are friendly and helpful and also run a travel agency (p251).

Hotel Lotus (☎ 227033; CT Rd; r Rs 100-150) Above Harry's Cafe (opposite), the friendly Lotus has a range of inexpensive, fan-cooled rooms, some with intact flywire and some with balconies that bizarrely front on to the neighbour's brick wall only centimetres away. The front rooms may suffer a bit of street noise.

Pink House Hotel (☎ 222253; off CT Rd; r with shared bathroom Rs 150-250, with private bathroom Rs 250-350) One of the closest to the beach with sand drifting to your front door, the Pink House and its outdoor restaurant (opposite) looks the part. The basic rooms, either on the beach side with little verandas, or round at the back, are passably clean. Mosquito nets are provided and the toilets are all squat.

Hotel Derby (☎ 223660; off CT Rd; r Rs 300-350) This is an older-style hotels, with 10 small, neat rooms with private bathrooms set around a cheerful garden close to the beach. Mosquito nets are provided and there's a great little restaurant, Golden Green (opposite), attached.

Hotel Ghandara (☎ 224117; www.hotelgandhara .com; CT Rd; dm Rs 40, dm women only Rs 50, s/d with shared bathroom Rs 110/150, s/d with private bathroom from Rs 350/450, with AC Rs 550/750; ✷ 💻) Ghandara has a wide range of rooms for different budgets. The rear five-storey block has some fine rooftop AC rooms catching breezes and views; other rooms are arrayed around a tree-shaded garden and have balconies. A nice touch is a daily newspaper to your room. There's a rooftop restaurant and a travel agency that does foreign exchange.

Z Hotel (☎ 222554; www.zhotelindia.com; CT Rd; dm women only Rs 60, s/d with shared bathroom Rs 200/300, with private bathroom Rs 500/600; 🖳) Z is a travellers' favourite and rightly so. Formerly the home of a maharaja, it has huge, spotless, airy rooms, many of them facing the sea. There are great common areas, including a big-screen TV showing movies nightly, a roof terrace, plus a restaurant. The two doubles with an enclosed balcony are well worth the splurge.

Puri Hotel (☎ 222114; www.purihotel.in; Marine Pde; d from Rs 300, with AC from Rs 800; 🖳) Saris and underwear adorn the balconies, while inside the place has the feel of crowded hospital ward, nevertheless the Puri Hotel is a Bengali holiday institution and the place to bring the whole family; room sizes go all the way to sleeping 10. Children under six stay free. Checkout is 24 hours.

MIDRANGE & TOP END

BNR (☎ 222063; CT Rd; s/d from Rs 400/650, with AC Rs 650/900; 🖳) BNR stands for Bengal National Railways, which explains the steam locomotive parked out the front. This remnant of the Raj is well worn, slightly senile and rattles around in a huge heritage building set at an angle to the sea. The capacious rooms are rather threadbare, but the liveried staff, billiard room (per hour Rs 40), dusty library and lethargic restaurant have a certain charm; and it welcomes credit cards old chap. Checkout is 24 hours.

Panthanivas Puri (☎ 222740; off CT Rd; r Rs 400-690, with AC Rs 990; 🖳) This government hotel is rather large and impersonal, but the nonchalant staff can be stirred into friendliness. The newer block gazes right onto the sea; best rooms and views are on the 1st floor. The cheaper rooms in the old block are worn and depressing. Checkout is 8am.

Hotel Lee Garden (☎ 223647, leegarden@rediffmail .com; VIP Rd; r Rs 500-800, with AC Rs 900-1200; 🖳) This welcoming hotel has a range of spacious, spotless rooms that boast cable TV and windows with unbroken flyscreens. A bonus of staying here is the excellent Chung Wah Chinese restaurant (right). Checkout is 7am!

Hotel Samudra (☎ 222705; www.samudrahotel.com; r Rs 550-750, with AC from Rs 900; 🖳) Backing onto the beach, off CT Rd, this hotel is the best of a bunch in the area. All rooms have balconies facing the sea, though those closest to the sea are the best, and all are very comfortable. However, avoid northern rooms at the front

with the smell wafting in from the malodorous creek.

Mayfair Beach Resort (☎ 227800; www.mayfair hotels.com; r from Rs 4000; 🖳 🖳) The benchmark for Puri luxury features spacious hideaway units nestled into lovely gardens dotted with carved stone statues. The swimming pool, which nonguests can use for Rs 200 when hotel occupancy is low, comes with a swim-up bar. The hotel backs onto a semiprivate beach and boasts an outstanding restaurant, gym and spa.

Eating & Drinking

Puri is a smorgasbord: there's excellent fresh seafood to be enjoyed in inexpensive beach-side eateries or plush hotel restaurants. In CT Rd there's muesli, filter coffee, pancakes, pizzas and puddings for homesick travellers and, refreshingly, most places can serve a cold beer. All the following are open for breakfast, lunch and dinner.

Peace Restaurant (CT Rd; mains Rs 20-130) 'Peace Restaurant world famous in Puri but never heard of anywhere else.' So reads the menu, which features curries, macaroni and tasty fish dishes. This restaurant, a simple row of tables with thatch canopies, is deservedly popular.

Xanadu Restaurant (☎ 227897; CT Rd; mains Rs 20-150) Another garden setting with a sandy floor, Xanadu is for the early riser – enjoy a breakfast fry-up or muesli from under the shade of coconut and banana palms. In the evening, over a cold beer and some crunchy pappadam, you can choose between prawns or fish curry or try one of numerous continental dishes.

Honey Bee Bakery & Pizzeria (☎ 320479; CT Rd; mains Rs 60-125) The pizzas aren't bad and the pastas and burgers are acceptable, while the lassis are excellent. Choose between filtered or espresso coffee to wash down the small range of bakery items.

Achha (☎ 9437304761; CT Rd; mains Rs 30-150) Another sand-floor garden restaurant, with lilting background sounds of Indian music. Sit under a thatched pavilion and choose seafood and veg dishes from the extensive Indian menu.

Pink House (☎ 222253; off CT Rd; mains Rs 60-100) Right on the beach the Pink House is an open-air restaurant that does all the things travellers seem to demand: muesli or pancakes for breakfast; and lots of fish and prawns for dinner.

ORISSA

Chung Wah Restaurant (☎ 223647; VIP Rd; mains Rs 55-135). The Chung Wah is a first-rate Chinese restaurant serving the real thing. There's lot's of favourites on the menu, including sweet and sours and a commendable Sichuan chicken.

Wildgrass Restaurant (☎ 9437023656; VIP Rd; mains Rs 50-100) Wildgrass is a secret garden gone wild with trees and shrubs, surrounding a small restaurant and a scattering of thatched canopies for alfresco dining. The Indian and continental menu is enlivened with excellent seafood dishes.

Also recommended:

Harry's Cafe (☎ 227033; CT Rd; mains Rs 20-60) Harry's serves tasty *Marwadi basa,* strictly vegetarian food without onions or garlic.

Golden Green Restaurant (☎ 223660; off CT Rd; mains Rs 15-100) A cosy little restaurant where the best, freshest seafood is not on the printed menu.

Shopping

Shops along Marine Pde sell fabric, beads, shells and bamboo work. Stalls at the eastern end of town, nearer the village, sell Kashmiri and Tibetan souvenirs.

Near Jagannath Mandir, many places sell palm-leaf paintings, handicrafts and Orissan hand-woven *ikat,* which you can buy in lengths or as ready-made garments. Popular souvenirs include cheap, silk-screen-printed postcards and Jagannath images – carved, sculpted or painted.

Getting There & Away

BUS

From the sprawling **bus station** (☎ 224461) near Gundicha Mandir, frequent buses serve Konark (Rs 20, 30 minutes), Satapada (Rs 39, three hours) and Bhubaneswar (Rs 25, two hours). For Pipli and Raghurajpur, take the Bhubaneswar bus. For other destinations change at Bhubaneswar.

TRAIN

Book well ahead if travelling during holiday and festival times. The booking counter at the train station can become incredibly crowded, but CT Rd agencies will book tickets for a small fee.

The *Purushottam Express* No 2801 travels to Delhi (non-AC sleeper/3AC sleeper/2AC sleeper Rs 501/1354/1924, 32 hours, 8.15pm), while Howrah can be reached on the *Puri-Howrah Express* No 2838 (Rs 247/641/895, nine hours, 7.35pm) and the *Sri Jaganath Ex-press* (Rs 227/611/865, 10 hours, 10.15pm). The *Neelachal Express* No 2875 goes to Varanasi (Rs 377/1005/1421, 21 hours, 10.40am), continuing to Delhi on Tuesday, Friday and Sunday. To Sambalpur, the *Puri-Sambalpur Express* No 8304 (2nd class/chair Rs 105/356, six hours, 4.30pm) is best.

Getting Around

Several places along CT Rd rent bicycles for Rs 20 per day and both mopeds and motorcycles for Rs 250.

RAGHURAJPUR

The artists' village of **Raghurajpur**, 14km north of Puri, is two streets and 120 thatched brick houses adorned with mural paintings of geometric patterns and mythological scenes – a traditional art form that has almost died out in Orissa.

Everyone in the village is apparently an artist and there are nine classical arts and crafts practised here. The village is famous for its *pattachitra* – work made using a cotton cloth coated with a mixture of gum and chalk and then polished. With eye-aching attention and a very fine brush, artists mark out animals, flowers, gods and demons, which are then illuminated with bright colours.

In *chitra pothi* images are etched onto dried palm-leaf sections with a fine stylus, after which the incisions are dyed with a wash of colour.

Take the Bhubaneswar bus and look for the 'Raghurajpur The Craft Village' signpost 11km north of Puri, then walk or take an autorickshaw for the last 1km.

KONARK

☎ 06758 / pop 15,020

The majestic Sun Temple at Konark – a Unesco World Heritage site – is, like the Taj Mahal, one of India's signature buildings and Konark exists purely for it. Most visitors are day-trippers from Bhubaneswar or Puri, but it's not a bad place to kick back in overnight.

Originally nearer the coast (the sea has receded 3km), Konark was visible from far out at sea and known as the 'Black Pagoda' by sailors, in contrast to the whitewashed Jagannath of Puri.

Orientation & Information

The road from Bhubaneswar swings around the temple and past a couple of hotels and a splash of eateries before continuing to meet Marine Dr, which follows the coast to Puri. To the north and east of the temple is the **post office** (10am-5pm Mon-Sat) and bus stand and numerous souvenir stands. There is also a **tourist office** (236821; Yatri Nivas hotel; 10am-5pm Mon-Sat).

Sights

SUN TEMPLE

The massive **Sun Temple** (Indian/foreigner Rs 10/250, video Rs 25, guides per hr Rs 100; dawn-dusk) was constructed in mid-13th century, probably by Orissan king Narashimhadev I to celebrate his military victory over the Muslims. In use for maybe only three centuries, the first blow occurred in the late 16th century when marauding Mughals removed the copper over the cupola. This vandalism may have dislodged the loadstone leading to the partial collapse of the 40m-high *sikhara;* subsequent cyclones probably compounded the damage.

As late as 1837 one half of the *sikhara* was still standing but collapsed completely in 1869. (An illustration in the Yatri Nivas foyer shows the Sun Temple with still half a *sikhara*

and gives an idea of its splendour.) Gradually, shifting sands covered the site, with only the *deul* and *jagamohan* rising proud of its burial mound. Excavation and restoration began in 1901; the *jagamohan* was closed off and filled with rocks and sand to prevent it from collapsing inwards.

The entire temple was conceived as the cosmic chariot of the sun god, Surya. Seven mighty prancing horses (representing the days of the week) rear at the strain of moving this leviathan of stone on 24 stone cartwheels (representing the hours of the day) positioned around the temple base. The temple was positioned so that dawn light would illuminate the *deul* interior and the presiding deity, which may have been moved to Jagannath Mandir in Puri in the 17th century.

The **gajasimha** (main entrance) is guarded by two stone lions crushing elephants and leads to the intricately carved **nritya mandapa** (dancing hall). Steps, flanked by straining horses, rise to the still-standing **jagamohan**. Behind is the spireless **deul** with its three impressive chlorite images of Surya aligned to catch the sun at dawn, noon and sunset.

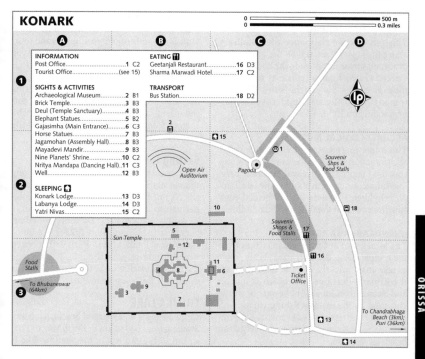

KONARK

0		500 m
0		0.3 miles

INFORMATION
Post Office....................................1 C2
Tourist Office..........................(see 15)

SIGHTS & ACTIVITIES
Archaeological Museum.............2 B1
Brick Temple................................3 B3
Deul (Temple Sanctuary)............4 B3
Elephant Statues.........................5 B2
Gajasimha (Main Entrance).........6 C3
Horse Statues..............................7 B3
Jagamohan (Assembly Hall).........8 B3
Mayadevi Mandir.........................9 B3
Nine Planets' Shrine...................10 C2
Nritya Mandapa (Dancing Hall)..11 C3
Well...12 B3

SLEEPING
Konark Lodge.............................13 D3
Labanya Lodge...........................14 D3
Yatri Nivas.................................15 C2

EATING
Geetanjali Restaurant................16 D3
Sharma Marwadi Hotel.............17 C2

TRANSPORT
Bus Station................................18 D2

Open Air Auditorium

Pagoda

Souvenir Shps & Food Stalls

Souvenir Shops & Food Stalls

Sun Temple

Food Stalls

To Bhubaneswar (64km)

Ticket Office

To Chandrabhaga Beach (3km); Puri (36km)

ORISSA

The base and walls present a chronicle in stone of Kalinga life, a storyboard of life and love in a continuous procession of carvings. Many are in the erotic style for which Konark is famous and include entwined couples as well as solitary exhibitionists. Sometimes they're minute images on the spoke of a temple wheel; at other times they're larger-than-life-sized figures higher up the walls.

Around the grounds are a small shrine called **Mayadevi Mandir**; a deep, covered **well**; and the ruins of a **brick temple**. To the north are a couple of **elephant statues**, to the south a couple of **horse statues**, both trampling soldiers.

If there's anywhere worth hiring a guide, it's here. The temple's history is a complicated amalgam of fact and legend, and the guides' explanations are thought provoking. They'll also show you features you might otherwise overlook – the woman with Japanese sandals, a giraffe (proving this area once traded with Africa) and even a man treating himself to venereal disease! Be sure your guide is registered. There are only 29 registered guides in Konark and the name board by the entrance has still to be updated. Unlicensed guides will dog your steps from arrival.

NINE PLANETS' SHRINE

This 6m-chlorite slab, once the architrave above the *jagamohan,* is now the centrepiece of a small shrine just outside the temple walls. Carved seated figures represent the Hindu nine planets – Surya (the sun), Chandra (moon), Mars, Mercury, Jupiter, Venus, Saturn, Rahu and Ketu.

ARCHAEOLOGICAL MUSEUM

This interesting **museum** (☎ 236822; admission Rs 5; ⏱ 10am-5pm Sat-Thu), 200m west of Yatri Nivas, contains many impressive sculptures and carvings found during excavations of the Sun Temple. Highlights include the full-bellied Agni (the fire god) and the fulsome Bina Badini.

CHANDRABHAGA BEACH

The local beach at **Chandrabhaga** is 3km from the temple down the Puri road. Walk, cycle or take an autorickshaw (Rs 50 return), or use the Konark–Puri bus. The beach is quieter and cleaner than Puri's, but beware of strong currents. To the east is a fishing village with plenty of boating activity at sunrise. Exploration to the west can give you a relatively clean beach all to yourself.

Sleeping & Eating

Konark Lodge (☎ 236502; Sea Beach Rd; r Rs 150) One among several bare-bones cheapies where you'll share your grim room with an army of mosquitoes, There's only four rooms. Bring your own mosquito net and insecticide.

Labanya Lodge (☎ 236824; Sea Beach Rd; s Rs 75, d Rs 150-250; 🖳) This laid-back option is the best budget choice, with a tropical garden and a fresh coconut drink to welcome guests. The comfortable rooms with private bathroom (squat toilets and no geyser) come in different sizes, and there's a pleasant rooftop terrace to spread out on. This is the only internet facility (per hour Rs 60) in town and there's bike hire (per day Rs 25). There's no restaurant but food can be ordered in.

Yatri Nivas (☎ 236820; r with/without AC from Rs 650/350; ❄) Set in large garden next to the museum, the Yatri Nivas is the best place to stay. The rooms are in two blocks; the rooms in the newer block have silent AC systems for a good night's sleep. The restaurant has a standard Indian menu (mains RS 30 to 75) plus a small selection of fresh seafood dishes. Staff may rent you their bike for Rs 50 per day.

Sharma Marwadi Hotel (mains Rs 30-50) Reputedly the best of the *dhabas* (snack bars), whose touts incessantly cajole worshippers and tourists into their fan-blown dining halls. Here you can select from eight generous and delicious thalis or order off the inexpensive menu.

Geetanjali Restaurant (mains Rs 30-75) Featuring the same menu as the Yatri Nivas hotel, this restaurant caters mostly to day-trippers who stagger from the temple entrance opposite desperate for refreshments.

Getting There & Away

Overcrowded minibuses regularly run along the coastal road between Puri and Konark (Rs 20, one hour). There are also regular departures to Bhubaneswar (Rs 40, two hours). Konark is included in OTDC tours from Bhubaneswar (p247) and Puri (p254). An autorickshaw will take you to Puri, with a beach stop along the way, for about Rs 200. Because the Puri–Konark road is flat, some diehards even cycle the 36km from Puri.

CHILIKA LAKE

Chilika Lake is Asia's largest brackish lagoon. Swelling from 600 sq km in April/May to 1100 sq km in the monsoon, the shallow lake is separated from the Bay of Bengal by a 60km-long sand bar called Rajhansa. Due to silting, a new mouth was dredged in 2000.

The lake is noted for the million-plus migratory birds – including grey-legged geese, herons, cranes and pink flamingos – that flock here in winter (from November to mid-January) from as far away as Siberia and Iran. Possibly the largest congregation of aquatic birds on the subcontinent, they concentrate in a 3-sq-km area within the bird sanctuary on Nalabana Island. Changes in salinity have caused some birds to move to Mangaljodi near the northern shore. Other problems, such as silting and commercial prawn farming, are also threatening this important wetland area and the livelihood of local fisherpeople.

Other attractions are rare Irrawaddy dolphins near Satapada, the pristine beach along Rajhansa, and Kalijai Island temple where Hindu pilgrims flock for the Makar Mela festival (p243) in January.

Satapada
☎ 06752
This small village, on a headland jutting southwestwards into the lake, is the starting point for most boat trips. There's an **Orissa Tourism office** (☎ 262077; Yatri Nivas hotel) here.

SIGHTS & ACTIVITIES
Boat trips from Satapada usually cruise towards the new sea mouth for a feed of fresh prawns, a paddle in the sea, and some dolphin- and bird-spotting en route. At the time of research, some of the better dolphin-spotting areas were made off-limits to tourist boats because of a dolphin fatality.

OTDC (☎ 262077; Yatri Nivas) has boats for hire (for large groups) or a three-hour tour (per person Rs 80) at 10.30am.

Dolphin Motor Boat Association (☎ 262038; Satapada jetty; 1-8hr trips per boat Rs 400-1000), a cooperative of local boat owners, has set-price trips mixing in dolphin spotting, the Nalabana Bird Sanctuary and Kalijai Island temple.

Chilika Lake Wetland Centre (☎ 262013; admission Rs 10; ✆ 10am-5pm) is an exhibition on the lake, its wildlife and its human inhabitants. The centre has an upstairs observatory with a telescope and bird identification charts.

A regular ferry (Rs 20, four hours, departs noon, returns 6am next day) plies between Satapada and Barkul.

SLEEPING & EATING
Yatri Nivas (☎ 262077; d Rs 250, with AC 650; ❷) A good option where the best rooms have balconies with lake views. The restaurant is OK (mains Rs 30 to 75), with a small selection of fresh seafood dishes as well as the standard Indian fare.

Several shops and food stalls line the road to the jetty. Don't forget to take water on your boat trip.

Barkul
☎ 06756
On the northern shore of Chilika, Barkul is just a scatter of houses and food stalls on a lane off NH5. From here boats go to Nalabana and Kalijai Islands. Nalabana is best visited in early morning and late afternoon, November to late February.

The OTDC (locally contact the Panthanivas hotel) runs a boat trip (per hour Rs 400, eight to nine hours) to the sea mouth with some dolphin spotting. With a minimum of 14 people OTDC runs tours to Kalijia (Rs 50), and Nalabana and Kalijia (Rs 150). Otherwise, a boat with a quiet engine (that doesn't scare birds) can be hired for Nalabana (Rs 900, two hours) or an ordinary boat for Kalijai (Rs 450, 1½ hours). Private operators (with no insurance and no safety gear) charge around Rs 350 an hour.

The **Panthanivas Barkul** (☎ 220488; r Rs 500, with AC Rs 900; ❷) has a great aspect with its clean, comfortable and renovated rooms overlooking the garden to the lake. This was the best Panthanivas we visited. The restaurant (mains Rs 30 to 80) is also good, with seafood specials, such as crab masala, always available.

Frequent buses dash along NH5 between Bhubaneswar (Rs 40) and Berhampur (Rs 70). You can get off anywhere on route.

A ferry goes to Satapada (left).

Rambha
The small town of Rambha is the nearest place to stay for turtle watching on Rushikulya beach. Not as commercial as Barkul, Rambha is also a very pleasant little backwater. Boat hire costs Rs 500 for a three-hour trip around the lake.

Panthanivas Rambha (☎ 06810-278346; dm Rs 50, d Rs 350, with AC Rs 750; ❷), about 200m off the main road and 1km west of Rambha centre, has reasonable rooms with balconies overlooking the lake. The restaurant (mains Rs 20 to 75) is

ORISSA

surprisingly good. Order the *khainga besara*: the local lake fish *(khainga)* simmered with mustard seed, garlic, chilli and curry leaves and only Rs 50!

There are regular buses to and from Bhubaneswar (Rs 70) and Berhampur (Rs 40), as well as several slow passenger trains (no express trains) stopping on the way to Bhubaneswar (2nd class Rs 25) and Berhampur (Rs 15).

Rushikulya

The nesting beach for olive ridley turtles is on the northern side of Rushikulya River, near the villages of Purunabandh and Gokharkuda. The nearest accommodation is in Rambha (p259), 20km away.

During nesting and hatching there will be conservationists on the beaches and activity takes place throughout the night. Do not use lights during hatching as they distract the turtles away from the sea.

GOPALPUR-ON-SEA
☎ 0680 / pop 6660

Gopalpur-on-Sea is a seaside town the British left to slide into history until Bengali holidaymakers discovered its attractions in the 1980s. Prior to this, it had a noble history as a seaport with connections to Southeast Asia.

It's no paradise, but its uncrowded, peaceful and relatively clean beach is great for a stroll and a paddle, or you can just relax and watch the fishing boats come and go.

Orientation & Information

The approach road from NH5 rushes straight through town and terminates in front of the sea. Around here are most of the hotels and restaurants. There is a Public Call Office (PCO) by Krishna's restaurant; the bus stand is 500m before the beach.

Dangers & Annoyances

Foreigners, especially women, are always an attraction for the curious, particularly men hoping to see a little flesh. It can be incredibly annoying. Remember to cover up, and if you go for a walk find a fellow traveller for company or just attach yourself to an obliging Indian family and bask under their general protection.

Swimming in the nasty shore break at Gopalpur, where there are undercurrents, is an untested activity; most visitors are content with a paddle.

Sights

Peering over the town is the **lighthouse** (admission Rs 5; ☉ 3.30-5.30pm) with its immaculate gardens and petite staff cottages. It's a late-afternoon draw card and after puffing up the spiral staircase you're rewarded with views, welcome cooling breezes and mobile-phone reception.

ORISSA'S OLIVE RIDLEY TURTLES

Olive ridley turtles, one of the smallest of the sea turtles and a threatened species, swim up from deeper waters beyond Sri Lanka to mate and lay their eggs en masse on Orissa's beaches. The main nesting sites are Gahirmatha within the Bhitarkanika National Park, Devi near Konark and Rushikulya.

Turtle deaths due to fishing practices are unfortunately common. Although there are regulations, such as requiring the use of turtle exclusion devices (TEDs) on nets and banning fishing from certain areas, these laws are routinely flouted in Orissa. Another threat has been afforestation of the Devi beach-nesting site with casuarina trees. While preserving the beaches, they take up soft sand necessary for a turtle hatchery. Other potential threats include oil exploration off Gahirmatha and seaport development near Rushikulya.

Turtles mass at sea between late October and early December. Then in January they congregate near nesting beaches and, if conditions are right, they come ashore over four to five days. If conditions aren't right, they reabsorb their eggs.

Hatching takes place 50 to 55 days later. Hatchlings are guided to the sea by the luminescence of the ocean and can be easily distracted by bright lights; unfortunately, NH5 runs within 2km of Rushikulya beach, so many turtles crawl the wrong way. However, villagers in the Sea Turtle Protection Committee gather up errant turtles and take them to the sea.

The best place to see nesting and hatching is at Rushikulya (above).

Sleeping & Eating

Gopalpur can be booked out during holiday and festival time. Prices below are for the high season (November to January); discounts are available at other times.

Hotel Rosalin (☎ 2242071; r with shared or private bathroom Rs 150) A small, single-storey house, opposite Sea Shell, with tiny rooms facing a 'garden'. It's for those who are over budget and who carry a mosquito net.

Hotel Green Park (☎ 2242016; greenpark016@yahoo .com; d Rs 200-400, with AC Rs 600; ✷) One street back from the beach, Green Park is a clean and friendly budget option, but note there is no bar or restaurant. Some rooms have front-facing balconies and there's a 24-hour checkout.

Hotel Sea Side Breeze (☎ 2242075; Main Rd; d from Rs 300) More like a guesthouse than a hotel, this friendly choice is located right on the sand with most rooms facing the beach. The rooms are bare but clean and spacious with private bathrooms. The restaurant (mains Rs 30 to 70) is also a simple affair but is good value serving one or two choices of simple, home-style curries.

Hotel Sea Pearl (☎ 2242556; d with side views Rs 600-700, with sea views Rs 750, with AC Rs 950-1200; ✷) Any nearer the sea and it'd be in it; the big and popular Sea Pearl has some great rooms, especially the upper-storey, beach-facing, non-AC rooms. There are two restaurants, with standard multicuisine menus (mains Rs 40 to 120); one is on the roof.

Swosti Palm Resort (☎ 2243718; www.swosti.com; Main Rd; s/d Rs 1980/2310; ✷) The Swosti has the best accommodation in town with luxurious and spacious, well-appointed rooms. The excellent multicuisine restaurant, Chilika, serves exquisite seafood, including authentic Odissi dishes (mains Rs 45 to 200).

Sea Shell (mains Rs 15-45) Camped on the beach, thatch roofed and with open sides for views and sea breezes, Sea Shell is an ideal place to while away the day with a good book, some snacks (Chinese, Indian) and a resuscitating ice cream or cold beer.

Krishna's (mains Rs 20-100) The folks at Krishna's have a keen eye for Western travellers and can make good pancakes, pasta and fried calamari or fish and chips in addition to their standard Indian offerings. Expect to pay Rs 100 and up for some of the seafood.

Getting There & Away

Frequent, crowded minibuses travel to Berhampur (Rs 7, one hour), where you can catch onward transport by rail or bus. Alternatively, an autorickshaw costs Rs 150.

WESTERN ORISSA

Although permits aren't usually needed, there are tribal areas in western and central Orissa where foreigners have to register their details with the police. This is all done for you if you are on a tour but independent visitors should check their plans with the police in the nearest city.

TAPTAPANI

Apart from the small **hot springs** in this peaceful village in the Eastern Ghats, there's not much else to see. The public baths (free) next to the sacred springs are particularly popular with people with skin diseases and other disorders.

For a great winter treat (December nights plunge to zero) book one of the two rooms at **Panthanivas Taptapani** (☎ 06816-255031; s/d Rs 450/600, with hot bath Rs 800). Hot spring water is channelled directly to vast tubs in its Roman-style bathrooms. Rooms can be rented for the day at half-price.

Buses go regularly to Berhampur (Rs 25, two hours).

BALIGUDA

This tiny one-street town is the base for visits to the Belghar region, home to fascinating and friendly Desia Kondh and Kutia Kondh villages. The State Bank of India ATM accepts Visa, and you can check email at **Mahakali Communication** (Main Rd; per hr Rs 15).

The nearby village of **Padar Sahi** makes interesting small statues using the lost wax process, which the villagers are keen to sell.

The only place to stay in Baliguda is the **Hotel Santosh Bhavan** (☎ 06846-243409; s Rs 150-300, d Rs 250-500), with clean rooms with soap, towel and mosquito coil. Unfortunately the staff start working and shouting at 3.30am! All the restaurants are *dhaba* style; the **Kalyani P Hotel** (mains Rs 15-40) has great fried chicken.

RAYAGADA

☎ 06856

Bustling Rayagada is the base for visiting the weekly Wednesday market at **Chatikona** (about 40km north). Here, highly ornamented

ORISSA

ORISSA'S INDIGENOUS TRIBES

Sixty-two tribal groups (Adivasi) live an area that encompasses Orissa, Chhattisgarh and Andhra Pradesh. In Orissa they account for one-quarter of the state's population and mostly inhabit the jungles and hilly regions of the centre and southwest. Regardless of their economic poverty, they have highly developed social organisations and distinctive cultures expressed in music, dance and arts.

Tribal influence on Indian culture is little recognised, but it is claimed that early Buddhist sanghas were modelled on tribal equality, lack of caste and respect for all life. Many of the Hindu gods, including Shiva and Kali, have roots in tribal deities. Many Adivasis have become integrated into Hindu society as menials, while others have remained in remote hilly or forested areas.

Most Adivasis were originally animists but have been the focus of attention for soul-seeking Christian missionaries over the last 30 years. In reaction, extreme Hindu groups have been aggressively converting the Adivasis to Hinduism. Naxalites have also exploited Adivasi powerlessness by using them as foot soldiers, while claiming to defend them.

The tribes have become something of a tourist attraction. Visits are possible to some villages and haats (village markets) that Adivasis attend on a weekly basis. There are arguments regarding the morality of visiting Adivasi areas. Usually you need to gain permission to visit the villages, whereas at the haats you are free to interact with and buy directly from the villagers. However, it remains the case that tourism still brings very little income to the tribes.

Of the more populous tribes, the Kondh number about one million and are based around Koraput in the southwest and near Sambalpur in the northwest. The Santal, with a population above 500,000, live around Baripada and Khiching in the far north. The 300,000 Saura live near Bolangir in the west. The Bonda, known as the 'Naked People' for wearing minimal clothing, have a population of about 5000 and live in the hills near Koraput.

It is important to visit these areas on an organised tour for the following reasons:

- Some areas are prohibited and others require permits, which are much more easily obtained by a tour operator.
- Some tribal areas are hard to find and often not accessible by public transport.
- Adivasis often speak little Hindi or Oriya, and usually no English.
- Some tribes can get angry, even violent, if foreigners visit their villages uninvited and without official permission.
- Some people do not allow themselves to be photographed.

Most tours start from Bhubaneswar (p247) or Puri (see p254), take in the more accessible areas in the southwest and can then go on to visit Similipal National Park. Options can include jungle trekking, staying at a village (tents and cooking supplied by the tour operator) and visiting one or more of the haats.

Dongria Kondh and Desia Kondh villagers from the surrounding Niayamgiri Hills bring their produce and wares to sell.

Hotel Jyoti Mahal (☎ 223015; Convent Rd; s/d Rs from 150/175, with AC from Rs 550; ✷) has the best budget rooms in town and a restaurant (mains Rs 20 to 70) that has 73 ways to serve the humble chicken. The friendly **Hotel Rajbhavan** (☎ 223777; Main Rd; r from Rs 350, with AC Rs 650; ✷) has bright and airy rooms and a good multicuisine restaurant (mains Rs 40 to 80).

There's a regular local bus from Rayagada to Chatikona (Rs 35, two hours).

JEYPORE
☎ 06854 / pop 77,000

Jeypore is the base for visiting the amazingly colourful Onkadelli market (opposite). The foreboding and derelict palace here was built in 1936 and is off limits. There's a State Bank of India ATM on Main Rd.

Hotel Madhumati (☎ 241377; NKT Rd; s/d Rs 275/300, with AC Rs 400/550; ✷) is in a quiet neighbourhood and surrounded by lawns. The spacious rooms are a little aged but well kept and the restaurant (mains Rs 35 to 100), serving Indian, Chinese and continental dishes, is OK.

Hello Jeypore (☎ 231127; www.hoteljeypore.com; NH Rd; s/d from Rs 400/500, with AC Rs 595/695; ❄ 🖥) is the best place to stay in town with clean, comfortable rooms and an excellent restaurant (mains Rs 35 to 100) serving fresh produce.

The new bus station is 2km out of town but buses still stop in town to pick up passengers. Frequent buses go to Koraput (Rs 15, one hour); others go to Berhampur (Rs 180, 12 hours), Bhubaneswar (Rs 280, 16 hours) and Rayagada (Rs 60, two hours).

Jeypore is on the scenic Jagdalpur–Visakhapatnam railway line. Slow passenger trains Nos 1VK and 2VK connect Jeypore with Visakhapatnam daily. The *Bhubaneswar Koraput Hirakhand Express* No 8447/8 plies daily between Bhubaneswar and Koraput stopping at Rayagada.

AROUND JEYPORE

The following towns are best accessed by hired car and Onkadelli should only be visited with a professional guide.

Koraput
☎ 06852

The **tourist office** (☎ 250318; Raipur–Visakhapatnam road; ⏲ 10am-5pm Mon-Sat, closed 2nd Sat in month) has information and can arrange car hire.

The **Tribal Museum** (admission Rs 1; ⏲ 10am-5pm) has an extensive static exhibit of tribal culture, including utensils, tools and clothes, as well as some paintings for sale. The useful *Tribes of Koraput* is for sale for Rs 90, and the museum will open out of hours if you can find the friendly caretaker.

For non-Hindus unable to visit Puri's Jagannath Mandir there's the opportunity to visit a **Jagannath temple** here that comes with an exhibition of gods of the different states of India. At the back of the temple is a series of apses containing statuettes of Jagannath in his various guises and costumes.

Onkadelli
This small village, 65km from Jeypore, has a most remarkable and vibrant **haat** (⏲ Thu, best time 11am-2pm) that throngs with Bonda, Gadaba and Didai villagers. Photographs should only be taken with the consent of the subject and will often come with a request for Rs 10 or more. Bring plenty of small demonination notes and other money to purchase souvenirs. Alcohol is an important ingredient in this social event; combined with the hunting bows

and arrows, it's a further incentive to make use of a professional guide.

Gupteswar Cave
Located 64km west of Jeypore is this cave temple, dedicated to Shiva on account of a handily shaped stalagmite serving as a lingam. Take a torch, as there are a few passages and chambers to explore alongside the lingam's grotto.

Kotpad
This town, 40km north of Jeypore on the road to Sambalpur, has a thriving home-based fabric-dyeing industry. Along the lanes you'll see ropes of thread in a rich range of colours from reds and burgundies to browns laid out to dry.

SAMBALPUR
☎ 0663 / pop 154,170

Sambalpur is the centre for the textile industry spread over western Orissa. If you haven't already bought examples of *ikat* or *sambalpuri* weaving, Gole Bazaar is the place to look. The town is important as a base for nearby Badrama National Park, and Debrigarh Wildlife Sanctuary on the edge of Hirakud Dam.

Orientation & Information
NH6 passes through Sambalpur to become VSS Marg. There are no moneychanging facilities but there are a couple of ATMs that advertise credit-card advances.

Internet Browsing Point (VSS Marg; per hr Rs 20; ⏲ 9am-9pm)

Orissa Tourism (☎ 2411118; Panthanivas Sambalpur, Brooks Hill; ⏲ 10am-5pm Mon-Sat, closed 2nd Sat in month) Can arrange tours to Debrigarh and Badrama.

State Bank of India (VSS Marg) MasterCard and Visa ATM next to Sheela Towers hotel.

Sleeping & Eating
Rani Lodge (☎ 2522173; VSS Marg; s/d Rs 100/140) A basic cheapie with adequately clean and well-cared-for rooms that come with a fan and mosquito nets.

Hotel Uphar Palace (☎ 2400519; fax 2522668; VSS Marg; s/d from Rs 300/350, with AC from Rs 600/650; ❄) An unexpected level of cleanliness characterises this friendly hotel, where the rooms are also spacious. The Sharda restaurant has an Indian and Chinese menu (mains Rs 45 to 130) plus daily specials.

Sheela Towers (☎ 2403111; www.sheelatowers.com; VSS Marg; s/d from Rs 795/845; ❄) This is Sambalpur's

ORISSA

top hotel, with a range of comfortable rooms. Checkout is 24 hours. The restaurant, Celebration (mains Rs 50 to 150), provides a buffet breakfast and there's a relaxing bar.

New Hong Kong Restaurant (☎ 2532429; VSS Marg; mains Rs 40-165; ⊙ Tue-Sun) For 15 years the Chen family has been providing authentic Chinese in Sambalpur. The menu also includes several tasty Thai dishes.

Shakti (VSS Marg; sweets per kg Rs 120-160; ⊙ 7am-10.30pm) This popular sweet shop usually sells Rasmulli and other delicacies by the kilo.

Getting There & Away

The **government bus stand** (Laxmi Talkies) has buses running to Jeypore (Rs 180, 14 hours), Bhubaneswar (Rs 178, eight hours) and Berhampur (Rs 194, 12 hours). Adjacent travel agencies book (usually more comfortable) buses leaving from the private **Ainthapali Bus Stand** (☎ 2540601), 3km from the city centre (Rs 25 by autorickshaw). Several buses go to Jeypore (Rs 210), Bhubaneswar (Rs 180), Raipur (Rs 150, eight hours) and Jashipur for Similipal (Rs 168, 10 hours).

The *Tapaswini Express* No 8451 goes to Puri (non-AC sleeper/3AC sleeper/2AC sleeper Rs 178/471/666, nine hours, 10.50pm) via Bhubaneswar (Rs 160/420/592, seven hours). The *Koraput-Howrah Express* No 8006 goes to Howrah (Rs 243/654/927, 10 hours, 9.25pm).

AROUND SAMBALPUR

Access to Huma, Khiching and Baripalli is only by organised tour.

Debrigarh & Badrama Wildlife Sanctuaries

The 347-sq-km **Debrigarh Wildlife Sanctuary** (☎ 0663-2402741; Indian/foreigner per day Rs 20/1000; ⊙ 8am-5pm 1 Oct-30 Jun), 40km from Sambalpur, is an easy day out. Mainly dry deciduous forest blankets the Barapahad Hills down to the shores of the vast Hirakud reservoir, a home for migratory birds in winter. Wildlife here includes deer, antelopes, sloth bears, langur monkeys, and the ever-elusive tigers and leopards. **Badrama Wildlife Sanctuary** (Ushakothi; Indian/foreigner per day Rs 20/1000; ⊙ 1 Nov–mid-Jun), 37km from Sambalpur, shelters elephants, tigers, panthers and bears.

Access to the sanctuaries usually requires a 4WD, which can be arranged through Orissa Tourism, a private tour agency, or your hotel in Sambalpur for about Rs 1000 for a half-day.

Huma

The leaning **Vimaleswar temple** at Huma, 32km south of Sambalpur, is a small Shiva temple where the *deul* slants considerably in two directions. The puzzle is that the porch of the temple appears square and there are no apparent filled-in gaps between the porch and *deul*. Was it built that way?

Khiching

On the way east to Similipal (north of the highway), about 50km west of Jashipur, is the 10th-century **Maa Kichakeswari temple** (⊙ 8am-noon & 3-8pm), reconstructed in 1934. Another of Shiva's avatars, Kichakeswari is resident in this single-room temple. Outside are several bands of sculptures, including Durga killing a buffalo demon.

Baripalli

The Costa Pada area in Baripalli, on the road to Jeypore, is where to discover how tie-dye *ikat* textiles are created. Skeins of threads separated into cords are wrapped around frames. Painstakingly, these cords are then tied in red cotton to mark out the dyeing pattern. Strips of rubber are then wound around to protect the undyed areas. Dyed and dried, the threads are then woven on the many looms you can see through open doorways. There's also a thriving terracotta industry here.

NORTHEASTERN ORISSA

SIMILIPAL NATIONAL PARK
☎ 06792

The 2750-sq-km **Similipal National Park** (Indian/foreigner per day Rs 40/1000; ⊙ 6am-noon day visitor, entry by 2pm with accommodation reservation 1 Nov-15 Jun) is Orissa's prime wildlife sanctuary.

The scenery is remarkable: a massif of prominent hills creased by valleys and gorges, and made dramatic by plunging waterfalls, including the spectacular 400m-high **Barheipani Waterfall** and the 150m-high **Joranda Waterfall**. The jungle is an atmospheric mix of dense sal forest and rolling open savanna. The core area is only 850 sq km and much of the southern part is closed to visitors.

The wildlife list is impressive: 29 reptile species, 231 birds and 42 mammals, including chital and sambar providing food for leopards and tigers. The tigers aren't tracked; the best chance to spot them will be at the **Joranda**

salt lick. What you may well see is your first wild elephant (there are over 400 in the park), most probably at the **Chahala salt lick**. The best time to visit is early in the season before the heavy visitation of the park impacts animal behaviour.

Orientation & Information

There are two entrances, **Tulsibani**, 15km from Jashipur, on the northwestside, and **Pithabata**, near Lulung, 25km west of Baripada. Options are a day visit or an overnight stay within the park.

Entry permits can be obtained in advance from the **assistant conservator of forests** (☎ 06797-232474; National Park, Jashipur, Mayurbhanj District, 757091), or the **field director, Similipal Tiger Reserve Project** (☎ 06792-252593; Bhanjpur, Baripada, Mayurbhanj District, 757002). Alternatively a day permit can be purchased from either gate.

Visitors either come on an organised tour or charter a vehicle (Rs 1200 to 2000 per day for 4WD); hiring a guide (around Rs 400) is advisable.

If you want to avoid the hassles of arranging permits, transport, food and accommodation, an organised tour is the answer; see p247, p254 and right for details.

Sleeping & Eating

Most accommodation is at 700m above sea level; in winter (November to February) overnight temperatures can plummet to zero.

Forest Department bungalows (d Indian/foreigner from Rs 440/880) Seven sets of bungalows with Chahala, Joranda and Newana being best for animal spotting and Barheipani for views. The very basic accommodation has to be booked well in advance (30 days) with the field director at Baripada – see above. You have to bring your own food and water.

Panthanivas Lulung (dm Rs 125, d with fan Rs 750) This comfortable lodge, 5km inside the Pithabata gate, is run by OTDC; book with Orissa Tourism in Baripada (right).

JASHIPUR
☎ 06797

This is an entry point for Similipal Park and a place to collect an entry permit and organise a guide and transport. Accommodation is very limited.

The **youth hostel** (☎ 232633; dm/d Rs 50/100) off Main Rd is bare-bones accommodation with no food available. For more comfort, **Sai Ram**

Hotel (☎ 232827; Main Rd; s Rs 70, d with/without AC Rs 500/200; ☒) has small singles, adequate non-AC rooms and bigger AC rooms. The owner can help arrange Similipal trips.

BARIPADA
☎ 06792

With the very helpful **Orissa Tourism** (☎ 252710; Baghra Rd; ☷ 10am-5pm Mon-Sat, closed 2nd Sat in month), this town is the better place to organise a Similipal visit.

Hotel Durga (☎ 253438; r Rs 180, with AC from Rs 550; ☒) has fan-cooled budget rooms, restaurant and bar. Better is **Hotel Ambika** (☎ 252557; ☒), a large rambling hotel set in pleasant gardens. The rooms are clean and comfortable, and there's a good bar and restaurant. It can organise Similipal trips.

Regular buses go to Kolkata (Rs 140, three hours) and frequently to Bhubaneswar (Rs 170, five hours) and Balasore (Rs 35, one hour).

CUTTACK
☎ 0671 / pop 535,140

Cuttack, one of Orissa's oldest cities, was the state capital until 1950; today it's a chaotic, crowded city. The **tourist office** (☎ 2612225; Link Rd; ☷ 10am-5pm Mon-Sat, closed 2nd Sat in month) is along the Bhubaneswar road. Shopping is great: saris, horn and brassware are crafted here, along with the famed, lace-like, silver filigree work (tarakasi). The best jewellers are on **Naya Sarak** and **Chowdary Bazaar**, while you can see pieces being crafted in **Mohammedia Bazaar**.

The 14th-century **Barabati Fort**, about 3km north of the city centre, once boasted nine storeys, but only some foundations and the moat remain. The 18th-century **Qadam-i-Rasool** shrine, in the city centre, is sacred to Hindus as well as Muslims (who believe it contains footprints of the Prophet Mohammed).

Bhubaneswar with its temples and better range of accommodation is less than an hour away, and Cuttack can easily be covered in a day trip. Express buses to Bhubaneswar leave every 10 minutes (Rs 14, 30 to 45 minutes).

BALASORE

Balasore, the first major town in northern Orissa, was once an important trading centre with Dutch, Danish, English and French warehouses. Now it's a staging post for Chandipur or Similipal National Park. **Orissa Tourism** (☎ 262048; 1st fl, TP Bldg, Station Sq; ☷ 10am-5pm

ORISSA

Mon-Sat, closed 2nd Sat in month) is 500m from the train station.

Several buses leave from Remuna Golai at around 10pm for Kolkata (Rs 190, seven to eight hours) and more frequently for Bhubaneswar (Rs 100, five hours). Infrequent buses to Chandipur makes an autorickshaw (Rs 150) a better option.

CHANDIPUR
☎ 06782

This delightful seaside village ambles down to the ocean through a short avenue of casuarina and palm trees. The place amounts to a couple of hotels, snack places and some souvenir shops. Chandipur has a huge beach at low tide when the sea is some 5km away; it's safe to swim here when there's enough water.

A bustling fishing village, the home of refugee Bangladeshis, is 2km further up the coast at a river mouth. In the early morning, walk up and watch the boats unloading fish and prawns.

Panthanivas Chandipur (☎ 272251; dm Rs 80, d with/without AC Rs 750/390;) has a great location overlooking the beach. Of the two blocks choose the one with sea views for a dramatic sunrise. Alternatively, there's the **Hotel Chandipur** (☎ 270030; d with/without AC from Rs 700/250;), a three-storey hotel with comfortable rooms overlooking a courtyard with a fountain and fragrant frangipani trees.

Regular buses ply the NH5 between Bhubaneswar and Balasore. From Balasore, taxis and autorickshaws can take you the 15km to Chandipur.

BHITARKANIKA WILDLIFE SANCTUARY

Three rivers flow out to sea at Bhitarkanika forming a tidal maze of muddy creeks and mangroves. Most of this 672-sq-km delta forms **Bhitarkanika Wildlife Sanctuary** (☎ 272460; permit Indian/foreigner per day Rs 20/1000). A significant ecosystem, it contains 63 of the world's 75 mangrove varieties. Hundreds of estuarine crocodiles, some 6m-plus monsters, bask on mud flats waiting for the next meal to swim by. Dangmar Island contains a successful breeding and conservation programme for these crocodiles. Less dangerous creatures are pythons, water monitors, wild boar and timid deer. The best time to visit is from December to February.

Bird-watchers will find eight species of brilliantly coloured kingfishers, plus 190 other bird species. A large heronry on Bagagaham Island is home for herons that arrive in early June and nest until November. Raucous open-billed storks have set up a permanent rookery here.

The sanctuary also protects the Gahirmatha nesting beach of the endangered olive ridley turtles (see the boxed text, p260). Gahirmatha is out of bounds due to a missile-testing site on one of the nearby Wheeler Islands. Rushikulya (p260) is a more accessible nesting beach.

Orientation & Information

Permits, accommodation and boat transport can all be organised in the small port of **Chandbali**. Organise a boat (per day Rs 2000, negotiable) with one of the private operators, such as the recommended **Sanjog Travels** (☎ 06786-220495; Chandbali Jetty), who can also help with obtaining the permit from the **Forest Officer** (☎ 9937324800; Chandbali Jetty; 6am-6pm).

Sights

First stop is a permit check at Khola jetty before chugging on to **Dangmar Island** for the crocodile conservation programme and an interesting **interpretive centre** (admission free; 8am-5pm) about the sanctuary. Binoculars can be useful to scan trees for birds, mud banks for crocs and lizards, and the undergrowth for monitors and deer.

The **heronry** at Bagagaham Island is reached by a wonky boardwalk leading to a watchtower, where you can spy on a solid mass of herons and storks nesting in the treetops.

Back at Khola, a 2km walk leads to Rigagada with its interesting 18th-century **Jagannath temple**, built with some passionate erotica in Kalinga style. While there, take an amble through this typical Orissan village.

Sleeping & Eating

Forest Rest Houses (dm Indian/foreigner Rs 40/80, d from Rs 150/400) These basic dorms and comfortable doubles are at Dangmal and Ekakula and have solar lights, mosquito nets and shared bathrooms. You need to bring your own drinking water and food, which staff will cook for you. The haphazard **divisional forest officer** (☎ 06729-272460; Rajnagar; 10am-5pm Mon-Sat, closed 2nd Sat in month) is the only place to make bookings, which must be paid in advance. These complications make going through a travel agent preferable.

Aranya Nivas (☎ 06786-220397; Chandbali; dm/d Rs 70/250) Set in a pleasant garden within 50m of the Chandbali jetty, the comfortable accommodation here is great value and the restaurant serves up some scrumptious food (mains Rs 30 to 75).

Hotel Orion (☎ 220397; NH 5 Bhadrak; s/d Rs 250/450, with AC Rs 350/550) The Orion is a good place to overnight on your way to Chandbali. The rooms are clean and come with TV and private bathrooms. The hotel has money-changing facilities, a multicuisine restaurant (mains Rs 40 to 90) and it can organise a car to Chandbali (Rs 450).

Getting There & Away
Chandbali is 55km southeast of Bhadrak on NH5. Buses go from Chandbali bazaar to Bhadrak (Rs 27), Bhubaneswar (Rs 72) and Kolkata (Rs 150). The *Howrah–Bhubaneswar Dhauli Express* Nos 2821/2 stops in Bhadrak at 10.27am going south to Bhubaneswar (2nd class/chair Rs 71/232, two hours); and at 3.35pm going north to Howrah (2nd class/chair Rs 104/346, five hours).

RATNAGIRI, UDAYAGIRI & LALITGIRI
These Buddhist ruins are on hilltops about 60km northeast of Cuttack. Currently there's no accommodation and inadequate transport, so the only feasible way to visit is by hired car organised in Bhubaneswar or Puri. However,

the OTDC was constructing a Panthanivas hotel opposite the museum in Ratnigiri at the time of research.

Ratnagiri
Ratnagiri has the most interesting and extensive **ruins** (Indian/foreigner Rs 5/100, video Rs 25; ☾ dawn-dusk). Two large monasteries flourished here from the 6th to 12th centuries and noteworthy are an exquisitely carved doorway and the remains of a 10m-high stupa. The excellent **museum** (admission Rs 2; ☾ 10am-5pm Sat-Thu) contains beautiful stone sculptures from the three sites.

Udayagiri
Another **monastery complex** is being excavated here. At present there's a large pyramidal brick stupa with a seated Buddha and some beautiful doorjamb carvings. Expect an entry fee soon.

Lalitgiri
Several **monastery ruins** (Indian/foreigner Rs 5/100, video Rs 25; ☾ dawn-dusk) are scattered up a hillside leading to a small museum and a hillock crowned with a shallow stupa. During excavations of the stupa in the 1970s, a casket containing gold and silver relics was found.

Excursions

The Northeast shares borders with Nepal, Bangladesh and Bhutan, and has a network of trains, planes and buses fanning out across the Indian plains, providing easy access to a string of famous sights and unique experiences. Don't feel restricted to just visiting West Bengal, Orissa, Sikkim and the Northeast states – it's easy to tag on a side trip to Varanasi, the sacred city on the Ganges, or take a ramble through the mountains to Kathmandu, the mystical capital of Nepal.

Within India, the easiest excursions are to the neighbouring states of Bihar and Uttar Pradesh. Trains run daily from Kolkata (Calcutta) and Guwahati to the Bihari capital, Patna – jumping-off point for Bodhgaya, where Buddha achieved enlightenment. In the south of the state, Betla (Palamau) National Park is one of the best places in India to spot wild elephants. A short hop west will take you to the holy city of Varanasi, opening up an interesting side trip to the ruined Buddhist city at Sarnath.

Venturing further afield, the easy availability of Nepali visas makes possible a fabulous circuit from Darjeeling to Kathmandu and Pokhara, crossing back into India at Sunauli near Varanasi. Alternatively, head overland from Kolkata to Tripura via Bangladesh, with stops in Dhaka, Khulna and the Sunderbans. With a little more cash in the bank, you can even cross into Bhutan, the mysterious Buddhist kingdom squeezed between Sikkim and Arunachal Pradesh.

HIGHLIGHTS

- Soak up the essence of Buddha at the serene Mahabodhi temple, then take a meditation class at a Buddhist monastery in **Bodhgaya** (opposite)

- Visit Patna Museum, with its oddities and Buddha ashes, then shop for Mithila paintings in **Patna** (p276)

- Take a pre-dawn boat ride along the bathing ghats that line the sacred Ganges at **Varanasi** (p278), then enjoy a rooftop yoga session before breakfast

- Trek in the company of sherpas and Himalayan snowpeaks on the **Everest Base Camp** trek (p287) or **Annapurna Circuit** (p287) in Nepal

- Experience the rush of river life at Sadarghat in **Dhaka** (p289), the bustling capital of Bangladesh

- Commune with Buddhist monks at ancient gompas (monasteries) and *dzongs* (temple fortresses) in Bhutan's **Chokksor Valley** (p291)

EXCURSIONS IN INDIA

RANCHI

☎ 0651 / pop 846,454

Jharkhand's capital, Ranchi was once the summer capital of Bihar under the British. The main reason for landing here is to transit to Betla National Park, or to tour the nearby waterfalls.

There's a **tourist office** (☎ 2310230; 5 Main Rd; ⏰ 10am-5pm Mon-Sat) at the Birsa Vihar Tourist Complex. The **State Bank of India** (Main Rd; ⏰ 10am-3.30pm Mon-Fri) changes cash and travellers cheques.

Suhara Tour & Travellers (☎ 3093808; Gurunanak Market, Station Rd) is a reliable travel agency that can organise day trips to local waterfalls (Rs 1200), two- or three-day trips to Betla National Park (from Rs 2500) and other transport ticketing.

Sights & Activities

If you're here for a day, visit the Hindu **Jagannath Temple**, a small version of the great Jagannath Mandir at Puri, 6km southwest of town. The **Tribal Research Institute Museum** (☎ 2541824; Morabadi Rd; admission free; ⏰ 10am-5pm Mon-Sat) covers the history of Jharkhand's many tribal groups.

There are several pretty waterfalls that can be visited on day trips from Ranchi, including the scenic **Hundru Falls**, 45km northeast of the city.

Sleeping & Eating

Hotel Birsa Vihar (☎ 2331828; Main Rd; dm/d Rs 70/300, d with AC Rs 500; 🍴) Jharkhand Tourism's hotel is welcoming and cheap enough but it's a bit gloomy and the rooms are sadly grubby. All private rooms have TV and hot-water geysers that sometimes work.

Hotel Embassy (☎ 2460813; Station Rd; s/d Rs 300/400, with AC Rs 650/850; 🍴) Staff are a little indifferent, but this is one of the few budget places to accept foreigners, and the comfortable air-con rooms are refreshingly contemporary and clean.

BNR Guesthouse-Southeastern Railway (☎ 2460584; Station Rd; s/d Rs 438/599, with AC from Rs 706/866; 🍴) Almost opposite the train station, this red-tiled terracotta-roofed Raj relic is a surprisingly pleasant haven, though the rooms are a little musty.

For meals, try **Planet Masala** (☎ 3291765; 56C Main Rd; mains Rs 30-80) in the centre or **The Nook** (☎ 2460128; Station Rd; mains Rs 45-95) near the train station, which also serves beer.

Getting There & Away

Air Deccan and Indian Airlines fly between Ranchi and Kolkata (from Rs 974, one hour) or Patna (from Rs 774, 50 minutes). Government buses to Gaya (Rs 101, six hours, hourly) and Patna (Rs 170, nine hours) leave from the main bus stand from 6.30am. To reach Ranchi from Kolkata, take the 6am *Shatabdi Express* (chair/executive Rs 645/1220, 7½ hours). Trains also run to Patna (sleeper/3AC Rs 218/612, 10 to 14 hours) and Gaya (sleeper/ chair Rs 133/291, seven hours).

For Betla (Palamau) National Park, the best option is an organised tour.

BETLA (PALAMAU) NATIONAL PARK

Part of Project Tiger, this undisputed natural gem of Jharkhand is 140km west of Ranchi. Although tiger sightings are comparatively rare, this is one of the best places in India to see wild elephants. The sanctuary covers 1026 sq km of sal and teak forest and bamboo thickets, providing shelter for some 37 tigers, 62 leopards, 210 elephants and 249 bison. There are several rickety observation towers where you can watch for wildlife, plus two ruined forts and the tiny villages of eight local tribes.

The best time to visit the **park** (☎ 06562-222650; admission per vehicle Rs 80, camera/video Rs 50/300; ⏰ 5am-7pm) is October through April. **Jeep safaris** (per hr about Rs 200) can be arranged privately at the park gate. You must also hire a local guide (per hour Rs 20) to bring in your vehicle. The park also offers **elephant safaris** (per hr up to 4 people Rs 100) that take you deeper into the jungle.

The government-run **Van Vihar Tourist Complex** (☎ 06567-226513; d Rs 400, with AC Rs 700; 🍴) is the best accommodation around the park entrance and it's the only option open all year. Spacious rooms are clean, bright and look onto the gardens. Jharkhand Tourism also runs the basic **Tourist House** (dm Rs 100).

It is possible to get to the park by public bus from Ranchi, but you'll still have to hire a taxi and security can be an issue on this stretch of highway. A better option is an organised tour from Ranchi – see left.

BODHGAYA

☎ 0631 / pop 30,883

Buddhist pilgrims from around the world are drawn to Bodhgaya. It was here, 26 centuries ago, that Prince Siddhartha Gautama attained enlightenment beneath a Bodhi tree and so became the Buddha. A beautifully serene

EXCURSIONS

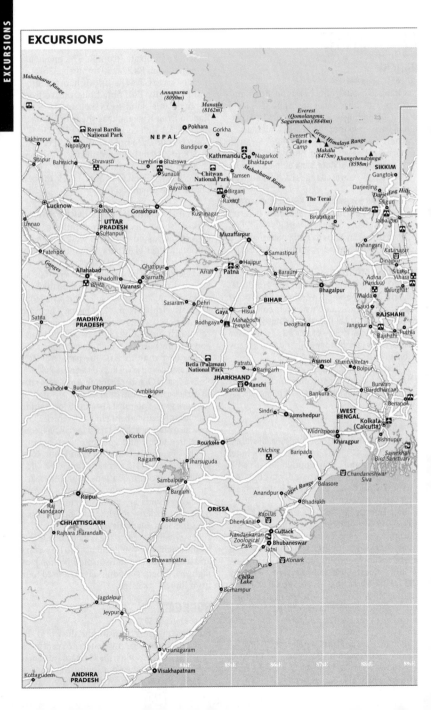

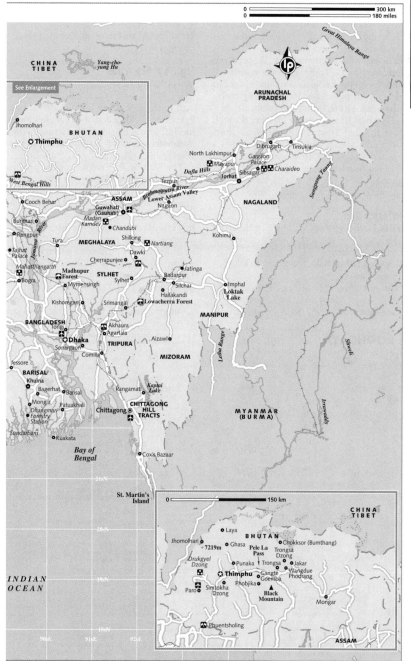

0 ——— 300 km
0 ——— 180 miles

CHINA
TIBET
Yang-cho-yung Hu

Great Himalaya Range

See Enlargement

Jhomolhari

BHUTAN

☉ Thimphu

West Bengal Hills

Cooch Behar

ASSAM
Guwahati
(Gauhati)

Burimari

Madan
Kamdev   ● Chandubi

ARUNACHAL
PRADESH

North Lakhimpur   Dibrugarh   Tinsukia
Mayapur   Gargaon
Palace
Dafla Hills   Sibsagar   Charaideo
Tezpur   Jorhat

Brahmaputra River
Lower Assam Valley
Nagaon

NAGALAND

Sangpong Topng

Rangpur
Jamuna River   Tura   Shillong   Nartiang
MEGHALAYA   Dawki
Cherrapunjee
Tajhat
Palace
Mahasthangarh
Bogra
Madhupur
Forest
Mymensingh
SYLHET
Sylhet
Kishoreganj
Srimangal
Lowacherra Forest
Badarpur   Jatinga
Silchar
Hailakandi

Kohima

Imphal
Loktak
Lake

MANIPUR

Lehia Range

Shweli

BANGLADESH
Tongi
☉ Dhaka
Sonargaon
Comilla

Akhaura
Agartala
TRIPURA   Aizawl

MIZORAM

Irrawaddy

Jessore

BARISAL
Khulna
Bagerhat   Barisal
Mongla   Patuakhali
Dhangmari
Forestry
Station
Sundarbans   Kuakata

Rangamati   Kaptai
Lake

CHITTAGONG
HILL
TRACTS
Chittagong

MYANMAR
(BURMA)

Bay of
Bengal

Cox's Bazaar

St. Martin's
Island

0 ——— 150 km

CHINA
TIBET

INDIAN
OCEAN

21°N

20°N

19°N

18°N

90°E   91°E   92°E

Jhomolhari   ● Laya
÷7219m   ● Ghasa   Pele La
Drukgyel   Pass
Dzong   ● Punaka   Trongsa
☉ Thimphu   Gangte
Paro   Simtokha   Goemba
Dzong   Phobjika
BHUTAN

Chokksor (Bumthang)
Trongsa
Dzong   ● Jakar
Wangdue
Phodrang

Black
Mountain
Mongar

☐ Phuentsholing

ASSAM

EXCURSIONS

temple marks the spot and a descendent of that original Bodhi tree remains, its roots happily clutching the same soil as its celebrated ancestor. Monasteries and temples, built by international Buddhist communities, are peppered around and attract pilgrims to study, meditate and absorb the ambience. Bodhgaya is not so much a town as a Buddhist working centre surrounded by farmland and rural villages.

The best time to visit is October through March, when Tibetan pilgrims come down from Dharamsala and Bodhgaya becomes a sea of maroon robes. However, accommodation can be in short supply so book rooms well ahead of time. The Dalai Lama himself often spends December and January here.

Information

BSTDC Tourist Complex (☎ 2200672; cnr Bodhgaya Rd & Temple St; ☯ 10.30am-5pm Tue-Sat) Little more than dusty brochures.
Magadh Internet Dhaba (Bodhgaya Rd; per hr Rs 40; ☯ 8am-9pm)
Main post office (☎ 2200472; cnr Bodhgaya & Godam Rds; ☯ 10am-3.30pm Mon-Fri, 10am-12.30pm Sat)
State Bank of India (☎ 2200852; Bodhgaya Rd; ☯ 10.30am-4pm Mon-Fri, to 1pm Sat) Foreign exchange and an ATM.
Verma Health Care Centre (☎ 2201101; ☯ 24hr) Emergency room and clinic.

Sights & Activities
MAHABODHI TEMPLE

The spiritual centrepiece of Bodhgaya, adjacent to the spot where Buddha attained enlightenment and formulated his philosophy of life, is the magnificent World Heritage–listed **Mahabodhi Temple** (Bodhgaya Rd; admission free, camera/video Rs 20/300; ☯ 5am-9pm).

The Mahabodhi Temple was constructed in the 6th century AD atop the site of a temple erected by Emperor Ashoka almost 800 years earlier. After being razed by 11th-century Muslim invaders, the temple underwent major restorations, the last occurring in 1882. Topped by a 50m pyramidal spire, the ornate structure houses a 2m-high gilded image of a seated Buddha. Four of the sculpted stone railings surrounding the temple date from the Sunga period (184-72BC).

Thankfully, before Ashoka's wife murdered the original **Bodhi tree**, a sapling from it was car-

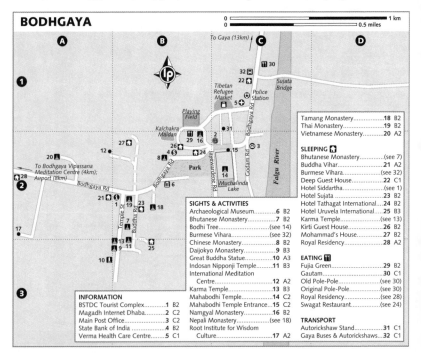

ried to Anuradhapura, Sri Lanka, by Sangha-mitta (Ashoka's daughter). That tree continues to flourish and from which, in turn, a cutting was carried back to Bodhgaya and planted where the original had stood. The red sandstone slab between the tree and the rear of the temple was placed there by Ashoka, and marks the spot of Buddha's enlightenment – it's referred to as the Vajrasan (Diamond Throne).

The temple complex is a serene network of paths, gardens, shrines, votive stupas and a meditation park. To the south is the **Muchalinda Lake**, a lotus pond surrounded by prayer flags and with a cobra statue rising from the centre. Legend has it Buddha meditated here on the sixth week after enlightenment and was sheltered from a violent storm by the snake god of the lake.

An **audio headset guide** (Rs 20), available from the camera ticket counter, offers a one-hour commentary in English, Hindi, Japanese or Korean.

MONASTERIES & TEMPLES

Thanks to most countries with a large Buddhist population having a temple or monastery here, Bodhgaya offers visitors a unique opportunity to peek into different Buddhist cultures. Head to the beautiful **Indosan Nipponji Temple** (Japanese temple) at 6am and 5pm daily for the free one-hour Zazen sessions (Zen meditation).

In an intriguing display of architecture, monasteries are designed in a representative style of their homeland. The most impressive is the **Thai Monastery**, a brightly coloured *wat* with shimmering gold leaf and manicured gardens. Meditation sessions are held here in the morning. The Tibetan **Karma Temple** and **Namgyal Monastery** each contain large prayer wheels, and the massive **Indosan Nipponji Temple** is donned with a Japanese pagoda roof. Other noteworthy monasteries include the **Chinese**, **Burmese, Bhutanese, Vietnamese, Tamang, Daijokyo** and **Nepali**.

OTHER SIGHTS

At the end of Temple St towers the 25m-high **Great Buddha Statue** (☼ 7am-noon & 2-5pm). The impressive monument was unveiled by the Dalai Lama in 1989 – the hollow statue is said to contain some 20,000 bronze Buddhas.

The **archaeological museum** (☎ 2200739; admission Rs 2; ☼ 10am-5pm Sat-Thu) contains a small collection of local Buddha figures, but pride

of place goes to part of the original granite railings and pillars rescued from the Mahabodhi Temple.

Courses

About 4km west of town, the **Bodhgaya Vipassana Meditation Centre** (Dhamma Bodhi; ☎ 220437; www.dhamma.org; Gaya-Dhoba Rd) runs intensive 10-day vipassana courses twice each month throughout the year (by donation).

Three nine-day vipassana meditation and spiritual inquiry retreats are held by **Insight Meditation Retreats** (www.insightmeditation.org) from 7 January to 6 February at the Royal Thai Monastery. Space is limited so book ahead. From mid-November you can inquire at the **Burmese Monastery** between 3pm and 4pm. Donations are requested.

The courses at the **International Meditation Centre** (☎ 2200707; per day Rs 100) are more informal and students can start and finish any time they choose year-round.

The popular introductory 10-day meditation courses run by the **Root Institute for Wisdom Culture** (☎ 2200714; www.rootinstitute.com) go from late October through March and are excellent for beginners – the website has prices and a full schedule.

Sleeping

Prices listed here are for the high season (November through March) – most places will drop prices by up to 50% in the off season, so be prepared to negotiate.

BUDGET

If you don't mind abiding by some simple rules and attending daily prayers, it's possible to stay at some of the monasteries. The **Bhutanese Monastery** (☎ 2200710; Buddha Rd; d with shared/private bathroom Rs 150/250) is a tranquil place typified by colourful surroundings, gardens and big rooms. The Tibetan **Karma Temple** (☎ 2200795; Temple St; d with shared bathroom Rs 200) has a similar feel. The **Burmese Vihara** (☎ 2200721; Bodhgaya Rd; r Rs 50) is popular with foreigners; there's a maximum stay of three days unless you're engaged in dharma studies.

Buddha Vihar (☎ 2200127; Bodhgaya Rd; dm Rs 75-100) The dormitory accommodation at the tourism complex is clean and cheap.

Mohammad's House (☎ 2200690; d with shared/private bathroom Rs 200/250) It may be a bit earthy for some, but just getting to this simple family homestay is an adventure. It's hidden

EXCURSIONS

among local homes north of the main road (ask directions). Rooms are very basic, but the rooftop terrace offers pleasant views of rice paddies, sunsets and the distant Mahabodhi Temple.

Deep Guest House (☎ 2200463; Bodhgaya Rd; d with shared/private bathroom Rs 200/300) Clean rooms and friendly service make this place near the bus stand a great choice. Rooms are bright and airy, and even the shared bathrooms are kept clean.

MIDRANGE

Hotel Siddartha (☎ 2200127; Bodhgaya Rd; d Rs 400, with AC 600) This is the best of the accommodation in the BSTDC tourism complex, though it's still a bit austere. Rooms are in an unusual circular building overlooking a quiet garden area. Rates are fixed year-round, making it good value from November to January.

Kirti Guest House (☎ 2200744; near Kalchakra Maidan; s/d Rs 700/850) Run by the Tibetan Monastery and one of the best of the midrange places, Kirti has clean, bright rooms behind a monastery-like façade. Go for one of the front rooms opening out onto the balcony. All have TV and hot water.

Hotel Uruvela International (☎ 2200235; s/d Rs 750/1000, with AC Rs 1000/1400; ❄) Spacious rooms, some a little ornate and over decorated, have the usual facilities at this quiet, friendly hotel near the Japanese temple. Off-season discount is 40%.

Hotel Tathagat International (☎ 2200106; www.hoteltathagatbodhgaya.net; Bodhgaya Rd; s/d Rs 1125/1350, with AC Rs 1350/1700; ❄) Simple and conservatively furnished rooms, but it's clean and efficiently run. Some rooms have balconies and all have TV and hot water.

TOP END

Hotel Sujata (☎ 2200761; www.hotelsujata.com; Buddha Rd; s/d/ste Rs 2400/2800/3600; ❄) Swish, spacious rooms with soft beds, an excellent restaurant and his and hers *o-furo* (communal Japanese baths) make this hotel, opposite the Thai monastery, best value in the top-end range. Unfortunately, the Japanese bath is only available to groups of 10 or more.

Royal Residency (☎ 2200124; www.theroyalresidency.net/bodhgaya; Bodhgaya Rd; s/d US$120/150; ❄) Bodhgaya's most luxurious hotel is in a quiet location about 1.5km west of the centre. Fine woodwork, rich marble, pleasant gardens and comfy rooms, but still overpriced.

Eating & Drinking

During the peak season from mid-November to February, when Tibetan pilgrims pour into Bodhgaya, temporary tent restaurants set up next to the Tibetan refugee market, at Kalchakra Maidan and near the Great Buddha Statue, serving a range of Tibetan dishes and sweets, such as apple pie and cinnamon rolls.

There are decent restaurants along the main road in the village centre, while the best dining experiences are in a handful of midrange and top-end hotels.

Opposite the Burmese Monastery are the long-running and popular semi-tent restaurants **Original Pole-Pole** (mains Rs 20–80), **Old Pole-Pole** (mains Rs 20–80) and the **Gautam** (mains Rs 20–80), serving a standard travellers' menu of breakfast fare, pancakes, pasta, and Indian and Chinese cuisine.

Fujia Green (Kalchakra Maidan; mains Rs 15–70) Another popular year-round tent restaurant, Fujia Green serves up wonderful Tibetan fare, such as *momos* (dumplings), *thukpas* and *thenthuks* (types of noodle soup), as well as tasty chicken dishes.

Swagat Restaurant (Bodhgaya Rd; mains Rs 50–150; ❄) At Hotel Tathagat International, this is a good choice with an innovative menu of veg and non-veg dishes, such as *mutton badam pasanda* (boneless mutton stuffed with almonds and cooked in an almond gravy).

Royal Residency Hotel (Bodhgaya Rd; mains Rs 70–150; ❄) Serves beers from the air-conditioned restaurant at the for a steep Rs 250.

Getting There & Away

The Gaya airport is 8km from town and Indian Airlines offers one flight a week to/from Kolkata (US$88).

Overly crowded shared autorickshaws (Rs 8) and occasional buses (Rs 5) leave the Burmese Monastery for the 13km to Gaya. A private autorickshaw to Gaya should cost Rs 80.

GAYA

☎ 0631 / pop 383,197

Gaya is a raucous, dusty town about 100km south of Patna. Although it's a centre for Hindu pilgrims, it's really only of interest to travellers as the transport hub for Bodhgaya, 13km away. Pilgrims come here to offer *pinda* (funeral cake) at the ghats along the river as part of the circuit of sacred Buddhist sites.

There's a **Bihar State Tourist Office** (☎ 2420155; Station Rd; ⊗ 10am–8pm Mon-Sat) and a State Bank of

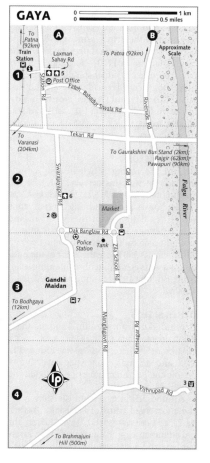

GAYA

preached the fire sermon; the views over Gaya and the surrounding plains are expansive.

Sleeping & Eating

Unless you arrive late or have an early departure, Bodhgaya is a better place to stay.

Hotel Akash (☎ 2222205; Laxman Sahay Rd; s/d Rs 175/250) A stand-out option among the concrete clone hotels down the lane opposite the station. The turquoise timber façade gives way to an Islamic-inspired inner courtyard. Basic rooms are reasonably clean with TV and there's a relaxing open-aired area upstairs.

Hotel Vishnu International (☎ 2431146; Swarajayapur Rd; s Rs 250, d Rs 350-600, d with AC Rs 1000; 🍽) With a castle-like façade, this reasonably new hotel is the best value in town. Clean, well kept and most rooms have TV and hot water.

Ajatsatru Hotel (☎ 2434584; Station Rd; d Rs 375, d with AC Rs 800; 🍽) Directly opposite the station, rooms here vary a lot and are comparatively overpriced. Its multicuisine restaurant (mains Rs 20 to80; ⏰7am to 11.30pm; 🍽) is a good place for a bite while waiting for a train.

Getting There & Away

Buses to Patna (Rs 50, three hours, hourly) and Ranchi (Rs 101, seven hours, hourly) leave from the Gandhi Maidan bus stand.

Gaya has regular trains to Kolkata (sleeper/3AC Rs 183/515, eight hours), and less frequent services to Varanasi (Rs 110/310, four hours) and Patna (Rs 101/188, two hours).

Persistent autorickshaw drivers charge Rs 80 for transfers to Bodhgaya. Alternatively, take a cycle-rickshaw to Kacheri stand and a crowded shared autorickshaw (Rs 8) from there.

India ATM at the train station. The nearest foreign exchange for cash and travellers cheques is in Bodhgaya. There are several **internet cafes** (per hr Rs 20) along Swarajayapur Rd.

Sights & Activities

Close to the banks of the Falgu River south of town, the *sikhara* (spired) **Vishnupad Temple** was constructed in 1787 by Queen Ahalya Bai of Indore and houses a 40cm 'footprint' of Vishnu imprinted in solid rock. Non-Hindus are not permitted to enter, but you can get a look at the temple from the pink platform near the entrance.

One thousand stone steps leads to the top of the **Brahmajuni Hill**, 1km southwest of the Vishnupad Temple, where Buddha is said to have

EXCURSIONS

Getting Around

From the train station, a cycle-rickshaw should cost Rs 12 to the Kacheri autorickshaw stand, Rs 15 to Gandhi Maidan or Gaurakshini bus stands, and Rs 20 to the Vishnupad Temple.

PATNA

☎ 0612 / pop 1,285,470

Bihar's busy capital spreads out over a vast area on the south bank of the swollen and polluted Ganges, just east of the river's confluence with three major tributaries. Patna was once the capital of the Magadha kingdom and later the capital of the Maurya emperors Chandragupta Maurya and Ashoka. As a regional hub, it has good transport links and a handful of interesting sights.

Orientation

The old and newer parts of Patna stretch along the southern bank of the Ganges for about 15km. The main train station, airport and hotels are in the western half, known as Bankipur, while most of the historic sites are in the teeming older Chowk area to the east.

Information

BSTDC Tourist Office (☎ 2225411; bstdc@sancharnet .in; Hotel Kautilya Vihar, Birchand Patel Path; ☼ 10am-5pm Mon-Sat) Books government accommodation.

Cyber World (Rajendra Path; per hr Rs 20; ☼ 9.30am-9pm)

General post office (Buddha Marg; ☼ 10am-5pm Mon-Fri, to 2pm Sat)

India Tourism Office (☎ 2345776; goitopatna@vsnl .net; Kankerbagh Rd; ☼ 9.30am-6pm Mon-Fri, 9am-1pm Sat) Helpful and knowledgeable office on 3rd floor.

Ruban Memorial Hospital & Ratan Stone Clinic (☎ 2320446; Gandhi Maidan; ☼ 24hr) Emergency room, clinic and pharmacy.

State Bank of India (☎ 2226134; Gandhi Maidan; ☼ 10.30am-4pm Mon-Fri, to 1.30pm Sat) Currency and travellers cheques exchanged; other ATMs nearby.

Dangers & Annoyances

Avoid walking alone at night, as robbery can be a real problem. Avoid carrying bags or valuables, which could encourage theft.

Sights & Activities

GANDHI MAIDAN AREA

For a dome with a view, head up to the landmark **Golghar** (Danapure Rd; admission free; ☼ 24hr), a short walk west of Gandhi Maidan. This massive and bulbous beehive of a granary was built by the British army in 1786, in the hope of avoiding a repeat performance of the vicious famine in 1770 – fortunately it was never required. Its dual spiralling staircases (250 steps each side) lead to an unparalleled view of the city and Ganges. Nearby is a diminutive **Gandhi Museum** (☎ 2225339; Danapure Rd; admission free; ☼ 10am-6pm Sun-Fri), devoted to the Mahatma.

PATNA MUSEUM

Behind the fading Mughal- and Rajput-inspired exterior, this **museum** (☎ 2235731; Buddha Marg; Indian/foreigner Rs 5/250; ☼ 10.30am-4.30pm Tue-Sun) houses a splendid collection of stone sculptures dating from the Mauryan and Gupta periods, plus various stuffed animals and ethnological displays. You must pay an additional Rs 500 to see the 'Relic of the Buddha' – a glass box reputedly containing ashes from Buddha's cremation, retrieved from Vaishali.

OTHER SIGHTS

Around 1km from Gandhi Maidan, **Khuda Baksh Oriental Library** (☎ 2300209; Ashok Raj Path; admission free; ☼ 9am-5pm Sat-Thu) was founded in 1900 and contains a renowned collection of Arabic and Persian manuscripts, Mughal and Rajput paintings.

Around 3.5km east from the station are the submerged ruins of **Pataliputra** (Kankerbagh Rd; Indian/foreigner Rs 5/100; ☼ 9am-5.30pm), the old Mauryan capital, surrounded by lovely gardens and a **museum** that details the site's historic past.

Behind a grand gate about 11km east of the centre is one of the nation's four holiest **Sikh shrines** (☎ 2642000). Its miniature marble domes, sweeping staircases and fine lattice work mark the spot where Guru Gobind Singh, the last of the 10 Sikh gurus, was born in 1660.

Nearby is **Qila House** (Jalan Museum; ☎ 2641121; Jalan Ave; ☼ by appointment only), a stately home overflowing with culturally significant antiques, from elaborate Mughal-period silverware to the humorously short bed of Napoleon Bonaparte.

Sleeping

The modern western half of the city has plenty of accommodation choices, mainly around Fraser and Station Rds.

PATNA

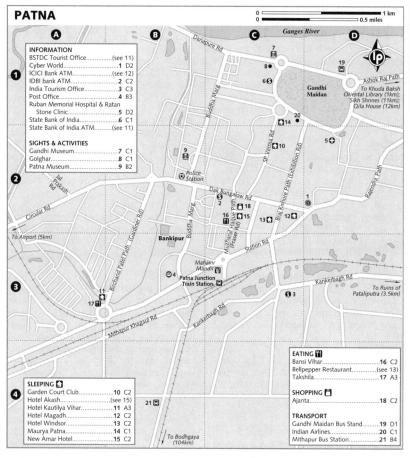

INFORMATION
BSTDC Tourist Office..............(see 11)
Cyber World..............................**1** D2
ICICI Bank ATM.....................(see 12)
IDBI bank ATM........................**2** C2
India Tourism Office.................**3** C3
Post Office.................................**4** B3
Ruban Memorial Hospital & Ratan
 Stone Clinic.........................**5** D2
State Bank of India....................**6** C1
State Bank of India ATM........(see 11)

SIGHTS & ACTIVITIES
Gandhi Museum......................**7** C1
Golghar.....................................**8** C1
Patna Museum.........................**9** B2

SLEEPING 🏠
Garden Court Club..................**10** C2
Hotel Akash.........................(see 15)
Hotel Kautilya Vihar................**11** A3
Hotel Magadh.........................**12** C2
Hotel Windsor.........................**13** C2
Maurya Patna.........................**14** C1
New Amar Hotel......................**15** C2

EATING 🍴
Bansi Vihar...............................**16** C2
Bellpepper Restaurant..............(see 13)
Takshila...................................**17** A3

SHOPPING 🛍
Ajanta.....................................**18** C2

TRANSPORT
Gandhi Maidan Bus Stand..........**19** D1
Indian Airlines.........................**20** C1
Mithapur Bus Station................**21** B4

BUDGET

New Amar Hotel (☎ 2224157; s/d Rs 170/246) The bright green New Amar is the best of several budget hotels down a small lane off Fraser Rd. Rooms are simple and cleanish.

Hotel Akash (☎ 2239599; d Rs 250) Try here if the New Amar Hotel next door is full.

Hotel Magadh (☎ 2321278; Station Rd; s/d Rs 350/500, with AC Rs 600/750; ﹡) Midrange comfort at a budget price makes this hotel the best value in Patna. The singles are small with squat toilet, but the doubles are spacious, bright and clean and all rooms have TV and hot water.

Hotel Kautilya Vihar (☎ 2225411; bstdc@sancharnet .in; Birchand Patel Path; dm Rs 75, d Rs 500-700, with AC Rs 800; ﹡) This sprawling government hotel has

a range of rooms that are clean and spacious. It lacks much atmosphere but there's a restaurant and bar and eager staff. The six-bed dorms are cramped.

MIDRANGE & TOP END

Garden Court Club (☎ 3096229; SP Verma Rd; s/d from Rs 600/800; ﹡) With only six rooms, the Garden Court Club is an intimate hotel tucked away in a small shopping complex. Comfortable rooms all have air-con and there's a communal lounge, but the biggest draw is the lovely open-air garden restaurant.

Hotel Windsor (☎ 2203250-58; www.hotelwindsor patna.com; Exhibition Rd; s/d/ste Rs 900/1100/1350; ﹡) Rooms in this thoughtfully designed hotel offer contemporary décor, fine woodwork,

EXCURSIONS

spotless bathrooms and air-con throughout, making this Patna's top midrange choice.

Maurya Patna (☎ 2203040-59; www.maurya.com; South Gandhi Maidan; s/d from Rs 2800/3500; 🖳 🕮 🏊) Fine appointments and luxurious surroundings are found throughout Patna's top business hotel. The large gardens host a tempting pool (Rs 350 for nonguests), and there are two good restaurants and a bar. Rooms are tastefully furnished and centrally air-conditioned.

Eating

Bansi Vihar (Fraser Rd; mains Rs 30-70) Locals crowd into this spotless air-con restaurant to enjoy cheap South Indian *masala dosas* (curried vegetables inside a crisp pancake), Chinese specials and friendly service.

Bellpepper Restaurant (Exhibition Rd; mains Rs 50-200; 🕑 noon-3.30pm & 7-11pm; 🍴) This intimate, contemporary restaurant in the Hotel Windsor is popular for its sublime tandoori specialities. No alcohol is served.

Takshila (☎ 2220590; Birchand Patel Path; mains Rs 80-375; 🕑 noon-3.30pm & 7.30-11pm) Inside Hotel Chanakya, Takshila exudes the ambience of the North West Frontier. The speciality is meat-heavy Mughlai, Afghan and tandoori dishes.

Shopping

Patna is one of the best places in Bihar to buy Mithila paintings – **Ajanta** (☎ 2224432; Hotel Satka Arcade, Fraser Rd; 🕑 10.30am-8pm Mon-Sat) has Patna's best selection.

Getting There & Away

Indian Airlines (☎ 2222554; Gandhi Maidan) flies to Ranchi (US$73) and **Air Deccan** (www.airdeccan.net) flies to Kolkata. About 2km south of the train station, the new bus stand (Mithapur bus station) has services to Gaya (Rs 50, three hours, hourly), Ranchi (Rs 180, 10 hours, 8pm and 9pm) and Raxaul (Rs 100, eight hours).

From the Gandhi Maidan bus stand government bus services go to Ranchi (Rs 170, 10 hours, four daily) and the Nepal border at Raxaul (Rs 109, eight hours, daily at 9.15am and 10pm).

Patna Junction station has eight daily trains to Kolkata (sleeper/3AC Rs 218/615, eight to 11 hours), and less frequent trains to New Jalpaiguri (Siliguri; sleeper/3AC Rs 195/549, nine to 12 hours), Varanasi (2nd class/sleeper Rs 65/112, five hours), Gaya (sleeper/chair Rs 101/142, 3½ hours) and Ranchi (sleeper/chair Rs 170/370, 10 hours).

Getting Around

The airport is 7km west of the city centre – autorickshaws charge Rs 80; taxis charge around Rs 180. Shared autorickshaws shuttle back and forth between the train station and Gandhi Maidan bus stand (Rs 3), or take a cycle-rickshaw.

RAXAUL
☎ 06255 / pop 41,347

Grimy, crowded Raxaul is the crossing point to Birganj in Nepal – see p324. Neither are places to hang around. If you must spend the night here, head to **Hotel Kaveri** (☎ 221148; Main Rd; d from Rs 250), which has the cleanest rooms.

There are several early morning buses from Raxaul to Patna (Rs 100, eight hours). The *Mithila Express* train runs daily from Kolkata to Raxaul (sleeper/3AC/2AC; Rs 256/723/1037).

VARANASI
☎ 0542 / pop 1,211,749

Few places in India are as colourful, charismatic or spiritual as the bathing ghats lining the Ganges in Varanasi. The city of Shiva is one of the holiest places in India, where Hindu pilgrims come to wash away a lifetime of sins in the Ganges or to cremate their loved ones along the banks of the sacred river. Varanasi, previously called Benares, has always been an auspicious place to die, since expiring here offers *moksha* – liberation from the cycle of birth and death. The city rose to prominence in the 8th century AD when the reformer Shankaracharya established Shiva worship as the principal sect. The Afghans destroyed Varanasi around AD 1300, and Aurangzeb waged a similar campaign of destruction in the 17th century, but a profound sense of antiquity and history still pervades the city.

Orientation

The old city of Varanasi is situated along the western bank of the Ganges and extends back from the riverbank ghats in a labyrinth of alleys called *galis* that are too narrow for traffic. Look for signposts to find hotels, or orient yourself using the ghats. Immediately south of the train station are the less congested areas of Lahurabir and Chetganj, while behind the station is the peaceful Cantonment area.

Information

For an online guide to the city, visit the website www.varanasi.nic.in, or www.visitvaranasi .com. Branches of **iway Internet** Assi Ghat (per hr Rs 25; 🕓 7.30am-10.30pm); Hotel Surya (per 45min Rs 25; h7.30am-10pm); Off Mandapur Rd (per hr Rs 25; 🕓 7am-10pm); Off Parade Kothi (per hr Rs 30; 🕓 9am-9pm Mon-Sat) across the city offer internet phone calls and broadband connections for Rs 25 to 30 per hour.

Bank of Baroda (☎ 2366150; 1st fl, Dasaswamedh Ghat Rd; 🕓 11am-6.30pm Mon-Fri, 11am-2pm Sat) Exchanges major currencies and travellers cheques.

Heritage Hospital (☎ 2368888) Located at the main entrance of Benares Hindu University, this private hospital has a 24-hour pharmacy and International Travellers Clinic.

India Tourism office (☎ 2226378; 191 The Mall 🕓 9am-5.30pm Mon-Fri, 9am-2pm Sat)

Post Office (☎ 2331398; Kabir Chaura Rd; 🕓 10am-6pm Mon-Sat) Also sub post offices near Dasaswamedh Ghat and Vishwanath temple.

State Bank of India (☎ 2343742; the Mall; 🕓 10am-2pm & 2.30-4pm Mon-Fri, 10am-1pm Sat) Exchanges cash and cheques; there's an ATM at Godaulia Crossing.

Tourist Police (☎ 2506670; UP Tourism office, Varanasi Junction train station; 🕓 6am-7pm)

UP Tourism office Tourist Bungalow (☎ 2206638; Parade Kothi; 🕓 10am-5pm Mon-Sat); Varanasi Junction train station (☎ 2506670; 🕓 7am-7pm)

Sights
GHATS

Spiritual life in Varanasi revolves around the ghats, the long string of bathing steps leading down to the water on the western bank of the Ganges. Most are used for bathing but there are also several 'burning ghats' where bodies are cremated in public. A stroll along the ghats provides a world-class opportunity for 'people watching' as you mingle with locals who come to the Ganges to bathe, offer *puja* (prayers), wash clothes, do yoga, chew *paan* (mix of betel nut and leaves for chewing), sell flowers, have massages, play cricket, improve their karma by giving to beggars or simply hang around. The best time to visit the ghats is at dawn when pilgrims come to perform *puja* to the rising sun, and at sunset when the main *ganga aarti* ceremony takes place at Dasaswamedh Ghat.

Around 80 ghats border the river, but the main group extends from Assi Ghat, near the university, northwards to Raj Ghat, near the road and rail bridge – there's a useful map online at varanasi.nic.in/phototalk/loc _and_maps.htm. Each ghat has its own unique history and rituals, linked to the rulers and

spiritual leaders who founded them. The easiest way to explore the ghats is on foot, but the ghats are equally fascinating from the water. Boatmen at Dasaswamedh Ghat and other boat stations offer one-hour tours south to Harishchandra Ghat and back for Rs 70 to 100 per hour (for up to four people), but foreign tourists will have to bargain down from marked-up prices like Rs 600 per hour.

The funeral ghats hold a particular fascination for visitors. **Manikarnika Ghat** and the smaller **Harishchandra Ghat** are the most auspicious places for a Hindu to be cremated. Dead bodies are handled by outcasts known as *dom*s, who also conduct the sale of firewood to cremate the bodies using giant scales. You can watch cremations but photography is strictly prohibited, and visitors should respect the solemnity of the occasion. Priests and 'guides' will invariably lead you to vantage points overlooking the ghats and demand a donation towards the cost of wood (in dollars) – make a donation but don't be pressured into giving outrageous sums.

VISHWANATH TEMPLE

About 300m inland from Manikarnika Ghat, this important Hindu temple is dedicated to Vishveswara – Shiva as lord of the universe. It's also known as the 'Golden Temple', because its tower and dome are plated in pure gold. Only Hindus can enter and there are strict security controls because of the risk of communal violence – non-Hindus can view the shrine for free from the 2nd floor of a shop across the street.

BENARES HINDU UNIVERSITY

Varanasi has long been a centre of learning and that tradition continues today at the attractively laid-out and well-regarded **Benares Hindu University** (BHU; www.bhu.ac.in), about 2km south of Assi Ghat on Assi Rd. On campus is **Bharat Kala Bhavan** (☎ 316337; Indian/foreigner Rs 10/100, camera Rs 20; 🕓 11am-4.30pm Mon-Sat), a roomy museum with a wonderful collection of miniature paintings, palm-leaf manuscripts, sculptures and local history displays.

The university is a 40-minute autorickshaw ride (Rs 150) from the train station and around 15 minutes from Assi Ghat (Rs 50).

RAMNAGAR FORT & MUSEUM

On the eastern bank of the Ganges, inside a crumbling 17th-century palace, is a haphazard **museum** (☎ 2339322; admission Rs 7; 🕓 9am-noon &

EXCURSIONS

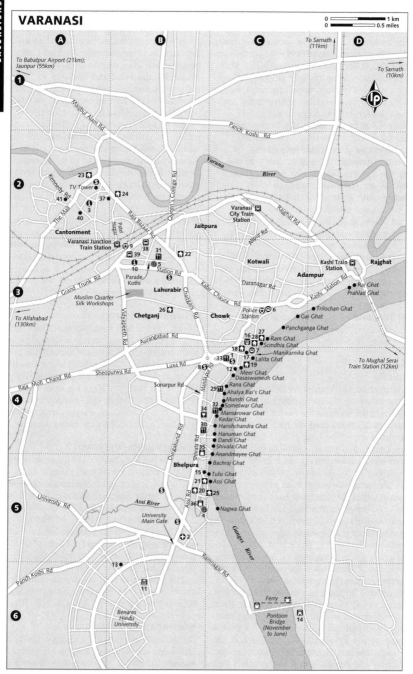

VARANASI

0 — 1 km
0 — 0.5 miles

To Babatpur Airport (21km);
Jaunpur (55km)

To Sarnath
(11km)

To Sarnath
(10km)

Maqbul Alam Rd

Panch Koshi Rd

Varuna River

23
TV Tower
41
37 24
3
40
Kennedy Rd
The Mall
Patel Nagar
Raja Bazaar Rd
Queen's College Rd

Cantonment

Varanasi Junction
Train Station

Varanasi
City Train
Station

Jaitpura

Alapur Rd

Rajghat Rd

9
38
31
39
5
10
22

Kotwali

Kashi Train
Station

Rajghat

Adampur

Kashi Station Rd

Parade
Kothi
Station Rd
Kabir Chaura Rd
Daranagar Rd

Raj Ghat
Prahlad Ghat

Grand Trunk Rd

Muslim Quarter
Silk Workshops

To Allahabad
(130km)

Lahurabir

Chetganj

Vidyapeeth Rd

26

Aurangabad Rd

Chowk

Police
Station

6

7

Trilochan Ghat

Gai Ghat

Panchganga Ghat

Ram Ghat
16 28
27
18 15
33 1
17 19
8
12
29
34
30
35
15
21
20 25
36
4

Scindhia Ghat
Manikarnika Ghat
Lalita Ghat
Meer Ghat
Dasaswamedh Ghat
Rana Ghat
Ahalya Bai's Ghat
Munshi Ghat
Someswar Ghat
Mansarowar Ghat
Kedar Ghat
Harishchandra Ghat
Hanuman Ghat
Dandi Ghat
Shivala Ghat
Anandmayee Ghat
Bachraj Ghat
Tulsi Ghat
Assi Ghat

To Mughal Serai
Train Station (12km)

Raja Moti Chand Rd

Sheopurwa Rd

Luxa Rd

Sonarpur Rd

Mandpur Rd

Durgakund Rd

Shivala Rd

Assi Rd

University Rd

Assi River

University
Main Gate

Nagwa Ghat

Ganges River

2

13

11

Ramnagar Rd

Panch Koshi Rd

Benares
Hindu
University

Ferry

Pontoon
Bridge
(November
to June)

14

2-5.30pm), with palanquins, howdahs, an astrological clock, clothing, weapons and other collectables.

Ferries (Rs 6 return, 10 minutes, from 5am to 8pm) operate a shuttle service across the river, but from November to June you can also cross on the somewhat unsteady pontoon bridge.

Activities

YOGA

Varanasi has plenty of centres offering yoga tuition, but beware of 'fake' yoga teachers who are mainly interested in a hands-on lesson with young females. Genuine places around the old city include the following:

International Yoga Clinic & Meditation Centre (☎ 2397139; gurujivyas@satyam.net.in) Classes cost Rs 100 per hour for one student (less if there are more students).

Malaviya Bhavan (☎ 2307208; Benares Hindu University) Four-week physical yoga certificate course (one hour per day) for Rs 5500.

Yoga Training Centre (☎ 9919857895; yoga_sunil@ hotmail.com; Sakarkand Lane) Three two-hour sessions a day (8am, 10am and 4pm; Rs 200).

Sleeping

Most budget hotels are concentrated in a tangle of narrow streets back from the ghats in Godaulia and the old city. Most of the top-end hotels are in the Cantonment area north of the train station, and there are more budget and midrange places in Lahurabir and Chetganj areas.

Varanasi also has an active paying guesthouse scheme – the UP Tourism office (p279) has a full list.

BUDGET

Old City & the Ghats

Yogi Lodge (☎ 2392588; yogilodge@yahoo.com; Kalika Gali; dm/s/d Rs 55/100/150) A long-running favourite with hippie types going for the bargain-basement prices and laid-back ambience. Rooms are pretty basic, and all have shared showers and squat toilets.

Shanti Guest House (☎ 2392568; varanasishanti@ yahoo.com; Manikarnika Ghat; dm Rs 55, s/d Rs 150/200, d with AC Rs 500; 🏊 💻) The biggest attraction here is the very social 24-hour rooftop restaurant, which overlooks Manikarnika Ghat. The restaurant has a free pool table, yoga classes can be arranged and free morning boat rides are organised for guests in the high season. Rooms are a bit gloomy and could do with a paint, but the price is right.

Scindhia Guest House (☎ 2420319; www.scindhia guesthouse.com; Scindhia Ghat; d with shared bathroom Rs 200, with private bathroom Rs 350-450, with AC Rs 600-1200; 🏊 💻) This well-kept and clean ghat-side hotel sets a high standard – the best rooms have great river views and balconies but are well into the midrange price bracket. There's a library and veg restaurant, and the hotel runs boat trips directly from Scindhia Ghat.

Ganga Fuji Home (☎ 3093949; raj327333@yahoo.com; Sakarkand Gali; s/d with shared bathroom from Rs 150/200, with private bathroom from Rs 300/350, d with AC from Rs 700; 🏊) Back from the ghats, Ganga Fuji is run by an exuberant and helpful family. The best and brightest rooms are at the top but all are clean, and the brand-new top-floor restaurant offers panoramic city views and live entertainment in the evenings.

Hotel Alka (☎ 2401681; www.hotelalkavns.com; Meer Ghat; r with shared bathroom Rs 200, with private bathroom Rs 250-700, with AC Rs 550-990; 🖳 🖳) With a lovely leafy terrace restaurant nudging over the river, Alka is the best of the ghat-side budget options. All rooms are clean and modern with TV, and the more expensive rooms offer wonderful views from the balconies.

MIDRANGE
Old City & the Ghats

Hotel Divya (☎ 2311305; www.hoteldivya.com; s/d Rs 600/750, with AC Rs 850/1000; 🖳 🖳) This new hotel set back from Assi Ghat is immaculate, stylish and well run by a charming lady manager. There's a good range of rooms, all with TV and hot water, an excellent restaurant as well as a rooftop terrace.

Hotel Ganges View (☎ 2313218; hotelgangesview@yahoo.com; Assi Ghat; r without/with AC Rs 1200/2500; 🖳) This beautifully restored and maintained traditional-style house overlooking Assi Ghat is crammed with artworks and antiques. Home-cooked meals are served in the charming dining room. Book ahead.

Other Areas

Hotel Surya (☎ 2508466; www.hotelsuryavns.com; 20/51 Mall Rd; s/d Rs 350/500, with AC Rs 600/800; 🖳 🖳 🖳) Rooms are built around an enormous garden and lawn area that makes this hotel popular with overlanding tour groups. It's an excellent-value and a well-designed place with clean, modern rooms, beautiful swimming pool, quality restaurant and massage centre.

Hotel Pradeep (☎ 2204963; www.hotelpradeep.com; Kabir Chaura Rd; s Rs 1100-2100, d Rs 1400-2600; 🖳) Behind the unusual classical façade are very smart air-con rooms with baths and minibars (some with balconies), but the standout feature here is the amazing rooftop garden restaurant Eden.

Pallavi International Hotel (☎ 2356939; Hathwa Pl; s/d Rs 850/950, with AC Rs 1200/1400; 🖳 🖳) The antique-filled former palace of the maharaja of Bahadur is now a slightly eccentric heritage hotel where every room is different. The gardens, interior courtyards and small pool help create a tranquil atmosphere.

TOP END

Palace on Ganges (☎ 2315050; www.palaceonganges.com; Assi Ghat; d Rs 2990; 🖳 🖳) This immaculate heritage accommodation is an interior decorator's dream with each room carefully themed on a regional Indian style – the colonial, Rajasthan and Jodhpur rooms are among the best. Some front rooms have balconies or views over Assi Ghat. The hotel has a quality multicuisine rooftop restaurant.

Hotel Taj Ganges (☎ 2503001; www.tajhotels.com; Raja Bazaar Rd; d/ste from US$175/220; 🖳 🖳 🖳) Still the number-one place by a long way in Varanasi, this five-star luxury hotel combines Western comforts and Indian style. You can walk, cycle or take a maharaja's buggy ride around the 5-hectare grounds, which contain fruit trees, a tennis court, pool, an outdoor yoga centre and the old maharaja's guesthouse.

Eating
OLD CITY & THE GHATS

Apsara Restaurant (☎ 3258554; 24/42 Ganga Mahal; meals around Rs 20-50; 🖳) This popular, reasonably priced air-con restaurant has a cosy feel with cushioned seats, good music and friendly staff. The endless menu tries to please everyone with Indian, Chinese, Continental, Japanese, Israeli and Korean food.

Vaatika Cafe (Assi Ghat; meals Rs 25-90) This outdoor *dhaba* (snack bar) almost in the river and overlooking Assi Ghat serves up pies, pasta and pizzas baked in a wood-fired oven and is a relaxing place for breakfast.

Bread of Life Bakery (☎ 2275012; www.bolbar.com; 322 Shivala Rd; bakery items Rs 10-65, meals Rs 55-110; 🕙 8am-9pm; 🖳) As well as tempting sweets and pastries from the bakery, there are Continental and Chinese dishes, soups, salads, pasta and sandwiches. Eat with a conscience as profits go to a local charity.

New Keshari Ruchikar Byanjan (Dasaswamedh Ghat Rd; meals Rs 40-100; 🖳) The upstairs pure veg restaurant is the brightest along this busy road and popular with families. Downstairs, premium ice creams are Rs 40.

Lotus Lounge (Mansarowar Ghat; mains Rs 20-140; 🕙 7am-10pm) Overlooking Mansarowar Ghat on the water's edge, this restaurant is hard to beat. With a mosaic floor and loungy furniture, it's a great place to relax and enjoy an ambitious menu of mostly Continental food, with dishes like Thai curry, Tibetan *momos* and Goan specialities thrown in.

Brown Bread Bakery (mains Rs 20-110; 🖳) In the alleys of the old city not far from Dasaswamedh Ghat, this laidback café is the perfect spot to relax on cushions at the low tables and enjoy homebaked bread, cakes, pastries and dynamite traveller food.

Yafah Restaurant (Hotel Divya; meals Rs 40-220) Middle Eastern flavours waft from this elegant restaurant. *Baba ghanoi, tahina,* mousaka and falafel share the menu with Indian and Chinese dishes. Occasional live classical music.

Dolphin Restaurant (dishes Rs 45-225; 🕑 6am-11pm) Perched high above Manmandir Ghat, this rooftop restaurant at Rashmi Guest House is a fine place for breakfast after a morning boat ride, or for an evening meal of solid traveller-oriented fare.

OTHER AREAS

Poonam & Eden Restaurant (Hotel Pradeep, Kabir Chaura Rd; meals Rs 75-130; 🔀) The rooftop Eden restaurant, complete with garden, manicured lawn and wrought-iron furniture, is a lovely place for a candlelit evening meal, while the downstairs Poonam features quality Indian specialities in smart surroundings.

El Parador (☎ 9839716157; off Parade Kothi; meals Rs 60-160; 🕑 8am-10pm) Fancy a buffalo steak, followed by waffles for dessert? Not far from the station this Nepali-run restaurant is pricey (most mains are over Rs 100) but with home-made pasta, chicken souvlaki, crepes and Tibetan *momos*, it's worthwhile.

Canton Restaurant (Hotel Surya, The Mall; meals Rs 30-120; 🔀) The air-con dining room at the Hotel Surya has a colonial elegance and on warm evenings you can eat out in the garden. The menu is probably a bit ambitious with Indian, Chinese, Continental, Korean and even Mexican dishes, but the food is good.

Varuna Restaurant (Hotel Taj Ganges, Raja Bazaar Rd; meals Rs 150-450; 🕑 7-10.30pm) One of Varanasi's top restaurants, Varuna is elegant without being stuffy and extravagant without being too expensive. The kitchen specialises in classic North Indian and Afghan dishes, and there's live sitar and tabla music nightly from 7.30pm.

Drinking

There's a discreet **wine shop** (Shivala Rd) between Godaulia Crossing and Assi Ghat, but otherwise head to midrange and top-end hotels away from the old city for the bars – **Prinsep Bar** (opposite; at Hotel Taj Ganges) has an air of class.

Shopping

Varanasi is justifiably famous for silk brocades and beautiful Benares saris, but being led by touts and rickshaw drivers to a silk shop is a fast-track to being taken for a ride. The following places are legit.

Ganga Silk (Shivala Rd) A good place to start is this small shop above the Bread of Life Bakery. Prices are fixed and the staff can explain the different types of silk.

Open Hand Shop & Cafe (☎ 2369751; www.openhandonline.com; 🕑 Mon-Sat) This shop near Assi Ghat offers a wide choice of quality handmade goods at fixed prices, including textiles, wood and paper products, plus good plunger coffee.

Benaras Art Culture (☎ 2313615; Shivala Rd) Although many of the artworks at this fixed-price gallery are expensive, it's worth a browse through the wonderful centuries-old *haveli* (traditional, ornately decorated residence) to see quality carvings, sculptures and art.

Varanasi is also a good place to shop for sitars and tablas.

Ankit Music House (☎ 9336567134; Sakarkand Gali) has locally manufactured sitars starting from Rs 3000 and tablas from Rs 2500.

Getting There & Away

AIR

There are no direct flights from the North-east, but you can reach Kolkata through Delhi on **Indian Airlines** (☎ 2502529; The Mall), **Jet Airways** (☎ 2506444; Krishnayatan Bldg, Kennedy Rd, Cantonment) or **Air Sahara** (☎ 2507872; Mint House, Cantonment). Indian Airlines also has a flight to Kathmandu.

BUS

Varanasi's chaotic **bus station** (☎ 2203476) is a few hundred metres east of Varanasi Junction train station. Frequent express buses run to Gorakhpur (Rs 121, seven hours) and one air-con bus goes to Bodhgaya (Rs 252, seven hours).

Buses to Sarnath (Rs 10, 40 minutes) leave from outside the Varanasi Junction train station, as do share jeeps (Rs 20) to Mughal Serai train station.

TRAIN

Luggage theft and drugged food are risks, so keep your wits about you.

Varanasi Junction train station (☎ 132), also known as Varanasi Cantonment (Cantt) train station, is the main station. Foreign tourist quota tickets must be purchased at the **Foreign**

Tourist Assistance Bureau (☺ 8am-8pm Mon-Sat, 8am-2pm Sun) in Varanasi Junction train station.

Many of the faster trains between Delhi and Kolkata stop at **Mughal Serai train station** (☎ 255703), 12km southeast of Varanasi, but you can make reservations at Varanasi. Share jeeps (Rs 20, 40 minutes) are the best way to travel between the two stations, but buses and taxis are also available.

Useful trains include the overnight *Doon Express* to Kolkata (sleeper/3AC/2AC Rs 253/716/1027, 14½ hours, 4.25pm) the *Howrah Mail* to Patna (Rs 112/315/452, five hours, 5pm) and the *Gorakhpur Express* to Gorakhpur (Rs 114/320/459, six hours, 1pm).

TO/FROM NEPAL

From Varanasi's bus station buses leave for Sunauli (Rs 172, 10 hours, nine daily), on the border with Nepal, from around 5am. Various travel agents sell 'through' bus tickets from Varanasi to Kathmandu or Pokhara for Rs 600, and partner agents in Pokhara and Kathmandu sell similar tickets in the opposite direction. In reality, *everyone* has to change buses at the border, and we receive regular reports of travellers being coerced into buying new tickets for onward travel. It's easier and safer to do the journey in two stages – agents offer tickets as far as Sunauli for Rs 300.

By train the best option is to get to Gorakhpur and then transfer to a local bus to Sunauli. Alternatively, fly direct from Varanasi to Kathmandu (US$110) with Indian Airlines.

Getting Around

Varanasi's **Babatpur airport** (☎ 2622081) is 22km northwest of the city. An autorickshaw should cost Rs 150 and a taxi Rs 350. Local buses charge just Rs 5, but routes can be confusing. You can pick them up outside the Varanasi Junction train station. The station also has prepaid booths for taxis and autorickshaws – to Dasaswamedh Ghat, you'll pay Rs 60/150 by autorickshaw/taxi; to Benares Hindu University, you'll pay Rs 80/200. When hailing an auto in the street, drivers always up the prices so bargain hard.

Cycle-rickshaws are useful for short distances or in the old city where motor vehicles are banned, but you'll have to fight to be taken to where you actually want to go and not a commission paying hotel. Prices are always elevated so bargain down – Rs 10 to 20 is fair for a short trip like Godaulia crossing to Assi Ghat.

SARNATH
☎ 0542

Buddha came to Sarnath, 10km northeast of Varanasi, to preach his message of the middle way to nirvana after he achieved enlightenment at Bodhgaya. He gave his famous first sermon here to a handful of followers in the 5th century BC and Ashoka raised a major Buddhist colony here 200 years later, marked by magnificent stupas and monasteries and an engraved Ashoka pillar. When the Chinese traveller Xuan Zang dropped by in AD 640, Sarnath boasted a 100m-high stupa and monasteries housing 1500 monks. However, soon after, Buddhism went into decline, and when Muslim invaders destroyed and desecrated the monasteries, Sarnath disappeared altogether. It was only rediscovered in 1835 by British archaeologists.

Today it's one of the four most important sites on the Buddhist circuit (along with Bodhgaya, Kushinagar and Lumbini in Nepal), and attracts followers from around the world. An easy day or half-day trip from Varanasi, Sarnath is a green and peaceful place to spend some time and learn about Buddhist history. There's tourist information at the Rahi UP Tourist Bungalow, but at the time of writing a new **Modern Reception Centre** (MRC; Ashoka Marg) was due to open opposite the archaeological museum, with internet café, tourist information and money-changing facilities.

Sights

DHAMEKH STUPA & BUDDHIST RUINS

Set in a peaceful **park** (Indian/foreigner Rs 5/100, video Rs 25; ☺ sunrise-sunset) of monastery ruins is the impressive 34m **Dhanekh Stupa**, which marks the spot where the Buddha preached his first sermon. Parts of the building date back to 200 BC and nearby is an **Ashoka pillar** engraved with one of the emperor's famous edicts. It was originally topped by the four-lion capital that provided the inspiration for the Indian national symbol, now housed in the nearby Archaeological Museum.

CHAUKHANDI STUPA

This large ruined **stupa** (☺ sunrise-sunset) dates back to the 5th century AD, and marks the spot where Buddha met his first disciples. The incongruous tower on top was built in the 16th century to commemorate the visit of Emperor Humayun.

MULGANDHA KUTI VIHAR & DEER PARK

This modern **temple** (☎ 2585595; ☯ 4-11am & 1.30-8pm) was completed in 1931 by the Mahabodhi Society. The walls inside are decorated with large frescoes by Japanese artist Kosetsu Nosi. Buddha's first sermon is chanted daily, starting between 6pm and 7pm depending on the season. A **bodhi tree** growing outside was transplanted in 1931 from the tree in Anuradhapura, Sri Lanka, reputedly an offspring of the original tree in Bodhgaya under which Buddha attained enlightenment.

Behind the temple is a large **deer enclosure** (admission Rs 2; ☯ sunrise-sunset), together with some aviaries and a crocodile pool.

ARCHAEOLOGICAL MUSEUM

This superb, modern **museum** (admission Rs 2; ☯ 10am-5pm Sat-Thu), which houses ancient treasures such as the famous lion capital from the Ashoka pillar, which has been adopted as India's national emblem. Other finds include bas reliefs, sculptures and Buddha images unearthed from the Sarnath region. Cameras, mobile phones, lighters and bags must be left in free lockers at the front gate.

Sleeping & Eating

Sarnath is only 10km from Varanasi so it's easy to day trip, but it's possible to stay in some of the modern temples, and there are several homestays, including the basic but friendly **Jain Paying Guest House** (☎ 2595621; d Rs 100-350) and **Agrawal Paying Guest House** (☎ 221007; r Rs 400-500), with a beautiful garden, eight spotless rooms and a refined owner.

Rahi UP Tourist Bungalow (☎ 2595965; dm/s/d Rs 100/500/550, s/d with AC Rs 700/750; ☒) UP Tourism place, with pleasant lawns, reasonable rooms and an airy restaurant.

Getting There & Away

Local buses (Rs 10, 40 minutes) depart regularly from the south side of Varanasi Junction train station. An autorickshaw (30 minutes) costs about Rs 100 return from the train station, or Rs 180 from the old city or Assi Ghat. A taxi costs around Rs 300 return.

GORAKHPUR

☎ 0551 / pop 624,570

For most travellers Gorakhpur is merely a waystation on the road between Varanasi and Nepal. There are no major tourist attractions in the city, but you can visit a **Buddhist museum** near the lake on the southern outskirts, and the important **Gorakhnath Temple**, devoted to Guru Gorakhnath, situated 4km west of the station.

Information

Gorakhpur's train station is a convenient onestop place for information. Inside is the **UP Tourism office** (☎ 2335450; ☯ 10am-5pm Mon-Sat) and just outside on the concourse is a State Bank of India ATM and the excellent **Railtel Cyber Express** (per hr Rs 23; ☯ 24hr; ☒). Hotel Bobina (below) can exchange travellers cheques and currency.

Sleeping & Eating

The street opposite the train station has a dozen or more cheap hotels, and while the area is noisy and grubby, some of the choices are surprisingly good. With the bus station close by, this is the area of choice for backpackers looking for a quick entry and exit.

Hotel Elora (☎ 2200647; s/d Rs 150/250, with AC Rs 350/450; ☒) Elora is an appealing cheapie with a breezy rooftop, and rooms with TV and hot water. Hotel Sunrise (☎ 2337458), next door, is virtually identical.

Hotel Bobina (☎ 2336663; bobina@ndb.vsnl.net.in; Nepal Rd; s/d Rs 500/600, with AC from Rs 700/800; ☒ ☒) This unusual hotel has all the trappings of a mini-resort – palm trees in the garden, a small pool, very serviceable gym, and a good restaurant and bar – and rooms are better than the price suggests. It's 1.5km west of the train station.

Bobi's Restaurant (Main Rd; meals Rs 30-80) Opposite Hotel President on the busy main street south of the train station, this place is clean and serves reliable food.

Getting There & Away

Hourly buses run from the main bus stand, about 300m south of the train station, to Sunauli (Rs 56, 2½ hours) on the Nepal border. Buses to Varanasi (Rs 112, seven hours) leave from the separate Katchari bus stand, south of the main bus stand, but the train is a better option.

Touts are dead keen to sell you 'through' bus tickets to Kathmandu or Pokhara from Rs 395, but everyone has to change buses at the border so these deals simply aren't worth it. There are no private buses to Sunauli – only local buses – and no through buses direct to Nepal.

Gorakhpur has direct train connections with Varanasi (2nd/sleeper/3A Rs 65/114/320, 5½ hours, four daily) and Kolkata (Rs 292/823, 23 hours, 1pm). Counter 811 serves foreign tourists.

SUNAULI & THE NEPAL BORDER

☎ 05522

Straddling the India–Nepal border, Sunauli is a dusty town that offers little more than a bus stop, a hotel, a few shops and a border post on the Indian side – it's just 4km on the other side to the more pleasant town of Bhairawa, leaping-off point for Lumbini, the birthplace of Buddha. Buses drop you 200m from the Indian immigration office, and there's a convenient Nepali bus stand just across the border. If you end up staying overnight, wear mosquito repellent – they swarm around here.

Rahi Tourist Bungalow (☎ 238201; rahiniranjana@up -tourism.com; dm Rs 75, s/d from Rs 250/300, with AC Rs 500/600; 🔀), located near the bus stand, is an UP Tourism concrete bunker and is the only recommended accommodation on the Indian side of Sunauli. There's a restaurant and the rooms are comfortable enough.

The Nepali side of Sunauli has a few cheap hotels, outdoor restaurants and a more upbeat atmosphere, but most travellers prefer to stay in Bhairawa, or get straight on a bus to Lumbini, Kathmandu or Pokhara.

Getting There & Away

Regular buses run from Sunauli to Gorakhpur (Rs 56, 2½ hours) until 9pm. Early morning and early evening buses run to Varanasi (Rs 150, 11 hours). A better option is to take the bus to Gorakhpur and a train from there.

Be wary of buying 'through' tickets from Kathmandu or Pokhara to Varanasi (or vice versa) – see p284 for more information.

EXCURSIONS AROUND INDIA

NEPAL

With the improving political situation in Nepal, this fabled mountain kingdom is once again becoming a favoured stop on the Indian overland trail. The border crossing at Kakarbhitta, near Darjeeling, is the eastern doorway to Nepal, opening up some fascinating side trips to the cities of the eastern Terai on the way west to Kathmandu. Many travellers head right across the country to Kathmandu and Pokhara, then cross back into India at Sunauli, continuing to Varanasi or back to the Northeast by train.

Information

Travel to Nepal is made easier by hassle-free border crossings and direct onward buses to major cities across Nepal. At the time this book went to print, the political situation in Nepal was stable, with Maoists leaders working as part of the interim government and the UN overseeing the disarmament of rebel forces. However, it makes sense to check the political situation before you travel, in case there has been any resumption of hostilities.

FOREIGN EXCHANGE

The Nepali currency is the Nepali rupee (NRs), divided into 100 paisa. The Nepali rupee is pegged to the Indian rupee at a fixed exchange rate of INRs 100 = NRs 160. Moneychangers along the Indian border can generally be relied upon to swap Indian rupees for Nepali rupees at the official rate, and hotels and shops in border towns often accept payment in either currency. You can exchange major international currencies at banks and exchange counters in most big towns in Nepal. ATMs are found in larger cities, but elsewhere, carry travellers cheques or cash. You'll need US dollars in cash if you intend to purchase a visa at any of the land borders between India and Nepal.

TOURIST INFORMATION

The Nepal tourism board offers extensive information through its website www.welco menepal.com. Information is arranged into practical tips, themed itineraries, and specialist sections on rafting, trekking and mountaineering. Other useful websites for information on Nepal:

Nepal Information (www.nepalinformation.com)
Nepal Tourism Department (www.tourism.gov.np)
Trek Info (www.trekinfo.com)
Visit Nepal (www.visitnepal.com)

VISAS

Indians can visit Nepal without a visa; for most other nationalities, single-entry tourist visas lasting 60 days are available on arrival at Kathmandu's Tribhuvan international airport or at any of the border crossings into Nepal for US$30 (two passport photos required). This fee should be paid in US dollars cash. You can also obtain a visa in advance from Nepali missions in India – see p324.

Multiple-entry visas cost US$80, but these tend to only be issued outside Nepal. Transit visas are free for visits of three days or less. Once inside Nepal, you can extend your tourist visa in 30-day increments up to a maximum of 150 days in any calendar year. For more information, see the **Department of Immigration website** (www.immi.gov.np).

Sights

With the snowcapped peaks of the Himalaya rising above every valley, the whole of Nepal is a 'sight'. Just walking through this magnificent countryside is a reason to visit all by itself and the country is fabulously well set up for trekkers, with agencies in all the major towns and inexpensive teahouse accommodation along the main trekking routes. However, you need permits for certain routes and you must pay a conservation fee for routes that pass through the Annapurna, Manaslu, Khangchendzonga and Makalu Himalaya, available in Kathmandu or Pokhara.

Every visitor to Nepal makes a stop in **Kathmandu**. There are few cities in the world that have such a mystical, medieval air. The Nepali capital is an atmospheric tangle of narrow alleyways, dotted with ancient Buddhist and Hindu temples and palaces. Must-sees include temple-fringed Durbar Sq, the winding lanes of Old Kathmandu, the sacred ghats at Pashupatinath, the iconic Buddhist stupas at Swayambhunath and Bodhnath, and traveller-tastic Thamel, where you'll find most of the restaurants, souvenir shops and traveller hotels.

There are more medieval cities dotted around the Kathmandu Valley, accessible by local bus and taxi. Just across the Bagmati River is ancient **Patan**, with its own temple-clogged Durbar Sq and 600 stupas and small Buddhist monasteries hidden away in the backstreets. About 4km east of Kathmandu is Bhaktapur, an even more pristine medieval city of cobbled, pedestrian streets. On the ridge behind Bhaktapur is Nagarkot, the best of the viewpoints around the Kathmandu Valley, offering uninterrupted views towards Mt Everest.

To the west of Kathmandu, a single snaking highway plunges into the valley of the Trisuli River, branching south to the Terai (Nepal's plains), and west to **Pokhara**, the start and end point for treks in the Annapurna range. En route, you can detour to historic Newari townships, like Bandipur and Gorkha, for a taste of what life was like in Nepal before tourism took off here. Pokhara itself has a stunning location on peaceful Phewa Tal, a millpond-calm lake that reflects the looming peaks of Mt Machhapuchhare and the Annapurnas.

From here, a network of trekking routes extends right around the Annapurna massif, including the nine-day Jomsom trek and the gruelling three-week **Annapurna Circuit**. If you just want the views, head to the viewpoint at Sarangkot, on the north shore of Phewa Tal, or hike through the forest to the Peace Pagoda on the ridge above the lake.

There are more epic treks in the foothills of Mt Everest – known to locals as Sagarmatha. The two- or three-week **Everest Base Camp** trek is arguably the most famous trek in the world, and smaller numbers of trekkers attempt the two-week Langtang trek to the foot of the Langtang glacier. Other trekking areas in the east and west of Nepal are slowly re-opening with the restoration of law and order following the Maoist ceasefire.

Down on the plains, **Chitwan National Park** is the other famous string in Nepal's bow. Sprawling along the banks of the Rapti and Narayani Rivers, this densely forested reserve has tigers, one-horned rhinos, wild buffalo, and numerous species of deer and crocodiles, best seen on guided walks or from the back of one of the park elephants. You can stay in lodges deep inside the park, or simpler backpacker lodges in the village of Sauraha.

Another highlight of the Terai is **Tansen**, an atmospheric medieval city on the back road between Pokhara and Sunauli. From here, you can continue south to Lumbini, the birthplace of the historical Buddha, just a short hop from the Indian border post at Sunauli. In the west of Nepal, **Royal Bardia National Park** has similar wildlife to Chitwan but sees far fewer visitors. Heading east, Janakpur is the former capital of the Mithila kingdom, and you can ride on the roof of the narrow-gauge train that runs down to the Indian border (only Indians can cross here). It's an easy stop on the way from Kakarbhitta to Kathmandu.

For more on all these sights, read Lonely Planet's *Nepal* and *Trekking in Nepal*.

Getting There & Around

Kathmandu is well connected to India by air and by road. Indian Airlines and Cosmic Air offer three weekly flights between Kolkata and Kathmandu, with one-way fares starting at just US$95. Travelling by land, several border crossings are accessible from the Northeast, but be wary of agents offering 'direct' bus tickets – everyone has to change buses at the border.

The easiest option is to take the train to Siliguri in West Bengal, then a share jeep to the border crossing at Kakarbhitta. Alternative crossings include Raxaul in Bihar and Sunauli in Uttar Pradesh – see p324 for details. There's a NRs 1695 departure tax if you leave Nepal by air (NRs 1356 if travelling to India, Bhutan, Pakistan or Bangladesh), but no tax if you leave by land.

For travel within Nepal, the main options are domestic flights, buses, minivans, share-jeeps, taxis and rented motorcycles. Avoid night buses wherever possible – Nepal has a shocking record when it comes to night-time road accidents.

BANGLADESH

The massive rise of tourism in the subcontinent has largely passed Bangladesh by. This is a massive oversight, as the country is a mesmerising blend of jungles and beaches, mosques and monasteries, heaving modern cities and silent ruins, with the same exotic air that suffuses life in India. Better still, you'll only have to share the sights with a handful of other tourists. Until 1947, this was the eastern half of the Indian state of Bengal, and Bengalis on both sides of the border share the same sense of regional pride. Travellers to the Northeast can easily squeeze in a trip through Bangladesh on the way from Kolkata to Tripura – in fact, next to taking the plane, this is the most direct way to reach the Northeast states.

Information

Transport from the Northeast to Bangladesh is fast and frequent, with daily buses and numerous flights from Kolkata and other regional hubs. The overland route from Kolkata to Dhaka and on to Agartala in Tripura provides a neat shortcut to the far Northeast, and there are also less used crossings to Meghalaya and the West Bengal hills. However, you may need to get a special endorsement on your visa to leave Bangladesh by land – see visas, below.

FOREIGN EXCHANGE

The currency of Bangladesh is the taka (Tk), which is divided into 100 paisa. Indian rupees and Bangladeshi taka are easy to exchange around the borders and shops, and hotels and buses often accept either currency as payment. When travelling around Bangladesh, the best currency to carry is US dollars, preferably in cash. Most moneychangers can change US dollars to taka, and taka back to US dollars when you leave (keep hold of enough taka to pay the departure tax before leaving Bangladesh). Standard Chartered and HSBC branches in major cities offer foreign exchange and have ATMs that accept international cards.

TOURIST INFORMATION

The **National Tourism Organisation of Bangladesh** (www.bangladeshtourism.gov.bd) provides information on planning a trip to Bangladesh, but the servers in Bangladesh are often offline due to bandwidth problems. More reliable sources of information include:

Bangladesh.com (www.bangladesh.com)
Bangladesh Online (www.bangladeshonline.com/tourism)
Discovery Bangladesh (www.discoverybangladesh.com)

VISAS

Visas for Bangladesh must be obtained in advance from Bangladeshi missions overseas – this is easily done in Kolkata (see p300) and **Agartala** (see the boxed text, p224). Fees vary considerably with nationality; for a 90-day single- or double-entry tourist visa, British citizens pay US$65, Americans US$100, Australians US$32 and Germans just US$15. Visas must be used within six months of the date of issue. A special reciprocal visa system exists for Indian citizens – contact local Bangladeshi missions for more information here.

To exit Bangladesh overland, you will need an additional road permit, or 'change of route' permit, issued by the Directorate of Immigration and Passports in Dhaka – see p323 for more information. Before leaving Bangladesh, you must pay your departure tax at a designated branch of Sonali Bank, which may be some distance from the actual border crossing.

Sights

There's more to see in Bangladesh than most people realise, including some stunning national parks, captivating coastal towns and traditional tribal culture in the Chittagong hills. Most visitors start off their trip in **Dhaka**, the fast and frenetic capital, which sprawls along the Buriganga River, a tributary of India's mighty Brahmaputra (known in Bangladesh as the Jamuna). The Buriganga is one of the busiest waterways in south Asia and the crush of boats at Dhaka's Sadarghat has to be seen to be believed. Dhaka is also jam-packed with interesting museums and historic architecture – including the Ahsan Manzil palace, Lalbagh Fort and numerous mosques, temples, Mughal ruins and gardens.

The ruins of the old capital at **Sonargaon** are an easy day trip from Dhaka, or you can take in some peaceful bird-watching in Madhupur Forest reserve, near Mymensingh. Southeast of Dhaka, Jessore is the gateway to the Bangladeshi half of the Sunderbans delta, and the closest town to Benapol, the main border crossing between India and Bangladesh. Most people start their explorations of the Sunderbans in Khulna, where agents offer multiday live-aboard boat trips through the creeks. A hidden gem in this corner of Bangladesh is Bagerhat, home to the largest medieval mosque in the country.

West of the Sunderbans is peaceful Barasil division, home to several interesting small towns with large Hindu populations. Nearby Kaukata is the nearest beach area to Dhaka, and much calmer than the more famous Cox's Bazaar. Further east is the busy port of Chittagong, Bangladesh's second city. Most of Bangladesh's Adivasis live in the surrounding **Hill Tracts**, an extension of the Mizo Hills. The Buddhist Chakma tribe live in small villages around Kaptai Lake – the regional capital, Rangamati, has numerous Buddhist shrines and you can arrange boat trips to traditional Chakma villages. **Chittagong** itself is interesting for its colonial relics – British and Portuguese – and the giant shipwrecking yards just outside town.

Down on the south coast, almost touching Myanmar, **Cox's Bazaar** is Bangladesh's most famous seaside resort, with an appealing, patrolled beach and several Burmese-style Buddhist monasteries. For those in the know, Inani Beach and the tiny coral island of **St Mar-**tin's are even better – St Martin's even offers top-notch diving and snorkelling.

In the north of Bangladesh, Rajshahi division is the rural heartland of Bangladesh. The bustling market town of Bogra is the starting point for excursions to **Mahasthangarh** – Bangladesh's oldest city, dating back to at least the 3rd century BC. Nearby, the ruined Somapuri Vihara temple at **Paharpur** was once the largest Buddhist temple south of the Himalaya. More historic ruins and *rajbaris* (landowners' palaces) can be seen at Puthia, close to Rajshahi, and at Gaud, the former capital of the Sena kings of Bengal. In the far northwest, Kantanagar Temple is a rare Bangladeshi example of the Bengali-hut style of Hindu architecture. Wedged against the Indian border on the north side of the Teesta River, the tiny town of Burimari offers a quick route to Siliguri and the West Bengal hills.

On the far side of the country, **Sylhet** was part of Assam before Partition, and it still has small communities of Khasi, Manipuri and Tripuri tribal people. Muslims from across Bangladesh make pilgrimages to Sylhet to pay their respects at the shrine of the 14th-century Sufi mystic Hazrat Shah Jalal. Nearby, **Srimangal** is the centre of the Bangladeshi tea industry and you can arrange tours to surrounding tea estates. Just 8km from town is Lowacherra Forest Reserve, home to rare Hoolock gibbons. Up against the Meghalayan border, tiny hamlet of Tamabil offers a backroute to Dawki, with connections on to Cherrapunjee and Shillong.

For more on all these sights, read Lonely Planet's *Bangladesh*.

Getting There & Around

Dhaka has good connections to Kolkata by bus and plane. Indian Airlines, Air Sahara, Biman Bangladesh and GMG Airlines all offer regular flights between the two cities, with fares starting from US$69 one way. GMG also has a useful flight from Kolkata to Chittagong. Travelling by land, express buses run from Kolkata all the way through to Dhaka, or you can change at Benapol. Heading on from Dhaka, trains run daily to Akhaura, about 9km from the Indian border post at Agartala. There's a Tk 2500 departure tax if you leave Bangladesh by air (Tk 1800 for travel to India, Bhutan, Pakistan or Nepal). Some border posts also charge a variable departure tax if you leave by land.

Local transport options include buses, trains, planes and boats, most famously the Bangladesh Rocket – an old-fashioned paddle-wheel steamer that runs upriver from Dhaka to Khulna. It's a great experience but the name is deceptive: the journey takes around 30 hours. When it comes to urban transport, autorick-shaws are known locally as 'Baby Taxis'.

BHUTAN

Perhaps the closest thing to real Shangri-La, Bhutan has managed to preserve its 1800-year old Buddhist culture by strictly managing the flow of tourists across its borders. All visitors to Bhutan must join a tour with an approved travel agent and there's a US$200 daily fee for every visitor (US$165 from July to August), which covers food, accommodation, transport and guides – see Visas on right. For those willing to dig deep, Bhutan offers a window onto a way of life that has changed little in centuries – a magical world of *dzongs* (monastery-fortresses), vivid Buddhist rituals and rugged Himalayan vistas.

Information

Informal day trips for foreigners across the border between Phuentsholing and Jaigon are no longer possible, so everybody who visits Bhutan must come via an organised trip with an approved agent. This doesn't mean that travel in Bhutan has to be boring! Although the tours follow set itineraries, there are plenty of ways to add in sights off the beaten track, and Bhutan is an increasingly popular destination for motorcycle tours – often combined with trips to Sikkim and Assam.

FOREIGN EXCHANGE

The currency of Bhutan is the ngultrum (Nu), divided into 100 chetrum. Exchange counters at the airport and branches of the Bhutan National Bank can change most international currencies into ngultrum. Travellers cheques are also widely accepted at banks and most hotels. The Bhutan National Bank branch in Thimpu has an ATM but it currently only accepts Bhutanese cards. It makes sense to carry US dollars cash for any major purchases – for example, buying paintings or Bhutanese weaving.

TOURIST INFORMATION

The main source of information on Bhutan is the state-run **Tourist Authority of Bhutan** (www

.tourism.gov.bt). Their website has a list of approved tour operators and extensive information on travel, culture and festivals in Bhutan – including the masked Tsechu dances at important monasteries. Other useful resources include:

Bhutan Tourism Corporation (www.kingdomofbhutan.com)
Bhutan Portal (www.bhutan.gov.bt)
Bootan (www.bootan.com)

VISAS

The US$200 per day visa system is part of a well-thought-out strategy to protect Bhutan's fragile culture from destructive foreign influences. Put simply, without the fee system, the traditional culture that people come to Bhutan to see probably wouldn't be here. Remember that the fee is all-inclusive, so your food, transport, guides and accommodation are all covered. Trekkers pay the same fee, inclusive of camping equipment, mountain guides and porters' fees. Around 35% of the fee goes towards social-welfare programmes that directly benefit the Bhutanese people. Note that solo travellers and small groups pay an additional surcharge of between US$40 and US$30 per person per day.

The Tourist Authority of Bhutan – see under Tourist Information on left – maintains a list of approved tour operators online at www.tourism.gov.bt. These agents will make all the arrangements for your itinerary and collect the daily fee (in advance). You will not be able to board a Druk Air flight into Bhutan unless you have prearranged your tour. There is an additional US$20 fee for the actual visa, which is stamped into your passport on arrival in Bhutan (bring two passport photos).

The initial visa is valid for a maximum of 15 days, but the exact duration will depend on your itinerary – extensions are possible in Thimphu for longer trips. Indian tourists are exempt from the daily fee but they still need a special entry permit from an approved tour operator. Special discounts apply to children (free for under five years old, half-price for children aged six to 12) and students get a 25% discount. For everyone else, there's a 10% discount if you stay more than 10 nights and a 20% discount if you stay more than 20 nights.

Sights

Until 1964, the kingdom of Bhutan was only accessible on foot, but these days, most visitors arrive by air at Paro, or by road at Phuentsholing. The first port of call for most visitors is the capital, **Thimphu**, which is dominated by Trashi Chhoe Dzong, the fortress-monastery that houses the offices of the government and the king of Bhutan (until the proposed parliamentary elections in 2008). The city is packed with *goembas* (monasteries), *chortens* (reliquary stupas) and cultural institutes preserving traditional Bhutanese literature, arts and medicine.

The Thimphu Valley is peppered with monasteries and forts that make easy day trips from the capital – **Tango Goemba**, **Chari Goemba** and **Simtokha Dzong** are all worth a visit. Venturing west, Paro has Bhutan's only airport, as well as the national museum and famous Paro Dzong, perhaps the finest example of monastery architecture in the country. Also in the area are the Kyichu Lhakhang temple, reputedly founded in AD 747 by Padmasambhava, and the restored Taktshang Goemba, perched on a sheer cliff-face above pine-clad hills.

Heading east from Thimphu, a scenic mountain road climbs over the 3150m Dochu La to the idyllic **Punakha valley**, a peaceful patchwork of fields and Buddhist villages. Historic Punakha Dzong was the former seat of the Bhutanese royal family. A challenging trekking route runs north from Punakha to Gasa and Laya village, home to the minority Laya people – this route can be trekked as a loop from Punakha, or tacked onto the end of the longer Jhomolhari Trek from Paro or Thimphu. It's also a stop on the breathless 23-day Snowman Trek, widely regarded as the hardest trek in the world.

From Punakha, the main road runs south to Wangdue Phodrang, gateway to the Phobjikha Valley. Half of the valley is set aside as **Black Mountain National Park**, a major conservation area for black-necked cranes, and there are sweeping views from Gangte Goemba. After leaving Gante, the road climbs over the 3400m Pele La, offering eagle-eye views of Jhomolhari (7219m), Bhutan's second-highest mountain. On the far side is **Trongsa**, a Tibetan-influenced market town lorded over by vast, sprawling Trongsa Dzong.

Another crossing over mountain passes takes you to **Jakar** at the mouth of the legendary Chokksor (Bumthang) Valley. Jakar has more temples and palaces and another fine *dzong* – reputedly the largest in Bhutan. The surrounding **Chokksor Valley** is crammed with temples and monasteries, all easy to reach on foot. Highlights include the temples of Jambey Lhakhang and Kurjey Lhakhang and Tamshing Goemba, founded by the Bhutanese lama Pema Lingpa in 1501. Heading east again, the road continues to **Mongar**, where a twisting mountain road cuts north to Lhuentse, a ridge-top village with a dramatic *dzong*, surrounded by sheer drops.

Heading on from Mongar, the main road continues to **Trashigang**, the largest town in eastern Bhutan. Trashigang has a handsome *dzong*, and there are numerous *goembas* and weaving projects in the surrounding hills. North of Trashigang, Trashi Yangtse province nestles up against Arunachal Pradesh; the Khora chorten here was styled after the famous stupa at Bodhnath in Nepal. Few travellers roam into the southern provinces of Bhutan, but **Phuentsholing** is the overland border crossing to India, accessible from Siliguri by bus, or by train and bus via Alipurduar. If you arrive in Bhutan overland, you'll get your first taste of Bhutanese scenery on the highway north to Thimphu – see p323 for more information.

For more on all these sights, read Lonely Planet's *Nepal, Bhutan* and *Trekking in Nepal*.

Getting There & Around

Druk Air (www.drukair.com.bt) is the only airline permitted to fly to Bhutan's Paro airport. The national carrier offers flights to Paro from Kolkata, Delhi, Bodhgaya, Kathmandu, Dhaka and Bangkok, but only to passengers who have prearranged a tour with an approved agent. Public buses run from Thimphu to Phuentsholing, Paro and Punakha, but most people travel in tour buses or rented cars and jeeps provided by their tour operator. A small die-hard group of travellers visit by mountain bike or on organised motorcycle tours – see p326 and p331 for more information.

Directory

CONTENTS

ACCOMMODATION

The Northeast has accommodation to suit all budgets, from basic backpacker hotels with concrete floors and cold showers to the former palaces of maharajas. Most towns have something for every pocketbook, but rates vary widely as you travel around the Northeast – see p294.

Accommodation listings in this book appear in price order under the Sleeping heading (sometimes divided into budget, midrange and top-end categories) – scroll through the

> **BOOK ACCOMMODATION ONLINE**
>
> For more accommodation reviews and recommendations by Lonely Planet authors, check out the online booking service at www.lonelyplanet.com. You'll find the insider lowdown on the best places to stay and reviews are thorough and independent.

listings to find places that meet your budget and accommodation preferences.

Unless otherwise stated, tariffs in this book are based on the cheapest room in each category. Rates don't include taxes unless otherwise indicated. If the rates are seasonal, this will be indicated in the Sleeping section. Note that hotels in resort towns can triple their rates in the high season – advance bookings may be essential at these times.

Room quality can vary within hotels, so try to inspect a few rooms first. Avoid carpeted rooms at cheaper hotels unless you like the smell of mouldy socks. For the low-down on hotel bathrooms, see the boxed text, p294. Sound pollution can be a real pain (especially in urban centres). Pack good-quality earplugs and request a room that doesn't face onto a busy road.

Credit cards are accepted at most top-end hotels and some midrange places; budget hotels require cash. Most hotels ask for deposit at check-in – ask for a receipt and be wary of any request to sign a blank impression of your credit card. Verify the checkout time when you check-in – some hotels have a fixed checkout time (usually 10am or noon), while others give you 24 hours. Reservations are usually fine by phone without a deposit, but confirm your booking the day before you arrive.

Be aware that in tourist hot spots, hotels often 'borrow' the name of a thriving competitor to confuse travellers, paying commissions to taxi and rickshaw drivers who bring them unsuspecting customers – see p299.

Accommodation Options

As well as conventional hotels, there are some charming guesthouses in traditional village homes and numerous old colonial properties that swim with faded Raj charm. Standout options are indicated with the Our Pick icon – **our pick** – in this book.

BUDGET & MIDRANGE HOTELS

Shared bathrooms are only found at the cheapest hotels; most places offer rooms with private bathrooms of varying standards. Most rooms have ceiling fans, and better rooms have electric mosquito killers or window nets. Bringing your own sheets (or a sleeping bag liner) is a sound policy – some cheap places have sheets with more holes and stains than a string vest at an oyster-eating contest. Away from tourist areas, cheaper hotels may not take foreigners because they don't have the necessary foreigner-registration forms.

Midrange hotels usually offer comforts like carpets and Indian cable TV. Some places offer noisy 'air-coolers' that cool air by blowing it over cold water, but it's worth paying more for real air-conditioning. Not all cheap hotels are characterless. Every so often you stumble across a budget or midrange gem – an old house from the colonial era, an idyllic mountain cottage or the fading wing of a maharaja's palace.

Note that some cheaper hotels lock their doors at night. Members of staff normally sleep in the lobby but waking them up can be a challenge. Let the hotel know in advance if you are arriving or coming back to your room late in the evening.

CAMPING & TREKKING ACCOMMODATION

Camping is the only accommodation option on many trekking routes, and larger hotels may let you camp in the grounds for a small charge. Sikkim has a network of rudimentary trekkers' huts – most just offer floor space for travellers with sleeping bags and few offer meals, but they provide shelter from the elements. These places are often booked out by groups in peak season, so a tent is always a useful back up.

DORMITORY ACCOMMODATION

Many hotels have cheap dormitories, though these are often mixed and may be full of drunk drivers – not ideal conditions for single women. Better dorms are found at the handful of hostels run by the YMCA, YWCA, and the Salvation Army and (HI) Hostelling International-associate hostels (see www.yhaindia.org for listings). Tourist Bungalows run by state governments and railway retiring rooms also offer cheap dorm beds.

GOVERNMENT ACCOMMODATION & TOURIST BUNGALOWS

The Indian government maintains a network of guesthouses in remote areas for travelling officials and public workers, known variously as Rest Houses, Dak Bungalows, Circuit Houses, Public Works Department (PWD) Bungalows and Forest Rest Houses. These places may accept travellers if no government employees need the rooms, but you usually need permission to stay from local officials. If you arrange a tour to tribal areas of the Northeast, your guide will make all the arrangements for you.

Many state tourism departments also run their basic 'tourist bungalows' and more

---

PRACTICALITIES

- Electricity is 230V to 240V, 50 Hz AC and sockets are the three round-pin variety (two-pin sockets are also found). Blackouts are common.

- Officially India is metric. Terms you're likely to hear are: lakhs (one lakh = 100,000) and crores (one crore = 10 million).

- National English-language dailies include the *Hindustan Times, Times of India, Indian Express, Pioneer, Asian Age, Hindu, Statesman, Telegraph* and *Economic Times*.

- Incisive current-affair reports are printed in *Frontline, India Today,* the *Week, Sunday* and *Outlook.* For India-related travel articles get *Outlook Traveller.*

- The national (government) TV broadcaster is Doordarshan. More people watch satellite and cable TV; English-language channels include BBC, CNN, Star Movies, HBO and MTV. TV (and radio) programme/frequency details appear in most major English-language dailies.

- Numerous private channels and government-controlled All India Radio (AIR) transmit local and international news, music and more.

upmarket hotels; bookings can be arranged through tourist offices.

HOMESTAYS & ACCOMMODATION FOR PAYING GUESTS
Staying with a local family is increasingly popular in India, and owners often provide blisteringly authentic home-cooked meals. Local tourist offices can provide lists of families involved in homestay schemes, particularly in Kolkata (Calcutta), Gangtok and Darjeeling.

RAILWAY RETIRING ROOMS
Most large train stations have basic rooms for travellers in possession of an ongoing train ticket or Indrail Pass. All are noisy from the sound of passengers and trains. But they're useful for early morning train departures, and most offer dormitories as well as private rooms (24-hour checkout).

RESORTS
Orissa has a small but growing number of upmarket seaside resorts offering standard resort facilities, including swimming pools. 'Resorts' in the mountains are normally just comfortable upmarket hotels, sometimes with adventure activities and cottages for accommodation.

Assam and Meghalaya have some unusual environmental resorts and you can stay at some fabulous old Raj-era tea estates in Assam – see the entries for Jorhat (p209) and Dibrugarh (p212).

TEMPLES & PILGRIMS' RESTHOUSES
Accommodation is available at some ashrams (spiritual communities), gurdwaras (Sikh temples) and *dharamsalas* (pilgrims' rest-houses) for a donation, but check to make sure they are happy with foreign guests and always abide by any local protocols about smoking, drinking and making noise.

TOP-END & HERITAGE HOTELS
The Northeast has plenty of comfortable top-end hotels, from five-star chain hotels to colonial-era palaces that don't even have a classification system (if they did, it would have to be five tiger-skin rugs). Most top-end hotels have rupee rates for Indian guests and separate US dollar rates for foreigners (including Non-Resident Indians, or NRIs). Officially, you are supposed to pay the dollar rates in foreign currency or by credit card, but many places will accept rupees adding up to the dollar rate.

Costs
Prices for accommodation vary widely as you travel around the Northeast, so it is hard to pinpoint exact accommodation costs, but most hotels fall somewhere within the following ranges:

Budget: single rooms from Rs 100 to 400, and doubles from Rs 200 to 600

Midrange: single rooms from Rs 300 to 1300, and doubles from Rs 450 to 1800

Top End: single and double rooms from around Rs 1900 to US$150 or more

Many hotels raise their room tariffs annually – be prepared for a slight increase on the rates we've provided.

HEATING
In winter, hotels in the mountains provide gas or electric heaters, or wood for the open fire,

---

KNOW YOUR BATHROOM

Top-end and midrange hotels in India generally have sit-down flush toilets with toilet paper supplied. In cheaper hotels, and off the tourist trail, squat toilets are the norm and toilet paper is rarely provided. Squat toilets are variously described as 'Indian style', 'Indian' or 'floor' toilets, while the sit-down variety may be called 'Western' or 'commode' toilets. In a few places, you'll find the curious 'hybrid toilet', a sit-down toilet with footpads on the edge of the bowl.

Terminology for hotel bathrooms varies across India. 'Attached bath', 'private bath' or 'with bath' means that the room has its own en suite bathroom. 'Common bath', 'no bathroom' or 'shared bath' means communal bathroom facilities down the hall. 'Running', '24-hour' or 'constant' water means that hot water is theoretically available around the clock. 'Bucket hot water' is only available in buckets (sometimes for a small charge). Many places use small, wall-mounted electric geysers (water heaters) that need to be switched on an hour before use.

In this book, hotel rooms have their own private bathroom unless otherwise indicated.

for an additional fee. Avoid charcoal burning fires because of the risk of fatal carbon monoxide poisoning.

SEASONAL VARIATIONS
Hotels in popular tourist hangouts crank up their prices in the high season – normally summertime in the mountains (June to October), and the period before and after the monsoon in the plains (April to June and September to October). At other times, these hotels offer significant discounts. It's always worth trying your luck and asking for a discount if the hotel seems quiet.

Many temple towns have additional peak seasons around major festivals and pilgrimages – see p301 and the Festivals boxed texts for individual states for festival details. Room rates in this book were generally collected outside the peak season, but the regional chapters have details on seasonal rates for individual areas.

TAXES & SERVICE CHARGES
State government taxes are added to the cost of rooms, except at the cheapest hotels. Taxes vary from state to state and are detailed in the regional chapters. Many upmarket hotels also levy an additional 'service charge' (usually around 10%). Rates quoted in this book's regional chapters exclude taxes unless otherwise indicated.

BUSINESS HOURS
Official business hours are from 9.30am to 5.30pm Monday to Friday, but many offices open later and close earlier. Government offices may also open on certain Saturdays (usually the first, second and fourth of the month). Most offices have a lunch hour from around 1pm. Shops generally open around 10am and stay open until 6pm or later; some close on Sunday. Note that curfews apply in some areas – particularly the Northeast states. airline offices generally keep to standard business hours Monday to Saturday.

Banks are open from 10am to 2pm on weekdays (till 4pm in some areas), and from 10am to noon (or 1pm) on Saturday. Foreign-exchange offices open longer seven days per week. Main post offices are open from 10am to 5pm on weekdays, till noon on Saturday. Some larger post offices have a full day on Saturday and a half-day on Sunday – see regional chapters for details.

Restaurant opening hours vary regionally – you can rely on most places to be open from around 8am to 10pm. Exceptions are noted in the Eating sections of the regional chapters.

CHILDREN
India is far more accepting of children than most Western nations, but extra caution is required as the normal risks are amplified in these hot and crowded conditions. Pay close attention to hygiene and be VERY vigilant around traffic. Also keep children away from monkeys and local dogs, which carry all sorts of diseases. See Lonely Planet's *Travel with Children,* and the travelling with children section of the Thorn Tree forum on **LonelyPlanet.com** (thorntree.lonelyplanet.com) for more advice.

Practicalities
ACCOMMODATION
Many hotels have 'family rooms' and almost all will provide an extra bed for a small additional charge. Upmarket hotels may offer baby-sitting facilities and cable TV with English-language children's channels (cheaper hotels only have cartoons in Hindi).

FOOD & DRINK
Children are welcome in most restaurants, but only upmarket places and fast-food chains have high-chairs and children's menus. Across India, nappy-changing facilities are usually restricted to the (often cramped) restaurant toilet. Western fast food is widely available and finger food, like pakora (deep-fried battered vegetables), dosas (thin lentil-flour pancakes) and finger chips (seasoned hot potato chips), goes down fairly easily. As long as it is peeled or washed in purified water, fruit can offset the unhealthiness of lots of fried food. Bottled water, cartons of fruit juice and bottles of soft drink are usually safe to drink.

HEALTH
Avoiding stomach upsets will be a daily battle – washing hands with soap or rubbing alcohol is your first line of defence (see p340 for more advice). If your child takes special medication, bring along an adequate stock. Note that rabid animals also pose a risk. Check with a doctor before departure about the correctly recommended jabs and drug courses for children in India.

TRANSPORT

Any long-distance road travel should include plenty of food and toilet stops, particularly on rough roads. Travel sickness is another problem – particularly on mountain roads in Sikkim and the hills of West Bengal and the Northeast states. Children normally travel on adults' laps; child seats – or indeed any kind of seatbelts – are extremely rare.

Discounts

On Indian trains, children under four years travel free and kids aged five to 12 pay half-price. Most airlines charge 10% of the adult fare for infants and 50% for under 12s. Many tourist attractions charge a reduced entry fee for children under 12 (under 15 in some states).

TRAVEL WITH INFANTS

Standard baby products such as nappies (diapers) and milk powder are available in most large cities. Also bring along high-factor sunscreen, a snug-fitting wide-brimmed hat and a washable changing mat for covering dirty surfaces. Breast-feeding in public is frowned upon by Indian society.

Sights & Activities

Some destinations are better for children than others – Kolkata has a number of child-friendly museums and the popular Nicco Park theme park – see p112. Old-fashioned planetariums are found in Kolkata (p103) and Guwahati (p200).

Kids will also enjoy spotting India's exotic beasties. Wildlife safaris, particularly those offering elephant rides, are also worth considering (see p76). There are better than average zoos in (or near) Darjeeling (p146) and Bhubaneswar (p250).

Beaches make great family outings, but you'll need to be careful of currents and tides. The Northeast's best beaches are found in Orissa – the sands at Puri (p251), Konark (p256) and Gopalpur-on-Sea (p260) are good for a paddle. Hill stations offer peaceful forest picnics, cooler weather and family-friendly activities, such as paddle boating and pony rides. Top spots in the Northeast include Darjeeling (p140), Mirik (p138) and Shillong (p214).

India's bounty of festivals may also capture your child's imagination, although some will be spooked by the crowds. For festival details, see p301 and the Festivals boxed texts at the start of regional chapters. For further destination-

specific sights and activities that may appeal to your children, read the regional chapters.

CLIMATE CHARTS

The Northeast is a vast area and climatic conditions vary considerably with the changing topography. Generally speaking, the country has a three-season year – the hot, the wet and the cool. For more details, see the charts on this page and p15.

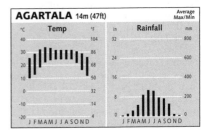

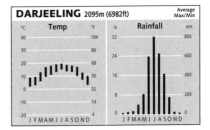

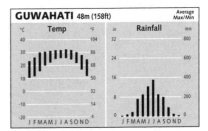

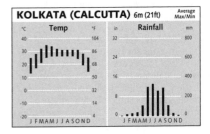

COURSES

You can learn all sorts of new skills in India, from yoga and meditation to Indian cooking and Hindi. To find out about local courses, inquire at tourist offices, ask fellow travellers, and browse local newspapers and noticeboards. See p77 for information on climbing courses and p92 for information on cooking courses.

Several centres in the Northeast offer yoga courses – see p80 for more information.

Languages

Language courses need time to give lasting benefits. Kolkata has several places offering long-term language courses – the **Ramakrishna Mission Institute of Culture** (☎ 033-24641303; www .sriramakrishna.org; Gol Park, Kolkata) in Kolkata runs six-month courses in Hindi for foreigners, beginning in April and November.

In Darjeeling in West Bengal, the Manjushree Centre of Tibetan Culture (p148) offers three- to nine-month Tibetan-language courses from March to December.

Music & Performing Arts

Most of the courses offered in the Northeast are for serious, long-term practitioners, but it's worth checking billboards in traveller centres for people offering private tuition.

Shakespeare Sarani in Kolkata is one of the best places in the country to buy Indian musical instruments – see Shopping (p310). One interesting option in Kolkata is the programme of courses in Indian classical dance offered at Kolkata's Aurobindo Bhawan (p112).

CUSTOMS

Visitors are allowed to bring 1L each of wine and spirits, and 200 cigarettes or 50 cigars or 250g of tobacco into India duty free. Officials may ask tourists to enter expensive items such as video cameras and laptop computers on a 'Tourist Baggage Re-export' form to ensure they are taken out of India. There are no duty-free allowances when entering India from Nepal.

Technically you're supposed to declare any amount of cash or travellers cheques over US$10,000 on arrival, and rupees should not be taken out of India. However, this is rarely policed. Exporting antiques and products made from animals is prohibited – see the boxed text, p308.

DANGERS & ANNOYANCES

Most problems in the Northeast can be avoided with a bit of common sense and a sensible level of caution. Scams change as dodgy characters try to stay ahead of the game, so chat with other travellers and tourism officials to stay abreast of the latest hazards. Also see the India branch of Lonely Planet's **Thorn Tree forum** (thorntree.lonelyplanet.com).

For region-specific scams and dangers, see the Dangers & Annoyances sections of the regional chapters. Women should also read the advice on p317.

Contaminated Food & Drink

In past years, some private medical clinics have provided patients with more treatment than necessary to procure larger payments from travel insurance companies – get a second opinion if possible. In the late 1990s, several travellers were killed after being fed food spiked with bacteria by restaurants linked to dodgy clinics. This scam has thankfully been quashed, but there's always the chance it could reappear.

Most bottled water is legit, but always ensure the lid seal is intact. Crush plastic bottles after use to prevent them being misused later, or better still, purify your own water with water-purification tablets or a filtration system.

Drugs

A few towns allow the legal sale of *bhang* (a derivative of marijuana) for religious reasons – including Puri in Orissa – but elsewhere, courts treat possession of cannabis as severely as possession of heroin, with a penalty of at least 10 years in prison. If you do choose to take drugs, be *extremely* circumspect. *Bhang* is frequently administered in food and drinks, which can be incredibly potent, leaving intoxicated travellers vulnerable to robbery or accidents. For more on the drug situation, see p304.

Festivals

The sheer mass of humanity at India's festivals provides an incredible spectacle, but every year pilgrims are crushed or trampled to death on temple processions and train platforms. Be extra careful at these times, and avoid special pilgrim trains.

Care is also needed during the Holi festival (p302). At the very least, you'll get a dousing with coloured dye – which can cause skin reactions – and at worst, women may get groped by intoxicated men. It's wise to seek a companion before venturing onto the streets at festival time.

Noise

Shouting, traffic noise, leaky plumbing and loud music can all add up to a waking nightmare for light sleepers. Bring earplugs and request rooms that face away from busy roads. Local holidaymakers often travel in large groups and knock randomly on hotel room doors looking for members of their party – lock your door if you don't want people to walk in uninvited.

Rebel Violence

Most of the time, the Northeast is no more dangerous than anywhere else, but certain areas are particularly prone to rebel violence. There are estimated to be more than a hundred insurgent armies operating in the Northeast, and bomb attacks on markets, public transport, religious centres and tourist sights are an ongoing risk, particularly in Manipur, Nagaland and upper Assam. In recent years, India has also been hit by a series of deadly bomb attacks on major cities, linked to the situation in Kashmir and global Islamic fundamentalism.

People involved in tourism rarely admit the dangers, while embassies often exaggerate the risks – the best sources of information are international charities and local news sources. Useful resources are listed in the Northeast States chapter (p194), and the website www .rediff.com/news/states.html has state by state listings of news stories for the whole of India.

Scams

India is notorious for the scams designed to separate travellers from their money, often with the promise of a chance to get rich quick. Don't be fooled. Any deal that sounds too good to be true, invariably is.

Be highly suspicious of claims that you can purchase goods cheaply in India and sell them easily at a profit elsewhere. Precious stones and carpets are favourites for this con. If anyone asks you to carry goods home to sell on to their 'representatives' in your home country, you are being set up for a scam. The company will often provide convincing-sounding testimonials from other satisfied customers, but without exception, the goods will be worthless.

It also pays to be cautious when sending goods home. Shops have been known to swap high-value items for junk, so send the package yourself from the post office to be safe. Be very careful when paying for souvenirs with a credit card. Government shops are usually legitimate; private souvenir shops have a reputation for secretly running off extra copies of the credit-card imprint slip, which will be used for phoney transactions after you have left the shop. To play it safe, visit the nearest ATM and pay in cash.

While it's only a minority of traders who are involved in dishonest schemes, many souvenir vendors are involved in the commission racket – see opposite.

Swimming

Beaches can have dangerous rips and currents, and there are drowning deaths each year – the beaches at Puri, Konark and Gopalpur-on-Sea in Orissa are particularly prone to undercurrents. Swimming in rivers is also a gamble – most locals prefer to stick to the safety of temple watertanks. Always check locally before swimming in unfamiliar waters.

Theft & Druggings

Theft is a risk in the Northeast as much as anywhere else in the world. On buses and trains, keep luggage securely locked (mini padlocks and chains are available at most train stations) and lock your bags to the metal baggage racks or the wire loops found under seats; padlocking your bags to the roof racks on buses is also a sensible policy.

Opportunistic thieves tend to target popular tourist train routes, such as Howrah to New Jalpaiguri. Armed bandits have been known to rob train passengers in rural parts of Assam and Bihar. Be extra alert just before the train departs – this is prime time for the snatch and run routine. Airports are another place you should exercise caution; after a long flight you're unlikely to be at your most alert.

Occasionally tourists (especially those travelling solo) are drugged and robbed during train or bus journeys. Typically, a seemingly friendly stranger will strike up a conversation, offer you a spiked drink, then make off with everything you have. Politely decline drinks or food offered by strangers – stomach upsets are a convenient excuse.

Unfortunately some travellers make their money go further by helping themselves to other peoples – take care in dormitories. For lost credit cards, immediately call the international stolen/lost number. For stolen/lost travellers cheques, contact the cheque issuing company – **Amex** (☎ 011-26145920) handles American Express and Thomas Cook cheques, while **Visa** (☎ 000-8001006475) has a country-wide toll-free number.

A good travel-insurance policy is essential (see p303) – keep the emergency contact details handy and familiarise yourself with the claims procedure. Keep photocopies of your passport, including the visa page, separately from your passport along with a copy of your airline ticket, or otherwise email scans to yourself via the internet.

PERSONAL SECURITY
The safest place for your money and your passport is next to your skin, either in a moneybelt or a secure pouch under your shirt. If you carry your money in a wallet, keep it in your front trouser pocket, never the back pocket. It may make sense to leave some backup currency in your luggage, but keep your main stash and other valuables on your person.

In dodgy-looking hotels, put your moneybelt under your pillow when you sleep and NEVER leave your valuable documents and travellers cheques in your hotel room when you go out. Better hotels will have a safe for valuables, and hostels normally provide a locker where you can use your own padlock. For peace of mind, use your own padlock in hotels where doors are locked with a padlock (common in cheaper hotels). If you cannot lock your hotel room securely from the inside at night, stay somewhere else.

It is usually wise to peel off at least US$100 and store it away separately from your main stash, just in case. Also, separate big notes from small bills so you don't publicly display large wads of cash when paying for services or checking into hotels.

Touts & Commission Agents
Many hotels and shops drum up extra business by paying commission to local fixers who bring tourists through the doors. These places tend to be unpopular for a reason and prices will be raised (by as much as 50%!) to pay the fixer's commission. To get around this, ask taxis or rickshaws to drop you at a landmark rather than a hotel, so you can walk in alone and pay the normal price.

Train and bus stations are often swarming with touts. If anyone asks if this is your first trip to India, this is usually a ruse to gauge your vulnerability – say you've been here several times.

You'll often hear stories about the hotels that refuse to pay commissions, being 'full', 'under renovation' or 'closed'. Check things out yourself. Be very sceptical of phrases like 'my brother's shop' and 'special deal at my friend's place'.

On the flip side, touts can be beneficial if you arrive in a town without a hotel reservation when some big festival is on, or during the peak season – they'll know which places have beds.

Transport Scams
Many private travel agencies make extra money by scamming travellers for tours and travel tickets. Make sure you are clear what is included in the price of any tour (get this in writing) to avoid charges for hidden 'extras' later on.

The Northeast is less prone to transport scams than many parts of India, but it pays to keep your wits about you. When buying a bus, train or plane ticket anywhere other than the registered office of the transport company, make certain you are getting the ticket class you paid for. Be wary of travel agents selling 'through tickets' to Nepal – everyone changes buses at the border and the second bus may not be the class you were expecting. Wherever possible, book tickets for buses and trains directly with the operating company.

Trekking
Trekking off the beaten track always carries risks and India is poorly set up for independent trekkers. We strongly recommend hiring local guides and porters or joining an organised trek before heading off into potentially dangerous terrain – see p78 for more information.

DISABLED TRAVELLERS
If you have a physical disability or you are vision impaired, the crowded public transport, crush of humanity and variable infrastructure in India can pose a serious challenge. However, many disabled travellers rise above these obstacles.

The Northeast has a limited number of wheelchair-friendly hotels (mostly top end). Some restaurants and offices have ramps, but most have at least one step. Staircases are often steep and lifts frequently stop at mezzanines between floors. Footpaths and pavements, where they exist at all, are riddled with holes and packed with pedestrians, hindering movement. Try to book ground-floor hotel rooms and if you use crutches, bring along spare rubber caps for the tips.

If your mobility is considerably restricted, you may like to consider travelling with an able-bodied companion. Additionally, hiring a car with driver will make moving around a whole lot easier (see p328).

Organisations that may offer further advice include the **Royal Association for Disability and Rehabilitation** (RADAR; ☎ 020-7250 3222; www.radar .org.uk; 12 City Forum, 250 City Rd, London EC1V 8AF, UK) and **Mobility International USA** (MIUSA; ☎ 541-3431284; www.miusa.org; 132 E Broadway, Ste 343, Eugene, OR 97401, USA). There are also some good sites on the web, including www.access-able .com.

DISCOUNTS
Seniors

Indian Airlines and Sahara Airlines offer 50% discounts on domestic air travel for foreign travellers aged 65 or over; Jet Airways offers 25% off. However, promotional fares and tickets on budget airlines are often cheaper than discounted full fares. If you're over 60, you're entitled to a 30% discount on the cost of train travel. Bring your passport as proof of age.

Student & Youth Travel

Hostels run by the **Indian Youth Hostels Association** (www.yhaindia.org) are part of the HI network; an HI card sometimes entitles you to discount rates. YMCA/YWCA members also receive discounts on accommodation.

Foreigners aged 30 or under receive a 25% discount on domestic air tickets. Again, this applies to full-price tickets, so standard budget airline fares may be cheaper still. Students studying in India get 50% off train fares.

EMBASSIES & HIGH COMMISSIONS
Embassies & High Commissions in India

Most foreign diplomatic missions are based in Delhi, but several nations operate consulates in Kolkata and other large cities. Most missions operate from 9am to 5pm Monday to Friday with a lunchbreak between 1pm and 2pm.

The following nations bordering the Northeast have missions in Kolkata:
Bangladesh (☎ 22475208; 9 Circus Ave).
Myanmar (☎ 22178273; 4th fl, Block D, White House, 119 Park St).
Nepal (☎ 24561224; 1 National Library Rd, Alipore).
Thailand (☎ 24407836; 18B Mandeville Gardens, Gariahat).

For other countries, or for more complicated consular matters, contact the main missions in Delhi (area code ☎ 011). Important embassies are listed below – for missions of other countries, see the local phone directory.
Australia (☎ 41399900; www.ausgovindia.com; 1/50G Shantipath, Chanakyapuri)
Bangladesh (☎ 24121389; www.bhcdelhi.org; EP39 Dr Radakrishnan Marg, Chanakyapuri)
Bhutan (☎ 26889230; Chandragupta Marg, Chanakyapuri)
Canada (☎ 41782000; www.dfait-maeci.gc.ca/new -delhi; 7/8 Shantipath, Chanakyapuri)
France (☎ 24196100; www.france-in-india.org; 2/50E Shantipath, Chanakyapuri)
Germany (☎ 26871837; www.new-delhi.diplo.de; 6/50G Shantipath, Chanakyapuri)
Ireland (☎ 24626741; www.irelandinindia.com; 230 Jor Bagh)
Israel (☎ 30414500; delhi.mfa.gov.il; 3 Aurangzeb Rd)
Italy (☎ 26114355; www.ambnewdelhi.esteri.it; 50E Chandragupta Marg, Chanakyapuri)
Japan (☎ 26876564; www.in.emb-japan.go.jp; 50G Shantipath, Chanakyapuri)
Malaysia (☎ 26111291; www.kln.gov.my/perwakilan /newdelhi; 50M Satya Marg, Chanakyapuri)
Maldives (☎ 41435701; www.maldiveshighcom.co .in; B-2 Anand Niketan)
Myanmar (Burma; ☎ 24678822; 3/50F Nyaya Marg)
Nepal (☎ 23327361; Barakhamba Rd)
The Netherlands (☎ 24197600; www.holland-in -india.org; 6/50F Shantipath, Chanakyapuri)
New Zealand (☎ 26883170; www.nzembassy .com; 50N Nyaya Marg, Chanakyapuri)
Pakistan (☎ 24676004; 2/50G Shantipath, Chanakyapuri)
Singapore (☎ 41019801; www.mfa.gov.sg/new delhi; N-88 Panchsheel Park)
South Africa (☎ 26149411; www.sahc-india.com; B18 Vasant Marg, Vasant Vihar)

Sri Lanka (☎ 23010201; www.slmfa.gov.lk; 27 Kautilya Marg, Chanakyapuri)
Switzerland (☎ 26878372; www.eda.admin.ch; Nyaya Marg, Chanakyapuri)
Thailand (☎ 26118104; www.thaiemb.org.in; 56N Nyaya Marg, Chanakyapuri)
UK (☎ 24192100; www.ukinindia.com; Shantipath, Chanakyapuri)
USA (☎ 24198000; www.newdelhi.usembassy.gov; Shantipath, Chanakyapuri)

FESTIVALS & EVENTS

India officially follows the European Gregorian calendar but most holidays and festivals follow the Indian or Tibetan lunar calendars, tied to the cycle of the moon, or the Islamic calendar, which shifts forward 11 days each year (12 days in leap years). As a result, the exact dates of festivals change from year to year.

The India-wide holidays and festivals listed here are arranged according to the Indian lunar calendar. Contact local tourist offices for exact dates or check the web – for listings, see http://festivals.iloveindia.com and www.festivalsofindia.in or the regional websites for the state governments, listed on www.india.gov.in/knowindia/districts.php.

The 'wedding season' falls in the cooler period from November to March. During this period you're likely to see at least one wedding procession on the street and you may well be invited to join in the festivities.

The following represent major festivals celebrated across the region – for details about regional festivals see the Festivals In… boxed texts at the beginning of regional chapters.

Chaitra (March/April)

Mahavir Jayanti Jain festival, commemorating the birth of Mahavira, the founder of Jainism.
Ramanavami Hindus celebrate the birth of Rama with processions, music and feasting, and enactments of scenes from the Ramayana.
Easter Christian holiday marking the Crucifixion and Resurrection of Jesus Christ.
Eid-Milad-un-Nabi Islamic festival celebrating the birth of the Prophet Mohammed; it falls on 20 March 2008, 9 March 2009 and 26 February 2010.

Vaisakha (April/May)

Buddha Jayanti Buddhists celebrate the life of the historical Buddha; it can fall in May, April or early June.

Jyaistha (May/June)

Only regional festivals fall in this period – see the regional chapters for details.

Asadha (June/July)

Rath Yatra (Car Festival) Effigies of Lord Jagannath (Vishnu) are hauled through cities on man-powered chariots; the biggest celebrations are at Puri in Orissa and Mahesh in West Bengal.

Sravana (July/August)

Naag Panchami Hindu festival dedicated to Ananta, the god of serpents. Snakes are venerated as totems against monsoon flooding and other evils.
Raksha Bandhan (Narial Purnima) On the full moon, girls fix amulets known as *rakhis* to the wrists of brothers and male friends to protect them in the coming year.

Bhadra (August/September)

Independence Day This exuberant public holiday on 15 August marks the anniversary of India's Independence in 1947.
Drukpa Teshi A Buddhist festival celebrating the first teaching given by Siddhartha Gautama.
Ganesh Chaturthi Hindus celebrate the birth of Ganesh by parading clay idols through the streets, then ceremonially immerse the effigies in rivers, water tanks or the sea.
Janmastami The anniversary of Krishna's birth is celebrated with gleeful abandon, by followers of Vishnu.
Shravan Purnima On this day of fasting, high-caste Hindus replace the sacred thread looped over their left shoulder.
Pateti The minority Parsi community celebrate the Zoroastrian new year at this time.
Ramadan (Ramazan) Thirty days of fasting marking the ninth month of the Islamic calendar, when the Koran was revealed to the Prophet Mohammed; the fast starts on 13 September 2007, 1 September 2008, 22 August 2009 and 11 August 2010.

Asvina (September/October)

Navratri (Festival of Nine Nights) This Hindu festival celebrates the goddess Durga in all her incarnations. Special dances are held and the goddesses Lakshmi and Saraswati also get special praise.
Durga Puja Symbolising the triumph of good over evil, Durga Puja commemorates the victory of the goddess Durga over buffalo-headed demon Mahishasura. This is the biggest annual festival in West Bengal and Assam, where thousands of images of the goddess are displayed then ritually immersed in rivers, tanks and the sea.
Dussehra Vaishnavites celebrate the victory of the Hindu god Rama over the demon-king Ravana on the same dates as Durga Puja.

Gandhi Jayanti This national holiday is a solemn celebration of Mohandas Gandhi's birth on the 2nd of October.

Eid al-Fitr Muslims celebrate the end of Ramadan with three days of festivities, starting 30 days after the start of the fast.

Kartika (October/November)

Diwali (Deepavaali) Hindus celebrate the 'festival of lights' for five days, giving gifts, lighting fireworks and burning butter and oil lamps to guide Rama home from exile.

Govardhana Puja A Vaishnavite Hindu festival celebrating the lifting of Govardhan Hill by Krishna.

Aghan (November/December)

Nanak Jayanti The birthday of Guru Nanak, the founder of Sikhism, is celebrated with prayer readings and processions.

Eid al-Adha Muslims commemorate Ibrahim's readiness to sacrifice his son to God; the festival falls on 20 December 2007, 8 December 2008, 27 November, 2009 and 16 November 2010.

Pausa (December/January)

Christmas Day Christians celebrate the birth of Jesus Christ on 25 December.

Losar Tibetan New Year – celebrated by Tibetan Buddhists in Sikkim, Arunachal Pradesh and West Bengal. Exact dates vary from region to region.

Loosong New Year for the people of Sikkim, with processions and monastery dances, celebrated by Sikkimese across the Northeast.

Muharram Shia Muslims commemorate the martyrdom of the Prophet Mohammed's grandson, Imam; the festival starts on 10 January and 29 December 2008, 18 December 2009 and 7 December 2010.

Magha (January/February)

Republic Day This public holiday on 26 January celebrates the founding of the Republic of India in 1950.

Bhogali Bihu (Makar Sankranti in Bengal) Farmers celebrate the winter rice harvest with buffalo fights and fires lit in honour of Agni, the Hindu god of fire.

Vasant Panchami Hindus honour Saraswati, the goddess of learning, by dressing in yellow and placing educational objects in front of idols of the goddess to receive her blessing.

Phalguna (February/March)

Holi Hindus celebrate the beginning of spring by throwing coloured water and *gulal* (powder – also known as *abeer*) at anyone in range. Bengalis celebrate the festival as Dol Yatra – when idols of Krishna and Radha are rocked on ritual swings.

Shivaratri This day of Hindu fasting recalls the *tandava* (cosmic dance) of Lord Shiva, ending in the anointing of linga (phallic symbols).

FOOD

Nowhere in the world makes such an inspired use of spices as India. To get a taste of what's on offer, see the Food & Drink chapter (p82) and the Eating sections of regional chapters. Places to eat are generally open from early morning (or lunchtime) to late at night – see p295 and the Eating sections for more information.

GAY & LESBIAN TRAVELLERS

Technically, homosexual relations for men are illegal in India and the penalties for transgression can theoretically be up to life imprisonment. In practice, gays are more vulnerable to harassment than arrest. There's a low-key gay scene in Kolkata and the city occasionally holds a small Gay Pride march. Physical contact and public displays of affection are generally frowned upon, for heterosexual couples as well as gay and lesbian couples. In fact, men holding hands is far more common than heterosexual couples holding hands, though this is generally a sign of friendship rather than sexual orientation.

See p46 for information on the campaign to legalise homosexuality in India.

Publications & Websites

The gay and lesbian magazine *Bombay Dost* is available from bookshops in more progressive Indian cities. Write to 105a Veena-Beena Shopping Centre, Bandra West, Mumbai – 400050, India or email info@bombay-dost .com for more information.

For further information about India's gay scene, point your web browser towards:

Indian Dost (www.indiandost.com/gay.php)

Humrahi (www.geocities.com/WestHollywood/Heights/7258)

Humsafar (www.humsafar.org).

Support Groups

In Kolkata the **Counsel Club** (☎ 033-23598130; counselclub93@hotmail.com; c/o Ranjan, Post Bag No 794, Kolkata 700017) provides gay, lesbian, bisexual and transgender support and arranges monthly meetings – contact them for details. The associated **Palm Avenue Integration Society** (pawan30@yahoo.com; C/o Pawan Post Bag No. 10237 Kolkata) offers health advice and runs a gay library service – opening times and directions by request.

HOLIDAYS

In India there are officially three national public holidays: Republic Day (26 January), Independence Day (15 August) and Gandhi Jayanti (2 October). Every state celebrates its own official holidays, which cover bank holidays for government workers as well as major religious festivals – usually Diwali, Durga Puja/Dussehra and Holi (Hindu), Nanak Jayanti (Sikh), Eid al-Fitr (Muslim), Mahavir Jayanti (Jain), Buddha Jayanti (Buddhist), and Easter and Christmas (Christian). For more on religious festivals, see p301.

Most businesses (offices, shops etc) and tourist sights close on public holidays, but transport is usually unaffected. Make transport and hotel reservations well in advance if you intend visiting during major festivals.

INSURANCE

Every traveller should take out travel insurance – if you can't afford it, you definitely can't afford the consequences if something does go wrong. Make sure that your policy covers theft of property and medical treatment, as well as air evacuation, as well as trekking and any other dangerous activities you might get involved in. When hiring a motorcycle in India, make sure the rental policy includes at least third-party insurance – see p331.

There are hundreds of different policies, so read the small print carefully. Some policies pay doctors and hospitals directly; others expect you to pay upfront and claim the money back later (keep all documentation for your claim). It is crucial to get a police report in India if you've had anything stolen, or your claim will be rejected. Also see Insurance in the Health chapter (p335).

Worldwide coverage to travellers from over 44 countries is available online at www.lonelyplanet.com/travel_services.

INTERNET ACCESS

Internet cafés are widespread in the Northeast, but connection speeds drop the further you get from large cities. Internet charges vary regionally (see individual chapters' Internet Access sections for exact costs) but most places charge between Rs 10 and Rs 50 per hour, usually with a 15-minute minimum.

It's a good idea to write and save your messages in a text application before pasting them into your browser in case of powercuts. Be wary of sending sensitive financial information from internet cafés – identity theft is on the rise. Using online banking on any non-secure system is generally a bad idea.

If you're travelling with a laptop, most internet cafés can supply you with internet access over a LAN Ethernet cable, or you can take out an account with a local ISP. Major ISPs in India include **Sify** (www.sify.com/products), **BSNL** (www.bsnl.co.in) and **VSNL/Tata Indicom** (www.vsnl.in). Make sure your modem is compatible with the telephone and dial-up system in India.

Another useful investment is a fuse-protected universal AC adaptor, to protect your circuit board from power surges. Wi-fi internet access is available in luxury hotels and some coffee shops in Kolkata and other large cities, but security is a consideration – never send credit card details or other personal data over a wi-fi connection. For more information on travelling with a portable computer, see www.teleadapt.com.

Hotels offering internet access to guests are marked with the internet icon – 🖳. See also p18 for useful India resources on the web.

LAUNDRY

Most hotels offer a same- or next-day laundry service, and private laundries are plentiful in tourist areas. Most employ the services of dhobi-wallahs – washermen and women who will diligently bash your wet clothes against rocks and scrubbing boards, returning them slightly more worn but spotlessly clean and ironed. If you don't think your gear will stand up to the treatment, wash them yourself or give them to a drycleaner.

Most laundries and hotels charge per item (you'll be required to submit a list with your dirty clothes) or by dry weight. Hand clothes in before 9am if you want them back the same day. It can take longer to dry clothes during the humid monsoon. Note that many hotels ban washing clothes in their rooms.

LEGAL MATTERS

If you're in a sticky legal situation, immediately contact your embassy (see p300). However, be aware that you are bound by Indian law – including the law on drugs – and all your embassy may be able to do is

---

BEWARE BHANG LASSIS!

Many restaurants in tourist centres will clandestinely whip up a *bhang lassi,* a yoghurt and iced-water beverage laced with cannabis. Commonly dubbed 'special lassi', this potent concoction can cause a drawn-out high that verges on delirium and lasts for many hours. Many travellers have been badly hurt in accidents or been robbed of all their possessions after drinking this risky brew. Drinkers beware!

---

monitor your treatment in custody and arrange a lawyer.

You should carry your passport at all times – police are entitled to ask you for identification in all sorts of situations. Corruption is rife, so the less you have to do with local police the better (unless getting a written police report for your insurance in the event of theft).

If you are asked for a bribe, the prevailing wisdom is to pay it, as the alternative can be a trumped-up prosecution. The problem is knowing how much to pay – it's better not to put yourself in risky situations.

Drugs

India has a global reputation for recreational drugs such as marijuana and hashish, and many travellers visit India specifically for this reason. We won't tell you not to take drugs, but be aware that possession of any illegal drug is treated as a serious criminal offence. If convicted, the *minimum* sentence is 10 years, with no chance of remission or parole, plus a hefty fine. The police have been getting particularly tough on foreigners who use drugs, so you should take this risk very seriously.

Note that travellers are sometimes targeted in sting operations (usually for bribes) in backpacker centres. Marijuana grows wild throughout India, but picking and smoking it is still an offence. *Bhang* (cannabis) is sold by government-licensed shops in Puri for religious rituals, but foreigners are still liable to prosecution if caught carrying the drug.

Anti-Social Behaviour

Smoking in public is now illegal in Sikkim, and a number of cities have also banned spitting and littering. The punishment for breaking these rules is a stiff (for locals) fine of at least Rs 100. This is variably enforced, but the police do have the power, so heed the street signs.

So far, restaurants are exempt from the smoking ban, but smoking is banned on many forms of public transport – including the Kolkata Metro. There are plans to eventually make the whole country smoke free, though this is highly unpopular with locals.

MAPS

Maps available inside India are very variable. Better map series include the following:

Eicher (maps.eicherworld.com) For street atlases and city maps.

Nelles (www.nelles-verlag.de) Also produces a good map covering the Northeast and Bangladesh (1:1500000).

Nest & Wings (www.nestwings.com) For maps and guidebooks.

Survey of India (www.surveyofindia.gov.in) Kolkata-based company also publishes decent city, state and country maps, but some titles are restricted for security reasons.

TTK Discover India Covers states and cities.

All of these maps are available at good bookshops or you can buy online from the **India Map Store** (www.indiamapstore.com).

YOUR OWN EMBASSY

It's important to realise what your own embassy – the embassy of the country of which you are a citizen – can and can't do to help you if you get into trouble.

Generally speaking, it won't be much help in emergencies if the trouble you're in is remotely your own fault. Remember that you are bound by the laws of India. Your embassy will not be sympathetic if you end up in jail after committing a crime locally, even if such actions are legal in your own country.

In genuine emergencies you might get some assistance, but only if other channels have been exhausted. Do not expect handouts. New passports can be issued, but a loan for travel home is exceedingly unlikely – the embassy would expect you to have insurance.

Throughout India, state government tourist offices stock local maps, which are often dated and lacking in essential detail, but good enough for general orientation.

MONEY

The Indian rupee (Rs) is divided into 100 paise (p), but paise coins are usually just used as alms for the poor. Coins come in denominations of 5, 10, 20, 25 and 50 paise and Rs 1, 2 and 5; notes come in Rs 10, 20, 50, 100, 500 and 1000 (this last bill can be hard to change outside banks). The rupee is linked to a basket of currencies and its value is generally stable – see the inside front cover for exchange rates.

ATMs linked to international networks are found in larger towns and cities in the Northeast. However, carry cash or travellers cheques as backup in case the power goes down, the ATM is out of order or you lose your card.

Remember, you must present your passport whenever changing currency and travellers cheques. Commission for foreign exchange is becoming increasingly rare – if it is charged, the fee is nominal. For information about costs, read p15.

See the Theft & Druggings heading under Dangers & Annoyances (p297) for tips on keeping your money safe.

ATMs

Modern 24-hour ATMs are found in many large towns and cities. The most commonly accepted cards are Visa, MasterCard, Cirrus, Maestro and Plus. The most reliable banks for ATMs are ICICI and the State Bank of India. Away from major towns, always carry cash or travellers cheques as a back up.

Banks impose higher charges on international ATM transactions, but this may be offset by the favourable exchange rates between banks. Always check in advance whether your card can access banking networks in India and check the charges. Indian ATMs take a long time to deliver the money and may snatch it back if you don't remove it quickly. If your card gets eaten by an ATM, contact bank staff immediately.

The ATMs listed in this book's regional chapters accept foreign cards (but not necessarily all types of cards). Always keep the emergency lost and stolen numbers for your credit cards in a safe place, and report any loss or theft immediately.

Black Market

Legal moneychangers are so common that there's no reason to use black market moneychangers, except to change small amounts of cash at land border crossings. As a rule, if someone comes up to you in the street and offers to change money, you're probably being set up for a scam.

Cash

Major currencies such as US dollars, UK pounds and euros are easy to change throughout the Northeast, though some bank branches insist on travellers cheques only. A few banks also accept Australian, New Zealand and Canadian dollars and Swiss francs. Private moneychangers accept a wider range of currencies, but Pakistani, Nepali and Bangladeshi currency can be harder to change away from the border. When travelling off-the-beaten track, always carry a decent stock of rupees.

Banks staple bills together into bricks, which puts a lot of wear and tear on the currency. Do not accept any filthy, ripped or disintegrating notes, as these may not be accepted as payment. If you get lumbered, you can change them to new bills at branches of the Reserve Bank of India. Nobody in India ever seems to have change, so it's a good idea to maintain a constant stock of smaller currency – try to stockpile Rs 10, Rs 20 and Rs 50 notes.

Officially, you cannot take rupees out of the country, but this is laxly enforced. However, you can change any leftover rupees back into foreign currency, most easily at the airport (some banks have a Rs 1000 minimum). You may require encashment certificates (see p306) or a credit card receipt and you may also have to show your passport and airline ticket.

Credit Cards

Credit cards are accepted at a growing number of shops, upmarket restaurants and midrange and top-end hotels, and you can also use them to pay for flights and train tickets. However, be wary of scams – see p298. MasterCard and Visa are the most widely accepted cards, and cash advances on major credit cards are possible at some banks without ATMs. Make sure you can access your account from India before you leave home.

Encashment Certificates

For every foreign exchange transaction, you will receive an encashment certificate, which will allow you to re-exchange rupees into foreign currency when departing from India (see p305). You'll need certificates for at least the sum you are trying to exchange. Printed receipts from ATMs may also be accepted as evidence of an international transaction at some banks.

Traditionally, money-exchange receipts have also been required when paying for tourist quota train tickets in rupees, but this requirement has recently been relaxed at most booking offices.

International Transfers

If you run out of money, someone at home can wire you money via moneychangers affiliated with **Moneygram** (www.moneygram.com) or **Western Union** (www.westernunion.com). To collect cash, bring your passport and the name and reference number of the person who sent the funds.

Moneychangers

Private moneychangers are usually open for longer hours than banks, and they are found almost everywhere. Compare rates with those at the bank, and check you are given the correct amount. In a scrape, some upmarket hotels may also change money, usually at well below the bank rate.

Tipping, Baksheesh & Bargaining

In tourist restaurants or hotels, a service fee is usually already added to your bill and tipping is optional. Elsewhere, a tip is appreciated. Hotel bellboys expect around Rs 20 to carry bags and bring up room service. It's not mandatory to tip taxi or rickshaw drivers, but we encourage tipping drivers who are honest about the fare to encourage good behaviour.

Baksheesh can be defined as a 'tip' and it covers everything from alms for beggars to unjustified demands for money for pointing out that the temple you are looking for is across the street. Beggars attach themselves to new arrivals in many Indian cities – whether you give or not is up to you, but try to treat people compassionately and consider what you might do if the positions were reversed.

Many Indians implore tourists not to hand out sweets, pens or money to children, as it is positive reinforcement to beg. To make a last-ing difference, donate to a school or charitable organisation (see Volunteer Work, p316).

Apart from at fixed-price shops, bargaining is the norm – see the boxed text, p311.

Travellers Cheques

All major brands are accepted in India, but some banks may only accept cheques from American Express (Amex) and Thomas Cook. Pounds sterling and US dollars are the safest currencies. Charges for changing travellers cheques vary from place to place and bank to bank.

Always keep an emergency cash stash in case you lose your travellers cheques, and keep a record of the cheques' serial numbers separate from your cheques, along with the proof of purchase slips, which you will need to replace lost or stolen cheques. If you are separated from your cheques, contact the emergency lost/stolen cheques number for the issuing company – see p298. Remember to get a police report as part of your claim.

PHOTOGRAPHY

For useful tips and techniques on travel photography, read Lonely Planet's *Guide to Travel Photography, Travel Photography: Landscapes* and *Travel Photography: People & Portraits*. Overexposure can be a problem in the mountains because of the bright light – a polarising filter can cut through the glare.

Digital

Memory cards for digital cameras are available from photographic shops in most large cities. However, some local memory cards do not carry the advertised amount of data. Expect to pay upwards of Rs 1000/1600 for a 512MB/1GB card. To be safe, regularly back up your memory card to CD – internet cafés offer this service for Rs 50 to 100 per disk. Some photographic shops make prints from digital photographs for roughly the standard print and processing charge.

Print & Slide

Colour print film-processing facilities are available almost everywhere. Film is relatively cheap and the quality is usually good, but you'll only find colour slide film in the major cities. On average, print and processing costs around Rs 6 per 4 x 6 colour print plus Rs 15 to 20 for processing. Passport photos are available from photo shops for around Rs 100 (10 to 12 shots).

Always check the expiry date on local film and slide stock. Make sure you get a sealed packet and that you're not handed a roll that's been sitting in a glass cabinet in the sunshine for the last few months. It's best to only buy film from reputable shops – and preferably film that's been refrigerated.

Restrictions

India is touchy about anyone taking photographs of military installations – this can include train stations, bridges, airports and sensitive border regions. On flights to strategically-important destinations, cameras may be banned from the cabin (or you may need to remove the batteries).

Many places of worship – monasteries, temples and mosques – also prohibit photography. Respect these proscriptions and always ask when in doubt to avoid causing offence. See p43 for etiquette about photographing people.

POST

India has the biggest postal network on earth, with over 155,600 post offices. Mail and poste restante services are generally good, although the speed of delivery will depend on the efficiency of any given office. Airmail is faster and more reliable than seamail, although it's best to use reputable international courier services (such as DHL) to send and receive items of value – expect to pay around Rs 2700 per kilo to Europe, Australia or the USA.

Receiving Mail

To receive mail in India, ask senders to address letters to you with your surname in capital letters and underlined, followed by: poste restante, GPO (main post office) and the city or town in question. When picking up mail, check under both your names and ask senders to provide a return address in case you don't collect your mail. Letters sent via poste restante are generally held for around one month before being returned. To claim mail, you'll need to show your passport. It's best to have any parcels sent to you by registered post.

Sending Mail

Posting postcards/aerogrammes anywhere overseas costs Rs 8/8.50 and airmail letters cost from Rs 15 (1g to 20g). Sending a letter by registered post adds Rs 15 to the stamp cost.

Posting parcels is quite straightforward; prices vary depending on weight and you have a choice of airmail (delivery in one to three weeks), seamail (two to four months) or Surface Air-Lifted (SAL; where parcels travel by air and sea; one month). Parcels must be packed up in white linen and the seams sealed with wax. Local tailors offer this service, or there may be a parcel service at the post office. Carry a permanent marker to write on any information requested by the desk. The post office can provide the necessary customs declaration forms and these must be stitched or pasted to the parcel. If the contents are a gift under the value of Rs 1000, you won't have to pay duty at the delivery end. Never try to send drugs by post – the police will track the package to your door and bust you when you open it.

Parcel post has a maximum of 20kg to 30kg depending on the destination, and charges vary depending on whether you go by air or sea. As an indication, a 1kg parcel costs the following prices (in Rs):

Destination	Airmail	SAL (Surface Air-Lifted)	Seamail
Australia	570	535	450
Europe	645	525	500
USA	645	595	480

You also have the option of Express Mail Service (EMS) – delivery is within three days and the cost is around 30% more than the normal airmail price.

Books or printed matter can go by inexpensive bookpost (maximum 5kg), but the package must be cloth wrapped with a hole that reveals the contents for the customs inspection – tailors know what to do. Overseas rates depend on the weight – a 1kg bookpost parcel costs just Rs 260 to any international destination. The **India Post website** (www.india post.gov.in) has an online calculator for other international postal tariffs.

Be cautious with shops that offer to mail things to your home address. Government emporiums are usually fine, but in most other places it pays to do the posting yourself – see p298.

SHOPPING

India is an Aladdin's cave of delights for shoppers, with markets and shops dripping with precious metals, gemstones, silks,

DIRECTORY

pearls, carpets and statues of Indian gods. Every region has its own special crafts – usually showcased in local state emporiums and cottage industry cooperatives. These shops normally charge very fair fixed prices; everywhere else, you'll have to bargain – see the boxed text, p311. Opening hours for shops vary – exceptions to standard hours are provided in the Shopping sections of the regional chapters.

Be very wary of shops that offer to deliver items to your country of residence, and be wary of being led to shops by touts – see the Dangers and Annoyances section (p299. Also see the warning on exporting antiques (p310).

Bronze Figures, Pottery & Stone-Carving

In Sikkim, West Bengal and many other parts of India, small images of deities are created by the age-old lost-wax process. A model is sculpted from wax and covered in plaster to create a mould – when molten metal is poured in, the wax melts away. The plaster is then chipped off to reveal the metal sculpture inside. Images of Shiva as dancing Nataraja are the most popular items, but you can find images of numerous other deities from the Hindu pantheon. In Buddhist areas, look for bronze statues of Buddha and the Tantric gods, finished off with finely polished and painted faces. The West Bengalese employ the lost-wax process to make Dokra tribal bell sculptures.

Kolkata also produces attractive terracotta work, including some fine images of deities and animal toys for children. At temple bazaars across the region you can buy small clay or plaster effigies of Kali, Durga and other deities, though these are fragile. Stone carvings of gods are produced all over India and sold across the Northeast. Prices vary depending on the quality of carving and the material – easy-to-carve soapstone is the cheapest, while premium prices are paid for granite and marble.

Many souvenir shops sell reproduction *pietra dura* – the ancient Mughal art of inlaying marble with semiprecious stones. The inspiration for most pieces comes from the Taj Mahal. Expect to pay about Rs 400 for a jewellery box or miniature model of the Taj; chess sets start at Rs 2000. Always consider the airline baggage allowance before filling your luggage with stone.

ETHICAL SHOPPING

Only a small proportion of the money brought to India by tourism reaches people in rural areas. You can make a greater contribution by shopping at community cooperatives, set up to protect and promote traditional cottage industries and provide education, training and a sustainable livelihood for rural families. Many of these projects focus on refugees, low-caste women, the disabled and other socially disadvantaged groups. Prices are usually fixed and a share of the money goes directly into social projects, like schools, healthcare and training. Shopping at the national network of Khadi & Village Industries emporiums will also contribute to rural communities. Community shops and cooperatives are recommended in the Shopping sections throughout the regional chapters of this book.

Carpets

Indian artisans have been producing carpets since at least the Mughal era and carpet-making is a living craft, with workshops across the country producing fine wool and silk work to traditional and modern designs. In the Northeast, Tibetan carpets predominate, using wool yarn, dyed into striking colours. Carpet-making is a major revenue earner for Tibetan refugees – most refugee settlements have cooperative carpet workshops. You can also find shops selling Iranian-style carpets and rustic folk rugs from Kashmir and reproductions of tribal Turkmen and Afghan designs from Uttar Pradesh. Antique carpets usually aren't antique – unless you buy from an internationally reputable dealer, stick to new carpets.

The price of a carpet will be determined by the number and the size of the hand-tied knots, the range of dyes and colours, the intricacy of the design and the material. Silk carpets cost more and look more luxurious but wool carpets last longer. Tibetan carpets are slightly cheaper than Kashmiri carpets, reflecting the relative simplicity of the designs – many refugee cooperatives sell 3ft by 5ft carpets for US$100 or less. A similar-sized Kashmiri carpet of decent quality will cost around US$200 in wool or US$2000 in silk.

Many people buy carpets under the mistaken belief that they can be sold for a profit back home. Unless you really know your carpets and the carpet market in your home country, buy a carpet because you love it. Many places can ship carpets home for a fee – though it may be safest to ship things independently to avoid scams.

If you can't stretch to a woven carpet, look out for coarse felt *numdas* (or *namdas*) embroidered with rustic designs in coloured wool, flat-weave *dhurries* (kilim-like cotton rugs) and striking *gabbas* (Kashmiri rugs) made from chain-stitched wool or silk.

Jewellery

Bangle shops abound in the Northeast, selling an extraordinary variety of bangles at minimal prices (as little as Rs 20 for a set of 12), made from plastic, glass, brass, bone, shell and wood. Traditionally, these are worn continuously until they break – Hindu widows break all their bangles as part of the mourning process.

Jewellery shops in big cities and tourist areas carry stock from all over India, including chunky Tibetan jewellery made from silver (or white metal) and semiprecious stones. Many pieces feature Buddhist motifs and text in Tibetan script – including the famous mantra 'Om Mani Padme Hum' (Hail to the Jewel in the Lotus). Real antiques are rare these days, so buy something because you like it, not for its antique value. If you feel like being creative, loose beads of agate, turquoise, carnelian and silver are widely available. Buddhist prayer beads made of gems, wood or inlaid bone also make highly portable souvenirs.

Gemstones from Rajasthan and the western deserts are sold all over India, either set into jewellery or loose as cut stones and carvings. However, be wary of gem scams (see Scams, p298). Cuttack in Orissa (p265) is famed for its lace-like, silver filigree work known as *tarakasi*. Silver and gold are also crafted into rings, anklets, earrings, toe-rings, necklaces and bangles.

Pearls are produced by most seaside states and sold at bargain prices at government emporiums in Kolkata and other state capitals. Prices vary depending on the colour and shape – you pay more for pure white pearls or rare colours like black and red. Perfectly round pearls are more expensive than misshapen or elongated pearls, but the quirky shapes of Indian pearls are often more alluring than the perfect round balls. A single strand of seeded pearls can cost as little as Rs 200, but better quality pearls start at Rs 600.

Leatherwork

As the cow is sacred in India, leatherwork is made from buffalo hide, camel, goat or some other substitute. Shops and markets in

---

CARPETS & CHILD LABOUR

Children have been employed as carpet weavers in India for centuries and many child-care charities from Europe and the USA are campaigning against the use of child labour by the carpet industry. There are thought to be at least 30,000 child carpet weavers in India, and 10% of these children are believed to have been trafficked from neighbouring countries.

Unfortunately, the issue is more complicated than it first appears. In many areas, education is often not an option, for both economic and cultural reasons, and the alternative to child labour may not be school but hunger for the whole family. We encourage travellers to buy from carpet-weaving cooperatives that employ adult weavers and provide education for their children, breaking the cycle of child labour.

The **Carpet Export Promotion Council of India** (www.india-carpets.com) is campaigning to eliminate child labour from the carpet industry by penalising factories that use children, and by founding schools to provide an alternative to carpet-making. Ultimately, the only thing that will stop child labour completely is compulsory education for children, but the economic and social obstacles are significant.

Unfortunately for the buyer, there is no easy way of knowing whether a carpet has been made by children. Shops are unlikely to admit using child labour and most of the international labelling schemes for carpets have been discredited. The carpets produced by Tibetan refugee cooperatives are almost always made by adults, while government emporiums and charitable cooperatives are also reputable.

Kolkata and Guwahati are full of well-made, moderately priced leather handbags, belts and other leather accessories.

Chappals, those wonderful curly toed leather sandals, are a particularly popular buy. They are sold in most cities and prices from around Rs 150. Look out for *jootis* (traditional pointed shoes with curling toes) from Punjab and Rajasthan – buy a pair, if only as part of your genie costume for fancy dress parties. Most big cities offer striking modern leather footwear at very competitive prices, often stitched with thousands of sequins – great party wear!

Metalwork
You'll find copper and brassware throughout the Northeast. Many Tibetan religious objects are created using copper inlaid with silver and other metals, including prayer wheels, document cases and ceremonial horns. Resist the urge to buy *kangling* (Tibetan horns) and *kapala* (ceremonial bowls) made from inlaid human leg bones and skulls – they are illegal!

No Assamese home would be complete without a *bota* – a brass platter on a stand with a dome-shaped cover known as a *xorai* – used to serve betel nut and paan to guests. These items are sold all over Assam; prices vary depending on the size and detail of the engraving.

In all Indian towns, you can find *kadai* (Indian woks, also known as *balti*) and other items of cookware for incredibly low prices. Beaten brass pots are particularly attractive, and steel storage vessels, copper-bottomed cooking pans and steel thali trays are also popular souvenirs.

Musical Instruments
Quality Indian musical instruments are available in larger cities in the Northeast, especially Rabindra Sarani in Kolkata (p121). Prices vary, but the higher the price the better the quality – and sound – of the instrument.

Decent quality tabla sets, with a wooden tabla (tuned treble drum) and metal *doogri* (bass tone drum), cost upwards of Rs 3000. Sitars range from Rs 4000 to 15,000 – a good starter sitar with quality-inlay work will cost upwards of Rs 7000. Every sitar sounds different so try a few – make sure the strings ring clearly and check the gourd carefully for damage. Spare string sets, sitar plectrums and a second screw-in 'amplifier' gourd are sensible additions.

Other popular instruments include the *shennai* (Indian flute; Rs 250 upwards), the *sarod* (like an Indian lute; from Rs 8,000), the harmonium (from Rs 3500) and the *esraj* (like an upright violin; from Rs 3000). Conventional violins are a bargain – prices range from Rs 3000 to 15,000.

Paintings
Reproductions of Indian miniature paintings are widely available, but quality varies –state emporiums (particularly branches of the Rajasthan State Emporium) have the best selection, particularly in Kolkata (p121). Beware of paintings purported to be antique – it's highly unlikely and export of antique paintings is banned.

The artists' community of Raghurajpur (p256) near Puri (Orissa) preserves the age-old art of *pattachitra* painting. Cotton or *tassar* silk cloth is painted with images of deities and scenes from Hindu legends, using ex-

PROHIBITED EXPORTS

To protect India's cultural heritage, the export of many objects over 100 years old is prohibited, including all old stone carvings. Reputable antique dealers know the laws and can make arrangements for an export clearance certificate for any ancient items that you are permitted to export. If in doubt, contact the **Archaeological Survey of India** (☎ 011-23010822; asi@del3.vsnl.net.in; Janpath; 🕑 10am-1pm & 2-5pm Mon-Fri) in Delhi. Quality reproductions of antiques are widely available, and buying these will help protect India's artistic legacy for future generations.

The Indian Wildlife Protection Act bans any form of wildlife trade. Don't buy products that endanger threatened species and habitats – doing so can result in heavy fines and even imprisonment. This includes shawls made from *shahtoosh* wool, ivory, and anything made from the fur, skin, horns or shell of any endangered species. Realistically, the only way to be sure is to avoid animal products completely. Products made from certain rare plants are also forbidden for export.

THE ART OF HAGGLING

Government emporiums, department stores and modern shopping centres usually charge fixed prices. Anywhere else you need to bargain, and bargain hard – foreigners are perceived to be wealthy, so shop keepers routinely double or triple the 'real' price. Souvenir shops are probably the least likely places of all to charge you the real going rate.

The first 'rule' to haggling is never to show too much interest in the item you want to buy. Decide how much you would be happy paying and then express a casual interest. If you have absolutely no idea of what something should really cost, start by slashing the price by half. The vendor will make a show of being shocked at such a low offer, but the game is set and you can now work up and down respectively in small increments until you reach a mutually agreeable price. You'll find that many shopkeepers lower their so-called 'final price' if you head out of the shop saying you'll 'think about it'.

Haggling is a way of life in India, but it should never be an angry process. Locals treat it like a game and so should you. Keep in mind exactly how much a rupee is worth in your home currency to put things in perspective. If a vendor seems to be charging an unreasonably high price, simply look elsewhere or find something cheaper.

ceedingly fine brushes. Orissa also produces *chitra pothi,* where dried palm-leaf sections are etched with a fine stylus.

In all Tibetan Buddhist areas, including Sikkim and parts of West Bengal, you can find exquisite *thangkas* (Tibetan cloth paintings) of Tantric Buddhist deities and ceremonial mandalas. Some perfectly reproduce the glory of the murals in India's medieval *gompas* (Buddhist monasteries); others look crude on closer inspection. Prices vary – bank on at least Rs 3000 for a decent quality *thangka* of A3 size, much more for large intricate *thangkas.* The selling of antique *thangkas* is illegal and you would be unlikely to find the real thing anyway. If you get caught with old *thangkas* at Indian customs, they will be confiscated.

Throughout the country (especially in capital cities) look out for shops and galleries selling brilliant contemporary paintings by local artists. A cheaper option are the fabulously colourful posters of religious deities and folk heroes, sold in every street market. Also keep an eye out for vendors selling colourful religious stickers – kids love them.

Shawls, Silk & Saris

Indian shawls are famously warm and lightweight. It's worth buying one to use as an emergency blanket on cold night journeys. You'll find shawls made from all sorts of wool, from lamb's wool to yak, *pashmina* goat and angora rabbit hair. However, *shahtoosh* shawls should be avoided as rare Tibetan antelopes are killed to provide the wool.

Shawls from the Northeast states are famously warm, with bold geometric designs that are specific to individual tribes. Naga shawls are particularly sought after for their bold black-and-red designs. In Sikkim and West Bengal, you can also find fantastically embroidered Bhutanese shawls.

In all big cities, you'll find shops selling shawls from Himachal Pradesh and other parts of the Himalaya. Prices range from about Rs 200 for a simple lamb's wool shawl to Rs 6000 for a stylish angora. Authentic *pashmina* shawls, made from soft goat wool, cost at least Rs 6000. Cheaper *pashminas* are usually made from a mixture of yarns.

Saris are a very popular souvenir, and they can be readily adapted to other purposes. Silk saris are the most expensive, and the silk usually needs to be washed before it becomes soft. Assam is renowned for its *muga, endi* and *pat* silks (produced by different species of silkworms), which are widely available in Guwahati (p202), You'll pay Rs 3000 or more for a quality embroidered silk sari.

For sophisticated designer saris, your best bet is Kolkata – shops there sell extravagant silk and cotton saris from all over India, often embroidered with silver and gold thread and sequins. Look out for *baluchari* saris from Bishnapur in West Bengal, made using a traditional form of weaving with untwisted silk thread.

Textiles

Textile production is India's major industry. Around 40% of textile output is *khadi* (homespun cloth) – hence the government-backed *khadi* emporiums around the country. These inexpensive superstores sell all sorts of items made from village cloth, including the popular 'Nehru jackets' (a collarless jacket, modelled on the Indian *sherwani*) and kurta pyjamas (a long shirt with loose-fitting cotton trousers), and sales benefit rural communities.

You will find a truly amazing variety of weaving and embroidery techniques around the country. In tourist centres, Indian textiles are stitched into handbags, wall hangings, cushion covers, bedspreads, clothes and more. Every village in India has at least one tailors shop and most will take on bespoke tailoring projects, so you can buy fabric at the market and have a suit, shirt or dress made to measure.

Appliqué is an ancient art in India, with most states producing their own designs. The traditional lampshades and *pandals* (tents) used in weddings and festivals such as Durga Puja are produced using the same technique. Souvenir shops often stock vivid bags, cushion covers and wall hangings embroidered with small pieces of mirrored glass from Gujarat and Rajasthan.

Orissa has a reputation for bright appliqué and *ikat* (a Southeast Asian technique where thread is tie-dyed before weaving). The town of Pipli (p251), between Bhubaneswar and Puri, produces some particularly eye-catching appliqué work. Women in West Bengal use chain stitches to make complex figurative designs called *kantha*.

Batik can be found throughout India. It is often used for saris and *salwar kameez* (a long dresslike shirt worn over trousers with a *dupatta* scarf). City boutiques produce trendy *salwar kameez* for women and the similar kurta Punjabi for men in a staggering array of fabrics and styles. Big Indian cities such as Kolkata are great places to pick up *haute couture* (high fashion) by talented Indian designers, as well as moderately priced Western fashions. Western brand names at Indian prices are becoming increasingly common in the flashy shopping malls of Kolkata (p121).

Woodcarving

Woodcarving is a living art in India. Sandalwood carvings of Hindu deities are sold all over the country. You'll pay a kings' ransom fortune for the real thing – a 4in-high Ganesh costs around Rs 3000 in sandalwood, compared to Rs 300 in *kadamb* wood – but it will

release fragrance for years. Wood-inlay work from Bihar is also sold widely in the Northeast, used in wooden wall hangings, tabletops, trays and boxes.

Buddhist woodcarvings are a speciality of Sikkim, Arunachal Pradesh and all Tibetan refugee areas, including Darjeeling (p140). You'll find wall plaques of the Buddhist eight lucky signs, *choktse* (low Tibetan tables) and *chaam* masks, used for ritual dances. Most of the masks are artless reproductions, but you can sometimes find genuine *chaam* masks, made of lightweight whitewood or papier-mâché.

The carved wooden massage wheels and rollers available at many Hindu pilgrimage sites are also good presents. In many towns, you can find printing blocks carved from teak wood – used to create traditional block-printed fabrics, but attractive in their own right. In Sikkim (p168), look out for traditional *tongba* pots – wooden tankards bound with metal, used to serve warm millet beer.

Other Buys

Markets across the Northeast sell most of the spices that go into *garam masala* (the 'hot mix' used to flavour Indian curries), and the Northeast states and Sikkim are famous for black cardamoms and cinnamon bark.

Attar (essential oil) shops can be found in many large cities, selling sandalwood oil and traditional fragrances prepared using aromatic oils from herbs, flowers and eucalyptus. Indian incense is exported worldwide and available across the Northeast, though most brands are manufactured in South India.

Sikkim has a special license from the government to produce liquor and the Sikkimese spirits are highly respected. Many come in funky-shaped bottles – the 1L bottle of Old Monk rum comes in a monk-shaped bottle with a screw-off head. Prices for Indian spirits start at around Rs 200 per litre.

Quality Indian tea is widely sold in Darjeeling and Kalimpong, Assam and Sikkim. The finest teas of all are the 'first flush' Golden Flowery Orange Pekoe teas from Darjeeling – you'll pay around Rs 1000 per 100g.

The Tibetan refugees of Darjeeling also produce quality handmade paper – often made up into cards, boxes and notebooks.

In most traveller centres, you'll find traditional clay pipe chillums and hookah pipes for smoking *bhang* . Drug paraphernalia is not illegal by itself but *used* paraphernalia can land you in a lot of trouble with customs when you get back home.

Markets sell some colourful fabric shopping bags, printed with Indian advertising in vivid colours. The Northeast states are noted for their beautiful handwoven baskets and wickerware – each tribe has its own unique basket shape. Basketware is also woven into furniture, lampshades, placemats and ornaments. The tribes of Meghalaya also produce bone-handled pocket knives and bamboo bows and arrows – easily purchased in Shillong (p214).

There are some fabulous antiques for sale in India, including window frames, ornaments and furnishings, but we recommend only buying reproductions as the export of many kinds of antiques is banned to preserve India's cultural heritage – see p310. As well as specialist antique shops, Kolkata's auction rooms throw up occasional Raj-era gems.

In towns with Buddhist populations, such as Gangtok, Kalimpong and Darjeeling, keep an eye out for 'Buddha shops' selling religious objects, such as prayer flags, wall hangings, trumpets, drums, singing bowls, handbells, prayer wheels and *thangkas* (see p310).

Most souvenir shops and many state emporiums sell lacquered papier-mâché from Kashmir in the form of bowls, boxes, letter holders, coasters, trays, lamps and Christmas decorations. Weight for weight, these are probably the most cost-effective souvenirs in India, but you need to transport them carefully. A small jewellery box will only cost around Rs 150.

Tribal hats are a popular buy through the Northeast – miniature *jaapi* (Assamese sun hats stitched with sequins) make great Christmas decorations. Tibetan refugees produce woollen hats, gloves and scarves, sold in shops across West Bengal and Sikkim.

You can find a phenomenal range of Indian books in Kolkata and other big cities – see the Bookshops sections of individual regional chapters. CDs by local musicians are also good value (Rs 100 or less). Pirate copies of Western CDs are available in tourist towns, along with original and pirate copies of DVD movies, both Bollywood and international.

SOLO TRAVELLERS

Tourist hubs such as Kolkata and Darjeeling in West Bengal and Gangtok and Pelling in Sikkim are good places for solo travellers to

network. Traveller hotels and restaurants are good places to swap stories and find people to travel with. You might also try advertising for travel companions on the **Lonely Planet Thorntree** (www.thorntree.lonelyplanet.com). Throughout India, people tend to move in the same direction, so you'll probably see the same faces over and over again on your trip.

Perhaps the most significant issue facing solo travellers is cost. Single-room rates at guesthouses and hotels are sometimes not much lower than double rates; some midrange and top-end places don't even offer a single tariff. However, it's always worth trying to negotiate a lower rate for single occupancy.

In terms of transport, you'll save money if you find others to share taxis and autorickshaws. This is also advisable if you intend hiring a car with driver. For important information specific to women, see p317.

TELEPHONE

There are few payphones in the Northeast, but private PCO/STD/ISD call booths do the same job, offering inexpensive local, interstate and international calls at much lower prices than calls made from hotel rooms. A digital meter displays how much the call is costing and provides a printed receipt when the call is finished. Faxes can be sent from some call centres or from the local telephone exchange or BSNL Customer Service Centre.

Call centres charge the full rate from around 9am to 8pm. After 8pm the cost slides – the cheapest time to call is 11pm to 6am. Interstate calls are half-rate on Sunday. Direct international calls from call booths range from Rs 22 to 40 per minute depending on the country you are calling. Hotels charge much more all the time. International calls for as little as Rs 5 per minute can be made through internet cafés using Net2phone, Skype and other net-phone services.

Some places also offer a 'call-back' service – you ring home, provide the phone number of the booth and wait for people at home to call you back, for a fee of Rs 5 to 10 on top of the cost of the preliminary call.

India has both **White Pages** (www.indiawhitepages.com) and **Yellow Pages** (www.indiayellowpages.com) online. Note that getting a line can be difficult in remote country and mountain areas – an engaged signal may just mean that the exchange is overloaded, so keep trying.

Mobile Phones

Mobile-phone numbers in India usually have 10 digits, typically starting with '9'. There is roaming coverage for international GSM phones in Kolkata and other large towns and cities, but anywhere else, it makes sense to invest in a local phone (or a local SIM card) as few companies covering the Northeast have roaming deals with international mobile-phone companies.

Mobiles bought in Western countries are often locked to a particular network; you'll have to get the phone unlocked, or buy a local phone (available from Rs 2300) to use an Indian SIM card. As soon as you have an Indian SIM, you can start making calls at local rates – which can be staggeringly cheap even for international calls.

In most towns you simply buy a prepaid mobile-phone kit (SIM card and phone number, plus a starter allocation of calls) for around Rs 150 from a phone shop or local PCO/STD/ISD booths. Thereafter, you must purchase new credits on that network, sold as scratch cards in the same shops and call centres.

Credit must usually be used within a set time limit and costs vary with the amount of credit on the card. For some networks, recharge cards are being replaced by direct credit, where you pay the vendor and the credit is deposited straight to your phone – ask which system is in use before you buy.

Calls made within the state/city in which you bought the SIM card are cheap – less than Rs 1 per minute – and you can call internationally for less than Rs 25 per minute. SMS messaging is even cheaper. However, some travellers have reported unreliable signals and problems with international texting.

The most popular (and reliable) companies are Airtel, Hutch (Orange in some states), Idea and BSNL. Note that most SIM cards are state specific – they can be used in other states, but you pay for calls at roaming rates and you will be charged for incoming calls as well as outgoing calls.

Phone Codes

Regular phone numbers have an area code followed by up to eight digits. The government is slowly trying to bring all numbers in India onto the same system, so area codes can change and new digits may be added to numbers at short notice – check locally.

To make a call to India from overseas, dial the international access code of the country you're in, then 91 (international country code for India), then the area code (drop the initial zero when calling from abroad), then the local number. See this book's regional chapters for area codes.

To make an international call from India, dial 00 (international access code from India), then the country code (of the country you are calling), then the area code and the local number.

Also available is the Home Country Direct service, which gives you access to the international operator in your home country for the price of a local call. The number is typically constructed ☎ 000 + the country code of your home country + 17 .

TIME

Indian Standard Time is 5½ hours ahead of GMT/UTC, 4½ hours behind Australian Eastern Standard Time (EST) and 10½ hours ahead of American EST. The floating half-hour was added to maximise daylight hours over such a vast country. See the Time Zones map, p374-5.

TOILETS

The cleanest toilets are at restaurants and fast-food chains, museums, upmarket shopping complexes and cinemas, but carry your own toilet paper in case there is just a tap and a jug – see the boxed text p294 for more on Indian toilets. Many towns also have public urinals and squat toilets (an entry fee of Rs 1 to 2 applies), but they tend to be quite filthy.

When it comes to effluent etiquette, locals prefer the 'hand and water' technique, which involves cleaning your bottom with a small jug of water and your left hand. If you choose to do the same, carry some soap or hand gel for hand washing. Alternatively, toilet paper is widely available in cities and towns. However, used paper (as well as sanitary napkins and tampons) goes in the rubbish bin beside the toilet, not into the easily blocked drains.

TOURIST INFORMATION
Local Tourist Offices

In addition to the excellent national (Government of India) tourist offices, each state maintains its own network of tourist offices, though these vary in their efficiency and usefulness. Most of the tourist offices have free brochures and often a free (or inexpensive) local map, plus booklets listing state-owned tourist bungalows and hotels.

The first stop should be the tourism website of the **Government of India** (www.incredibleindia.org), with information in English, French, German, Spanish, Korean and Hindi. For international and regional offices, click the 'Held Desk' bar; for details of state tourism offices, click on 'Links' at the bottom of the homepage. You can also find useful information on the official state government websites – there's a list on india.gov.in/knowindia/districts.php. Also see the Information sections of this book's regional chapters.

TRAVEL PERMITS

Access to certain parts of India – particularly disputed border areas – is controlled by a complicated permit system. A permit known as an Inner-Line Permit (ILP) is required to visit northern parts of Sikkim that lie close to the disputed border with China/Tibet. Obtaining the ILP is basically a formality, but travel agents must apply on your behalf for certain areas, including many trekking routes passing close to the border. ILPs are issued by regional magistrates and district commissioners, either directly to travellers (for free) or through travel agents (for a fee). See the Sikkim chapter (p162) for more information.

Entering the Northeast states of Arunachal Pradesh, Nagaland, Manipur and Mizoram is much harder – tourists require a Restricted Area Permit (RAP), which must be arranged through Foreigners' Regional Registration Offices (FRRO; p316) offices. Ultimately, permission comes from the Ministry of Home Affairs in Delhi – without exception, your best chance of gaining a permit is to join an organised tour and let the travel agent make all the arrangements. See the Northeast States chapter for details (p192).

Most permits officially require you to travel in a group of four (married couples are also permitted in certain areas). This is enforced in some places, not in others – travel agents normally have tricks to help solo travellers get around these restrictions. Note that you can only travel to the places listed on the permit, often by set routes, and this is hard to change after the permit is issued.

It's not a bad idea to double check with tourism officials to see if permit requirements have undergone any recent changes before you head out to these areas.

VISAS

You must get a visa *before* arriving in India and these are easily available at Indian missions worldwide. Most people travel on the standard tourist visa, which is more than adequate for most needs. Student and business visas have strict conditions and also restrict your access to tourist services, such as tourist quotas on trains. An onward travel ticket is a requirement for most visas, but this is not always enforced, except for the 72-hour Transit Visa. Check the current requirements before you apply.

Six-month multiple-entry tourist visas (valid from the date of issue) are granted to nationals of most countries regardless of how long you intend to stay. You can enter and leave as often as you like, but you can only spend a total of 180 days in the country, starting from the date of issue. There are additional restrictions on travellers from Bangladesh and Pakistan, as well as certain Eastern European, African and Central Asian countries. Check any special conditions for your nationality with the Indian embassy in your country.

Visas are priced in the local currency – Brits pay UK£30, Americans pay US$60, Australians pay A$75 (an extra A$15 service fee applies at consulates) and Japanese citizens pay just ¥1200.

Extended visas (up to five years) are possible for people of Indian descent (excluding those in Pakistan and Bangladesh) who hold a non-Indian passport and live abroad. Contact your embassy for more details.

For visas lasting more than six months, you need to register at the Foreigners' Regional Registration Office (FRRO; see p316) within 14 days of arriving in India – inquire about these special conditions when you apply for your visa.

Visa Extensions

Delhi's **Ministry of Home Affairs** (☎ 011-23385748; 26 Jaisalmer House, Man Singh Rd; ☺ inquiries 9-11am Mon-Fri) has the power to grant 14-day visa extensions, but permission is rarely granted. The only circumstances where this might conceivably happen is if you were robbed of your passport just before you planned to leave the country at the end of your visa. If you run low on time, consider doing the 'visa run' over to

DIRECTORY

Bangladesh or Nepal and applying for another six- month tourist visa there.

If you do need to apply for an extension, or if you need a replacement visa after losing your passport, contact the **Foreigners' Regional Registration Office** (FRRO; Map p104; ☎ 033-22473301; 237A AJC Bose Rd, Kolkata; ☒ 10am-5pm Mon-Fri) in Kolkata. Although it has the authority to grant extensions, in all likelihood, you will be referred on to the Delhi **office** (☎ 011-26195530; frrodelhi@hotmail.com; Level 2, East Block 8, Sector 1, RK Puram; ☒ 9.30am-1.30pm & 2-3pm Mon-Fri).

If by some remote chance you meet the stringent criteria, extensions of 14 days are free for nationals of all countries except Japan (Rs 390), Sri Lanka (Rs 135 to 405, depending on the number of entries), Russia (Rs 1860) and Romania (Rs 500). You must bring your confirmed air ticket, one passport photo and a photocopy of your passport (information and visa pages). Note that this system is designed to get you out of the country promptly with the correct official stamps, not to give you two extra weeks of travel.

VOLUNTEER WORK

There are growing opportunities for foreign volunteers in the Northeast, but there is a major backlash against the casual volunteering that exists mainly for the benefit of the volunteer rather than the host community. Better volunteer agencies will work to make small, sustainable changes, letting the process be guided and informed by local people.

Always look for longer-term opportunities that require your specific skills – a month is a reasonable minimum time period to volunteer. It is possible to find a placement after you arrive in India, but most charities and NGOs prefer volunteers who apply in advance. Be aware that some Christian charities have a religious agenda that may conflict with the interests of local people.

Agencies Overseas

There are hundreds of international volunteering agencies, and it can be bewildering trying to assess which ones have ethical policies. The organisation **Ethical Volunteering** (www.ethical volunteering.org) has some excellent guidelines for choosing an ethical sending agency. Look for projects where you use your existing skills, rather than signing up for something that just sounds like a fun thing to do.

There are some tried and tested international projects, such as Britain's **Voluntary Service Overseas** (VSO; www.vso.org.uk), that place volunteers in serious professional roles, though the time commitment can be as much as two years. The international organisation **Indicorps** (www.indicorps.org) matches volunteers to projects across India in all sorts of fields, particularly social development. Many Indian NGOs also offer volunteer work – for listings click on www.indianngos.com.

To find sending agencies in your area, look at Lonely Planet's *Volunteering, Gap Year* and *Career Break* books, or search for 'Volunteering' on Google. Some good starting sites include:

- **Working Abroad** (www.workingabroad.com)
- **World Volunteer Web** (www.worldvolunteerweb .org)
- **Worldwide Volunteering** (www.worldwidevolunt eering.org.uk)

Aid Programmes in India

Following are listings of programmes in India that may have opportunities for volunteers. Always contact them in advance, rather than turning up on the doorstep unannounced. Donations of money or clothing from travellers may also be welcome. Note that unless otherwise indicated, volunteers are expected to cover their own costs (accommodation, food, transport etc).

KOLKATA

Founded by Mother Teresa, the Missionaries of Charity has opportunities at several care homes around Kolkata, including Nirmal Hriday (home for the dying), Prem Dan (for the sick and mentally ill) and Shishu Bhavan (for orphaned children). The administrative centre for volunteers is the **Motherhouse** (☎ 033-22497115; 54A AJC Bose Rd, Kolkata); register and get more information about placements at 3pm Monday, Wednesday and Friday. Note that this organisation has been criticised over sustainability issues and its religious agenda.

Also in Kolkata, the **Situational Management & Inter-Learning Establishment** (SMILE; ☎ 033-30956494; www.smilengo.org; Udayrajpur, Madhyamgram, No 9 Rail Gate, Kolkata 700129) runs a residential children's home and provides direct assistance to homeless children at Sealdah train station. Volunteers are accepted for two-week work camps and longer stays lasting up to a year (you pay a fee to participate, which covers meals and accommodation).

Started in 1979, **Calcutta Rescue** (☎ /fax 033-22175675; www.calcuttarescue.com; 4th fl, 85 Collins St, Kolkata 700016) provides medical care and health education for the poor and disadvantaged of Kolkata and West Bengal. The organisation has six- to nine-month openings for experienced medical staff, teachers and administrators – contact them directly for current vacancies.

The **Calcutta Society for the Prevention of Cruelty to Animals** (CSPCA; ☎ 033-22367738; cspca@rediffmail.com; 276 BB Ganguly St, Kolkata) has opportunities for qualified vets to help abused animals in Kolkata, but a minimum of one month is preferred.

ORISSA

The **Wildlife Society of Orissa** (☎ 0671-2311513; A-320, Sahid Nagar, Bhubaneswar 751007) accepts volunteers to help with its work to save endangered species in Orissa, especially the olive ridley turtle (see the boxed text, p260).

SIKKIM

Placements for volunteer teachers at schools in Sikkim – including the Denjong Pedma Choling Academy near Pelling – can be arranged through the British-based charity **Himalayan Education Lifeline Programme** (HELP; ☎ 012-2726 3055; www.help-education.org; Mansard House, 30 Kingsdown Park, Whitstable, Kent CT5 2DF, UK). Placements last two months and volunteers make a donation to towards running costs. English speakers over 20 years old are preferred.

Teaching placements in Sikkim can also be arranged through the **Muyal Liang Trust** (☎ 020-7229 4774; 53 Blenheim Crescent, London W11 2EG UK).

WEST BENGAL

In Darjeeling, **Hayden Hall** (☎ 2253228; haydenhall@cal.vsnl.net.in; 42 Laden La Rd, Darjeeling) has volunteer opportunities (minimum six months) for people with health-care and preschool-teaching backgrounds.

The **Tibetan Refugee Self-Help Centre** (☎ 0354-52346; 65 Gandhi Rd, Darjeeling) has occasional openings for volunteer nursery- and early-primary school teachers, medical staff, and geriatric- and child-care workers. Pervious experience is preferred.

Human Wave (☎ 033-26852823; humanwav@cal3.vsnl.net.in; 52 Tentultala Lane, Mankundu, Hooghly 712136)

runs community projects in the Sunderbans and youth projects in Kolkata. The minimum period for volunteers is 15 days and you pay a small fee for food and accommodation. Contact the organisation directly for opportunities.

WOMEN TRAVELLERS

Although things are changing, particularly in the big cities, India remains a conservative country, particularly when it comes to the role of women. Combined with local attitudes to sex, the skimpy clothing and culturally inappropriate behaviour of a minority of foreign women have had a ripple effect on the perception of foreign women by Indian men. The situation hasn't been helped by the Hollywood film industry constantly portraying Western women as sexual objects.

One unfortunate consequence is that many female travellers experience sexual harassment in India – predominantly lewd comments and invasion of privacy, though groping is not uncommon. Most cases are reported in urban centres and prominent tourist towns; the problem is much less prevalent in tribal and Buddhist areas in the hills.

While there's no need to be paranoid, you should be aware that that local men may be watching your behaviour and interpreting it in unintended ways. Getting constantly stared at is something you'll have to get used to. Just be thick-skinned and try to rise above it. It's best to refrain from returning male stares, as this may be considered a come-on; dark glasses can help.

Other harassment women have encountered include provocative gestures, jeering, getting 'accidentally' bumped into on the street and being followed. Be particularly careful at festivals – see p297. Women travelling with a male partner are less likely to be harassed. However, mixed couples of Indian and non-Indian descent may get disapproving stares, even if neither individual actually lives in India.

Ultimately, there are no sure-fire ways of shielding yourself from sexual harassment, even if you do everything 'right' – use your instincts and err on the side of caution if you are unsure. The warnings in this section may seem a little daunting, but most men are not out to bother you and thousands of female travellers rise above these challenges every year.

DIRECTORY

Sanitary towels and tampons are available from pharmacies in all large cities and most tourist centres. Carry additional stocks for travel off the beaten track.

Clothing

Avoiding culturally inappropriate clothing is a sure-fire way to reduce harassment. Steer clear of sleeveless tops, shorts, miniskirts (ankle-length skirts are recommended) and any other skimpy, see-through or tight-fitting clothing. Baggy clothing that hides the contours of your body is the way to go.

Although Orissa has beaches, take your cues from local women, who wear saris, *salwar kameez,* or long shorts and a T-shirt whenever swimming in public view. When returning from the beach, use a sarong to avoid stares on the way back to your hotel.

Indian dress, when done properly, can also help. The *salwar kameez* is regarded as respectable attire and wearing it will reflect your respect for local dress etiquette. The flowing outfit is also surprisingly cool in the hot weather, and the *dupatta* (long scarf) worn with it is very handy if you visit a shrine that requires your head to be covered.

Going into public wearing a *choli* (small tight blouse worn under a sari) or a sari petticoat (which many foreign women mistake for a skirt) is rather like strutting around half dressed – don't do it. Read personal experiences proffered by fellow women travellers on the India page at www.journeywoman.com.

Staying Safe

Women have reported being molested by masseurs and other therapists, especially in traveller centres. Try to check the reputation of any teacher or therapist and if you feel uneasy at any time, leave. For gynaecological health issues, seek out a female doctor.

Keep conversations with unknown men short, as idle chat may be interpreted as a come-on. Questions such as 'do you have a boyfriend?' or 'you are looking very beautiful' are indicators that the conversation may be taking a steamy tangent. Some women prepare in advance by wearing a pseudo wedding ring, or by announcing early on in the conversation that they are married or engaged (even if it isn't true).

If you still get the uncomfortable feeling that a man is encroaching on your space, he probably is. A firm request to keep away is usually enough, especially if your voice is loud enough to draw the attention of passers-by. Alternatively, the silent treatment (not responding to questions at all) can be remarkably effective.

When interacting with men on a day-to-day basis, adhere to the local practise of not shaking hands. Instead, say 'namaste' – the traditional, respectful Hindu greeting – and bow slightly with the hands brought together at the chest or head level.

Female film goers will probably feel more comfortable (and decrease the chances of potential harassment) by going to the cinema with a companion. Lastly, it's wise to arrive in towns before dark and, of course, always avoid walking alone at night, especially in isolated areas.

Taxis & Public Transport

Officials recommend that solo women prearrange an airport pick-up from their hotel if their flight is scheduled to arrive late at night. If that's not possible, catch a prepaid taxi and make a point of (in front of the driver) writing down the car registration and driver's name and giving it to one of the airport police. Many female travellers prefer to wait until daybreak before leaving the airport. Avoid taking taxis alone late at night (when many roads are deserted) and never agree to having more than one man (the driver) in the car.

On trains and buses, being a woman has some advantages. Women are able to queue-jump without consequence and on trains there are special women-only carriages. Solo women have reported less hassle by opting for the more expensive classes on trains, especially for overnight trips. If you're travelling overnight in a three-tier carriage, try to get the uppermost berth, which will give you more privacy (and distance from potential gropers).

On public transport, don't hesitate to return any errant limbs, put some item of luggage in between you and, if all else fails, find a new spot. Expensive-looking jewellery and handbags are a green light to muggers – casual wear will draw less attention.

WORK

Obtaining paid work in India is harder than you might expect, and local wages rarely make this cost effective for travellers. Business trips are easy, but working for an Indian company requires visa sponsorship from an Indian employer and finding a job before you travel. Although not strictly legal, casual opportunities exist at some tourist resorts teaching adventure sports and holistic therapies. However, this may deprive locals of much needed employment.

There may be opportunities with international package holiday companies for tour reps in Goa and Kerala (though you normally need to complete seasons in Europe to qualify), and opportunities for drivers and guides with the big overland tour companies.

Transport

CONTENTS

GETTING THERE & AWAY

The following sections contain information on transport to and around Northeast India. Flights, tours and rail tickets can also be booked online at www.lonelyplanet.com .travel_services.

ENTERING THE COUNTRY

Entering India by air or land is relatively straightforward, with standard immigration and customs procedures (p297).

THINGS CHANGE…

The information in this chapter is particularly vulnerable to change. Check directly with the airline or a travel agent to make sure you understand how a fare (and the ticket you may buy) works and be aware of the security requirements for international travel. Shop carefully. The details given in this chapter should be regarded as pointers and are not a substitute for your own careful, up-to-date research.

Passport

To enter India you need a valid passport, visa (see p315) and an onward/return ticket. If your passport is lost or stolen, immediately contact your country's representative (see p300). It's wise to keep photocopies of your airline ticket and the identity and visa pages from your passport in case of emergency. There are restrictions on entry for some nationalities – see the Visa section, p315.

AIR
Airports

The main gateway to the Northeast is **Kolkata** (CCU; Netaji Subhas Chandra Basu International Airport; ☎ 033-25118787; www.calcuttaairport.com), but a handful of international flights land in **Guwahati** (GAU; Lokpriya Gopinath Bordoloi International Airport; ☎ 0361-2840068) in Assam. You can also fly into Delhi, Mumbai (Bombay), Chennai (Madras) or Bengaluru (Bangalore) and pick up transfers to the Northeast with India's new budget airlines.

Larger airports have free luggage trolleys; elsewhere, porters will eagerly lug your load for a negotiable fee. For flights originating in India, hold bags must be passed through the X-ray machine in the departures hall before you check in. Baggage tags are required for the security check for all cabin bags, including cameras.

Airlines

India's national carrier is **Air India** (code AI; www .airindia.com; hub: Indira Gandhi International Airport, Delhi), but the state-owned domestic carrier **Indian Airlines** (www.indian-airlines.nic.in) also offers flights to 20 countries in Asia and the Middle East (though it has a poor record when it comes to safety and reliability).

The more dependable private airlines **Jet Airways** (www.jetairways.com) and **Air Sahara** (www .airsahara.net) offer flights from Delhi to Colombo, Kathmandu and the Maldives, with connections through to Kolkata (Calcutta), Guwahati, Agartala, Bhubaneswar and other towns in the northeast. Jet Airways has recently started long-haul flights to London, Bangkok, Kuala Lumpur and Singapore. For details about India's domestic airlines, see p325.

Most airlines no longer require reconfirmation of international tickets, though it's still a good idea to call to check that flight times haven't changed. The standard check-in time is about three hours before international departures, but remember to factor in the Indian traffic when planning your trip to the airport.

Security regulations change all the time – contact your airline in advance for the latest requirements.

AIRLINES FLYING TO FROM NORTHEAST INDIA

Foreign airlines flying directly to Kolkata include (websites have contact details):

Biman Bangladesh Airlines (code BG; www.bimanair .com) Hub: Zia international airport, Dhaka

British Airways (code BA; www.british-airways.com) Hub: Heathrow airport, London

Cosmic Air (code F5; www.cosmicair.com) Hub: Kathmandu airport

Druk Air (code KB; www.drukair.com.bt) Hub: Paro airport

Emirates (code EK; www.emirates.com) Hub: Dubai international airport

GMG Airlines (code Z5; www.gmgairlines.com) Hub: Zia international airport, Dhaka

Gulf Air (code GF; www.gulfairco.com) Hub: Bahrain international airport

Kuwait Airways (code KU; www.kuwait-airways.com) Hub: Kuwait international airport

Lufthansa Airlines (code LH; www.lufthansa.com) Hub: Frankfurt international airport

Singapore Airlines (code SQ; www.singaporeair.com) Hub: Changi airport, Singapore

Thai Airways International (code TG; www.thaiair.com) Hub: Bangkok international airport

Tickets

An onward or return air ticket is a condition of the tourist visa, so few visitors buy international tickets inside India. Only designated travel agents can book international flights, but fares are normally the same if you book directly with the airlines. The departure tax of Rs 500 (Rs 150 for most subcontinent and Southeast Asian countries) and the Rs 200 passenger service fee is included in the price of almost all tickets.

The fares we've given in this section represent average starting fares available at the time of research. Contact a travel agent or surf the web to get up-to-the-minute fares and flight schedules. Note that fares on airline websites are often cheaper than going through an agent.

AFRICA

There are direct flights to Delhi or Mumbai from South Africa and East Africa, but you'll have to pick up a connecting flight to the Northeast. Return fares to Delhi or Mumbai

TRANSPORT

CLIMATE CHANGE & TRAVEL

Climate change is a serious threat to the ecosystems that humans rely on, and air travel is one of the fastest-growing contributors to the problem. Lonely Planet regards travel, overall, as a global benefit, but we believe that everyone has a responsibility to limit their personal impact on global warming.

Flying & Climate Change

Every form of motorised travel generates CO_2 but planes are far and away the worst offenders, not just because of the fuel they consume, but because they release greenhouse gases high into the atmosphere. Two people taking a return flight between Europe and the US will contribute as much to climate change as an average household's gas and electricity consumption over a whole year.

Carbon Offset Schemes

Climatecare.org and other websites use 'carbon calculators' that allow travellers to offset the level of greenhouse gases they are responsible for with financial contributions to sustainable travel schemes and tree-planting projects that offset the effects of global warming – including projects in India.

Lonely Planet, together with *Rough Guides* and other concerned partners in the travel industry, support the carbon offset scheme run by climatecare.org. Lonely Planet offsets all of its staff and author travel. For more information check out our website: www.lonelyplanet.com.

start at US$600 from Nairobi (Kenya) and US$500 from Cape Town or Johannesburg (South Africa).

ASIA
India has excellent connections to the rest of Asia.

Bangladesh
Dhaka is the air hub for Bangladesh. Biman Bangladesh, GMG Airlines and Indian Airlines offer flights between Dhaka and Kolkata (from US$200 return) or Delhi (from US$500 return). GMG also has a flight from Kolkata to Chittagong (US$178 return).

Japan
Tokyo/Narita is the main hub for flights between Japan and India. Flights to Delhi, Chennai, Kolkata and Mumbai start from US$540, flying direct or with a stop in Southeast Asia.

Maldives
Most flights leave from the west coast of India. Excursion fares to Malé from Thiruvananthapuram (Trivandrum) in Kerala start at US$200 return; several Indian airlines offer connections from Kolkata via Chennai or Bengaluru.

Myanmar (Burma)
Return flights between Yangon (Rangoon) and Kolkata cost around US$350. Alternatively, you can connect through Bangkok, Singapore or Kuala Lumpur for around US$500.

Nepal
Royal Nepal Airlines, Indian Airlines and several private carriers provide inexpensive flights from Kathmandu to Kolkata, Delhi, Mumbai, Bengaluru and Varanasi. One-way/return fares from Kolkata start from US$120/240, but cheap deals as low as US$90 are offered by the budget carrier Cosmic Air.

Pakistan
There are regular air connections between Delhi or Mumbai to Lahore or Karachi, with connections on to Kolkata. However, flights between India and Pakistan are often suspended when relations between the two countries sour. At the time of research, return fares cost around US$300 to Delhi and US$200 to Mumbai from Karachi.

Singapore, Malaysia, Hong Kong & China
There are several useful air routes from Southeast Asia to Kolkata, or you can connect through Delhi, Mumbai, Bengaluru or Chennai. Return flights between Kolkata and Singapore, Hong Kong or Kuala Lumpur start from US$550. Several airlines have recently started flights from Beijing and Shanghai to Delhi or Mumbai (from around US$550), where you can pick up onward connections to Kolkata.

Sri Lanka
There are no direct flights, but Sri Lankan Airlines and several Indian carriers offer flights from Colombo to Mumbai (US$390), Delhi (US$450), Bengaluru (US$270) and Thiruvananthapuram (US$200), with easy connections on to the Northeast.

Thailand
Numerous carriers offer flights from Bangkok to Kolkata, Guwahati (Indian Airlines only) and other Indian hubs. Return fares from Bangkok include: Kolkata (US$400), Guwahati, Delhi or Mumbai (US$500), and Chennai (US$700).

AUSTRALIA & NEW ZEALAND
Qantas has a flight from Sydney to Mumbai via Darwin, but the best way to reach the Northeast is through Kolkata with a stop in Southeast Asia. Return fares to Mumbai or Kolkata range from A$1200 and A$1700, depending on the season.

Flights between India and New Zealand go via Southeast Asia. Return tickets from Auckland to Kolkata start at NZ$1500, or you can fly to Delhi or Mumbai for around NZ$1200 and pick up an onward flight to Kolkata.

CONTINENTAL EUROPE
There are flights to Kolkata from most European capitals, either direct or with a stop in another European country or the Middle East. Expect to pay €600 to €1000 from Paris, Frankfurt, Madrid, Amsterdam or Rome. From Helsinki, Stockholm, and other Scandinavian capitals, fares start at €560 (or equivalent).

UK & IRELAND
Flights from London or Manchester to Kolkata range from UK£350 to UK£600, depending on the season, or you can connect through Delhi, Mumbai, Chennai, Bengaluru or Amritsar.

USA & CANADA

There are no direct flights between the USA and Kolkata, but there are easy connections through Europe and Asia. Fares vary – bank on US$1100 or more from the East Coast and US$1300 or more from the West Coast.

Canada also has no direct flights to Kolkata, but you can connect through Delhi or Mumbai for around C$1600. From eastern and central Canada, most flights go via Europe; from Vancouver and the west coast, flights go via Asia.

LAND
Border Crossings

Although most visitors fly into India, the Northeast has land borders with Nepal, Bhutan, Bangladesh, Tibet (China) and Myanmar (closed to foreigners). A small number of travellers also enter India on the classic overland route though Europe, the Middle East and Pakistan – consult Lonely Planet's *Istanbul to Kathmandu*, or see the 'London to India' section on www.seat61.com/India .htm for more on this route.

If you enter India by bus or train, you'll be required to disembark at the border for standard immigration and customs checks. You must have a valid Indian visa in advance as no visas are available at the border.

Drivers of cars and motorcycles will need the vehicle's registration papers, liability insurance and an International Driving Permit. You'll also need a *Carnet de passage en douane*, which acts as a temporary waiver of import duty. To find out the latest requirements, contact your local automobile association.

See p328 and p329 for more on car and motorcycle travel.

BANGLADESH

Foreigners can use four of the land crossings between Bangladesh and India, all in West Bengal or the Northeast states. Exiting Bangladesh overland is complicated by red tape – if you enter by air, you require a road permit (or 'change of route' permit) to leave by land. This free permit can be obtained in Dhaka at the **Directorate of Immigration and Passports** (☎ 02-9131891/9134011; Sher-e-Bangla Nagar, Agargaon Rd; ✆ 9am-5pm Sun-Thu) in two to three working days; bring several passport photos. Some travellers have also reported problems exiting Bangladesh overland with the visa issued on arrival at Dhaka airport.

Visas for Bangladesh can be obtained in advance from the Bangladeshi missions in Kolkata (see p300) and Agartala (see the boxed text, p224). Most offices issue visas in two working days with two passport photos; fees vary depending on nationality.

Heading from Bangladesh to India, you must prepay the exit tax at a designated branch of the Sonali Bank, which may be some distance from the border post.

Kolkata to Dhaka

There are daily bus services from Kolkata to Dhaka, crossing the India–Bangladesh border at Benapol – see p122 for more information. Plans for a train link between Kolkata and Dhaka have dragged on for years – inquire locally for progress reports.

Siliguri to Burimari (Chengrabandha)

This minor northern border crossing is accessible from Siliguri in West Bengal. You must take a private bus from outside Tenzin Norgay central bus station to Jalpaiguri (Rs 40, two hours) and change there for the border post at Burimari (Chengrabandha). See p138 for more details.

Shillong to Sylhet

This little-used crossing offers a handy back route from Meghalaya to Bangladesh. Share jeeps run every morning from Bara Bazaar in Shillong to the border post at Dawki, a short walk or taxi ride from Tamabil, which has regular buses to Sylhet – see the boxed text, p219 for more information.

Agartala to Dhaka

The Bangladesh border is 4km from Agartala and several daily trains run on to Dhaka from Akhaura on the Bangladesh side of the border. See the boxed text, p224, for more details.

BHUTAN

Phuentsholing in West Bengal is the main entry and exit point between India and Bhutan, but you now need a full Bhutanese visa to enter the country, which must be obtained at least 15 days before your trip from a registered travel agent listed under the **Bhutan Department of Tourism** (www.tourism.gov.bt).

Visitors to Bhutan pay an obligatory daily fee of US$200 per person per night (US$165 from July to August), which includes tours, meals, accommodation and local transport.

TRANSPORT

CROSSING INTO NEPAL

Border Hours

Border crossings between India and Nepal are generally open 24 hours but border staff stop work from around 10pm to 5am. If you arrive outside these hours, you may have to wake someone up to complete the entry and exit formalities or find a hotel until the office reopens in the morning.

Foreign Exchange

Most border crossings have banks or foreign-exchange desks that can change Indian and Nepali rupees, but not much else. Bhairawa and Kakarbhitta have moneychangers that accept US dollars, euros and UK pounds.

Visas

Two-month single-entry visas for Nepal (US$30) are available at all the border crossings, but payment is due in US dollars and you need two passport photos. Alternatively, obtain a single-entry or six-month multiple-entry (US$80) visa in advance from a Nepali mission. In Kolkata, the **Nepali consulate** (☎ 033-24561224; 1 National Library Ave, Alipore; ♱ 9am-4pm Mon-Fri) issues visas while you wait.

Siliguri/Kolkata to Phuentsholing

Buses from Kolkata and Siliguri to the border post at Phuentsholing are run by Bhutan Transport Services. From Kolkata, there's a direct bus at 7pm on Tuesday, Thursday and Saturday (Rs 300, 20 hours). See the boxed text, p138, for information on travel from Siliguri. There's also a rail route from Siliguri via Alipurduar (on the main train line between Siliguri and Guwahati) connecting with local buses to the border.

NEPAL

Although the security situation in Nepal has improved massively since the ceasefire in 2006, it makes sense to check the security situation before crossing into Nepal by land – local newspapers and international news websites are good places to start.

Political and weather conditions permitting, there are five land border crossings between India and Nepal:

- **Raxaul** in Bihar to **Birganj** in central Nepal
- **Panitanki** in West Bengal to **Kakarbhitta** in eastern Nepal
- **Sunauli** in Uttar Pradesh to **Bhairawa** in central Nepal
- **Jamunaha** in Uttar Pradesh to **Nepalganj** in western Nepal
- **Banbassa** in Uttaranchal to **Mahendranagar** in western Nepal

Only the Panitanki–Kakarbhitta crossing is really convenient for the Northeast, but quite a few people enter Nepal using one crossing and leave via another. Be cautious of buying a 'through ticket' to Kathmandu – all passengers must change buses at the border and there are numerous scams involving run-down local buses at deluxe bus prices. See the boxed text, above, for general information on crossing into Nepal.

Panitanki

The handiest crossing for Darjeeling, Sikkim and the Northeast states. Buses and share jeeps run to the border from Siliguri and other towns in West Bengal, and there are regular buses on to Kathmandu. See the boxed text, p138, for details on crossing the border.

Raxaul

This crossing in Bihar is reasonably convenient for Kolkata. The most comfortable way to reach Raxaul is the daily *Mithila Express* from Kolkata's Howrah train station (sleeper/3AC/2AC Rs 256/723/1037). From Raxaul, it's a Rs 30 autorickshaw ride to Birganj, which has onward buses to Kathmandu (NRs 250 to NRs 500, eight hours) and Pokhara (NRs 250 to NRs 500, 10 hours).

Sunauli

The easiest crossing for Varanasi or Delhi, with connections on to Kathmandu, Pokhara and Lumbini. Coming from Kolkata, the easiest option is to take a train from Howrah to Gorakhpur in Uttar Pradesh, then a bus to

Sunauli (Rs 56, 2½ hours). On the far side, private buses run to Kathmandu and Pokhara (NRs 180 to NRs 220, 10 hours).

Jamunaha
This little-used western crossing is a useful gateway for Nepal's Royal Bardia National Park and there are good connections to Pokhara and Kathmandu. Coming from Kolkata, take the train to Lucknow in Uttar Pradesh, then the bus to Rupaidha Bazar (Rs 160, seven hours), a short rickshaw ride from the Jamunaha border post. On the far side, buses run to Kathmandu (NRs 450 to NRs 540, 12 hours) and Pokhara (NRs 400 to NRs 520, 12 hours).

Banbassa
The little-used crossing between Banbassa in Uttaranchal and Mahendranagar in western Nepal is too far away to be of much use to travellers in the Northeast, but it's a possible exit point from Nepal. Buses run to Mahendranagar from Pokhara (Rs 730, 16 hours), and Kathmandu (NRs 750, 16 hours) and there are onward buses from Banbassa to Delhi (Rs 210, 10 hours). Check the roads are open before attempting this crossing.

PAKISTAN
All the border crossings between India and Pakistan are in the far west of the country – far from Kolkata and the Northeast. To leave India via Pakistan, you will have to travel right across the country. Unfortunately, crossing between the two countries depends on good diplomatic relations between India and Pakistan. Security is also a concern – trains and buses between the two countries have been repeatedly targeted by militant groups.

You must have a visa to enter Pakistan, and it is usually easiest to obtain this in the Pakistan mission in your home country. At the time of writing, the **Pakistan embassy** (☎ 24676004; 2/50G Shantipath, Chanakyapuri; ✉ applications 8.30am-11.30am Mon-Fri) in Delhi was issuing double-entry, two-month tourist visas for most nationalities in around two days, but applicants need a letter of recommendation from their home embassy as well as the usual application forms and passport photos.

The most popular option is to take the direct bus or the slow, crowded *Samjhauta Express* train between Delhi and Lahore. However, security is a serious concern – the Delhi–Lahore

train was bombed by militants in February 2007. Alternatively, take the train to Amritsar, then a bus to Attari and a second bus on from Wagah to Lahore. A third option is the *Thar Express* train from Jodhpur in Rajasthan to Munabao/Khokrapar and on to Karachi. Check locally for details of all these routes.

SEA
There are several sea routes between India and surrounding islands but none leave Indian sovereign territory – see p327. There has been talk of a passenger ferry service between southern India and Colombo in Sri Lanka but this has yet to materialise.

GETTING AROUND

AIR
Indian Airlines, Jet Airways and Air Sahara charge rupee fares for Indian citizens and higher US dollar fares for foreigners (usually payable in rupees). Most budget airlines charge the same low rupee fares to everyone. Budget airline seats can be booked by telephone, through travel agents or cheaply online. Fares change daily, but you get a better deal the further you book in advance – check the airline websites for details.

Reconfirmation is normally only required if your ticket was bought outside India, but call a few days ahead to be safe. For details of discounts on airfares, see p300.

Check-in for domestic flights is an hour before departure, and hold luggage must be X-rayed and stamped before you check-in. Every item of cabin baggage needs a baggage label, which must be stamped as part of your security check. Note that batteries may need to be removed from all electronic items and placed in the hold.

The baggage allowance is 20kg (10kg for smaller aircraft) in economy class, 30kg in business.

Airlines in India
In recent years, there has been a massive surge in domestic flights around India. Although it has a poor record on safety and reliability, state-owned carrier **Indian Airlines** (www.indian-air lines.nic.in) has the largest network, but the private airlines **Jet Airways** (www.jetairways.com) and **Air Sahara** (www.airsahara.net) are catching up fast.

TRANSPORT

Then there are India's new budget airlines, offering discounted rupee fares for flights around the country over the internet. As a rough indication, fares for a one-hour flight range from US$150 on an established carrier to Rs 1000 with a budget airline.

In fact, the whole aviation industry is seriously overinflated and there is no guarantee that all the airlines will still be around by the time you read this. At the time of writing, the airlines listed below were serving destinations across India – the regional chapters and the airline websites have details of routes, fares and booking offices.

Air Deccan (www.airdeccan.net) Budget carrier serving Bhubaneswar and numerous cities in the Northeast states.

Air India (www.airindia.com) Operates a few domestic flights from the international terminal in Kolkata.

Indian Airlines (www.indian-airlines.nic.in) With its subsidiary Alliance Air, the state-domestic carrier serves destinations across the Northeast.

IndiGo (www.goindigo.in) A growing budget carrier, with flights to Kolkata and Guwahati.

Jet Airways (www.jetairways.com) India's favourite private airline, serving Kolkata, Guwahati, Imphal, Agartala, Jorhat and Bagdogra (for Sikkim).

Kingfisher Airlines (www.flykingfisher.com) Yep, it's an airline owned by a beer company, serving Kolkata, Guwahati, Dibrugarh and Agartala.

Sahara Airlines (www.airsahara.net) A similar domestic and international network to Jet Airways; Northeast stops include Kolkata, Guwahati, Dibrugarh and Bhubaneswar.

Spicejet (www.spicejet.com) Discount seats to hubs across India, including Guwahati and Kolkata.

Air Passes

The big three Indian airlines – Indian Airlines, Jet Airways and Air Sahara – all offer

---

HELICOPTER SERVICES IN INDIA

Several companies offer helicopter shuttle services around the Northeast. The state-subsidised carrier **Pawan Hans Helicopters** (www.pawanhans.nic.in) connects the regional capitals of Northeast India, and there are also flights from Siliguri in West Bengal to Gangtok in Sikkim (see p136). However, helicopter travel in India has a shocking safety record, with four major accidents since 2002, and numerous minor crashes. We won't say don't use them, but be aware of the risks.

---

air passes. However, these rarely work out cheaper than buying individual discounted tickets.

Indian Airlines offers the reasonably useful 'Discover India' pass for US$630/895 for 15/21 days, plus US$21 tax for each flight sector. You can travel on any flight, except the flight to the Lakshadweep Islands, but you can't visit the same place twice.

Air passes are also available from Jet Airways (foreigners and Indians) and Air Sahara (Indian nationals only).

BICYCLE

The quiet backroads of the Northeast are a pleasure to cycle and there are no restrictions on bringing a bicycle into India, though it may be cheaper to hire or buy a bike after you arrive. Contact your airline for information about transporting your bike and customs formalities in your home country. Mountain bikes with off-road tyres give the best protection against India's potholed and puncture-prone roads, particularly if you plan to tackle steeper mountain roads.

Roadside cycle mechanics abound but bring spare tyres and brake cables, lubricating oil and a chain repair kit, and plenty of puncture repair patches. Bikes can often be carried for free, or for a small luggage fee, on the roofs of public buses. You can also carry your bike in the luggage car on trains – see the instructions for transporting motorcycles on p330.

Read up on bicycle touring before you travel – Rob van de Plas's *Bicycle Touring Manual* (Bicycle Books, 1987) and Stephen Lord's *Adventure Cycle-Touring Handbook* (Trailblazer Publications, 2006) are good places to start. The **Cycle Federation of India** (☎ /fax 011-23392578 in Delhi) can provide general advice on cycling in India.

Road rules are virtually nonexistent in India and cities and national highways are hazardous places to cycle, so stick to quieter backroads wherever possible. However, be wary of cycling into rebel-held areas in the Northeast states (see p298). Always be conservative about the distances you expect to cover – an experienced cyclist can cover 60km to 100km a day on the plains, 40km to 60km on sealed mountain roads and 40km or less on dirt roads.

See p77 for more on cycling in the Northeast.

Rental

There are only a handful of places in the Northeast with bicycles for hire, and these tend to be only good for local sightseeing. Expect to pay Rs 30 to 100 per day for a roadworthy, Indian-made bike. Hire places may require cash or an ID card as a security deposit.

Purchase

Kolkata has its share of bicycle shops, particularly along Bentinck St, just east of BBD Bagh (Map p106). Mountain bikes from reputable brands like Hero, Atlas, Hercules or Raleigh start at Rs 2000, and extras like panniers, stands and bells are readily available.

Reselling is quite easy – ask at local cycle shops or put up an advert on traveller noticeboard boards. You should be able to get 50% of what you originally paid back if it was a new bike and is still in reasonably good condition.

BOAT

Regular scheduled ferries connect mainland India to Port Blair in the Andaman Islands. The journey takes around 56 hours from Kolkata (see p122).

There are also numerous ferry services across rivers, from chain pontoons to wicker coracles, and boat cruises along the Sunderbans delta in West Bengal and the Brahmaputra River in Assam – see the regional chapters and the Activities chapter (p76) for more information.

BUS

Buses are the cheapest way to get around the Northeast, though trains are much more comfortable. State government-run bus companies are usually the safest and most reliable option, and seats can be booked up to a month in advance. Private buses tend to be cheaper, but drivers take reckless risks and conductors cram as many passengers on as possible to maximise profits.

On any bus, sit between the axles to minimise the effect of bumps and potholes. All buses make regular snack and toilet stops, providing a break from the rattle and shake but adding hours to journey times. Share jeeps supplement the bus service in mountainous areas – see p332.

Avoid night buses unless there is no alternative – drivers use the quieter roads as an excuse to take even more death-defying risks. Note that buses must travel in armed convoys through some parts of the Northeast, particularly in northern Tripura – check the latest security situation before you travel (see p298).

Luggage is either stored in compartments underneath the bus (sometimes for a small fee) or it can be carried free of charge on the roof. Conductors will carry your bags up for a modest tip, or you can scramble up yourself and have piece of mind that your luggage is secure. Riding on the roof on public buses used to be a thrilling way to see the Indian countryside but the authorities have decided that it is a) dangerous and b) too much fun. It's now only possible on local buses between outlying villages.

If your bags go on the roof, make sure they are locked shut and securely tied to the metal baggage rack – some unlucky travellers have seen their belongings go bouncing off the roof on bumpy roads! Theft is a minor risk so keep an eye on your bags at snack and toilet stops, and never leave your day pack unattended inside the bus.

Classes

Both state and private companies offer 'ordinary' buses – ageing rattletraps with wonky windows that blast in dust and cold air – or more expensive 'deluxe' buses, which range from less decrepit versions of ordinary buses to flashy Volvo tour buses with air-con and reclining two-by-two seating. Try to book at least one day in advance. Be warned that travel agents have been known to book people onto ordinary buses at super-deluxe prices.

Costs

On ordinary-class buses, expect to pay Rs 40 to 60 for a three-hour daytime journey and Rs 200 to 300 for an all-day or overnight trip. Add around 50% to the ordinary fare for deluxe services, double the fare for air-con and triple or quadruple the fare for a two-by-two service.

Reservations

Deluxe buses can usually be booked in advance – up to a month in advance for government buses – at the bus stand or local travel agents. Reservations are rarely possible on 'ordinary' buses and travellers often get left behind in the mad rush for a seat – try sending

TRANSPORT

a travelling companion ahead to grab some space while you deal with the luggage or pass a book or article of clothing through an open window and place it on an empty seat.

At many bus stations there is a separate women's queue, although this isn't always obvious as signs are often in Hindi and men frequently join the melee. Local women will merrily push to the front and few people will object if female travellers do the same.

CAR

Few people bother with self-drive car rental, but hiring a car with a driver is surprisingly affordable, particularly if several people share the costs. Seatbelts are rarely working – if they are use them, or hold on to handrails.

Hiring a Car & Driver

Hiring a car and driver is an excellent way to see several places in one day, and the cost comes down dramatically if you can find other travellers to split the fare. Some taxi companies will only operate in a designated area, dictated by their government permit. If you cross a state border, there may be an additional fee.

Try to find a driver who speaks some English and knows the region. For multiday trips, the fare should cover the driver's meals and accommodation, but confirm this when you book (preferably in writing). Drivers make their own sleeping and eating arrangements in the evening. Offering to buy the driver a meal is a nice gesture but it can cause embarrassment – use your judgement.

Finally, it is *essential* to set the ground rules from day one. Many travellers have complained of having their holiday completely dictated by their driver. Politely, but firmly, let the driver know from the outset that you're the boss!

COSTS

The cost of charter trips depends on the distance and the terrain (driving on mountain roads uses more petrol, hence the higher cost). One-way trips often cost as much as return trips to cover petrol for the driver's return trip.

Expect to pay Rs 1500 to Rs 2000 for a day trip, including petrol and waiting time at sights along the way. Some taxi unions set a time limit or a maximum kilometre distance for day trips – if you go over, you'll have to pay extra. To avoid problems later, confirm in advance that the fare covers petrol, sightseeing stops, all your chosen destinations, and meals and accommodation for the driver.

You generally pay the fee at the end of the trip, though the driver may ask for an advance to cover petrol (ask for a written record of this at the time). A moderate tip is customary at the end of your journey.

Self-Drive Hire

Self-drive car hire is possible in Kolkata, but given the hair-raising driving conditions most travellers opt for a car with driver. International rental companies with representatives in India include **Budget** (www.budget.com) and **Hertz** (www.hertz.com), and you'll need an International Driving Permit.

HITCHING

Truck drivers supplement the bus service in some remote areas for a fee, but as drivers rarely speak English, you may have difficulty explaining where you want to go and working out how much is a fair price to pay. As anywhere, women are strongly advised against hitching alone.

LOCAL TRANSPORT

Buses, cycle-rickshaws, autorickshaws, taxis, boats and urban trains provide transport around India's cities. On any form of transport without a fixed fare, agree on the fare *before* you start your journey and make sure that it covers your luggage and every passenger. If you don't, expect heated altercations when you get to your destination.

Even where local transport is metered, drivers may refuse to use the meter, demanding an elevated 'fixed' fare. If this happens, hail another taxi – moving taxis are more likely to charge a fair price than taxis parked at tourist sights. On some routes, particularly to airports, it may be impossible to get a metered fare.

Costs for public transport vary from town to town. Fares usually increase at night (by up to 100%) and some drivers charge a few rupees extra for luggage. Carry plenty of small bills for taxi and rickshaw fares as drivers rarely have change. Taxis in the Northeast states often pick up extra passengers along the way to earn a little more on the side.

Many taxi/autorickshaw drivers are involved in the commission racket – for more information, see p299.

Autorickshaw, Tempo & Vikram

The Indian autorickshaw is basically a three-wheeled motorcycle with a tin or canvas cab, providing room for two passengers and luggage. You may also hear autorickshaws called autos, scooters, tuk-tuks or Bajaj (after the company that makes them). Autorickshaws tend to be cheaper than taxis and they are usually metered, though getting the driver to turn the meter on can be a challenge.

Tempos and *vikrams* are basically outsized autorickshaws with room for more passengers, running on fixed routes for a fixed fare. In country areas, you may also see the fearsome-looking 'three-wheeler' – a crude, tractor-like *tempo* with a front wheel on an articulated arm.

Bus

Urban buses, particularly in the big cities, are fume-belching, human-stuffed, mechanical monsters that travel at breakneck speed (except during morning and evening rush hour, when they can be endlessly stuck in traffic). It's usually more convenient and comfortable to opt for an autorickshaw or taxi.

Boat

Various kinds of local ferries offer transport across and down rivers in the Northeast, from big car ferries to wooden canoes and wicker coracles – see the regional chapters for details. Most boats will also carry bikes and motorcycles for a fee.

Cycle-Rickshaw

A cycle-rickshaw is a pedal cycle with two rear wheels, supporting a bench seat for passengers. Most have a canopy that can be

raised in wet weather, or lowered to provide extra space for luggage. As with taxis and autorickshaws, fares must be agreed upon in advance.

Locals invariably pay lower fares than foreigners, but considering the effort put in by the rickshaw-wallahs, it's hard to begrudge them a few extra rupees. Around Rs 20 to 40 is a fair price to pay for a 1km to 2km journey in town and tips are always appreciated.

Kolkata is the last bastion of the human-powered rickshaw, a handcart pulled directly by the rickshaw-wallah, though some people feel that being towed around by a local is a little too colonial for comfort.

Taxi

Most towns have taxis, and these are usually metered. However, getting drivers to use the meter can be a major hassle. Drivers often claim that the meter is broken and request a hugely elevated fixed fare. Threatening to get another taxi will often miraculously fix it. It is usually less hassle to use a prepaid taxi from the airport or train station.

Getting a metered ride is only half the battle. Meters are almost always outdated, so fares are calculated using a combination of the meter reading and a complicated 'fare adjustment card'. Predictably, this system is open to abuse. If you spend a few days in any town, you'll soon get a feel for the difference between a reasonable fare and a rip-off. Many taxi drivers supplement their earnings with commissions – refuse any unplanned diversions to shops, hotels or private travel agencies.

Other Local Transport

In some towns, tongas (horse-drawn two-wheelers) and *victorias* (horse-drawn carriages) still operate. Kolkata has a tram network and a fast and efficient underground train network. See regional chapters for further details.

MOTORCYCLE

With its quiet backroads and amazing scenery, the Northeast is an amazing part of the country for long-distance motorcycle touring. However, riding in India can be quite an undertaking – there are some excellent motorcycle tours (see p331) that will save you the rigmarole of going it alone.

The classic way to motorcycle round India is on an Enfield Bullet, still built to the original

---

PREPAID TAXIS

Most Indian airports and many train stations have a prepaid-taxi booth, normally just outside the terminal building. Here, you can book a taxi to town here for a fixed price (which will include baggage) and hopefully avoid price hikes and commission scams. However, it makes sense to hold on to the payment coupon until your reach your chosen destination, in case the driver has any other ideas! Smaller airports and stations may have prepaid autorickshaw booths instead.

TRANSPORTING MOTORCYCLES BY RAIL

You can cut out some tedious long-distance journeys in India by putting your bike on the train. First, buy a standard train ticket for the journey, then take your bike to the station parcel office with your passport, registration papers, International Driving Permit and insurance documents. Packing-wallahs will wrap your bike in protective sacking for around Rs 100 and you must fill out various forms and pay the shipping fee – around Rs 1600 for a 350cc or smaller bike – plus an insurance fee of 1% of the declared value of the bike. Just bring the same paperwork to collect your bike from the goods office at the far end.

1940s specifications. As well as making a satisfying chugging sound, these bikes are fully manual, making them easy to repair (parts can be found everywhere in India). On the other hand, Enfields are less reliable than many of the newer, Japanese-designed bikes.

Sikkim, West Bengal and Assam are popular destinations for motorcycle expeditions, and it's possible to cross into Nepal, Bangladesh and Bhutan with the correct paperwork – contact the relevant diplomatic mission for details. At the time of research, it wasn't possible to cross into Pakistan by motorcycle, but check locally in case the rules have changed.

The most popular starting point for motorcycle tours is Delhi, partly because this is the easiest place to buy or rent a motorcycle. Even if your final destination is the Northeast, it probably makes sense to fly into Delhi to rent or buy a bike before you travel across the country.

Driving License

You're technically required to have a valid International Driving Permit to hire a motorcycle in India; however, many places are happy with the driving license from your home country. In tourist areas, you may be able to rent a small motorcycle without a driving license, but you definitely won't be covered by insurance in the event of an accident.

ROAD DISTANCES (KM)

	Agartala	Bhubaneswar	Bodhgaya	Darjeeling	Delhi	Guwahati	Kohima	Kolkata	Puri	Shillong	Varanasi
Agartala	---										
Bhubaneswar	2179	---									
Bodhgaya	1443	745	---								
Darjeeling	468	819	454	---							
Delhi	2584	1745	1015	1559	---						
Guwahati	599	1483	1044	550	1959	---					
Kohima	683	1822	1383	889	2298	339	---				
Kolkata	1680	441	456	681	1461	1081	1420	---			
Puri	1196	93	552	889	1538	2022	2361	1524	---		
Shillong	499	1583	781	650	2059	100	439	1181	2122	---	
Varanasi	1778	965	270	779	780	1179	1518	680	843	1279	---

Fuel & Spare Parts

Spare parts for Indian and Japanese machines are widely available in larger towns and cities, but it makes sense to carry spares (valves, fuel lines, piston rings etc). Seek local advice about fuel availability before setting off into remote regions.

For all machines, make sure you regularly check and tighten all nuts and bolts, as Indian roads and engine vibration tend to make things loose quickly. Check the engine and gearbox oil level regularly (at least every 500km) and clean the oil filter every few thousand kilometres. Trips to puncture-wallahs are par for the course – start your trip with new tyres (around Rs 1500) and carry spanners to remove your own wheels.

Rental

Long-term bike rental is not widely available in the Northeast, so you may be better off renting a bike in Delhi and transporting it to the Northeast by train – see opposite.

Delhi's Karol Bagh is the best place in India to rent bikes, and Japanese and Indian-made bikes in the 100cc to 150cc range are cheaper than the big 350cc to 500cc Enfields. As a deposit, you'll need to leave your passport, air ticket or a big cash lump sum.

One consistently reliable company for long-term rentals is **Lalli Motorbike Exports** (☎ 011-25728579; www.lallisingh.com; 1740-A/55 Basement, Hari Singh Nalwa St, Abdul Aziz Rd, Karol Bagh Market, Delhi) – a 500cc Enfield costs Rs 13,000/23,000 for three/eight weeks, and the price includes excellent advice and an invaluable crash course in Enfield mechanics and repairs.

Insurance

Only rent a bike with third-party insurance – if you hit someone without insurance, the consequences can be severe. Reputable companies will include third-party cover in their policies. Those that don't probably aren't reputable.

You must also arrange insurance if you buy a motorcycle. The minimum level of cover is third-party insurance – available for Rs 300 to 500 per year. Comprehensive insurance (recommended) costs Rs 500 to 2000 per year.

Organised Motorcycle Tours

Several companies offer organised motorcycle tours around Sikkim, Assam and West Bengal (often combined with trips to Bhutan), with a support vehicle, mechanic and a guide. Below are some reputable companies (see websites for contact details, itineraries and prices):

Classic Bike Adventures (www.classic-bike-india.com)
Ferris Wheels (www.ferriswheels.com.au)
H-C Travel (www.hctravel.com)
Himalayan Roadrunners (www.ridehigh.com)
Indian Shepherds (www.asiasafari.com)
Lalli Singh Tours (www.lallisingh.com)
Moto Discovery (www.motodiscovery.com)
Saffron Road Motorcycle Tours (www.saffronroad.com)

Purchase

If you are planning a longer tour, consider purchasing a motorcycle. Second-hand bikes are widely available from bike-repair shops and the paperwork is a lot easier than buying a new machine.

Again, Delhi's Karol Bagh is the best place to purchase a motorcycle. Hari Singh Nalwa St has dozens of motorcycle and parts shops, but we consistently receive good reports about Lalli Motorbike Exports, see left

COSTS

A well-looked-after second-hand 350cc Enfield will cost Rs 18,000 to 40,000; the 500cc model will cost Rs 35,000 to 65,000. You should be able to resell the bike for 50% to 60% of the original price if it's still in decent condition. Prices for new Enfield models are listed on www.royalenfield.com. Shipping an Indian bike overseas is complicated and expensive – ask the shop you bought the bike from to explain the process.

As well as the cost of the bike, you'll have to pay for insurance – see left. Helmets are available for Rs 1000 to 1500, and extras like panniers, luggage racks, protection bars, rearview mirrors, lockable fuel caps, petrol filters and extra tools are easy to come by. An Enfield 500cc gives about 25km/L and the 350cc model gives slightly more.

OWNERSHIP PAPERS

There is plenty of paperwork associated with owning a motorcycle. The registration papers are signed by the local registration authority when the bike is first sold and you'll need these papers when you buy a second-hand bike. Foreign nationals cannot change the name on the registration. Instead, you must fill out the forms for a change of ownership and transfer of insurance. If you buy a new bike, the company selling it must register the machine for you, adding to the cost.

For any bike, the registration must be renewed every 15 years (for around Rs 5000) and you must make absolutely sure that there are no outstanding debts or criminal proceedings associated with the bike. The whole process is extremely complicated and it makes sense to seek advice from the company selling the bike. Allow around two weeks to get the paperwork finished and get on the road.

Road Conditions

Given the road conditions in India, this is not a country for novice riders. Hazards range from cows and chickens crossing the carriageway to broken-down trucks, pedestrians on the road, and perpetual potholes and unmarked speed humps. Rural roads sometimes have grain crops strewn across them to be threshed by passing vehicles – a serious sliding hazard for bikers.

Try not to cover too much territory in one day and avoid travelling after dark if at all possible. On busy national highways expect to average 50km/h without stops; on winding back roads and dirt tracks this can drop to 10km/h.

Road Rules

Traffic in India nominally drives on the left-handside, but in reality, it seems everyone drives all over the road. Observe local speed limits (these vary from state to state) and give way to any larger vehicles. Locals tend to use the horn more than the brake, but travellers should heed the advice of the Border Roads Organisation – it is better to be Mr Late than the late Mr! Alcohol and riding never go together – it's illegal as well as dangerous.

SHARE JEEPS

In mountain areas, such as Sikkim, West Bengal and Arunachal Pradesh, share jeeps supplement the bus service, charging similar fixed fares. Although nominally designed for five to six passengers, most share jeeps squeeze in as many as 11. The seats beside and immediately behind the driver are more expensive than the cramped bench seats at the rear. Jeeps only leave when full, but drivers will leave immediately if you pay for all the empty seats in the vehicle.

Jeeps run from jeep stands and 'passenger stations' at the junctions of major roads; ask

locals to point you in the right direction. In some states, jeeps are known as 'sumos' after the TATA Sumo, India's favourite 4WD. See the regional chapters for routes and fares. Be warned that many locals suffer from travel sickness – be prepared to give up your window seat to queasy fellow passengers.

TOURS

Tours are available all over India, run by tourist offices, local transport companies and travel agencies. Organised tours can be an inexpensive way to see several places on one trip, through you rarely get much time at each place. If you arrange a car and driver through the local taxi office, you'll have more freedom about where you go and how long you stay.

Drivers typically double as guides, or you can hire a qualified local guide for a fee. However, be wary of touts claiming to be professional guides in tourist towns – ask the local tourist office for advice on reputable guides. Assess the experience of trekking guides by asking about routes, distances and the type of terrain involved – vague answers should set off alarm bells.

On any overnight tour or trek, ensure that all the necessary equipment is provided (eg first aid, camping gear) and inspect everything before you set off. Always confirm exactly what the quoted price includes (food, accommodation, petrol, trekking equipment, guide fees etc).

See the Tours sections in the regional chapters for information on local tours. For more on treks and tours, read the Activities chapter (p75).

TRAIN

Train travel is one of the joys of India. Around 14 million passengers travel by train in India every day – the network is extensive, prices are reasonable and the experience of travelling on an Indian train is a reason to travel all by itself.

From Kolkata, main-line trains fan out across the Northeast. New Jalpaiguri station near Siliguri is the gateway to Darjeeling, Kalimpong and Sikkim, while Guwahati is the starting point for branch lines to Nagaland and Upper Assam. Winding up through the hills from Siliguri, the toy train to Darjeeling is one of the most famous rail journeys in India.

| EXPRESS TRAIN FARES IN RUPEES | | | | | | |
Distance (km)	1AC	2AC	3AC	Chair car (CC)	Sleeper (SL)	Second (II)
100	400	226	158	122	56	35
200	653	269	256	199	91	57
300	888	502	348	271	124	78
400	1107	626	433	337	154	97
500	1325	749	519	404	185	116
1000	2159	1221	845	657	301	188
1500	2734	1546	1070	832	381	238
2000	3309	1871	1295	1007	461	288

At first, the process of booking a train seat can seem bewildering, but behind the scenes things are incredibly well organised – see Reservations on p334 for tips on buying a ticket. Trains are far better than buses for long-distance and overnight trips – you can lie down, walk around and use the bathroom whenever you need to.

Train services to certain destinations are often increased during major festivals but the crowds make this a risk time to travel (see p297). Something else to be aware of is passenger drugging and theft – see p298.

We've listed useful trains throughout this book but all the routes are listed in *Trains at a Glance* (Rs 45), available at train station bookstands and city newsstands. Alternatively, you can use the train search engine on the **Indian Railways website** (www.indianrail.gov .in). Another useful resource is www.seat61 .com/India.htm.

Larger stations often have English-speaking staff who can help with picking the best train. At smaller stations, midlevel officials such as the deputy station master usually speak English.

Classes

Trains and seats come in a variety of classes. Express and mail trains usually have general (2nd-class) compartments with unreserved seating – usually a real free-for-all – and a series of more comfortable compartments that you can reserve. On day trains, there may be a chaircar with padded reclining seats and (usually) air-con, or an executive chair car with better seats and more space.

For overnight trips, you have several choices. 'Sleeper' berths are arranged in groups of six, with two roomier berths across the aisle, in fan-cooled carriages. Air-conditioned carriages have either three-tier air-con

(3AC) berths, in the same configuration as sleepers, or two-tier air-con (2AC) berths in groups of four on either side of the aisle. Some trains also have flashier 1st-class air-con (1AC) berths, with a choice of two- or four-berth compartments with locking doors.

Bedding is provided in all air-con sleeping compartments and there is usually a meal service, plus regular visits from the coffee and chai-wallah. In sleeper class, bring your own bedding (an Indian shawl is perfect for the job). For an excellent description of the various train classes (including pictures) see www .seat61.com/India.htm. In all classes, a padlock and a length of chain are useful for securing your luggage to the baggage racks.

In sleeping compartments, the lower berths convert to seats for day-time use. If you'd rather sleep, book an upper berth. Note that there is usually a locked door between the reserved and unreserved carriages – if you get trapped on the wrong side, you'll have to wait till the next station to change.

There are also special train services connecting major cities. Shatabdi express trains are same-day services with seating only. They're fast and comfortable, but the tinted glass windows cut down the views considerably. Rajdhani express trains are long-distance overnight services between Delhi and state capitals.

Costs

Fares are calculated by distance and class of travel – as shown in the box, above. Rajdhani and Shatabdi express trains are slightly more expensive, but the price includes meals. Most air-conditioned carriages have a catering service (meals are bought to your seat); in unreserved classes, carry samosas or other portable snack foods. You can search for exact fares on

TRANSPORT

www.indianrail.gov.in. Seniors get discounted train tickets – see p300.

Major stations offer 'retiring rooms', which can be handy if you have a valid ticket or Indrail Pass – see p294. Another useful facility is the left-luggage office (cloakroom). Locked bags (only) can be stored for a small daily fee if you have a valid train ticket. For peace of mind, chain your bag to the baggage rack and check the opening times to make sure you can get your bag when you need it.

Reservations

No reservations are required for general (2nd-class) compartments. You can reserve seats in all chair car, sleeper, and 1AC, 2AC and 3AC carriages up to 60 days in advance – book ahead for all overnight journeys.

The reservation procedure is fairly simple – obtain a reservation slip from the information window and fill in the starting station, the destination station, the class you want to travel in, and the name and number of the train (this is where *Trains at a Glance* comes into its own). You then join the long queue to the ticket window, where your ticket will be printed.

In larger cities, there are dedicated ticket windows for foreigners and credit-card payments. Elsewhere, you'll have to join a general queue and pay in rupees cash. A special tourist quota is set aside for foreign tourists travelling between popular stations. These seats can only be booked at special reservation offices in Kolkata (see p123) and other major cities, and you need to show your passport and visa as ID.

You can pay for tourist quota seats in rupees, UK pounds, US dollars or euros, in cash or Thomas Cook and Amex travellers cheques (change is given in rupees). How-ever, some offices may ask to see foreign-exchange certificates before accepting payment in rupees.

Trains are frequently overbooked, but many passengers cancel. You can buy a ticket on the 'wait list' and try your luck – a refund is available if you fail to get a seat. Refunds are available on any ticket, even after departure, with a penalty – the rules are complicated so check when you book.

If you don't want to go through the hassle of buying a ticket yourself, many travel agencies and hotels will purchase your train ticket for a small commission, though ticket scams abound.

Internet bookings are also possible on the website www.irctc.co.in, and you can choose an e-ticket, or have the tickets sent to you inside India by courier. See the 'How to buy tickets – from outside India' heading on the website www.seat61.com/India.htm for more booking tips.

Reserved tickets show your seat/berth number (or wait-list number) and the carriage number. When the train pulls in, keep an eye out for your carriage number written on the side of the train. A list of names and berths is also posted on the side of each reserved carriage – a beacon of light for panicking travellers!

Train Passes

The Indrail pass permits unlimited rail travel for the period of its validity, but it offers limited savings and you must still make reservations. Passes are available for one to 90 days of travel and you can book through overseas travel agents or station ticket offices in major Indian cities – click on the Information/International Tourist link on www.indianrail.gov .in for prices and conditions.

Health

There is huge geographical variation in India, from tropical beaches to the Himalayan mountains. Consequently, environmental issues such as heat, cold, and altitude can cause significant health problems. Hygiene is generally poor in India, so food and water-borne illnesses are common. Many insect-borne diseases are present, particularly in tropical areas. Medical care is basic in many areas, so it is essential to be well prepared before travelling to India.

Travellers tend to worry about contracting infectious diseases when in the tropics, but these rarely cause serious illness or death in travellers. Pre-existing medical conditions and accidental injury (especially traffic accidents), account for most life-threatening problems. Becoming ill in some way, however, is very common. Fortunately most travellers' illnesses can be prevented with some common-sense behaviour or treated with a well-stocked traveller's medical kit.

The following advice is a general guide only and does not replace the advice of a doctor trained in travel medicine.

BEFORE YOU GO

Pack medications in their original, clearly labelled containers. A signed and dated letter from your physician describing your medical conditions and medications, including generic names, is very useful. If carrying syringes or needles, be sure to have a physician's letter documenting their medical necessity. If you have a heart condition, bring a copy of your ECG taken just prior to travelling.

If you take any regular medication, bring double your ordinary needs in case of loss or theft. You'll be able to buy many medications over the counter in India without a doctor's prescription, but it can be difficult to find some of the newer drugs, particularly the latest antidepressant drugs, blood pressure medications and contraceptive pills.

INSURANCE

Even if you are fit and healthy, don't travel without health insurance – accidents do happen. Declare any existing medical conditions you have – the insurance company will check if your problem is pre-existing and will not cover you if it is undeclared. You may require extra cover for adventure activities such as rock climbing and scuba diving. If your health insurance doesn't cover you for medical expenses abroad, consider getting extra insurance. If you're uninsured, emergency evacuation is expensive; bills of over US$100,000 are not uncommon.

It's a good idea to find out in advance if your insurance plan will make payments directly to providers or if it will reimburse you later for overseas health expenditures. (In many countries doctors expect payment in cash.) Some policies offer lower and higher medical-expense options; the higher ones are chiefly for countries that have extremely high medical costs, such as the USA. You may prefer a policy that pays doctors or hospitals directly rather than you having to pay on the spot and claim from your insurance company later. If you do have to claim later, make sure you keep all relevant documentation. Some policies ask that you telephone back (reverse charges) to a centre in your home country where an immediate assessment of your problem will be made.

VACCINATIONS

Specialised travel-medicine clinics are your best source of information; they stock all available vaccines and will be able to give specific recommendations for you and your trip. The doctors will take into account factors such as past vaccination history, the length of your trip, activities you may be undertaking and underlying medical conditions, such as pregnancy.

Most vaccines don't give immunity until at least two weeks after they're given, so visit a doctor four to eight weeks before departure. Ask your doctor for an International Certificate of Vaccination (otherwise known as the 'yellow booklet'), which will list all the vaccinations you've received.

Recommended Vaccinations
The World Health Organization (WHO) recommends these vaccinations for travellers to India (as well as being up-to-date with measles, mumps and rubella vaccinations):

Adult diphtheria and tetanus Single booster recommended if none in the previous 10 years. Side effects include sore arm and fever.

Hepatitis A Provides almost 100% protection for up to a year; a booster after 12 months provides at least another 20 years' protection. Mild side effects such as headache and sore arm occur in 5% to 10% of people.

Hepatitis B Now considered routine for most travellers. Given as three shots over six months. A rapid schedule is also available, as is a combined vaccination with Hepatitis A. Side effects are mild and uncommon, usually headache and sore arm. In 95% of people lifetime protection results.

Polio In 2007 polio was still present in India. Only one booster is required as an adult for lifetime protection. Inactivated polio vaccine is safe during pregnancy.

Typhoid Recommended for all travellers to India, even if you only visit urban areas. The vaccine offers around 70% protection, lasts for two to three years and comes as a single shot. Tablets are also available; however, the injection is usually recommended as it has fewer side effects. Sore arm and fever may occur.

Varicella If you haven't had chickenpox, discuss this vaccination with your doctor.

These immunisations are recommended for long-term travellers (more than one month) or those at special risk:

Japanese B Encephalitis Three injections in total. Booster recommended after two years. Sore arm and headache are the most common side effects. Rarely, an allergic reaction comprising hives and swelling can occur up to 10 days after any of the three doses.

Meningitis Single injection. There are two types of vaccination: the quadravalent vaccine gives two to three years' protection; meningitis group C vaccine gives around 10 years' protection. Recommended for long-term backpackers aged under 25.

Rabies Three injections in all. A booster after one year will then provide 10 years' protection. Side effects are rare – occasionally headache and sore arm.

Tuberculosis (TB) A complex issue. Adult long-term travellers are usually recommended to have a TB skin test before and after travel, rather than vaccination. Only one vaccine given in a lifetime.

Required Vaccinations
The only vaccine required by international regulations is yellow fever. Proof of vaccination will only be required if you have visited a country in the yellow fever zone within the six days prior to entering India. If you are travelling to India from Africa or South America, you should check to see if you require proof of vaccination.

INTERNET RESOURCES
There is a wealth of travel health advice on the internet – www.lonelyplanet.com is a good place to start. Some other suggestions:

Centers for Disease Control and Prevention (CDC; www.cdc.gov) Good general information.

MD Travel Health (www.mdtravelhealth.com) Provides complete travel health recommendations for every country, updated daily.

World Health Organization (WHO; www.who.int/ith/) Its superb book *International Travel & Health* is revised annually and available online.

FURTHER READING
Lonely Planet's *Healthy Travel – Asia & India* is a handy pocket size and packed with useful information, including pretrip planning, emergency first aid, immunisation and disease information, and what to do if you get sick on the road. Other recommended references include *Travellers' Health* by Dr Richard Dawood and *Travelling Well* by Dr Deborah Mills – check out the website **Travelling Well** (www.travellingwell.com.au).

HEALTH ADVISORIES

It's usually a good idea to consult your government's travel-health website before departure, if one is available:

Australia (www.dfat.gov.au/travel/)
Canada (www.travelhealth.gc.ca)
New Zealand (www.mfat.govt.nz/travel)
South Africa (www.dfa.gov.za/travelling)
UK (www.doh.gov.uk/traveladvice/)
US (www.cdc.gov/travel/)

MEDICAL CHECKLIST

Recommended items for a personal medical kit:

- Antifungal cream, eg Clotrimazole
- Antibacterial cream, eg Muciprocin
- Antibiotic for skin infections, eg Amoxicillin/Clavulanate or Cephalexin
- Antihistamine – there are many options, eg Cetrizine for daytime and Promethazine for night
- Antiseptic, eg Betadine
- Antispasmodic for stomach cramps, eg Buscopam
- Contraceptive method
- Decongestant, eg Pseudoephedrine
- DEET-based insect repellent
- Diarrhoea medication – consider an oral rehydration solution (eg Gastrolyte), diarrhoea 'stopper' (eg Loperamide) and antinausea medication (eg Prochlorperazine). Antibiotics for diarrhoea include Norfloxacin or Ciprofloxacin; for bacterial diarrhoea Azithromycin; for Giardia or amoebic dysentery Tinidazole.

- First-aid items such as scissors, elastoplasts, bandages, gauze, thermometer (but not mercury), sterile needles and syringes, safety pins and tweezers
- Ibuprofen or another anti-inflammatory
- Indigestion tablets, eg Quick Eze or Mylanta
- Iodine tablets (unless you are pregnant or have a thyroid problem) to purify water
- Laxative, eg Coloxyl
- Migraine medication if you suffer from them
- Paracetamol
- Pyrethrin to impregnate clothing and mosquito nets
- Steroid cream for allergic/itchy rashes, eg 1% to 2% hydrocortisone
- Sunscreen and hat
- Throat lozenges
- Thrush (vaginal yeast infection) treatment, eg Clotrimazole pessaries or Diflucan tablet
- Ural or equivalent if prone to urine infections

HEALTH

IN TRANSIT

DEEP VEIN THROMBOSIS (DVT)

Deep vein thrombosis (DVT) occurs when blood clots form in the legs during plane flights, chiefly because of prolonged immobility. The longer the flight, the greater the risk. Though most blood clots are reabsorbed uneventfully, some may break off and travel through the blood vessels to the lungs, where they may cause life-threatening complications.

The chief symptom of DVT is swelling or pain of the foot, ankle or calf, usually but not always on just one side. When a blood clot travels to the lungs, it may cause chest pain and difficulty in breathing. Travellers with any of these symptoms should immediately seek medical attention.

To prevent the development of DVT on long flights you should walk about the cabin, perform isometric compressions of the leg muscles (ie contract the leg muscles while sitting), drink plenty of fluids, and avoid alcohol and tobacco.

JET LAG & MOTION SICKNESS

Jet lag is common when crossing more than five time zones; it results in insomnia, fatigue, malaise or nausea. To avoid jet lag try drinking plenty of fluids (nonalcoholic) and eating light meals. Upon arrival, seek exposure to natural sunlight and readjust your schedule (for meals, sleep etc) as soon as possible.

Antihistamines such as dimenhydrinate (Dramamine), promethazine (Phenergan) and meclizine (Antivert, Bonine) are usually the first choice for treating motion sickness. Their main side effect is drowsiness. An herbal alternative is ginger, which works like a charm for some people.

IN INDIA

AVAILABILITY OF HEALTHCARE

Medical care is hugely variable in India. Some cities now have clinics catering specifically to travellers and expatriates. These clinics are usually more expensive than local medical facilities, but are worth utilising, as they will offer a superior standard of care. Additionally, they understand the local system, and are aware of the safest local hospitals and best specialists. They can also liaise with insurance companies should you require evacuation. Recommended clinics are listed under Information in the regional chapters in this book. It is difficult to find reliable medical care in rural areas.

Self-treatment may be appropriate if your problem is minor (eg traveller's diarrhoea), you are carrying the relevant medication and you cannot attend a recommended clinic. If you think you may have a serious disease, especially malaria, do not waste time; travel to the nearest quality facility to receive attention. It is always better to be assessed by a doctor than to rely on self-treatment.

Before buying medication over the counter, always check the use-by date and ensure the packet is sealed. Don't accept items that have been poorly stored (eg lying in a glass cabinet exposed to the sun).

INFECTIOUS DISEASES

Avian Flu

'Bird Flu' or Influenza A (H5N1) is a subtype of the type A influenza virus. This virus typically infects birds and not humans; however, in 1997 the first documented case of bird-to-human transmission was recorded in Hong Kong. Currently very close contact with dead or sick birds is the principal source of infection and bird to human transmission does not easily occur.

Symptoms include high fever and typical influenza-like symptoms with rapid deterioration leading to respiratory failure and death in many cases. The early administration of antiviral drugs such as Tamiflu is recommended to improve the chances of survival. At this time it is not routinely recommended for travellers to carry Tamiflu with them – rather immediate medical care should be sought if bird flu is suspected. At the time of writing there have been no recorded cases in travellers or expatriates.

There is currently no vaccine available to prevent bird flu. For up-to-date information check these two websites:

▪ www.who.int/en/
▪ www.avianinfluenza.com.au

Coughs, Colds & Chest Infections

Around 25% of travellers to India will develop a respiratory infection. This usually starts as a virus and is exacerbated by environmental conditions such as pollution in the cities, or cold and altitude in the mountains. Commonly a secondary bacterial infection will intervene – marked by fever, chest pain, and coughing up discoloured or blood-tinged sputum. If you have the symptoms of an infection, seek medical advice or commence a general antibiotic.

Dengue Fever

This mosquito-borne disease is becomingly increasingly problematic in the tropical world, especially in the cities. As there is no vaccine available it can only be prevented by avoiding mosquito bites. The mosquito that carries dengue bites day and night, so use insect avoidance measures at all times. Symptoms include high fever, severe headache and body ache (dengue was previously known as 'breakbone fever'). Some people develop a rash and experience diarrhoea. There is no specific treatment, just rest and paracetamol – do not take aspirin as it increases the likelihood of haemorrhaging. See a doctor to be diagnosed and monitored.

Hepatitis A

A problem throughout the region, this food- and water-borne virus infects the liver, causing jaundice (yellow skin and eyes), nausea and lethargy. There is no specific treatment for hepatitis A, you just need to allow time for the liver to heal. All travellers to India should be vaccinated against hepatitis A.

Hepatitis B

The only sexually transmitted disease that can be prevented by vaccination, hepatitis B is spread by body fluids. The long-term consequences can include liver cancer and cirrhosis.

Hepatitis E

Transmitted through contaminated food and water, Hepatitis E has similar symptoms to hepatitis A, but is far less common. It is a severe problem in pregnant women and can result in the death of both mother and baby. There is currently no vaccine, and prevention is by following safe eating and drinking guidelines.

HIV

HIV is spread via contaminated body fluids. Avoid unsafe sex, unsterile needles (including in medical facilities) and procedures such as tattoos. The growth rate of HIV in India is one of the highest in the world.

Influenza

Present year-round in the tropics, influenza (flu) symptoms include fever, muscle aches, runny nose, cough and sore throat. It can be severe in people over the age of 65 or in those with medical conditions such as heart disease or diabetes – vaccination is recommended for these individuals. There is no specific treatment, just rest and paracetamol.

Japanese B Encephalitis

This viral disease is transmitted by mosquitoes and is rare in travellers. Like most mosquito-borne diseases it is becoming a more common problem in affected countries. Most cases occur in rural areas and vaccination is recommended for travellers spending more than one month outside of cities. There is no treatment, and a third of infected people will die while another third will suffer permanent brain damage.

Malaria

For such a serious and potentially deadly disease, there is an enormous amount of misinformation concerning malaria. You must get expert advice as to whether your trip actually puts you at risk. For most rural areas, the risk of contracting malaria far outweighs the risk of any tablet side effects. Before you travel, seek medical advice on the right medication and dosage for you.

Malaria is caused by a parasite transmitted by the bite of an infected mosquito. The most important symptom of malaria is fever, but general symptoms such as headache, diarrhoea, cough or chills may also occur. Diagnosis can only be made by taking a blood sample.

Two strategies should be combined to prevent malaria – mosquito avoidance, and antimalaria medications. Most people who catch malaria are taking inadequate or no antimalarial medication.

Travellers are advised to prevent mosquito bites by taking these steps:

- Use a DEET-containing insect repellent on exposed skin. Wash this off at night, as long as you are sleeping under a mosquito net. Natural repellents such as citronella can be effective, but must be applied more frequently than products containing DEET.
- Sleep under a mosquito net impregnated with pyrethrin.
- Choose accommodation with screens and fans (if not air-conditioned).
- Impregnate clothing with pyrethrin in high-risk areas.
- Wear long sleeves and trousers in light colours.
- Use mosquito coils.
- Spray your room with insect repellent before going out for your evening meal.

There are a variety of medications available. The effectiveness of the chloroquine and Paludrine combination is now limited in many parts of South Asia. Common side effects include nausea (40% of people) and mouth ulcers.

The daily tablet doxycycline is a broad-spectrum antibiotic that has the added benefit of helping to prevent a variety of tropical diseases, including leptospirosis, tick-borne disease and typhus. The potential side effects include photosensitivity (a tendency to sunburn), thrush (in women), indigestion, heartburn, nausea and interference with the contraceptive pill. More serious side effects include ulceration of the oesophagus – you can help prevent this by taking your tablet with a meal and a large glass of water, and never lying down within half an hour of taking it. It must be taken for four weeks after leaving the risk area.

Lariam (mefloquine) has received much bad press, some of it justified, some not. This weekly tablet suits many people. Serious side effects are rare but include depression, anxiety, psychosis and having fits. Anyone with a history of depression, anxiety, other psychological disorder, or epilepsy should not take Lariam. It is considered safe in the second and third trimesters of pregnancy. Tablets must be taken for four weeks after leaving the risk area.

The new drug Malarone is a combination of atovaquone and proguanil. Side effects are uncommon and mild, most commonly nausea and headache. It is the best tablet for scuba divers and for those on short trips to high-risk areas. It must be taken for one week after leaving the risk area.

Rabies

Around 30,000 people die in India each year from rabies. This uniformly fatal disease is spread by the bite or lick of an infected animal –

most commonly a dog or monkey. You should seek medical advice immediately after any animal bite and commence postexposure treatment. Having pretravel vaccination means the postbite treatment is greatly simplified. If an animal bites you, gently wash the wound with soap and water, and apply iodine-based antiseptic. If you are not prevaccinated you will need to receive rabies immunoglobulin as soon as possible, and this is almost impossible to obtain in much of India.

STDs
Sexually transmitted diseases most common in India include herpes, warts, syphilis, gonorrhoea and chlamydia. People carrying these diseases often have no signs of infection. Condoms will prevent gonorrhoea and chlamydia but not warts or herpes. If after a sexual encounter you develop any rash, lumps, discharge or pain when passing urine, seek immediate medical attention. If you have been sexually active during your travels, have an STD check on your return home.

Tuberculosis
While TB is rare in travellers, those who have significant contact with the local population (such as medical and aid workers and long-term travellers) should take precautions. Vaccination is usually only given to children under the age of five, but adults at risk are recommended pre- and post-travel TB testing. The main symptoms are fever, cough, weight loss, night sweats and tiredness.

Typhoid
This serious bacterial infection is also spread via food and water. It gives a high and slowly progressive fever, headache, and may be accompanied by a dry cough and stomach pain. It is diagnosed by blood tests and treated with antibiotics. Vaccination is recommended for all travellers who are spending more than a week in India. Be aware that vaccination is not 100% effective, so you must still be careful with what you eat and drink.

TRAVELLER'S DIARRHOEA
This is by far the most common problem affecting travellers – between 30% and 70% of people will suffer from it within two weeks of starting their trip. In over 80% of cases, traveller's diarrhoea is caused by a bacteria (there are numerous potential culprits), and

therefore responds promptly to treatment with antibiotics. Treatment with antibiotics will depend on your situation – how sick you are, how quickly you need to get better, where you are etc.

Traveller's diarrhoea is defined as the passage of more than three watery bowel actions within 24 hours, plus at least one other symptom such as fever, cramps, nausea, vomiting or feeling generally unwell.

Treatment consists of staying well hydrated; rehydration solutions like Gastrolyte are the best option. Antibiotics such as norfloxacin, ciprofloxacin or azithromycin will kill the bacteria quickly.

Loperamide is just a 'stopper' and doesn't get to the cause of the problem. It can be helpful, though (eg if you have to go on a long bus ride). Don't take loperamide if you have a fever, or blood in your stools. Seek medical attention quickly if you do not respond to an appropriate antibiotic.

Amoebic Dysentery
Amoebic dysentery is very rare in travellers but is often misdiagnosed by poor-quality labs. Symptoms are similar to bacterial diarrhoea, ie fever, bloody diarrhoea and generally feeling unwell. You should always seek reliable medical care if you have blood in your diarrhoea. Treatment involves two drugs: Tinidazole or Metronidazole to kill the parasite in your gut and then a second drug to kill the cysts. If left untreated, complications such as liver or gut abscesses can occur.

Giardiasis
Giardia is a parasite that is relatively common in travellers. Symptoms include nausea, bloating, excess gas, fatigue and intermittent diarrhoea. The parasite will eventually go away if left untreated but this can take months; the best advice is to seek medical treatment. The treatment of choice is Tinidazole, with Metronidazole being a second-line option.

ENVIRONMENTAL HAZARDS
Air Pollution
Air pollution, particularly vehicle pollution, is an increasing problem in most of India's major cities. If you have severe respiratory problems, speak with your doctor before travelling to any heavily polluted urban centres. This pollution also causes minor respiratory problems such as sinusitis, dry throat and

---

DRINKING WATER

- Never drink tap water
- Bottled water is generally safe – check the seal is intact at purchase
- Avoid ice
- Avoid fresh juices – they may have been watered down
- Boiling water is the most efficient method of purifying it
- The best chemical purifier is iodine. It should not be used by pregnant women or those with thyroid problems.
- Water filters should also filter out viruses. Ensure your filter has a chemical barrier such as iodine and a small pore size, eg less than four microns.

---

irritated eyes. If troubled by the pollution, leave the city for a few days and get some fresh air.

Diving & Surfing

Divers and surfers should seek specialised advice before they travel to ensure their medical kit contains treatment for coral cuts and tropical ear infections, as well as the standard problems. Divers should ensure their insurance covers them for decompression illness – get specialised dive insurance through an organisation such as **Divers Alert Network** (DAN; www.danasiapacific.org). Have a dive medical before you leave your home country – there are certain medical conditions that are incompatible with diving.

Food

Eating in restaurants is the biggest risk factor for contracting traveller's diarrhoea. Ways to avoid it include eating only freshly cooked food, and avoiding shellfish and food that has been sitting in buffets. Peel all fruit, cook vegetables and soak salads in iodine water for at least 20 minutes. Eat in busy restaurants with a high turnover of customers. See p90 for more on safe eating.

Heat

Many parts of India are hot and humid throughout the year. For most people it takes at least two weeks to adapt to the hot climate. Swelling of the feet and ankles is common, as are muscle cramps caused by excessive sweating. Prevent these by avoiding dehydration and excessive activity in the heat. Take it easy when you first arrive. Don't eat salt tablets (they aggravate the gut); drinking rehydration solution or eating salty food helps. Treat cramps by stopping activity, resting, rehydrating with double-strength rehydration solution and gently stretching.

Dehydration is the main contributor to heat exhaustion. Symptoms include feeling weak, headache, irritability, nausea or vomiting, sweaty skin, a fast, weak pulse and a normal or slightly elevated body temperature. Treatment involves getting out of the heat and/or sun, fanning the sufferer and applying cool wet cloths to the skin, laying the sufferer flat with their legs raised and rehydrating with water containing ¼ teaspoon of salt per litre. Recovery is usually rapid and it is common to feel weak for some days afterwards.

Heat stroke is a serious medical emergency. Symptoms come on suddenly and include weakness, nausea, a hot dry body with a body temperature of over 41°C, dizziness, confusion, loss of coordination, fits, and eventually collapse and loss of consciousness. Seek medical help and commence cooling by getting the person out of the heat, removing their clothes, fanning them and applying cool wet cloths or ice to their body, especially to the groin and armpits.

Prickly heat is a common skin rash in the tropics, caused by sweat being trapped under the skin. The result is an itchy rash of tiny lumps. Treat it by moving out of the heat and into an air-conditioned area for a few hours and by having cool showers. Creams and ointments clog the skin, so they should be avoided. Locally bought prickly heat powder can be helpful.

Tropical fatigue is common in long-term expatriates based in the tropics. It's rarely due to disease and is caused by the climate, inadequate mental rest, excessive alcohol intake and the demands of daily work in a different culture.

High Altitude

If you are going to altitudes above 3000m, you should get information on preventing, recognising and treating Acute Mountain Sickness (AMS). The biggest risk factor for developing altitude sickness is going too high too quickly – you should follow a conservative acclimatisation schedule such as can be found in all good trekking guides – and you should *never* go to a higher altitude when you have any symptoms that could be altitude related. There is no way to predict who will get altitude sickness and it is often the younger, fitter members of a group who succumb.

Symptoms usually develop during the first 24 hours at altitude but may be delayed up to three weeks. Mild symptoms include headache, lethargy, dizziness, difficulty sleeping and loss of appetite. AMS may become more severe without warning and can be fatal. Severe symptoms include breathlessness, a dry, irritative cough (which may progress to the production of pink, frothy sputum), severe headache, lack of coordination and balance, confusion, irrational behaviour, vomiting, drowsiness and unconsciousness.

Treat mild symptoms by resting at the same altitude until recovery, which usually takes a day or two. Paracetamol or aspirin can be taken for headaches. If symptoms persist or become worse, however, immediate descent is necessary; even 500m can help. Drug treatments should never be used to avoid descent or to enable further ascent.

The drugs acetazolamide and dexamethasone are recommended by some doctors for the prevention of AMS; however, their use is controversial. They can reduce the symptoms, but they may also mask warning signs; severe and fatal AMS has occurred in people taking these drugs.

To prevent acute mountain sickness:
- Ascend slowly – have frequent rest days, spending two to three nights at each rise of 1000m.
- It is always wise to sleep at a lower altitude than the greatest height reached during the day, if possible. Also, once above 3000m, care should be taken not to increase the sleeping altitude by more than 300m per day.
- Drink extra fluids. The mountain air is dry and cold and moisture is lost as you breathe.
- Eat light, high-carbohydrate meals.
- Avoid alcohol and sedatives.

Insect Bites & Stings
Bedbugs don't carry disease but their bites are very itchy. They live in the cracks of furniture and walls and then migrate to the bed at night to feed on you. You can treat the itch with an antihistamine. Lice inhabit various parts of your body but most commonly your head and pubic area. Transmission is via close contact with an infected person. They can be difficult to treat and you may need numerous applications of an antilice shampoo such as pyrethrin. Pubic lice are usually contracted from sexual contact.

Ticks are contracted after walking in rural areas. Ticks are commonly found behind the ears, on the belly and in armpits. If you have had a tick bite and experience symptoms such as a rash at the site of the bite or elsewhere, fever or muscle aches, you should see a doctor. Doxycycline prevents tick-borne diseases.

Leeches are found in humid rainforest areas. They do not transmit any disease, but their bites are often intensely itchy for weeks afterwards and can easily become infected. Apply an iodine-based antiseptic to any leech bite to help prevent infection.

Bee and wasp stings mainly cause problems for people who are allergic to them. Anyone with a serious bee or wasp allergy should carry an injection of adrenaline (eg an Epipen) for emergency treatment. For others pain is the main problem – apply ice to the sting and take painkillers.

Skin Problems
Fungal rashes are common in humid climates. There are two common fungal rashes that affect travellers. The first occurs in moist areas such as the groin, armpits and between the toes. It starts as a red patch that slowly spreads and is usually itchy. Treatment involves keeping the skin dry, avoiding chafing and using an antifungal cream such as clotrimazole or Lamisil. *Tinea versicolor* is also common – this fungus causes small, light-coloured patches, most commonly on the back, chest and shoulders. Consult a doctor.

Cuts and scratches become easily infected in humid climates. Take meticulous care of any cuts and scratches to prevent complications such as abscesses. Immediately wash all wounds in clean water and apply antiseptic. If you develop signs of infection (increasing pain and redness), see a doctor. Divers and surfers should be particularly careful with coral cuts, as they become easily infected.

Sunburn
Even on a cloudy day sunburn can occur rapidly. Always use a strong sunscreen (at least factor 30), making sure to reapply after

a swim, and always wear a wide-brimmed hat and sunglasses outdoors. Avoid lying in the sun during the hottest part of the day (10am to 2pm). You can get burnt very easily when you are at high altitudes, so be vigilant once above 3000m. If you become sunburnt, stay out of the sun until you have recovered, apply cool compresses and take painkillers for the discomfort. One-percent hydrocortisone cream applied twice daily is also helpful.

WOMEN'S HEALTH

In most places in India, supplies of sanitary products (pads, rarely tampons) are readily available. Birth control options may be limited, so bring adequate supplies of your own form of contraception. Heat, humidity and antibiotics can all contribute to thrush. Treatment is with antifungal creams and pessaries such as clotrimazole. A practical alternative is a single tablet of Fluconazole (Diflucan). Urinary tract infections can be precipitated by dehydration or long bus journeys without toilet stops; bring suitable antibiotics. For gynaecological health issues, seek out a female doctor.

Pregnant women should receive specialised advice before travelling. The ideal time to travel is in the second trimester (between 16 and 28 weeks), when the risk of pregnancy-related problems is at its lowest and pregnant women generally feel at their best. Always carry a list of quality medical facilities available at your destination and ensure you continue your standard antenatal care at these facilities. Avoid rural travel in areas with poor transport and substandard medical facilities. Most of all, ensure that your travel insurance policy covers all pregnancy-related possibilities, including premature labour.

Malaria is a high-risk disease for pregnant women, and WHO recommends that they do *not* travel to areas with Chloroquine-resistant malaria. None of the more effective antimalarial drugs are completely safe in pregnancy.

Traveller's diarrhoea can quickly lead to dehydration and result in inadequate blood flow to the placenta. Many of the drugs used to treat various diarrhoea bugs are not recommended in pregnancy. Azithromycin is considered safe.

HEALTH

Language

CONTENTS

Northeast India's official languages are Assamese (state language of Assam), Bengali (state language of West Bengal), Hindi (the most predominant of India's languages, although only spoken as a mother tongue by about 20% of the population), Manipuri (spoken in the state of Manipur), Nepali (the predominant language of Sikkim, where around 75% of the people are ethnic Nepalis).

While English is widely spoken throughout much of northern India, Bengali and Hindi will be the most useful indigenous languages for travel in the region.

For a far more comprehensive guide to Bengali and Hindi, get a copy of Lonely Planet's *Hindi, Urdu & Bengali Phrasebook*.

BENGALI

While Hindi is understood to some degree across most of Northeast India, Bengali is actually the most effective and widely spoken common language in the region; apart from anything else, a few words in Bengali will win you smiles from the locals you meet.

PRONUNCIATION

Pronunciation of Bengali is made difficult by the fact that the language includes a variety of subtle sounds with no equivalents in English. To make this language guide easier to use for basic communication we haven't tried to cover all the sounds, instead using nearest English equivalents – you're unlikely to have any trouble making yourself understood.

With regard to word stress, a good rule of thumb is to place the emphasis on the first and last syllables of words.

a	as in 'father'
b	as English 'b' or 'v'
ch	as in 'chant'
e	as in 'bet'
i	as in 'police'
j	as in 'jet'
o	similar to the 'o' in 'hold'
th	as in 'thing'
u	as in 'put'
v/w	a cross between English 'v' and 'w'
y	as in 'boy'

USEFUL VERBS

Two verbs that will undoubtedly come in very handy are *achhe* (there is, has), and *lagbe* (need). You can ask *khana a·che?* (Is there food?) or *bangti a·che?* (Do you have change?) The negative form of *a·che* is simply *nai*. Saying *baksheesh nai* means you don't have any baksheesh to give. You can say *pani lagbe* (lit: water is needed), or say *lagbe na* (lit: don't need) to turn down any unwanted offer.

ACCOMMODATION

Is there a hotel/ guesthouse nearby?	kache kono hotel/guesthouse a·che ki?
Do you have a room?	rum a·che?
May I see the room?	rum dekte pari?
Is there a toilet?	paikana/toilet a·che?
mosquito net	moshari
towel	toale

ACHA

Acha, the subcontinent's ambiguous 'OK/Yes/ I see' is used widely, but the local slang equivalent is *tik assay* or just *tik*. The words *ji* or *ha* are more positive – if the rickshaw-wallah answers *acha* to your offered price, expect problems at the other end; if it's *tik* or *ji* he's unlikely to demand more money.

I'd like to book a room ...	*ami ekta rum buk ... korbo*
for one person	*ekjon thakbe*
for two people	*duijon thakbe*
How much is it ...?	*... thakte koto taka lagbe?*
per person	*ek jon*
per night	*ek ra·te*
per week	*ek soptaho*

CONVERSATION & ESSENTIALS

If you travel to Bangladesh you should be aware that Bengali greetings vary according to religion and custom. The Muslim greeting is *asalam walekum* (peace be on you). The response is *walekum asalam* (unto you, also peace). In Northeastern India you're unlikely to hear the Muslim greeting, and the Hindu *nomashkar* will be far more common (including when saying goodbye). This is accompanied by the gesture of joining the open palms of both hands and bringing them close to the chest.

'Please' and 'Thank you' are rarely used in Bengali. Instead, these sentiments are expressed indirectly in polite conversation. The absence of these shouldn't be misread as rudeness. If you want to thank someone, you may use the Bengali equivalent for 'Thank you (very much)', *(onek) donyobad*, or, alternatively, pay them a compliment.

Hello/Goodbye.	*nomashkar* (Hindu greeting and response)
See you later.	*po·re dakha ho·be*
See you again.	*abar deka ho·be*
Excuse/Forgive me.	*maf korun*
Thank you (very much).	*(onek) don·nobad*
Yes.	*ji* (polite)/*ha* (commonly used, with the 'a' given a very nasal pronunciation)
No.	*na*
How are you?	*(apni) kamon achen?*

I'm well.	*bhalo achi*
friend (often used in greetings)	*bondhu*
What's your name?	*apnar nam ki?*
My name is ...	*amar nam ...*
Where are you from?	*apnar desh ki?*
My country is ...	*amar desh ...*
Not any/None.	*nai*
It's all right/ No problem.	*tik a·che*
Do you like ...?	*apnar ... bhalo lagge?*
I like it (very much).	*amar eta (khub) bhalo lagge*
I don't like ...	*amar ... bhalo lagge na*
What do you want?	*ki lagbe?*
It's available.	*pawa jai*
It's not available.	*pawa jai na*

DIRECTIONS

Where is ...?	*... kotai?*
How far is ...?	*... koto dur?*
I want to go to ...	*ami ... jabo*
Go straight ahead.	*shoja jan*
left	*ba·me*
right	*da·ne*
here	*ekha·ne*
there	*okhane*
north	*uttor*
south	*dokkin*
east	*purbodik*
west	*posh·chim*

HEALTH

I need a doctor.	*amar daktar lagbe*
antiseptic	*savlon*
nausea	*bomi-bhab*
sanitary napkins	*softex/modess* (brand names)
I'm a ...	*amar ... a·che*
diabetic	*diabetes*
epileptic	*mirghi rog*
I'm allergic to ...	*amar ... allergy a·che*
antibiotics/	*antibiotikeh*
penicillin	*penisillineh*

LANGUAGE DIFFICULTIES

I understand.	*ami bujhi*
I don't understand.	*ami bujhi na*
Do you speak English?	*apni english/ingreji bolte paren?*
I speak a little Bengali.	*ami ektu bangla bolte pari*
Please write it down.	*likhte paren*
How do you say ... in Bengali?	*banglai ... ki bo·le?*

EMERGENCIES

Please help me!	amake shahajjo koren!
Call a doctor!	daktar lagbe!
Call the police!	pulish lagbe!
I'm lost.	aami hariye gachi
Where is the toilet?	paikhana/toilet kotai?
Go away!	jao!

NUMBERS

Counting up to 20 is easy, but after that it becomes complicated, as the terms do not follow sequentially. In Bengali 21 isn't *bish-ek* or *ek-bish* as you might expect, but *ekush*; 45 is actually *poy-tal·lish*, but the simpler *pach-chollish* is understood.

0	shun·no
1	ek
2	dui
3	tin
4	char
5	pach
6	ch-hoy
7	shat
8	at
9	noy
10	dosh
11	egaro
12	baro
13	tero
14	chod·do
15	ponero
16	sholo
17	shotero
18	at·haro
19	unish
20	bish
30	tirish
40	chollish
50	ponchash
60	shatt
70	shottur
80	ashi
90	nob·boi
100	eksho
1000	ek hajar
100,000	ek lakh
10 million	ek koti
½	sha·re
1½	der
2½	arai

After two, the word *sha·re* is used before the number to indicate half, eg 3½ is *sha·re tin*.

SHOPPING & SERVICES

For many words, such as 'station', 'hotel' and 'post office', the English word will be understood.

Where is the ...?	... kotai?
bank	bank
chemist/pharmacy	oshuder dokan
embassy	embassy
hospital	hashpatal
market	bajar
palace	rajbari
post office	post offish
town	taun
village	gram

What time does it open/close?	kokhon khole/bondo-hoy
How much is it?	dam koto?
It's too expensive.	eta onek beshi dam
I'd like my change, please.	aami amar bhangti chai pleez
It's available.	pawa jai
It's not available.	pawa jai na

TIME & DATES

What is the time?	koto ba·je?
When?	kokhon?
2.45	po·ne tin ta (quarter to three)
1.30	der ta (one thirty)
4.15	shoa char ta (quarter past four)
hour	ghonta
day	din
week	shopta
month	mash
year	bochor

date (calendar)	tarikh
today	aj
tonight	aj ra·te
tomorrow	agamikal
yesterday	gotokal
in the morning	shokale
in the afternoon	bika·le
night	rat
every day	proti din
always	shob shomoy
now	ekhon
later	po·re

Monday	shombar
Tuesday	mongolbar
Wednesday	budhbar

Thursday	*brihoshpotibar*
Friday	*shukrobar*
Saturday	*shonibar*
Sunday	*robibar*

TRANSPORT

I want to go to ...	*ami ... jabo*
Where is this bus going?	*ey bas kotai ja·be?*

When does the ... leave/arrive?	*kokhon ... charbe/pochabe?*
boat	*nouka/launch*
bus	*bas*
car	*gari*
rickshaw	*riksha*
train	*tren*

HINDI

PRONUNCIATION

Most Hindi sounds are similar to their English counterparts, but there are a few tricky ones. The transliteration system we've used for Hindi in this language guide is designed to be as simple as possible, and for this reason it doesn't distinguish between all the sounds of spoken Hindi.

It's important to pay attention to the pronunciation of vowels and especially to their length, eg **a** compared to **aa**. The combination **ng** after a vowel indicates that it is nasalised (ie pronounced through the nose).

Vowels

a	as the 'u' in 'sun'
aa	as in 'father'
ai	as in 'hair' before a consonant; as in 'aisle' at the end of a word
au	as in 'haul' before a consonant; as the 'ou' in 'ouch' at the end of a word
e	as in 'they'
ee	as the 'ee' in 'feet'
i	as in 'sit'
o	as in 'shot'
oo	as the 'oo' in 'fool'
u	as in 'put'

Consonants

ch	as in 'cheese'
g	always as in 'gun', never as in 'age'
r	slightly trilled
y	as in 'yak'
g	as in 'go'

EMERGENCIES

Help!	*mada keejiye!*
Call a doctor!	*daaktar ko bulaao!*
Call the police!	*pulis ko bulaao!*
I'm lost.	*maing raastaa bhool gayaa/ gayee hoong* (f/m)
Where is the toilet?	*gusalkaanaa kahaang hai?*
Go away!	*jaao!*

ACCOMMODATION

Where is the (best/cheapest) hotel?
sab se (achaa/sastaa) hotal kahaang hai?
Please write the address.
zaraa us kaa pataa lik deejiye
Do you have any rooms available?
kyaa koee kamraa kaalee hai?

How much for ...?	*... kaa kiraayaa kitnaa hai?*
one night	*ek din*
one week	*ek hafte*

I'd like a ...	*mujhe ... chaahiye*
double room	*dabal kamraa*
room with a bathroom	*gusalkaanevaalaa kamraa*
single room	*singal kamraa*

CONVERSATION & ESSENTIALS

Hello.	*namaste/namskaar*
Goodbye.	*namaste/namskaar*
Yes.	*jee haang*
No.	*jee naheeng*

'Please' is usually conveyed through the polite form of the imperative, or through other expressions. This book uses polite expressions and the polite forms of words.

Thank you.	*shukriyaa/danyavaad*
You're welcome.	*koee baat naheeng*
Excuse me/Sorry.	*kshamaa keejiye*
How are you?	*aap kaise/kaisee haing?* (m/f)
Fine, and you?	*maing teek hoong aap sunaaiye?*
What's your name?	*aap kaa shubh naam kyaa hai?*
Where's a/the ...	*... kahaang hai?*
Is it far from/near here?	*kyaa voh yahaang se door/ nazdeek hai?*

HEALTH

I'm sick.	*maing beemaar hoong*
antiseptic	*ainteeseptik*
antibiotics	*ainteebayotik*
diarrhoea	*dast*

LANGUAGE

medicine	*davaa*
nausea	*gin*
tampons	*taimpon*
Where is a/the ...?	*... kahaang hai?*
clinic	*davaakaanaa*
doctor	*daaktar*
hospital	*aspataal*

LANGUAGE DIFFICULTIES

Do you speak English?
  kyaa aap ko angrezee aatee hai?
Does anyone here speak English?
  kyaa kisee ko angrezee aatee hai?
I understand.
  maing samjhaa/ee
I don't understand.
  maing naheeng samjhaa/ee
Please write it down.
  zaraa lik deejiye

NUMBERS

Whereas we count in tens, hundreds, thousands, millions and billions, the Indian numbering system uses tens, hundreds, thousands, hundred thousands and ten millions. A hundred thousand is a *laakh*, and 10 million is a crore. These two words are almost always used in place of their English equivalents.

Once in the thousands, written numbers have commas every two places, not three.

1	*ek*
2	*do*
3	*teen*
4	*chaar*
5	*paangch*
6	*chai*
7	*saat*
8	*aat*
9	*nau*
10	*das*
11	*gyaarah*
12	*bara*
13	*terah*
14	*chaudah*
15	*pandrah*
16	*solah*
17	*satrah*
18	*attaarah*
19	*unnees*
20	*bees*
21	*ikkees*
22	*baaees*

30	*tees*
40	*chaalees*
50	*pachaas*
60	*saat*
70	*sattar*
80	*assee*
90	*nabbe/navve*
100	*sau*
1000	*hazaar*
100,000	*ek laak* (written 1,00,000)
10,000,000	*ek krore* (written 1,00,00,000)

SHOPPING & SERVICES

Where's the nearest ...?
sab se karib ... kah hai?

bank	*baink*
bookshop	*kitaab kee dukaan*
chemist/pharmacy	*davaaee kee dukaan*
general store	*dukaan*
market	*baazaar*
post office	*daakkaanaa*
public phone	*saarvajanik fon*
public toilet	*shauchaalay*

How much is this?
  is kaa daam kyaa hai?
I think it's too expensive.
  yeh bahut mahegaa/i hai (m/f)
Can you lower the price?
  is kaa daam kam keejiye?
Do you accept credit cards?
  kyaa aap vizaa kaard vagairah lete ha?

TIME & DATES

What time is it?
  kitne baje haing?/taaim kyaa hai?
It's (ten) o'clock.
  (das) baje haing
It's half past two.
  daaee baje haing

When?	*kab?*
now	*ab*
today	*aaj*
tomorrow/	*kal* (while *kal* is used for both, the
yesterday	meaning is made clear by context)
day	*din*
evening	*shaam*
month	*maheenaa*
morning	*saveraa/subhaa*
night	*raat*
week	*haftaa*
year	*saal/baras*

LANGUAGE

Monday	*somvaar*
Tuesday	*mangalvaar*
Wednesday	*budvaar*
Thursday	*guruvaar/brihaspativaar*
Friday	*shukravaar*
Saturday	*shanivaar*
Sunday	*itvaar/ravivaar*

TRANSPORT

How do we get to ...?	*... kaise jaate haing?*
A ticket to ...	*... keliye tikat deejiye*

When is the ... bus?	*... bas kab jaaegee?*
first	*pehlaa/pehlee*
next	*aglaa/aglee*
last	*aakiree*

What time does the ... leave/arrive?	*... kitne baje jaayegee/ pahungchegee?*
boat	*naav*
bus	*bas*
train	*relgaaree*

Also available from Lonely Planet:
Hindi, Urdu & Bengali Phrasebook

Glossary

This glossary is a sample of the words and terms you may come across during your Indian wanderings. For definitions of food and drink, see p93.

abbi – waterfall
Abhimani – eldest son of Brahma
Abhimanyu – son of Arjuna
acha – 'OK' or 'I understand'
acharya – revered teacher; spiritual guide
Adivasi – tribal person
agarbathi – incense
Agasti – legendary Hindu sage, revered in the south, as he is credited with introducing Hinduism and developing the Tamil language
Agni – major deity in the Vedas; mediator between men and the gods; also fire
ahimsa – discipline of nonviolence
AIR – All India Radio, the national broadcaster
air-cooler – big, noisy water-filled fan
Amir – Muslim nobleman
amrita – immortality
Ananda – Buddha's cousin and personal attendant
Ananta – snake on which Vishnu reclined
Andhaka – 1000-headed demon, killed by Shiva
angrezi – foreigner
anikut – dam
anna – 16th of a rupee; no longer legal tender
Annapurna – form of Durga; worshipped for her power to provide food
apsara – heavenly nymph
Aranyani – Hindu goddess of forests
Ardhanari – Shiva's half-male, half-female form
Arishta – *daitya* who, having taken the form of a bull, attacked Krishna and was killed by him
Arjuna – Mahabharata hero and military commander who married Subhadra, took up arms and overcame many demons. He had the Bhagavad Gita related to him by Krishna, led Krishna's funeral ceremony and finally retired to the Himalaya.
Aryan – Sanskrit for 'noble'; those who migrated from Persia and settled in northern India
ashram – spiritual community or retreat
ashrama – Hindu system; there are three stages in life recognised by this system: *brahmachari, grihastha* and *sanyasin* but this kind of merit is only available to the upper three castes
ASI – Abbreviation for the Archaeological Survey of India; an organisation involved in monument preservation
atman – soul

attar – essential oil; used as a base for perfumes
autorickshaw – noisy, three-wheeled, motorised contraption for transporting passengers, livestock etc for short distances; also known as Bajaj and autos
Avalokiteshvara – in Mahayana Buddhism, the bodhisattva of compassion
avatar – incarnation, usually of a deity
ayah – children's nurse or nanny
Ayurveda – the ancient and complex science of Indian herbal medicine and healing
azan – Muslim call to prayer

baba – religious master or father; term of respect
badmash – villain or hooligan, a reoccurring character in Bollywood action films
bagh – park or garden; also the local name for the Bengal tiger
bahadur – brave or chivalrous; an honorific title
baksheesh – tip, donation (alms) or bribe
Balarama – brother of Krishna
bandar – monkey
bandh – general strike
bandhani – tie-dye
banian – T-shirt or undervest
baniya – moneylender or trader
banyan – Indian fig tree; spiritual to many Indians
baori – well, particularly a step-well with landings and galleries
bearer – like a butler
begum – Muslim princess or woman of high rank
Bhagavad Gita – Hindu Song of the Divine One; Krishna's lessons to Arjuna, the main thrust of which was to emphasise the philosophy of *bhakti*; it is part of the Mahabharata
Bhairava – the Terrible; refers to the eighth incarnation of Shiva in his demonic form
bhajan – devotional song
bhakti – surrendering to the gods; faith
bhang – dried leaves and flowering shoots of the marijuana plant
bhangra – rhythmic Punjabi music/dance
Bharat – Hindi for India
Bharata – half-brother of Rama; ruled while Rama was in exile
bhavan – house, building; also spelt *bhawan*
bheesti – see *bhisti*
Bhima – Mahabharata hero; he is the brother of Hanuman and renowned for his great strength
bhisti – water carrier
bhoga-mandapa – Orissan hall of offering

bhojanalya – see *dhaba*

bidi – small, hand-rolled cigarette

bindi – forehead mark (often dot-shaped) worn by women

BJP – Bharatiya Janata Party

Bodhi Tree – tree under which the Buddha sat when he attained enlightenment

bodhisattva – literally 'one whose essence is perfected wisdom'. In Early Buddhism, bodhisattva refers only to the Buddha during the period between his conceiving the intention to strive for Buddhahood and the moment he attained it; in Mahayana Buddhism, one who renounces nirvana in order to help others attain it.

Bollywood – India's answer to Hollywood; the booming film industry of Mumbai (Bombay)

Brahma – Hindu god; worshipped as the creator in the Trimurti

brahmachari – chaste student stage of the *ashrama* system

Brahmanism – early form of Hinduism which evolved from Vedism (see *Vedas*); named after Brahmin priests and Brahma

Brahmin – member of the priest/scholar caste, the highest Hindu caste

Buddha – Awakened One; the originator of Buddhism; also regarded by Hindus as the ninth incarnation of Vishnu

Buddhism – see *Early Buddhism*

bugyal – high-altitude meadow

bund – embankment or dyke

burka – one-piece garment used by conservative Muslim women to cover themselves from head to toe

bustee – slum

cantonment – administrative and military area of a Raj-era town

caravanserai – traditional accommodation for camel caravans

Carnatic music – classical music of South India

caste – a Hindu's hereditary station (social standing) in life; there are four castes: the Brahmins, the Kshatriyas, the Vaishyas and the Shudras

cenotaph – a monument honouring a dead person whose body is somewhere else

chaam – ritual masked dance performed by Buddhist monks in gompas to celebrate the victory of good over evil and of Buddhism over pre-existing religions

chaitya – Sanskrit form of 'cetiya', meaning shrine or object of worship; has come to mean temple, and more specifically, a hall divided into a central nave and two side aisles by a line of columns, with a votive stupa at the end

chakra – focus of one's spiritual power; disclike weapon of Vishnu

chalo, chalo, chalo – 'let's go, let's go, let's go'

Chamunda – form of Durga; a real terror, armed with a scimitar, noose and mace, and clothed in elephant hide, her mission was to kill the demons Chanda and Munda

chandra – moon, or the moon as a god

Chandragupta – Indian ruler, 3rd century BC

chappals – sandals or leather thonglike footwear; flip-flops

charas – resin of the marijuana plant; also referred to as 'hashish'

charbagh – formal Persian garden, divided into quarters (literally 'four gardens')

charpoy – simple bed made of ropes knotted together on a wooden frame

chedi – see *chaitya*

chela – pupil or follower, as George Harrison was to Ravi Shankar

chhatri – cenotaph (literally 'umbrella')

chillum – pipe of a hookah; commonly used to describe the pipes used for smoking *ganja*

chinkara – gazelle

chital – spotted deer

chogyal – Sikkimese king

choli – sari blouse

chomos – Tibetan Buddhist nuns

chorten – Tibetan for stupa

choultry – pilgrim's rest house; also called *'dharamsala'*

chowk – town square, intersection or marketplace

chowkidar – night watchman, caretaker, particularly of a government rest house

chuba – dress worn by Tibetan women

Cong (I) – Congress Party of India; also known as Congress (I)

coolie – labourer or porter, from the Hindi *quli*

CPI – Communist Party of India

CPI (M) – Communist Party of India (Marxist)

crore – 10 million

dacoit – bandit (particularly armed bandit), outlaw

dada – paternal grandfather or elder brother

dagoba – see *stupa*

dais – raised platform

daitya – demon or giant who fought against the gods

dak – staging post, government-run accommodation

Dalit – preferred term for India's Untouchable caste; see also *Harijan*

Damodara – another name for Krishna

dargah – shrine or place of burial of a Muslim saint

darshan – offering or audience with someone; auspicious viewing of a deity

darwaza – gateway or door

Dasaratha – father of Rama in the Ramayana

Dattatreya – Brahmin saint who embodied the Trimurti

desi – local, Indian

deul – temple sanctuary

devadasi – temple dancer

Devi – Shiva's wife; goddess

dhaba – basic restaurant or snack bar
dham – holiest pilgrimage places of India
dharamsala – pilgrim's rest house
dharma – for Hindus, the moral code of behaviour or social duty; for Buddhists, following the law of nature, or path, as taught by the Buddha
dharna – nonviolent protest
dhobi – person who washes clothes; commonly referred to as *dhobi*-wallah
dhobi ghat – place where clothes are washed
dhol – traditional, large, two-sided drum
dholi – man-carried portable 'chairs' or palanquins; people are carried in them to hill-top temples etc
dhoti – like a lungi, but the ankle-length cloth is then pulled up between the legs; worn by men
dhurrie – rug
Digambara – 'Sky-Clad'; Jain group that demonstrates disdain for worldly goods by going naked
dikpala – temple guardian
Din-i-Ilahi – Akbar's philosophy asserting the common truth in all religions
diwan – principal officer in a princely state; royal court or council
dorje – the celestial thunderbolt, from Tibetan Buddhist mythology
dowry – money and/or goods given by a bride's parents to their son-in-law's family; it's illegal but still widely exists in many arranged marriages
Draupadi – wife of the five Pandava princes in the Mahabharata
Dravidian – general term for the cultures and languages of the deep south of India.,
dukhang – Tibetan prayer hall
dun – valley
dupatta – long scarf for women often worn with the *salwar kameez*
durbar – royal court; also a government
Durga – the Inaccessible; a form of Shiva's wife, Devi, a beautiful, fierce woman riding a tiger/lion; a major goddess of the Shakti sect
dwarpal – doorkeeper; sculpture beside the doorways to Hindu or Buddhist shrines

Early Buddhism – any of the schools of Buddhism established directly after Buddha's death and before the advent of Mahayana. A modern form is the Theravada (Teaching of the Elders) practised in Sri Lanka and Southeast Asia. Early Buddhism differed from the Mahayana in that it did not teach the bodhisattva ideal.
elatalam – small hand-held cymbals
election symbols – identifying symbols for the various political parties, used to canvas illiterate voters
Emergency – period in the 1970s during which Indira Gandhi suspended many political rights
Eve-teasing – sexual harassment

fakir – Muslim who has taken a vow of poverty; may also apply to *sadhus* and other Hindu ascetics
ferengi – the Hindi word for foreigner, later used as the name for a race of aliens in Star Trek!
filmi – slang term describing anything to do with Indian movies
firman – royal order or grant

gabba – appliquéd Kashmiri rug
gaddi – throne of a Hindu prince
gali – lane or alleyway
Ganesh – Hindu god of good fortune; popular elephant-headed son of Shiva and Parvati, he is also known as Ganpati and his vehicle is a ratlike creature
Ganga – Hindu goddess representing the sacred Ganges River; said to flow from Vishnu's toe
ganga aarti – river worship ceremony, when leaf boats with candles are floated on the river at sunset
ganj – market
ganja – dried flowering tips of the marijuana plant
gaon – village
garh – fort
gari – vehicle; 'motor gari' is a car and 'rail gari' is a train
Garuda – man-bird vehicle of Vishnu
gaur – Indian bison
Gayatri – sacred verse of Rig-Veda repeated mentally by Brahmins twice a day
geyser – hot-water unit found in many bathrooms
ghat – steps or landing on a river, range of hills, or road up hills
ghazal – Urdu song derived from poetry; poignant love theme
gherao – industrial action where the workers lock in their employers
giri – hill
Gita Govinda – erotic poem by Jayadeva relating Krishna's early life as Govinda
godmen – commercially minded gurus; see also *export guru*
godown – warehouse
gompa – Tibetan Buddhist monastery
Gonds – aboriginal Indian race, found in remote jungles of Orissa
goonda – ruffian or tough; political parties have been known to employ them in gangs
Gopala – see Govinda
gopi – milkmaid; Krishna was fond of them
gopuram – soaring pyramidal gateway tower of Dravidian temples
gora – white person, European
Govinda – Krishna as a cowherd; also just cowherd
grihastha – householder stage of the *ashrama* system; followers discharge their duty to ancestors by having sons and making sacrifices to the gods
gufa – cave

gumbad – dome on an Islamic tomb or mosque
gurdwara – Sikh temple
guru – holy teacher; in Sanskrit literally *'goe'* (darkness) and *'roe'* (to dispel)
Guru Granth Sahib – Sikh holy book

haat – village market
haj – Muslim pilgrimage to Mecca
haji – Muslim who has made the *haj*
halal – literally 'permissable'; foods that have been prepared in accordance with Islamic law
hammam – Turkish bath; public bathhouse
Hanuman – Hindu monkey god, prominent in the Ramayana, and a follower of Rama
Hara – one of Shiva's names
Hari – another name for Vishnu
Harijan – name (no longer considered acceptable) given by Gandhi to India's Untouchables, meaning 'children of god'
hartal – strike
hashish – see *charas*
hathi – elephant
haveli – traditional, often ornately decorated, residences, particularly those found in Rajasthan and Gujarat
havildar – army officer
hijab – headscarf used by Muslim women
hijra – eunuch, transvestite
Hinayana – see *Early Buddhism*
Hind – an alternative name for India; part of the patriotic chant *Jai Hind* (Victory to India)
hindola – swing
Hiranyakasipu – *daitya* king killed by Narasimha
hookah – water pipe used for smoking ganja or strong tobacco
howdah – seat for carrying people on an elephant's back

iftar – breaking of the Ramadan fast at sunset
ikat – fabric made with thread which is tie-dyed before weaving
imam – Muslim religious leader
imambara – tomb dedicated to a Shiite Muslim holy man
IMFL – Indian-made foreign liquor
Indo-Saracenic – style of colonial architecture that integrated Western designs with Islamic, Hindu and Jain influences
Indra – significant and prestigious Vedic god; god of rain, thunder, lightning and war
Ishwara – another name given to Shiva; lord

Jagadhatri – Mother of the World; another name for Devi
jagamohan – assembly hall
Jagannath – Lord of the Universe; a form of Krishna, famously worshipped at Puri in Orissa

jali – carved lattice (often marble) screen, also used to refer to the holes or spaces produced through carving timber or stone
Janaka – father of Sita
jataka – tale from Buddha's various lives
jauhar – ritual mass suicide by immolation, traditionally performed by Rajasthani Rajput women at times of military defeat to avoid being dishonoured by their captors
jawan – policeman or soldier
jheel – swampy area
jhuggi – shanty settlement; also called *bustee*
jhula – bridge
ji – honorific that can be added to the end of almost anything as a form of respect; thus 'Babaji', 'Gandhiji'
jihad – holy war (Islam); most commonly associated with Islamic militants
JKLF – Jammu & Kashmir Liberation Front
jooti – traditional, often pointy-toed, slip-in shoes; commonly found in north India
juggernaut – huge, extravagantly decorated temple 'car' dragged through the streets during certain Hindu festivals
jumkahs – earrings
jyoti linga – most important shrines to Shiva, of which there are 12

kabaddi – traditional game (similar to tag)
Kailasa – sacred Himalayan mountain; home of Shiva
Kali – the ominous-looking evil-destroying form of Devi; commonly depicted with black skin, dripping with blood, and wearing a necklace of skulls
Kalki – White Horse; future (10th) incarnation of Vishnu which will appear at the end of Kali-Yug, when the world ceases to be; has been compared to Maitreya in Buddhist cosmology
Kama – Hindu god of love
kameez – woman's shirtlike tunic
kangling – sacred Tibetan flute made from a human thigh bone
Kanyakumari – Virgin Maiden; another name for Durga
kapali – sacred bowl made from a human skull, still used by followers of the extreme Hindu *aghori* sect
karma – Hindu, Buddhist and Sikh principle of retributive justice for past deeds
karmachario – workers
Kartikiya – Hindu god of war, Shiva's son
kata – Tibetan prayer shawl, traditionally given to a *lama* when pilgrims come into his presence
kathputli – puppeteer; also known as *putli*-wallah
Kedarnath – name of Shiva and one of the 12 *jyoti linga*
khadi – homespun cloth; Mahatma Gandhi encouraged people to spin this rather than buy English cloth
Khalistan – former Sikh secessionists' proposed name for an independent Punjab
Khalsa – Sikh brotherhood
Khan – Muslim honorific title for a ruler

kho-kho – traditional game (similar to tag)
khol – black eyeliner
khur – Asiatic wild ass
kirtan – Sikh devotional singing
koil – Hindu temple
kolam – see *rangoli*
kompu – C-shaped, metal trumpet
kos minar – milestone
kot – fort
kothi – residence or mansion
kotwali – police station
Krishna – Vishnu's eighth incarnation, often coloured blue; he revealed the Bhagavad Gita to Arjuna
Kshatriya – Hindu caste of soldiers or administrators; second in the caste hierarchy
kund – lake or tank
kurta – long shirt with either short collar or no collar
Kusa – one of Rama's twin sons

lakh – 100,000
Lakshmana – half-brother and aide of Rama in the Ramayana
Lakshmi – Vishnu's consort, Hindu goddess of wealth; she sprang forth from the ocean holding a lotus
lama – Tibetan Buddhist priest or monk
lathi – heavy stick used by police, especially for crowd control
Laxmi – see *Lakshmi*
lehanga – very full skirt with a waist cord
lhamo – Tibetan opera
lingam – phallic symbol; auspicious symbol of Shiva; plural 'linga'
LOC – 'Line of Control'; the de facto border between India and Pakistan in Kashmir
lok – people
Lok Sabha – lower house in the Indian parliament (House of the People)
loka – realm
Losar – Tibetan new year
lungi – worn by men, this loose, coloured garment (similar to a sarong) is pleated by the wearer at the waist to fit

machaan – observation tower
madrasa – Islamic seminary
maha – prefix meaning 'great'
Mahabharata – Great Hindu Vedic epic poem of the Bharata dynasty; containing approximately 10,000 verses describing the battle between the Pandavas and the Kauravas
Mahabodhi Society – founded in 1891 to encourage Buddhist studies
Mahadeva – Great God; Shiva
Mahadevi – Great Goddess; Devi
Mahakala – Great Time; Shiva and one of 12 *jyoti linga* (also one the Tibetan protector deity)

mahal – house or palace
maharaja – literally 'great king'; princely ruler
maharana – see *maharaja*
maharao – see *maharaja*
maharawal – see *maharaja*
maharani – wife of a princely ruler or a ruler in her own right
mahatma – literally 'great soul'
Mahavir – last *tirthankar*
Mahayana – the 'greater-vehicle' of Buddhism; a later adaptation of the teaching which lays emphasis on the bodhisattva ideal, teaching the renunciation of *nirvana* (ultimate peace and cessation of rebirth) in order to help other beings along the way to enlightenment
Mahayogi – Great Ascetic; Shiva
Maheshwara – Great Lord; Shiva
Mahisa – Hindu demon
mahout – elephant rider or master
maidan – open (often grassed) area; parade ground
Maitreya – future Buddha; the successor to the historical Buddha who will appear on earth ushering in a new age of enlightenment
Makara – mythical sea creature and Varuna's vehicle; crocodile
mala – garland or necklace
mali – gardener
mandal – shrine
mandala – circle; symbol used in Hindu and Buddhist art to symbolise the universe
mandapa – pillared pavilion a temple forechamber
mandi – market
mandir – temple
mani stone – stone carved with the Tibetan-Buddhist mantra *'Om mani padme hum'* ('Hail the jewel in the lotus')
mani walls – Tibetan stone walls with sacred inscriptions
mantra – sacred word or syllable used by Buddhists and Hindus to aid concentration; metrical psalms of praise found in the Vedas
Mara – Buddhist personification of that which obstructs the cultivation of virtue, often depicted with hundreds of arms; also the god of death
Maratha – central Indian people who fought the Mughals and British
marg – road
Maruts – Hindu storm gods
masala – spice mix, also a genre of Bollywood action films
masjid – mosque
masti – fun
mata – mother
math – monastery
maund – unit of weight now superseded (about 20kg)
maya – illusion
mehndi – henna; ornate henna designs on women's hands (and often feet), traditionally for certain festivals or ceremonies (eg marriage)

mela – fair or festival
memsahib – Madam; respectful way of addressing women (literally 'Mrs Sir')
Meru – mythical mountain found in the centre of the earth; on it is Swarga
mihrab – mosque 'prayer niche' that faces Mecca
misthan bhandar – South Indian sweet shop and vegetarian restaurant, found all over India.
mithuna – pairs of men and women; often seen in temple sculpture
Moghul – see *Mughal*
Mohini – Vishnu in his female incarnation
moksha – liberation from *samsara*
monsoon – rainy season
morcha – mob march or protest
mudra – ritual hand movements used in Hindu religious dancing; gesture of Buddha figure
muezzin – one who calls Muslims to prayer, traditionally from the minaret of a mosque
Mughal – Muslim dynasty of emperors from Babur to Aurangzeb
mujtahid – divine
mullah – Muslim scholar or religious leader
mund – village
murti – statue, often of a deity

nadi – river
Naga – mythical serpentlike beings capable of changing into human form
namaskar – see *namaste*
namaste – traditional Hindu greeting (hello or goodbye), often accompanied by a respectful small bow with the hands together at the chest or head level; also *namaskar*
namaz – Muslim prayers
namkeen – savoury (often spicy) nibbles (also *namkin*)
Nanda – cowherd who raised Krishna
Nandi – bull, vehicle of Shiva
Narasimha – man-lion incarnation of Vishnu
Narayan – incarnation of Vishnu the creator
Narsingh – see *Narasimha*
natamandir – dancing hall
Nataraja – Shiva as the cosmic dancer
nautch – dance
nautch girls – dancing girls
nawab – Muslim ruling prince or powerful landowner (also *nabob*)
Naxalites – ultra-leftist political movement characterised by violence in support of rural peasant farmers
Nilakantha – form of Shiva; his blue throat is a result of swallowing poison that would have destroyed the world
nilgai – antelope
nirvana – this is the ultimate aim of Buddhists and the final release from the cycle of existence
niwas – house, building
noth – the Lord (Jain)

NRI – Non-Resident Indian: Indians living abroad, who make a huge contribution to the Indian economy
nullah – ditch or small stream

Om – sacred invocation representing the essence of the divine principle; for Buddhists, if repeated often enough with complete concentration, it leads to a state of emptiness
Osho – the late Bhagwan Shree Rajneesh, a popular, controversial guru

padma – lotus; another name for the Hindu goddess Lakshmi
padyatra – 'foot journey' made by politicians to raise support at village level
pagal – insane, crazy; often said in jest
pagoda – see *stupa*
paise – the Indian rupee is divided into 100 paise
palanquin – boxlike enclosure carried on poles on four men's shoulders; the occupant sits inside on a seat
Pali – the language, related to Sanskrit, in which the Buddhist scriptures were recorded; scholars still refer to the original Pali texts
palia – memorial stone
palli – village
Panchatantra – series of traditional Hindu stories about the natural world, human behaviour and survival
panchayat – village council
pandal – marquee
pandit – expert or wise person; sometimes used to mean a bookworm
Parasurama – Rama with the axe; sixth incarnation of Vishnu
Parsi – adherent of the Zoroastrian faith
Partition – formal division of British India into two separate countries, India and Pakistan, in 1947
Parvati – another form of Devi
pashmina – fine woollen shawl
patachitra – Orissan cloth painting
PCO – Public Call Office from where you can make local, interstate and international phone calls
peepul – fig tree, especially a bo tree
peon – lowest grade clerical worker
pietra dura – marble inlay work characteristic of the Taj Mahal
pinjrapol – animal hospital run by Jains
pir – Muslim holy man; title of a Sufi saint
POK – Pakistan Occupied Kashmir
pradesh – state
pranayama – study of breath control; meditative practice
prasad – temple-blessed food offering
puja – literally 'respect'; offering or prayers
pujari – temple priest
pukka – proper; a Raj-era term
pukka sahib – proper gentleman

punka – cloth fan, swung by pulling a cord

Puranas – set of 18 encyclopaedic Sanskrit stories, written in verse, relating to the three gods, dating from the 5th century AD

purdah – custom among some conservative Muslims (also adopted by some Hindus, especially the Rajputs) of keeping women in seclusion; veiled

Purnima – full moon; considered to be an auspicious time

putli-wallah – puppeteer; also known as *'kathputli'*

qawwali – Islamic devotional singing

qila – fort

Quran – the holy book of Islam, also spelt Koran

Radha – favourite mistress of Krishna when he lived as a cowherd

raga – any of several conventional patterns of melody and rhythm that form the basis for freely interpreted compositions

railhead – station or town at the end of a railway line; termination point

raj – rule or sovereignty; British Raj (sometimes just Raj) refers to British rule

raja – king; sometimes *rana*

rajkumar – prince

Rajput – Hindu warrior caste, former rulers of north-western India

Rajya Sabha – upper house in the Indian parliament (Council of States)

rakhi – amulet

Rama – seventh incarnation of Vishnu

Ramadan – the Islamic holy month of sunrise-to-sunset fasting (no eating, drinking or smoking); also referred to as Ramazan

Ramayana – the story of Rama and Sita and their conflict with Ravana is one of India's best-known epics

rana – king; sometimes *raja*

rangoli – elaborate chalk, rice-paste or coloured powder design; also known as *kolam*

rani – female ruler or wife of a king

ranns – deserts

rasta roko – roadblock set up for protest purposes

rath – temple chariot or car used in religious festivals

rathas – rock-cut Dravidian temples

Ravana – demon king of Lanka who abducted Sita; the titanic battle between him and Rama is told in the Ramayana

rawal – nobleman

rickshaw – small, two- or three-wheeled passenger vehicle

Rig-Veda – original and longest of the four main Vedas, or holy Sanskrit texts

rishi – any poet, philosopher, saint or sage; originally a sage to whom the hymns of the Vedas were revealed

Road – railway town which serves as a communication point to a larger town off the line, eg Mt Abu and Abu Road

rudraksh mala – strings of beads made from seeds of the rudraksha tree, used in *puja*

Rukmani – wife of Krishna; died on his funeral pyre

sadar – main

sadhu – ascetic, holy person, one who is trying to achieve enlightenment; often addressed as *'swamiji'* or *'babaji'*

safa – turban

sagar – lake, reservoir

sahib – respectful title applied to a gentleman, equivalent to 'sir'

salai – road

salwar – trousers usually worn with a *kameez*

salwar kameez – traditional dresslike tunic and trouser combination for women

samadhi – in Hinduism, ecstatic state, sometimes defined as 'ecstasy, trance, communion with God'; in Buddhism, concentration; also a place where a holy man has been cremated/buried, usually venerated as a shrine

sambalpuri – Orissan fabric

sambar – deer

samsara – Buddhists, Hindus and Sikhs believe earthly life is cyclical; you are born again and again, the quality of these rebirths being dependent upon your karma in previous lives

sangam – meeting of two rivers

sangeet – music

sangha – community of monks and nuns

Sankara – Shiva as the creator

sanyasin – like a *sadhu;* a wandering ascetic who has renounced all worldly things as part of the *ashrama* system

Saraswati – wife of Brahma, goddess of learning; sits on a white swan, holding a *veena*

Sati – wife of Shiva; became a *sati* ('honourable woman') by immolating herself; although banned more than a century ago, the act of *sati* is still occasionally performed

satra – Hindu Vaishnavaite monastery and centre for art

satsang – discourse by a swami or guru

satyagraha – nonviolent protest involving a hunger strike, popularised by Mahatma Gandhi; from Sanskrit, literally meaning 'insistence on truth'

Scheduled Castes – official term used for the Untouchables or Dalits

sepoy – formerly an Indian solider in British service

serai – accommodation for travellers

seva – voluntary work, especially in a temple

shahadah – Muslim declaration of faith ('There is no God but Allah; Mohammed is his prophet')

Shaivism – worship of Shiva

Shaivite – follower of Shiva

shakti – creative energies perceived as female deities; devotees follow Shaktism

sharia – Islamic law

sher – the Hindi word for tiger, as in Sher Khan (tiger king) from the Jungle Book

Sheshnag – the supernatural snake on which Vishnu reclines

shikhar – hunting expedition

shirting – material from which shirts are made

Shiva – Destroyer; also the Creator, in which form he is worshipped as a lingam

shola – virgin forest

shree – see *shri*

shri – honorific male prefix; Indian equivalent of 'Respected Sir'

shruti – heard

Shudra – caste of labourers

sikhara – Hindu temple-spire or temple

Singh – literally 'lion'; a surname adopted by Sikhs

sirdar – leader or commander

Sita – the Hindu goddess of agriculture; more commonly associated with the Ramayana

sitar – Indian stringed instrument with resonant strings and a gourd soundbox

Siva – see *Shiva*

Skanda – another name for Kartikiya

sonam – karma accumulated in successive reincarnations

sree – see *shri*

sri – see *shri*

stupa – Buddhist religious monument composed of a solid hemisphere topped by a spire, containing relics of the Buddha; also known as a 'dagoba' or 'pagoda'

Subhadra – Krishna's incestuous sister

Subrahmanya – another name for Kartikiya

Sufi – Muslim mystic

Sufism – Islamic mysticism

suiting – material from which suits are made

Surya – the sun; a major deity in the Vedas

sutra – string; list of rules expressed in verse

swami – title of respect meaning 'lord of the self'; given to initiated Hindu monks

swaraj – independence

Swarga – heaven of Indra

sweeper – lowest caste servant, performs the most menial of tasks

tabla – twin drums

tal – lake

taluk – district

tandava – Shiva's cosmic victory dance

tank – reservoir; pool or large receptacle of holy water found at some temples

tantric Buddhism – Tibetan Buddhism with strong sexual and occult overtones

tatty – woven grass screen soaked in water and hung outside windows to cool the air

tempo – noisy three-wheeler public transport vehicle; bigger than an autorickshaw

thakur – nobleman

thangka – Tibetan cloth painting

theertham – temple tank

Theravada – orthodox form of Buddhism practiced in Sri Lanka and Southeast Asia which is characterised by its adherence to the Pali canon; literally, 'dwelling'

thiru – holy

tikka – a mark Hindus put on their foreheads

tilak – auspicious forehead mark of devout Hindu men

tirthankars – the 24 great Jain teachers

tonga – two-wheeled horse or pony carriage

topi – cap

torana – architrave over a temple entrance

toy train – narrow-gauge train; mini-train

Trimurti – triple form; the Hindu triad of Brahma, Shiva and Vishnu

Tripitaka – classic Buddhist scriptures, divided into three categories, hence the name 'Three Baskets'

tripolia – triple gateway

Uma – Shiva's consort (an avatar of Kali); light

Untouchable – lowest caste or 'casteless', for whom the most menial tasks are reserved; the name derives from the belief that higher castes risk defilement if they touch one; formerly known as Harijan, now Dalit

Upanishads – esoteric doctrine; ancient texts forming part of the Vedas; delving into weighty matters such as the nature of the universe and soul

urs – death anniversary of a revered Muslim; festival in memory of a Muslim saint

vaastu – creation of a cosmically favourable environment

Vaishya – member of the Hindu caste of merchants

Valmiki – author of the Ramayana

Vamana – fifth incarnation of Vishnu, as the dwarf

varku – sacred flute made from a thigh bone; known as *kangling* in Tibetan Buddhism

varna – concept of caste

Varuna – supreme Vedic god

Vedas – Hindu sacred books; collection of hymns composed in preclassical Sanskrit during the second millennium BC and divided into four books: Rig-Veda, Yajur-Veda, Sama-Veda and Atharva-Veda

veena – outsized sitar-like stringed instrument

vihara – Buddhist temple, usually with a Buddha shrine at one end

vikram – tempo or a larger version of the standard tempo

vimana – principal part of Hindu temple

vipassana – the insight meditation technique of Theravada Buddhism in which mind and body are closely examined as changing phenomena

Vishnu – part of the Trimurti; Vishnu is the Preserver and Restorer who so far has nine avatars: the fish Matsya; the tortoise Kurma; the wild boar Naraha; Narasimha; Vamana; Parasurama; Rama; Krishna; and Buddha

wadi – hamlet
wallah – man; added onto almost anything, eg *dhobi-wallah*, chai-wallah, taxi-wallah
wazir – title of chief minister used in some former Muslim princely states

yagna – self-mortification
yakshi – maiden
yali – mythical lion creature

yantra – geometric plan said to create energy
yatra – pilgrimage
yatri – pilgrim
yogini – female goddess attendants
yoni – female fertility symbol

zakat – tax in the form of a charitable donation, one of the five 'Pillars of Islam'
zamindar – landowner
zari – gold or silver thread used in weaving
zenana – area of a home where women are secluded; women's quarters

Behind the Scenes

THIS BOOK
This is the 1st edition of *Northeast India*. The regional chapters, apart from Northeast States and Excursions, have been taken directly from the 12th edition of *India*. The front matter, Directory and Transport chapters are based on text written by Joe Bindloss and Sarina Singh for *India* 12. Lindsay Brown wrote the West Bengal and Orissa chapters, and Mark Elliot wrote the Kolkata, Sikkim and Northeast States chapters. For the Excursions chapter, Paul Harding wrote the text on Bihar and Uttar Pradesh, while Joe Bindloss repurposed the text appearing in the *Bangladesh, Bhutan* and *Nepal* books. Dr Trish Batchelor wrote the Health text. This guidebook was commissioned in Lonely Planet's Melbourne office, and produced by the following:

Commissioning Editor Sam Trafford, Stefanie Di Trocchio
Coordinating Editor Trent Holden
Coordinating Cartographers Amanda Sierp, Erin McManus
Coordinating Layout Designer Yvonne Bischofberger
Managing Editor Suzannah Shwer
Managing Cartographer Shahara Ahmed
Managing Layout Designer Celia Wood
Assisting Cartographer Josh Geoghegan
Assisting Editors Gennifer Ciavarra, Melissa Faulkner
Assisting Layout Designer Wibowo Rusli
Cover Designer Pepi Bluck
Project Manager Sarah Sloane
Proofreader Kristin Odijk
Language Content Coordinator Quentin Frayne

Thanks to Sally Darmody, Ryan Evans, Jim Hsu, Wayne Murphy, Averil Robertson, Tashi Wheeler

THANKS
JOE BINDLOSS
In Assam, thanks to Ashish Phookan and the staff of Jungle Travels in Guwahati for opening up doors in the Northeast States. Thanks also to the dedicated authors who contributed to this book, and all the readers who wrote in with tips. In London, thanks to Linda Nylind, for putting up with my work trips and tight deadlines.

LINDSAY BROWN
Firstly, thank you Sam Trafford and the editors and cartos at Lonely Planet. Special thanks to fellow travellers Stephen Nicholson, Stan Armington, Sarina Singh and Samantha Marshall. In West Bengal, thanks go to Jamling Tenzing Norgay in Darjeeling, Norden Pempahishey in Kalimpong, and Dhiraj and Jennifer in Kurseong. In Orissa, thanks go to Tutu, Sarat and Bijay of Discover Tours.

MARK ELLIOTT
My greatest thanks are always to my wife (Dani Systermans) and parents whose love and support makes my bizarre life so delightful. Thanks to the whole team at LP and to hundreds of helpful people in India including Rupak Adhikary for his insight, patience and inscruitible accent, Bonalama for his hospitality, Neelam, Ashish, Nemo, Bhaswati, Sanjay and the Jungle Gang, Jai Chand in Kolkata, Wangyal Bhutia in Jorethang, Dipsara and Sudim in Tura, Bansbari's one-and-only wing commander, Romesh for pegs and yarns, Manju and co at Wild Grass, Naran Tami Gaobora in Hong, eccentric water-wizzard Suresh Kalita in Guwahati,

Subhratanu and Shyamal for Manipur tips, Pritam Majumder in Agartala, Phuphi Bhutia in Yuksam, Shantanu Biswas, Saniel the mysterious 'angel' in Siliguri, Lubo and the ubiquitous Slovak gang, Nicola, Jesse, Rich and Vic(toria) for their Mekhikan skills and ferrous phosphate, Raj the red panda, and of course the brave, fearless BRO.

ACKNOWLEDGMENTS

Many thanks to the following for the use of their content:

Globe on title page ©Mountain High Maps 1993 Digital Wisdom, Inc.

SEND US YOUR FEEDBACK

We love to hear from travelers – your comments keep us on our toes and help make our books better. Our well-traveled team reads every word on what you loved or loathed about this book. Although we cannot reply individually to postal submissions, we always guarantee that your feedback goes straight to the appropriate authors, in time for the next edition. Each person who sends us information is thanked in the next edition – and the most useful submissions are rewarded with a free book.

To send us your updates – and find out about Lonely Planet events, newsletters and travel news – visit our award-winning website: **www.lonelyplanet.com/contact**.

Note: we may edit, reproduce and incorporate your comments in Lonely Planet products such as guidebooks, websites and digital products, so let us know if you don't want your comments reproduced or your name acknowledged. For a copy of our privacy policy visit www.lonelyplanet.com/privacy.

364

Index

INDEX

INDEX

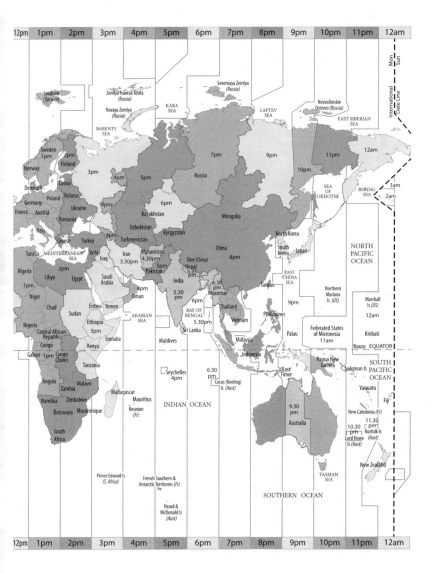

MAP LEGEND

ROUTES

Tollway	Mall/Steps
Freeway	Tunnel
Primary	Pedestrian Overpass
Secondary	Walking Tour
Tertiary	Walking Tour Detour
Lane	Walking Trail
Under Construction	Walking Path
Unsealed Road	Track
One-Way Street	

TRANSPORT

Ferry	Rail
Metro	Rail (Underground)
Bus Route	Tram

HYDROGRAPHY

River, Creek	Canal
Intermittent River	Water
Swamp	Lake (Dry)
Mangrove	Lake (Salt)
Reef	Mudflats

BOUNDARIES

International	Regional, Suburb
State, Provincial	Ancient Wall
Disputed	Cliff

AREA FEATURES

Airport	Land
Area of Interest	Mall
Beach, Desert	Market
Building	Park
Campus	Reservation
Cemetery, Christian	Rocks
Cemetery, Other	Sports
Forest	Urban

POPULATION

◎ CAPITAL (NATIONAL)	◉ CAPITAL (STATE)
● Large City	● Medium City
● Small City	● Town, Village

SYMBOLS

Sights/Activities
- Beach
- Buddhist
- Castle, Fortress
- Christian
- Hindu
- Islamic
- Jain
- Jewish
- Monument
- Museum, Gallery
- Point of Interest
- Pool
- Ruin
- Sikh
- Skiing
- Trail Head
- Zoo, Bird Sanctuary

Eating
- Eating

Drinking
- Drinking
- Café

Entertainment
- Entertainment

Shopping
- Shopping

Sleeping
- Sleeping
- Camping

Transport
- Airport, Airfield
- Border Crossing
- Bus Station
- General Transport
- Parking Area
- Petrol Station
- Taxi Rank

Information
- Bank, ATM
- Embassy/Consulate
- Hospital, Medical
- Information
- Internet Facilities
- Police Station
- Post Office, GPO
- Telephone
- Toilets

Geographic
- Lighthouse
- Lookout
- Mountain, Volcano
- National Park
- Pass, Canyon
- River Flow
- Waterfall

LONELY PLANET OFFICES

Australia
Head Office
Locked Bag 1, Footscray, Victoria 3011
☎ 03 8379 8000, fax 03 8379 8111
talk2us@lonelyplanet.com.au

USA
150 Linden St, Oakland, CA 94607
☎ 510 893 8555, toll free 800 275 8555
fax 510 893 8572
info@lonelyplanet.com

UK
72–82 Rosebery Ave,
Clerkenwell, London EC1R 4RW
☎ 020 7841 9000, fax 020 7841 9001
go@lonelyplanet.co.uk

Published by Lonely Planet Publications Pty Ltd
ABN 36 005 607 983

© Lonely Planet Publications Pty Ltd 2007

© photographers as indicated 2007

Cover photograph: A young Konyak man performing a traditional dance, Thierry Falise/OnAsia Images. Many of the images in this guide are available for licensing from Lonely Planet Images: www.lonelyplanetimages.com.

Printed through Colorcraft Ltd, Hong Kong
Printed in China